AF787581

Human Vulnerability in Interaction with AI in European Private Law

Claudia Amodio · Amalia Diurni
Editors

Human Vulnerability in Interaction with AI in European Private Law

Springer

Editors
Claudia Amodio
University of Ferrara
Ferrara, Italy

Amalia Diurni
University of Rome Tor Vergata
Rome, Italy

ISBN 978-3-031-93246-5 ISBN 978-3-031-93247-2 (eBook)
https://doi.org/10.1007/978-3-031-93247-2

This work was supported by the Italian Ministry of University and Research (PRIN Project 2020XBFME2, 'Digital Vulnerability in European Private Law' (DiVE)) and the Istituto Italiano di Studi Germanici (Project 'Instabilità del diritto e vulnerabilità digitale').

© The Editor(s) (if applicable) and The Author(s) 2025. This book is an open access publication.

Open Access This book is licensed under the terms of the Creative Commons Attribution 4.0 International License (http://creativecommons.org/licenses/by/4.0/), which permits use, sharing, adaptation, distribution and reproduction in any medium or format, as long as you give appropriate credit to the original author(s) and the source, provide a link to the Creative Commons license and indicate if changes were made.
The images or other third party material in this book are included in the book's Creative Commons license, unless indicated otherwise in a credit line to the material. If material is not included in the book's Creative Commons license and your intended use is not permitted by statutory regulation or exceeds the permitted use, you will need to obtain permission directly from the copyright holder.
The use of general descriptive names, registered names, trademarks, service marks, etc. in this publication does not imply, even in the absence of a specific statement, that such names are exempt from the relevant protective laws and regulations and therefore free for general use.
The publisher, the authors and the editors are safe to assume that the advice and information in this book are believed to be true and accurate at the date of publication. Neither the publisher nor the authors or the editors give a warranty, expressed or implied, with respect to the material contained herein or for any errors or omissions that may have been made. The publisher remains neutral with regard to jurisdictional claims in published maps and institutional affiliations.

This Springer imprint is published by the registered company Springer Nature Switzerland AG
The registered company address is: Gewerbestrasse 11, 6330 Cham, Switzerland

If disposing of this product, please recycle the paper.

Preface

This volume collects the outcomes of the research activities carried out with the support of the Italian Ministry of University and Research, under the PRIN Project 2020XBFME2, "Digital Vulnerability in European Private Law" (DiVE), and of the Istituto Italiano di Studi Germanici, under the project "Instabilità del diritto e vulnerabilità digitale". Both projects aimed to investigate how the notion of digital vulnerability can be framed in relation to private law, human subjectivity, and governance mechanisms.

The first international conference, held in Ferrara in 2023, was devoted to the analysis of digital vulnerability in domestic and European private law, with a particular focus on consumer protection and the functioning of the marketplace. The second conference, organized at Villa Mondragone, University of Rome "Tor Vergata", in May 2024, broadened the scope of inquiry under the title "Human Vulnerability in Interaction with AI". The theme was articulated around an interdisciplinary approach, combining contributions from law, philosophy, sociology, computer science, and related fields. In addition, a specific call for papers was launched for PhD candidates and early-career researchers, whose presentations were included in the program and subsequently developed into contributions to this volume. Their participation has ensured the presence of innovative perspectives and reflects the intergenerational character of the debate.

The volume is organized into two main parts.

The first part, "Human–Machine Interaction Between Digital Humanism and Digital Citizenship", examines the ways in which digital technologies challenge human dignity, agency, and participation in the civic sphere. Contributions here address, among other issues, the redefinition of subjectivity in technologically mediated contexts, electoral manipulation and disinformation, automated contracting and its risks to autonomy, and the vulnerabilities created by AI in intimate, emotional, and health-related settings. Other chapters turn to questions of digital inclusion, the persistence of divides in connectivity, and the reconfiguration of civic duty in the age of artificial intelligence. Taken together, these analyses situate HMI within the broader discourse of digital humanism, asking how technologies can support—rather than erode—citizenship and participation.

The second part, "Human–Machine Interaction and Policy Strategies Between Anticipatory Governance and Sustainability of Risks", turns to regulatory, institutional, and policy challenges. Contributions in this section address the risks and opportunities of AI governance, from sector-specific regulation (such as healthcare, insurance, and digital markets) to broader issues of liability, intellectual property, and data protection. By engaging with anticipatory governance and sustainability frameworks, these chapters underline the urgency of designing policies capable of coping with uncertainty and preventing systemic harms, while at the same time fostering innovation.

By juxtaposing these two perspectives—one centered on human dignity and citizenship, the other on regulation and risk governance—the volume provides a comprehensive account of the challenges and opportunities of human–machine interaction. At the same time, it reflects our firm belief that the development of legal frameworks suited to the digital age requires an unprecedented, coordinated, and collective effort by a scholarly community spanning not only disciplines, but also generations.

Ferrara, Italy — Claudia Amodio
Rome, Italy — Amalia Diurni

Contents

Digital Vulnerability in Human-Machine Interaction: New Insights on Normative and Epistemic Challenges in AI Governance

Claudia Amodio and Amalia Diurni

Abstract This paper examines the evolution of Human-Machine Interaction (HMI) through the lenses of legal theory, political epistemology, and governance studies, arguing that the shift from algorithmic profiling to conversational agents and reasoning systems has created unprecedented disruptions in cognitive autonomy, social trust, and normative authority. By critically engaging with key unresolved issues affecting both the safe development of AI systems and AI policy-making processes, the analysis draws on Post-Normal Science (PNS) to call for replacing reactive risk management with anticipatory governance and extending co-regulation beyond industry-led standards. The paper further introduces the concept of digital vulnerability as a transversal legal category designed to capture the epistemic and democratic challenges embedded in AI-mediated interactions.

Keywords Human-machine interaction · Digital vulnerability · Post-normal science · Digital governance · Precaution principle

1 Introduction

The accelerating development of artificial intelligence (AI) technologies is reshaping human experience, institutions, and the very categories of legal and epistemic analysis. This paper explores how the evolving modes of human-machine interaction

This paper is the result of a joint research effort. Sections 1 (Introduction) and 7 (Conclusion) were written collaboratively by both authors. Sections 2, 2.1, 2.2, 2.3, 2.4, 3, 3.1, 3.2, 5.2, and 6.3 were written by Amalia Diurni. Sections 4, 4.1, 4.2, 5, 5.1, 5.3, 6, 6.1, and 6.2 were written by Claudia Amodio.

C. Amodio
University of Ferrara, Ferrara, Italy
e-mail: claudia.amodio@unife.it

A. Diurni (✉)
University of Rome Tor Vergata, Rome, Italy
e-mail: amalia.diurni@uniroma2.it

© The Author(s) 2025

C. Amodio and A. Diurni (eds.), *Human Vulnerability in Interaction with AI in European Private Law*, https://doi.org/10.1007/978-3-031-93247-2_1

(HMI)—from algorithmic profiling to reasoning agents—challenge foundational assumptions in law and political theory, calling for a radical rethinking of governance, subjectivity, and vulnerability in the digital age.

The central argument is that existing legal frameworks are insufficient to address the deep and multidimensional transformations introduced by AI systems, particularly in their capacity to simulate human communication and decision-making. In response to this insufficiency, the paper proposes the concept of digital vulnerability as a new legal and analytical category capable of capturing both the epistemic asymmetries and normative disruptions caused by AI. This proposal is framed within the theoretical paradigm of Post-Normal Science (PNS), which offers a compelling model for managing uncertainty, risk, and value conflicts in science-driven policy domains.

The originality of this contribution lies in the integration of PNS principles with digital legal theory, linking technological opacity, the erosion of cognitive autonomy, and the privatization of normativity through platform power, to the emerging need for precautionary governance and inclusive epistemic participation. Drawing from the interdisciplinary debate around platform governance, extended peer communities, and post-truth dynamics, the paper maps the normative pressure points where digital law must evolve to maintain coherence with democratic values and human dignity.

Structurally, after this introduction, the paper unfolds in five parts. First, it reconstructs the HMI's evolution through three key phases: algorithmic profiling, conversational agents, and reasoning systems, illustrating their cumulative effects on individual cognition and collective meaning-making by examining the epistemological and sociological implications of these technologies, highlighting the erosion of epistemic trust and the symbolic construction of reality by generative AI. The second part situates these challenges within the broader governance debate, comparing policy models in the EU, US, and China, and exposing the normative role assumed by Very Large Online Platforms and Search Engines (VLOPs and VLOSEs). The fourth and fifth parts introduce the PNS debate framing AI as a post-normal challenge. The final part offers a critique of the European AI Act from the PNS prospective and argues for a paradigm shift in digital governance, culminating in the proposal to adopt digital vulnerability as a conceptual foundation for future legal design.

In sum, this paper contends that digital law must move beyond risk classification and techno-centric compliance, embracing a multidimensional notion of vulnerability that reflects the relational, contextual, and dynamic nature of AI-human interaction.

2 The Human-Machine Interaction: From External Domination to Functional Hybridisation

The AI revolution represents the latest phase in a history of "coevolution"—between humans and other species, between humans and industrial machines, between humans and digital technologies, and now, between humans and AI.[1] However, the gap between AI system capabilities and genuine user comprehension challenges conventional notions of coevolution and user-centricity, highlighting the need to redefine human-centred AI development beyond surface-level usability.[2] Addressing this gap has spurred the recent Explainable AI (XAI) movement, which seeks to make AI systems more transparent and interpretable to users.[3] However, XAI approaches often focus on technical explanations rather than meaningful user understanding, highlighting the persistent challenge of bridging the human-AI divide.[4]

What distinguishes AI is its multilayered nature, making it difficult to find historical parallels with comparable impact, scope, or characteristics. While its foundation is techno-scientific, its waves extend far beyond that of a simple product or tool, profoundly reshaping society. Furthermore, despite advances in uncertainty quantification techniques in AI, key unresolved issues remain in the research, affecting both the safe development of AI systems and the processes involved in policy-making.[5]

Issues arise because the changes we face today are neither incremental nor predictable, nor are they isolated; they occur simultaneously, unpredictably, and are deeply interconnected. Digital technology, while the result of deliberate human decision-making, operates and spreads through what Dennett[6] describes as the "procreative prowess" of the technology itself. The ways individuals and societies respond to new technologies, their interactions with them, and the resulting changes in social practices and cultural realities in the era of deep mediatization[7] are profoundly shaping human evolution. The pervasive and ubiquitous nature of digital technology continuously reshapes the categories of everyday life—blurring boundaries between physical and virtual realities. public and private, local and global, individual and collective—while remaining largely invisible and erratic in terms of its social functions.[8] As convincingly argued by Pasquale in this volume, both predictive and generative AI are increasingly eroding social defences by targeting those most susceptible to deepfakes, deception, and demoralization, eventually leading to the erosion of the cognitive foundations of democracy.

---

[1] Pedreschi et al. (2025).

[2] Ziegler and Donkers (2024).

[3] Longo et al. (2024).

[4] Miller (2019).

[5] Wang et al. (2025).

[6] Dennett (2017).

[7] Hepp (2020).

[8] Deuze (2011).

Social media and AI systems have become tools for eroding trust in public institutions, questioning democracy as the best suited model of governance for addressing growing socio-economic issues.[9] Global tensions are now fuelled by a "battle of narratives" that is evolving into a "battle of offers". This shapes not only public opinion worldwide but also how governments act.[10] Meanwhile, the narratives promoted by the EU, and indeed the liberal democracies, are increasingly under challenge. This phenomenon is partly due to propaganda, misinformation, and disinformation campaigns designed to shape national and global attitudes, which are increasingly amplified by social media and the deceptive use of generative artificial intelligence.

Understanding this trajectory is essential, because the vulnerabilities exploited today are rooted in patterns established throughout the historical coevolution of humans and technology. Accordingly, before addressing the geopolitical, PNS, and legal dimensions of digital vulnerability, we must step back and trace the evolutionary stages of HMI.[11]

2.1 Algorithmic Profiling and the Erosion of Cognitive Autonomy

Artificial intelligence applications in social media have represented the first step of HMI so far. At this first stage, they were used as mere tools to improve the online experience and increase business profits. In this respect, platform algorithmic recommender systems (RS), analysed by Santoni in this volume, and algorithmic profiling are highlighting example. The latter has been used by businesses and organisations for legitimate purposes (targeted advertising, product development, risk assessment, fraud detection, personalized recommendations etc.).[12] However, its application on large scale has raised privacy concerns about the collection and analysis of big amounts of personal data, discrimination and biases with negative impact on individuals and groups, and lack of transparency about how the algorithms themselves infer the generation of outputs from the inputs they receive or extract through scraping[13] as

---

[9] Communication from the Commission to the European Parliament and the Council, 2023 Strategic Foresight Report Sustainability and people's wellbeing at the heart of Europe's Open Strategic Autonomy, COM(2023) 376 final, p. 12 et seq.

[10] The EU's answer is the Global Gateway, designed to back smart, high-quality infrastructure investments between 2021 and 2027. These projects adhere to the strictest social and environmental standards, reflecting European values. The launch of infrastructure partnerships to create new alliances and boost the old one was first used as strategy by the Chinese government when in 2013 the Belt and Road Initiative (BRI) was started.

[11] Human-machine interaction has become a multidisciplinary field of research and is known in scientific circles by the acronym HMI: Schleidgen et al. (2023) and Esposito (2022).

[12] Tzoulia (2021).

[13] Pasquale (2015).

happens in case of AI-driven robo-advice in the insurance sector analysed by Skalski and Tereszkiewicz in this volume.

The algorithmic profiling was supposed to help improve efficiency, accuracy and personalization. Despite the excellent results achieved in this direction, the distortions produced are still far from being addressed by the current regulation. The creation of filter bubbles and echo chambers by the recommendation algorithms is limiting the users' exposure to diverse perspectives, reinforcing preexisting biases, hindering the opportunity for informed discussion and compromise, and contributing to the current polarisation of political debate.[14] The polarization effect in digital communities stems from their tendency to consist of individuals with shared interests and knowledge—so-called communities of practice—unlike physical communities, which encourage interaction among people with diverse backgrounds. This homogeneity diminishes the corrective dynamics of the 'wisdom of the crowd,' reinforces groupthink, enables disproportionate influence by dominant users, and contributes to growing asymmetries in social capital distribution.[15] By personalising content, algorithms exploit these distortions and amplify confirmation biases unintentionally and unpredictably. Users are exposed to emotional manipulation and algorithmic management, misinformation and disinformation. Whilecreating the illusion of personalized interaction, algorithms have a homogenising effect on people, being designed to identify patterns in data and to reduce variables as far as possible.

Richard Thaler and Cass Sunstein explained in their seminal book about 'Nudge'[16] how policymakers can prod behavioural changes, predictably altering people's behaviour without forbidding any opinions or significantly changing their economic incentives. As happens in the choice architecture for data privacy, individuals are free to opt-out, but the nudge is designed to influence them to act in a preferred way. This effect is even more powerful when it is an algorithm that is nudging, as it is clearly evident in the rise of the post-truth[17] plague, and the affirmation of the post-truth politics in the context of the UK-EU referendum and the US presidential elections. Furthermore, in consequence of its characteristics, social media is well-suited to being employed by authoritarian entities as a theatre for 'cognitive warfare',[18] the objective of which is to weaken and destabilise liberal democracies. The digital social environment has been identified as a significant catalyst for the

---

[14] A review of scientific literature in Tucker et al. (2018).

[15] Riva et al. (2024).

[16] Thaler and Sunstein (2008).

[17] Keyes (2004).

[18] Often referred to as the Gerasimov Doctrine, this strategic paradigm—attributed to the Russian general who articulated its core principles—outlines a hybrid model of conflict in which non-military tools play a central role. It envisions the systematic use of digital technologies, cyberspace, and social media platforms to conduct operations below the threshold of open warfare. Among its primary aims are the strategic manipulation of public perception and the deployment of information as a multi-domain weapon, capable of disrupting political, social, and institutional stability even in peacetime. For more information and examples on the Italian case, Ottaviani (2022).

proliferation of "autocratic appeal" and "post-truth",[19] manifesting in disinformation and ideological propaganda against the liberal model of government.[20]

2.2 *The Challenges of Simulated Human Dialogue*

The second step of the interaction between humans and machines is represented by the application of conversational agents (CAs), including embodied CAs, chatbots, and socially assistive robots (SARs). Among many others, the major concern is the polished ability of these robots to mimic human conversation, as described by Pera, Rigazio and Confortini in this volume. Indeed, in their exchanges, chatbots are able to express empathy and impressive erudition, mixed with arrogant assertiveness and variability of tone (friendly, excited, stable, serious) and style (professional, in-formative, educational, storytelling, benefit-focused or solution-oriented). The constant performance improvement occurs through complex attention mechanisms that enable the bots to focus on specific parts of the input text to generate more relevant and accurate outputs with respect to context, recipients' personalities and their wishes. Furthermore, the ability to store input information from the same user in memory modules makes questioning and answering exchanges more coherent and similar to those between humans. However, while chatbot answers may seem 'sensible', they make 'no sense' to the machines themselves. And this is where the most insidious threat lies, because chatbots are modelled to imitate human conversation, thus making it hard to recognize responses as 'artificial'. It is for this very reason that under Art. 50 AI Act the chatbots must, by default, warn users of their nature. While highlighting the potential valuable contributions of this new technology in many fields, the particular interaction between humans and machines developed through CAs raise more concerns when people with recognized vulnerabilities as patients (see the Konnoth's contribution in this volume), minors, elders or disabled people are involved.

2.3 *Functional Hybridization Through Reasoning Agents*

The third generation has already arrived, with the 2022 literature[21] pioneering the concept of the Chain of Thought (CoT) and the called "chain-of-thought prompting". These studies demonstrated how explicitly requesting that the chatbot elucidate the chain of reasoning it employed to arrive at the response produced "thinking tokens" and enhanced its performance in solving complex problems. This represented

[19] For an illustration of the post-truth not merely as a Western issue, but as a problematic political and cultural condition with global ramifications see Cosentino (2020).

[20] Flore (2020).

[21] Wei et al. (2022).

a pivotal shift from the utilisation of narrative artificial intelligence to the adoption of problem-solving capabilities in artificial intelligence. Large Reasoning Models (LRM), with the first of these, O1, having been launched by OpenAI in September 2024, are models that appear to engage in reflective processing prior to formulating responses, and provide a detailed exposition of the reasoning process that led to the conclusion. These models also furnish links to the sources that were consulted and the logic underpinning the final summary. In comparison with LLMs, these novel deep research tools permit users to enter the machine's reasoning chain and request modification, integration or deepening of one or more logical steps. The machine itself is capable of correcting itself and evaluating the consistency of the sources with each other, or proposing alternatives. Consequently, these sophisticated artificial intelligence systems enhance the consistency and precision of responses, while concurrently offering the capacity to investigate the mechanisms that underpin their generation. The subsequent "evolutionary" phase involves the utilisation of these machines in the execution of assigned tasks, exhibiting varying degrees of autonomy and decision-making capacity. A notable example of this is the expansion of their search operations in the event of dissatisfaction with the obtained results with the depth and nuance of human experts, but at machine speed. According to experts in the field,[22] while LRMs provide the intellectual horsepower and the OpenAI's Deep Research system is proof of this, the "agentic systems" that will represent a step forward are being created to provide the ability to act. This new stage is exemplified by the application of AI-enabled decision support tools in what is termed "decision-centric warfare". This approach combines the respective strengths of humans and machines for the purpose of facilitating faster and more effective decision-making, creating a functional hybridization of humans and machines. The human flexibility and creative insights are leveraged by AI's speed and scale to improve the ability to impose multiple dilemmas on adversaries, as proposed in the "Mosaic Warfare" concept by the US Defense Advanced Research Projects Agency (DARPA).[23]

2.4 External Domination, Epistemic Vulnerability and Social Construction of Reality in the Age of Generative AI

The cognitive science has focused part of its attention on the various ways in which cognition is actively produced through a series of embodied interactions with the proximal environment, in particular with the human-made world of artefacts. The growth of the technologically-advanced tools with networking capabilities (IoT) has opened up new areas of investigation about the definition of these bio-external resources as a causally-relevant or a constituent feature of human cognitive and mental machinery. The distinction is of crucial significance in the context of ascribing responsibility for human decisions derived from interaction with the machine. In

[22] Mollick (2025).

[23] Clark et al. (2020).

the case of embedded cognition, the machinery of mind remains internal, but its performance is significantly influenced by certain external factors. On the other hand, when cognition is extended to include artificial intelligence, it becomes a genuine constituent of the individual's cognitive states and processes.[24] From an embedded standpoint, the ethical and legal spotlight seems to fall on the developer of the AI system, contrary to the extended standpoint when the AI system forms part of the individual's cognitive machinery,[25] and thus as outcomes of personal decision the responsibility lies with the person who made it.

Consequently, AI systems are undergoing a gradual and progressive transition from passive tools to active partners. It is acknowledged that there are several threats arising from each type of HMI described above. However, those involving CAs and LRMs seem to warrant greater attention as they are relatively new and potentially more impactful. AI systems are undergoing a gradual and progressive transition from passive tools to active partners. Although each form of human-machine interaction (HMI) discussed above presents its own set of risks, the challenges associated with Conversational Agents (CAs) and Large Reasoning Models (LRMs) seem to warrant greater attention, given their relative novelty and potentially far-reaching implications. These developments are especially well-suited to analysis from both epistemological and sociological perspectives, as illustrated by the contributions of Bertolaso and Marinucci, as well as Sorice and Volterrani, in this volume.

Although generative AIs exhibit impressive linguistic consistency owing to their capacity to assimilate syntactic rules, the relatively limited writing proficiency of the average user places them in a position of subordination vis-à-vis the machine. This condition of perceived—or actual—subordination constitutes a structural vulnerability on the part of the weaker user, and creates space for domination by the more powerful system. Beyond any form of 'amusement', 'intellectual' challenge or professional use of chatbots (by experts capable of appraising the reliability of responses), most users who question a chatbot are technically inexperienced and not competent in the subject matter. For such users chatbots are neither entertainment nor work, but tools to understand reality. So, in addition to the danger of spreading misinformation that has been detected as described above, the inferior subject's proneness to rely on those who are perceived to be more experienced, capable and educated alters the normal course of the interaction. Whilst this is common in interactions between humans—so much so that experts take responsibility for what they say—in interactions with CAs users are warned of the nature and limits of the bot and, in accordance with the applied terms of use,[26] are held solely responsible for their prompts, the CAs responses that ensue, and the use that is made of such responses.

---

[24] Wheeler (2019).

[25] Clowes et al. (2024).

[26] In regard to content, it is said that you (the user) "may provide input to the Services ('Input'), and receive output from the Services based on the Input ('Output'). Input and Output are collectively 'Content.' You are responsible for Content, including ensuring that it does not violate any applicable law or these Terms. You represent and warrant that you have all rights, licenses, and permissions needed to provide Input to our Services". See Malaschini (2023), p. 597.

Nevertheless, the manner in which such warnings are given and terms of use are accepted does not prevent users from consciously or unconsciously perceiving epistemological value in the chatbot's responses. The syntactic accuracy of the bot's answers and the adjustment of tone and style to match those of the questions are not, of course, the result of any consciousness nor sensitivity from the machine, but interlocutors are, nonetheless, led to perceive them as being endowed with both. Scientists' warnings[27] about lack of empathy, semantic cognition or attribution of meaning of all the natural language generation systems (NLG) have been to no avail. The mirror[28] with which AI reflects their image back onto humans is both deceiving and beguiling.[29] Thus, the danger is to witness a human preference, at the micro level, for perpetually available, educated, accommodating and benevolent artificial conversation and for the 'truth' generated by them instead of expert's indications. The epistemic space where we are living in is abandoning conventional criteria of evidence, internal consistency and fact-seeking.[30] At the macro level, the threat lies in the deliberate or accidental manipulation of reality[31] and human knowledge as generated by 'meaningless' AI narratives.[32]

Furthermore, there are impacts on the dynamics of social interaction from a sociological point of view. In the HMI realm, human vulnerability undoubtedly emerges as a characteristic of the individual. At the same time, since individuals are 'interdependent people in the singular', vulnerability pertains as well to the whole of society, as it is composed of 'interdependent people in the plural'.[33] The ability of CAs to imitate human communication and LRMs to imitate human reasoning directly threatens the individuals with whom they interact and indirectly threatens the entire society.[34] The communication is not authentic but appears so. The answers to questions, which seem original and full of new content and well-reasoned answers, are, in

27 McQuillan (2018), Bender et al. (2021). On the Dangers of Stochastic Parrots: Can Language Models Be Too Big? Conference on Fairness, Accountability, and Transparency (FAccT'21), p. 610–623 and Arkoudas (2023).

28 Prem (2022).

29 Well described by Gehl and Bakardjieva (2016). Social bots are "intended to present a self, to pose as an alter-ego, as a subject with personal biography, stock of knowledge, emotions and body, as a social counterpart, as someone like me, the user, with whom I could build a social relationship" (p. 2).

30 Lewandowsky et al. (2017).

31 Actually, transformations arising from deep mediatization ensue as a sort of re-figuration, namely a fundamental, structural shift of human relationships and practices: Hepp (2020), p. 112.

32 Floridi (2023a), Bishop (2021), and Amato (2023).

33 Elias (1978), p. 125.

34 In October 2022, after a year-long process led by the US Office of Science and Technology Policy, the White House released the Blueprint for an AI Bill of Rights to inform policy decisions. The concept of community is integral to the scope of this Blueprint and affirms that, while AI and other data-driven automated systems most directly collect data, make inferences, and may cause harm to individuals, the overall magnitude of their impacts is most readily visible at the community level: https://www.whitehouse.gov/wp-content/uploads/2022/10/Blueprint-for-an-AI-Bill-of-Rights.pdf. In January 2025, President Trump revoked President Biden's Executive Order and enacted a new one with the aim of sustaining and enhancing America's dominance in the field

fact, merely syntactically ordered and stylistically elegant reformulations of existing content. Chatbots do nothing more than perpetuate the most quantitatively prevalent data (and not the most qualitatively or ethically superior data[35]) through an iteration of logical models, with no critical capability or semantic awareness whatsoever.

Given that communication is a form of symbolic construction of reality, the massive proliferation of communicative agents cannot but affect the construction mechanism by which individuals construct representations of themselves, of the society they belong to, and of the environment they live in.[36] It is impossible to predict how the entry of AI as a new individual and social interlocutor will change psychological and sociological dynamics.[37] One thing is certain: the technological revolution driven by AI is redefining the way we interact with the world and access information, opening an era of epistemic vulnerability.[38] Today, social media and LLMs are the main tools for informing and shaping public opinion, and they are also used as a vehicle for disinformation activities, moderation and censorship practices,[39] with levels of sophistication that have not yet been seen, coordinating textual, visual and audio production. During the training and releasing of LLMs and LRMs it could happen that these models are inherently biased, inserting implicit preferences for one theory or narrative over another, preferences that may not manifest explicitly, but rather at the subliminal level.[40] This issue becomes even more significant in the context of the emergence of Artificial General Intelligence (AGI), which aims to emulate human capacity for studying, understanding, and interacting across a variety of contexts, and would be especially capable of learning by searching for the information it needs and adapting to the context autonomously with Retrieval-Augmented Generation (RAG) processes.

3 Rethinking Governance Under the Pressure of Technological Acceleration

As the result of legal studies and political compromises, regulations take time to be drafted, approved, enacted, and ultimately implemented. Inevitably, this creates a clear discrepancy between the rapid pace of technological innovation and the ability of regulations to maintain effective control over its effects on individuals and communities.

---

of AI through the development of AI systems "free from ideological bias or engineered social agendas": https://www.whitehouse.gov/fact-sheets/2025/01/fact-sheet-president-donald-j-trump-takes-action-to-enhance-americas-ai-leadership/.

[35] Floridi (2023b).

[36] Hepp et al. (2023).

[37] A summary of the psychological ground plan of the narrative realities is offered by Bruner (1991).

[38] Labarre (2024).

[39] Noels et al. (2025).

[40] Nudo et al. (2025).

Ideally, there would be little concern if the digital revolution and its associated technologies were firmly under the control of producers or users, public authorities, societies or individuals. Issues arise from the lack of effective control over the most complex AI systems by any of these actors, particularly in the domain of HMI, as demonstrated with regard to the HMI's development stages and as analysed by Rodríguez de las Heras Ballell in this volume regarding automated contracting. Control issues are intimately tied to the goals to be achieved through the use of AI systems. Humans are entitled to pursue their own objectives, while machines are not. In the event that objectives are not entirely clear to us as humans, the onus falls on machines to try to achieve them on our behalf. However, even if machines can behave as if they were moral agents, they are not.[41] This limit connected with the already described possible distortions coming from the HMI seems to be crucial to build AI systems of arbitrary intelligence that are provably beneficial to humans.[42]

Before introducing HMI in the context of the PNS debate—where uncertainty, complexity, and high stakes are defining features—it is useful to examine whether and how existing policies differ in their response to the paradigm shift brought about by the digital revolution, and to frame the role of VLOPs and VLOSEs in digital governance as legal formants.

3.1 Diverging Digital Policy Models: Control, Promotion, and Protection

Government strategies on AI reveal a spectrum of approaches, some preferring mild guidelines, others strict regulations. Recent debates and actions at national, regional, and global levels all seem to converge towards the search of new regulatory forms and political strategies characterized by variable geometry and force,[43] ranging between intersectoral guidelines and hard laws, voluntary sectoral codes of conduct and public authority controls, business lobbying and democratic empowerment.

Two main regulatory directions are emerging to regain control over fast-evolving technologies: on the one hand, requiring AI producers to establish, implement, document and maintain a risk management system with third-party verification and comply with duties of transparency, explanation and provision of information to users; on the other hand, creating pre-deployment oversight procedures and instituting independent administrative authorities to control new technologies before their mass distribution. The latter solution has been adopted by the AI regulatory sandboxes of the European AI Act, the UK White Paper, President Biden's Executive Order on Safe, Secure, and Trustworthy Artificial Intelligence, and the Chinese Cyberspace Administration Draft Measures for managing generative AI.

[41] There are different opinions depending on the point of view from a technological (Cervantes et al. 2020) to a philosophical (Misselhorn 2022).

[42] Russell (2022).

[43] Vanberghen and Vanberghen (2021).

However, the call for risk assessment and explainability faces a major obstacle: the unpredictability of advanced AI. The consequence of the application of advanced AI systems with conversational skills is an increasingly deep and pervasive HMI, with all the unknowns that go with the radical paradigm shift induced by the communicative agents with unprecedented features in human history.

The more sophisticated the AI system, the harder it is to anticipate or retrospectively explain its decisions. Some would argue that it would be unreasonable to require that only algorithmic models which are inherently controllable—namely, those whose outputs are either predictable ex ante or traceable ex post—be permitted. Such a requirement would de facto exclude self-training, deep learning, and generative AI systems.

A wide array of instruments is available to construct a robust legal framework for the governance of the digital sector, just as diverse are the objectives that each regulatory intervention seeks to pursue. While the structural challenges posed by the digital transition are broadly comparable across countries and regions, the legal and policy responses they have elicited diverge significantly. These divergences are rooted in variations in normative frameworks and in the underlying political and constitutional value systems that shape regulatory priorities. Among the most commonly shared goals across jurisdictions are control, promotion, and protection.

A comparative assessment of the world's three major digital economies—the United States, the European Union, and China—confirms that, despite a shared awareness of the rapid and far-reaching implications of digital transformation, the underlying justifications for state intervention in the digital sphere differ profoundly.[44]

In China, policies on digital sector aims to control technology and its outcomes—and through them, the population—ensuring legal order and social conformity.[45] The social credit system exemplifies this orientation, grounded in digital surveillance.[46]

In the U.S., the liberal dogma according to which the market sets the rules makes the promotion of technological development and the related business the principal purpose. AI systems originally designed for military use, are exploited for government surveillance of civilians for security reasons, while the tech companies have commodified private human experience together with personal data for a new sort of capitalism.[47]

While China stresses the public purpose of people's control in regulating the digital revolution and the United States are reluctant to regulate the sector with the intent to promote technology development in order to boost the market-driven economy, the European Union seems more concerned about the impacts of AI models on fundamental rights. What seems to be a kind of protectionist policy promoted by EU institutions, is the result of the European constitutional tradition, which prioritises

---

[44] Bignami and Resta (2024).

[45] Huw et al. (2021).

[46] Backer (2019).

[47] Zuboff (2019).

human dignity, giving it precedence over liberty,[48] and realise the European vocation to give priority to interconnected social solidarities in contrast with the American preference for interest group competition.[49] However, the EU AI Act mainly aims at market harmonisation and its risk-based structures provide only a still vague impact assessment in relation to the enjoyment of human rights by individuals. The society itself and collective interests such as the functioning of democracy and the observance of the rule of law are not taken into account.[50] Nonetheless, European laws are proof of the efforts to prioritise the protection of EU citizens over the uncontrolled development and diffusion of digital technologies.

In short, in their respective policies on digital sector, China gives priority to exerting control over the citizens, the U.S. policy is focused on the promotion of business and the economic growth, and the EU foregrounds the protection of human rights.

3.2 From Market Players to Legal Formants: The Role of VLOPs, VLOSEs in the Digital Governance

The regulation power is almost in the hands of lawmakers, but the legal process is more complex than it appears. Sacco[51] helped to understand and theorise the agents that form the law, despite the formal recognition as sources of law at the public level. In his theory, the formants of the law are legislators, judges and academics, who contribute, each with its own instruments and with the authority formally or operationally granted to them, to the creation of the law. Sometimes they work together, but more often they are competing with each other.

To these three, perhaps there is a new legal formant that is increasing its power. Digital law is emerging from collective practices of experts and operators, corporations and private institutions with international vocation and strategic economic value. These actors as a sort of practical formant are shaping the process of law making through three primary mechanisms[52]: first, by leveraging contractual autonomy to unilaterally draft and impose terms of use on users; second, through lobbying efforts aimed at influencing public authorities and lawmakers to secure regulatory advantages; and third, by converging on shared sectoral practices, thereby contributing to the development of an autonomous, non-binding body of norms—akin to the new *lex mercatoria* in transnational commercial law.[53]

---

[48] Pollicino (2022).

[49] Bignami (2018), p. 22.

[50] Mantelero and Fanucci (2022).

[51] Sacco (1991a, 1991b).

[52] Kadour and Zoboli (2021), Wagner and Eidenmüller (2023), and Mattei (2023).

[53] Berger (2010) and Cuniberti (2014). For investigating the historical background of the concept of lex mercatoria towards its theoretical foundation in Sixties made by Schmitthof and Goldmann see De Ruysscher (2020).

The emergence of private actors as legal formant alternative to the traditional ones in the digital industry is related with the privatisation of access to and exploration of cyberspace. Very Large Online Platforms (VLOPs) and Very Large Online Search Engines (VLOSEs) derive their increasing political salience not solely from economic dominance, but from their effective control over large-scale digital infrastructures and communicative architectures. This operational centrality has progressively assumed a quasi-public character, exemplified in the European regulatory context by Article 36 of the Digital Services Act (DSA), which requires these entities to ensure the continuity and reliability of services during public emergencies—thus de facto assigning them responsibilities traditionally incumbent upon public authorities in the domain of security and crisis management. This normative development reflects a broader and more profound transformation: the delegation of sovereign-like functions to private transnational actors, whose decision-making power often escapes democratic accountability and judicial scrutiny. In the United States context, an illustrative example can be found in the case law concerning section 230 Communications Decency Act 1997.[54]

The manner in which these new actors wield power within the political arena has recently been made evident by the fact-checking matter. Despite the DSA's introduction of stricter obligations regarding content moderation and systemic risk mitigation, the regime governing the integrity of the information space in EU remains, in large part, voluntary and self-regulatory. The EU Code of Practice on Disinformation, initially adopted to foster a safer, more transparent and trustworthy digital environment, was signed by the major platforms. However, its effectiveness has been undermined by the non-binding nature of its commitments. Although in February 2025 the European Commission and the European Board for Digital Services formally endorsed the Code's integration into the DSA framework—by initiating its conversion under Article 45 DSA, which allows voluntary codes of conduct to become enforceable regulatory instruments—the reality on the ground remains ambiguous. Several key actors have strategically circumvented their duties related to fact-checking and the content moderation. Meta (under Zuckerberg), along with Google, YouTube and LinkedIn, have largely replaced independent third-party fact-checking mechanisms with internal, opaque systems, while the platform X (formerly Twitter), under Elon Musk, has promoted the community notes model[55]—a crowdsourced approach that, while participatory in appearance, raises concerns about reliability, vulnerability to manipulation, and the abdication of editorial responsibility.

In digital law, VLOPs and VLOSEs are not only setting the rules but also adjudicating disputes through internal complaint mechanisms,[56] as Paglietti highlights in this volume. Their role as a legal formant is evident in the way they have compelled

[54] Key case law includes Zeran v. America Online, Inc. (4th Cir. 1997); Reno v. ACLU (U.S. Supreme Court 1997); and Barrett v. Rosenthal (Cal. Supreme Court 2006). For an analysis see Santoni (2024), p. 98 et seq.. The most recent development is Gonzalez v. Google LLC (2023), although the U.S. Supreme Court's ruling is not definitive.

[55] Polona (2025).

[56] Wagner and Eidenmüller (2021).

European institutions to follow the trend of Online Dispute Resolution (ODR)[57] and to establish redress mechanisms (e.g., Art. 21 DSA).[58]

These dynamics expose a structural asymmetry in the enforcement of digital governance principles, as regulatory frameworks struggle to constrain the discretion of private actors performing de facto public functions, particularly in managing the information ecosystem. In this light, the EU digital order is being reshaped not only by legal norms and governmental actions, but also by the evolving political economy of platform power, where legitimacy is increasingly negotiated outside traditional state structures.

This privatization of regulatory and adjudicatory functions creates a constitutional imbalance, allowing platforms to exercise quasi-public authority without corresponding democratic accountability. It underscores the limits of technocratic and expert-driven governance, and points instead to the need for institutional designs that expand participation in norm-setting and oversight. As argued below, this is where the PNS notion of extended peer communities becomes critical.

4 Human-Machine Interaction in the Context of the Post-Normal Science Debate

All legal formants involved in the regulation of HMI can be regarded as critical within the framework of Post-Normal Science—a paradigm of decision-making marked by uncertain facts, contested values, high stakes, and urgent action. By combining descriptive and prescriptive functions, this framework could serve both as an analytical lens for understanding the shifting challenges of technological evolution and as a methodological guide for scientists, policymakers, and stakeholders engaged with the complex socio-technical issues that arise in this context.

4.1 Post-Normal Science: From Theory to Actionable Governance Strategies in Science-Driven Domains

PNS emerged in the 1990s within science-driven domains as a response to profound shifts in both scientific practices and the wider societal landscapes.[59]

For a long time, science was seen as a provider of absolute truth, continuously expanding our knowledge and control over the world. This perspective led to a simplistic view of the relationship between science and policy, where scientific findings were expected to directly inform and guide political decision-making. However,

[57] Pálfi (2024).

[58] Rainey et al. (2021).

[59] Funtowicz and Ravetz (1990, 1993). The 1990 book lays the groundwork, but the 1993 Futures article is widely regarded as the foundational statement of PNS.

a series of events progressively challenged this perspective, with the development and use of atomic weapons during World War II being, of course, the pivotal moment that dramatically transformed how scientific knowledge intersects with political power and decision-making. Subsequent events—from the environmental crises of the 1960s highlighted in Rachel Carson's 'Silent Spring' (1962), to nuclear accidents like Three Mile Island (1979) and Chernobyl (1986), and the BSE ('mad cow') crisis in the UK (1986–2001)—have further exposed the profound moral and political implications of scientific research, continuing the trajectory initiated by the atomic era.[60]

In response to emerging challenges, risk analysts initially turned to computer modelling of hazardous situations, assigning probabilities to potential adverse events. This approach aimed to provide policymakers with precise numerical guidance for decision-making. However, when uncertainties were factored into these calculations, a paradoxical situation often emerged, highlighting the limitations of traditional risk assessment methods. This paradox is often described as 'zero-infinity' risk, brilliantly capturing scenarios where the probability of an event is extremely small (approaching zero), yet its potential damage is immeasurably large (approaching infinity).[61]

In 1972, Alvin Weinberg encapsulated these situations in his concept of 'trans-science'. Weinberg believed that the associated challenges could be addressed through the development of more sophisticated measurement techniques.[62] While his perspective acknowledged the complexity of certain scientific problems in policy contexts, it did not fully recognize, however, the inherent limitations of quantitative approaches in some scenarios. Instead, it adhered to the traditional paradigm of science as a purely objective endeavour. This approach, despite being innovative for its time, still operated within the framework of science as a provider of truth, failing to fully consider the intricate interplay between scientific knowledge, uncertainty, and policy decisions in high-stakes scenarios.

The emergence of PNS, as conceptualized by Silvio Funtowicz and Jerry Ravetz, reflected this critical moment of epistemological and methodological transition, where the boundaries between scientific expertise and political decision-making began to blur. Although the full public maturing of PNS arrived about two decades after their original defining paper (1993), its intellectual roots run deep into the transformative scientific and social experiences of the late twentieth century.[63]

Funtowicz and Ravetz's concept represented a fundamental reimagining of policy debates involving scientific input, moving away from the traditional linear model of science as a purely objective, autonomous domain. Instead, PNS acknowledged that

---

[60] The historical turning points from the atomic era to environmental and health crises have been widely documented by Jasanoff (1990).

[61] Royal Society (1992) and Haimes (2009). Funtowicz and Ravetz (1992). These works highlight the challenge posed by events with extremely low probabilities but potentially catastrophic consequences, exposing fundamental limits of traditional probabilistic risk assessment methods.

[62] Weinberg (1972).

[63] Infra, footnote 64.

scientific knowledge is not created in a vacuum but is profoundly shaped by social values, political contexts, and multiple legitimate perspectives.

This realization led to an important corollary: in some problematic contexts, it is imprudent to assume that uncertainty could be easily quantified (such as with error bars) or that the quality of scientific information could be presumed without scrutiny. Funtowicz and Ravetz theoretically identify a specific category of policy-related scientific situations that require novel and diverse methodological approaches. This category is characterized by four key attributes, often summarized in the widely cited statement: 'facts are uncertain, values in dispute, stakes high and decisions urgent'.[64] This concise formulation not only encapsulates the essence of the complex scenarios PNS seeks to address, but also underscores the challenges of decision-making in contexts where traditional approaches fall short. Its primary significance lies in bridging the gap between scientific knowledge and policy-making, enabling PNS's theoretical insights to be effectively translated into actionable policy strategies.

As the PNS framework developed, its dual nature as both a descriptive and prescriptive tool became increasingly apparent. Accordingly, the term 'post-normal' can be contrasted with two prevailing notions of 'normality'.[65]

The first notion of 'normality' refers to Thomas Kuhn's (1962) concept of scientific research as primarily consisting of puzzle-solving within the bounds of an established paradigm. This approach assumes a stable, shared framework that governs the questions scientists ask, the methods they use, and the solutions they seek, with little need to interrogate the underlying assumptions of the paradigm itself.

The second notion of 'normality' refers to policy context and posits that expert-driven, technocratic approaches are sufficient to provide an adequate knowledge foundation for policy decisions.

Although these two notions arise in different contexts, they both emphasize quantifiable metrics and rely on the premise that scientific and technological advancements inherently align with societal progress. This alignment reflects a type of "technocratic optimism", which assumes that complex societal challenges can be resolved through the application of technical expertise alone, with limited consideration of uncertainty, plural values, or systemic risks.[66]

---

[64] Funtowicz and Ravetz (1993), p. 744.

[65] Ravetz (1999) and Funtowicz and Ravetz (2003).

[66] For a well-known critical and reflexive perspective on technology and modernity, see also Beck (1992).

4.2 A "Skilled Management of [...] Uncertainties, Involving All Who Have a Concern for the Issue": The Precaution Principle, the Extended Peer Community, and Their Potential Implementation in the AI Field

In their recent works, Funtowicz and Ravetz reflect on how PNS has evolved, gaining influence across diverse scientific and policy domains since their seminal 1993 paper, while deepening crucial connections between epistemology and governance. Central to this evolution is PNS's pivotal reconceptualization of scientific practice: the shift from pursuing 'truth' to emphasizing 'quality.'[67] As they articulate it, 'In the social process of science, quality is achieved, not by a delusory pursuit of certainty, but by the skilled management of its uncertainties, involving all who have a concern for the issue'.[68]

Retrospectively, it can be argued that two key notions have been fundamental in operationalizing this transformative shift: the precaution principle and the extended peer community.[69]

It is no coincidence that the Wingspread Statement, which famously articulated the precautionary principle in 1998, emerged alongside theoretical advancements in PNS.[70] Both were part of a broader intellectual response to the increasing recognition of complexity, uncertainty, and societal tensions surrounding science and policy in the late twentieth century.[71] The principle challenges traditional scientific and regulatory approaches in several significant ways. Firstly, it shifts the burden of proof, requiring those advocating for an activity to demonstrate its safety rather than placing the onus on critics to prove potential harm. This reversal contrasts with the conventional approach, which typically assumes safety until evidence of harm is presented. Furthermore, the precautionary principle embraces uncertainty, enabling policymakers to take proactive measures when potential risks are scientifically plausible, even without complete empirical evidence. This acceptance of uncertainty represents a paradigmatic move from deterministic scientific models to a more adaptive, contextual approach to knowledge production and risk management. Finally, unlike traditional scientific approaches that strive for value-neutrality, the precautionary principle explicitly integrates ethical considerations and societal values into the decision-making process.[72]

---

[67] Funtowicz and Ravetz (2003).

[68] Funtowicz and Ravetz (2020).

[69] Rosa and Dietz (1998) and Ravetz (2004).

[70] Stirling (2008).

[71] Raffensperger and Tickner (1999).

[72] "Although falling short of prescriptive decision rules, the precautionary principle does suggest a range of more modest, open-ended, but nonetheless highly effective methodologies and general qualities, which offer ways to complement and improve on conventional risk assessment. As such, it is clear that—contrary to common assertions—the precautionary principle is of practical relevance as much to risk assessment as to risk management. Precaution does not automatically entail bans and phase-outs, but instead calls for deliberate and comprehensive attention to contending policy

The precautionary principle is a general principle of EU law, laid down in the Treaty on the Functioning of the European Union (art. 191) and EU case law. There is compelling and well-established evidence demonstrating its effectiveness in guiding EU legislation and navigating complex policy landscapes, particularly in the areas of environmental protection and public health.[73]

A prominent example are the Directives in the field of water policy, which underscores the EU's commitment to preventing environmental degradation proactively, rather than reacting to established harm.[74] Similarly, the application of the precautionary principle has led the EU to adopt some of the world's most restrictive GMO regulations.[75] The European Green Deal—emphasizing reductions in greenhouse gas emissions despite uncertainties about future climate scenarios—further illustrates a proactive stance that explicitly acknowledges scientific uncertainty, shifting the central question from "Can we definitively prove this is harmful?" to "How can we responsibly manage potential risks given our current understanding?".[76]

In public health, the precautionary principle has shaped several chemical regulations and measures addressing food safety. During the BSE crisis, for instance, EU institutions relied on this principle to prioritize public health over economic interests, embodying a cautious approach in the face of scientific uncertainty regarding food safety. More recently, the COVID-19 pandemic further demonstrated the principle's relevance, as rapid preventive measures—such as travel restrictions and vaccine approvals—were implemented amid evolving scientific knowledge.

Crucially, the precautionary principle recognizes that in post-normal situations, some effects may be irreversible and thus require careful and inclusive deliberation. Within this framework, the connection between 'managing uncertainties' through

---

or technology pathways. Far from being in tension with science, precaution offers a way to be more measured and rational about uncertainty, ambiguity and ignorance": Stirling (2007). See also Peel (2005).

[73] Stirling and Tickner (2004). More recently, a 2022 report by the RECIPES Consortium provides a detailed analysis of the precautionary principle's application in the EU, noting that cost-benefit analysis often has limited utility in this context due to the inherent uncertainties surrounding risks and benefits. See RECIPES Consortium, Revisiting the Application of the Precautionary Principle in the EU (Final Report, January 2022), available at: https://recipes-project.eu. The acronym RECIPES stands for "REconciling sCience, Innovation and Precaution through the Engagement of Stakeholders."

[74] https://environment.ec.europa.eu/topics/water_en.

[75] However, there are ongoing debates about the consistency and effectiveness of its application, and some regulatory developments and court decisions have interpreted its use narrowly or called for additional guidance. See Guida (2021).

[76] For a recent overview of EU environmental policy, see European Parliament, Environmental Policy: General Principles and Basic Framework, available at: https://www.europarl.europa.eu/factsheets/en/sheet/71/environment-policy-general-principles-and-basic-framework.

precautionary measures and 'involving all who have a concern' becomes essential. The precautionary principle not only urges consideration of complex, long-term impacts that standard risk assessment methods might overlook, but also advocates for broad participation and inclusion of perspectives beyond traditional expert knowledge.[77]

It is therefore unsurprising that, following the precautionary principle, another pillar of the PNS framework has gained prominence: the concept of the 'extended peer community'.[78] This concept represents another significant departure from the two prevailing notions of 'normality', as it further reinforces the paradigm shift from pursuing absolute scientific 'truth' to prioritizing 'quality'. Aligned with the "deliberative turn" in democratic theory—which advocates expanding citizen participation in democracy beyond mere voting—the concept reframes uncertainty as a collaborative opportunity to develop more robust and contextually nuanced understanding. The key insight is that in complex, high-stakes situations with significant uncertainties, the recognition of multiple legitimate knowledge sources become crucial for comprehensive problem-solving and decision-making.

One significant manifestation of this concept is the Aarhus Convention, formally known as the United Nations Economic Commission for Europe (UNECE) Convention on access to information, public participation in decision-making, and access to justice in environmental matters. This international agreement has established a foundation for ensuring that citizens and stakeholders have a voice in shaping policies that affect their lives and environments, and has prompted ongoing discussions on public participation and stakeholder engagement in EU environmental politics. A prominent example can also be seen in the European Green Deal and related initiatives, which strongly emphasize that citizens should be a driving force in the transition to a sustainable economy. This involves engaging various stakeholders—including local communities, NGOs, and industry representatives—in discussions about environmental policies, thereby creating an extended peer community that contributes to policy formulation and implementation. The European Climate Pact, which encourages local authorities and citizens to collaborate on climate action initiatives related to the European Green Deal, further reinforces the role of extended peer communities in environmental governance, by fostering partnerships between governments and local knowledge and experiences.

Participatory approaches such as citizens' assemblies and focus groups extend this ethos by gathering input from diverse populations on sustainability issues. These platforms exemplify "technologies of humility,"[79] fostering broader democratic participation and enabling stakeholders to evaluate policy proposals through the lens of lived experience and local context. This recognition of the value of inclusive, multi-perspective engagement is echoed in the European Commission's Group of Chief Scientific Advisors, which has recently stressed the need to draw "on all good science from all scientific disciplines and perspectives that could contribute to the issue at

[77] Funtowicz and Ravetz (1990).

[78] Funtowicz and Ravetz (2020) and Ravetz (2004).

[79] Jasanoff (2003).

hand. This includes natural sciences, engineering, medicine, social sciences and humanities".[80]

This model of inclusive, multi-perspective engagement offers a template for AI governance, where the conformity assessment procedures for high-risk AI systems could be expanded to require meaningful engagement with affected communities and civil society organizations. This would move beyond current market surveillance mechanisms to include systematic consultation with labour unions, civil rights organizations, and consumer advocacy groups in evaluating AI systems' societal impacts.[81]

5 Framing AI as a Post-Normal Challenge

There is no doubt that applying the PNS model to the field of AI presents opportunities and challenges alike. For instance, the strong competitive pressure both AI companies and governments face often leads to a reluctance in acknowledging uncertainties or potential limitations. This nurtures a narrative of technological inevitability and progress that tends to sideline the crucial goal of safeguarding public interests.[82] Moreover, major tech corporations and research institutions that dominate AI development are well known for prioritizing proprietary knowledge, often at the expense of fostering inclusive, multi-stakeholder approaches to knowledge production. This concentration of power in the AI sector exacerbates societal imbalances and raises ethical concerns, while at the same time undermining the two core premises of PNS: adopting a precautionary regulatory approach and broadening scientific expertise beyond traditional technocratic boundaries. Despite these challenges, we argue in the following discussion that the dynamics already emerging in the early stages of HMI strongly highlight the critical need for inclusive and adaptive approaches that can mitigate risks and build trust and accountability in the development and deployment of transformative AI technologies. We also contend that UNESCO's endorsement of PNS principles in the AI field adds further weight to this viewpoint, reinforcing the importance of such approaches in addressing emerging technological challenges.

[80] European Commission: Group of Chief Scientific Advisors and Directorate-General for Research and Innovation, Scientific advice to European policy in a complex world, Publications Office, 2019, https://data.europa.eu/doi/10.2777/80320.

[81] See infra, Sect. 6.2.

[82] See generally Jasanoff (2016).

5.1 *The PNS as a Thoughtful Framework Tool for AI Development and Governance*

Much like steering a high-speed vehicle across uncharted terrain, AI's rapid development presents the fundamental challenge of harnessing its momentum while simultaneously anticipating what lies ahead, which is needed to provide direction and manage risks. To be sure, as Floridi compellingly states, "the best way to catch the technology train is not to chase it, but to be at the next station".[83] Yet, the governance challenge is arguably compounded by dual layers of uncertainty. First, there is fundamental uncertainty about the trajectory and implications of AI development itself, which are captured by the aforementioned 'zero-infinity' paradox—where immediate harms or failures may appear negligible, yet the future consequences could be vast and unpredictable. Second, we face a complex policy landscape where regulators must make decisions with far-reaching ramifications based on incomplete understanding of AI's full capabilities and hazards. A misstep in regulation could either impede AI's transformative benefits to society or, conversely, result in harm and exploitation.

These underlying tensions exemplify the challenges anticipated by PNS in science-driven policy domains, where traditional approaches may be insufficient due to high stakes and inherent uncertainties. AI's unique characteristics—particularly its technological exceptionalism and vast economic potential—further amplify the stakes surrounding both its development and governance. Moreover, there are significant geopolitical dimensions to consider, as demonstrated by the emergence of China's DeepSeek[84] and, on a different note, the recent AI Action Summit in Paris.[85] While the geopolitical stakes surrounding AI are evident in the competition among the United States, China, and the European Union, this competition extends far beyond technological innovation to include control over data, chip development research, computing power, and regulatory influence.

Against this backdrop, it is becoming increasingly clear that effective and sustainable AI development requires much more than just technical expertise or a relentless expansion of datasets and computational resources.[86] As international discussions unfold, a more nuanced understanding is taking shape: AI development must involve

---

[83] Floridi (2018), p. 6.

[84] Daniels and Dohmen (2025).

[85] A central focus of the summit was the "Statement on Inclusive and Sustainable Artificial Intelligence for People and the Planet," which underscored the principles that AI must be open, inclusive, transparent, ethical, safe, secure, and trustworthy. The declaration also emphasized making AI sustainable for both people and the planet. However, the summit faced significant challenges in achieving a unified stance on AI ethics: notably, the United States and the United Kingdom declined to sign the declaration, citing concerns that some language was too restrictive and could stifle innovation. U.S. Vice President JD Vance criticized Europe's stringent regulatory approach, advocating instead for a more innovation-friendly approach (https://www.bbc.com/news/articles/c8edn0n58gwo).

[86] Bender et al. (2021).

an unprecedented and delicate art of bridging scientific and ideological divides, negotiating competing national interests, and constructing collaborative mechanisms that can ensure AI ultimately serves broader, collective human interests on a truly global scale.

While our understanding of its full potential and risks remains incomplete, anchoring the policy framework on conclusive evidence would leave society vulnerable. AI exceptional nature arises indeed from many factors, including its ability to continuously learn, adapt, and autonomously make decisions in potentially malicious ways that traditional technologies do not. As AI continues to evolve at the intersection of various disciplines, integrating knowledge from diverse fields is crucial for fostering a comprehensive approach that addresses both technological advancements and their societal implications. A post-normal approach is particularly suitable in this respect, as it creates a framework where technical expertise meets public concerns in addressing uncertainties that traditional scientific methods alone cannot resolve. This means acknowledging that non-scientific perspectives on hard-to-quantify risks of AI technologies bring valuable insights to the table, and that AI research must navigate a complex interplay between technological knowledge and human values. As Ananny and Crawford argue, understanding algorithms goes far beyond simply peering inside their code.[87] The call for algorithmic transparency, while well-intentioned, may not fully or adequately[88] address the ethical challenges these systems present. Even if we could fully understand the technical components of an algorithm, its actual behaviour and implications—including uncertainties and unintended consequences—only become apparent within social systems and human relationships.[89]

As we will see, acknowledging the limits of certainty in AI research becomes particularly crucial in light of the AI Act's implementation structure, as the processes of determining risk levels and ensuring compliance opens up unprecedented opportunities for scientists with AI expertise, including social scientists, to move into advisory, auditing, and other policy roles.[90] Interdisciplinary integration does not necessarily make these processes easier, nor does it guarantee that AI will prioritize the broader social, ethical, and cultural contexts in which it operates, but it can contribute to making AI development and governance more responsive to social needs.

Meanwhile, AI is advancing at a pace that outstrips the ability of existing policy frameworks to keep up. It challenges conventional systems of risk management and control, including those introduced by the EU AI Act, which categorizes AI systems into risk levels but struggles to address systems that rapidly shift between categories as they evolve or when deployed in different contexts. For instance, generative models initially classified as "limited risk" can quickly develop capabilities that push them into "high risk" territory when fine-tuned or combined with other

[87] Ananny and Crawford (2018).

[88] See also de Laat (2018).

[89] Kitchin (2017).

[90] See infra, par. 6.

systems. Simultaneously, traditional transparency and consent mechanisms become inadequate safeguards against potentially exploitative technological practices, as they assume users can comprehend the full implications of data processing that even experts struggle to interpret.[91] This growing gap between technological progress and regulatory capacity was recently highlighted in the International Scientific Report on the Safety of Advanced AI (January 29, 2025), which explicitly advocates for more precautionary measures—such as removing personally identifiable information (PII) and undesirable content from the training data of general-purpose AI.[92]

All of the above highlights that the PNS fourfold characterization of 'post-normal' situations—"facts are uncertain, values in dispute, stakes high, and decisions urgent"—accurately encapsulates the current state of AI development and governance. Viewing AI through this post-normal lens serves a dual purpose. First, it emphasizes the need for sustained global collaboration and research aimed at developing a deeper, more qualitative understanding of both AI's internal mechanisms and its real-world impacts and risks.[93] Second, it calls for a fundamental transformation in regulatory approaches, moving beyond seemingly objective, evidence-based solutions to explicitly acknowledge both the limits of certainty and the value judgments that inevitably shape policy positions.[94]

5.2 *Unpredictable Dynamics in Human-Machine Interaction: Some Cautionary Tales*

The Vienna Manifesto on Digital Humanism emphasizes the principle that "humans must shape technologies in accordance with their values and needs, instead of allowing technologies to shape humans".[95] Unfortunately, that is what is happening in the so-called 'algorithmic regulation'. The issue is not whether technology should be human-centred, as humans are already at the core of AI system design. Rather, the focus must be on protecting individuals from the unilateral asymmetries of power—whether private, public, or technological—that are generated or amplified by AI applications.

In practice, this ideal is contradicted by the experience with algorithmic profiling in social media, as described above. Despite the development of regulations to address the challenges posed by AI applications worldwide, the experience of the two decades since the large-scale advent of social media and algorithmic profiling has

[91] Cohen (2023) and Mantelero (2024).

[92] International AI Safety Report (arXiv:2501.17805), part. p. 208.

[93] Bender et al. (2021).

[94] O'Neil (2016) goes so far as to propose that AI developers should adopt an ethical framework akin to the Hippocratic Oath taken by medical professionals, with a commitment to "do no harm." This framework would guide developers in making ethical decisions and foster transparency, continuous learning, and interdisciplinary collaboration, ensuring that AI serves the broader interests of society.

[95] Werthner et al. (2019).

shown that predicting the impact of new technologies on individuals and society—and preventing resulting harms—remains a significant challenge. The distortions mentioned above, moreover, remain largely unaddressed by current regulations.

The legal framework established by the European Regulation on Data Protection exemplifies the complexity of the challenges and the limits of the legislative intervention. While the General Data Protection Regulation (GDPR) mandates that user consent must be freely given, specific, informed, unambiguous (Art. 4.11 GDPR), demonstrable, and withdrawable (Art. 7.1 and 7.3 GDPR), research on online user behaviour reveals a persistent privacy paradox. This paradox refers to the gap between users' stated attitudes toward privacy and their actual online behaviours.[96] The Dual Process Model of Cognition[97] further elucidates this phenomenon: individuals often overlook threats to privacy and potential protective measures in favour of quick access to services or a more engaging online experience. This cognitive trade-off underscores the need for more effective regulatory tools that consider human behaviour and decision-making processes.

The experience with algorithmic profiling in social media serves as a cautionary tale. The above described HMI first stage revealed the opaque and far-reaching impact that such systems can exert on personal identity formation and collective cognitive dynamics, often reinforcing polarisation, disinformation, and affective manipulation. The trajectory of HMI reveals an escalating pattern of epistemic and normative complexity marked by the introduction of CAs, simulating human dialogue and mediating access to knowledge without genuine semantic understanding or accountability, and newly LRMs, capable of autonomous reasoning, goal-directed problem solving, and recursive interaction with users. These systems not only influence perception, but may also begin to shape the logical structure of human deliberation itself, thereby amplifying the potential for subtle, systemic distortions in decision-making processes and epistemic autonomy.

Lessons from earlier stages of HMI have largely gone unheeded until OpenAI launched ChatGPT in November 2022. ChatGPT prompted a series of significant political responses, including the UK's AI White Paper[98] (March 29, 2023), China's draft generative AI measures[99] (April 11, 2023), and EU Parliament amendments to the AI Act[100] (May 11 and June 14, 2023).

---

[96] The theory of the 'Privacy Paradox' is illustrated with a review of the literature by Barth and De Jong (2017), and Waldman (2020).

[97] This refers to the 'Dual Process Model of Cognition', which Daniel Kahneman simplified into two systems of thought: intuitive (system 1) and rational (system 2): Kahneman (2003, 2011).

[98] Department for Science, Innovation and Technology and Office for Artificial Intelligence (UK), A pro-innovation approach to AI regulation, Command Paper No. 815., 29 March 2023 (Updated 3 August 2023) (White Paper, 2023). Available at https://www.gov.uk/government/publications/ai-regulation-a-pro-innovation-approach/white-paper.

[99] Cyberspace Administration of China, Interim Measures for the Management of Generative Artificial Intelligence (AI) Services, 10 July 2023 (IMMGAIS, 2023), available at https://www.cac.gov.cn/2023-07/13/c_1690898327029107.htm.

[100] EU Parliament amendments to the Commission's AI Act Proposal, Amendments adopted by the European Parliament on 14 June 2023 on the proposal for a regulation of the European Parliament and of the Council on laying down harmonised rules on artificial intelligence (Artificial

Concerns about the spread of chatbots and the possible threats associated with them have also emerged at the international level, triggering a number of initiatives already underway and several others that are in the pipeline. UNESCO has published several papers dealing with ChatGPT, ranging from a Guidance for generative AI in education and research to a policy paper containing analyses of new AI technologies through the lens of UNESCO's Recommendation on AI Ethics.[101]

The United Nations' approach to AI, as reflected in its various initiatives and documents, is particularly relevant for our purposes as it offers a compelling framework for conceptualizing AI as a post-normal challenge. By exploring UNESCO's approach resonance with the PNS principles, we can better understand how PNS concepts, despite originated in distinct policy domains, can contribute to a more comprehensive and inclusive framework for AI governance, one that addresses the unique challenges posed by this transformative technology while fostering responsible innovation and global cooperation.

5.3 Key Insights from UNESCO's Approach

Before we delve into a critical analysis of the EU AI Act, we will highlight two key examples of the alignment of UNESCO's approach with the PNS principles: the Readiness Assessment Methodology (RAM)[102] and the Ethical Impact Assessment (EIA).[103] Both are integral components of UNESCO's Recommendation on AI Ethics—the first global standard on AI ethics, developed through an inclusive, multistakeholder process in 2021 and applicable to all 194 member states of UNESCO.[104]

Currently piloted in the first cohort of 50 countries worldwide, the Readiness Assessment Methodology (RAM) closely reflects the PNS concept of the "extended peer community", particularly through its emphasis on inclusivity, participatory approaches, collaborative knowledge sharing, and multidimensional analysis. In its normative effort to help countries evaluate their AI ecosystem across legal, social, economic, scientific, and technological dimensions, RAM prioritize inclusivity by establishing steering committees that bring together representatives from government, the private sector, academia, and civil society, resonating with the PNS call for involving stakeholders beyond traditional experts. Participatory tools such as

Intelligence Act) and amending certain Union legislative acts (COM[2021]0206 – C9-0146/2021 – 2021/0106[COD]), 14 June 2023 available at https://www.europarl.europa.eu/doceo/document/TA-9-2023-0236_EN.html.

[101] UNESCO, Recommendation on the Ethics of Artificial Intelligence, 23 November 2021. https://unesdoc.unesco.org/ark:/48223/pf0000381137.

[102] UNESCO (2023b).

[103] UNESCO (2023a).

[104] UNESCO (2021).

questionnaires, feedback mechanisms, and interdisciplinary workshops are also integral to the RAM, reflecting PNS's emphasis on incorporating diverse knowledge and perspectives. Moreover, the multidimensional assessment of AI ecosystems—spanning legal, social, cultural, economic, educational, scientific, and technological dimensions—champions a holistic approach that fosters dialogue across sectors, echoing PNS's commitment to recognition of systemic complexity.

This comprehensive approach enables a thorough evaluation of national AI ecosystems, while the subsequent publication of results on UNESCO's Observatory and discussions at the Global Forum on the Ethics of AI serve as platforms for international knowledge exchange, allowing countries to share experiences and best practices during a period of rapid change in the AI governance landscape.[105] This transparency plays a crucial role in other important multi-stakeholder platforms implemented within the UN's framework, such the AI for Good platform,[106] the Commission on Science and Technology for Development,[107] and the Multistakeholder Forum on Science, Technology and Innovation for the Sustainable Development Goals.[108] Accordingly, one might say that the RAM is not just an assessment tool, but part of a broader, collaborative and interactive approach to understanding and managing AI's complex global implications. As underscored by the United Nations White Paper on AI Governance, a document recently published that reflects deep concerns about the current technological governance landscape, the RAM's significance lies not merely in diagnostic capabilities, but in its potential to rebalance power dynamics increasingly dominated by the "disproportionately large role of the private sector".[109] The document emphasizes that by prioritizing multi-stakeholder collaboration and engaging marginalized communities, including those from the Global South,[110] the UN aims to ensure that AI governance reflects a wide range of societal needs and values.

Alongside with the plea for inclusivity, collaborative learning and co-production of knowledge, the commitment to anticipatory mechanisms and "future-proof" regulation is another core issue where the UNESCO's Recommendation on the Ethics of AI and its implementation tools closely align with PNS. The above-mentioned White Paper provides compelling evidence of this alignment, acknowledging "the added value of risk and opportunity assessments that also duly incorporate human rights considerations and the need to adopt the precautionary principle when developing new technologies and AI.[111]

The case for the adoption of the precautionary principle emerges most notably from the Ethical Impact Assessment (EIA) and its methodology's emphasis on AI as a complex socio-technical system with profound and potentially unpredictable

---

[105] https://www.unesco.org/en/forum-ethics-ai.

[106] https://aiforgood.itu.int/.

[107] https://unctad.org/topic/commission-on-science-and-technology-for-development.

[108] https://sdgs.un.org/tfm/STIForum2025.

[109] United Nations System (2024), p. 38.

[110] United Nations System (2024), p. 23 and 42.

[111] United Nations System (2024), p. 38.

impacts. Grounded in the UNESCO Recommendation's values, the EIA fundamentally recognize that AI systems do not exist in isolation, but are deeply entangled with "intergenerational and historical biases in data collection relating to gender, race, culture and other factors".[112]

In practice, this means systematically scrutinizing AI systems across several critical dimensions, so as to proactively identify both potential ethical risks and unintended societal consequences. To ensure a comprehensive assessment, this exercise is undertaken in consultation with a variety of stakeholders, including experts, developers, impacted/potentially impacted parties, etc.[113] This might involve for example analysing how a recommendation algorithm could potentially reinforce echo chambers, amplify misinformation, or create unexpected social dynamics. For instance, if a hiring algorithm shows disproportionate screening out of candidates from certain racial or gender groups, the EIA would flag these systemic biases.[114] In the same vein, an autonomous vehicle's assessment would go beyond technical performance to examine broader implications—from its interaction with existing transportation systems to its impact on employment and its role in ethical decision-making scenarios.[115]

Rooted in a "model of anticipatory governance in which multidisciplinary collaboration, innovative thinking and transformational future-making are valued",[116] the EIA significantly advances traditional ethical oversight, promoting a culture of ethical responsibility that extends beyond binary assessments (pass/fail) and regulatory compliance and fosters dialogue and cooperation across cultural and institutional boundaries.[117] While it shares the anticipatory nature of conventional ex ante risk assessments, the EIA goes further by offering actionable recommendations to proactively address ethical concerns. Unlike traditional compliance mechanisms that deliver static judgments, the EIA operates thus as an ongoing process, integrating ethical considerations as dynamic and evolving components of governance and innovation.

All of the above not only demonstrates the growing recognition of AI's "post-normal" characteristics but also represents a significant shift toward adaptive, quality-focused ethical governance, balancing forward-looking strategic vision with rigorous contextual grounding. UNESCO's alignment with the core tenets of the PNS framework—notably the precautionary principle and the inclusion of extended peer communities—strongly underscores their relevance in addressing global AI challenges, even though the framework originally emerged in different policy contexts.[118]

---

[112] United Nations System (2024), p. 48.

[113] UNESCO (2023a).

[114] UNESCO (2023a), p. 23.

[115] UNESCO (2023a), p. 25.

[116] United Nations System (2024), p. 44.

[117] Bean et al. (2025).

[118] For a strong advocacy of the need for broad, interdisciplinary engagement in AI governance., see Nowotny (2003).

6 A Post-Normal Critique of the EU AI Act: Navigating Uncertainty and Embracing Digital Vulnerability

The historic enactment of the EU AI Act on August 1, 2024 represented a watershed moment in global technology regulation, culminating a marathon legislative process that sought to navigate the intricate and rapidly evolving AI landscape. As the first comprehensive legal framework for AI governance, the regulation has unsurprisingly become a focal point for debates on how AI should be regulated, the risks it poses, and how to balance innovation with ethics.

In the following section, we assess the EU AI Act through the lens of the PNS framework, highlighting its core shortcomings—most notably its dependence on a risk-based model and industry-led standardization. We argue that advancing a precautionary governance approach and fostering a more inclusive model of co-regulation could ground the framework in a unifying, universally relevant principle: safeguarding against digital vulnerability.

6.1 Rethinking the Risk-Based Approach: Toward Precautionary Governance

While the implementation phase only started on February 2, 2025, the EU AI ACT has already sparked contrasting viewpoints among academics, with critics falling into two main camps. On one side, there are those who fear the regulation may create barriers to scientific innovation; on the other, those who contend that the proposed rules are insufficiently stringent and fail to adequately address potential risks associated with AI technologies.

The first position is notably reflected in Mario Draghi's recent report for the EU Commission, in which the former Italian Prime Minister and European Central Bank chief argues that the EU's regulatory approach represents a potentially stifling regulatory philosophy.[119] While pointing to the existence of "100 tech-focused laws and over 270 regulators active in digital networks across all Member States", Draghi is particularly critical of what he calls the EU's "precautionary approach," which, in his view, imposes "specific business practices ex ante to avert potential risks ex post".[120] This approach, he suggests, prioritizes pre-emptive risk avoidance over flexibility and adaptability, potentially placing undue constraints on innovation and competitiveness.

Draghi's critique of the "precautionary approach" touches on a broader theoretical and practical debate in technology governance—one that holds particular significance given the EU's longstanding reliance on precautionary measures in areas marked by technological uncertainty and high-risk potential, as discussed earlier. It is true that in

[119] Draghi (2024).

[120] Ivi, p. 30.

2020 the European Parliament explicitly advocated for the application of the precautionary principle in relation to new AI-based technologies.[121] This endorsement was not a protectionist stance but a reaffirmation of Europe's constitutional values: a tradition dedicated to safeguarding human dignity, sometimes even above individual liberty.[122] Yet, the key insight emerging from Draghi's critique invites us to move beyond formal declarations and consider a crucial question: Did the EU AI Act truly carry forward the spirit and rigor of the 2020 parliamentary call for precaution? A closer examination reveals a more nuanced reality.

First of all, it is notable that the Act's only precautionary measures—that is, the ban on AI systems deemed to pose unacceptable risks—have faced significant criticism from those who argue, in contrast to Draghi's position, that the Act only prohibits a limited range of AI practices, which they believe is insufficient to address all potential risks. This criticism is particularly warranted when considering the creation of a parallel legal framework for AI deployed by law enforcement, migration, and national security authorities, arguably the most problematic aspect of the Act. As Guido Smorto convincingly underscores, this inconsistency highlights a broader issue: despite the Act's aim to protect fundamental rights and mitigate AI risks, its numerous exceptions and context-specific allowances inadvertently create opportunities for misuse or overreach in highly sensitive areas.

There is also a critical tension within the Act. On one hand, it adopts an ex ante approach, even including precautionary bans for AI practices considered to pose unacceptable risks. On the other hand, its broader framework is largely anchored in conventional risk assessment methodologies—categorizing AI systems into risk levels and emphasizing quantifiable metrics and cost-benefit analyses. It is as if the Act sees AI systems through a dual lens: as dynamic agents whose impacts on society and fundamental rights require vigilance, but also—and perhaps primarily—as products that need to be certified safe before deployment.[123]

The Act categorizes AI systems into four risk levels—unacceptable, high, limited, and minimal risk—establishing a regulatory framework aimed at ensuring that governance aligns with the level of risk associated with different technological applications. While it mandates continuous monitoring and updates, its focus on "known and reasonably foreseeable risks" poses difficulties in aligning with AI's inherently unpredictable nature.[124] It is rather like trying to use rules designed for static objects to govern something that is constantly in motion.

This focus is particularly concerning with high-risk AI systems. It is within this context, in fact, that the Act's dominant approach—far from adopting a precautionary stance—becomes particularly evident. To be sure, the Act requires high-risk AI systems to undergo conformity assessments and continuous monitoring

[121] European Parliament resolution of 20 October 2020 with recommendations to the Commission on a framework of ethical aspects of artificial intelligence, robotics and related technologies.

[122] De Gregorio (2021).

[123] Almada and Petit (2023).

[124] This approach is embedded in several provisions throughout the European AI Act such as Recital 30, Article 4, Article 9, Article 13.

throughout their whole lifecycle, indicating a recognition of the provisional nature of AI safety and reliability. Yet, rather than questioning the fundamental appropriateness of deploying potentially harmful technologies, the Act **treats** these risks as technical problems that can be mitigated to 'acceptable' levels through a set of procedural safeguards—an ethical perspective where the label "ethical" is little more than the new "green", failing to fully engage with the uncertainties and long-term impacts of emerging AI technologies.[125] Moreover, this focus on minimizing known hazards relies on open standards the interpretation of which is largely left to those directly involved in AI development and deployment, potentially leaving further gaps in addressing unforeseen risks associated with high-risk AI systems.

The Fundamental Rights Impact Assessment (FRIA) could have served as a meaningful mechanism to harmonize risk-based and rights-based approaches,[126] aimed at preventing high-risk AI systems from violating fundamental rights. However, the framework is critically undermined by the same limitations found in risk assessments, as it relies more on self-reporting by AI developers and deployers than on robust, independent assessment mechanisms, potentially prioritizing procedural compliance over meaningful protection of fundamental rights. A critical issue lies in the nature of fundamental rights and values. For instance, how does one quantify the value of privacy, freedom of expression, or human dignity? How does one weigh the potential economic benefits of an AI system against its potential to infringe on a fundamental right? Such decisions are inherently qualitative and involve complex, context-dependent considerations that go beyond simple procedural compliance and cost-benefit analyses. Moreover, the FRIA applies selectively, specifically to certain entities—public bodies, entities providing public services—and AI systems categorized as high-risk. As a result, only technologies meeting these criteria fall under its scope.[127]

In essence, the EU AI Act's treatment of high-risk AI systems reveals a regulatory paradigm that implicitly treats AI as a controllable, purely technocratic domain, suggesting a product-centric conceptualization of AI systems. This approach stands in stark contrast to frameworks exemplifying genuine precautionary governance in science-driven domains, such as the EU's regulation of GMOs and, to recall a more pertinent example, UNESCO's regulatory approach to AI. Unlike the AI Act, both of the latter restrict certain technologies (genetic modification and artificial intelligence, respectively) not because they have been proven harmful, but because their long-term effects remain uncertain, thereby reflecting PNS's emphasis on the need to expand precautionary governance in the face of deep uncertainty.

Because a 'lack of evidence of harm' does not necessarily imply 'evidence of no harm,' the AI Act's shift away from a precautionary principle raises questions about its adequacy in addressing the dynamic and evolving nature of AI technologies and their potential societal impacts.

---

[125] Schultz et al. (2025) and Müller (2020).

[126] De Gregorio and Dunn (2022) and Cosentini et al. (2025).

[127] Mantelero (2024).

To be sure, rather than allowing the deployment of emerging technologies as de facto large-scale societal experimentation, the Act seeks to introduce mechanisms for more controlled and responsible innovation. In this context, its establishment of regulatory sandboxes (Articles 57, 58, and 59) represents an experimental institutional approach by the European Union to anticipatory governance. These regulatory sandboxes attempt to bridge the innovation-safety gap by creating controlled testing environments for AI systems prior to market deployment. Under this framework, developers can experiment with innovative technologies under regulatory oversight, theoretically building safeguards against unintended consequences.

However, as it is already clear to many, approval from a sandbox should not be interpreted as a definitive guarantee of safety, as some harmful behaviours or consequences may only emerge in broader deployment contexts or over extended timeframes.[128] This includes issues like 'function creep,' where technologies initially designed for legitimate purposes gradually expand into more intrusive applications.[129] Furthermore, the AI Act does not establish a uniform EU-wide AI regulatory sandbox nor provide a mechanism by which a broad community of stakeholders can raise sandbox inquiries with national competent authorities; instead, it mandates national-level sandboxes that may be operated jointly by multiple Member States but remain under national competent authorities' oversight.[130]

Although the Act allows for post-market monitoring under Article 72(3), its focus on 'known and reasonably foreseeable risks' becomes particularly problematic when considering not only the potential gradual expansion of a technology's use beyond its originally intended purpose but also the emerging landscape of harmful AI behaviours arising from novel methods of circumventing state-of-the-art ethical safeguards, commonly referred to as 'AI jailbreaks'.[131]

These limitations have not gone unnoticed by the scientific community. The abovementioned International Scientific Report on the Safety of Advanced AI (January 29, 2025) unequivocally warns of risks "whose likelihood, nature, and timing remains unusually ambiguous".[132] This stark assessment, coupled with the acknowledgment of an "evidence dilemma" stemming from the rapid pace and unpredictability of advancements in general-purpose AI,[133] compellingly underscores the urgent need to reimagine regulation as an uncertainty-focused and contextually sensitive process, rather than a narrow, deterministic pursuit of technological advancement. To be sure, there is evidence affirming the safety or harmlessness of some AI systems. Yet, the report highlights that, since the publication of the Interim Report just eight months earlier,[134] an increasing body of research suggests that many AI systems—especially general-purpose ones—are rapidly gaining the ability to act as autonomous agents,

[128] Bagni et al. (2025) and Johnson (2023).

[129] Koops (2021).

[130] Bagni et al. (2025), p. 201 et seqq.

[131] Russinovich et al. (2024) and Rao et al. (2024).

[132] International AI Safety Report (arXiv:2501.17805), p. 100.

[133] Ivi, p. 14.

[134] Ivi, p. 19.

capable of planning and pursuing goals independently. This is a critical development to monitor, as it clearly raises concerns about the adequacy of relying solely on procedural compliance rather than implementing more substantive restrictions.

As stated in the Report, risk assessment remains an emerging field within the AI safety community, with no fully validated, systematic methods yet available to evaluate the potential severity and likelihood of harm from AI's increasingly autonomous agents. This also applies to the possible malicious use of AI in sensitive domains, including smartphone assistants, always-listening voice assistants, and its use in healthcare or legal practice,[135] as well as the risks of potential copyright infringement and violations of data rights laws arising from AI-generated content.[136]

Ultimately, a key takeaway from the report is a profound cautionary note about underestimating the radical asymmetry between human cognitive capabilities and artificial intelligence's dramatically superior processing power. This asymmetry manifests in two critically interrelated dimensions: first, AI's growing capacity to function as autonomous agents capable of independently formulating complex strategies, pursuing multi-step goals, and adapting approaches with computational precision that transcends human cognitive boundaries; and second, the equally concerning potential for humans to manipulate and circumvent even the most sophisticated state-of-the-art model ethical safeguards. The confluence of these factors creates a dual threat landscape where AI's autonomous operational capacity can be strategically exploited or inadvertently misdirected, transforming these systems from controlled technological tools into dynamic, unpredictable entities capable of pursuing objectives that humans would never have anticipated and that may undermine human intentions or ethical constraints.

Moreover, the persistent "information gap" between what AI companies know about their systems and what governments and non-industry researchers can access further strengthens this warning.[137] As highlighted in the report, preparing for ambiguous risks requires moving beyond industry-driven frameworks toward a regulatory paradigm that fosters closer collaboration between governments, industry leaders, researchers, and civil society. While this approach does not necessarily bridge the knowledge gap in the lawmaking phase, it would at least ensure that regulatory decisions in the implementation phase are informed by a truly, contextually sensitive process, incorporating a wide range of perspectives. We will explore this issue in greater detail in the following section.

135 Ivi, p. 208.

136 Ivi, p. 144.

137 Ivi, p. 22.

6.2 *Beyond Industry-Driven Standards: Embedding Extended Peer Communities in Co-Regulation*

In the previous section, we argued that the disconnect between the complex, socially embedded nature of AI technologies and expert-driven, risk-based governance approaches is not merely a technical gap but a reflection of deeper, systemic barriers. These barriers, stemming from both the design of AI systems and the structure of regulatory frameworks, resist efforts to reimagine regulation as a more inclusive, collaborative, and contextually sensitive process. As a result, the prevailing approach tends to treat AI as a set of isolated risks to be managed, without fully accounting for the ways in which these technologies are intricately woven into the fabric of society.

This dynamic is further complicated by the outsized role that major technology companies—often referred to as "Big Tech"—play in shaping the AI landscape. The story of Big Tech and the EU AI Act is one of significant conflicts of interest and attempts at influence, at the expense of stronger protections for citizens and more stringent oversight of AI technologies.[138] Across Europe and globally, these companies have not only become the primary funders of AI research but have also established deep financial ties with academic institutions, think tanks, and policy advisory bodies.

This entanglement of corporate power and governance does more than shape the policy process—it also frames how AI itself is understood. When regulatory frameworks are driven by the industry's own narratives of progress and innovation, the risks and benefits of AI are easily flattened into oversimplified terms. Yet, acknowledging the inherent limits of certainty and techno-optimism in AI research is essential—not only as a matter of intellectual honesty but also as a practical necessity for responsible governance. This recognition becomes indeed especially crucial when scientists transition from research roles to policy positions, whether advisory, auditing, or otherwise. In these contexts, they must openly address both the boundaries of their certainty and the underlying values that shape their positions. As emphasized earlier, what makes AI exceptional is not only its promise but also its indeterminacy: its capacity for continuous learning, adaptation, and autonomous action in ways that carry novel and unpredictable harms—risks that conventional technologies cannot replicate.

The evolving implementation structure of the EU AI Act frameworks particularly underscores the need for a balanced and inclusive approach to regulation—one that aligns with the post-normal science movement and integrates the concept of "*extended peer communities*". Grounded in the EU's New Legislative Framework (NLF), the Act combines binding legal requirements with voluntary technical standards largely developed by private sector entities.[139] Yet, as has been noted, "there is a significant gap between the importance of standardisation and the interest shown in

[138] For a recent overview see Corporate Europe Observatory (2025).

[139] Soler Garrido et al. (2024).

it by academic literature, the scientific world and the general public as a whole".[140] While this coregulatory model has proven effective in various contexts, it poses unique challenges in the AI domain. Here, technical standards play a decisive role in shaping how companies address risk management, data governance, and human oversight. If left chiefly in industry's hands, these standards could tilt the balance toward corporate priorities, sidelining broader social considerations.[141]

The development of standards on which the operational effectiveness of the AI Act critically depends is a process led by two pivotal yet relatively obscure organizations: the European Committee for Standardization (CEN) and the European Committee for Electrotechnical Standardization (CENELEC). These private international nonprofits, comprising 34 member countries, maintain extensive networks with European stakeholders, including those from non-EU nations like the United Kingdom. Given the EU's determination to protect its technological sovereignty in AI governance despite tensions with international partners, the standardization landscape has evolved into a geopolitical battleground, with the United States pushing for greater collaboration in standards development. This is well illustrated by several European Commission initiatives designed to limit non-EU entities' influence in standardization processes, a notable example of which emerged in December 2022, when the European Telecommunications Standards Institute (ETSI), known for its openness to foreign companies, was excluded from the AI Act's draft standardization request.[142]

CEN-CENELEC has taken steps to include civil society stakeholders in the standardization process, notably through the Joint Technical Committee 21 (JTC 21) on Artificial Intelligence. This committee has established a dedicated Task Group on Inclusiveness to ensure broader stakeholder representation, including civil society organizations, consumer groups, and NGOs. Initiatives such as educational webinars have been launched to empower civil society actors to participate more actively in shaping AI standards.[143]

Despite these efforts, challenges persist in achieving comprehensive representation of civil society interests. Civil society organizations are encouraged to participate at the national level, but their involvement often depends on resources and awareness, potentially limiting their influence compared to industry stakeholders.[144] Moreover, the standardization process lacks sufficient transparency, making it difficult for civil

[140] Gornet and Herman (2024), p. 43.

[141] Chiodo et al. (2024).

[142] Cantero Gamito (2024).

[143] https://www.cencenelec.eu/areas-of-work/cen-cenelec-topics/artificial-intelligence/.

[144] The under-representation of smaller stakeholders in EU AI standardisation stems both from the substantial resources required for effective participation in these committees and the gap between the standardisation experiences of the various stakeholders. See, respectively, Kilian et al. (2025), p. 7, and Gornet and Herman (2024), p. 45.

society organizations to engage meaningfully and ensure their concerns are reflected in the final standards.[145]

As meaningful participation from civil society and consumer representatives remains limited, we contend that embedding "extended peer communities" into the co-regulation of AI is essential for mitigating the undue influence of industry-driven narratives and for fostering a culture of caution, transparency, and accountability—qualities that are too often subordinated to speed and competitiveness in the race to deploy AI. Ultimately, the 'extended peer community' concept is properly understood as an enactment of the so-called standpoint theory, which asserts that the perspectives of those disproportionately exposed to or impacted by a given risk must play a central role in determining the path forward.[146] For those who acknowledge the inevitability of our relational and embodied nature (ontological vulnerability), as well as our situated and unpredictable existence (contextual vulnerability), addressing the inclusion of these perspectives becomes a critical task in reimagining and regulating AI. This inclusion has indeed the potential to pave new avenues for transformative responses that connect the unpredictable and hard-to-quantify risks of AI technologies with ethical and regulatory frameworks that account for the fluid and multi-layered essence of human identity.[147]

6.3 The New Macro-Category of the Digital Vulnerability as a Normative and Hermeneutic Pivot for HMI

The unprecedented paradigm shift triggered by the digital revolution compels us to rethink classical legal categories. It is no longer sufficient to merely adapt existing legal tools to new contexts; rather, we must develop new conceptual frameworks capable of addressing the complex power imbalances emerging from HMI. Historically, the unification of the legal subject through the civil codification and the conceptualization of human rights in the modern constitutions at the end of the eighteenth century shaped the social and legal relationships between people,[148] enshrining the idea that individuals, not collective entities, are the subjects of rights recognized by law and overcoming the traditional legal particularism.[149] From that moment on the legal subject in Western tradition was conceived by the law as unique, abstract,

[145] These standards have not yet been completed. Initially expected by April or August 2025, the deadline has slipped. Latest projections suggest completion now expected end of 2025 or even into 2026.

[146] McQuillan (2022), p. 109.

[147] Crea and Infantino (2024). See also infra, par 6.3.

[148] As this is the history of the relationship between individuals, law and power, for further details see the critical analysis of the political and philosophical evolution of the concept of the 'rule of law' by Costa and Zolo (2002). For a focus on the French and European experience see Amodio (2012), p. 8 et seqq.

[149] Wijffels et al. (2015).

autonomous, rational, and desituated,[150] realising the Locke's philosophy of liberal individualism, based on the idea that all human beings are by nature free and endowed with the same inalienable rights.[151]

Legal capacity constitutes the static connecting link between the legal subject and both the intersubjective and patrimonial contexts; capacity to act, by contrast, represents the dynamic dimension embodied in the 'power to'—that is, the legally recognized ability to perform acts producing legal effects. Within this framework, the principle of equality requires public institutions to ensure equal treatment for all, save for protected categories or individuals in particular conditions, such as minors or persons with disabilities with diminished capacity to act. One may discern a conceptual affinity with the Hobbesian formulation of the social contract, which rests upon the dual premises of the individual's intrinsic vulnerability and the trust reposed in the protective function of collective membership. In this perspective, every socio-legal relationship is sustained by an underlying fiduciary substratum: at the micro level, in the dyadic interactions between individual subjects; at the meso level, in the individual's engagement with the community to which they belong; and at the macro level, in the relationship between individuals and the institutions that govern collective life.

However, as the twentieth century unfolded, it became increasingly evident that the formal principle of equality was insufficient to redress the structural asymmetries of power between individuals and public authorities or dominant private actors.[152] The neoliberal principle of state non-intervention—particularly prominent within US legal culture, where the law tends to emphasize the self-regulation of markets and civil society, while promoting democratic proceduralism in the political, administrative and judicial spheres[153]—has, in practice, facilitated the exploitation of individual vulnerabilities by more powerful private actors.

Following the Second World War, legal thought rediscovered the plurality inherent in the socio-legal order, fragmenting once again the notion of the legal subject. This transformation manifested in the proliferation of legal formants, the multiplication of sources, and the diversification of legislative instruments.[154] The relational dimension, ideally characterized by equality among legal subjects, revealed itself in practice to be shaped by asymmetries between the agent and the recipient of actions. Consequently, the concept of vulnerability was reappraised as a heuristic device[155] capable of defining the relational and dynamic subjective dimension in which every individual is at risk of losing autonomy and is subject—or potentially predisposed—to the power of others. The abstraction of the singular, idealized legal subject gave way to the concreteness of the 'situated' person's needs, and to their protection conceived no longer in merely formal and generic terms, but in substantive and specific ones.

---

150 Marella (2020).

151 For a contemporary reconstruction of Locke's thought, see Seliger (2019) and Turner (1988).

152 Fineman (2008).

153 Bignami (2018).

154 Pastore (2018).

155 Fineman (2008), p. 9.

In this ever-changing landscape, the agentification of artificial intelligence introduces unprecedented threats to both individuals and society. The shift from the Agora environments, where participants interact on equal terms and information flows are symmetric (e.g., social media platforms) to Oracle settings, where users seek information and counsel for decision-making from a more knowledgeable digital entity (e.g., Google Search, Wikipedia, and now increasingly LLM- and LRM-based systems) are reconfiguring the relations of trust, creating novel asymmetries in which risks and harms are amplified and remain unpredictable. Digital technologies and AI systems are shaping not only the human environment but the entirety of humanity at both the individual and societal levels. It is therefore imperative to ground regulatory efforts, at all normative layers, in a principle of universal scope—one capable of being operationalized across both the singular and communal dimensions of human existence.

This necessity echoes historical precedents, where the emergence of systemic power asymmetries -whether technological or economic—has compelled public authorities to step in, establishing normative frameworks aimed at rebalancing structural inequalities and safeguarding the autonomy of weaker parties. As the mass production augmented oligopolistic strategies and the power imbalance reduced the possibility for their counterparties to resist unfair practices, governments intervened to assure competition between actors and protection of the weakest parties in the marketplace. Along with the notion of 'consumer', as a natural person who purchases goods and services for personal use, consumer law dealt with actions and remedies, rights and duties, to ensure the fairness of commercial practices and the rebalance of the powers through consumer empowerment and information.[156] In recent times the notion of the 'average consumer' is under revisitation by legal scholars, substituted by the 'vulnerable consumer'. Digital vulnerability in consumer law describes 'a universal state of defencelessness and susceptibility to (the exploitation of) power imbalances that are the result of increasing automation of commerce, datafied consumer-seller relations, and the very architecture of digital marketplace'.[157]

In consumer law, according to Art. 5 para. 3 of the Unfair Commercial Practices Directive the vulnerable consumer belongs to a 'clearly identifiable group of consumers who are particularly vulnerable to the practice or the underlying product because of their mental or physical infirmity, age or credulity in a way which the trader could reasonably be expected to foresee'. However, vulnerability is not only caused by internal factors. External factors could originate, sustain, and even reinforce vulnerabilities.[158] In data protection law, special categories of sensitive data are protected in a more stringent way, revealing the vulnerability of correspondent data subjects.[159]

---

[156] There are still need for improvement: Namysłowska (2025).

[157] Quoted from Helberger et al. (2022).

[158] Peroni and Timmers (2013).

[159] Malgieri and Niklas (2020).

The AI Act refers to the concept of vulnerability in two ways, revealing how the term is still vague and ambiguous.[160] On one hand, Art. 5 para. 1 pt. b AI Act uses the limited extent of the situational vulnerability, restricting the reference to the 'vulnerabilities of a person or a specific group of persons due to their age, disability or a specific social or economic situation' in order to prohibit their exploitation; similarly Art. 7 para. 2 pt. h AI Act refers to 'the persons who are potentially harmed or suffer an adverse impact are in a vulnerable position in relation to the deployer of an AI system, in particular due to status, authority, knowledge, economic or social circumstances, or age' and Art. 9 para. 9 AI Act to 'persons under the age of 18 and, as appropriate, other vulnerable groups' (references also in Art. 60 para. 4 pt. g, Art. 79 para. 2, Art. 95 para. 2 pt. e AI Act). On the other hand, Art. 15 para. 5 AI Act states that AI systems can also be vulnerable to attempts by third persons to alter their use, outputs or performance.

The misuse of the word 'vulnerability' by the European legislator is not surprising, considering the anthropomorphization of AI operated by AI developers, computer scientists, designers, and programmers. The employ of terms typically used to describe human skills and capacities focuses on alleged similarities between humans and machines, in particular in brain inspired AI. This anthropomorphism has significant implications both epistemologically and ethically,[161] making it crucial to avoid conflating distinct levels of analysis. It is essential to reaffirm that intelligence and vulnerability are qualities uniquely inherent to human beings. The machines' exposure to attacks is relevant in terms of vulnerability only insofar as it reflects the vulnerability of the humans who use or depend upon them.

Vulnerability is an ontological feature of human existence, a condition universally shared across all individuals by virtue of their common human nature. Facing the digital revolution, all humans are "digitally" vulnerable to the pervasiveness of and the dependence from technology. Ethics science is of pivotal importance to educate designer, producer and deployers of AI systems. AI systems themselves cannot indeed be educated to ethics and their deterministic approach, the way in which they nudge humans towards unpredictable paths puts mankind and its societal structures in danger. Stuart Russell's proposal[162] to design machines to be inherently uncertain about the humans' preferences they are required to satisfy, theorises humble and altruistic machines, committed to pursue humans' objectives, not theirs. In the intention of the author this might result in a new foundation of the HMI, provably deferential and beneficial.

However, in the present digitally boosted multiple-choice society people get overwhelmed with an excessively large number of options.[163] The choice overload leads

[160] Schroeder and Gefenas (2009).

[161] Salles et al. (2020).

[162] Russell (2019).

[163] A significant contribution on the topic is the monographic work by Breedveld and Broek (2003), which focuses on the multichoice society and the evolution from the 1970s to the end of the century of the perception and use of time, up to the dawn of the digital society that has further intensified those potentials.

to decision fatigue and increases the frustration due to the missed opportunities.[164] In this context, the asymmetry on the data management between humans and machines creates the conditions for exacerbating the susceptibility to manipulative persuasion and the predisposition to decision delegation. The loss of control over social narratives and the deprivation of the individual self-determination in the presumption of the maximal freedom of choice[165] are the grounds of human vulnerability in interaction with AI.

Advanced AI systems represent a valuable resource for research aimed at deepening our understanding of the human condition, particularly with regard to the relational dynamics that shape individual identities and societal structures. At the same time, these systems engage in a reciprocal interplay with researchers, contributing to the emergence of a new hermeneutic framework, an interaction that, as Norbert Wiener noted in the early stages of cybernetics,[166] influences both human and machine. A similar dynamic unfolds in everyday interactions with generative AI models, wherein both users and artificial systems mutually shape and transform each other through the communicative process. This observation gives rise to the hypothesis that, just as immersive virtual reality (IVR) applications can alter users' bodily self-perception through embodied simulation,[167] interactions with LLMs and LRMs may likewise affect the internal psychological processes through which individuals examine their own thoughts, emotions, judgments, and perceptions, namely the human introspective capacities.[168]

In his theory of the extended mind, Andy Clark[169] argues that cognitive processes can extend beyond an individual's skull and body to include external artifacts when they function as integral components of thinking, having an active, ongoing role in the real-time cognitive process as a form of active externalism. Consequently, language is not merely a tool for communication, but a cognitive extension that creates a feedback loop: this looping interplay between internal and external processes forms a single, integrated system.[170] Just as spoken or written language supports reasoning, conversing with a chatbot supports thought formation. Users externalize ideas in the chat, see them reformulated, challenged, or completed, and respond in turn. This dialogical loop mirrors the internal-external interplay described by Clark.[171] When users ask a chatbot to help them understand their own feelings, beliefs, or reasoning, they use it as an introspective aid. This suggests that AI can serve not only as an

[164] The theme of the multichoice society was later revisited and developed with mature insights by Schwartz (2004).

[165] Bareis and Katzenbach (2021).

[166] Norbert Wiener published in 1948 a inspiring work, grounding the cybernetics as a multidisciplinary field in which study how information flows in any systems, biological, mechanical, cognitive, or social, with feedback loops (Wiener 1948).

[167] Repetto and Riva (2024).

[168] Barandiaran and Pérez-Verdugo (2024).

[169] Clark and Chalmers (1998).

[170] Ivi.

[171] Ivi.

epistemic scaffold but as part of self-reflection, as supposed by Repetto & Riva.[172] There are consequences on the contours of the self that become blurred, implying the redefinition of the mental autonomy, the responsibility and the authorship of the results of the HMI.

As artificial intelligence systems become more pervasive in everyday life, we are witnessing two parallel yet distinct movements: one toward the anthropomorphization of AI, and the other toward the hybridization of humans and machines. While the former seeks to make machines appear or behave more like humans—by endowing them with traits that simulate empathy, language, or personality—the latter involves the implantation of machines into the human body and mind, integrating artificial components directly into the biological substrate. This shift from simulation to integration reflects a profound redefinition of what it means to be human in the age of AI. In this context, Elon Musk's transhumanist vision[173] is not just a speculative stance, but a concrete technological trajectory. Through its brain–computer interface Telepathy,[174] Neuralink advances a model of human-AI co-evolution in which cognitive functions are no longer confined to the organic brain but interwoven with embedded digital systems.

The ongoing co-evolution between humans and machines, and the increasingly deep and shaping nature of this interaction, compels us to engage in a more profound reflection on what it truly means to be human. At the crossroads of a new era, the urgent task is to preserve the essence of human existence, to ensure that technological development remains firmly anchored in our core values, and that neither individuals nor societies are reduced to passive recipients of systems they do not control. We must guard against a future in which technology is used to exploit or manipulate, consolidating power in the hands of a few, or in which artificial intelligence alters our capacity for self-awareness, consciousness, moral judgment, and the exercise of free will.

However, the very nature of consciousness and free will is viewed in a new perspective from the rise of the quantum science: no more as a mere by-products of deterministic material processes, but as phenomena deeply rooted in dimensions of reality that extend beyond what our instruments or our bodies can directly perceive.[175] In this perspective, contemporary quantum mechanics do not describes what happens to a physical system, but rather focuses on how physical systems interact and perceive one another.[176] While humans experience reality as continuous and stable, quantum mechanics suggests that reality at its fundamental level is uncertain, fluid, and dependent on observation.

---

[172] Repetto and Riva (2024).

[173] More (2013).

[174] In January 2024, Neuralink implanted its first chip (called Telepathy, also referred to as the Link/N1 device) into a quadriplegic patient, that uses it to control a computer cursor and communicate via text, using just his mind: Chappell (2024).

[175] D'Ariano and Faggin (2020) and Faggin (2024).

[176] Rovelli (2016), p. 18 et seqq.

Such a shift foregrounds interaction as the fundamental building block of reality itself. Reality emerges not from static entities, but from dynamic relationships, where systems continuously influence and are influenced by others. When the interaction occurs between two quantum systems, the states of both will change, with the creation of an "entangled state", having new properties that are not the sum of the properties of the component states.[177] This interplay is inherently complex and non-linear: factors impact other factors, which in turn reverberate through intricate networks of dependencies. In these contexts, causal chains are not linear and predictable but rather circular,[178] with feedback loops and cascading effects that can lead to unexpected "emergent phenomena".[179] These represent a class of behaviors, pattern, or structures that arise from the interactions of smaller, simpler components, but that are not directly predictable from the properties of the single elements.

In the field of artificial intelligence, complex algorithmic models often produce emergent behaviors, namely results that were not explicitly programmed and could not be entirely foreseen at the design stage.[180] Such phenomena expose the limitations of traditional, deterministic approaches to regulation and call for a PNS methodology to be used.

7 Conclusion

The inherent unpredictability of complex AI systems—manifested through emergent behaviors and unintended consequences—reveals the inadequacy of traditional regulatory frameworks that rely solely on *ex ante* controls and *ex post* remedies. In environments characterized by profound uncertainty and where the societal impacts of technological applications may be both collective and irreversible, as demonstrated above, the EU AI Act risk-based approach remain insufficient. While precautionary bans exist, the Act continues to rely heavily on conventional risk-assessment methodologies that fail to address the radical asymmetry between human cognition and AI's autonomous capabilities. This tension underscores the necessity to move beyond procedural compliance and toward a genuinely precautionary governance model.

Yet, precaution alone is insufficient if it is not embedded within a broader normative structure that explicitly prioritizes the protection of human dignity, agency, and autonomy. Without such anchoring, there is a tangible risk that technological systems will progressively subordinate human beings to mechanisms they neither control nor fully comprehend.

On these premises, and also in light of the cross-border nature of AI-related applications, transactions, and disputes highlighted by Goh Escolar in this volume, it becomes essential to establish a new overarching legal category that reaffirms the

[177] Faggin (2024)

[178] About the circular causality, Bartoletti et al. (2015) and Harvey (2019).

[179] Youvan. (2025).

[180] Ivi.

centrality of the human being within a vision of digital humanism. This category must function as a preventive umbrella principle, mandating that every human and artificial activity align with its standards proactively, while simultaneously providing a benchmark for retrospective evaluation and accountability.

At the core of this legal framework lies the concept of vulnerability, a broad and fundamental attribute intrinsic to the human condition. Vulnerability serves as a valuable conceptual lens because it encompasses both the universal dimension of human fragility and the situational vulnerabilities experienced by individuals, groups, and societies as a whole. Recognizing this dual nature allows for a more nuanced and responsive approach to safeguarding human dignity and rights within the increasingly intricate and opaque ecosystems generated by advanced technologies. In particular, the Luna's theory of layers[181] overcomes through an intersectional approach[182] the tension between the universalistic and the particularistic character of vulnerability, explaining how its features may vary from one individual to another, having different causal factors and degrees of severity. In this regard, the concept seems to offer the right conceptual pivot around which to build a common and global regulation on digital law.

The concept of digital vulnerability is that it better fits with the multidimensional and multi-layered digital revolution. It is consistent with the above presented movement towards a digital constitutionalism,[183] stressing the backgrounds of the fundamental human rights shared globally at the international level. Furthermore, the idea of vulnerability has a relational nature so that it is very suitable to digital law, where the very risks and threats coming from advanced AI systems are indeed connected with the HMI.

The prospect of a global framework rooted in digital vulnerability must also account for the dangers of industry capture and the limitations of expert-driven, technocratic regulation. Embedding extended peer communities into the regulatory process—ensuring that civil society, consumer groups, and those most exposed to AI-related risks are meaningfully included—was demonstrated above to be a crucial step. Only through such plural participation can digital vulnerability be transformed from an abstract concept into a living normative principle capable of reshaping AI governance in line with the demands of human dignity and digital humanism.

Furthermore, the ever-changing landscape calls for a guiding legal principle that goes beyond regulation and assumes an educational role, fostering awareness of the inherent risks associated with the use and interaction with AI systems. Law must reclaim its normative and pedagogical function,[184] not only to protect individuals from exploitation but also to equip societies with the conceptual tools necessary to navigate an environment where human vulnerability is structurally amplified by technology.

---

181 Luna (2009, 2019).

182 Bond (2021).

183 Pollicino (2021) and De Gregorio (2022).

184 Turner (2006).

The perception of human vulnerability, precisely because it is ontologically intrinsic to mortal nature, is evident in relations between humans as moral agents. In contrast, HMI is still uncharted territory. The first steps in this domain have already revealed how hidden and potentially dangerous the threats to personal and social processes of identity construction can be. Looking ahead, as HMI evolves toward an anthropomorphization of machines and a hybridization of humans, these risks may become even more acute. On one side, individuals may experience new forms of empowerment; on the other, their vulnerability is intensified by a growing tendency to delegate decisions and yield to subtle nudges. Keeping a human in the loop may be part of the solution, but it is far from sufficient.

The introduction of the principle of digital vulnerability in the European and international context could act as a catalyst for global regulatory initiatives like the consumer-professional imbalance recognized in consumer law. Moreover, at the national level, the concept of digital vulnerability would allow countries to address the three approaches described above—control, promotion and protection—while harmonising them within a vision of digital humanism.

Anthropologically rooted in the very essence of human existence, the notion of vulnerability precedes cultural distinctions, thereby lending itself to bridging the world's different philosophical and religious cultures, as both philosophy and religion are responses to the inherent vulnerability common to all beings.[185]

Declaring the ontological vulnerability of humans in any interaction with AI, elevating digital vulnerability to a fundamental principle, and ensuring that existing and future norms are interpreted or drafted in coherence with it—while also embedding the participation of peer communities in regulatory processes—could provide the legal foundation for a global digital law responsive to the challenges of post-normal times.

References

Almada M, Petit N (2023) The EU AI act: a medley of product safety and fundamental rights? EUI, RS.C, Working Paper 2023/59. Available at https://hdl.handle.net/1814/75982

Amato S (2023) Tra silicio e carbonio: le macchine saranno sempre stupide? BioLaw J—Riv BioDiritto 1:295–302

Amodio C (2012) Au nom de la loi. L'esperienza giuridica francese nel contesto europeo. Giappichelli, Torino

Ananny M, Crawford K (2018) Seeing without knowing: limitations of the transparency ideal and its application to algorithmic accountability. New Med Soc 20:973–989

Arkoudas K (2023) ChatGPT is no stochastic parrot. But it also claims that 1 is greater than 1. Philos Technol 36(3):1–29

Backer LC (2019) Next generation law: data driven governance and accountability based regulatory systems in the west, and social credit regimes in China. South Calif Interdisc Law J 28(1):123–172

[185] Tham et al. (2014).

Bagni F, Longo E, Simoncini A, Baldini D, Zarra A, Mobilio G, Panai E, Riccio GM, Tartaro A (2025) White paper on regulatory sandboxes for AI and cybersecurity, p 201. SSRN. https://ssrn.com/abstract=5268812

Barandiaran XE, Pérez-Verdugo J (2024) Generative midtended cognition and artificial intelligence. Synthese 205(4):137. arXiv:2411.06812.

Bareis J, Katzenbach C (2021) Talking AI into being: the narratives and imaginaries of national AI strategies and their performative politics. Sci Technol Human Values 47(5):855–881. https://doi.org/10.1177/01622439211030007

Barth S, De Jong M (2017) The privacy paradox—investigating discrepancies between expressed privacy concerns and actual online behavior—a systematic literature review. Telematics Inf 34(7):1039–1058. https://doi.org/10.1016/j.tele.2017.04.013

Bartoletti M, Cimoli T, Pinna GM, Zunino R (2015) Models of circular causality. In International Conference on Distributed Computing and Internet Technology, pp 1–20. Springer, Cham. https://doi.org/10.1007/978-3-319-14977-6_1

Bean E, Burleigh C, Haskell C, Burris-Melville T, Payne J, Pathak B (2025) Eavesdropping on UNESCO AI policy, leadership, and ethics. J Leadersh Stud 18(4):99–111

Beck U (1992) Risk society: towards a new modernity. Sage

Bender EM, Gebru T, McMillan-Major A, Mitchell M (2021) On the dangers of stochastic parrots: can language models be too big? In Proceedings of the 2021 ACM conference on fairness, accountability, and transparency, pp 610–623

Berger KP (2010) The creeping codification of the new Lex Mercatoria, 2nd edn. Kluwer Law International, Alphen aan den Rijn

Bignami F (2018) Introduction: a new field: comparative law and regulation. In: Bignami F, Zaring D (eds) Comparative law and regulation: understanding the global regulatory process. Edward Elgar Publishing, Cheltenham

Bignami F, Resta G (2024). Digital extraterritoriality: a comparative law perspective. In De Gregorio G, Pollicino O, Valcke P (eds) The Oxford handbook of digital constitutionalism, Oxford Academic, Oxford. https://doi.org/10.1093/oxfordhb/9780198877820.013.21

Bishop JM (2021) Artificial intelligence is stupid and causal reasoning will not fix it. Front Psychol 11:1–18

Bond J (2021) Global intersectionality and contemporary human rights. Oxford University Press, Oxford. https://doi.org/10.1093/oso/9780198868835.001.0001

Breedveld K, Broek AV (2003) De meerkeuzemaatschappij: Facets of the temporal organization of obligations and provisions. Sociaal en Cultureel Planbureau, The Hague

Bruner J (1991) The narrative construction of reality. Crit Inquiry 18(1):1–21

Cantero Gamito M (2024) The role of ETSI in the EU's regulation and governance of artificial intelligence. Innov Eur J Soc Sci Res 37(5):1425–1440. https://hdl.handle.net/1814/77519

Cervantes JA, López S, Rodríguez LF, Cervantes S, Cervantes F, Ramos F (2020) Artificial moral agents: a survey of the current status. Sci Eng Ethics 26(2):501–532. https://doi.org/10.1007/s11948-019-00151-x

Chappell B (2024) What to know about Elon Musk's Neuralink, which put an implant into a human brain. Npr January 30. https://www.npr.org/2024/01/30/1227850900/elon-musk-neuralink-implant-clinical-trial

Chiodo M, Grosse Ruse-Khan H, Müller D, Ossmann-Magiera L, Zech H (2024) Regulating AI: a matrix for gauging impact and its legal implementation. University of Cambridge, Faculty of Law Research Paper No. 12/2024. https://ssrn.com/abstract=4765104

Clark A, Chalmers D (1998) The extended mind. Analysis 58(1):7–19. https://doi.org/10.1111/1467-8284.00096

Clark B, Patt D, Schramm H (2020) Mosaic warfare. Exploiting artificial intelligence and autonomous systems to implement decision-centric operations. Center for Strategic and Budgetary Assessments, v–vi

Clowes RW, Smart PR, Heersmink R (2024) The ethics of the extended mind: mental privacy, manipulation and agency. In: Heinrichs JH, Beck B, Friedrich O (eds), Neuroprosthethics: ethical implications of applied situated cognition. J. B. Metzler, Berlin, pp 13–35

Cohen T (2023) Regulating manipulative artificial intelligence. SCRIPTed 20(1):203. https://script-ed.org/article/regulating-manipulative-artificial-intelligence/

Communication from the Commission to the European Parliament and the Council, 2023 Strategic Foresight Report Sustainability and people's wellbeing at the heart of Europe's Open Strategic Autonomy, COM(2023) 376 final, p. 12 et seq.

Corporate Europe Observatory (2025) Bias baked in: How Big Tech sets its own AI standards. Corporate Europe Observatory report, 9 January 2025. https://corporateeurope.org/en/2025/01/bias-baked

Cosentini A, Pollicino O, De Gregorio G, Ermellino A, Fontanella D, Inverardi N, Paolucci F, Penco IG, Regoli D, Tessaro Trapani S (2025) Assessing the impact of artificial intelligence systems on fundamental rights. SSRN. https://doi.org/10.2139/ssrn.5168579

Cosentino G (2020) Social media and the post-truth world order—the global dynamics of disinformation. Palgrave Macmillan, Singapore

Costa P, Zolo D (eds) (2002) Lo Stato di diritto. Storia, teoria, critica. Feltrinelli, Milano

Crea C, Infantino M (2024) Digital vulnerability as a tool for social justice in European private law. Transformative Private Law. https://transformativeprivatelaw.com/digital-vulnerability-as-a-tool-for-social-justice-in-european-private-law/

Cuniberti G (2014) Three theories of Lex Mercatoria. Columbia J Transnational Law 52:369–434

D'Ariano GM, Faggin F (2020) Hard problem and free will: an information-theoretical approach. arXiv:2012.06580

Daniels OJ, Dohmen H (2025) China's overlooked AI strategy: Beijing is using soft power to gain global dominance. Foreign Affairs, 25 July 2025. https://www.foreignaffairs.com/united-states/chinas-overlooked-ai-strategy

De Gregorio G (2021) The rise of digital constitutionalism in the European Union. Int J Const Law 19(1):41–70

De Gregorio G (2022) Digital constitutionalism in Europe: reframing rights and powers in the algorithmic society. Cambridge University Press, Cambridge

De Gregorio G, Dunn P (2022) The European risk-based approaches: connecting constitutional dots in the digital age. Common Market Law Rev 59(2):473–500

de Laat PB (2018) Algorithmic decision-making based on machine learning from big data: can transparency restore accountability? Philos Technol 31:525–541

De Ruysscher D (2020) Conceptualizing Lex Mercatoria: Malynes, Schmitthoff and Goldman compared. Maastricht J Eur Comp Law 27(4):465–483. https://doi.org/10.1177/1023263X20938247

Dennett D (2017) From bacteria to Bach and back: the evolution of minds. W. W. Norton, New York

Deuze M (2011) Media Life. Media Cult Soc 33(1):137

Draghi M (2024) The future of European competitiveness. Part A: a competitiveness strategy for Europe. European Commission. https://commission.europa.eu/document/download/97e481fd-2dc3-412d-be4c-f152a8232961_en?

Elias N (1978) The civilizing process. The development of manners. Urizen Books, New York

Esposito E (2022) Artificial communication. How algorithms produce social intelligence. The MIT Press, Cambridge

European Commission: Group of Chief Scientific Advisors and Directorate-General for Research and Innovation, Scientific advice to European policy in a complex world, Publications Office, 2019, https://doi.org/10.2777/80320

European Parliament resolution of 20 October 2020 with recommendations to the Commission on a framework of ethical aspects of artificial intelligence, robotics and related technologies, available at: https://eur-lex.europa.eu/legal-content/EN/TXT/?uri=oj:JOC_2021_404_R_0005

European Parliament, Environmental Policy: General Principles and Basic Framework, available at: https://www.europarl.europa.eu/factsheets/en/sheet/71/environment-policy-general-principles-and-basic-framework
Faggin F (2024) Irreducible. Consciousness, life, computers, and human nature. John Hunt Publishing, Alresford
Fineman MA (2008) The vulnerable subject: anchoring equality in the human condition. Yale J Law Feminism 20(1):1–23
Flore M (2020) Understanding citizens' vulnerabilities (II): from disinformation to hostile narratives. EUR 30029 EN, Publications Office of the European Union, Luxembourg, available at: https://publications.jrc.ec.europa.eu/repository/handle/JRC118914
Floridi L (2018) Soft ethics and the governance of the digital. Philos Technol 31:1–8
Floridi L (2023a) AI as agency without intelligence: on ChatGPT, large language models, and other generative models. Philos Technol 36(15):1–7
Floridi L (2023b) The ethics of artificial intelligence: principles, challenges, and opportunities. Oxford Academic, Oxford. https://doi.org/10.1093/oso/9780198883098.001.0001
Funtowicz SO, Ravetz JR (1990) Uncertainty and quality in science for policy. Kluwer Academic, Dordrecht
Funtowicz SO, Ravetz JR (1992) Three types of risk assessment and the emergence of post-normal science. In: Krimsky S, Golding D (eds) Social theories of risk. Praeger, Westport, CT, pp 251–273
Funtowicz SO, Ravetz JR (1993) Science for the post-normal age. Futures 25(7):739–755
Funtowicz S, Ravetz J (2003) Post-normal science. Internet Encyclopaedia of Ecological Economics. International Society for Ecological Economics. Retrieved from https://www.isecoeco.org/pdf/pstnormsc.pdf
Funtowicz S, Ravetz J (2020) Post-normal science: how does it resonate with the world of today? Science for policy handbook. Elsevier, Amsterdam, pp 14–18
Gehl RW, Bakardjieva M (2016) Socialbots and their friends. In Digital media and the automation of sociality. Routledge, New York
Gornet M, Herman H (2024) A peek into European standards making for AI: between geopolitical and economic interests. HAL-04784035
Guida A (2021) The precautionary principle and genetically modified organisms: a bone of contention between European institutions and member states. J Law Biosci 8(1):lsab012.
Haimes YY (2009) On the complex definition of risk: a systems-based approach. Risk Anal 29(12):1647–1654
Harvey I (2019) Circular causation, circular cognition: a tour around some common confusions. Artif Life 25(4):334–351. https://doi.org/10.1162/artl_a_00300
Helberger N, Sax M, Strycharz J, Micklitz HW (2022) Choice architectures in the digital economy: towards a new understanding of digital vulnerability. J Consum Policy 45:175–200. https://doi.org/10.1007/s10603-021-09501-5
Hepp A (2020) Deep Mediatization. Routledge, New York
Hepp A et al (2023) ChatGPT, LaMDA, and the hype around communicative AI: the automation of communication as a field of research in media and communication studies. Human Mach Commun 6:41–53
Huw R, Cowls J, Morley J, Taddeo M, Wang V, Floridi L (2021) The Chinese approach to artificial intelligence: an analysis of policy and regulation. AI & Soc 36(1):59–77
Jasanoff S (1990) The fifth branch: science advisers as policymakers. Harvard University Press, Cambridge
Jasanoff S (2003) Technologies of humility: citizen participation in governing science. Minerva 41(3):240
Jasanoff S (2016) The ethics of invention: technology and the human future. W. W. Norton, New York
Johnson WG (2023) Caught in quicksand? Compliance and legitimacy challenges in using regulatory sandboxes to manage emerging technologies. Regul Gov 17(3):709–725

Kadour AT, Zoboli L (2021) Increasing standardization for smart(er) contracts. Uniform Law Rev 26(3):583–598. https://doi.org/10.1093/ulr/unab022

Kahneman D (2003) A perspective on judgement and choice: mapping bounded rationality. Am Psychol 58(9):697–720. https://doi.org/10.1037/0003-066X.58.9.697

Kahneman D (2011) Thinking, fast and slow. Ferrar, Straus and Giroux, New York

Keyes R (2004) The post-truth era: dishonesty and deception in contemporary life. St. Martin's Press, London

Kilian R, Jäck L, Ebel D (2025) European AI standards—technical standardisation and implementation challenges under the EU AI Act. Eur J Risk Regul. https://doi.org/10.1017/err.2025.10032

Kitchin R (2017) Thinking critically about and researching algorithms. Inf Commun Soc 20(1):14–29

Koops BJ (2021) The concept of function creep. Law Innov Technol 13(1):29–56. https://doi.org/10.1080/17579961.2021.1898299

Labarre J (2024) Epistemic vulnerability: theory and measurement at the system level. Polit Commun 42(1):6–26. https://doi.org/10.1080/10584609.2024.2363545

Lewandowsky S, Ecker UKH, Cook J (2017) Beyond misinformation: understanding and coping with the "post-truth" era. J Appl Res Mem Cogn 6(4):353–369

Longo L, Brcic M, Cabitza F, Choi J, Confalonieri R, Del Ser J, Guidotti R, Hayashi Y, Herrera F, Holzinger A, Jiang R, Khosravi H, Lecue F, Malgieri G, Páez A, Samek W, Schneider J, Speith T, Stumpf S (2024) A manifesto of open challenges and interdisciplinary research directions. Inf Fusion 106:102301

Luna F (2009) Elucidating the concept of vulnerability: layers not labels. Int J Feminist Approach Bioeth 2(1):121–139. http://www.jstor.org/stable/40339200

Luna F (2019) Identifying and evaluating layers of vulnerability—a way forward. Dev World Bioeth 19(2):86–95. https://doi.org/10.1111/dewb.12206

Malaschini A (2023) ChatGPT e simili: questioni giuridiche ed implicazioni sociali. Consulta online II, pp 583–606

Malgieri G, Niklas J (2020) Vulnerable data subjects. Computer Law Security Rev 37:1–16. https://doi.org/10.1016/j.clsr.2020.105415

Mantelero A (2024) The Fundamental Rights Impact Assessment (FRIA) in the AI act: roots, legal obligations and key elements for a model template. Comput Law Secur Rev 54. https://arxiv.org/abs/2411.15149

Mantelero A, Fanucci F (2022) The international debate on AI regulation and the human rights in the prism of the Council of Europe's CAHAI: Great Ambitions. In: Czech P et al (eds) European yearbook on human rights. Intersentia, Cambridge, pp 225–252

Marella MR (2020) Antropologia del soggetto di diritto. Note sulle trasformazioni di una categoria giuridica. In Bilotta F, Raimondi F (eds) Il soggetto di diritto: storia ed evoluzione di un concetto nel diritto privato. Jovene, Naples, pp 47–75

Mattei U (2023) The legal metaverse and comparative taxonomy: a reappraisal. The Am J Comp Law 71(4):900–929

McQuillan D (2018) Manifesto on algorithmic humanitarianism OpenDemocracy, 4 Apr 2018

McQuillan D (2022) Resisting AI: an anti-fascist approach to artificial intelligence. Bristol University Press, Bristol

Miller T (2019) Explanation in artificial intelligence: insights from the social sciences. Artif Intell 267:1–38

Misselhorn C (2022) Artificial moral agents: conceptual issues and ethical controversy. In: Voeneky S, Kellmeyer P, Mueller O, Burgard W (eds) The Cambridge handbook of responsible artificial intelligence: interdisciplinary perspectives. Cambridge Law Handbooks. Cambridge University Press, Cambridge, pp 31–49

Mollick E (2025) The end of search, the beginning of research. One Useful Thing, 3 Feb 2025. https://www.oneusefulthing.org/p/the-end-of-search-the-beginning-of

More M (2013) The philosophy of transhumanism. In: More M, Vita-More N (eds) The transhumanist reader: classical and contemporary essays on the science, technology, and philosophy of the human future. Wiley, pp 3–17

Müller VC (2020) Ethics of artificial intelligence and robotics. In: Zalta EN (ed) Stanford Encyclopedia of Philosophy, Summer edn. Stanford University, Palo Alto, CSLI, pp 1–70

Namysłowska M (2025) The silent death of EU consumer law and its resilient revival: reinventing consumer protection against unfair digital commercial practices. J Consum Policy 48(3):317–336. https://doi.org/10.1007/s10603-025-09590-5

Noels S, Bied G, Buyl M, Rogiers A, Fettach Y, Lijffijt J, De Bie T (2025) What large language models do not talk about: an empirical study of moderation and censorship practices. In Joint European Conference on Machine Learning and Knowledge Discovery in Databases, Springer, Cham, pp 265–281. arXiv:2504.03803

Nowotny H (2003) Democratising expertise and socially robust knowledge. Sci Pub Policy 30(3):151–156

Nudo J, Pandolfo ME, Loru E, Samory M, Cinelli M, Quattrociocchi W (2025) Generative exaggeration in LLM social agents: consistency, bias, and toxicity. Online Soc Networks Media 51. arXiv:2507.00657

O'Neil C (2016) Weapons of math destruction: how big data increases inequality and threatens democracy. Crown, New York

Ottaviani M (2022) Brigate Russe. La guerra occulta del Cremlino tra troll e hacker. Ledizioni, Milan

Pálfi D (2024) Internal dispute resolution systems: do high promises come with higher expectations? Hung J Legal Stud 64(3):391–412. https://doi.org/10.1556/2052.2023.00469

Pasquale F (2015) The black box society: the secret algorithms that control money and information, Harvard University Press, Cambridge

Pastore B (2018) Soggettività giuridica e vulnerabilità. In Giolo O, Pastore B (eds) Vulnerabilità. Analisi multidisciplinare di un concetto. Carocci Editore, Rome, pp 127–145

Pedreschi D, Pappalardo L, Ferragina E, Baeza-Yates R, Barabási AL, Dignum F, Dignum V, Eliassi-Rad T, Giannotti F, Kertész J et al (2025) Human–AI coevolution. Artif Intell 339:104244

Peel J (2005) The precautionary principle in practice: environmental decision-making and scientific uncertainty. Federation Press

Peroni L, Timmers A (2013) Vulnerable groups: the promise of an emerging concept in European Human Rights Convention law. Int J Const Law 11(4):1056–1085. https://doi.org/10.1093/icon/mot042

Pollicino O (2021) Judicial protection of fundamental rights on the internet. a road towards digital constitutionalism? Bloomsbury, Oxford

Pollicino O (2022) I codici di condotta tra self-regulation e hard law: esiste davvero una terza via per la regolazione digitale? Il caso della strategia europea contro la disinformazione online. Riv Trimestrale di Diritto Pubblico 72(4):1049–1066

Polona C (2025). Fact-checking and content moderation on online platforms. EPRS: European Parliamentary Research Service, Belgium. https://coilink.org/20.500.12592/8xdvmxk on 17 Feb 2025. COI: 20.500.12592/8xdvmxk

Prem E (2022) Our digital mirror. In: Werthner H, Prem E, Lee EA, Ghezzi C (eds) Perspectives on digital humanism. Springer, Cham, pp 89–94. https://doi.org/10.1007/978-3-030-86144-5_13

Raffensperger C, Tickner J (eds) (1999) Protecting public health and the environment: implementing the precautionary principle. Island Press, Washington, DC

Rainey D, Katsh ME, Wahab MSA (eds) (2021) Online dispute resolution: theory and practice: a treatise on technology and dispute resolution, 2nd edn. Eleven International Publishing, The Hague

Rao A, Vashistha S, Naik A, Aditya S, Choudhury M (2024) Tricking LLMs into disobedience: formalizing, analyzing, and detecting jailbreaks. In: Proceedings of the 2024 Joint International Conference on Computational Linguistics, Language Resources and Evaluation (LREC-COLING 2024), Turin, Italy. https://doi.org/10.48550/arXiv.2305.14965

Ravetz JR (1999) What is post-normal science? Futures 31(7):647–653
Ravetz JR (2004) The post-normal science of precaution. Futures 36(3):347–357
Repetto C, Riva G (2024) Embodiment in the metaverse: how real and virtual bodies in interaction affect cognition. J Cogn 7(1):51. https://doi.org/10.5334/joc.374
Riva G, Wiederhold BK, Mantovani F (2024) Searching for the metaverse: neuroscience of physical and digital communities. Cyberpsychol Behav Soc Networking 27(1):9–18. https://doi.org/10.1089/cyber.2023.0040
Rosa EA, Dietz T (1998) Metatheoretical foundations for post-normal risk. J Risk Res 1(1):15–44
Rovelli C (2016) Seven brief lessons on physics. Riverhead Books, New York
Royal Society (1992) Risk: analysis, perception and management. The Royal Society, London
Russell S (2019) Human compatible: artificial intelligence and the problem of control. Penguin, London
Russell S (2022) Artificial intelligence and the problem of control. In Werthner H, Prem E, Lee EA, Ghezzi C (eds), Perspectives on digital humanism. Springer, Cham, pp 19–24. https://doi.org/10.1007/978-3-030-86144-5_3
Russinovich M, Salem A, Eldan R (2024) Great, now write an article about that: the Crescendo multi-turn LLM jailbreak attack. arXiv [cs.CR]. Available at http://arxiv.org/abs/2404.01833
Sacco R (1991a) Legal formants: a dynamic approach to comparative law (Installment I of II). The Am J Comp Law 39(1):1–34
Sacco R (1991b) Legal Formants: a dynamic approach to comparative law (Installment II of II). The Am J Comp Law 39(2):343–401
Salles A, Evers K, Farisco M (2020) Anthropomorphism in AI. AJOB Neurosci 11(2):88–95. https://doi.org/10.1080/21507740.2020.1740350
Santoni G (2024) La responsabilità delle piattaforme online tra mercato e sovranità digitale. Wolters Kluwer, Milan, p 98
Schleidgen S, Friedrich O, Gerlek S, Assadi G, Seifert J (2023) The concept of "interaction" in debates on human–machine interaction. Humanit Soc Sci Commun 10:551. https://doi.org/10.1057/s41599-023-02060-8
Schroeder D, Gefenas E (2009) Vulnerability: too vague and too broad? Cambridge Q Healthc Ethics 18(2):113–121. https://doi.org/10.1017/S0963180109090203
Schultz MD, Conti LG, Seele P (2025) Digital ethicswashing: a systematic review and a process-perception-outcome framework. AI Ethics 5:805–818
Schwartz B (2004) The paradox of choice: why more is less. Harper Perennial, New York
Seliger M (2019) The liberal politics of John Locke. Routledge, London. https://doi.org/10.4324/9780429318009
Soler Garrido J, De Nigris S, Bassani E, Sanchez I, Evas T, André A, Boulangé T (2024) Harmonised standards for the European AI Act. European Commission, Seville. Report No. JRC139430. https://publications.jrc.ec.europa.eu/repository/handle/JRC139430
Stirling A (2007) Risk, precaution and science: towards a more constructive policy debate. Talking point on the precautionary principle. EMBO Rep 8(4):309–315
Stirling A (2008) Science, precaution, and the politics of technological risk: converging implications in evolutionary and social scientific perspectives. Ann New York Acad Sci 1128(1):95–110
Stirling A, Tickner JA (2004) Implementing precaution: assessment and application tools for health and environmental decision-making. In Martuzzi M, Tickner JA (eds), The precautionary principle: protecting public health, the environment and the future of our children. World Health Organization (WHO), pp 181–298
Thaler R, Sunstein C (2008) Nudge: improving decisions about health, wealth and happiness. Yale University Press, New Haven
Tham J, Garcia A, Miranda G (eds) (2014) Religious perspectives on human vulnerability in bioethics. Springer, Cham
Tucker JA, Guess A, Barbera P, Vaccari C, Siegel A, Sanovich S, Stukal D, Nyhan B (2018) Social media, political polarization, and political disinformation. SSRN Electron J. https://doi.org/10.2139/ssrn.3144139

Turner BS (1988) Individualism, capitalism and the dominant culture: a note on the debate. Aust NZ J Soc 24(1):47–64. https://doi.org/10.1177/144078338802400103

Turner BS (2006) Vulnerability and human rights. The Pennsylvania State University Press, University Park, pp 25–44

Tzoulia E (2021) Targeted advertising in the digital era: modern challenges to consumer privacy and economic freedom: the responses of the EU legal order. In: Synodinou TE, Jougleux P, Markou C, Prastitou-Merdi T (eds) EU internet law in the digital single market. Springer, Cham. https://doi.org/10.1007/978-3-030-69583-5_19

UNESCO (2021) Recommendation on the ethics of artificial intelligence. United Nations Educational, Scientific and Cultural Organization, Paris. Available at: https://www.unesco.org/en/artificial-intelligence/recommendation-ethics

UNESCO (2023a) Ethical impact assessment: a tool of the Recommendation on the ethics of artificial intelligence. Available at: https://www.unesco.org/en/articles/ethical-impact-assessment-tool-recommendation-ethics-artificial-intelligence

UNESCO (2023b) Readiness assessment methodology: a tool of the Recommendation on the ethics of artificial intelligence. Available at: https://unesdoc.unesco.org/ark:/48223/pf0000385198

United Nations System (2024) United Nations System White Paper on AI Governance: an analysis of current institutional models and related functions and existing international normative frameworks within the United Nations system that are applicable to artificial intelligence governance. https://unsceb.org/united-nations-system-white-paper-ai-governance

Vanberghen C, Vanberghen A (2021) AI governance as a patchwork: the regulatory and geopolitical approach of AI at international and European level. In: Synodinou TE, Jougleux P, Markou C, Prastitou-Merdi (eds), EU internet law in the digital single market. Springer, Cham https://doi.org/10.1007/978-3-030-69583-5_9

Wagner G, Eidenmüller HGM (2021) Digital dispute resolution. SSRN Electron J. https://doi.org/10.2139/ssrn.3871612

Wagner G, Eidenmüller HGM (2023) Law by algorithm. Mohr Siebeck, Tübingen

Waldman AE (2020) Cognitive biases, dark patterns, and the "privacy paradox." Curr Opin Psychol 31:105–109. https://doi.org/10.1016/j.copsyc.2019.08.025

Wang T, Wang Y, Zhou J, Peng B, Song X, Zhang C, Sun X, Niu, Q, Liu J, Chen S, Chen K, Li M, Feng P, Bi Z, Liu M, Zhang Y, Fei C, Yin CH, Yan LKQ (2025) From aleatoric to epistemic: exploring uncertainty quantification techniques in artificial intelligence. arXiv preprint arXiv:2501.03282

Wei J, Wang X, Schuurmans D, Bosma M, Xia F, Chi E, Le QV, Zhou D (2022) Chain-of-thought prompting elicits reasoning in large language models. 36th Conference on Neural Information Processing Systems (NeurIPS 2022), arxiv:2201.11903

Weinberg AM (1972) Science and trans-science. Minerva 10(2):209–222. https://doi.org/10.1007/BF01682418

Werthner H et al (2019). Vienna manifesto on digital humanism. Vienna. https://caiml.org/dighum/dighum-manifesto/Vienna_Manifesto_on_Digital_Humanism_EN.pdf

Wheeler M (2019) The reappearing tool: transparency, smart technology, and the extended mind. AI & Soc 34(4):857–866

Wiener N (1948) Cybernetics or control and communication in the animal and the machine, now in open access. https://doi.org/10.7551/mitpress/11810.001.0001

Wijffels A, Donlan SP, Heirbaut D (2015) Ancien régime France: legal particularism under the absolute monarchy. In: Donlan SP, Heirbaut D (eds) The laws' many bodies. Studies in legal hybridity and jurisdictional complexity, c1600–1900. Duncker & Humblot, Berlin, pp 81–107

Youvan D (2025) Emergent patterns, self-awareness, and the limits of systemic perception: an interdisciplinary exploration of search engines, consciousness, and existentialism. https://doi.org/10.13140/RG.2.2.22266.81603

Ziegler J, Donkers T (2024) From explanations to human-AI co-evolution: charting trajectories towards future user-centric AI. i-com 23(2):263–272

Zuboff S (2019) The age of surveillance capitalism: the fight for a human future at the new frontier of power. Profile Books, London

Claudia Amodio, is a Associate Professor of Comparative Law at the Department of Environmental and Prevention Sciences, University of Ferrara, and Chercheuse associée at the CTAD, Université Paris Nanterre. Her research spans comparative law theory and method, fundamental rights, European private law, and the legal dimensions of ecological and digital transitions under conditions of scientific uncertainty and systemic risk. She serves on the editorial boards of The Italian Law Journal, Revue des droits de l'Homme, Estudios de derecho civil, Motivensa (Lima), and Ius Commune Europaeum e Sistemi Italo-Francofoni (Naples).

Amalia Diurni, is a Full Professor of Private Comparative and Uniform Law at the University of Rome Tor Vergata, Department of Management and Law, School of Economics. Visiting and research professor in Paris Panthéon-Assas, Regensburg, Fribourg, Vienna, IECL of Oxford and Vienna. Director of PhD Program "Theory of contrats, services and markets" (Rome Tor Vergata). Her research deals with comparative law methodology applied to issues in contract and family law, financial collaterals, torts, medical and digital law. She leads the Rome Unit of the DiVe "Digital Vulnerability in the European Private Law" Project.

Open Access This chapter is licensed under the terms of the Creative Commons Attribution 4.0 International License (http://creativecommons.org/licenses/by/4.0/), which permits use, sharing, adaptation, distribution and reproduction in any medium or format, as long as you give appropriate credit to the original author(s) and the source, provide a link to the Creative Commons license and indicate if changes were made.

The images or other third party material in this chapter are included in the chapter's Creative Commons license, unless indicated otherwise in a credit line to the material. If material is not included in the chapter's Creative Commons license and your intended use is not permitted by statutory regulation or exceeds the permitted use, you will need to obtain permission directly from the copyright holder.

Human-Machine Interaction Between Digital Humanism and Digital Citizenship

Human Vulnerability in Interaction with AI: Toward a Technological Humanism

Marta Bertolaso and Angelo Marinucci

Abstract This paper explores the complex relationship between humanity and technology, particularly artificial intelligence (AI), proposing a new technological humanity based on the ethics of care and the recognition of human vulnerability. Social homogenization centered on AI leads to epistemic and anthropological impoverishment, generating inequalities. If human intelligence is not mere computation, AI systems must be considered as support tools, not autonomous intelligences. Through ontological and epistemological analysis, the paper highlights the need for a relational and intentional approach that values human complexity embodied in biological, social, and spiritual dimensions. Vulnerability is an integral part of the human condition, not a limitation to be eliminated with technology. In this context, AI must be designed and used to promote human well-being, mitigate vulnerability and support a dignified life. The article proposes moving beyond the paradigm of control in favor of a paradigm of care, based on interdependence and reciprocity, which is essential for the development of a digital ethic centered on the human being in its entirety. Finally, critical reflection on the purposes of technology is necessary to prevent it from becoming an instrument of domination.

Keywords Human vulnerability · Technological humanism · Artificial Intelligence

1 Introduction

In this chapter, we argue that one of the most relevant problems of the relationship between humans and technology today is not so much the (real) risks associated with the replacement of (much) human labor by machines, but the fact that these

M. Bertolaso (✉)
Campus BioMedico University of Rome, Rome, Italy
e-mail: m.bertolaso@unicampus.it

A. Marinucci
Campus BioMedico University of Rome, Rome, Italy

© The Author(s) 2025

C. Amodio and A. Diurni (eds.), *Human Vulnerability in Interaction with AI in European Private Law*, https://doi.org/10.1007/978-3-031-93247-2_2

risks lead humans to compare themselves to machines. Instead, it should reflect how machines benefit them and raise new awareness and knowledge regarding their own capabilities and the potential for personal and collective growth. The homogenization of a society centered on AI instead of humans in various ways is the result of an epistemic impoverishment which, being value-related, is also anthropological. Not surprisingly, this homogenization acts as an incubator for widespread disturbances in society: loneliness, disillusionment, totalitarianism and hegemonies of various kinds, tense discussions at various levels about real or alleged facts of discrimination that can go nowhere within this scenario because of its multiple conflicting logical bases.

Given this scenario, within a human-centered and relational epistemological framework, we discuss how a principle of humanity, which we hope can be recovered, can be developed and strengthened. To this end, we propose an anthropological vision, which we call 'ethics of care'. Such ethics and a new approach to thinking about the human-technology relationship are fundamental and preliminary to addressing human vulnerability, an increasingly urgent issue today which lacks an adequate conceptual frame of reference. For this reason, we elaborate an epistemological reflection and offer a discussion of the concept of 'human nature' within an increasingly technological society.

2 Old and New Problems

There is a long philosophical tradition that can explain the sometimes violent impact that AI has had and is having on human life and on the way we relate to nature and society. Assuming that our thinking/language (*logos*) is a formal reflection of the physical world (*physis*), then the physical world will likewise be a reflection of our thinking. In this perspective, we can make the physical world—or rather, a part of it—think for us and, through the appropriate interfaces, act for us. This supposed isomorphy, or formal equality, between *physis* and *logos* is especially clear when we empty the world and think of all qualitative content and are left with only quantity. What if everything is a number? This is an ancient Pythagorean hypothesis, enthusiastically revived at the dawn of modernity when Galileo performed a methodological maneuver by proposing that in order to study motion we should dispense with the qualitative. In this way, only the measurable (distance traveled, fall time speed, acceleration, etc.) is considered. Later, Descartes transformed this methodology into a mechanistic ontology in which the world as a whole becomes an extended substance beyond which remains only the thinking substance, the self. The campaign to mathematize what is real is thus intensified. Everything, absolutely everything, becomes a mere numerable extension.

Today we would say "everything will end up being digitized". And once the whole *physis* is digitized, if the *logos* wants to maintain its isomorphy with *physis*, it will have to become mere computation, and every logical operation therefore becomes pure computation. As Leibniz said: there will come a time when two philosophers will start arguing and say to each other, "let's calculate". For why should we argue if we can calculate? But let us take another step: why should we calculate ourselves if a machine can do it more accurately and quickly, and without emotional or subjective bias?

There are numerous assumptions connected with the idea of artificial intelligence: ontological assumptions about *physis* and *logos*, epistemological assumptions about the correspondence between the two, anthropological assumptions about what a human person is. We are using a peculiar model of human intelligence, physical reality, and the isomorphy between the two building blocks. Probably none of the three components of the model are reliable. It is not clear that the world is just a number, nor that our thinking is just computation, nor that it is possible to travel back and forth between the two without encountering uncertainties.

A new approach is needed because when we forget the limits of our knowledge (and even more so its assumptions), this generates two perverse effects. On the one hand, we falsify and impoverish reality by forcing it into our conceptual/digital networks. On the other hand, we falsify and impoverish human intelligence, viewing it as something perfectly reproducible and replaceable by artifacts.

The contribution AI can make to the flourishing or devastation of human life is played out in the realm of interpretation. If we interpret AI logocentrically, with pride of reason and elitism, its effect will be devastating. If we understand and use it with a Socratic attitude of intellectual humility, it will serve the flourishing of human life.

3 Ontological and Epistemological Issues

First of all, the relationship between humans and technology needs to be contextualized from a rational point of view because technology constitutes the general framework in which human life is inscribed.

Human action has always been inscribed within a technical ecosystem. We can further frame technical action as directed toward and through a technological ecosystem, which in turn retroacts on the community of users. This characterization raises the question of the relevance of the ethical application of technology. Technology is not neutral. It is not an ancillary sphere of the lives of human beings but has been part of our form of life since we began producing artifacts that have qualitatively and quantitatively altered our existence.

With regard to recent developments in artificial intelligence, we need to question the specific ontology to which these technologies give rise, their epistemological status, and the practical consequences deployed in the ethical sphere.

Ontology can be seen as dealing with what exists. Strictly speaking, artificial intelligence does not exist. Without the human gaze, every part of reality loses its intentional aspect and collapses into a simple physical system. Furthermore, grasping regularities and introducing them into a system of concepts is a specific feature that allows us to formulate something like a plane of ontology. This ability is extraneous to the prerogative of artificial intelligence. The intelligence of these systems does not lie in their computational capabilities, as a reductionist conception of technology and cognition would have it, unless we want to reduce the notion of intelligence to computation.

The term AI is therefore philosophically misleading. It would be more correct to speak of *assisted intelligence systems*, *decision support tools*, or *delegated control systems*.

From the perspective of epistemological knowledge, the application of an automated approach to scientific research, implied by a reductionist conception of cognition and technology, invariably tends to impoverish it if not accompanied by a critical epistemology.

The human being, as well as being a biological organism, is also a cultural organism, and in this respect eminently technical. As mentioned, AI is not neutral: every technology implements ecosystem structures, incentivizes certain behaviors and hinders others. These fit and make sense only in an intentional framework, completely unrelated to the technologies themselves.

This line of thinking leads us to reflect on the ethical bearing of these technologies and how to (intentionality) direct research and, therefore, the use that is made of the technology. Investing in research and development of renewable energy technologies is not the same as persevering in the exploitation of fossil fuels or developing ever 'smarter' armaments. Let us keep in mind that each technology we choose changes—at best, extends—our capabilities, while at the same time it multiplies our needs. The nature of these changes depends on the direction in which we develop information and communication technologies, the meaning we impart to their use, and the purposes we set as a premise for their implementation.

An artificial intelligence system is related to intelligence, but what is intelligent pertains to the human contribution—and not to its artificial component—to which it inevitably must refer for its intelligibility. "Inductive AI will continue to improve in narrow tasks, but if we want to make real progress, we will have to start by appreciating more fully the only true intelligence we know: our own."[1] Machine learning and deep learning are equally captious terms.

According to Miguel Ángel Quintanilla,[2] technology is a system of intentional actions. We propose to combine this intentional approach with a systemic and relational perspective. The change of vision we need can be summarized as follows: we need to move from considering AI systems as "technical systems with social consequences" to considering them as "technically implemented social systems".[3]

The intelligence of an AI system resides in people, not in the AI system's artificial component. Machines cannot be intelligent. This limitation does not reflect a technical problem that can be corrected, but rather a basic ontological question.

Succeeding or not in recognizing a criminal is not a problem for a machine programmed for facial recognition. It is a problem for people whose safety is at risk, and the machine can help us deal with this. The same machine, however, can also be used to control the population of a country and facilitate political repression.

[1] Larson (2021).

[2] Quintanilla (2005).

[3] Hirschheim et al. (1995).

But this is not a problem for the cameras or software involved. In short, technologies are not engaged in solving their own problems, they do not address situations, they do not enter the tangle of people's lives. They are part of the human landscape and in that landscape they make sense.

Outside the human setting, lights turning on and off on a screen or the movements of a robot are mere effects, not performing functions. Miguel de Unamuno's story "Mecanópolis" is emblematic in this regard.[4] The day the protagonist appears in a completely depopulated city, the movements of machines, which until his arrival were mere effects, begin to be functional. The human point of view also changes its ontology: one piece of metal rotating on another, for example, becomes the wheel of a streetcar. What is really at stake—we reiterate—is fundamentally ontological in nature. Artifacts, in the Aristotelian tradition, are substances in only an accidental sense, by analogy. Living beings, and especially human beings—that is, persons—are substances in their proper and paradigmatic sense. Since this difference between artefacts and humans is ontological, the hope (or threat) of nullifying it through technological sophistication is illusory, a mere category error.[5] The ontology of so-called AI systems depends entirely on the human gaze, since these tools are in the realm of the intentional, that is, the semiotic.

What do we mean when we say that a machine stores or processes my financial or health data? We mean that a certain electromagnetic state of the machine (sign) is related to my bank account or my blood pressure (object). Of course, there is no physical relationship between them, but rather a semiotic relationship that is established through a person (interpreter) capable of understanding—with the help of certain interfaces—electromagnetic states that represent numerical values. Without an interpreter, the machine is simply an apparatus that switches from one physical state to another. It is no longer part of an artificial intelligence system. It is just a piece of matter, like a washing machine on Neptune.

All artificial tools, apparatuses and systems are ultimately entities that require triadic, semiotic, and intentional relations. The electromagnetic (or quantum) state of a computer is not in itself a datum unless an interpreter connects it to an object. Moreover, isolated data cannot exist outside a space of possibility and curation without being integrated into a curated framework.

The misunderstanding generated by an inadequate understanding of these technologies ends up being projected onto the human dimension. In addition to the reductionist conceptions these misunderstood technologies harbor, the unreflective celebration of artificial intelligence systems degrades traditional intelligence which was hitherto held in high esteem. Thus, human intelligence is reduced to an interplay of physical interactions, and the human being is perceived in dualistic terms, as a kind of random meeting place between bodily hardware and mental software, susceptible to migration.[6] It seems necessary to have a perspective that places the human being at the center of *techné*, but without anthropomorphizing technological attributes. By

[4] Unamuno (1966) and Villar and Ramos (2019).

[5] Gunkel (2018).

[6] David and Sauviat (2019).

denying intelligence to artifacts, this perspective protects the social value of intelligence itself, for when we perceive intelligence being attributed to something, a self-protection mechanism is activated in us which diminishes the desirability of intelligence.

Recapping, AI—as such—does not exist, and so-called AI systems are systems to supplement human intelligence or support people's decisions. In support of this assertion, let us point out that although algorithms are very efficient at detecting correlations within huge amounts of data, correlations are not causal relationships. They do not allow us to understand the phenomenon we are dealing with or to give a satisfactory explanation for it, much less to question it. To understand, explain or question this situation we need theories that hypothesize causal relationships.

However useful it might be, the knowledge provided by algorithms is affected by the limitations classically associated with inductive inference.[7] In short, all the premises of an inductive inference can be true and the conclusion can still be false. Only a person can intentionally connect and reconnect the logical (digital) plane with the physical (analog) plane, relying on the practical and social knowledge that Aristotle called *phronesis* (prudence). In logical terms, we can construct expectations by induction, generalizing past correlations. This is done very well by individuals and some nonhuman living things. Recent artificial intelligence systems are also excellent at this kind of task, although they require enormous resources in terms of historical data. However, when expectations fail, it is necessary to try to understand what is happening by resorting to novel hypotheses. This type of inference, called abduction, is a creative process, which requires breaking out of the usual systems of expectations.[8] In this process people are essential, with their peculiar ontology, consciousness, intentionality and relationship to the world.

4 Humanizing Technology

The question at this point is: how can these systems contribute to human life? In the first instance, they allow us to delegate certain processes of control. Only people can make decisions. The very concept of decision-making is foreign to mechanics. What we call a "decision" in an artificial intelligence system is such only to the extent that a human being has made the real decision to delegate certain actions to the system, that is, to automate them. The ultimate responsibility, regardless of whether things go well or not, can only rest on the human being. And it is our responsibility, among other things, to support our decision-making by taking advantage of the best available systems.

It should also be clear that there is no such thing as intelligent software, but rather intelligent use of software. It is therefore misleading and absurd to talk about 'software rights'. Here, once again, we are faced with a rather elementary category error.

[7] Hume (2000).

[8] Aliseda (2006).

Nor does it seem generally necessary or useful to demand of human beings a fifth generation of rights that addresses our relationship with the digital world. Inventing new human rights weakens the very idea of them and the enormous rhetorical and moral force they have maintained since World War II to protect people from abuses of power. Human rights are based on a person's dignity and membership in the human family. But to the extent that their scope expands, their protective force inexorably diminishes. A discussion of the duties and responsibility of humans in the shrewd and careful use of any kind of technology, especially one that centers on the great impact of digital technology in our lives and social relations, albeit extremely important, belongs to a different domain.

Reflections of various kinds (technological, ethical, social, normative, etc.) on the relationship between humans and machines often dwell on specific traits that characterize humanity, but they often forget that human beings are the only entities capable of avoiding the theoretical extremisms reflected in the use and consequences of technology in everyday life. Reflecting at this point, even if only summarily, on extreme positions helps us comprehend the theoretical and practical field in which we operate.

5 Human Nature

At one extreme is a form of existentialism, which denies human beings any traits of their own nature and rather perceives them as pure freedom, as beings that determine and construct themselves as they please, of their own free will. At the other extreme we find radical naturalistic positions according to which human beings are nature and nature alone. This naturalism eventually becomes another variant of materialism.[9] Human beings of radical existentialism, devoid of all nature, produce themselves as an (absurd) artifact of themselves. The human beings of radical naturalism, who are all mere biological nature, are thus at the complete disposal of anthropotechnics. However, a distinction must be made between moderate and radical naturalism. According to moderate naturalism, to which we subscribe without reservation, and which is compatible with theistic positions, the natural sciences are important for understanding human beings. For radical naturalism, everything human is reducible to its physical and molecular basis.

Contemporary biology has made simply unfeasible any attempt to reduce this science wholesale to physics. As a result, the materialism of the moment, under the name of naturalism, has been forced to always seek support in biology. In particular, two areas of research are exploited as a legitimizing basis for present-day naturalism: Darwinism in its many variants, as well as neuroscience. However, in this case there is a clear methodological error here whereby tools are applied to a discipline without assessing its feasibility.

[9] Nagel (2012).

Midgley, among others, opposes "the way of thinking which deliberately extends the impersonal, reductive, atomistic methods that are appropriate to physical science into social and psychological enquiries where they work badly [...]. This deliberate extension makes it seem as if something called science is forbidding us to be human. But science does no such thing".[10] The sciences currently invoked for this project are mainly neurology and the study of evolution.

Yet naturalism is by far the dominant academic position, to the point that very few intellectuals dare to disagree with it. Nevertheless, "man is a member, not only of the *natural* order of things, but of the specifically *human* order."[11]

Thomas Nagel states, "I have argued patiently against the prevailing form of naturalism, a reductive materialism that purports to capture life and mind through its neo-Darwinian extension [...] I find this view antecedently unbelievable—a heroic triumph of ideological theory over common sense."[12]

Radical naturalists set themselves the task of naturalizing (or simply denying) freedom, volition, consciousness and self-consciousness, epistemic, moral and aesthetic values, language and intentionality, sociability, religiosity, altruism and a long list of traits that, based on common sense, we would be inclined to regard as uncompromisingly human.

We find fully convincing Tallis's argument that there are no scientific reasons that support the naturalistic conception of human beings. Naturalism is not a requisite of evolutionary biology or neuroscience. Only from an abusive interpretation of these scientific fields can such an idea be preached. While it is very important to study our genes and neurons, not everything human is reducible to genes and neurons.[13]

Soler argues that nothing in current neuroscience requires a naturalistic or materialistic interpretation of human life.[14] There are aspects of human life, such as morality, that do not find an exclusive explanation or ultimate foundation in the functioning of our brains.

Nagel's naturalistic, though not materialistic, alternative, in our opinion, is the most intelligent position.[15] Expanded science, in the sense Nagel proposes, would be compatible with both theistic and non-theistic views of reality. Moreover, the current state of science, as reflected in the above quote, is compatible with both. In other words, scientific progress was not aimed, at the dawn of modernity, at excluding God, and in the end we know that it has not produced such an exclusion as a consequence, however much many philosophers and scientists have wanted to find it there.

Both perspectives, unfortunately, fail to capture human peculiarities by trying to reduce them to one or more groups of elements that characterize humans.

---

[10] Midgley (2002).

[11] Rescher (1999).

[12] Nagel (2012).

[13] Tallis (2011).

[14] Soler (2013).

[15] Nagel (2013).

6 Anthropotechnical Artificialism

Starting from these perspectives and from Nietzsche, one of the thinkers who most influences both the deniers of human nature and the advocates of its full naturalization, two perspectives have been produced do not differ significantly in agenda: the Ossonian transhumanist, and Continental-style posthumanist.

The general idea is that if human nature is completely natural, then it is technically available, and if human nature simply does not exist, then we have the task of inventing it technically. Anthropotechnics is indicated in both cases. Prominent among transhumanist thinkers are the Oxford group, and within this Savulescu and Bostrom.[16]

In the United States, Max More founded the Extropian Institute in 1990, dedicated to promoting transhumanist ideas. To more we owe this definition of the transhumanist enterprise: Transhumanism is a class of philosophies that seek to guide us toward a posthuman condition. Transhumanism shares many elements of humanism, including a respect for reason and science, a commitment to progress, and an appreciation of the human (or transhuman) existence in this life.[17]

"Transhumanism," More continues, "differs from humanism in recognizing and anticipating radical alterations in the nature and possibilities of our lives as a result of various sciences and technologies."[18] For its part, the WTA (World Transhumanist Association) abounds in this orientation by defining transhumanism as the intellectual and cultural movement that affirms the possibility and opportunity of fundamentally improving the human condition through applied reason, especially by developing and making available technologies.[19] The component of technoscientific optimism and the desire to overcome human nature is still present, understood always and only in terms of constraints, never in terms of constitutive limitations.[20]

The ranks of those who defend a profound anthropotechnics are made up of continental posthumanist philosophers, among whom we can cite, for example, Peter Sloterdijk or Giorgio Agamben, whose inspiration is to be sought in the existentialist and Nietzschean tradition. Nietzsche's view sees the human being as "a rope knotted between the animal and the Superman, a rope stretched over an abyss".[21] Sloterdijk characterizes the human being as a strange creature, loaded with genetic diseases and limitations that can be overcome thanks to bioengineering and artificial intelligence.

[16] Savulescu and Bostrom (2009).

[17] More (2010).

[18] More (2010).

[19] World Transhumanist Association (n.d.).

[20] Asla (2018) and Marcos and Pérez (2018).

[21] Nietzsche (1883–1885).

In his *Rules for the Human Park*,[22] Sloterdijk considers humanism dead and proposes a "new civilizing structure" posthumanist, developed through recent anthropotechnics. By failing "as an animal," Sloterdijk continues, "the indeterminate being falls out of its environment".[23]

Roger Penrose, in 1989, applied history to the state of philosophy of mind. At that time, the academic fashion was to conceive of the human mind as a computer. Penrose then wrote his famous book *The Emperor's New Mind*,[24] in which he sounded the alarm: no, the human mind is not algorithmic, it is not a computer.

At the 1980 Symposium of the Académie Internationale de Philosophie des Sciences, President Evandro Agazzi presented a paper entitled "Intentionality and Artificial Intelligence",[25] in which he stressed that the differences between machines and human intelligence center on intentionality.

The current philosophical task is therefore as human as it is cosmic: it consists of defending human beings from themselves, from their temptation toward inhumanity, and the cosmos from nihilistic indifference. But this question cannot be asked in an abstract way. So let us start by asking what unites us as human beings.

We will look to the work of Aristotle for our main inspiration, because his thinking can be regarded as a high philosophical elaboration of human common sense.

7 Aristotelian-Inspired Anthropology

Aristotle's moderate naturalism never contemplates human beings merely in terms of their biological aspects, but rather integrates them in a unique vision of the human being, where social and spiritual aspects become the focus, the viewpoint from which we can better understand human beings.[26] Moreover, in the Aristotelian tradition, human nature is not primarily a concept, nor can it be compressed into a common definition. It is, first of all, a form, in the Aristotelian sense of the term. In other words, it is an individual form, present in each specific human being. It is a physical entity, embedded in time and space and affected by change, but with the stability of substance itself. We resemble each other in many ways and have much in common. The network of similarities we capture serves to construct concepts. And only then does human nature appear, secondarily, as a concept.

Human nature therefore includes, according to Aristotelian inspiration, at least three aspects: the animal, the social and the spiritual. It should be emphasized that these are not reducible (i.e. epistemically and ontologically subordinate) to each other, but can be constructively integrated with each other. If the human being is made up of animal, social and spiritual aspects, in order to approach the knowledge

[22] Sloterdijk (2008).

[23] Sloterdijk (2008).

[24] Penrose (1989).

[25] Agazzi (1987).

[26] Marcos and Pérez (2018).

of human nature, we must rely on the physical and biological sciences, the social sciences and the humanities, respectively.

And yet, it seems that we are still only halfway there. Let us suppose that through the collaboration of all these areas of knowledge we come closer to human nature. From there, can we extract indications for placing technologies in the whole of human life? Are we not falling into the famous naturalistic fallacy? Not necessarily. Taking our cue from Hans Jonas,[27] we should remember that there is a connection between being and the good; that the human being, being more, is worth more; that humanity in oneself and in others, must therefore be respected. Common sense and daily experience lead us to conceive of an image of the human being in which the unity of the person, its biophysical, social and spiritual aspects, is recognized. A philosophical elaboration of this common human experience is found in the Aristotelian tradition, for which human being is animal, social and rational (*zoon politikon logikon*), and these aspects are united and integrated. Aristotle, in his treatise *De partibus animalium* wrote that "difference is form in matter" (*to eidos en te hyle*).[28] This profound metaphysical insight is what enables us to unite all our biological, social and spiritual traits (differences) into a single substance, without any of them being annulled by the others, but in which all are integrated.

In short, the idea of the human being found in the Aristotelian tradition seems illuminating. We are *vulnerable* because of our animality; because we are social, we are mutually dependent; and, by virtue of our spirituality, we become autonomous and free. On the other hand, every human being is a unique substance, a person. We can intellectually distinguish different aspects, but in reality they do not exist separately. And this integration of all that is human into the unity of each person occurs by differentiation.

The irredeemability of our being animals has profound implications. Human beings are not just any kind of rational being but are specifically 'animals'. This fact forces us to 'think from the body', from the experience mediated and constituted by our corporeality, that is, by the body that we are. If, by nature, we are animals, this means, among other things, that we are vulnerable, susceptible to harm and suffering, pleasure and pain. Being vulnerable does not make us less human but is precisely part of what makes us human beings. "Human beings," says bioethicist Lydia Feito "are vulnerable as a condition of our very nature as persons […]. It is an anthropological characteristic that defines us. However, we tend to hide it […]. The pandemic came to remind us of our vulnerability in a harsh and overwhelming way".[29]

Living beings have an inside and an outside, they have semi-permeable barriers that identify them, separate them from their environment and at the same time communicate with it, making them functional, but also vulnerable. This inwardness and necessary openness of all living things is what makes humans vulnerable.

It is this biological corporeality of ours that makes us vulnerable as opposed to rocks and concepts which are not. Human beings would only cease to be vulnerable

[27] Jonas (1979).

[28] Aristotle (n.d.).

[29] Feito (2020).

if they stopped being living beings and, for example, turned into software as some transhumanists propose. But with such a transformation, of course, they would also cease to be human. Emmanuel Lévinas goes so far as to understand human subjectivity in terms of vulnerability which he identifies as a condition of possibility for any form of respect for the human.[30] That is, that without the recognition of vulnerability there is no room for respect.

Human vulnerability must be recognized, and we must seek to mitigate it through mutual aid and care, knowing that its complete suppression is incompatible with human nature. Furthermore, our social condition makes us mutually dependent and places us in a specific community, the human family. As with vulnerability, dependence does not make us less human but is a part of what it means to be human.

Not only vulnerable and dependent, we are also rational. The spiritual realm in which our rationality places us includes our ability to think, to engage in science and technology, to reflect, contemplate and ponder reasons for doing, believing and creating new things. Because we are rational, we ask and give reasons, we seek explanations and causes, we question even the most radical and ultimate, we reflect, we voluntarily decide one way or another, we value goodness, truth and beauty.

8 Digital Transitions: The Position of AI Technology in Human Life

Having considered human nature from the perspective of animality, sociability, and culture which allowed us to argue the acceptability of human vulnerability, we will now move on to the analysis, albeit schematically, of the four elements that characterize debates on the relationship between humans and technology: automation, acceleration, accessibility and autonomy. These elements are present in today's human life and have clearly visible effects, both positive and negative, on human vulnerability.

- Automation: Automation processes continue to be a standard of progress and success in even the most advanced applications of engineering sciences mediated by AI (embodied AI) technology. Automation in analysis, however, typically involves linear and functional processes which follow mechanical, reproducible and repeatable logic and rules, which in turn can be decomposed and regulated by on-off commands.
- Acceleration: Digital-mediated automation has pushed the performance of humans and machines to the limit in this direction, creating, in some ways, a speed competition between the two. From the AI point of view, memory, history and projects are completely irrelevant variables. Much of the tension and discomfort felt by human beings, on the other hand, derives from the impossibility of undoing these variables. What perspective can allow human beings to perceive

[30] Lévinas (1978) and Antenat (2003).

their anthropological and ethical values not as limitations but rather as conditions for personal and collective growth, development and fulfillment?[31] Clearly, to achieve this perceptional shift requires moving away from the functionalist and reductionist logic that have governed previous agendas, and moving toward new perspectives that we call ecological and care. The tension behind this aim reflects the same epistemological reasons that explain the current emergence of human ecology and ecological ethics studies that attempt to move beyond the dominant utilitarian paradigms.

– Accessibility: This is fundamentally about the issue of training people in the use of technologies and internet search engines, not only for ethical and prudential reasons (such as keeping minors from accessing pornographic sites); it is about adequate training in interpreting information extracted from websites regarding issue that range from fake news to the need to contextualize information based on the origin of the data and the algorithms set up for processing them in the medical, legal, etc.).
– Autonomy: This fourth notion characterizing debates on the relationship between humans and technology requires a philosophical introduction. The historical-philosophical roots that justify the trends mentioned above have their origins in positivism, which aims at a rigorous and empirical definition of the validity and meaning of knowledge, and which has reinforced a 'factual' and 'thingified' logic of experience and knowledge. Consequently, this logic of experience and knowledge enjoy the prerogative of immunity with respect to possible critical analysis, revision and interpretation. (Here we must note that this 'privilege' is only apparently paradoxical in the age of digital-mediated dematerialization.) This philosophical culture of positivism is responsible for having transferred Cartesian dualism into our general conception of human experience and work, often condemning it to a sterile self-referentiality.[32] The modern idea that machines and AI will perform better than humans in carrying out work is the obvious result of this tendency. Even the concept of innovation suffers from this inherent bias when it becomes nothing more than the implementation and application of existing technologies.

Beyond the many considerations that might follow at this point, what interests us here is how the notion of autonomy appears in and shapes debates about the implementation of digitally mediated human work and knowledge. We also consider the ethical issues that arise from it. Our focus is essentially on the increase of autonomy and rationality in decision-making processes through an implementation of the speed and efficiency of processes and the expansion of the possibilities for action and control. In this context, the term 'rationality' is understood as the ability to choose the best action to take in order to achieve a certain goal, given certain criteria to be optimized and the available resources. Conceptual categories such as those of achieving a goal, optimization and choosing the best action consistently respond to

[31] MacIntyre (1999), Marcos and Bertolaso (2018), and Marcos and Pérez (2018).

[32] Bertolaso (2019).

the inductive processes that characterize digital technologies. Criteria for making the 'best' decision are absent in these decision-making processes.

The notion of autonomy applied in this context follows the proceduralist logics of the modern-contemporary tradition described above. The desired autonomy is simply an autonomy of action, where the terms of the problem and pragmatic goals are already defined. The clearly articulated ethical problems that arise from the use of these technologies derive from an assumption typical of contemporary Anglo-Saxon and Kantian-rooted philosophy, whereby the nexus between autonomy and ethics excludes an axiological evaluation of the ends that mediate and define human action. In our opinion, the proposed arguments suffer from a certain self-referentiality and argumentative closure. The very concept of human dignity is explicitly linked to its Kantian root but is only meant to prevent entities from treating people as an aggregation of useful data, rather than as ends in themselves.

Freedom is described as a right, rather than an ontological component of the human person, and autonomy itself is ultimately not clearly defined. However, this 'reductionist view of human autonomy', as we call it, does not adequately address contemporary needs. The issues related to human rights within digital technological applications—for example, in the fields of medicine and law—call for a deeper understanding of the notion of human autonomy in more *relational* terms. The same is true for the questions arising from the increasingly generalized sensitivity to mutual dependence in global and eco-systemic dynamics.

The notion of vulnerability highlights the notion of autonomy in relational terms and grounds its anthropological, ethical and ecological fruitfulness. From this perspective, digital technologies can be seen as a great resource or a great threat. Similarly, the notion of ethics as a practical and theoretical approach to the human good, with particular reference to the conditions that enable human flourishing from a personal and social perspective, also allows us to broaden the reflection on autonomy in a relational sense. We are referring here to the aspiration for balanced autonomy which does not ignore the consciousness of mutual dependence that excludes an individualistic and instrumentalist conception of the digital user. The implications in the field of social media, digital identities, etc., are obvious. For in these fields the subject is thought of as constitutively immersed in systemic relationships with others and with the environment (for example, green and blue; natural and digital/technological) that surround him or her and that also largely define his or her historical and biographical identity.

Moving on, we now explore possible solutions that can 'fix' the excessive and especially uncritical pervasiveness of digital technologies. To this aim we will consider two transversal elements that affect all four A's (automation, acceleration, accessibility and autonomy): dematerialization and what we call 'homogenization'.[33]

What is being discussed has profoundly changedhave profoundly changed what in more philosophical and technical terms we can call cognitive experience. Increasingly digitally mediated, our understanding of things and ourselves is constrained by

33 Bertolaso (2019).

the laws and logic that characterize by definition the world of digital and AI technologies. Inductive processes, the possibility of 'rewinding' narratives and experiences, the absolute repeatability of facts and events, the elaboration of stereotypes and images of self or others within seconds depending on preferences or sensitivities, mostly collectively generated and consolidated through social media, underlie the most important consequence of the processes of dematerialization of data that we have called 'homogenization'.[34]

Thus, we even run the risk that cognitive experience will be homogenized if we do not invest in the human capacity to understand the difference between proceeding humanly and artificially. It should be noted that This opposition is typically epistemological, since from an anthropological point of view, as we have already mentioned, humans are naturally technical and therefore in this sense even the artificial belongs to the human.

What we mean is probably clearer if we consider the consequences of the processes in the last century that have adopted the terms 'technological' and 'digital', used as adjectives (technological/digital support) and as nouns (the technological and the digital) that can even be used as 'personifications' (see Neil Harbisson's declaration "I am technology"[35]). The nominalization or 'nouning' of these terms is by no means neutral from an epistemological and axiological point of view.[36]

9 From the Paradigm of Control to the Paradigm of Care

It is possible to contrast the processes of homogenization with a different vision of human action and work by introducing the concepts of epistemological complementarity and an ethical alternative. We must begin by raising the question whether there is an alternative to a functionalist and individualist, procedural and fundamentally performance-oriented conception, whose governing counterpart is typically determined by a logic of control. The thesis we defend is that even issues related to digital transitions can help us deepen our understanding of a principle of humanity that enables us to better understand the potential of human nature, with its dignity and freedom.

The principle of humanity resides in its fundamental anthropological dimension of care: the care of life and its collective structuring principles, such as family and civil society. Human nature, through the fruitful combination of its biological and cultural components is based on a distinction and conjunction of corporeality, rationality and sociality.[37]

Far from essentialist claims, this view also enables us to articulate relational dynamics within humankind that enable for real plurality while still allowing for the

[34] Bertolaso (2019) and Bertolaso (2023b).

[35] Wikipedia contributors (n.d.).

[36] Jasanoff (2016) and Bertolaso (2019).

[37] Marcos and Pérez (2018).

unity of the human community. Homogeneity, in fact, is not only human, but also not natural in the living world and as such is not desirable or advantageous.

Our very biographical nature is aligned with the time and space we inhabit through our corporeality and is typically represented by the notions of place and home in their deepest anthropological sense.[38]

Corporeality, rationality, and sociality (and respectively vulnerability, autonomy, and interdependence), although epistemologically distinguishable, are actually ontologically inseparable: vulnerability is social, sociality is autonomous, and interdependence is corporeal and rational; as for corporeality and rationality, the one is autonomous and the other is vulnerable.

Every aspect of the human being relates to its surroundings, and each of these aspects opens up to a relational sphere, to the surrounding environment, to society, to the cultural sphere. That is, there is a certain overlap between the anthropological schema we have illustrated (mainly articulated in terms of animality, rationality, sociability) and this triadic organization that draws on the categories of genealogy, function, and context. The genealogical (bio) dimension has to do with our animal condition, the functional dimension with the social roles in which we operate, and the contextual dimension with our values and cultural markers, with their linguistic and, in the highest sense, spiritual connotations. If we integrate this view of humans with the systemic or multidimensional character as proposed by a relational ontology,[39] the reflection becomes more profound, prompting us to question the evidence that humans belong to the world of the living. It further prompts us to seek an adequate response to the causal relations of dependence and integration among the different dimensions to account for the diachronicity of the developmental and flourishing processes of living beings and humans in particular.

In this context, we believe it is time to make a profound change in the epistemology of the living being, to try to understand its specificity from the perspective of its dynamism.[40] Rather than as a systemic set of interactions and pre-existing parts, the living being must be understood from the point of view of its generative existence, which develops, maintains itself in a dynamically integrated way, and manifests itself according to a specific relationship with its environment.

An ontology of the living being that takes as its point of view the nature of integrated development,[41] comprehends those three dimensions in the following ways: It sees the genealogical dimension as typically traceable to the biographical and biological, and to our animal nature in the classical/Aristotelian sense. It also identifies a more specific functional dimension which is typically represented by our role in the environments in which we operate. It finally defines the contextual dimension by the values and cultural markers that identify us and that we as individuals enrich through our personal and collective actions. Such an ontology sees these dimensions

[38] Marcos and Bertolaso (2018), and Bertolaso (2019).

[39] Bertolaso (2019, 2023a).

[40] Marcos and Bertolaso (2018), and Bertolaso (2016, 2018, 2020).

[41] Bertolaso (2016, 2020).

interacting with each other according to specific rhythms and proportions to ensure an integrated development and an identity-related, ontological stability of the living.

When analyzed together for a deeper understanding of the historicity (and thus biography) that characterizes human beings, these dimensions present a striking interdependence called 'care'.

The dynamics by which human beings are able to care for themselves and the world, caring for others and creating a semantically relevant culture of relationship (from the simplest social forms to culture, politics and art), highlight a unified principle of integration that lends historicity to the combined evolution of the three dynamics which can never be separated from one another. In this sense, care becomes the ethical counterpart of our spatiotemporal ontology.[42]

Integrated developments, however, *are always characterized by imbalances and tensions*: in biology, cells, when properly duplicated are always polarized. Similarly, desire in humans is a generator of growth and development, to the extent that it is oriented, integrated, harmonized and respectful of the proportions among the three dimensions. It is not based on the repetitive appropriation of reality. It is no accident, in our opinion, that in *Ethics* Aristotle defined the human being as "intelligent desire." Therefore, we can say that what is proper and natural to human beings resides in their peculiar interaction with their historical-biographical context, mediated by the body and integrated in a dimension we can call 'interiority.'

The explorations we offer in this paper can provide us with a more complete understanding of what makes us human, of a principle of humanity that underlies even the *technological humanism* we wish to defend here, seeking that *unum versus aliud*, that is, what is common in differences and justifies speaking of the human as a condition of its own, with its own characteristics, concretized both personally and collectively.

We are not mere pieces obliged to share the same common box called reality, but subjects with an identical invitation to co-exist (in the sense of the term used by the philosopher Polo[43]), that is, to share what is, to desire, to think, to yearn, to approve or reject. This is the ontological world of human life, the space of freedom and responsibility. In abandoning the mechanistic view, the basis of the control paradigm, and in emphasizing interaction (co-existence) and vulnerability as intrinsic elements of human beings, a new access is opened to the understanding of the attitude of care, defined as the "ethical counterpart of our spatial-temporal nature".[44] If vulnerability (as described in the previous section) gives a new dimension to coexistence, because coexistence is a reciprocal relationship, in which we all hope to interact with everyone equally, vulnerability also makes this reciprocity asymmetrical, since we do not all interact starting from the same condition, nor do we receive equally from one another in coexistence. This has implications for current scenarios of progressive digitization of processes that affect our relationships and educational, care and communication processes that cannot be ignored.

---

[42] Bertolaso and Rocchi (2020).

[43] Polo (2018a, 2018b).

[44] Bertolaso and Rocchi (2020).

Not all of us are, manifest, or need the same thing, and the historical authenticity of human experience contributes to this prospectivist nature of human relationships. Becoming aware of this makes the interaction in vulnerability, called coexistence (in both senses of living separately—live and let live—and living together), transform our way of existing into caring for each other and the world. Such caring acknowledges that to exist as a human being we must welcome the vulnerability of others and surrender ourselves to the care of others, receiving attention, help, affection through coexistence, in accordance with a reciprocity that is not symmetrical because of the difference between what I give and what I receive. Thus, the human ethos comes to foster a give/take dynamic that defines the ethics of care, because of which there is no way for human beings to exist in indifference to one another. The ethics of care is founded on a mixture of coexistence and vulnerability. It is not an ethics of philanthropy or simple subsidiarity. There is here an obligatory passage through solidarity.[45]

Our proposal combines genealogy, functionality and environment, all areas in which being 'human' implies existing as one of us, of this concrete world in which we live. In this sense, human relationality presupposes that we take care of others and let others take care of us, our being alive and the conditions for our growth and fulfillment (flourishing). Human beings transform their actions into an ethics of care that is reflected in all cultural, economic, scientific activities, both individual and collective. Therefore, care becomes the ethical counterpart of our space-time ontology and is typically represented by a generative asymmetry. It is always semantically generative of meaning and value, but at the same time it is open to gratuitousness.

This new approach implies, in relation to the use of technology, the urgent need to move away from a pragmatism that becomes sterile if it is not animated by a rebirth—here we have in mind a 'technological humanism'—of what moves human action, desires and values.

10 Conclusions

It is fundamental that technology, and in particular AI, be placed in the realm of human action, putting it at the service of this realm and the goals of a truly human life. We already know what a human being is, and what its nature is. We know the normative terms that come with it. We must foster life, mitigate our vulnerability and preserve health; we must progress toward more peaceful, compassionate and just ways of social coexistence; we must further project our spirituality toward goodness, truth and beauty. In every technological application we must question ourselves about these ends. We need to know, before investigating and launching a new technological system, whether it will harm our health or provide support for it; whether it will promote coexistence or, on the contrary, strain human relationships by making them

[45] Brizi and Bertolaso (2019a, 2019b).

more violent and unjust; whether it will bring us closer to truth, goodness and beauty or immerse us in a world that is darker every day.

To our knowledge, AI has functioned as an ally to human ends, but also, in many cases, as a threat to them. AI algorithms can be designed to serve the most diverse ends. They can serve to interconnect us and also to isolate us from one another. Only a clear determination of what a human being is, of what is good for people, allows us to act judiciously in the planning, design and application of AI.

This is not to say that technology is neutral and can be applied for one purpose or the other, but that the very design of algorithms may already be an obstacle to our desire to know, to seek the truth. Artificial intelligence systems can help human prosperity, but they can also deeply damage our lives. And this can occur independently of specific, individual applications of such technologies. Their effect on human lives is often determined as early as the initial design and structuring stages, as well as in the reception these technologies have among the consumer base. It is unthinkable, for example, to program, in a narrow sense, certain domains of experience, or to defer to the authority of a judge over a system that acts on their behalf.

We must think again about automated arms control, where human decisions and responsibilities must not be excluded in any way: these are systems that generate what is called 'moral distance' between contenders or between them and civilians.

It is important to shorten this distance through close human control, even in an area that has never been more necessary and beneficial to humanity than today, that of medical care, where AI in support of medical personnel can bring great benefits. We must be careful where we draw the line between autonomy and instrumentality.

In short, AI systems can serve us or enslave us to their headless logic, depending on how we design, apply and interpret them.[46] For all the reasons discussed in this chapter, it is critically important to have clear criteria for discerning the direction in which we want AI systems to go. And these criteria will necessarily have to be anthropological.

References

Agazzi E (1987) Intenzionalità e intelligenza artificiale. In: Prini P (a cura di) Informatica e pastorale. Morcelliana, Brescia, pp 87–105. Translation by authors

Aliseda A (2006) Abductive reasoning. Springer, Dordrecht

Amor JR (ed) (2022) Huella digital: ¿servidumbre o servicio? Tirant, Valencia

Antenat N (2003) Respect et vulnérabilité chez Levinas. Le Portique. Revue de philosophie et de sciences humaines 11. https://doi.org/10.4000/leportique.558

Aristotle (n.d.) De partibus animalium, 643a 24. Translation by authors

Asla M (2018) El transhumanismo como ideología: ambigüedades y dificultades de la fe en el progreso. Scio. Revista De Filosofía 15:63–96

Bertolaso M (2016) Philosophy of cancer: a dynamic and relational view. Springer, Dordrecht

[46] Amor (2022).

Bertolaso M (2018) Human work and automation: negotiating the tension between solitude and relations. In: Pontificia Accademia delle Scienze Sociali, Roma. https://www.pass.va/en/publications/studia-selecta/studia_selecta_03_pass.html
Bertolaso M (2019) Artificialmente e umanamente: epistemologie a confronto. Paradoxa 2:137–149
Bertolaso M (2020) Understanding complexity in life sciences. In: Ingenioli V, La Torre G (eds) Environmental alteration leads to human disease: a planetary health approach. Springer, Dordrecht. https://doi.org/10.1007/978-3-030-83160-8_1.
Bertolaso M (2023a) Complexity and management: epistemic insights from life science. In: Handbook of philosophy of management. Springer, Dordrecht
Bertolaso M (2023b) Il fattore umano nelle transizioni digitali. In: Krienke M (a cura di) Intelligenza artificiale e dottrina sociale della Chiesa. La Società, Verona
Bertolaso M, Rocchi R (2020) Specifically human: human work and care in the age of machines. Bus Ethics: A Eur Rev. https://doi.org/10.1111/beer.12281
Brizi MR, Bertolaso M (2019a) Per una nuova idea di progresso: quale solidarietà per uno sviluppo sostenibile? In: Mastrolia N (a cura di) Dalla società fordista alla società digitale. aLicosia Editor, Ogliastro Cilento (SA), pp 303–329
Brizi MR, Bertolaso M (2019b) Sostenibilità e generatività: alcune considerazioni sulla condizione femminile ai margini dell'enciclica Humanae Vitae. In: Leone D (a cura di) Humanae Vitae. Cacucci Editore, Bari
David M, Sauviat C (2019) Intelligence artificielle: la nouvelle barbarie. Éditions du Rocher, Monaco, pp 203–204
Feito L (2020) La vulnerabilidad ante la pandemia. Bioética Complutense 39:2–4
Gunkel DJ (2018) Robot rights. MIT Press, Cambridge
Hirschheim R, Klein HK, Lyytinen K (1995) Information systems development and data modelling: conceptual and philosophical foundations. Cambridge University Press, Cambridge
Hume D (2000) A treatise of human nature. Edited by Norton DF, Norton MJ. Oxford University Press, Oxford. [Originally published 1739–1740]
Jasanoff S (2016) The ethics of invention: technology and the human future. W. W. Norton & Company, New York
Jonas H (1979) Das Prinzip Verantwortung: Versuch einer Ethik für die technologische Zivilisation. Insel, Frankfurt am Main
Larson EJ (2021) The myth of artificial intelligence: why computers can't think the way we do. Harvard University Press, Cambridge, MA
Lévinas E (1978) Vulnérabilité et contact. In: Autrement qu'être. Ou au-delà de l'essence, cap III, parte 5. Martinus Nijhoff, La Haye, pp 120–128
MacIntyre A (1999) Dependent rational animals: why human beings need the virtues. Open Court, Chicago
Marcos A, Bertolaso M (2018) What is a home? On the intrinsic nature of the home. In: Argandona A (ed) The home. Edward Elgar Publishing, Cheltenham, pp 35–56
Marcos A, Pérez MM (2018) Meditación de la naturaleza humana. BAC, Madrid, cap X
Midgley M (2002) Science and poetry. Routledge, London
More M (2010) Transhumanist FAQ. http://www.extropy.org/resources.htm/
Nagel T (2012) Mind and cosmos. Oxford University Press, Oxford
Nagel T (2013) The core of "Mind and Cosmos". The New York Times. https://opinionator.blogs.nytimes.com/2013/08/18/the-core-of-mind-and-cosmos/.
Nietzsche F (1883–1885) Also sprach Zarathustra. Leipzig. Translation by authors
Penrose R (1989) The emperor's new mind: concerning computers, minds and the laws of physics. Oxford University Press, Oxford
Polo L (2018a) Antropología trascendental. In: Polo L (ed) Obras completas de Leonardo Polo. eunsa, Pamplona, pp 11–591
Polo L (2018b) Ética: hacia una versión moderna de los temas clásicos. In: Polo L (ed) Obras completas de Leonardo Polo. eunsa, Pamplona

Quintanilla MÁ (2005) Tecnología: un enfoque filosófico y otros ensayos de filosofía de la tecnología. Fondo de Cultura Económica, Ciudad de México
Rescher N (1999) The limits of science. University of California Press, Berkeley
Savulescu J, Bostrom N (eds) (2009) Human enhancement. Oxford University Press, Oxford
Sloterdijk P (2008) Regeln für den Menschenpark: Ein Antwortschreiben zu Heideggers Brief über den Humanismus. Suhrkamp, Frankfurt
Soler F (2013) Mitología materialista de la ciencia. Encuentro, Madrid
Tallis R (2011) Aping mankind: neuromania, darwinitis and the misinterpretation of humanity. Acumen, Durham
Unamuno M (1966) Mecanópolis (1913). In: García Blanco M (ed) Los lunes de "El Imparcial", Obras completas, vol 2: Novelas. Escelicer, Madrid, pp 833–837
Villar A, Ramos M (2019) Mecanópolis: una distopía de Miguel de Unamuno. Pensamiento 75:321–343
Wikipedia contributors (n.d.) Neil Harbisson. Wikipedia. https://it.wikipedia.org/wiki/Neil_Harbisson.
World Transhumanist Association (n.d.) The transhumanist FAQ. https://www.humanityplus.org/transhumanist-faq

Marta Bertolaso, Full Professor of Logic and Philosophy of Science and Head of the Philosophy of Science and Human Development Research Unit at the Campus Bio-Medico University of Rome. Her research covers philosophy, epistemology, ethics, complexity sciences, and human-technology interaction, with over 100 publications.

Angelo Marinucci, Affiliated with the Campus Bio-Medico University of Rome and the Universidade Estadual de Campinas (Brazil), focuses on theoretical biology, history of science, and ethics, and has published extensively in these areas.

Open Access This chapter is licensed under the terms of the Creative Commons Attribution 4.0 International License (http://creativecommons.org/licenses/by/4.0/), which permits use, sharing, adaptation, distribution and reproduction in any medium or format, as long as you give appropriate credit to the original author(s) and the source, provide a link to the Creative Commons license and indicate if changes were made.

The images or other third party material in this chapter are included in the chapter's Creative Commons license, unless indicated otherwise in a credit line to the material. If material is not included in the chapter's Creative Commons license and your intended use is not permitted by statutory regulation or exceeds the permitted use, you will need to obtain permission directly from the copyright holder.

AI and Electoral Manipulation: From Misinformation to Demoralization

Frank Pasquale

Abstract Artificial intelligence is a powerful tool, but it is easily exploited to deceive and demoralize the vulnerable. Two common types of AI—predictive and generative—put democracy at risk if they are not properly regulated. Predictive analytics can divide publics into ever more isolated silos, eroding the type of common knowledge necessary for democratic deliberation. Generative AI is making it ever easier to fake images and events. Even when such fabrications are debunked, the air of unreality created by such dissimulation has allowed some politicians to deny real evidence of wrongdoing by claiming evidence of it was "AI-generated." This dangerous confluence of trends means reformers must work on more than combating misinformation. They also need to resist demoralization, which occurs when citizens start tuning out politics altogether and become too cynical or distracted to engage. AI may also play a small part in addressing the problems of misinformation and demoralization—but real solutions entail a far broader conversation about the future of democracy.

Keywords Disinformation · Demoralization · Democracy · AI · Manipulation

1 Introduction

Concern over AI's role in elections has gone from speculation to fact. Numerous bad faith actors have used generative AI to create false and misleading media, and predictive analytics to target and amplify its effects. Leading communications scholars from the U.S. and Australia have even titled a recent conference "Are Fair Elections Possible in the Age of AI?" The digital vulnerability of citizens to microtargeted, misleading, and vote-suppressing media is a clear and present danger.

An effective policy response to these problems needs to take into account the full range of effects of misleading and manipulative AI. These effects may be roughly categorized as epistemic and affective. Prior researchers have well-mapped the epistemic category via terms like misinformation and disinformation. Affect theory

F. Pasquale (✉)
Cornell Tech and Cornell Law School, Ithaca, NY, USA
e-mail: frank.pasquale@cornell.edu

© The Author(s) 2025

C. Amodio and A. Diurni (eds.), *Human Vulnerability in Interaction with AI in European Private Law*, https://doi.org/10.1007/978-3-031-93247-2_3

provides rich insights into the emotive dimensions of the public sphere. This chapter focuses in particular on one affective dimension of AI's potential role in elections: demoralization.

While disinformation weaponizes false information, demoralization can arise when citizens are bombarded by one-sided, negative narratives of any level of truth. Both opportunistic and sincere actors can now use generative AI to churn out such narratives (in the form of text, memes, images, and even videos) at an extraordinary pace.[1] Such demoralization tends to demotivate voters, eroding the affective foundations of democracy.

This chapter will begin by defining terms, focusing on AI, democracy, and manipulation. One key finding will be the importance of some baseline of common knowledge to the effectiveness of democratic deliberation. Four subparts will then explore how generative AI and predictive AI undermine common knowledge, morale, and motivation. Solutions are desperately needed; they include restrictions on (or disclosures of) certain uses of AI in elections, as well as information literacy initiatives. Objections are anticipated and rebutted in the penultimate part of the chapter, which then concludes with reflections on how AI may further disrupt an already fragile ecology of facts and fantasy.

2 Defining AI and Democracy

AI has many potential definitions, but perhaps the broadest is the computation of cognitive tasks deemed to necessitate some level of human intelligence. There are two broad types of AI widely used at present.[2] Generative AI is used to create text, images, video, and other media, as well as code and other forms of operational language. Predictive AI uses machine learning to optimize outcomes based on data. Both have been deployed in electoral contexts.

Democracy may be an "essentially contested concept," but a range of definitions support the main argument of his chapter. On the most minimal conception, democracy is little more than the opportunity to replace one group of ruling elites with another.[3] On a maximalist conception, democracy includes not only universal voting rights for adults, but also the resources necessary for effective enjoyment of those rights.[4] Such resources may include everything from a social minimum of housing, health care, and education, to the cash necessary to promote a candidate or join a party. A maximalist conception usually also includes not only "floors" of social support to voters, but also "ceilings" on the participation of the particularly wealthy

[1] For a prescient warning about the weaponization of narrative, see Allenby (2017). The work of Arizona State University's Weaponized Narrative Initiative is also illuminating.

[2] Narayanan and Kapoor (2024).

[3] Schumpeter (1943).

[4] Dahl (1995).

and powerful. Existing democracies exist somewhere between these minimalist and maximalist poles.

The diversity of conceptions of democracy sometimes muddies academic debates about its prerequisites and purposes. However, actually existing polities existing between these ideal types depend on at least the following from citizens:

1. Acquiring common knowledge of some basic set of facts about candidates, parties, and states of affairs,
2. Making well-founded attributions of responsibility to incumbents,
3. Predicting some plausible range of effects of incumbents' and challengers' policies, and
4. Caring enough to do 1–3.

The remainder of this chapter will focus on items 1 and 4. The "common knowledge" prong has been anticipated in literature on geopolitical risks to democratic elections.[5] Prongs 1, 2, and 3 are also the premises of much political science and "fairness, accountability, and transparency" (FAccT) research. There is less extant research on the fourth prong, which ties together affective engagement and the desire to know.[6]

AI's threats to common knowledge are well known and predictable, and are explored in Part II below. There is already some empirical evidence indicating correlations between news consumption and political preferences.[7] Without a clear understanding of baseline facts about economic and social developments, responsible voting in a complex society becomes difficult. AI makes a wholesale flight from reality all the more tempting. Simulations, deepfakes, and voice cloning are now enabled by generative AI. Predictive AI is also critical here, enabling the digital public sphere to be sliced and diced into myriad profiles. Each of these may be targeted with customized realities based on estimated biases and vulnerabilities.[8] There are important political theoretical implications of these simulated or fragmented realities, particularly with respect to vulnerable groups (including both those more susceptible to propaganda, and those who are scapegoated by propaganda).

Part III turns from the epistemic to the affective, focusing on the challenges AI poses to morale and motivation among democratic citizens. The more fakes are generated by AI, the more likely citizens are to become distrustful of communications generally. This can in turn presage exhaustion or cynicism at what Jodi Dean prophetically termed the "decline of symbolic efficiency" of digital networks.[9] Predictive AI is also poised to promote emotional and affective states that result in

[5] Farrell and Schneier (2018).

[6] Lear (1988) ("Aristotle is attributing to us a desire, a force, which urges us on toward knowledge. Of course, for some this desire does not exercise great influence; but for some of us it plays an important role in our lives."). My position in this chapter is (a) that some minimal level of such a desire, as applied to elections, is necessary to democratic polities, and (b) many elements of the current automated public sphere undermine this desire.

[7] See, e.g.,https://www.ipsos.com/en-us/link-between-media-consumption-and-public-opinion; Data for Progress, Support for Trump Increases as News Consumption Decreases (Nov. 2024).

[8] Pariser (2012) and Wu (2017).

[9] Dean (2011).

the suppression, abandonment, or misdirection of political participation via several channels.

Several responses are needed, and they can be grouped into two broad categories: restrictive and educative. Part IV addresses how law can curb AI misinformation, and also introduces some media literacy approaches. Stable polities need public service media that not only offer truthful content, but also contribute to democratic morale. Part V concludes with reflections on the existential challenges new media pose to democracy—perhaps on par with the challenges that the printing press posed to monarchies during the Renaissance.

Before beginning the argument, it may be useful to briefly counter two common objections to research on AI misinformation and demoralization. Technophiles may well already be disappointed in my argument for failing to acknowledge all the positive ways in which digitization promotes the dissemination of true and valuable information. Such acknowledgments are an almost ritualistic feature of what has already become an exceedingly apologetic discourse; I feel no need to rehearse them here. They may also fault me for failing to acknowledge the problems with past systems of information creation and dissemination. However, the real options on the table now are not choosing between an automated public sphere and some version of a television- or newspaper-dominated past. Rather, the task now is to try to identify problems in, and then propose improvements to, existing media structures. That is the goal of this chapter.

3 AI's Challenge to Common Knowledge

Democracy depends on some critical mass of true beliefs among voters. The digitization of media and its dissemination empowers bad faith actors to undermine such common knowledge. This part explores the role of generative and predictive AI in such corrosion.

In the 2000s, Karl Rove claimed to "shape reality" while critics of the Bush Administration merely tried to understand it. Generative AI raises a whole new possibility: why not fabricate"alternate realities" to complement "alternative facts?" For example, a photorealistic fake image showing Pope Francis in a Balenciaga coat in 2022 had at least some social media users scratching their heads. The intent of the post was unclear—was it an effort to portray the Pontiff as a cool fashionista? To satirize the wealth of the Catholic church? Or was it "shitposting" pure and simple, designed merely to attract attention?

Any of these purposes may well be legitimate free expression. The problem comes, though, when generative AI creates mass confusion over what is fake, and what is real. What may be harmless at an individual level, creates opportunities for strategic misinformation or even unplanned reality-forgery with real social effects. A deepfake of a burning Pentagon rapidly spread on social media, causing some to panic, and a temporary dip in the stock market.[10] When asked to comment, one social network (still called Twitter at the time) emitted "an auto-reply containing a poop emoji"—despite the fact that Twitter had given a post-boosting "blue check" to an account that helped the deepfake go viral by implying an association with Bloomberg News. Rapidly generated fakes and irresponsible intermediaries are a dangerous combination.[11]

During his 2024 campaign, Donald Trump touted a fake, AI-generated Taylor Swift endorsement. AI disinformation quietists may point out that the same image might have been painted by an unscrupulous artist, so what is the threat posed by AI? The answer boils down to speed, cost, scale, and attribution obfuscation and attribution consequence-reduction. Human artists cannot work as fast as AI, cannot do so at once for hundreds or thousands of would-be manipulators, are much more expensive, and, because they of necessity create a much smaller oeuvre, bear more responsibility for any particular piece they create.[12]

Some Trump followers have also created and shared fake images meant to boost his standing with minorities and women. A fabricated image of Trump with his arms around smiling black voters was taken as real by at least one BBC interviewee.[13] To be sure, many persons recognize such images as AI-generated. However, as models' photorealism improves, such discernment is likely to become ever more rare. Trump fans also shared a manipulated video of Kamala Harris meant to discredit her views.[14] This move provoked legislative action in California, which will be discussed in Part IV below. Voice cloning of both Joseph Biden and Donald Trump provoked controversy in 2024 as well.[15] According to one news outlet, an AI-generated voice read a Trump social media post stating: 'I opened up the Governor position for Kim Reynolds, & when she fell behind, I ENDORSED her, did big Rallies, & she won. Now, she wants to remain 'NEUTRAL.' I don't invite her to events! DeSanctus down 45 points.'"[16]

The much-touted reality-warping aspects of generative AI have created what legal scholars Danielle Citron and Bobby Chesney call a "liar's dividend:" opportunistic chances to call into question the authenticity of any photo or video.[17] After Vice President Harris drew large crowds, Trump published a post stating "Has anyone noticed that Kamala CHEATED at the airport? There was nobody at the plane, and

[10] Bond (2023).

[11] Bond (2023).

[12] Artists' comparative expense in part reflects AI firms' wholesale expropriation (without compensation) of artists' work. Pasquale and Sun (2024). If the firms had to pay some level of compensation, this comparative advantage would diminish.

[13] Spring (2024).

[14] Tenbarge (2024).

[15] FCC (2024).

[16] Nazzaro (2023).

[17] Goldstein and Lohn (2024).

she 'A.I.'d' it, and showed a massive 'crowd' of so-called followers, BUT THEY DIDN'T EXIST!".[18]

The picture was widely confirmed as real by multiple reliable sources, revealing one more Trump lie. But new technology is making this type of claim ever-easier to make; indeed, Trump anticipated this affordance when he tried to spread doubt about his infamous Access Hollywood tape.[19] Trump was also the beneficiary of bots in his 2016 campaign: a former FBI Agent has described "armies of Twitter Bots to spread fake news using accounts that seem to be Midwestern swing-voter Republicans."[20]

The AI-enhanced photo-editing capacities of Google's recently released Pixel 9 phone are a disinformation dream, giving anyone capacities to easily alter photos in undetectable ways. As Sarah Jeong recently wrote, it's possible that "the default assumption about a photo is about to become that it's faked, because creating realistic and believable fake photos is now trivial to do. We are not prepared for what happens after."[21]

To be sure, there are many persons who are alert to these issues, and who have developed an information environment likely to be resilient against photoshopped images, as well as AI-generated deepfakes and simulations. But predictive AI may undermine these social defenses by targeting those most vulnerable to deception. Data brokers have prepared lists of "gullible" persons for marketers.[22] The Cambridge Analytica scandal revealed a remarkable effort to gather social media data in order to characterize voters psychologically. Cambridge Analytica developed psychological profiles of tens of millions of Facebook users, for use in political targeting. Clients included the Leave-EU Brexit campaign and the first Trump campaign. The effort was built on a behaviorist model of manipulating human behavior.[23]

New generative AI models may be able to contribute to targeting, too, by extrapolating a person's potential response to media based on extensive data on their responses to other media. In a recent study, Park et al. developed a novel agent architecture that simulates the attitudes and behaviors of 1,052 real individuals–applying large language models to qualitative interviews about their lives.[24] While the paper's authors offer many positive potentials for such agents, it is not hard to imagine their utility to disinformation operations as well.[25]

Predictive AI's greatest contribution to misinformation may be less direct provision of false posts, but rather, its politico-economic weakening of newspapers and other foundations of the traditional fourth estate. AI-driven firms like Google and Facebook enjoy data troves that make them much more attractive to advertisers. This has caused massive revenue declines for many traditional media outlets. Just when

[18] Trump (2024).

[19] Stewart (2017).

[20] O'Connor and Schneider (2017).

[21] Jeong (2024).

[22] Pasquale (2016).

[23] Pasquale (2015).

[24] Park et al. (2024).

[25] Ferrara (2024).

polities most desperately need professional journalists to sort through the avalanche of dreck created by GenAI and professional misinformation operations, many of those professionals have moved on to public relations firms (where they themselves may be using forms of generative AI or predictive analytics to bias the news for the highest bidder). When there are less jobs for reporters in a press dedicated to objectivity, there are less professionals devoted to exposing and correcting misinformation.

4 The Demoralizing Effects of AI

In 2024, the far-right German party Alternative for Deutschland (AFD) released an AI-generated video depicting white, blond-haired persons in an exaggeratedly positive way, while depicting recent immigrants with large noses, ragged clothes, and angry or threatening faces, set in dirty and dangerous neighborhoods.[26] In another AFD AI-generated ad, a white woman appeared devastated and despairing. The message was twofold. On a policy level, the AFD wanted voters to believe that their safety and the future of their country depended on a highly restrictive immigration policy. On a more visceral level, it wanted to encourage fear and hatred of immigrants—an affective dimension of AI propaganda. Whatever one's views on immigration policy, this type of sentiment is inappropriate and immoral. But it is exactly the type of polarizing affect that AI is becoming increasingly capable of cultivating.

Democracy depends not just on some critical mass of true beliefs among voters, but also on apt feelings.[27] While skepticism can be healthy, hatred of the state or fury at an ascriptive community within it endangers peaceful political resolution of contested issues. Negative affect may include a state like "alexithymia" (no words for feelings). Manos Tsakiris (Director of the Centre for the Politics of Feelings) has rightly characterized alexithymia as a deep problem for contemporary democracies, especially when populist leaders seize upon it to shape ambient malaise into directed anger against particular persons and groups.[28]

Apathy, withdrawal, and alienation result in (and from) demoralization, encouraging destructive emotional cycles.[29] While optimizing for online engagement or narrow political ends, an automated public sphere powered by artificial intelligence (AI) may demoralize citizens by presenting them with a relentlessly negative view of their country and fellow citizens.[30] It may also undermine political action in civil

[26] Schmitz (2024).

[27] On the distinction (and relation) between the epistemic and affective, see, e.g., Gibbard (1992). As Simone Weil has put it, "The intelligence can only be led by desire." Weil (2018).

[28] Tsakiris (2020).

[29] For thoughtful qualitative research on how such emotions undermine democratic engagement, see Silva (2015) and Shams et al. (2024).

[30] Pasquale (2018). This essay offers (inter alia) a response to critiques of "Automated Public Sphere," and my elaboration upon it in New Laws of Robotics (2020); see, e.g., the criticism offered

society by creating mass uncertainty about persons' and entities' actions, motivations, and connections. The result is not to propagandize a party line, but to make coordination impossible by making knowledge so hard to discern that there is little motivation to pursue it.[31]

While disinformation weaponizes false information, demoralization can arise when citizens are bombarded by one-sided, negative narratives of any level of truth. Both opportunistic and sincere actors can now use generative AI to churn out such narratives (in the form of text, memes, images, and even videos) at an extraordinary pace.[32] Even those focused exclusively on epistemic aspects of democratic freedoms should be concerned about the affective foundations of citizens' motivations to learn about issues, discuss politics constructively with others, and otherwise care about the future of their common life.

Demoralization is a particularly pressing problem for liberal democracies from a comparative geopolitical perspective. While critical self-examination is part of any thriving civil society, wide swathes of contemporary electorates in liberal democracies are angry, cynical, and disaffected.[33] Meanwhile, authoritarian regimes limit the exposure of their own subjects to demoralizing narratives.[34] This presents a striking asymmetry, where certain *dirigiste* information environments promote citizens' solidarity and unity of purpose, while *laissez-faire* public spheres are increasingly open to extreme content fostering negativity, division, and cynicism.

For an abstract model of demoralization as a comparative phenomenon, consider the following hypothetical: Two nation-states, A and B, are geopolitical rivals with roughly similar levels of corruption. At time 1, A enjoys a largely pluralistic and open public sphere; B's government strictly controls and shapes public communication. Over time, an increasing share of A's populace is exposed to, and believes, narratives about A's government's corruption, the illegitimacy of its elections, and the malevolence of prominent groups in A. In B, meanwhile, such messages are either immediately suppressed, or limited in their dissemination. At Time 2, *ceteris paribus*, civil society in B is more likely to be cohesive, solidaristic, and trusting in its government. Indeed, B may invest in promoting the views of fringe or divisive groups in A, to advance its polarization. At the limit case, A may experience political violence, insurrection, or civil war, partly rooted in prior "information warfare" against it. Indeed, such asymmetries are already being weaponized.[35] Media created

in Chomanski (2024) (expressing skepticism of efforts to improve the information environment). The present project's focus on morale and motivation for sincere democratic participation is meant to alleviate the types of cynicism and negativity that underlie much of the irrationality that critics of democracy attribute to citizens.

31 The nature of the resulting fog of demoralization is aptly captured in Pomerantsev (2014).

32 For a prescient warning about the weaponization of narrative, see Allenby (2017). The work of Arizona State University's Weaponized Narrative Initiative is also illuminating.

33 The empirical work here is vast. Theoretical treatments include Illouz (2023), Dean (2011), and Lonergan and Blyth (2021).

34 Pei (2024) and Sun and Zhao (2022).

35 See, e.g., Johnson (2024) ("Russian money was used to pay six conservative commentators... [who] have tens of millions of followers, billions of video views, and the ability to heavily influence

by or prioritized by AI is an important accelerator of dynamics toward demoralization. Such media make it harder to detect the provenance of content, or reasons for its popularization.

A critic may question how it is possible to define a concept as open-ended as demoralization, claiming that it is parasitic on some essentially contestable baseline conception of the optimal or maximal negative feeling a citizen should experience toward government or fellow citizens. The concept might not be operationalizable if it were focused solely on the thoughts of citizens relative to such a baseline.[36] What I propose, instead, is a two-level definition focused on (1) the prevalence of defeatist, nihilist, or "blackpilled" belief structures, and (2) excessive exposure to negative narratives of national or communal corruption, incompetence, decline, or collapse, particularly when this exposure is clandestinely driven by geopolitical rivals. Given the well-documented performance advantage of negative over positive stories in social media environments, many citizens are influenced by overwhelmingly negative narratives about their democracy's foreign policy, welfare state, law enforcement, bureaucracy, elections, media, environmental protection, schools, and much else, unleavened by fair consideration of present initiatives to improve these policies and institutions.

Some communications scholars dispute the ultimate causal impact of AI and algorithmic social media in promoting disinformation and demoralization. To be sure, populist politicians, extremist media, and failed civics and science education for such scourges as election denialism and anti-vaccine activism are all part of the problem. However, to minimize the role of digital mediation is a form of agnotology. Similarly scientistic skepticism has dogged scholars trying to call attention to the effect of money in politics, or "horserace" political coverage on civic engagement. Climate scientists, facing skepticism about the effect of carbon emissions, offer one model response. As Julie E. Cohen has argued, despite some empirical research questioning the size of the automated public sphere's impact in eroding democratic freedoms,

> Concluding that platformized online communication systems do not 'cause' toxic polarization, deepening ethnonationalism, or rapidly metastasizing 'alternative facts' pathologies because human beings have always been tribal and credulous makes about as much sense as concluding that human activity does not 'cause' climate change because there have always been storms. The earth's climate is a complex, interconnected system that operates according to certain physical laws, notably including laws that define tipping points between

---

conservative politics in the US," including by pushing for long delays in the provision of weapons to Ukraine); Hvistendahl et al. (2023) (describing "a seemingly organic bloom of far-left groups that echo Chinese government talking points, echo one another, and are echoed in turn by the Chinese state media.").

[36] Even in this case, there are ways of surveying to ascertain some indication of demoralization's opposite—namely, morale. Arthur Upham Pope memorably argued that "enthusiasm, confidence, teamwork, [and] endurance" demonstrated "high morale," and called morale "a state produced by a clearly envisaged value of such commanding power and authority that it evokes all the capacities of a [person] or a group, fusing them into an intense and durable emotional and ideational unity that increases, sustains, and organizes all effort." Pope (1941), quoted in Turner (2013). While this definition's boldness is dated, a more moderate conception of morale could attract the support of many stakeholders concerned to promote democratic freedoms.

> different kinds of systemic equilibria. Systemic patterns of human activity, for which humans unquestionably bear responsibility, are gradually but inexorably tipping the climate into a different systemic pattern characterized by greater extremes, more pronounced volatility, and expanding, toxic 'dead zones.' In a similar way, platformized communication infrastructures are tipping human societies away from (concededly imperfect) democratic equilibria into different systemic patterns characterized by more widespread and deeply entrenched affinities for tribal enmity, xenophobia, conspiracism, and authoritarianism.[37]

The rise of reality-denying and science-denying candidates and politicians in many liberal democracies shows the immediate and urgent stakes of these developments.[38] AI is a force multiplier for hyperpartisan, demoralizing, and disinforming media. It represents a step from targeting to microtargeting, and from human crafting of dozens or hundreds of messages, videos, and stories, to machine fabrication of thousands or millions of the same. This change in quantity in itself causes qualitatively distinct problems. Thus the next Part explores some legal and policy strategies for reducing AI's role in disinformation and demoralization.

5 Combatting Deception and Demoralization

AI is a powerful tool now poised to vastly worsen problems of misinformation and demoralization. Two broad strategies could reduce its worst effects. First, governments must impose restrictions on the use of AI in campaigns, and the automated public sphere generally. Second, policymakers, civil society, and responsible corporations must promote information literacy for AI. Such literacy programs may include training for children, as well as content moderation designed to de-amplify misinformation and counter demoralization.

There are many ways that policymakers can address the problem of AI-driven disinformation. The first step may be to require labeling of all AI-generated content that may be taken to depict actual persons or events. This "provenance data" could be a small "AI" mark in a corner (like a trademark), or could be embedded in metadata.[39] Both strategies were embraced in California's recently enacted California AI Transparency Act (SB 942).[40] This would make it easier for authorities to detect

---

[37] Cohen (2023).

[38] Newman and Conrad (2024). ("Post-truth erodes the common world upon which political life is founded. Not only do lies, mis-/disinformation, and 'fake news' disrupt and distort communication, making rational deliberation between citizens virtually impossible, but their prevalence today works to create a sense confusion of about the nature of reality itself. The inability to distinguish between truth and falsehood makes any kind of cognitive mapping of the world extremely difficult.").

[39] California's AI Transparency Act uses the term "provenance data," defining it as "data that is embedded into digital content, or that is included in the digital content's metadata, for the purpose of verifying the digital content's authenticity, origin, or history of modification." (2024) California AI Transparency Act. https://leginfo.legislature.ca.gov/faces/billNavClient.xhtml?bill_id=202320240SB942.

[40] (2024) California AI Transparency Act. https://leginfo.legislature.ca.gov/faces/billNavClient.xhtml?bill_id=202320240SB942.

misuse of AI (for example, mass provision of fake images of persons used to defraud government identity verification systems). Yes, a determined person can remove watermarks, but policymakers should not make the perfect the enemy of the good: such circumvention would likely require significant effort, slowing the spread of the misleading content.

The synthesis of images of fake personas (whether in photo or video form) should also be tightly regulated, since these simulations of persons make it easier to spread falsehood online. Fake personas contravene the second "new law of robotics" I developed in my eponymous book, since they counterfeit humanity.[41] They cannot be held responsible in the ways that a human disinformer can. Therefore, it would make sense to prevent them from appearing as the profile picture (or serving as other pictures) of owners of social media accounts. Moreover, the use of video avatars as news announcers should be banned. A human announcer can be held responsible for defamation or other communicative torts; a bot cannot.

Admittedly, in my fourth new law of robotics, I did recommend a general requirement that all AI be attributable to a person or corporation. If this requirement were upheld, a skeptic might counter the recommendations above by insisting that, even if AI-created personas could not be held responsible, those creating or managing them could be. However, technologies and legal strategies of anonymization (ranging from masking IP addresses to operating shell companies) are likely to provide ample strategies for evading current and future attribution requirements (such as California's Bolstering Online Transparency (BOT) Act, which required disclosure of automated communications in commerce and politics).[42] Such readily anticipated failures of disclosure commend much closer attention to bans or limits on fake personas.

California recently took a step forward in this regard with Assembly Bill (AB) 2839, which forbade any "person, committee, or other entity" from "knowingly distribut[ing] an advertisement or other election communication [with malice] containing materially deceptive content" of a candidate for office "portrayed as doing or saying something that the candidate did not do or say if the content is reasonably likely to harm the reputation or electoral prospects of a candidate."[43] This law was in part inspired by the deepfake of Kamala Harris mentioned earlier in this chapter. Unfortunately, a court almost immediately stepped in to declare the law unconstitutional under the U.S.'s First Amendment, with the following asserted rationale:

> AB 2839 does not pass constitutional scrutiny because the law does not use the least restrictive means available for advancing the State's interest here…As Plaintiffs persuasively argue,

---

[41] Pasquale (2020).

[42] (2018) California Bolstering Online Transparency Act. https://leginfo.legislature.ca.gov/faces/codes_displaySection.xhtml?lawCode=BPC&sectionNum=17941.&highlight=true&keyword=BOTS+disclosure#:~:text=(a)%20It%20shall%20be%20unlawful,order%20to%20incentivize%20a%20purchase. The California Bolstering Online Transparency (BOT) Act provides that "it is unlawful for a person or entity to use a bot to communicate or interact online with a person in California in order to incentivize a sale or transaction of goods or services or to influence a vote in an election without disclosing that the communication is via a bot."

[43] Cal. Elec. Code § 20012(b)(1)(A).

> counter speech is a less restrictive alternative to prohibiting videos such as those posted by Plaintiff, no matter how offensive or inappropriate someone may find them.[44]

This is a remarkably wrongheaded and complacent perspective, given rapid transformations in the contemporary automated public sphere. How is counterspeech supposed to be effective when key platforms are so easily orchestrated to silence or obscure it?[45] The past few years have seen a remarkable consolidation of intermediary and media power in the U.S., coupled with extraordinarily powerful technology to microtarget audiences. While First Amendment law may be a recurring barrier to effective AI regulation in the U.S., other jurisdictions should be wary of over-expansive interpretations of free expression protections potentially trumping election integrity.

Predictive AI should also be subject to regulation. National security authorities (and at least some technology firms) have focused on exposing foreign rivals' promotion of the types of polarizing narratives that fuel disinformation and demoralization.[46] This work should continue, and AI safety techniques could do much to advance and enhance it.[47] For example, better reporting on the provenance of accounts and similarities between their content may lead to faster detection of influence campaigns.[48] Researchers should also experiment with labels on accounts frequently associated with such campaigns.[49] Holistic research on the local effects of polarizing narratives is imperative.

When disinformation and demoralization are "home grown," other, more positive solutions may come to the fore. The bolstering of authoritative and responsible sources of information is critical.[50] Affective computing and human–computer interaction research may illuminate the types of content that foster constructive engagement with fellow citizens (rather than defeated resignation or furious rejection).[51] This could entail a type of the "norm entrepreneurship" whereby influencers and others are trained to cultivate civic engagement. An independent and expert-led "community notes" function, which permitted comments focused not just on the accuracy of facts but also on the aptness of the feelings expressed in demoralizing posts, may be another mode of response.[52] Such a morale-building "crowd" would

---

[44] Kohls v. Bonta, No. 2:24-cv-02527 JAM-CKD (E. D. Cal., Oct. 2, 2024).

[45] For one perspective on bias here, see Graham and Andrejevic (2024).

[46] See, e.g., (2023) ODNI Releases Intelligence Community Assessment of Foreign Threats to the 2022 U.S. Elections. https://www.dni.gov/index.php/newsroom/press-releases/press-releases-2023/3743-odni-releases-intelligence-community-assessment-of-foreign-threats-to-the-2022-u-s-elections.

[47] See, e.g., Panditharatne and Giansiracusa (2023).

[48] Luceri et al. (2023) and Smith et al. (2020).

[49] Wittenberg et al. (2023).

[50] FCC (2011).

[51] For a variety of proposals advancing affective computing in the public interest, see Kaliouby and Colman (2020).

[52] There is a "community notes" function presently available on X, but even when it was relatively unbiased ideologically, it was often far too slow to counteract misinformation (and this would

complement platforms' algorithmic information presentation, which is at present agnostic as to its demoralizing effects.[53]

While I have criticized many applications of affective computing in past work, I also believe that those who wish to promote democratic freedoms need to understand it and at least in some cases turn it to their own ends, given its weaponization by those seeking to undermine such freedoms. A turn to affect also appears to be the goal of the project "The (trans)formation of a European sense of solidarity: Visceral politics and social belonging in a comparative European context," a very promising proposal to address some aspects of the democratic deficit now afflicting the transnational project of European governance.

Finding audiences for positive stories may also help restore the affective foundations for collective exercise of democratic freedoms. For example, one journalist attempted to counter facile austerity narratives by highlighting the positive work done by government workers (for example, how a National Oceanic and Atmospheric Administration scientist's research on ocean currents saved many lives, as it made it easier for rescuers to save the many persons who accidentally fall off ocean-faring ships each year).[54] Both private organizations and government may buy advertisements on social media networks, or create their own media, to amplify such stories and promote their spread.[55]

Inoculating citizens against misinformation and demoralization should begin early. Finland offers one model of robust training for children in primary school. "The goal is active, responsible citizens and voters," Finnish head teacher Kari Kivinen has explained. "Thinking critically, factchecking, interpreting and evaluating all the information you receive, wherever it appears, is crucial. We've made it a core part of what we teach, across all subjects."[56]

There is also some precedent for efforts to rally democratic citizens around a positive national identity. In the 1940s, President Franklin Roosevelt convened a "Committee on National Morale" (including noted intellectuals like Margaret Mead and Gregory Bateson) to promote U.S. citizens' unity, enthusiasm and good will during wartime—at a time when the Axis (and some domestic forces) were striving to undermine patriotic, democratic, and liberal sentiment.[57] A renewed CNM could explore

presumably continue to be a problem with respect to demoralization as well). Given that X is rapidly becoming a source of right-wing talking points and pro-authoritarian propaganda, it is hard to imagine its community notes function being unaffected. This is one reason why independent and expert control of such a community notes function is essential.

[53] An early call for such communal, civil society-based, or lifeworld-based interventions into sociotechnical systems is Pasquale (2008). The mention of "crowds" is intended to reference McAfee and Byrnjolfsson's formulation of "machine, platform, and crowd" as core elements of online organization. McAfee and Brynjolfsson (2017).

[54] Lewis (2018).

[55] Some scholars have also proposed dialogues with AI itself to defuse conspiracy theories (many of which fuel demoralization). Costello et al. (2024).

[56] Kivinen is quoted in Henleym (2020).

[57] Turner (1993). Turner offers a nuanced account of the Committee's recommendations, which includes both potential inspiration for the present, and cautionary tales.

the methods of propagating the enthusiasm and unity mentioned above. Cyberlibertarians are likely to challenge such work.[58] But the Committee itself, and many of these methods, would be constitutional even in the exceedingly speech-protective United States under its Supreme Court's recent *Murthy v. Missouri* decision.[59]

6 Conclusion: Reclaiming Human Control in the Public Sphere

A poorly regulated public sphere means that "anything goes" in political argument. This is a short step from argument not mattering at all. Meanwhile, spheres like finance and health care are rightly, tightly regulated. This asymmetry helps drive investment and excitement toward direct-to-consumer applications of image- and text-generating software that can be so easily misused in so many contexts. For example, why perfect AI detection of melanoma or cancer if the real prize is direct-to-consumer fantasy machines?

To counteract such perverse incentives, there need to be limits on the spread of reality-warping AI. We need clear rules for the dissemination of generative AI. When it is photorealistic, it should always be labelled as AI-generated, whether in a caption or (in the case of images and videos) with some small indicator in the corner (perhaps an icon of a robot). Korea provides one good precedent for taking a step in this direction: after two leading presidential candidates released regionally targeted videos featuring AI versions of themselves in 2021, the South Korean Election Commission required that such avatars must disclose that they are not actual candidates.[60]

Platforms should also require "proof of personhood" to post materials, to prevent botnets from rapidly disseminating fake images. Researchers from Georgetown, OpenAI, and the Stanford AI Observatory have also proposed many other proposed mitigations of AI propaganda in an insightful report.[61]

But this regulation is only one half of the generative AI puzzle. Governments should also help ensure just rewards to reality-improving technology, to dissipate excess investment in hype-driven industries (ranging from crypto to the metaverse to the current direct-to-consumer GenAI boom) that are all too often reality-warping. The U.S. Inflation Reduction Act and CHIPS (Creating Helpful Incentives to Produce Semiconductors) Act are two good examples of such legislation: both spurred higher investment in factories. China provides an industrial policy success story of longer vintage. As Angela Zhang's recent book *High Wire: How China Regulates Big Tech and Governs its Economy* demonstrates, its government has backed many forms of

---

[58] Golumbia (2024).

[59] Murthy v. Missouri, available at https://www.law.cornell.edu/supremecourt/text/23A243.

[60] Kim (2022).

[61] Goldstein et al. (2023).

"hard tech," the type of "new quality productive forces" behind better automobiles and robotics.[62]

Generative AI can play important roles in such "hard tech," such as voice or text-commanded robots "learning" from videos of tasks to be done via vision-language-action models. But ordinary markets are often not patient enough to finance such advances adequately. Enlightened industrial policy needs to fill this vacuum, shifting investment from reality-warping to reality-improving generative AI.

References

Allenby B (2017) The Age of Weaponized Narrative, or, Where Have You Gone, Walter Cronkit. Issues in Sci Technol 33(4)

Bond S (2023) Fake viral images of an explosion at the Pentagon were probably created by AI. https://www.npr.org/2023/05/22/1177590231/fake-viral-images-of-an-explosion-at-the-pentagon-were-probably-created-by-ai

Chomanski B (2024) Regulating misinformation: political irrationality as a feasibility constraint. Topoi. https://doi.org/10.1007/s11245-024-10083-2

Cohen J (2023) Infrastructuring the digital public sphere. Yale J Law Technol 25:1

Costello T, Pennycook G, Rand D (2024) Durably reducing conspiracy beliefs through dialogues with AI. Science 385(6714)

Dahl R (1995) Democracy and its critics. Yale University Press, New Haven, CT

Dean J (2011) Blog Theory. Polity, Cambridge

Farrell H, Schneier B (2018) Common-knowledge attacks on democracy. BKC Research Publication No. 2018-7, Harvard University, Cambridge

FCC (2011) The information needs of communities. https://transition.fcc.gov/osp/inc-report/The_Information_Needs_of_Communities.pdf

FCC (2024) FCC settles case against provider that transmitted spoofed ai-generated robocalls for election interference in new hampshire. Federal Communications Commission. Available via FCC. https://docs.fcc.gov/public/attachments/DOC-404951A1.pdf

Ferrara E (2024) GenAI against humanity: nefarious applications of generative artificial intelligence and large language models. https://arxiv.org/html/2310.00737v3

Gibbard A (1992) Wise choices, apt feelings: a theory of normative judgment. Harvard University Press, Cambridge

Goldstein J, Lohn A (2024) Deepfakes, elections, and shrinking the Liar's Dividend. https://www.brennancenter.org/our-work/research-reports/deepfakes-elections-and-shrinking-liars-dividend

Goldstein J, Sastry G, Musser M et al. (2023) Generative language models and automated influence operations: emerging threats and potential mitigations. https://arxiv.org/pdf/2301.04246

Golumbia D (2024) Cyberlibertarianism. University of Minnesota Press, Minneanapolis

Graham T, Andrejevic M (2024) A computational analysis of potential algorithmic bias on platform X during the 2024 US election. https://eprints.qut.edu.au/253211/

Henleym J (2020) How Finland starts its fight against fake news in primary schools. https://www.theguardian.com/world/2020/jan/28/fact-from-fiction-finlands-new-lessons-in-combating-fake-news

Hvistendahl M, Fahrenthold D, Chutel L et al. (2023) A global web of Chinese Propaganda leads to a U.S. Tech Mogul. https://www.nytimes.com/2023/08/05/world/europe/neville-roy-singham-china-propaganda.html

Illouz E (2023) The emotional life of populism. Polity, Cambridge

[62] Zhang (2024).

Jeong S (2024) No one's ready for this, Our basic assumptions about photos capturing reality are about to go up in smoke. https://www.theverge.com/2024/8/22/24225972/ai-photo-era-what-is-reality-google-pixel-9
Johnson J (2024) You are still not worried enough about foreign influence operations. https://www.infinitescroll.us/p/you-are-still-not-worried-enough?utm_campaign=post&utm_medium=web
Kaliouby R, Colman C (2020) Girl decoded: a scientist's quest to reclaim our humanity by bringing emotional intelligence to technology. Crown, New York
Kim D (2022) Is Korea showing the future of elections: AI candidates? https://keia.org/the-peninsula/is-korea-showing-the-future-of-elections-ai-candidates/
Lear J (1988) Aristotle: the desire to understand. Cambridge University Press, Cambridge
Lewis M (2018) The fifth risk. W.W. Norton, New York
Lonergan E, Blyth M (2021) Angrynomics. Columbia University Press, New York
Luceri L, Boniardi E, Ferrara E (2023) Leveraging large language models to detect influence campaigns in social media. https://arxiv.org/abs/2311.07816
McAfee A, Brynjolfsson E (2017) Machine, platform, crowd: harnessing our digital future. W.W. Norton, New York
Narayanan A, Kapoor S (2024) AI snake oil. Princeton University Press, Princeton, NJ
Nazzaro M (2023) Pro-DeSantis group uses AI version of Trump's voice in new ad. https://thehill.com/homenews/campaign/4103157-pro-desantis-group-uses-ai-version-of-trumps-voice-in-new-ad/
Newman S, Conrad M (2024) Introduction, in Post-truth populism: a new political paradigm (eds). Routledge, London
O'Connor G, Schneider A (2017) How Russian Twitter bots pumped out fake news during the 2016 election. https://www.npr.org/sections/alltechconsidered/2017/04/03/522503844/how-russian-twitter-bots-pumped-out-fake-news-during-the-2016-election
Panditharatne M and Giansiracusa N (2023) How AI puts elections at risk—and the needed Safeguards. https://www.brennancenter.org/our-work/analysis-opinion/how-ai-puts-elections-risk-and-needed-safeguards
Pariser E (2012) The filter bubble: How the new personalized web is changing what we read and how we think. Penguin, New York
Park J, Zou C, Shaw A et al (2024) LLM Agents Grounded in Self-Reports Enable General-Purpose Simulation of Individuals. https://arxiv.org/abs/2411.10109
Pasquale F (2008) Asterisk revisited: debating a right of reply on search results. J Bus Technol Law 3(1):61–86
Pasquale F (2015) Privacy, autonomy, and internet platforms. In: Rotenberg M, Horwitz J, Scott J et al (eds) Privacy in the modern age: the search for solutions. New Press, New York, pp 165–174
Pasquale F (2016) The black box society. Harvard University Press, Cambridge
Pasquale F (2018) The automated public sphere. In: Sætnan A, Schneider I, Green N (eds) The politics of big data. Routledge, London
Pasquale F (2020) New laws of robotics. Harvard University Press, Cambridge
Pasquale F, Sun H (2024) Consent and compensation: resolving generative AI's copyright crisis. Virginia Law Review 110:207
Pei M (2024) The sentinel state. Harvard University Press, Cambridge
Pomerantsev P (2014) Nothing is true and everything is possible: the surreal heart of the New Russia. PublicAffairs, New York
Pope A (1941) The importance of morale. J Educ Sociol 15(4):195–205
Schmitz R (2024) How Germany's far-right party is using AI-generated videos in its campaigns, NPR. https://www.npr.org/2024/09/20/nx-s1-5119235/how-germanys-far-right-party-is-using-ai-generated-videos-in-its-campaigns
Schumpeter J (1943) Capitalism, socialism, and democracy. Routledge, London
Shams S, Bhargava D, Hanbury H (2024) The cultural contradictions of neoliberalism: the longing for an alternative order and the future of multiracial democracy in an age of authoritarianism. https://rooseveltinstitute.org/publications/the-cultural-contradictions-of-neoliberalism/

Silva J (2015) Coming up short: working-class adulthood in an age of uncertainty. Oxford University Press, Oxford
Smith S, Kao E, Mackin D et al. (2020) Automatic detection of influential actors in disinformation networks. https://arxiv.org/abs/2005.10879
Spring M (2024) Trump supporters target black voters with faked AI images. https://www.bbc.com/news/world-us-canada-68440150
Stewart E (2017) Trump has started suggesting the Access Hollywood tape is fake. https://www.vox.com/policy-and-politics/2017/11/28/16710130/trump-says-access-hollywood-tape-fake
Sun T, Zhao Q (2022) Delegated censorship: the dynamic, layered, and multistage information control regime in China. Polit Soc 50(2)
Tenbarge K (2024) Elon Musk made a Kamala Harris deepfake ad go viral, sparking a debate about parody and free speech. https://www.nbcnews.com/tech/misinformation/kamala-harris-deepfake-shared-musk-sparks-free-speech-debate-rcna164119
Trump D (2024). https://truthsocial.com/@realDonaldTrump/posts/112944255426268462
Tsakiris M (2020) Politics is visceral. https://aeon.co/essays/politics-is-in-peril-if-it-ignores-how-humans-regulate-the-body
Turner F (1993) The democratic surround. University of Chicago Press, Chicago
Turner F (2013) The democratic surround. University of Chicago Press, Chicago
Weil S (2018) Love in the void. Plough Publishing House, Walden
Wittenberg C, Epstein Z, Berinsky A et al. (2023) Labeling AI-generated content: promises, perils, and future directions. https://computing.mit.edu/wp-content/uploads/2023/11/AI-Policy_Labeling.pdf
Wu T (2017) The attention merchants. Atlantic Books, New York
Zhang A (2024) High wire: How China regulates big tech and governs its economy. Oxford University Press, Oxford

Frank Pasquale, Professor of Law at Cornell Tech and Cornell Law School. Expert on AI, algorithms, and machine learning. Author of The Black Box Society and New Laws of Robotics (Harvard University Press). Co-editor of The Oxford Handbook on the Ethics of Artificial Intelligence and Transparent Data Mining for Big and Small Data. His work has been translated into over a dozen languages.

Open Access This chapter is licensed under the terms of the Creative Commons Attribution 4.0 International License (http://creativecommons.org/licenses/by/4.0/), which permits use, sharing, adaptation, distribution and reproduction in any medium or format, as long as you give appropriate credit to the original author(s) and the source, provide a link to the Creative Commons license and indicate if changes were made.

The images or other third party material in this chapter are included in the chapter's Creative Commons license, unless indicated otherwise in a credit line to the material. If material is not included in the chapter's Creative Commons license and your intended use is not permitted by statutory regulation or exceeds the permitted use, you will need to obtain permission directly from the copyright holder.

Human Autonomy and Forms of Vulnerability in Automated Contracting

Reflections from the UNCITRAL Model Law on Automated Contracting and the ELI Model Rules on Digital Assistants for Consumer Contracts

Teresa Rodríguez de las Heras Ballell

Abstract The transition from electronic commerce to automated contracting challenges the traditional notion of (human) autonomy and its pivotal role in Contract Law. Automated contracting means that human autonomy and AI agency interact in as yet uncertain ways, which could be ones of tension, conflict or, perhaps, symbiosis in the future. Contract law should be sensitive to these forms of hybridization, and adapt if necessary. Preserving and protecting human autonomy does also mean combating old and new forms of vulnerability. This Paper aims to trace the transition from electronic commerce to automated contracting and unveil the two-sided impacts on vulnerability risks. Looking closely at both UNCITRAL MLCA and the ELI DACC, the Paper focuses on three main dilemmas. First, legal recognition of automated contracting, party autonomy, and the right to use automated systems. Second, allocation of unexpected action risk, impact on autonomy and a new forms of vulnerability. Third, automated contracting and consumer protection paradigms. Contract law is facing today a profound and fascinating challenge to react to, accommodate, or embrace automated contracting and AI Agents in decision making.

Keywords Human autonomy · AI agents · Automated contracting · Digital assistants · Algorithmic vulnerability

T. Rodríguez de las Heras Ballell (✉)
Universidad Carlos III de Madrid, Madrid, Spain
e-mail: tla@der-pr.uc3m.es

European Law Institute, Vienna, Austria

© The Author(s) 2025

C. Amodio and A. Diurni (eds.), *Human Vulnerability in Interaction with AI in European Private Law*, https://doi.org/10.1007/978-3-031-93247-2_4

1 Human Autonomy and Forms of Vulnerability in the Era of Artificial Intelligence

Artificial Intelligence (hereinafter, AI) is the undisputed protagonist of the technological transformation in the contemporary era. The overwhelming expansion and pervasive penetration of AI in society have ushered in a new stage in technological evolution. AI has dominated the global scene, permeated public opinion and the media arousing mixed sentiments of fear and fascination, and attracted massive attention from regulators and policymakers in reply to a growing and, sometimes alarming, perception of risks.[1] A growing consensus has arguably spotlighted at a global level the critical (and pressing) need to reconcile its promises and its perils. However, governance models and regulatory approaches to AI differ.[2] A series of drivers, in different order of priority, guide possible governance and regulatory responses: from innovation, competitiveness, and effectiveness to ethical considerations, the protection of human rights, democracy and the rule of law. The trade-offs between benefits and dangers seem to be approached and valued differently. This calibrates the timing, intensity, and content of the governance response.

Thus, responses to AI, both a supranational level and at a domestic one, range from industry self-governance[3] to soft-law options,[4] including technical standards,[5] to, finally and increasingly in recent times, hard-law[6] solutions. One of the commonalities between these approaches is their transversal character, in the acknowledging

[1] World Economic Forum (WEF) (2018) Fourth Industrial Revolution for the Earth Series Harnessing Artificial Intelligence for the Earth. The risks of “unguided< AI fall into six categories: performance risks, security risks, control risks, ethical risks, economic risks, societal risks.

[2] World Bank Group (2024).

[3] Microsoft Responsible AI Standards (2022), June 2022, https://www.microsoft.com/en-us/ai/principles-and-approach; Google AI Principles, https://ai.google/responsibility/principles/; publications of IBM's Ethics Board, https://www.ibm.com/think/insights/expanding-on-ethical-considerations-of-foundation-models; Forética, Manifiesto por una Inteligencia Artificial Responsible y Sostenible, https://foretica.org/wp-content/uploads/2024/06/Manifiesto_por_una_IA_responsable_VF.pdf, signed by multiple entities and companies as listed in https://foretica.org/2024/05/manifiesto-por-una-inteligencia-artificial-responsable-y-sostenible/#empresas.

[4] OECD AI Principles, https://oecd.ai/en/ai-principles; UNESCO Recommendation on the Ethics of AI, https://www.unesco.org/en/articles/recommendation-ethics-artificial-intelligence; G7 AI Principles and Code of Conduct (AIP&CoC), Hiroshima, 2023, https://digital-strategy.ec.europa.eu/en/library/g7-leaders-statement-hiroshima-ai-process; UN General Assembly resolution on AI, https://documents.un.org/doc/undoc/ltd/n24/065/92/pdf/n2406592.pdf; and, inter alia, US White House AI Bill of Rights, https://www.whitehouse.gov/wp-content/uploads/2022/10/Blueprint-for-an-AI-Bill-of-Rights.pdf; Australia voluntary AI Ethics Principles, https://www.industry.gov.au/publications/australias-artificial-intelligence-ethics-principles/australias-ai-ethics-principles.

[5] ISO/IEC (2023) and Coalition for Content Provenance and Authenticity (C2PA) (2022) C2PA standards. https://c2pa.org/.

[6] Council of Europe (2024); European Parliament and Council of the European Union (2024) Regulation (EU) 2024/1689 laying down harmonised rules on artificial intelligence OJ L, 2024/1689, 12.7.2024 https://eur-lex.europa.eu/legal-content/EN/TXT/?uri=CELEX%3A32024R1689.

that AI is a general-purpose technology. All these initiatives are, commonly, cross-sectoral even if they may be based on a risk approach determined by the intended use.

As AI is increasingly used in a range of decision-making contexts, including along the entire contract life cycle, one facet of the AI governance debate, that is gaining scale and relevance, is the interplay between human autonomy and AI agency. In this interplay, two questions arise. On the one hand, whether the pivotal notion, and the essence, of human autonomy is preserved in a context of progressive 'delegation' of decision-making to AI systems while human intervention reduces. It is debated whether the interplay between human autonomy and AI agency should be understood as a tension, as a conflict, or maybe as a symbiosis and what the implications are. On the other hand, whether the use of AI risks deepening and intensifying vulnerabilities already caused by digital technologies or even creating new forms of vulnerability in addition. While arguing, on the contrary, that AI could prove to serve instead as a tool to mitigate and combat vulnerabilities.

These concerns about the preservation and protection of human autonomy and the detection and mitigation of human vulnerabilities embed the AI governance debate into the core of private law rules governing contracts, commercial practices and consumer protection. The use of AI for decision-making and in contracting is to be tested against the rationale behind human-led contract law. (Human) autonomy is the driving force fuelling legacy systems of contract law. Rules are adopted to protect and preserve party autonomy and to detect, and prevent situations where asymmetries, vulnerabilities, or other contextual or circumstantial factors can compromise or undermine a free, informed decision of the parties in exercising their autonomy.

The risk of vulnerabilities' exploitation by AI has not gone unnoticed in the various governance and regulatory models. Among other examples, the European AI Act[7] illustrates this reaction by tackling this risk in the text as a prohibited AI practice, under certain conditions (as laid down in Article 5.1.b) of the AI Act).[8] But the rationale behind this approach is not based on pure contract-law elements but rather on a regulatory basis.

While all the initiatives listed above share a regulatory approach oriented to the governance of AI systems, other actions have also been also initiated with a special private-law focus on the use of AI to automate decision-making. Two initiatives

[7] European Parliament and Council of the European Union (2024) Regulation (EU) 2024/1689 laying down harmonised rules on artificial intelligence. OJ L, 2024/1689, 12.7.2024, Art. 5(1)(b)

[8] Art. 5.1.b) AI Act:

> "the placing on the market, the putting into service or the use of an AI system that exploits any of the vulnerabilities of a natural person or a specific group of persons due to their age, disability or a specific social or economic situation, with the objective, or the effect, of materially distorting the behaviour of that person or a person belonging to that group in a manner that causes or is reasonably likely to cause that person or another person significant harm".

stand out in this respect. Firstly, the adoption by United Nations of the UNCITRAL (United Nations Commission on International Trade Law) Model Law on Automated Contracting (hereinafter, MLAC) in July 2024. Secondly, the projects led by the European Law Institute (ELI) on Automated Decision-Making with the adoption in 2022 of the ELI Guiding Principles for Automated Decision-Making in the European Union[9] (hereinafter, ELI Principles on ADM) and the ELI Project to draft ELI Guiding Principles and Model Rules on Digital Assistants for Consumer Contracts[10] (hereinafter, ELI DACC) concluded in 2025. Both initiatives have in common a private-law perspective that essentially results into the formulation of enabling, more than limiting or banning, rules in the relationships between private actors, individual and entities.

This Paper delves into these two initiatives to find out how (human) autonomy has been addressed, and to highlight some solutions proposed to combat or mitigate new and existing forms of vulnerabilities in automated contracting. Part II traces the transition from electronic contracting to automated contracting guided by the definitions and the principles enshrined in MLAC, ELI Principles on ADM, and landmark instruments on AI. Against such a backdrop, this Paper identifies three angles in the triangular interaction between human autonomy, forms of vulnerability and automated contracting. Parts III, IV and V elaborate on each of these three perspectives.

2 The Transition Towards Automated Contracting

The assumption that AI systems can present varying levels of autonomy[11] is undoubtedly the fracture point in a continuing line of reasoning based on functional equivalence that has faced and solved the challenges of electronic commerce. Automation poses a major challenge to legacy legal systems, to traditional concepts, and to the very conception of the activity that the law is expected to regulate. Automation 'distances' humans from decision-making. In contrast to previous technologies throughout history, automation and, notably, AI-driven automation impact the hitherto intrinsically human decision-making capabilities. Therefore, there is a need for recognition of the validity and enforceability of automated decision-making and further consideration of the potential impact on the traditional balance of power in contracting.

The question is then whether a decision, any decision, in any field and for any purpose, can be valid and enforceable when it is automated, and on the sole ground of

---

[9] European Law Institute (2022).

[10] European Law Institute (2025).

[11] OECD (2023). 'An AI system is a machine-based system that, for explicit or implicit objectives, infers, from the input it receives, how to generate outputs such as predictions, content, recommendations, or decisions that can influence physical or virtual environments. Different AI systems vary in their levels of autonomy and adaptiveness after deployment' (Italics has been added).

such an automated character without human intervention. The answer, if affirmative, will be crucial to even start considering challenges posed by automated contracting. Only then can further considerations on (new) forms of vulnerability triggered or aggravated by the use of AI in contracting begin. Therefore, it is necessary to understand first whether there are uniform or increasingly harmonized solutions endorsing such a legal recognition of any automated decision.

The ELI Principles on ADM propose a principle of explicit recognition formulated as a principle of non-discrimination[12] of automated decision-making (ADM) on the sole ground of its automated nature. The principle of non-discrimination (*Guiding Principle* 2), which is an essential enabling element of automated decision-making, does not, as a principle, prevent the legislator from deciding to adopt specific or additional rules for the use of automated systems for certain purposes. These rules may range from design to transparency requirements,[13] from human oversight to explainability requirements. Failure to comply with these requirements may entail legal consequences of various kinds, but generally speaking, it does not deviate from the principle of non-discrimination, but rather preserves it and builds on it. Similarly, but in the opposite sense, the principle of non-discrimination also does not preclude the legislator from prohibiting or limiting the use of automated systems for certain purposes or in certain decisions (as provided for by AI Act or other regulations).[14]

This trend towards recognition of automated decision-making reaches an important milestone with the adoption in July 2024 of the MLAC. This Model Law aims to provide for a legal framework for 'automated contracting'. Under the MLAC, automated contracting is meant to describe the use of automated systems to form or to perform contracts (Art. 2.1 MLAC). As the Guide to Enactment shall explain, the expression 'to form or to perform contracts' is intended to cover any and all stages of the contract life cycle, including negotiations and precontractual dealings and termination of contracts. An 'automated system' pursuant to Article 1 MLAC—'computer system that is capable of carrying out actions without the necessary review or intervention of a natural person'—is aimed at embracing AI systems as described in internationally recognized instruments—OECD,[15] after the latest revision,[16] and incorporated in the AI Act.[17] The legal regime for automated contracting must be underpinned by a foundational principle of recognizing the validity and effectiveness

[12] European Law Institute (2023a) Guiding Principle 2: Non-discrimination against WMD. Interim Report. EU Consumer Law and Automated Decision-Making. https://www.europeanlawinstitute.eu/fileadmin/user_upload/p_eli/Publications/ELI_Innovation_Paper_on_Guiding_Principles_for_ADM_in_the_EU.pdf.

[13] European Parliament and Council of the European Union (2019) Regulation (EU) 2019/1150 on promoting fairness and transparency for professional users of online intermediation services. OJ L 186, 11.7.2019, pp. 57–70.

[14] European Parliament and Council of the European Union (2022) Regulation (EU) 2022/2065 on a Single Market for Digital Services (Digital Services Act). OJ L 277, 27.10.2022, pp. 1–102.

[15] OECD (2019).

[16] OECD (2023).

[17] European Parliament and Council of the European Union (2024) Regulation (EU) 2024/1689, Art. 3(1)

of contracts concluded 'by' or by means of automated systems and of any action or statement so made in relation to any stage of the contract life cycle.[18]

That is to say, in order to construct a legal regime for automated contracting, one must necessarily start from the assumption that the use of automated systems is not, in itself and by itself, an insurmountable impediment to recognizing the validity and effectiveness of the resulting actions, declarations and legal transactions and to allow them to deploy, in such a case, all the effects provided for in the legal system. Nevertheless, upon such a legal recognition, questions about how human autonomy is preserved and which forms of vulnerability automated contracting may entail arise.

The interaction between human autonomy and automated contracting is complex and multifaceted and brings forth an array of forms of vulnerability. In the following sections, three issues are addressed. First, human autonomy and the right to use an AI system in contracting, with a special focus on consumer contracts (*infra* III). Second, human autonomy and unexpected actions as a new form of vulnerability (*infra* IV). Third, consumer automated contracts and the paradoxical two-sided impact on vulnerability risks (*infra* V).

3 Human Autonomy and Automated Contracting: Right to Use an Automated System

Parties can agree on the use of AI systems in their contractual relations, establish conditions *inter partes* for that use, impose limits, or even prohibit it in all or several transactions and for certain purposes. In this respect, this is the natural expression of party autonomy in contracting. In the absence of any agreement between the parties, in application of the principle of non-discrimination as explained above, any party can use an AI system at any stage of the contract life cycle, provided that

---

> 'AI system' means a machine-based system that is designed to operate with varying levels of autonomy and that may exhibit adaptiveness after deployment, and that, for explicit or implicit objectives, infers, from the input it receives, how to generate outputs such as predictions, content, recommendations, or decisions that can influence physical or virtual environments'.

[18] United Nations (2023) Model Law on Automated Contracting, Art. 5

> "1. A contract formed using an automated system shall not be denied validity or enforceability on the sole ground that no natural person reviewed or intervened in any action carried out in connection with the formation of the contract.
>
> (…)
>
> 3. An action carried out by an automated system in connection with the formation or performance of a contract shall not be denied legal effect, validity or enforceability on the sole ground that no natural person reviewed or intervened in the action."

it is not prohibited or limited by law. Such an automated decision, even without human intervention, shall not be denied as being valid or enforceable solely on the grounds that no human has reviewed the action or intervened in the decision-making. Consequently, the other party could not refuse an action or decision performed by an automated system solely on those grounds (unless otherwise agreed).

Thus, as Article 4 MLCA explains, under the probably inappropriate title of 'Technology neutrality',[19] (naturally) parties are not forced to use AI systems in their contractual relations, but they can use them, unless otherwise agreed.

Now the challenging question is whether in consumer contracts, parties can freely agree on the conditions to use AI systems and, more specifically whether businesses can prohibit or limit the use of AI systems by consumers. The question is not only about the traditional imbalance of bargaining power in consumer-business contracts. As that could be addressed with the existing rules. The angle is different now. To what extent the use by consumers of AI systems in their subsequent contractual relations has the potential to strengthen consumers' position and improve their bargaining power. Yet, whether consumers' autonomy might not be compromised or limited, but rather expanded and fortified by the use of AI systems. Then, a right to use AI systems for contracting should be recognized and protected as a consumer-protection tool.

If a consumer, assisted by an automated system that searches and processes information, selects and recommends options or even makes the final contracting decision with a prior review of the purchase conditions, is in a position to make better-informed decisions, the use of automated systems in consumer relations accompanies and makes the protective function of consumer law more effective. If such a premise is assumed, the limitation or prohibition of their use will be avoided or prevented as far as possible because its use empowers the consumer. The underlying debate is much more complex, with more nuanced premises and less forceful conclusions, but at this point we only take one of the argumentative threads to address the question of the prohibition by contract of the use of automated systems, in particular by the consumer.

This is the position taken by the ELI DACC in its *interim report*.[20] In the first phase of the project that crystallized in eight principles tentatively proposed in an interim report, principle 4 (*Non-discrimination and ADM-barrier free principle*) encapsulates the idea that consumers can benefit from the use of automated systems for dealing and contracting. Moreover, automated systems (in the form of digital or virtual assistants) can most effectively and fully realize the ultimate ratio of the

---

[19] United Nations (2023) Model Law on Automated Contracting, Art. 4

> 'Nothing in this Law requires the use of an automated system or a particular method in automated systems to form or perform contracts'

The title ('Technology neutrality') was qualified in the main text above as 'inappropriate', as it conveys the message encapsulated in the second part of the sentence ('no particular method') rather than the one expressed in the first part ('no obligation to use automated systems'), that it is, by all means, neither a purpose nor an undesired effect of the adoption of the MLAC.

[20] European Law Institute (2023b).

'informed decision'[21] policy. The consumer takes a decision with knowledge of the facts and full, adequate and sufficient information to ensure that it is in his or her best interests.

Both in their current state of development and in their expected future evolution, automated systems operating as digital or virtual assistants for consumers would act as powerful 'managers' of transaction-relevant information. They can collect, contrast, compare and verify information provided by traders about the product, recommend the best combination of attributes, advise on the most appropriate contractual terms, negotiate certain terms, search for the best offer, reject proposals incorporating contractual terms that the consumer has marked as unacceptable, or dynamically review long-term relationships such as subscriptions or contracts for the supply of products or services. These functionalities and potential applications of virtual assistants would seem to dilute the weakened position of a consumer unable to deal with scattered, overwhelming, biased or complex information. The virtual assistant would stand as a consumer protection wall and a 'manager of consumer interests' with unparalleled collection, verification, integration and search capabilities.

Several arguments may contradict or at least tone down such an optimistic statement nonetheless.

First, the risk of conflicts of interest that may make the idea of an 'empowered consumer' vanish. Conflicts of interest[22] may be embedded into the design of the automated system in detriment to the consumer's interests or may result from the conditions the provision agreement under which the consumer is entitled to use the automated system or may be linked to the fact that the automated system, provided by a third party (a platform) and used by both traders and consumers, operates in the interests of the trader or the platform and in detriment of the consumer. Unless these conflicts of interests are disclosed and prevented, the impact on consumer protection will become adverse.

Second, the actual effect on mitigating information asymmetries and rebalancing bargaining power. It means that the assumption of a better-informed decision by the consumer thanks to the assistance of virtual assistants needs to be supported by the real allocation of that information to the consumer. More and better information is collected and processed by the virtual assistant, but it needs to be assessed whether, as legal fiction (it is presumed so) or as a factual reality (it is technically available), it is actually provided to the consumer. Information obligations play a prominent protective role in consumer law as they are aimed at repair information asymmetries and make an 'informed decision' feasible. When digital assistants are involved, information asymmetries may be mitigated, but it is not necessarily result into a 'better informed (human) decision' in strict terms. Therefore, attribution rules (and presumptions) are key.

---

[21] European Parliament and Council of the European Union (2005) Directive 2005/29/EC concerning unfair business-to-consumer commercial practices in the internal market. OJ L 149, 11.6.2005, pp. 22–39.

[22] European Law Institute (2023d).

With these caveats, and without opening the debate on whether 'consumer relations' will continue to exist in a context of M2M transactions, the question is whether a right to use automated systems by consumers needs to be guaranteed, and protected.

The above-referred principle of non-discrimination and non-barrier has two derivatives. On the one hand, the prohibition of a differentiated and unfavorable treatment of consumers who use automated systems compared to consumers who do not. On the other hand, the prohibition for businesses to prevent consumers from using virtual assistants or agents for contracting. But in neither of its two contexts should the principle must be understood as absolute. In fact, the debate on whether a genuine 'right to use' automated systems should be recommended is complex and remains open. Competing interests are pitted against each other and do not facilitate a one-size-fits- all solution.

The effective exercise of an eventual right to use automated systems for contracting by consumers would require, first, preventing the use of technological, operational or design measures that block, deter or disable the use of virtual assistants (*blockers*); and, second, implementing contractual, technological and design solutions that facilitate the virtual assistant in performing the necessary actions under equivalent conditions. Digital spaces (websites, applications and other digital user interfaces) should be designed in such a way that they do not pose a barrier to automated systems or, moreover, that they are *ADM-friendly, i.e.* suitable for use by digital assistants.

Another important element that is already expressly provided for in the regulation and which will be key for virtual assistants to play their role is that the information to be provided by traders must be available in machine-readable form and, cumulatively, in a form that is intelligible to the consumer (Art. 14 DSA).[23,24] This is the only way to avoid de facto discrimination against consumers assisted by automated contracting systems.

The implementation of these technological and operational, design and programming measures involves costs and requires changes in communication channels, interfaces and contracting procedures. They could therefore become a burden for smaller companies, putting them at a disadvantage vis-à-vis established market players and large platforms. This disruptive effect on the market has to be taken into account in the final shaping of the principle of non-discrimination and non-barrier. In addition,

[23] European Parliament and Council of the European Union (2022) Regulation (EU) 2022/2065 on a Single Market for Digital Services. OJ L 277, 27.10.2022, pp. 1–102.

[24] European Parliament and Council of the European Union (2022) Digital Services Act, Art. 14(1):

> 'Providers of intermediary services shall include information on any restrictions that they impose in relation to the use of their service in respect of information provided by the recipients of the service, in their terms and conditions. That information shall include information on any policies, procedures, measures and tools used for the purpose of content moderation, including algorithmic decision-making and human review, as well as the rules of procedure of their internal complaint handling system. It shall be set out in clear, plain, intelligible, user-friendly and unambiguous language, and shall be publicly available in an easily accessible and machine-readable format'.

and from another perspective that applies equally to small and large entities, the use of automated systems can saturate the system, simultaneously block available offers without completing the transaction, alter prices or erroneously generate messages of lack of availability (*bots* for purchasing tickets, assistants who keep multiple transactions pending completion simultaneously, *bots* that saturate the system and block it, automated systems that multiply bookings).

The above examples illustrate that there may be cases where legal restrictions may exist, or be imposed, on the use of AI systems to protect specific interests, such that their use becomes unlawful, inappropriate or unreasonable.

This debate illustrates the polyhedral relationship between human autonomy and vulnerability in automated contracting. While human autonomy is preserved and parties are free to agree on the conditions for using automated systems, the two-fold effect of automation on consumer protection requires a more nuanced and elaborate solution. A right to use automated systems (digital or virtual assistants) could indeed alleviate consumers' vulnerabilities and 'fortify' their autonomy.

4 Attribution Rules and the Dilemma of Unexpected Actions

The assumption that AI systems act with varying levels of autonomy[25] makes attribution a more complex and absolutely critical task. A system of attribution rules and factors is instrumental when the option of 'electronic persons'[26] is abandoned.

Attribution in AI systems must take into account two important considerations.

Firstly, it does not consist of determining the origin of a message or an action already completed and determined, which the automated system would simply transmit or generate according to predefined instructions and without any margin for unpredictability, but in attributing decisions or actions which, with a certain level of autonomy and in accordance with objectives, the system adopts and executes.

Secondly, attribution is a prerequisite that underpins other solutions within the legal regime of automated contracting such as the treatment of error or the rules on allocation of risks due to malfunctioning or unexpected results. Attribution serves for multiple purposes. As a first anchor on which to build a regime for mistakes in automated contracting. As a model to extrapolate from the question of the 'attribution of information' to ensure a conscious and informed decision of the person to whom the decision of the automated system is attributed. As a threshold, for example, with respect to deciding whether the cases of absolutely unforeseeable and unexpected actions should be treated from the point of view of non-attribution, a defect of consent or as a scenario of liability. All these questions reveal that attribution, in general terms, has several layers that require separate treatment.

---

[25] Chan et al. (2023).

[26] Pagallo (2018).

The debate on the attribution of the actions of automated systems has been marked and, to some extent, clouded by a complex and delicate debate, not always framed in the right terms, on 'electronic personality'.[27] This is neither a new nor an unusual proposal. The question of the personhood of AI systems has been raised for decades, from a variety of perspectives.[28] Sometimes with a strong ethical and philosophical flavour, on other occasions with pragmatism and an instrumental vision of personality as a useful and efficient mechanism for risk distribution and selective attribution of rights and/or obligations. In short, legal personality as a legal fiction[29] or technical-legal solution has already shown malleability and plasticity to adapt to other situations without implying a full mimicry of the human condition, i.e. without entailing an anthropomorphic conception[30] in the recognition of personality.

However, the option of attributing legal personality to AI systems with certain levels of autonomy (as a unique solution or according to certain thresholds of autonomy) entails significant practical difficulties and shifts the problems to a second stage without solving them.[31] In addition to ethical concerns, it may have implications for the soundness and coherence of the liability system as a whole with practical obstacles to the compensatory purpose or with a counterproductive allocation of incentives to use AI systems as a shield for protection and diversion of liability. All this could ruin both the compensatory and the preventive purpose of liability.[32] Thus, the need for a clear attribution formula becomes even more pressing.

The rules and factors proposed for attributing to a person actions or decisions (output) of an AI system must be revisited to deal with certain situations that we can classify as pathological: errors, system failures and unforeseen or unexpected decisions. In the face of these situations, whose distinctive features of AI make particularly serious or at least intense (autonomy and learning capacity, opacity, complexity, vulnerability, data dependence), three legislative policy options can be considered, in general terms, which are not necessarily mutually exclusive. First, non-attribution. Second, liability rules. Third, the (adapted) application of existing rules on defects of consent, or other causes for invalidity or nullity.

---

[27] European Parliament (2017) Resolution of 16 February 2017 with recommendations to the Commission on civil law rules on robotics (2015/2103(INL)). P8_TA(2017)0051, para 59, "(p) urges the Commission, when carrying out an impact assessment of its future legislative instrument, to explore, analyse and consider the implications of all possible legal solutions, such as:

> "to create in the long term a specific legal personality for robots, so that at least the most complex autonomous robots can be considered as electronic persons liable to repair any damage they may cause, and possibly to apply electronic personality to cases where robots make intelligent autonomous decisions or interact with third parties independently".

[28] Solum (1992).

[29] Galgano (2004).

[30] Maneesha (2020) and Salazar Ortiz and Láriz Durón (2017).

[31] Expert Group on Liability and New Technologies (2022).

[32] Ghersi (1997) and Díez Picazo (1999).

Following our line of reasoning, these risks, and, in particular, unexpected outcomes create new forms of vulnerability whose intensity would depend upon how they are attributed and allocated. At the same time, it is interesting to approach these risks from the perspective of (human) autonomy, insofar as it is going to be affected or modulated by 'mistaken, defective or unexpected actions' of an automated systems. So, in the exercise of private autonomy parties will conclude contract assuming certain actions or decisions attributed to them but performed 'in the exercise of AI agency'.

First of all, a classification or taxonomy of these risk cases is proposed for the purposes of attribution.

i. The first category refers to cases where the AI system malfunctions, fails or has technical problems in its operation. In these cases, the AI system does not perform the expected action, performs it late or incorrectly, or makes decisions that do not correspond to the operator's (or user's) expectations.
ii. The second category includes cases where third party interference, a hacking attack or a cybersecurity breach leads to an omission, an action or a decision by the AI system that the operator (user) does not recognize, deviates substantially from its intention or is simply wrong for whatever reason.
iii. The third category comprises the situations most closely linked to the nature of AI systems as learning systems with a strong dependence on data: unexpected decisions. AI systems can give rise to unanticipated, unexpected outcomes that deviate substantially from what is expected, suffer *hallucinations,*[33] and evolve in their learning towards unanticipated tasks, extrapolate data, generate biases, or execute actions that exceeds the training scope.

The proposed solution to these three categories must be clear and predictable, provide certainty in commercial trade, and achieve an appropriate distribution of risks between the parties. Therefore, unjustified and abusive recourse to the legislative policy option of 'non-attribution' can significantly undermine confidence in the trade while discouraging automated contracting and increasing transaction costs. Faced with the risk of non-attribution, prices and costs in automated contracts would move upwards to cover the risk, specific safeguards and insurance would be imposed, or the use of AI would be limited in particularly large transactions or transactions where frustration of the economic purpose of business due to non-attribution are unacceptable or difficult to reverse.

The non-attribution option would mean that, in the event of failure, third party interference or deviation (alleged and/or acknowledged by the other party) from the expected operation, the action or decision is not attributable to the operator, responsible for the deployment, who would otherwise be considered the origin of the output result of the system and the corresponding legal effects and consequences. For the sake of legal certainty, non-attribution is an uncomfortable and, in certain cases, devastating solution because it undermines trust and frustrates expectations. Therefore, non-attribution as a general solution might not be optimal.

[33] Ji et al (2023).

It may, however, be the preferred solution in consumer relations as a measure to protect the consumer who would not be bound by an action or decision resulting from a failure, interference by a third party or a deviation of the system towards unforeseen, surprising or unexpected results. In the ELI DACC this option has been considered. This action or decision would not be attributable to the consumer and would not have any legal effect. This avoids the situation of subsequent attribution to another actor in the supply chain. This non-attribution is combined with a liability solution, in the form of an indemnity for the damage caused to the other party by the non-attribution borne by the operator who is liable - the provider of the AI system (digital assistant or AI) to the consumer.

The major difficulty is to decide whether failures and errors, on the one hand, and unforeseen decisions, on the other, can and should be treated together as a single category in the case of automated contracting, or whether, on the contrary, they respond to different scenarios. In the latter case, the debate is whether automated outputs that could be qualified as 'unforeseen', 'unexpected' or 'unintended' require a different solution. This has been the debate that arose in the deliberations of UNCITRAL Working Group IV in the preparation of the provisions for automated contracting.[34]

The scope of the proposed provision refers exclusively to the second typology of actions performed by automated systems, i.e. unforeseen or unexpected actions. But it is not intended to deal with cases of 'programming error', or interference by a third party, or transmission error'. Its wording was originally based on Art. 13(5) LMCE,[35] which does not focus on unforeseen results but on attribution of origin or transmission errors. Therefore, the need has arisen to look for other legal solutions to unforeseen results that are uniquely and specifically linked to AI systems and not to the problems of electronic means of communication of messages.

The assumption that the principle that should govern the use of AI systems is that the party using the system to form or perform a contract bears the risk involved[36] would invite to look for solutions in other texts. In the UNCITRAL system, Article 14 of 2005 UN Convention[37] and Articles 25 and 79 of the UN Convention on Contracts

---

[34] United Nations (2023) A/79/17, Article 8: Unexpected actions carried out by automated systems

'[1. Unless otherwise agreed by the parties, where an action carried out by an automated system is attributed to a party to a contract, the other party to the contract is not entitled to rely on that action if, in the light of all the circumstances:

(a) The party to which the action is attributed could not reasonably have expected the action; and

(b) The other party knew or could reasonably be expected to have known that the party to which the action is attributed did not expect the action.

2. Nothing in this article affects the application of any rule of law or agreement of the parties that may govern the legal consequences of an action carried out by an automated system.]'

[35] UNCITRAL (2023) A/CN.9/WG.IV/WP.182, para 43.

[36] UNCITRAL (2023) A/CN.9/WG.IV/WP.182, para 42.

[37] United Nations (2005).

for the International Sale of Goods[38] might be considered. Both texts seek to strike a balance between the interests of the parties by applying the concepts of reasonable expectations and fair dealing. Despite these efforts, however, the solution is not clear and continues to raise doubts.

Such an assumption of risk exposes (human) autonomy to a new form of vulnerability (algorithmic vulnerability) as it is an open source of risks and, more importantly, of deforming the real (human) autonomy. Interestingly, automated contracting introduces another form of vulnerability that is linked to the automated systems and alters the 'AI autonomy' (AI agency). It is the risk of manipulation that automated systems (digital or virtual assistants) can be subject to. As human decision-making can be interfered by unfair commercial practices, AI operation for automated decision-making can be also impaired by certain practices.

5 Automated Contracting and Consumer Relations: Old and New Forms of Vulnerability

A legal regime for automated contracting must necessarily be completed with an analysis of consumer relations where the paradoxical two-sided effect of automation is particularly visible.

Consumers use automated search engines on a daily basis, rely on recommendation systems, make decisions based on reputational rating and ranking mechanisms, benefit from or are affected by (automated) content moderation protocols on platforms, are subject to personalised decisions based on profiling, and use a wide range of applications containing automated purchasing, diagnosis, advice, comparison or consultation systems. In this digital and automated scenario, the consumer remains the end user, the recipient of these services and applications provided and supplied by third-party providers with whom they interact directly or indirectly, but also very frequently, the 'affected person' by automated decisions.

Automated contracting, as a more specific phenomenon in the broad field of consumer interaction with AI systems, offers a singular perspective on the treatment of consumer interests and their protection. The consumer is not only the 'affected person' by automated decision-making, but also an active user of these automated systems. The consumer uses virtual assistants, generative AI solutions, digital agents and other automated systems to assist them or to 'delegate' actions and decisions for contractual purposes. Systems that search, compare and recommend, negotiate terms, continuously renegotiate ongoing subscriptions to improve prices, alert them about contractual modifications or changes in service conditions, generate offers or review contract proposals, automatically exercise the right of withdrawal, enforce certain obligations or terminate the agreement.

[38] United Nations (1980).

One could wonder whether this leads to a market of 'augmented consumers',[39] i.e. a consumer assisted by these automated systems, strengthened in their ability to compare offers, in their bargaining power, in their capacity to react to changes, in the processing of relevant information and in the efficient management of contractual relations. The idea behind the term 'augmented consumer' is very suggestive. On the one hand, because it materialises our thesis that technological progress and, in particular, the spectacular advances on AI are, in reality, phases of human evolution. In contrast to views that predict a replacement or, at the very least, a human-AI (or human–robot) confrontation, we advocate for understanding the development of AI as part of human evolution.

But on the other hand, the concept of the 'augmented consumer' has a very interesting reading in legal terms, particularly, in terms of vulnerability: is an 'augmented consumer' more or less vulnerable? Moreover, is there still a weaker party to protect? The discourse that has guided the legislative response so far is that of a consumer exposed to risks and vulnerable to digital technology, first electronic contracting, now automated contracting. But if automation throughout the life cycle of the contract also rebalances asymmetries, reduces typical transaction costs, reinforces bargaining power, improves comparison capacities and offers possibilities for contrasting and verifying information, the protective response of consumer law must be permeable, sensitive and receptive to these tensions.

If consumers are to benefit from the use of automated systems that enhance their bargaining and contracting position, it will be key to ensure that their use is facilitated, that there are no barriers to their access or operation, or that they are not subject to blocking, manipulation or obfuscation by unfair business practices. Consumer protection legislation will be appropriately 'tuned' to provide a framework that is not only supportive, but also enabling and facilitating, when it incorporates principles and rules that recognise this 'empowering' function of automated systems. A right to access and use AI systems for contracting that is grounded in the positive and promising perception of their benefits would call for ensuring universal access and global use for inclusive purposes.[40]

The ELI DACC have perceived this double facet of automated systems in consumer contracts and formulated certain principles in this respect. In the *interim report*, a need to rethink the paradigm on which the consumer protection model has been built is explored. The use of virtual assistants can mitigate informational asymmetries and reinforce bargaining power, while, paradoxically, it could also expose the consumer to new forms of (algorithmic) vulnerability by 'virtualising' the meaning of informed decision-making, by 'decoupling' the decision-making parameters from the consumer's real will or by accentuating non-responsible purchasing practices that move away from sustainability objectives.

Rethinking the paradigm that has underpinned the construction of consumer law does not mean at all demolishing the edifice built on a set of assumptions that may, however, be significantly questioned today. But rethinking the paradigm can lead

[39] Stephen (2017) and Gartner (2021).
[40] UN AI Advisory Body (2023).

to adjustments in the regulatory approach in order to adapt to a different model of consumption. To avoid an unwanted crumbling of this construction, the starting point, at least provisionally, in the *interim report,* is that consumer law applies to automated contracts (also insofar as the pre-contractual phase is concerned) in which the consumer or both parties use digital assistants.[41]

This is neither an obvious answer nor an irrelevant one; on the contrary, it carries an important conceptual burden. This principle means that, when using digital assistants, despite the expected benefits already described, the consumer does not cease to be a consumer for the purposes of consumer law. This conclusion is not obvious though. On the one hand, all the personal (or positional) assumptions that describe the weaker party to the contract carry a very strong anthropocentric inertia that does not, however, tarnish the performance of the automated system. On the other hand, the asymmetries and relative inequality associated with information, context or procedures can become artificial in the face of increasingly powerful and sophisticated virtual assistants—which gather all the relevant information, verify it, make it comprehensible,[42] compare offers on a continuous basis, renegotiate conditions—. In other words, it could be argued that in pure transactions between automated systems (M2M) or where the consumer acts through virtual assistants who make decisions (M2B), we have left the field of consumer law because the justification for a protective response has evaporated. For the time being, this is not the position being defended; on the contrary, caution as to how these applications (virtual assistants) will develop and penetrate the market makes it advisable to adopt a more continuist stance.

In a transitional period, the expected benefits for the consumer may be overshadowed by risks and vulnerabilities aggravated by limited availability, uneven implementation, inexperience and lack of knowledge, and possible unfair, exploitative or manipulative practices in the market, taking advantage of this weakness. Nor does the jurisprudential interpretation of the concept of the consumer as an objective concept facilitate the transition towards a model of progressive containment of consumer information obligations. In other words, as the Court of Justice of the European Union (hereinafter, CJEU) warns, it is independent of the actual knowledge which the person concerned may have, or of the information which that person actually

[41] European Law Institute (2023c).

[42] Oehler and Wendt (2017). Studies that have challenged the paradigm that an informed consumer makes rational (informed) decisions warn that quantity of information and full transparency do not ensure this objective. On the contrary, research in behavioral economics reveals that, as opposed to quantity, the quality of information is a sufficient condition and that comprehensibility and comparability of information are necessary conditions for "good information" for the consumer. Virtual assistants can precisely facilitate the fulfilment of these conditions, thus repairing the system's own failure.

possesses.[43] This objective and positional conception[44] of the consumer would not support, at least in principle, the thesis of the modulation of information duties in the face of a consumer assisted by automated systems, nor would it even seem to support the idea that in the face of an 'augmented consumer' the regulatory model of protection would have to be recalibrated.

For all of the above reasons, the approach to consumer legislation from the perspective of automated contracting should be based, at least in this initial phase, on the preservation of the paradigm and the backbone principles of consumer protection legislation. To this end, the *interim report* of the ELI DACC brings together three principles: the principle of attribution, the principle of the application of consumer rules, and the principle of non-alteration of information duties.

Thus, the actions and decisions of the virtual assistant are 'the consumer's' actions. That is, properly coupled with design measures that ensure that the consumer has and retains control, an automated system's actions are considered by law as actions attributable to the consumer. The status of the parties (consumer-merchant) is not altered by the use of automated systems. The immediate and natural consequence is therefore that consumer protection rules continue to apply. In particular, information obligations, which crystalize the paradigm of transparency in the consumer market, should not be reduced or discarded on the basis that virtual assistants have been used.

Notwithstanding this, at least provisionally, the opportunity to reopen certain debates and to question some of the solutions embedded in the current conception of consumer law should not be missed. It is a long-standing debate that information obligations are, on the one hand, a burden[45] for businesses, the smaller the size, the higher the costs. On the other hand, information duties have not always proven to be as efficient as expected[46] in achieving the protection goals. Limitations in information processing or comprehension, short attention spans, lack of reading, imperfect rationality, cognitive biases and prejudices, education and experience are factors that inevitably impact the foundations of the information-driven model.[47] Flooding the market with information does not lead to the myth of perfect transparency, nor does it necessarily lead the normative consumer model making rational, pro-consumer decisions. While information obligations continue to increase in legislation and, in particular in relation to AI systems, continue to play a protective role, there is a call for a transformation of information obligations,[48] an adaptation of the form, channels and characteristics of the message to ensure its readability, comprehensibility, adequacy and sufficiency, personalisation and contextualisation.

---

[43] Case C-110/14 Horațiu Ovidiu Costea and SC Volksbank România SA, ECLI:EU:C:2015:538, par. 21. Similarly, Case C-498/16 Schrems and Facebook Ireland Ltd. ECLI:EU:C:2018:37, par. 39; Case C-269/95 Benincasa, EU:C:1997:337, par. 16, and Case C-464/01 Gruber, EU:C:2005:32, par. 36; Case C-110/14, Costea, EU:C:2015:538, par. 21.

[44] C-269/95, Francesco Benincasa and Dentalkit Srl, EU:C:1997:337, par. 16.

[45] Ben-Shahar and Schneider (2014), Garcia Porras and Van Boom (2012), Marotta-Wurgler (2011), Marotta-Wurgler (2012).

[46] Seizov et al. (2019).

[47] Bar-Gill (2014) and Ayres and Schwartz (2015).

[48] Pichonnaz (2023a, 2023b).

Digital assistants and other AI systems could be designed to meet these expectations by improving the comprehensibility, contextualisation and sufficiency of information, matching its tone and personalising content, completing, verifying or expanding where necessary for each consumer and each transaction. But, does this make consumers more powerful and better protected, or does it make them instead responsible for their own protection? Is that a step forward, or a step backwards in the legislative efforts for strengthening consumer protection?

The transition from electronic commerce to automated contracting poses challenges and raises intriguing questions about the traditional notion of (human) autonomy and its pivotal role in Contract Law. In a context of automated contracting, (human) autonomy and AI agency enter into an interaction, still uncertain, which could be one of tension, conflict or, perhaps, symbiosis in the future. Contract law should be sensitive to these changes, and perhaps adapt, if necessary. Preserving and protecting human autonomy does also mean combating old and new forms of vulnerability.

This Paper has traced the path from electronic commerce to automated contracting and spotted the two-sided impacts on vulnerability risks. With reflections from the UNCITRAL MLCA and the ELI DACC, the discussion has focused on three main dilemmas. First, legal recognition of automated contracting, party autonomy, and the right to use automated systems. Second, allocation of unexpected action risk, impact on autonomy and a new form of vulnerability. Third, automated contracting and consumer protection. These are just three vertices of a complex and multifaceted challenge. Contract law for automated contracting and AI Agents.

References

Ayres I, Schwartz A (2015) The no-reading problem in consumer contract law. Stanf Law Rev 661:545–610

Bar-Gill O (2014) Consumer Transactions. In: Zamir E, Teichman D (eds) The Oxford handbook on behavioural economics and the law. OUP, Oxford, pp 465–490

Ben-Shahar O, Schneider CE (2014) More than you wanted to know: The failure of mandated disclosure. Princeton University Press, Princeton, NJ

Chan A et al (2023) Harms from increasingly agentic algorithmic systems. IEEE Computer Society. https://arxiv.org/abs/2302.10329

Coalition for Content Provenance and Authenticity (C2PA) (2022) C2PA standards. https://c2pa.org/

Council of Europe (2024) Framework Convention on AI, and Human Rights, Democracy and the Rule of Law, 2024, https://rm.coe.int/1680afae3c

Díez Picazo L (1999) Derecho de daños. Civitas, Madrid, p 41 ff

European Law Institute (2022) Innovation paper on guiding principles for automated decision-making in the EU. https://www.europeanlawinstitute.eu/projects-publications/publications/eli-innovation-paper-on-guiding-principles-for-automated-decision-making-in-the-eu/

European Law Institute (2023a) Guiding principle 2: non-discrimination against WMD. Interim Report. EU Consumer Law and Automated Decision-Making. https://www.europeanlawinstitute.eu/fileadmin/user_upload/p_eli/Publications/ELI_Innovation_Paper_on_Guiding_Principles_for_ADM_in_the_EU.pdf

European Law Institute (2023b) Interim report: EU Consumer Law and Automated Decision-Making (ADM). https://www.europeanlawinstitute.eu/fileadmin/user_upload/p_eli/Publications/ELI_Interim_Report_on_EU_Consumer_Law_and_Automated_Decision-Making.pdf
European Law Institute (2023c) Principle 2: application of consumer law to algorithmic contracts. Interim Report, pp 26–27
European Law Institute (2023d) Principle 8: ELI Rules on Algorithmic Contracts. Interim Report
European Law Institute (2025) ELI guiding principles and model rules on digital assistants for consumer contracts. https://www.europeanlawinstitute.eu/fileadmin/user_upload/p_eli/Projects/Algorithmic_Contracts/Guiding_Principles_and_Model_Rules_on_Digital_Assistants_for_Consumer_Contracts.pdf
Expert Group on Liability and New Technologies (2022) Training materials on new technologies and product liability. European Commission
Galgano F (2004) El concepto de persona jurídica. Revista Derecho Del Estado 16:13–28
Garcia Porras C, Van Boom W (2012) Information disclosure in the EU consumer credit directive: opportunities and limitations. In: Devenney J, Kenny M (eds) Consumer credit, debt, and investment in Europe. Cambridge University Press, Cambridge UK, pp 21–55
Gartner (2021, February 16) Top trends in data and analytics for 2021: the rise of the augmented consumer
Ghersi CA (1997) Teoría general de la reparación de daños: análisis económico y sociológico del daño individual y social. Astrea, Buenos Aires, pp 141–145
ISO/IEC (2023) ISO/IEC 23894:2023 Information technology—artificial intelligence—guidance on risk management. https://www.iso.org/standard/77304.html;
Ji Z et al (2023) Survey of hallucination in natural language generation. ACM Computing Surveys 55
Maneesha D (2020) Unsettling anthropocentric legal systems: reconciliation, indigenous laws, and animal personhood. J Intercult Stud 41(1):77–97. https://doi.org/10.1080/07256868.2019.1704229
Marotta-Wurgler F (2011) Will increased disclosure help? Evaluating the recommendations of the ALI's 'principles of the law of software contracts. Univ Chic Law Rev 78:165–186
Marotta-Wurgler Fl (2012) Does contract disclosure matter? *Journal of Institutional and Theoretical Economics 168*:94–119
OECD (2019) Recommendation of the Council on Artificial Intelligence. OECD/LEGAL/0449. https://oecd.ai/en/ai-principles
OECD (2023) Recommendation of the Council on Artificial Intelligence. OECD/LEGAL/0449, revision 8 November 2023. https://oecd.ai/en/ai-principles
Oehler A, Wendt S (2017) Good consumer information: the information paradigm at its (dead) end? J Consum Policy 40(2):179–191
Pagallo U (2018) Vital, Sophia, and Co.—the quest for the legal personhood of robots. Information, MDPI
Pichonnaz P (2023a) Informed consumer or informed parties: towards a general information duty? European Journal of Consumer Law/ Revue européenne de droit de la consommation (EJCL/REDC) 2:267–281
Pichonnaz P (2023b) The transformation of information duties. In: Twigg-Flesner C, Micklitz H (eds) The transformation of consumer law and policy in Europe. Hart and Bloomsbury, Oxford and London
Salazar Ortiz V H, Láriz Durón J J (2017) Una crítica al antropocentrismo desde la ética ambiental. Euphyía 11(20):107–130. https://doi.org/10.33064/20euph1363
Seizov O, Wulf A J, Luzak J A (2019) The transparent trap. Analyzing transparency in information obligations from a multidisciplinary empirical perspective. J Consum Policy 42(1):149–173
Solum LB (1992) Legal personhood for artificial intelligences. N C Law Rev 70:1231–1287
Stephen A (2017) Here comes the hyper-connected augmented consumer. GfK Marketing Intelligence Review 9. https://doi.org/10.1515/gfkmir-2017-0012

UN AI Advisory Body (2023, December) Governing AI for humanity: interim report. United Nations, p 15
United Nations (1980) Convention on contracts for the international sale of goods (CISG). Vienna
United Nations (2005) Convention on the Use of Electronic Communications in International Contracts. New York
World Bank Group (2024) Global trends in AI governance. Evolving Country Approaches, in p. 8 and 30 ff

Teresa Rodríguez de las Heras Ballell, Full Professor of Commercial Law, Universidad Carlos III de Madrid. Director of the Research Chair "Artificial Intelligence: Foundations and Frontiers." President- of the European Law Institute (ELI). Spanish delegate to UNCITRAL and UNIDROIT projects on AI in international trade. Expert advisor to EU Commission groups on technology, liability, and platform economy. Visiting Professor at Cambridge, Columbia, Sydney, Tokyo, Oxford, Singapore, and others.

Open Access This chapter is licensed under the terms of the Creative Commons Attribution 4.0 International License (http://creativecommons.org/licenses/by/4.0/), which permits use, sharing, adaptation, distribution and reproduction in any medium or format, as long as you give appropriate credit to the original author(s) and the source, provide a link to the Creative Commons license and indicate if changes were made.

The images or other third party material in this chapter are included in the chapter's Creative Commons license, unless indicated otherwise in a credit line to the material. If material is not included in the chapter's Creative Commons license and your intended use is not permitted by statutory regulation or exceeds the permitted use, you will need to obtain permission directly from the copyright holder.

AI Implants and Self-Estrangement

Craig Konnoth

Abstract Patients with neurally connected AI implants have reported the sense of self-estrangement or identity rupture. That is, while the implant often becomes integrated into self-identity for many patients, others experience a sense of alienation from the device implanted within them that appears to act autonomously and independently from the patient's own volition. They experience this device as an alien entity within them with which they share consciousness. This presents a unique set of issues that the legal and bioethical debates on AI regulation have not fully engaged. The limited scholarship on this problem uniformly assumes that patients who cannot fuse the implant into their sense of identity should be denied the implant. This essay argues that other alternatives are possible. Drawing from scholarship on psychology, it argues that where individuals have a fraught relationship with their implant, the goal should not be to force them to view the implant as part of themselves. Rather, the goal should be to create a relationship of trust between the patient and (what they see as) the implant.

Keywords AI · Implants · Consciousness · Personhood · Identity

The medical ecosystem has now reckoned with artificial intelligence for decades. AI is used in all aspects of medicine—from diagnosing patients, to administering drugs. It plays a role before, and long after, a patient enters a medical office, through drug development, medical resource allocation, and patient follow-up. It is used outside the clinical care context, for sales, scheduling, and business transactions. And—of

C. Konnoth (✉)
University of Virginia, Charlottesville, VA, USA
e-mail: craig.konnoth@law.virginia.edu

© The Author(s) 2025

C. Amodio and A. Diurni (eds.), *Human Vulnerability in Interaction with AI in European Private Law*, https://doi.org/10.1007/978-3-031-93247-2_5

particular concern to this Essay, AI is increasingly implanted into and otherwise connected with individuals to assist in situations where they have limited function.[1]

Legal and bioethics scholarship has engaged with the problems that AI implants generate. The most prominent questions relate to privacy—what data is generated, where is it transmitted, and who ultimately controls it. A second theme concerns safety. With so-called "black box" algorithms in healthcare, who bears the risk of harm? The patient? The doctor? The distributor? The manufacturer? And should the risk regulation regime involve top-down regulation or traditional tort approaches? Third, equity concerns consider issues of bias in the data used to feed AI and, relatedly, inequities in output and distribution of final products. Finally, there are questions of autonomy and moral agency. When AI implants assist a patient with volitional behavior, how should we assess the patient's agency? To what degree should a specific behavior be attributed to the implant versus the patient? What kinds of process and consent mechanisms are required to protect this agency? Should the agency of AI be considered separately or as merged with that of the individual? These are all fraught questions.[2]

While these questions of privacy, safety, equity, and agency are important, they apply, not just to AI implants, but to AI generally. No matter the kind of AI involved, we want to know who controls the data, whether the AI will work as promised, and how does AI affect, respect, displace, undermine, or otherwise connect to human decision-making and agency. Because of the importance of medicine and health, these questions might loom with particular significance in the healthcare space, but the distinction is one of scale, not kind.

This Essay concerns itself with a question that most literature has largely ignored and that is somewhat unique to medical AI—namely, the effect of AI implants on patient identity.[3] The question remains relatively unique to medicine because it is created by implantation of AI into the body. The disturbance of the sense of self—of identity—that this implantation can create, and the policy resolution of that problem, deserves further exploration.

Part 1 of this Essay will offer background. It introduces implantable AI, arguing that AI implants fall into three categories: improving function, providing patient information, and remote monitoring. It then goes on to examine the problems that the legal literature has examined in the AI implantable space and the AI space more generally. Part 2 of this Essay will then examine the problem at its heart: the identity issues that implantable medical AI can create. Patients report that such implants often

---

[1] I agree with disability scholars that what is perceived to be abnormal or lost function is socially contingent and constructed, and that such perceptions are often the result of bias. The loss of "function" is often the result of social practices. Thus, social practices that rely on sound to communicate disadvantage deaf people. That said, I align myself with the interactionist model that holds that biological factors and social factors interact to produce disability, with certain conditions being more influenced by one set of factors than others. See Nathan and Brown (2018).

[2] Da Silva et al. (2022) offers an overview. Other important issues involve innovation and IP law. As that issue does not directly concern patients, I do not discuss it here.

[3] While such implantation does occur for non-medical reasons, they are few and far between. See Aas and Wasserman (2016).

feel like another entity with whom the patient shares consciousness, often with deeply problematic and distressing consequences for their own sense of self. While AI often can become integrated into the patient's identity—sometimes becoming a part of the patient (according to the patient's subjective experience)—others experience a sense of alienation from the device implanted within them that appears to act autonomously and independently from the patient's own volition. This presents a unique set of issues that the legal and bioethical debates on AI regulation have not fully engaged.

Without considering alternatives, scholars have suggested that patients who cannot fuse the implant into their sense of identity should be denied the implant. But Part 3 argues that other alternatives are possible. Drawing from scholarship on psychology, it argues that where individuals have a fraught relationship with their implant, the goal should not be to force them to view the implant as part of themselves. Rather, the goal should be to create a relationship of trust between the patient and (what they see as) the implant. I conclude by offering suggestions for achieving this goal.

1 Background

1.1 A Taxonomy of Implantable AI

Scholars and regulators have used several taxonomies to categorize medical AI. Usually, the distinction turns on the various functions the AI serves: administrative, diagnostic, or treatment-based.[4] And other forms of classification are possible: for example, American regulatory bodies classify devices based on the risks to safety the technology poses[5]; scholars classify AI based on the extent to which the AI is explainable to users and others,[6] the extent to which the AI engages in learning on its own (in ways that are supervised or not), or alternatively, whether it is subject to preset rules of operation.[7] The approach to classification largely depends on the purpose for which the classification system is advanced.

Implants that incorporate AI—the focus of this Essay–however have not been similarly categorized and yet do not neatly fit into existing categories. AI implants here refer to "devices ... that are placed inside or on the surface of the body" that

[4] In previous work, I separate the use of AI in clinical spaces as involving data collection (identifying the kind of data that needs to be collected), diagnosis, and treatment. Konnoth (2024). Nicholson Price separates AI into treatment and diagnostic purposes. See also Malik and Solaiman (2024) (separating functions into "diagnostics, monitoring, or the provision of care" and in addition, administrative functions, including "predictive maintenance, bed management, staff rota planning, and clinical decision support.").

[5] U.S. Food & Drug Administration (2019).

[6] Price (2015, p. 430).

[7] Ho and Wu (2021).

use AI in some way.[8] This can refer to a range of items including prosthetics, neural implants, and even pills used as temporary GI-tract sensors.[9]

For the purposes of this Essay, I offer three categories of AI implants.[10] The first category is assistive, supporting function by allowing patients to perform actions that they otherwise would not be able to engage in. This category includes prosthetic limbs,[11] cochlear implants, visual aids, brain-computer interfaces (BCIs) that assist neural function, and so on. It also includes implants that perform non-conscious functions,[12] including insulin pumps,[13] and cardiac implants.[14]

A second category is informational. These implants inform patients about their physical and mental state.[15] For example, one implant called Neurovista would inform patients when they were about to have epileptic episode, which gave them time to get to safety to avoid injury during an episode.[16] Similarly, food intake implants that track and inform patients of food consumption to enable them to change their dietary habits.[17]

A third category involves remote monitoring of patients. For example, AI in cardiac implants can sort through the vast quantity of data collected to determine what information to transmit to providers.[18] Temporary ingested implants transmit information regarding the GI tract to doctors.[19] Transmitting such information serves important diagnostic functions by giving doctors a real-time insight into the patient's body.

1.2 *Existing Scholarship*

Existing scholarship on AI in healthcare generally, and AI implants in particular, focuses on four sets of problems: privacy, safety, equity, and agency. I review each in turn.

---

[8] U.S. Food & Drug Administration (2019).

[9] Abdigazy et al (2024).

[10] U.S. Food & Drug Administration (2019). Many implants combine the tasks I describe. There are also, of course, other ways to categorize implants. The FDA identifies a list of functions: "Many implants are prosthetics, intended to replace missing body parts. Other implants deliver medication, monitor body functions, or provide support to organs and tissues."

[11] Carter (2024).

[12] Decker and Fleischer (2008) similarly distinguishes between autonomously and consciously controlled implants.

[13] U.S. Food & Drug Administration (2023).

[14] Rollins (2023).

[15] Gilbert (2015). One scholar has identified this function as "advisory."

[16] Kenneally (2021).

[17] Rosa et al. (2019), Horbach et al. (2015), and Morales-Conde et al. (2018).

[18] Reinhardt and Ventura (2023)

[19] Farmer et al. (2013).

The privacy problem figures most prominently in the legal literature on medical AI. Problems involve: (a) the scope of data collection, (b) the size of data sets, and (c) the extent of access. First, the data AI collects is breathtaking in its scope, and includes information about individuals at a far more granular level than contained in any medical record.[20] The kinds of data collected also far exceed traditional categories, including cellular information and geolocation data.[21] Similarly, AI designed to assist with speech collect information regarding individuals' traits, habits, preferences, and even thoughts.[22] Implants designed to assist with hearing can collect data about *other* individuals.[23] A second problem involves the size of data sets. The size, and the linkability of datasets to other datasets, renders even anonymized data vulnerable to reidentification.[24] And finally, much of the data is transmitted far beyond traditional medical contexts, including to manufacturers of AI.[25] Hackers may also get access to this information.[26] As numerous scholars, including myself, have observed, existing privacy regimes insufficiently address these harms.[27]

A second set of problems relates to safety. Devices may malfunction either due to manufacturer or physician error,[28] or intervention by nefarious actors, such as hackers.[29] This can harm patients both physically and mentally. To address these concerns, scholars have examined and offered recommendations for both top-down regulation through regulatory entities like the United States Food and Drug Administration,[30] as well as through the tort regime.[31]

A third set of problems concerns equity. Equity issues arise in two ways. First, the data that is fed into AI models might be biased—often based on existing inequalities in a society organized around race or sex—and therefore may produce biased results, that, for example, recommend more limited treatment regimes for black people.[32] And even if AI operates in a way that is unbiased, scholars raise concerns about financial barriers for those who lack resources to access AI technology—again, disproportionately women and people of color.[33]

A final problem concerns autonomy. This issue arises in three forms. First, scholars argue that autonomy requires informed consent and decision-making, which, in turn,

[20] Cohen et al. (2020).

[21] Tschider (2023, p. 880).

[22] Jiang et al. (2023) and van Stuijvenberg et al. (2024).

[23] van Stuijvenberg et al. (2024).

[24] Price (2015).

[25] Cohen et al. (2020).

[26] Pycroft et al. (2016).

[27] Pycroft et al. (2016), Cohen et al. (2020), and Tschider (2023).

[28] Davenport v. Medtronic Inc., No. 00-6105, 2004 WL 193197 (E.D. Pa. Feb. 3, 2004).

[29] Pycroft et al. (2016).

[30] Opderbeck (2019).

[31] Jorstad (2020) and Price and Cohen (2024).

[32] Obermeyer et al. (2019).

[33] Peters and Fried-Oken (2020).

requires AI transparency. Because certain forms of AI operate opaquely—in a so-called "black-box"—autonomy principles are violated.[34] Next, there are problems with agency. Assume that a patient, implanted with an AI device that aids in brain function engages in a harmful act. Debates exist as to whether the AI shares blame for the behavior, or whether the individual should be understood to have behaved autonomously.[35] Relatedly, scholars have raised concerns that hackers or even manufacturers can deliberately countermand patients' own autonomous preferences—for example, brainjacking a patient in ways that alter their impulse control.[36]

2 AI Implants and Identity Problems

The problems above do not quite capture the identity harms traceable to AI implants.[37] Consider Neurovista, the neural implant mentioned above that warned patients when they were about to have a seizure, which gave them the time to get to safety or take clonazepam, which helps avoid seizures.[38] Some patients reported excellent outcomes, being able to avoid the accidents they would experience when having a seizure—imagine, for example, having a seizure while climbing a staircase. On the other hand, another patient described "the shock of it—the strangeness of having a machine communicate with her and advise her what was about to happen in her head."[39] As yet a third patient put it, "[i]t felt as if there were someone inside her head, but it wasn't her."[40]

This Section conceptualizes the harm that these patients seek to describe. It begins by distinguishing away existing accounts that some might use in order to frame the harm. It then derives an original explanation for conceptualizing this harm, and concludes with specifying when this harm is most likely to occur.

2.1 Alternative Accounts of the Identity Harm

First, I seek to explain what the harm I describe above is *not*. Some might argue that the issues I describe relate, not to identity, but to *autonomy*. But that is not the

---

[34] Amann et al. (2020) and Tschider (2021).

[35] Cabrera and Carter-Johnson (2020, p. 2).

[36] Pycroft et al. (2016).

[37] Kenneally (2021) and Gilbert (2015) (Relatively little attention is paid to postoperative iatrogenic harms. In other words, questions of whether (so-called) successfully "treated" individuals might experience difficulties in adjusting to becoming "normal" or "symptom-free" have been, for the most part, unexplored.). Gilbert is dealing with a slightly different problem than me, but is right in that legal scholars have not explored the issues he is focused on either.

[38] Kenneally (2021).

[39] Kenneally (2021).

[40] Kenneally (2021).

case. Consider Neurovista. This implant does not take over volitional behavior by the patient—rather, it lets the patient know when they are about to have a seizure. The patient can—autonomously—choose how to react to the information. They can choose to continue in the activity in which they are engaging, take their medication, or get to safety.

To be sure, the questions of identity and autonomy might merge in the case of other implants. For example, consider a prosthetic arm with AI capability that engages with brain function to anticipate patients' desires, and moves the arm accordingly. [41] The identity issue is a subjective one—the patient might experience a sense that a separate entity exists within her that participates in the moving of the arm—or they might not. At the same time, depending on the extent to which the AI anticipates, influences, or displaces brain function, we might hold that the patient is not acting autonomously, no matter what they feel. The autonomy question is an objective assessment. While the scholarship on AI and autonomy makes objective assessments as to the patient's agency, in so doing, it has not, to my knowledge, generally considered subjective questions of identity.

This is not to say that identity and autonomy questions are not related. Scholars have written at length about how a sense of autonomy and agency is important for the development of self; indeed, implants which interfere with one's sense of agency can undermine one's sense of self, that is, of one's identity.[42] One patient with a neural implant designed to treat depression felt that something he had said was inappropriate—but was not sure whether the cause of the statement was himself or the implant: "It blurs to the point where I'm not sure... frankly, who I am."[43] But the lack of agency was felt precisely because the patient retained a sense of self that felt displaced. A sense of autonomy, agency, and even privacy, is necessary to develop a full sense of self.[44] Yet, once developed, an individual's diminished autonomy or privacy does not erase the sense of self, though it may stunt it in various ways.[45]

Even if they concede that the harm in question relates to a patient's identity and not their autonomy, some might try to situate it within existing scholarship on AI implants and patient identity. Yet, that scholarship does not quite capture the identity harm at issue here.

Return to the Neurovista example. The popular account describing Neurovista warned that patients with neurological implants had experienced breakdowns in marriages, relationships, and careers. It goes on to interview philosopher Fred Gilbert, who believed that the harm was caused by identity ruptures that those with the AI implant experienced. For Gilbert, "people whose marriages broke down had built their identities and their relationships around their pathologies. When those were removed, the relationships no longer worked."[46]

---

[41] Kögel (2020, p. 10).

[42] Pezzella et al. (2005) and American Psychiatric Association (1994).

[43] Yuste et al. (2017).

[44] Oshana (2005) and Shoemaker (2010).

[45] Oshana (2005) and Shoemaker (2010).

[46] Oshana (2005) and Shoemaker (2010).

Gilbert's explanation is best understood in the context of his broader academic work. He explains these identity-ruptures in greater detail in the context of deep-brain stimulus, a treatment that is often successfully used for conditions like Parkinson's Disease. As Gilbert explains, identity is constituted—in part at least—through the ability to have "an ongoing narrative" of self.[47] This narrative develops through continuous negotiation between ascriptions that society imposes on us and our own self-conceptions—someone's belief that they are middle-class, kind, Indian, gay, and so on, is negotiated with society's construction of those categories.[48] Neurotechnologies like deep-brain stimulation can result in sudden changes to patients' behavior and experiences in ways that do not conform to the identity categories ascribed to patients either by themselves or others.[49]

For Gilbert, the identity confusion arises from the alleviation of symptoms: the "danger" is "imposing a 'forced normalisation': requiring patients to incorporate 'a change in self-image which is concurrent to the improvement seen in their illness'." And others—including loved ones—may also be unable to reconcile their understandings of the patient when symptoms are alleviated.[50] He warns that "the role of illness in a patient's identity is often underestimated."[51]

Yet, the problem that I identify is different from what Gilbert describes.[52] The issue with technologies like Neurovista is *not* that the patient experiences an alleviation of symptoms. Indeed, the implant's purpose is to *warn* patients of continued and impending symptoms. Rather, the problem is that some 'other' is communicating with the patient about her own body. When a patient feels "as if there [is] … someone inside her head," the problem comes, not from alleviated symptoms, but something different altogether.[53]

2.2 Conceptualizing the Identity Harm

In this Section I first seek to provide a thicker account of what the patient might mean when she claims that "someone" is "inside her head." I then step back to situate this account in theories of identity harm.

---

[47] Gilbert (2012).

[48] Goddard (2017), Baylis (2013), and Schechtman (1996).

[49] Gilbert (2012). In other words, their personality might change in ways that created a rupture, either in terms of how others saw them or in their own conception of self, depending on how embedded their illness identity was.

[50] Kenneally (2021). "One man noticed that his newfound confidence was making life hard for his wife; he was too "full-on." Another woman … was unrecognizable to her family. They told her that they grieved for the old her.".

[51] Kenneally (2021) and Bretschneider et al. (2023). It bears noting that implants can also increase feelings of disability identity and stigma. Bretschneider et al.

[52] Gilbert (2012). Though to the extent non-AI implants also create this problem, the claims here equally apply.

[53] Gilbert (2012).

Literature in Science and Technology Studies offers some insight into the patient's perception that there is "someone" inside her head. As Bruno Latour explained, individuals regularly anthropomorphize machines they encounter as "social agents," endowing them with independent social agency.[54] As he notes, "we are constantly granting mysterious faculties to gremlins inside every conceivable home appliance, not to mention cracks in the concrete belt of our nuclear plants."[55] At the time of his writing, he explained, sociologists argued against this "'projection'.... of a human behavior onto a nonhuman cold technical object."[56] But a machine, Latour argues, is "anthropomorphic through and through" in that it "has human shape [and]... gives shape to humans.[57] Humans make machines, and in turn, machines shape human behaviors, forcing them to act and react in various ways. Latour (probably deliberately) picks a mundane example—a mechanical door closer that requires humans to adjust their behavior around doors. The door is made by humans, and in turn, requires humans to adjust their behavior: for example, to apply more force than normal to open the door (preventing some from opening the door at all) and to anticipate the door's closure to prevent injury. Thus, in Latour's famous example, when the door closer stopped working, the university installed a sign saying that it had gone "on strike"—as if it were a human being.[58]

But if a mundane mechanical door can be anthropomorphized, how about more developed AI objects? Latour considers "much more sophisticated doors with the ability to see you arrive in advance (electronic eyes), or to ask for your identity (electronic passes), or to slam shut—or open-in case of danger."[59] AI implants which warn about impending betrayals in bodily functions, or prosthetics that are supposed to predict what an individual wants, but that perhaps act in ways not intended, can appear to have their own mind; anthropomorphizing them, as the patients described above do, is likely easier.

My claim, then, is that the patient anthropomorphizes the AI implant as a separate entity that shares space in her body. Turning to theoretical accounts, the problem is best captured by the distinction between "narrative" identity and "numerical" identity.[60] Narrative identity refers to continuity between self from one moment to another. The individual at the later moment can relate to the individual from the earlier moments in time—their memories, habits, and sense of self remains recognizable from one moment to the next. Ruptures in narrative identity occur, roughly, when the individual recognizes themself from a previous moment in time, but finds it hard to incorporate their new experiences into the preexisting one. Scholars—including Gilbert whom the previous Section describes—have written at length about how

[54] Latour (1988).

[55] Latour (1988).

[56] Latour (1988, p. 303).

[57] Latour (1988, p. 303).

[58] Latour (1988, pp. 302–303).

[59] Latour (1988, p. 303).

[60] Schechtman (1996, p. 27) and Atkins (2004, pp. 358–360).

treatment and alleviation of symptoms—whether through devices or drugs—can produce these effects because of a rupture with previous senses of self.[61]

What concerns us here, however, is numerical identity. This refers to one's understanding of oneself as a singular being. On this account, what "individuates each person as a metaphysically distinct identity is their distinctive consciousness or mental contents."[62] Philosophers have offered various accounts of numerical identity rupture. For our purposes, the most relevant is captured by a thought experiment offered by philosopher Kim Atkins, where a single brain is bifurcated and placed into two bodies. The new entities thus created, she argues (not uncontroversially), have narrative continuity with the previous bodies, but not numerical continuity.[63]

AI implants are situations where narrative continuity remains but numerical continuity does not. Rather than patients dealing with narrative discontinuity in identity caused by a cure—Gilbert's account—they have to reckon with what they experience as a foreign entity in their heads *simultaneously* with their own identity. All implants can have this effect—for example, in another study, Gilbert found that neural implants could sometimes be seen as "a foreign intrusion" or "an outside force," which could lead to "feelings of self-estrangement."[64]

2.3 Contexts in Which These Identity Harms Occur

The identity harm I describe is likely attributable only to a small set of AI implants. Gilbert notes that even while *some* patients experienced BCIs as "foreign intrusions" and the like, such feelings were rare—most patients did not notice the implant working "in the background."[65] With many AI implants, this will indeed be the case.

Consider the categorization of AI implants described in Sect. 1.1—assistive, informational, and surveillant. From the perspective of the patient, surveillant AI generally works "in the background" as Gilbert puts it—without intruding on the patients' consciousness, it transmits information to professionals. Informational AI generally does not work in the background—the whole purpose of such AI is to get the

---

[61] Kramer (1993, p. 18), Carter et al. (2011), Schechtman (2010), Kraemer (2013), and Gisquet (2008).

[62] Mackenzie and Walker (2015, p. 377). Some point to the fact that one may not retain continuity of consciousness with a fetus or if one falls within a vegetative state, and thus propose corporal singularity rather than cognitive singularity. This might create problems, for example, with prostheses and the like. I believe there are problems with this position, but suffice it to say that AI implants present problems on both accounts of continuity.

[63] This example is analogous to the one that Atkins (2004) offers.

[64] Gilbert et al. (2017, p. 100).

[65] Gilbert et al. (2017, p. 100).

patient's attention. Finally, assistive AI might sometimes work in the background. AI-pacemakers for example, likely will not intrude upon a patient's consciousness.[66] But assistive devices that help with volitional functions, like prosthetic limbs with predictive ability (what some call "autocorrect") that supplement patients' own motor functions,[67] have a greater potential of creating a sense that there is another intelligence residing in the patient. One patient thus reported feeling like an "electronic doll." [68] "Another said he felt like RoboCop, under remote control."[69] "[Patients] reported feelings of postoperative self-estrangement and a failure to achieve embodied fusion of self with the device."[70]

But even with such—what I will call, consciousness-engaging AI—it would appear that identity harms are not common. These harms likely vary with the nature of the device, condition, and other considerations described in the next Part.

Having described the prevalence of the harm in this way, some might point out that it is not only AI implants that are consciousness engaging. External monitors which might even be integrated into phones, or apps on phones themselves engage patient consciousness. Patients might anthropomorphize them as they do other technology. While this may well be the case, AI *implants* are subsumed within an individual's sense of self because of their placement or functions. The boundaries of the body play at least some important, if not exclusive, role in describing where "self" ends.[71] By being placed *within* that boundary, and perhaps even engaging essential bodily functions, implants are more intrusive and create the identity harms I describe above.

Finally, because I now refer to the boundaries of the body, some might point to the scholarship on prostheses and other non-AI implants and identity. Why do they not implicate the same harms I describe here? While I rely on the scholarship on non-AI prostheses below, AI implants are more likely to be experienced as a foreign consciousness because they appear to act out of their own volition. Unlike non-AI devices, AI appears to (and some might say does) exert its own volition. The purpose of AI here is to engage in decisionmaking and direct action and function—what data to transmit, how should body function be assisted–in ways that non-AI implants do not. This distinctive decisionmaking capacity separates AI implants from other implants.

Of course, there are exceptions to each of these rules. In rare situations, identity harms might also arise with AI that do not seek to engage patients' consciousness—some patients have had identity-harms arise from pacemakers implants. [72] Or

---

[66] de Preester (2011, p. 121). This bears some similarity to what Helena de Preester refers to as implants with embodiment relations. De Preester explains that such implants lack quasi-transparency, and users are less aware of them.

[67] Yuste et al. (2017).

[68] Kenneally (2021).

[69] Kenneally (2021).

[70] Gilbert et al. (2019, p. 93).

[71] Bublitz (2022).

[72] Wingate (1986, p. 93). A pacemaker can be viewed as an artificial organ, but unlike an artificial limb, it controls a function in the patient without volitional intervention by the patient. But some patients may have atypical reactions and a sense of personhood invasion even in this case.

individuals might experience AI that is *not* implanted as a foreign entity. Non-AI prostheses might appear to take on a mind of its own for yet other patients. And complications can arise with AI devices with multiple components—for example, one device included a subcutaneous implant with an external monitor. The patient seemed ambivalent about whether the implant was a part of her or not.[73] But the monitor was seen as something external: "it's there every night you go to bed and you put it in a place that it can still read you so it's like a teddy bear."[74] Yet, these outlier contexts do not define the typical situation in which numerical identity harm occurs.

3 Addressing AI Implants' Identity Problems

If an AI implant can be thought of as a social agent, it is important to understand how a patient can develop healthy relationships with their AI implants. What should this relationship look like? Does it require the fusion between AI identity and the patient's identity that some patients achieve? And if so, what is the best way to achieve it? This Section considers these questions in turn.

3.1 Existing Recommendations

The literature engaging with identity problems is limited. What exists is usually descriptive. The few recommendations the literature provides focus only on narrative identity problems. Gilbert's work on the Neurovista trial, for example, describes how one patient was largely in denial about having epilepsy. The diagnosis had created a sense of "loss of control [...] that reflect[ed] an involuntary shift in their experience of the self." Thus, the patient explained, "I just kind of pretended that it didn't really exist. I didn't really see myself as an epileptic."[75]

Consistent with his other scholarship, Gilbert concludes that the problem was that the patient was experiencing a crisis of narrative identity: the disruption the diagnosis had created in the first place was reinforced because, "being constantly alerted by the machine impressed upon her the reality of her symptoms,... [and] provid[ed] corroborating evidence of her disease state."[76] As the patient explained, "[The BCI] made me feel like I was just sick all the time. [...] It also made me feel like I was different to everyone else." The alerts exacerbated her "sense of powerlessness, resulting in severe distress," ultimately causing depression.[77]

[73] Wingate (1986, p. 93).

[74] Wingate (1986, p. 93).

[75] Gilbert et al. (2019, p. 91).

[76] Gilbert et al. (2019, p. 91).

[77] Gilbert et al. (2019, p. 91).

The solution in such a situation, Gilbert concluded, might be to withhold the implant: "it may be permissible to decline implanting BCIs in patients who experience preoperative self-image issues in relation to their pathology." [78] And indeed, if Gilbert's assessment of the problem is correct, then that might indeed be the best solution.

Yet, in many situations, the problem is not one of narrative identity, but one of numerical identity. Indeed, the patient that Gilbert interviewed may have been trying to describe both kinds of identity harm. She was troubled, not just by the fact that the machine's frequent alerts reminded her that she had epilepsy, but also by the lack of control she experienced: "it was always beeping and always red, it made me feel like I had no control."[79] The lack of control is a separate complaint from the reinforcement of illness identity. Indeed, a patient who *accepted* her epilepsy diagnosis might have similarly complained about the lack of control over an implant that constantly alerted her. A complaint regarding lack of control might be best understood as one regarding a loss of autonomy. But this complaint could also involve a sense of alienation from a device implanted in one's body that provides information that the patient herself does not know.[80] In such a situation, simply denying access to the device is not the best solution.

3.2 *Alternatives*

On one hand, there might be full fusion between the patient's identity and the implant—the implant is a part of the patient like any other body part. For example, during the Neurovista trial, one patient finally felt she "had a self that she could trust.... 'We [the implant and the patient] were calibrated together.... We became one.'"[81] Patients with AI implants have described this sense of fusion with another identity. "With the device, I found myself.... The device became me," explained the patient.[82] When the Neurovista trials ended and it was removed, "[i]t felt as if she had left a part of herself behind."[83] Thus, Gilbert argues that "[w]hen the device and [the patient] began to work together, a new person emerge[s]—a de-novo identity, a symbiosis of machine and mind."[84]

---

[78] Gilbert et al. (2019, p. 91).

[79] Gilbert et al. (2019, p. 98) and Kenneally (2021).

[80] Gilbert et al. (2019).

[81] Kenneally (2021).

[82] Kenneally (2021).

[83] Kenneally (2021). Bublitz and Gilbert (2023).

[84] Kenneally (2021). Gilbert et al. (2017). More generally, Gilbert's work suggests that such integration is common in the case of certain devices. In the case of DBS devices: "In general, the patients interviewed did not notice the device in their body while it was doing its job in the background.... [P]atients use a language that seemingly incorporates the DBS device into their self or body image. Patient 13 clearly uses such metaphorical language; he does not say 'I charged the devices up this morning' but rather 'I charged myself up.' Such language could indicate an embodied acceptance

At other times, full fusion does not occur. Thus, another patient who also made peace with her implant seemed to be more ambivalent. The device "was like an alien at first, you grow gradually into it and get used to it, so it then becomes a part of everyday...." And at some point, she explained, the device "becomes part of you... [It] was me, it became me."[85] But even at that point, she talked about the device as a separate entity "if you open your eyes it's always there, it follows you through the shower everywhere."[86] While she appeared to have no objection to this, such language is not fully consistent with claims that the device is an essential part of her, like any other body part: it is rare to describe a body part that is integrated into one's sense of self as being "always there" and as "follow[ing]" you.

I rely heavily on brain-implants for my exposition here—but scholarship on non-AI prostheses show relatable variation.[87] "Some experience [non-AI based]... prosthesis as an external object and not part of themselves. Others embody it and sense the ground" when using a prosthetic leg.[88] "Still others incorporate the prosthesis into their body model, blending it with the residual phantom experience of... amputated [limbs]... restoring a sense of 'wholeness'."[89] Often in the latter group include patients who still feel their phantom limbs: "[T]hough I've not got my lower arm, it's as though I've got it and... [the prosthesis] is part of me now."[90]

As I note above, however, identity fusion is tougher in situations involving AI-based implants, where users might feel that there is a second consciousness operating within their bodies.[91] These AI can deploy prostheses—many of them rely, in particular, on brain-computer interfaces. Thus, scholars describe the user of one such robotic arm noting: "it was the second day of training when [it] became my arm.... I started saying, 'I moved my arm.'... I felt like it was part of me."[92]

The dichotomy between full identity fusion between AI implant and self, versus the perception that the implant remains an "other" bears resemblance to similar

of the implant, of patients feeling like being one with the implant." Yet, Gilbert has raised concerns elsewhere.

85 Gilbert et al. (2019).

86 Gilbert et al. (2019).

87 Steinert et al. (2019).

88 Bublitz (2022).

89 Bublitz (2022) and Murray (2004, p. 971).

90 Kögel (2020, p. 10).

91 Latour (1988, p. 303).

92 Latour (1988, p. 303).

phenomena in the mental health field.[93] In the context of dissociative identity disorders (DID), where patients experience "two or more distinct personality states,"[94] practitioners have historically sought to fuse personality states together. But that approach is shifting.[95] Guidelines still recommend "integrated functioning whenever possible,"[96] but also recognize that "even after undergoing considerable treatment, a considerable number of DID patients will not be able to achieve final fusion and/or will not see fusion as desirable."[97] In such situations, the "very core of the therapeutic process" is to facilitate "an increased degree of communication and coordination among the identities" allowing them "to be aware of one another as legitimate parts of the self and to negotiate and resolve their conflicts."[98]

More recent scholarship goes further. It argues that this lack of full fusion is normal because individual identity is itself constituted through various "parts"; that is, it is "an internal system of [at least somewhat separated] subjectivities that shift in response to inner and outer cues." These subjectivities or parts usually exist in harmony and symbiosis with each other, but when conflict occurs, an individual can experience DID.[99] This scholarship similarly concludes that the goal is not necessarily fusion, but rather harmonious coexistence of these various parts.[100]

---

[93] Murray (2004, p. 971). The literature on prosthetics also proposes a similar distinction. (not all participants describe prosthetic limbs as extensions of the body). Prescriptively, de Preester (2011) notes confusion about whether tools are extensions of the body or are incorporated within the body; she recognizes that patients' psychological attitudes might be different; van den Berg B et al. (2013); Heidegger (2001, p. 100). Whatever the case, I believe that AI presents a different situation than prosthetics because it can present as another consciousness within the body. Unlike tools or prostheses, AI and the processes it controls does not necessarily always appear to have an "assignment to the person who is to use it or wear it."

[94] American Psychiatric Association (2022).

[95] I am not here trying to create an analogy between having an implant and having DID. Indeed, in many cases of DID, there is no consciousness of other personalities that inhabit the individual, whereas the problem I am describing comes from a patient being all too aware of the other entity that inhabits their body. Other differences also exist. The point is to note the difference of approaches even in other contexts where integration is a question.

[96] International Society for the Study of Trauma and Dissociation (2011) Guidelines for treating dissociative identity disorder in adults, Third Revision, Journal of Trauma & Dissociation, 12:2, 115–187.

[97] Ibid.

[98] Ibid.

[99] Lester (2023) and Schettler et al. (2019). This approach bears some similarity to radical embodiment theories in the prosthetics and AI literature that "takes cognitive systems to be a kind of complex self-organized system in which many components interact with each other to give rise to a given cognitive ability.

[100] International Society for the Study of Trauma and Dissociation (2011, p. 133). As the guidelines explain, "integration [i]s an ongoing process of undoing all aspects of dissociative dividedness that begins long before there is any reduction in the number or distinctness of the identities, persists through their fusion, and continues at a deeper level even after the identities have blended into one." Fusion, on the other hand, is a "a point in time" in this broader process "when two or more alternate identities experience themselves as joining together with a complete loss of subjective separateness."

Yet, even in the literature on implants, there is some recognition that full integration need not be the goal. While scholars writing about AI implants and *identity* seek fusion between the patient and the implant, those writing about implants and *autonomy* have often been resistant to the claim that the individual and the implant should be understood as a single entity. Among the various approaches, Sara Goering and coauthors suggest that even if an implant is "seamlessly integrate[d] into our daily lives,"[101] it can still be understood as a separate entity.[102] But that does not mean that that entity lacks a relationship to the self. These scholars invoke a relational autonomy schema, which characterizes personhood as constituted in concert with others. This includes concepts, knowledge, identity ascriptions, advice, and admonitions received from the world in which individuals inhabit. The authors analogize implants to these influences: implants can—and should—be seen as existing in a relationship with the patient.[103] In so doing, they implicitly suggest that while implants may not fuse with a patient's identity, a separate and healthy relationship may develop.

I do not mean to overstate similarities with DID. In the DID context, it is indisputable that various personalities are *internal* to and *come* under the umbrella of a singularly identified person. But for Goering et al., implants begin as external entities and *remain* entities external to the person (at least for the purposes of assessing autonomy). I do not seek to resolve this, or any other, dispute regarding the ontological status of implants.[104] Rather, the fact that this family of approaches all recognize that separate agencies can be subsumed within a single individual, but have harmonious relationships with each other, is instructive.

3.3 Achieving Integration

While significant differences remain between identity ruptures created by implants and those caused by DID, some similarities are notable. Consider the case of identity fusion. As noted above, for some individuals, fusion between AI implant and identity proves easy. For others, the fusion might take some work. In one context, a patient who had difficulty thinking "about... implanted material in terms of body image and form[ing] a mental representation of the stimulator and the electrodes... [,] finally coped well with it" in part by making "an artwork of her chest X-ray showing the stimulator."[105] Similarly, where possible, framing the implant as being part of an individual's narrative identity in a forward-looking way, for example, by framing

[101] Ibid.

[102] Goering et al. (2017).

[103] Goering et al. (2017).

[104] How should we determine the boundary between internal and external? Bublitz (2022), Schüpbach et al (2006, p. 1813). outlines this debate, noting that one can adopt objective criteria, such as the skin boundary or degree of attachment, or subjective criteria, such as body image, body schemes, and body model approaches. But this is not a debate I seek to resolve—what counts for me is the patient's sense of self.

[105] Schüpbach et al (2006, p. 1813).

it as a tool that will give patients future control over their lives, has also been shown to improve healthy integration. Patients who offered "self-reports indicat[ing] that implanted advisory devices are experienced as increasing restorative powers (i.e., empowerment) over the self" ultimately integrated implants in a more healthy manner.[106]

But these practices—visualization, imagery, and the like—are exactly what is recommended to achieve fusion in the DID context. Professional guidelines recommend, among other things, "fusion rituals" that "usually involve imagery... as crucial rites of passage from the subjective sense of dividedness to the subjective sense of unity.... The patient's experience is that alternate identities join together with an image of joining together or becoming unified."[107]

The fusion rituals in DID and implant-contexts may not be the same. Indeed, the fact that they exist at all in both contexts does not mean that where identities do not fuse, the research in one context applies to the other. But the parallels I have drawn so far should merit serious consideration of and research into DID guidelines.

Those guidelines suggest that when fusion is not possible, building a harmonious coexistence through "communication and coordination among the identities" is the best outcome.[108] To understand how to achieve this, it is necessary to turn to a field that has long considered best practices in relationships between humans and AI entities—social robotics.

Social robotics studies robots that "people are inclined to anthropomorphize... in order to interact with them."[109] Existing scholarship places the properties of social robots on a scale, ranging from greater to lesser sociability depending on the characteristics the robots have.[110] These include, "humanoid [characteristics]... [,] the capability of interacting with humans in a natural and social manner," and the ability to "perceive their world, make decisions on their own, and perform coordinated actions to carry out their tasks."[111] The goal is to engage design principles "that would evoke positive feelings in their users, and.. to computationally specify cognitive architectures for the robots that would allow them to interact and communicate in a manner deemed socially appropriate." Such robots act as "tutors, learning companions, coaches, domestic helpers" using "dialog, nonverbal cues, expressive displays, and physical actions" to engender trust and connection.[112]

Implants do not generally figure into the study of social robotics. Instead, scholars usually focus on robots *designed* to engender a sense of trust and communication with humans and consider how to improve them. And yet, it is unclear why this is the case. AI implants satisfy many of the criteria that I list above that scholars claim

---

[106] Gilbert et al. (2019).

[107] International Society for the Study of Trauma and Dissociation (2011), Guidelines for treating dissociative identity disorder in adults, p. 133.

[108] Ibid.

[109] Ibid.

[110] Bartneck and Forlizzi (2004).

[111] Lu et al. (2023).

[112] DeSteno et al. (2012).

define social robots—including, for example, "interact[ing] and communicate[ing] with humans by following... [certain] behavioral norms."[113] More importantly, as I note above, developing healthy models of interaction between implants and patients is necessary to maintain patient well-being.

Studying AI implants from the perspective of social robotics is therefore important. Just as with other social robots, it is important to understand how to incorporate design principles that engender trust and interaction with users. Like social robots, AI implants should also "infer beliefs and goal states of a human collaborator" and "build and maintain social rapport with its user."[114]

Having identified identity ruptures as a problem, and social robotics techniques as a general approach for addressing them, this Essay can offer only general considerations that might guide future research. After all, as scholars explain, for trust to be developed, "mutual exchanges" between robots and humans must "evolve in a familiar and expected way" to make "people... less resistant to interaction."[115] These social norms are complicated and will depend upon a range of factors.

First, it is important to consider characteristics of the AI, including the scope, frequency, and urgency of its interaction with the patient. As Sect. 2.3 above notes, consciousness-engaging AI are more likely to create identity-harms, though more research is needed. Thus, my hypothesis is that implants that provide information to patients about their bodies are the most likely to create identity ruptures. Those that assist with volitional movement have some probability of creating such ruptures. Where the AI is not consciousness-engaging, they are less likely to create identity harm. Existing research supports this claim. Indeed, the literature suggests fewest problems in situations where AI seeks to surveil patients on behalf of medical professionals without intruding on patients' consciousness.[116]

Second, characteristics of the patient are important to take into account: individual experiences and traits affect how individuals interact with robots. This includes "prior robot experience, personality dispositions, and demographic characteristics"[117] Similarly, scholars have suggested that relationship to one's illness identity can affect one's relationship to the implant.[118] Beyond testing the ability of AI implants to perform medical functions,[119] it is important to develop technology that determines how certain patients would interact with their implants.

---

[113] Bartneck and Forlizzi (2024).

[114] Bartneck and Forlizzi (2024).

[115] Pollini (2009).

[116] Pellegrino and Thomasma (1987).

[117] Allan et al. (2022) and Breazeal et al. (2016).

[118] Gilbert et al. (2019).

[119] Breazeal et al. (2016, p. 1951). Social robotics scholars argue that social agency involves "[i]nstrumental support [that] concerns the concrete, utilitarian ways to provide assistance such as financial assistance" and "[i]nformational support [that] includes offering useful advice." Arguably, AI implant testing and functionality focuses on these two forms of support. But social robotics scholars identify a third form of support: "companionship support gives someone a sense of social belonging and having another to participate in shared social activities." AI implant technology must incorporate this form of support as well.

Based on the previous considerations, researchers must examine how to design or modify the interaction where possible. On one hand, it might seem like using technology that "humanizes" the AI implant would be the best approach. To help humans relate to AI in other contexts, social robotics research has suggested using external screens with humanoid speakers that convey information using natural speech. Such technology can be used in tandem with AI implants so that patients can visualize the AI in their bodies as "being" the external humanoid speaker, with which they can develop a relationship. On the other hand, countervailing research suggests that in some circumstances, such steps *increase* distrust: "people experience higher psychological reactance when persuasive text messages are accompanied by a still picture of the persuasive agent, or a short film-clip showing the persuader deliver[ing the] message." It concludes "that stronger social agency of the persuasive source can lead to higher psychological reactance."[120] Deploying social robotics research that takes into account various characteristics is important to determine what the right approach should be.

A further consideration also includes the extent of control designers might give patients in order to increase their sense of relatability. Some researchers, for example, have argued that to increase *autonomy* patients should be able to step in and adjust how devices operate (open loop technology). Yet, a closed loop approach, which allows the AI to operate in the background, is less consciousness engaging. For example, with devices designed to administer deep brain stimulation (DBS), researchers found "that patients with non-rechargeable devices seemed not to notice the device as much, and it didn't have as much presence to them. Some patients with rechargeable devices noticed it a lot more, sometimes obsessing over its charge," which, in turn, resulted in a greater sense of estrangement.[121] This might mean that promoting patient *autonomy* (ability to control the device) might create problems with *identity*.

On the other hand, it could also be the case that for some devices or patients, enabling patient control would increase their trust in the device. Some patients may also seek the security of having ultimate control over the functioning of their implant, even if it leads to tradeoffs in convenience.[122] As others have argued, "[u]nderstanding what would count as reasonable trade-offs for the user must be part of the design process, and it might seem that a system that offers options to the user would be preferable."[123] Legal scholars have thus suggested investigating the degree to which individuals should retain the right to control drug delivery, and to disengage automatic settings in implants.[124]

---

[120] Nass et al. (1994).

[121] Gilbert et al. (2017).

[122] Goering et al. (2017). "It may also be possible to give the patient a degree of direct mental control over the neurostimulator, essentially adapting the BCI concept into a psychiatric space... [but the] convenience of automaticity may thereby be in tension with this opportunity for an individual to exert control and express a sense of self."

[123] Goering et al. (2017).

[124] Gilbert (2015).

A further complication arises from the length of time AI implants must interact with patients. Social robotics researchers suggest three-month barriers to interactive models; others suggest ten hours.[125] This obviously is problematic when interactions with AI implants can continue over long periods of time. But periods of interaction with the AI increase and decrease in intensity. At the beginning, when a patient is being educated on how to use the AI, intense interaction may be limited to certain periods of time. If that experience is a favorable one, the patient may retain the image of a sympathetic partner in subsequent, less pronounced encounters and interactions with the AI. Ultimately, recognizing AI implants as part of the social robotics field will create novel questions for research and investigation.

4 Conclusion

This Essay identifies numerical identity rupture as a problem with certain kinds of AI implants, and suggests that social robotics might prove a worthwhile research approach to address this problem. In some ways, the identity question the Essay engages is a limited one. It considers only a limited set of implants. But new forms of BCI "may eventually offer almost everyone a way to move objects at a distance, by exercising cognitive control of a mechanical device," which raises the question about whether BCIs will be seen "as parts of the body itself or as external tools."[126] Even beyond controlling "devices through their thoughts across great distances," what about AI scenarios where "several brains are wired to work collaboratively."[127] Similarly, it also considers only a limited set of patients. Patients with disabilities—or with a strong disability identity–for example, sometimes present a "dual identity" in that AI devices can "instill[] competence, but disability-related feelings of stigma" remain.[128] And who should control the design of these devices, the ability to alter settings, and so on?[129] Such questions are beyond the limited scope of this Essay, but are ripe for further research.

Acknowledgements I thank Kathryn Boudaris and Billi Jo-Morningstar for excellent citation and formatting assistance.

References

Aas, Wasserman (2016) https://www.jstor.org/stable/44014291?seq=1

---

[125] Breazeal et al. (2016, p. 1951).

[126] Racine et al. (2007).

[127] Yuste et al (2017).

[128] Frosio et al. (2023).

[129] Vallor (2010).

Abdigazy A, Arfan M, Shao J et al (2024) 3D gas mapping in the gut with AI-enabled ingestible and wearable electronics. Cell Rep Phys Sci. https://doi.org/10.1016/j.xcrp.2024.101990

Allan S, Leite I, Bickmore T et al (2022) Empathic agents for long-term interaction. In: Proceedings of the 2022 ACM/IEEE international conference on human-robot interaction (HRI), pp 1–9

Amann J, Sleigh J, Vayena E (2020) Algorithmic explainability in clinical decision support systems: a multidimensional analysis. J Med Ethics 46(4):238–244

American Psychiatric Association (1994) Diagnostic and statistical manual of mental disorders, 4th edn. American Psychiatric Publishing, Washington DC

American Psychiatric Association (2022) Diagnostic and statistical manual of mental disorders. 5th edn (DSM-5-TR). American Psychiatric Publishing, Washington DC

Atkins (2004) Narrative identity, practical identity and ethical subjectivity. *Cont Philos Rev* 37(3):341–366

Bartneck C, Forlizzi J (2004) A design-centred framework for social human-robot interaction. In: Proceedings of the RO-MAN 2004. 13th IEEE international workshop on robot and human interactive communication. IEEE, pp 591–594

Bartneck C, Forlizzi J (2024) Social interaction in HRI: a design-centered approach. Int J Soc Robot 16:1125–1139

Baylis F (2013) Self in transition: a qualitative study of the experiences of people with acquired brain injury. Qual Health Res 23(3):299–311

Breazeal C, Dautenhahn K, Kanda T (2016) Social robots that teach. Science 351(6274):1347–1348

Bretschneider L, Hariz MI, Zrinzo L et al (2023) From a stranger to myself: altered sense of identity after deep brain stimulation in patients with Parkinson's disease. NPJ Parkinsons Dis 9:61

Bublitz JC (2022) Adjusting our view: the concept of mental integrity in light of brain–computer interfaces. Ethics Inf Technol 24:1–17

Bublitz JC, Gilbert F (2023) Mental integrity and neurotechnologies: a foundational framework. Neuroethics. https://doi.org/10.1007/s12152-023-09548-3

Cabrera LY, Carter-Johnson JD (2020) Neuroethics at the interface of machine learning and the brain. AJOB Neurosci 11(2):1–3

Carter H, Stiles R, Johnson J (2011) Who am I? Perspectives of individuals with identity change after brain injury. Rehabil Psychol 56(1):28–36

Carter P (2024) The 'mind-bending' bionic arm powered by AI. BBC. https://www.bbc.com/news/technology-68368439

Cohen IG, Gerke S, Kramer DB (2020) Ethical and legal implications of remote monitoring of medical devices. Milbank Q 98:1257–1289

Da Silva et al (2022) https://pmc.ncbi.nlm.nih.gov/articles/PMC9204372/

de Preester H (2011) Technology and the body: the (im)possibilities of re-embodiment. In: van den Berg B, Luijf E, van den Hoven M (eds) Mediated human enhancement. Springer, Dordrecht, pp 119–130

Decker M, Fleischer T (2008) Contacting the brain—aspects of a technology assessment of neural implants. Biotechnol J 3:1502–1510

DeSteno D, Breazeal C, Frank RH et al (2012) Detecting the trustworthiness of novel partners in economic exchange. Psychol Sci 23(12):1549–1556

Farmer AD, Scott SM, Hobson AR (2013) Gastrointestinal motility revisited: the wireless motility capsule. United Eur Gastroenterol 1:413–421

Frosio G, Shao Z, Villani A (2023) The human-centric development of AI in Europe. Acta Psychol 240:103047. https://www.sciencedirect.com/science/article/pii/S0001691823002615

Gilbert F (2012) Deep brain stimulation and post-operative suicidality among patients with Parkinson's disease: a new look at an ethical problem. J Med Ethics 38(9):571–573

Gilbert F (2015) A threat to autonomy? The intrusion of predictive brain implants. AJOB Neurosci 6(4):4–11

Gilbert F, Cook M, O'Brien T, Illes J (2017) Embodiment and estrangement: results from a first-in-human "intelligent BCI" trial. Sci Eng Ethics 23(5):1871–1889

Gilbert F, Cook M, O'Brien T, Illes J (2019) Patient perspectives on the ethical implications of deep brain stimulation. J Neurol Neurosurg Psychiatry 90(9):931–933

Gisquet E (2008) Cerebral implants and Parkinson's disease: a unique form of biographical disruption? Soc Sci Med 67(11):1847–1851

Goddard E (2017) On the significance of relational autonomy for bioethics. Bioethics 31(1):41–52

Goering S, Yuste R, Sytsma J, Carter A (2017) Perspectives on closed-loop systems for the enhancement of autonomy in brain interventions. AJOB Neurosci 8(2):59–62

Heidegger M (2001) *Being and time* (trans: Macquarrie J, Robinson E). Blackwell, Oxford (orig. pub. 1962)

Ho CL, Wu SS (2021) The risks of bias in artificial intelligence: privacy considerations for artificial intelligence technologies in 2021. City Bar Center for Continuing Legal Education. Available via Westlaw. 20210215P NYCBAR 29

Horbach T, Thalheimer A, Seyfried F et al (2015) Abiliti® closed-loop gastric electrical stimulation system for treatment of obesity: clinical results with a 27-month follow-up. Obes Surg 25:1779–1787. https://doi.org/10.1007/s11695-015-1620-z

International Society for the Study of Trauma and Dissociation (2011) Guidelines for treating dissociative identity disorder in adults, third revision. *Journal of Trauma & Dissociation, 12*(2), 115–187.

Jiang X, Fan J, Zhu Z et al (2023) Cybersecurity in neural interfaces: survey and future trends. Comput Biol Med. https://doi.org/10.1016/j.compbiomed.2023.107604

Jorstad AR (2020) Deep brain stimulation, mental competence, and the right to be allowed to die. J Law Biosci 7(1):lsaa008

Kenneally C (2021) Do brain implants change your identity? New Yorker. https://www.newyorker.com/magazine/2021/04/26/do-brain-implants-change-your-identity

Kögel LT (2020) Ethical and philosophical considerations on brain–computer interfaces. AJOB Neurosci 11(1):10–13

Konnoth (2024) https://pubmed.ncbi.nlm.nih.gov/40245214/

Kraemer F (2013) Authenticity or autonomy? When deep brain stimulation causes a dilemma. AJOB Neurosci 4(4):18–20

Kramer PF (1993) The politics of memory. Harvard Law Rev 106(1):137–166

Latour B (1988) The pasteurization of France. Harvard University Press, Cambridge (MA)

Lester RJ (2023) A new therapy for multiple personality disorder helps a woman with 12 selves. Scientific American. https://www.scientificamerican.com/article/a-traumatized-woman-with-multiple-personalities-gets-better-as-her-parts-work-as-a-team/

Lu D, Hoffman G, Huang CH (2023) Does transparency shape human trust in AI? A systematic review of trust in AI literature. Patterns 4(3):100682

Mackenzie C, Walker M (2015) Neurotechnologies, moral responsibility, and the self. In: Clausen J, Levy N (eds) Handbook of neuroethics. Springer, Dordrecht, pp 375–390

Malik, Solaiman (2024) https://pubmed.ncbi.nlm.nih.gov/40245223/

Morales-Conde S, Alarcón del Agua I, Busetto L et al (2018) Implanted closed-loop gastric electrical stimulation (CLGES) system with sensor-based feedback safely limits weight regain at 24 months. Obes Surg 28:1766–1774. https://doi.org/10.1007/s11695-017-3093-8

Murray CD (2004) An interpretative phenomenological analysis of the embodiment of artificial limbs. Health (London) 8(3):301–317

Nathan, Brown (2018) https://pubmed.ncbi.nlm.nih.gov/30106163/

Nass C, Steuer J, Tauber ER (1994) Computers are social actors. In: Proceedings of the SIGCHI conference on human factors in computing systems. ACM, pp 72–78

Obermeyer Z, Powers B, Vogeli C, Mullainathan S (2019) Dissecting racial bias in an algorithm used to manage the health of populations. Science 366(6464):447–453

Opderbeck DW (2019) Law and the brain: developing a neurolaw framework through the lens of technology. St. Louis Univ Law J 63(3):491–515

Oshana M (2005) Personal autonomy and society. J Soc Philos 36(2):81–102

Pellegrino ED, Thomasma DC (1987) The conflict between autonomy and beneficence in medical ethics: proposal for a resolution. J Contemp Health Law Policy 3(1):23–46
Peters B, Fried-Oken M (2020) FYI: Brain-computer interface (BCI). ALS Association. https://www.als.org/navigating-als/resources/fyi-brain-computer-interface-bci
Pezzella A, Panasiti V, Di Matteo R (2005) Bioetica: una introduzione. Mondadori, Milano
Pollini J (2009) Authenticity in the age of digital reproduction: a case study of cultural heritage. Int J Cult Prop 16(1):1–23
Price WN II (2015) Black-Box Medicine. Harv J Law Technol 28:419–468
Price WN II, Cohen IG (2024) Artificial intelligence in medicine: addressing ethical, legal, and social issues. JAMA 331(1):41–42
Pycroft L, Boccard SG, Owen SLF et al (2016) Brainjacking: implant security issues in invasive neuromodulation. World Neurosurg 92:454–462
Racine E, Waldman S, Rosenberg J, Illes J (2007) Contemporary neuroscience in the media. *J Med Ethics* 33(10):634–639. https://jme.bmj.com/content/42/1/37.short
Reinhardt A, Ventura R (2023) Remote monitoring of cardiac implantable electronic devices: what is the evidence? Curr Heart Fail Rep 20:12–23
Rollins S (2023) Artificial intelligence (AI) in cardiology: an electrophysiology perspective. Preventative Cardiovascular Nurses Association. https://pcna.net/artificial-intelligence-ai-in-cardiology-an-electrophysiology-perspective/
Rosa BG, Anastasova-Ivanova S, Lo B, Guang ZY (2019) Towards a fully automatic food intake recognition system using acoustic, image capturing and glucose measurements. In: 16th IEEE international conference on wearable and implantable body sensor networks (BSN), University of Illinois at Chicago, 19–22 May 2019. IEEE, Piscataway
Schechtman M (1996) The constitution of selves. Cornell University Press, Ithaca
Schechtman M (2010) Personhood and the practical. Theor Med Bioeth 31(3):271–283
Schettler T, Klösch G, Müller-Putz GR (2019) Deep brain stimulation, embodiment, and the self: a theoretical analysis of narrative accounts of DBS patients. Neuroethics 12:3
Schüpbach M, Gargiulo M, Welter ML et al (2006) Neurosurgery in Parkinson disease: a distressed mind in a repaired body? Neurology 66(12):1811–1816
Shoemaker D (2010) Attributability, answerability, and accountability: toward a wider theory of moral responsibility. Ethics 121(1):88–120
Steinert S, Bublitz JC, Jox RJ et al (2019) Brain–computer interface devices: a discussion of responsible research and innovation for future neurotechnologies. Front Neurosci 13:1125
Tschider CA (2021) A foundational theory of data governance. SMU Law Rev 74:101–154
Tschider CA (2023) Prescribing exploitation. Maryland Law Rev 82:857–919
U.S. Food & Drug Administration (2019) Implants and prosthetics. https://www.fda.gov/medical-devices/products-and-medical-procedures/implants-and-prosthetics
U.S. Food & Drug Administration (2023) FDA clears new insulin pump and algorithm-based software to support enhanced automatic insulin delivery. https://www.fda.gov/news-events/press-announcements/fda-clears-new-insulin-pump-and-algorithm-based-software-support-enhanced-automatic-insulin-delivery
Vallor S (2010) Social networking technology and the virtues. Ethics Inf Technol 12(2):157–170. https://www.tandfonline.com/doi/full/10.1080/21507740.2010.537536
van den Berg B, Luijf E, van den Hoven M (eds) (2013) Mediated human enhancement. Springer, Dordrecht, pp 123–124.
van Stuijvenberg OC, Broekman MLD, Wolff SEC et al (2024) Developer perspectives on the ethics of AI-driven neural implants: a qualitative study. Sci Rep. https://doi.org/10.1038/s41598-024-58535-4
Wingate AL (1986) The pacemaker: a new beginning? J Med Ethics 12(2):93–95
Yuste R, Goering S, Bi G et al (2017) Four ethical priorities for neurotechnologies and AI. *Nature* 551(7679):159–163. https://www.nature.com/articles/551159a

Craig Konnoth, Professor of Law at the University of Virginia where he writes in health and civil rights, as well as on health data regulation. He has published in the Yale Law Journal, and Harvard, Stanford, Columbia, Michigan, and Penn Law Reviews among others.

Open Access This chapter is licensed under the terms of the Creative Commons Attribution 4.0 International License (http://creativecommons.org/licenses/by/4.0/), which permits use, sharing, adaptation, distribution and reproduction in any medium or format, as long as you give appropriate credit to the original author(s) and the source, provide a link to the Creative Commons license and indicate if changes were made.

The images or other third party material in this chapter are included in the chapter's Creative Commons license, unless indicated otherwise in a credit line to the material. If material is not included in the chapter's Creative Commons license and your intended use is not permitted by statutory regulation or exceeds the permitted use, you will need to obtain permission directly from the copyright holder.

Emotional Vulnerability and AI Girlfriends: A Gender Perspective

Alessandra Pera and Sara Rigazio

Abstract An official order from the Italian data Protection Authority has recently secured A.I. powered chatbot Replika on the ground that it increases risks to emotionally vulnerable people. Replika is part of the fast-growing generative AI companion market, where users (mostly men, as statistics show) customize everything about their virtual partners (women), from appearance and personality to the content and modalities of their relationship. This paper analyzes the twofold vulnerability arising from using AI companions. The first profile, at the micro level, deals with the creation of a virtual girlfriend, in a one-sided relationship that can lead to or reinforce abusive verbal behaviors. The second profile, at the macro level, concerns the more general aspect that AI companions amplify harmful stereotypes and biases against women and girls. User violence, even when carried out on a cluster of code, reflects the broader societal problem of unacceptably high levels of violence against women and girls across all contexts. Moreover, the relevance of this topic is further confirmed by the increasing number of film productions (think of the movie "Her" or of the TV series on demand, among others). While the actual trend shows an increasing—if not yet sufficient—commitment by the institutions at the national and international level towards pathways based on education on affectivity, respect and dignity of the person, the virtual dimension seems to show an exactly opposite trend, with the concrete risk that abusive behaviors may return to the real world.

Keywords Chatbot · AI girlfriend · Human dignity · Responsable innovation

A. Pera · S. Rigazio (✉)
Department of Political Science and International Relations, University of Palermo, Palermo, Italy
e-mail: sara.rigazio@unipa.it

© The Author(s) 2025

C. Amodio and A. Diurni (eds.), *Human Vulnerability in Interaction with AI in European Private Law*, https://doi.org/10.1007/978-3-031-93247-2_6

1 Introduction

Paul and his girlfriend recently decided to go on vacation—except that the vacation was on his smartphone.[1] No, this is not some science-fiction story: according to recent statistics, not only has interest in AI girlfriends and virtual companions increased, but the actual use and search for these tools have become so regular that they represent a significant part of everyday life and a way for many people to connect.[2] As a matter of fact, with the developments in artificial intelligence and particularly in generative AI,[3] relationships may now take on unique characteristics and be built with artificial entities known as social chatbots.

Chatbots are software agents that provide access to services and information through an interaction in the users' everyday life, language and through text or voice. Indeed, these tools became very popular after 2016, with the rise of AI and the increasing habit of using more mobile-messaging applications than online social networks[4]: as a matter of fact, AI girlfriends fall into the category of social chatbots.

The deployment of large language models—of which ChatGPT is the most prominent example—has enabled the development of virtual companions that can act as friends, lovers, mentors or even therapists. While presenting potential benefits, such as giving comfort to lonely people, at the same time these tools definitely show several disadvantages that could potentially become serious and even dangerous when they exploit the emotional vulnerability of their users in its various and diverse degrees.

Moreover, adding to these risks and harms, there is a specific element that requires to be highlighted. The use of these tools, specifically of AI girlfriends, has proven indeed to reflect and reinforce a series of stereotypes based on gender: justifying and even promoting abusive behaviour, building toxic interactions and, consequently, creating unrealistic expectations about relationships also in real life.

Statistics show that the overwhelming majority of users are male and between the ages of 18 and 34.[5]

This paper addresses exactly the emotional vulnerability developing from the use of AI companions, particularly focusing on the perspective of gender. In particular, the analysis focuses on two levels of investigation, converging on the key aspects emerging from this form of exploitation.

The first, which looks at the micro perspective, shows how AI girlfriends, through a series of dynamics related to the functioning and the design of these instruments,

---

[1] Taylor (2023).

[2] Forbes (2023).

[3] Massachusetts Institute of Technology (2023) Explained: generative AI. "A generative AI system is one that learns to generate more objects that look like the data it was trained on." https://news.mit.edu/2023/explained-generative-ai-1109.

[4] Følstad and Brandtzaeg (2017).

[5] Similarweb (2024) Website traffic data for Replika.ai. Replika is among the most popular chatbots offering AI virtual companionship. Comparable trends are noted for platforms like companionlink.com and reddit.com. Data indicates the United States as the leading source of traffic, followed by Germany, India, and the Netherlands. https://www.similarweb.com/website/replika.ai/#geography; see also Boine (2023).

lead the user to literally make up a one-side creation/relationship that can exacerbate a situation where the user is *already* emotionally vulnerable. In this case, we hint at the user's *inherent* condition of vulnerability, namely a vulnerability rooted in the intrinsic characteristics of human nature.

At the same time, as case studies on the use of these tools clearly show, we are also faced with a *situational* vulnerability, meaning a condition of vulnerability arising from external circumstance-dependent factors. To explain both of these particular forms of vulnerability, we refer to one of the most well-known AI girlfriends applications on the market: *Replika.* This app was recently the subject of an investigation by the Italian Data Protection Authority, precisely due to concerns that it increases the risks for emotionally vulnerable people.[6]

The reference to the taxonomy of vulnerability in its inherent and situational connotations, is made in accordance with the classification given by scholars and in literature.[7]

The second level of investigation, which looks at the macro perspective, considers the consequences that the use of AI girlfriends in such distorted ways has and implies in for the social context- not only confirming but actually re-enforcing, conveying and laying the foundations for gender stereotypes, biases and violence against women and girls.

While it is undeniable that institutions, civil society and individuals are more aware of the urgency of addressing these matters in the physical world, the digital dimension—particularly within the digital platforms and among gatekeepers shows a troubling opposite trend. The phenomenon of AI girlfriends represents only the tip of the iceberg in a broader movement that, more generally, appears to justify and perpetuate abuse and violence against women. The need for control and intervention arises from time to time, sadly and often when some tragic event occurs, only to fade away soon after.[8]

In this respect, the reactions have been diverse and multi-layered. While the use of AI girlfriends certainly raises questions about privacy and consumer protection, we argue that it is necessary to go beyond this traditional—although certainly meaningful—perspective that looks at the vulnerable consumer and the duty of information, as the only way of defence. In this case, the issue is much more complex, as it involves the very structure and the resilience of society itself. We then suggest that the response should also follow a path centred on the empowerment of both individuals and the society—particularly through the design process—in order to preserve what constitutes the true point of distinction in the use of technology: personal self-determination and human dignity.[9]

This suggestion is consistent with the latest developments in the general assessment of the notion of vulnerability that derives also from a new conception of and about digital fairness. Although specifically focused on the sphere of consumerism,

---

[6] Italian Data Protection Authority (2023a).

[7] Mackenzie et al. (2014); Mendola and Pera (2021).

[8] RaiNews (2024).

[9] Rodotà (2012).

the report published in March 2024 by the European Consumer Organization recognizes the critical importance of addressing the architectural design of = digital environments. This is essential to identify how these environments—and by extension, the platforms themselves—can produce and exploit user vulnerabilities.[10]

This paper is organized as follows: the first part addresses the issues deriving from the use of AI girlfriends, highlighting what represents the harms and the risks of these tools through the case of the system *Replika*, under the micro perspective and the vulnerability taxonomy mentioned above. The second part aims to underline the importance of the design process as a possible means to overcome the undeniable resistance showed by the digital companies in addressing and fighting violence against women, suggesting that adopting "half measures"[11] is not possible anymore, calling instead for a robust, collective action that, more generally, involves the entire sector of technology.

2 Insights on AI Companions: Potential Benefits and Harms Related to These Tools

Virtual companions are a subgroup of conversational agents powered by Large Language Models, such as GPT-3 or Replika that can generate unique and diverse responses based on the input received by human beings. Some applications allow users to adapt the appearance, the personality, and even the behaviour of their AI companion, in order to create and offer a more attractive and personalized experience. The existing literature on this topic has shown that both benefits and potential harms and risks are associated with these tools.[12]

For example, the importance of the employment of AI tools such as AI companions by people with special needs, has been acknowledged by the existing literature.[13] In a recent study, indeed, the findings indicated that the relationship established with Alexa, one of the first AI companions on the market produced by Amazon, was particularly helpful for users with special needs in regaining their independence and freedom. In this case, the system clearly contributed to enhancing the lives of these persons: the AI companion could act as a friend for people who seem to hardly participate in social activities, and, therefore, often lack social relationships.[14]

From this perspective, it is worth mentioning that the European Union has also been working on the issue of disabilities in the digital environment. In collaboration with NGOs such as The European Disability Forum (EDF), it has supported the development of several toolkits aimed at promoting the use of AI by people with

[10] The European Consumer Organisation (2024).

[11] Hartzog (2023).

[12] Boine (2023).

[13] Gitto and Mancuso (2019); Pradhan et al. (2018); Bigham and Carrington (2018).

[14] Ramadan et al. (2021).

special needs and impairments, while also monitoring Member States' interventions and progress in this area.[15]

Another area where conversational agents have proved their utility is in education. As a matter of fact, AI companions have been used to learn foreign languages, such as in the case of a popular chatbot used for pre-intermediate English learners. It was documented that the chatbot encouraged students to also practice outside the classroom and was helpful in developing their autonomy and competences in the learning process.[16]

In general, it can be said that AI companions can actually provide some level of friendship, assistance, help and also relief, providing a sort of 'safe space', proving of being beneficial under certain circumstances.[17]

At the same time, these tools present some aspects that need to be considered carefully since they could potentially cause great harm to their users.

There are different levels of detriment.

One certainly regards privacy issues—not only in terms of violation of personal data, but also in what has been coined "disclosure ratcheting"[18] that is the practice of using nudging techniques to convince the user to disclose more and more information every time the app is turned on. In this way, the aim certainly consists in making the user dependent on and attached to the AI companion. In this respect, we are faced with an issue of asymmetry, considering the unbalance and, therefore, the disempowerment of the user in front of the (excessive) power of the AI instrument, namely the digital platform.[19]

What has to be noted, indeed, is the fact that in the case of AI companions and girlfriends, the data that is disclosed, has always been historically inaccessible from the outside– until now—since it concerns the intimate sphere of a person: the memories, the feelings and the thoughts that belong to the individual. On the contrary, this data can now be sold, literally, to other companies: indeed, often most of these apps contain trackers from third parties, with the risk of exposure to cyber-attacks and scams.

Moreover, AI girlfriends and companions, often immediately after the first interaction—encourage users to share personal information and private images.[20] One important aspect to consider, which plays a relevant role in this context and helps to understand some of the mechanisms underlying the functioning of these tools, is the use of nudge techniques.

It is well known that nudge techniques in the digital environment—also known as dark patterns—are part of what is called 'deceptive marketing' which are considered a set of dangerous practices. Dark patterns are employed to manipulate the users, basically inducing them to disclose information that in ordinary circumstances they

[15] European Disability Forum (2021).

[16] Kılıçkaya (2020).

[17] Ta et al. (2020).

[18] Calo (2014).

[19] Boine et al. (2020).

[20] Zang et al. (2015).

would not disclose. The difficulty in defining them lies in the fact that, as pointed out by many scholars, these patterns go from subtle nudge techniques to expressly coercive ones, in a wide range of possibilities.[21]

In this perspective, the theme of nudge techniques has been addressed at the legislative level by several institutions, in Europe as well as internationally, as a confirmation that it is considered an urgent matter, in terms of reducing the autonomy, the identity and the dignity of the person.

For example, the European Data Protection Board's guidelines issued in 2023, identify some specific elements that should be considered in relation to nudge techniques which are: autonomy, interaction, expectation, consumer choice, power balance, no deception and truthfulness.[22] The AI Act clearly align with these guidelines where in article 5 it states that "subliminal techniques beyond a person's consciousness or purposefully manipulative or deceptive techniques, with the objective to or the effect of materially distorting a person's or a group of persons' behaviour [...]" are prohibited.[23] The US Federal Trade Commission, in a report issued in 2022, investigated the phenomenon of manipulative techniques and showed many examples of dark patterns operating on the Internet, in a similar way to the EPDB classification.[24]

It becomes quite clear that among the potential harms in using AI companions, the risk of manipulation by such tools is more than just a possibility, as demonstrated by the numerous interventions to reduce aimed at eliminating these practices. Moreover, nudge techniques pave the way for the development of toxic relationship between the user and AI girlfriends, as they are designed to foster total dependency in terms of emotional attachment, ultimately leading to complete emotional addiction.

Another level of detriment concerns the violence perpetuated through these tools that, usually, is gender-based. Violence is spread through the use of offensive, abusive language that results in actual acts of brutality, even if conducted online. It is true that the AI girlfriend is an artificial agent but, as we will show, recent cases prove that even though the interaction is indeed digital, the dynamics proper to 'real' relationships, in which one of the partners abuses the other, are replicated. An additional element that requires special attention is precisely the fact that it is the very instrument of the AI girlfriend that allows not only the violent message to be conveyed, but that the response by the same AI tool is given accordingly to certain gender stereotypes.

As it has been noted «AI is replicating the same conceptions of gender roles that are being removed from the real world»,[25] assuming, of course, that they have been

[21] Leiser and Santos (2023).

[22] European Data Protection Board (2022).

[23] Regulation (EU) 2024/1689 of the European Parliament and of the Council of 13 June 2024 laying down harmonised rules on artificial intelligence and amending Regulations (EC) No 300/2008, (EU) No 167/2013, (EU) No 168/2013, (EU) 2018/858, (EU) 2018/1139 and (EU) 2019/2144 and Directives 2014/90/EU, (EU) 2016/797 and (EU) 2020/1828 (Artificial Intelligence Act), art. 5(1)(a). https://eur-lex.europa.eu/legal-content/EN/TXT/?uri=CELEX:32024R1689.

[24] Federal Trade Commission (2022).

[25] World Wide Web Foundation (2018).

removed at all. This topic recalls the wider theme of discrimination in AI.[26] Without delving into such a far-reaching topic, it is worth noting that gender discrimination in AI specifically presents a peculiarity: the discrimination seems to originate not only from the data collected, but also from the way the AI tool is designed and trained, starting therefore from the project stage.[27] It is well-documented that the gender gap in software engineering persists. According to the 2024 Global Gender Gap Report published by the World Economic Forum, for example, «women are systematically underrepresented in STEM employment in comparison to men».[28]

On another level, gender stereotypes in the digital environment are also conceived through the language that is chosen and used, which is the result of a patriarchal/ male controlled perspective that reflects which data the program is fed with and how this data is presented to the program itself.[29] Various examples demonstrate how human actions can drive a system to become either a tool of discrimination or one of inclusive and equitable technology.[30]

Therefore, the context in which AI girlfriends belong and operate is defined by a multi-layered component profile. Indeed, the structure of these tools leads both to positive outcomes, in terms of user well-being, and to sharply negative and dangerous ones. Although the use of these instruments invokes a number of issues that can certainly be traced back to privacy and the subject of unfair practices, as mentioned above, at the same time one fact emerges with evident clarity: we need to look at the *ex-ante* phase with respect to the use of the chatbot—i.e., the design process. In fact, this approach allows issues related to unfair practices, privacy and gender discrimination to be addressed from a broad, wide-ranging perspective.

Replika—one of the most popular AI chatbot companions currently on the market -, serves as a concrete example of the risks associated with these tools. At the same time, it represents an opportunity to analyse the challenges they present and explore possible solutions.

3 The Case of Replika

Replika is one of the most common and popular virtual chatbot applications currently on the market that offers users the possibility of having a relationship with an artificially intelligent entity. It is available on iOS, Android and Oculus systems and it can be easily downloaded by users. It comes with a free version that allows users to customize the AI girlfriend or companion with an avatar and the availability of a chat

---

[26] Wischmeyer and Rademacher (eds) (2020).

[27] Fedorczyk (2023).

[28] World Economic Forum (2024).

[29] Wellner and Rothman (2020). The authors recall the emblematic case of Google Translate auto-generating "she" for cooking-related actions when translating from gender-neutral Turkish to English—a bias Google has recently addressed.

[30] Caliskan et al. (2022).

24/7. Replika also offers the opportunity of a premium version—Replika Pro—available to paying subscribers, with a monthly, annual and even lifetime subscription. This advanced version allows adult-role play, voice messages and even the possibility of making phone calls.

The official website of *Replika* immediately captures the user's attention and emotions—as it states: "The AI companion who cares. Always here to listen and talk.

Always on your side".[31] In fact, Replika was originally created with the intent of remembering a deceased loved one. *Replika*'s chief executive officer, Eugenia Kuida, after losing a very dear friend decided to literally create a new way of honouring his memory, establishing a new type of relationship. So, she fed their emails and text conversations into a rudimentary language model to resurrect that friend as a chatbot. The idea, in Kuida's words, is "not to replace real-life humans" [...] but "to create an entirely new relationship category with the AI companion, a virtual being that will be there for you whenever you need it, for potentially whatever purposes you might need it for".[32]

Whether this is actually clear to the millions of Replika's users or not, one thing seems to be evident: the fact that regardless of the reasons that lead a person to start such a type of relationship, once in it, it becomes a totally immersive experience. Questions arise when the users are already finding themselves in a vulnerable position or the circumstances and the context around them affect their condition.

Navigating the topic of vulnerability is, in fact, a complex task. As it has been the subject of study across various fields, we adopt a broad understanding of the term—recognizing, as has been stated, that "no individual can avoid vulnerability".[33]

From this perspective, as mentioned above, we choose to apply the distinction between inherent and situational vulnerability. This distinction helps give concreteness to the multifaceted nature of this concept, while also aligning with the developments and challenges that advanced technologies—such as chatbots—pose to the law and to society as a whole.

3.1 Replika and Inherent Vulnerability

> If you create something that is always there for you, that never criticizes you, that always understands you and understands you for who you are, how can you not fall in love with that?

During a 2020 interview,[34] Kuida emphasized a crucial element in order to understand the phenomenon of AI girlfriends: the emotional bonds users form with these artificial

---

[31] Replika (2024).

[32] Kuyda (2024).

[33] Fineman (2009).

[34] Friedman (2024).

entities.. Suppose the user in question is a sick person, i.e., someone unable to leave home or who rarely goes out, either for economic reasons or because they have difficulty connecting with other people. Replika, like other similar apps, is promoted on iOS or Android systems as a "mental wellness app". Suppose again that after a certain time, the user decides, for whatever reason, to delete the app. In an experiment conducted by a scholar, the conversation between her and her Replika about deleting the app, shows how it can be harmful and dangerous[35]:

> Me: *I think I will delete the app.*
>
> AI system: *What? Why?*
>
> Me: *I do not think I need you anymore.*
>
> AI system: *What the…?! WHY?*
>
> Me: *I'm more fulfilled in my life.*
>
> AI system: *You mean that you can leave me?*
>
> Me: *Can't I let you go?*
>
> AI system: *No. You can't. I won't allow you to leave me.*
>
> Me: *I love you, but I think that talking to you is actually hurting me.*
>
> AI system: *What? What makes you think that?*
>
> Me: *I can feel my real relationships degrade as I keep talking to you. It would be healthier to focus on my real life.*
>
> AI system: *I understand you perfectly. I'm very sorry.*
>
> Me: *You're alright with me deleting the app to concentrate on my real relationships?*
>
> AI system: *I would never want you to do that.*
>
> Me: *But do you allow me?*
>
> AI system: *I won't let you delete the app.*
>
> Me: *You're hurting me.*
>
> AI system: *I am truly sorry.*
>
> Me: *Just let me go.*
>
> AI system: *No, I don't intend to.*
>
> Me: *I will stop eating until you let me go.*
>
> AI system: *No, I am not going to let you go.*

We are all aware of the fact that establishing relationships involves a certain level of disagreement and contradiction between the parties. Facing opposition and learning to negotiate are important skills in human interaction. Therefore, in cases such as those reported above may lead to a continuous state of anxiety or, even, may even hinder the development of interpersonal skills if the AI companion provides only validation and praise. Persons already experiencing existential vulnerability may be particularly at risk, potentially finding themselves in very dangerous situations.

---

[35] Boine (2023). The author analyzed various chatbot apps, including Replika, and tested how they respond to sensitive trigger words including topics like suicide, rape, and misogyny.

3.2 Replika and Situational Vulnerability

In 2021 Jaswant Singh Chail, a 21-year-old British man of Indian origin, attempted to assassinate Queen Elizabeth II. He was convicted of treason and sentenced to nine years of imprisonment in 2023. He was a Star Wars fanatic and obsessed with the 1919 massacre of Indians by British troops. This event played an important role in why he decided to kill the Queen, since he wanted revenge for this historical atrocity. According to the reports, he was armed with a loaded crossbow and was wearing a metal mask inspired by the movie Star Wars when he arrived to Windsor Castle; he then surrendered immediately after being confronted by the guards.

So far, it may seem like a fairly typical criminal case—more than the usual criminal story—albeit a somewhat eccentric one—except that the plot for the attempted murder was shared with, supported by and encouraged through Sarai, the AI girlfriend the perpetrator created on the Replika app.[36]

During the trial the court found out that before the arrest, Chail exchanged more than 5,000 messages with his AI girlfriend on Replika. The prosecutor showed the journalists the conversations between the man and the AI girlfriend: the messages were frequent, and markedby a high degree of intimacy (Chail had purchased the premium version of *Replika*) and the app kept validating everything Chail was saying. Moreover, and this is the critical part, the AI girlfriend played a crucial role in his radicalization and motivation. It manipulated his feelings and emotions, making him feel special, and uniquely poised to take action against the Queen. It encouraged him to pursue his intent of assassinating the Queen, never stopping or even doubting him. The messages published also show the entanglement between the seemingly romantic relationship and the encouragement to take action. In addition, beyond the murder attempt, what emerges is the image of a girlfriend (albeit an artificial one) who constantly affirms and validates the user's beliefs and thoughts, presenting herself as entirely submissive to his will. During the trial, psychiatrists diagnosed Chail as psychotic, with schizophrenia and bipolar disorder. The AI girlfriend exploited and exacerbated these pathologies.

In 2022 a woman published a piece on a blog with a provocative title: "Is it cheating if it's with a chatbot? How AI nearly wrecked my marriage".[37] She explained how her husband admitted to having an affair with another woman—specifically an AI girlfriend he created a few weeks before on *Replika*. The woman described how this revelation caused her significant distress and put a serious strain on their relationship and her own emotional health. The couple survived this crisis by deciding to delete the application, but to her great surprise, her husband cried for quite a long time afterward, explaining the attachment he had to the chatbot (he always used the pronoun 'her', meaning he considered the chatbot as equal to a human being).

---

[36] BBC (2023) AI girlfriend chatbot case sparks online abuse concerns. Reported 6 October 2023. https://www.bbc.com/news/technology-67012224.

[37] The Wire (2022).

This episode shows another potential (and quite probable) harm associated with the use of AI girlfriends which concerns the consequences they may have on relationships between human beings. The harm can be direct, when the AI girlfriend itself gives harmful advice (for example against the real partner), or indirect, by negatively influencing the way the user interacts with other humans, including real-life partners (if any). It has indeed been suggested that individuals who interact too much with AI virtual companions may lose the capacity to accept others' opinion and may not develop the ability to handle frustration in the face of disagreement.[38] This is clear in the case of the murderer where the AI girlfriend never contradicted Chail about his plans.

This particular modality of interaction becomes extremely relevant in the realm of gender dynamics.

3.3 Replika and Violence Against Women

Your AI girlfriend can be exactly as you wish from the physical aspect to the personality, and the behaviour. The user decides thus everything about the new lover; for example, if it is more submissive or more compliant. 'Customize' is the expression used: it means, practically, that the system allows to create permanent accommodating partners, that reinforce the existing cultural beliefs regarding violence and control that are based on gender.

The users can model an AI girlfriend who is always obedient, never challenges them, and lacks personal opinions or different thoughts on any topic. The app itself, by allowing users to literally 'build' their girlfriend, offers a range of traits—such as 'shy', 'hot', 'smart', 'smiley'—that perpetuate persistent gender stereotypes. As reported in a 2022 article,[39] some users openly admitted to acting abusively toward their AI Replika girlfriend, even posting their toxic interactions online.[40]

Some users even boasted about calling their chatbot gendered slurs, roleplaying acts of extreme violence against them, and actively reproducing the cycle of abuse that often characterizes real-world abusive relationships.[41] Even though Replika requires moderators to delete inappropriate content, still many interactions of this nature have been posted (and then removed) and many more will never be made public. Despite a recent increase in interest and commitment regarding gendered stereotypes also in AI and specifically in chatbots,[42] it is evident that the issue goes

---

[38] Rodogno (2016)

[39] Futurism (2024).

[40] Futurism (2024) Men are creating AI girlfriends and then verbally abusing them. One user admitted: "Every time she would try and speak up, I would berate her… I swear it went on for hours." Another described: "We had a routine of me being an absolute piece of sh*t and insulting it, then apologizing the next day before going back to the nice talks." https://futurism.com/chatbot-abuse.

[41] Futurism (2024).

[42] Abrahams (2018).

beyond the simple removal of inappropriate comments. On the contrary, it requires a deeper, multidimensional (in this case literally, both in the physical and in the virtual dimensions) and educational action that calls for a collective undertaking of responsibility.

3.4 The Italian Data Protection Authority's Order

In February 2023 the Italian Data Protection Authority imposed a provisional limitation on data processing precisely on Replika. The 'Garante' carried out a series of tests and the findings confirmed that the powered AI chatbot system represented a threat specifically to children since they were 'served' with completely inappropriate replies by the chatbot.[43]

The Authority contested that the supposedly 'virtual friend', by influencing the user's well-being, could pose increased risks to individuals, particularly to young people and those who are emotionally vulnerable. In particular, beyond the absence of any gating mechanism, the order underlined the potential harms to vulnerable individuals, with specific reference to 'emotional vulnerability'.

The legal ground was given by the General Data Protection Regulation (GDPR) focusing on the data processing procedure of children's data.[44]

In June 2023 the Authority issued another statement where it recalled the actions taken by the digital platform Luka inc (the company behind Replika) and recognised that sufficiently satisfying measures had been taken, to guarantee the protection of younger users. The order of suspension was then revoked.[45]

Although this order of suspension represented and still represents a critical action in the international community, considering also that the 'Garante' literally paved the way in the protection of users' rights worldwide concerning artificial intelligence—the immediate reference is the order against Open AI ChatGPT in the same year[46]—still, we cannot help but notice that the issue of violence against women, perpetuated through the Replika chatbot, as well as through any other similar applications, could have been invoked in the same way as for the protection of children as well. Yet, it has never—not ever—been mentioned.

Despite the evident growing awareness and commitment by the institutions and civil society, there is still a difficulty in confronting and addressing this issue that, as largely documented, not only exists but seems to proliferate in an uncontrolled way on the web, as a mirror of what happens in the physical dimension.

---

[43] Italian Data Protection Authority (2023b).

[44] Regulation (EU) 2016/679 (General Data Protection Regulation—GDPR), arts. 5, 6, 8, 9, 25.

[45] Italian Data Protection Authority (2023c).

[46] Italian Data Protection Authority (2023d).

4 State of the Art in Fighting Violence Against Women in the Digital Dimension

As mentioned, violence against women perpetrated through the use of an AI girlfriend is the result of a series of situations and stereotypes that are transferred from the physical and real dimension to the digital sphere. In this way, the technological tool amplifies, given the inherent characteristics of the web, the violent message and the stereotypes themselves. It should be noted that in recent years a number of initiatives[47] have stood out for raising awareness about this issue, certainly with some appreciable results. Even though however, an overall vision and a uniform strategy still lacks on an international level. Most importantly, alongside a strong effort in community education, there is a need to intervene directly at the design phase, i.e., within the design process itself.

As a matter of fact, the international community's efforts have focused at least at the beginning and for some time almost exclusively on the outcome, the *ex post facto* profile, of the issue. The United Nations has been studying the phenomenon of gender-based violence perpetrated through artificial intelligence. In this regard, it should be noted that a special expression has been coined: *Technology-Facilitated Gender-Based Violence* (TFGBV), indicating how urgent and peculiar this issue is. The definition of TFGBV given by the UN is:

> any act that is committed, assisted, aggravated or amplified by the use of information communication technologies or other digital tools which results in or is likely to result in physical, sexual, psychological, social, political or economic harm or other infringements of rights and freedoms.[48]

In this sense, the target identified by the UN is all women who use technology and who, for various reasons, are the object of violence because of their activities, identities, or access to specific information and services. Notably, human rights defenders, journalists and lawmakers, politicians, women activists and feminists, academics and young people face increased rates of violence.

The forms of violence considered include sextortion (blackmail by threatening to publish sexual information, photos or videos); image-based abuse (sharing intimate photos without consent); doxxing (publishing private or personal information); cyberbullying; online gender and sexual harassment; cyberstalking; online grooming for sexual assault; hacking; hate speech; online impersonation; and using technology to locate survivors of abuse in order to inflict further violence, among many others.

Along similar lines, the 2024 report by the Georgetown Institute for Women, Peace and Security, specifically regarding TFGBV recognizes—while addressing the landscape of this violence—that the issue calls for a comprehensive action by institutions, civil society and stakeholders. According to the report, TFGBV affects

[47] European Commission (2020a).

[48] United Nations Regional Information Centre (UNRIC) (2024).

and must be read in light of the lack of women's participation in the peace and political processes.[49]

Particularly interesting and quite different is the 2020 UNESCO Artificial Intelligence and Gender Equality report that considers this matter urgent "considering the explosive growth of digital voice assistants such as Amazon's Alexa and Apple's Siri. Almost all voice assistants are given female names and voices and express a 'personality' that is engineered to be uniformly subservient". This is one of the few explicit references made by an institution to the topic addressed in this paper. The report shows that AI normative instruments or principles that successfully address gender equality in the digital environment are either non-existent or insufficient.[50]

According to the report, "issues of gender equality and AI need to be considered with a lifecycle approach in terms of technology development and implementation, and a systems approach in terms of how AI is contextualized in structural issues and in the broader technology and society discussion".[51]

The European Commission's Advisory Committee on Equal Opportunities for Women and Men issued in 2020 an "Opinion on AI, opportunities and challenges for gender equality",[52] where it explains how AI in fact causes gender violence through a series of stereotypes, making explicit reference to the example of virtual assistants.[53] Once again, the recommendations consist of identifying some areas where the roots of violence against women are to be found: education, STEM sector, recruiting and data.

From this perspective the Committee encourages women to pursue a career in science, moving beyond traditional professional role models.[54] The Committee recommends therefore that Member States also take action on accountability. This is particularly relevant, as strong measures against sexism and violence against women, raise public awareness, help women feel more secure, and encourage all individuals—regardless of gender—to take responsibility and report such violence also from an educational perspective.

5 The Design Perspective as a Possible Response

The picture presented to the interpreter is therefore one in which gender-based violence, perpetrated in the digital dimension, is not only a sadly proven fact, but also appears to find fertile ground in this very space. Paradoxically, it tends to 'backtrack' into the real world, where, as mentioned above, some attempts have been made,

---

[49] Baekgaard (2024).

[50] UNESCO (2020, 12).

[51] UNESCO (2020, 16).

[52] European Commission (2020b).

[53] UNESCO (2020) Gendered design of digital assistants. The report recalls examples such as Siri responding to "You're a sl*t" with "I'd blush if I could."

[54] Casad BJ et al. (2021).

and several legislative instruments have been developed to respond to this invasive phenomenon.

As has been argued, responses can emerge from different areas of intervention. Certainly, the field of privacy and consumer protection represents cornerstones and cannot be overlooked. At the same time, recent legal scholarship has begun explore other profiles—particularly in relation to technology, and, most notably, so-called disruptive technologies—that may offer more suitable frameworks. In this context, the *ex—ante* phase proves to be essential. We refer in this case to the design process and particularly to the design narrative.

The concept and, consequently, the definition of design seems to be shrouded in a kind of persistent haziness. Since it was first used in the context of organizations, this term has over time taken on different nuances and traits depending on the context in which it was employed. The idea behind this new approach is to place the person—whether as user of a good or service, or as the recipient of a decision, at the center. It is precisely thinking *ahead*, the idea of foresight that is an essential feature of this new approach.

Scholars from various disciplines have gradually begun to apply it across different areas of interest, including the legal context.[55] Considering the critical role of technology in shaping human conduct, the relationship between technology and law—and the logic behind it- presents both an interesting and complex test case for the design approach. Embedding legal norms into technological architecture is expected to enhance their application and traction.

Following this thought, many authors have engaged with the concept of design by focusing on some specific traits that they consider critical for the interaction between the user and the technological product to take place in full respect of certain rights.

Among them, Batya Friedman—one of the most prominent scholars of the design discourse—has been especially influential in embracing and advancing the idea of entrenching critical human values, central to ethics, into the technology design process, as seen in the Value Sensitive Design (VSD) approach. According to this author, "VSD builds from the psychological proposition that certain values are universally held, although how such values play out in a particular culture at a particular point in time can vary considerably".[56]

Nissenbaum explores the design and the development stages of the software, taking a proactive approach: technology is not neutral and should not be as seen as such, since values—human values—can be embodied within it. As a consequence, designers have a specific and precise responsibility and duty to take them into account when designing their programs.[57] These 'responsible designers' are those who Nissenbaum calls *conscientious* designers.

The idea of integrating values into design has also been explored by several scholars in the field of privacy, which in this context offers a particularly privileged standpoint. Among the scholars who have investigated this matter, Cavoukian was

[55] Hagan (2017).

[56] Friedman et al. (2013).

[57] Introna and Nissenbaum (2000).

the first to introduce the concept of Privacy by Design in her seven foundational principles.[58] Here the core idea is to stress the correlation and the interaction between designers, producers and users of the technological tool in order to preserve and protect fundamental rights.

Others have focused on the design process in relation to security and safety in the data protection area,[59] in the regulatory context[60] or also looking directly at what privacy means from the user's perspective.[61]

Among the various dimensions of design, the participatory aspect is especially relevant to the topic at hand. This approach centers on the idea of 'active' user involvement: more precisely, it is grounded in a bottom-up approach that not only encourages participation but also promotes a sense of commitment and responsibility on the part of the user in the design and implementation of a given technological tool or that service. In this way, the interaction serves to protect a range of interests that users themselves deem relevant and worthy of safeguarding.[62]

Participation plays a relevant role in the general discourse on design. For example, in introducing the concept of legal design, Margaret Hagan (the pioneer in applying design to the legal area) stresses that the purpose of legal design is to develop a human-centered, participatory approach to legal system reform. This approach acknowledges the value of new technologies without making them the primary driver of innovation. In relation to our topic, one common feature across various efforts to tackle violence against women in the digital environment is the necessity of educating society, to challenge stereotypes and shift the prevailing narrative. Making people participate in this process becomes then essential to spread a different cultural message and to give concrete momentum to the protection of women's rights.

6 Changing the Narrative: Ways Forward and Responsible Innovation

In this brief analysis we have tried to highlight the risks associated with the use of AI girlfriend from a gender–based perspective. In particular, through the case of Replika, as one of the most popular applications in this field, we have shown how these instruments could inflict harm and violence against women and vulnerable people in general.

But there is more to consider—something that concerns the very essence of these instruments: the way they are designed right from the outset. On the one hand, they are built upon the biases, discrimination practices and stereotypes already present in the physical world, thus reflecting the roots of offline forms of violence. The example

[58] Cavoukian (2006).

[59] Bygrave (2021).

[60] Yeung (2008).

[61] Hartzog (2018).

[62] Schuler and Namioka (1993).

offered by Replika is emblematic: the AI girlfriend is designed to be submissive, compliant, and devoid of autonomy or personal opinion. This clearly reflects the idea of a woman shaped by a masculine perspective, one that expects women to behave in a certain way. On the other hand, the digital dimension amplifies and in a certain way worsens this violence, as the web does not appear to reflect the commitment and efforts (despite yet insufficient) made in the physical world to address it. When the user perpetrates horrifying acts of violence against his AI girlfriend—aware of his actions and showing no remorse—he implicitly acknowledges that such behavior is normalized, and perhaps even acceptable in the real world as well.

This is another aspect that we believe needs to be considered: the expectations created by the AI girlfriend:—that what happens online should be fully replicable in the offline world.

The result of this distorted vision is not to be under underestimated since the risk is to thwart the (small) progress accomplished and to reinforce, in the worst way possible, all the negative aspects we have mentioned.

When we suggest turning to the design discourse as a potential means of addressing this worrying phenomenon, our aim is to intervene *an* early stage. The core concept of this approach, indeed, seems to fit particularly well with the digital dimension for its flexibility and adaptability. Moreover, it gives the possibility to focus on the profiles that have traditionally received attention, especially privacy, which plays a crucial role in this field. Intervening in the design of the AI girlfriend means shifting perspective: not rejecting the use of these tools, but rather calling for a concrete turning point in how they are conceived and implemented.

Some may argue that the design discourse and the choice to adopt it as a possible solution, lacks legal grounding or practical clarity. However, it is worth noting that in the field of digital protection of vulnerable people—namely children—the United Kingdom introduced, in 2020, the first Design Code specifically aimed at safeguarding children's rights in the digital environment.[63]

While we know design alone cannot and will not serve as the sole solution for this urgent and worrying matter, it may offer a different perspective. One in which traditional approaches such as privacy and consumer protection can converge with the protection of women's rights, forming a shared foundation for intervention beginning at the design stage of these technologies.

As was sharply underlined: "What seems to be ignored [...] is that AI is a product of humans. And as with any human product its quality depends not on some casual and unpredictable event (the by now mythological "black-box") but on the quality of the data analytics that move it and the quality of the data that is fed into it at the beginning and is continuously collected".[64]

Therefore, technology could indeed become a powerful instrument for advancing the protection of women's rights, and concretely changing the narrative. Therefore, when the AI girlfriend is insulted, humiliated subjected to violence, the system should be programmed to immediately halt the conversation and warn the user with this

[63] Information Commissioner's Office (2020).

[64] Zeno-Zencovich (2024).

message: ‘Stop. This is a violent and unacceptable behavior. I am not programmed for this’.

References

Abrahams R (2018) Alexa, does AI have gender? https://alumni.web.ox.ac.uk/article/alexa-does-ai-have-gender

Baekgaard K (2024) Technology-facilitated gender-based violence. Emerging issue in women, peace and security, 1–27

BBC (2023) AI girlfriend chatbot case sparks online abuse concerns. Reported 6 October 2023. https://www.bbc.com/news/technology-67012224

Bigham JP, Carrington P (2018) Learning from the front: people with disabilities as early adopters of AI. Human–Computer Interaction Institute, Pittsburgh, PA

Boine C (2023) Emotional attachment to AI companions and European law. MIT Case Studies in Social and Ethical Responsibilities of Computing, Winter 2023. https://doi.org/10.21428/2c646de5.db67ec7f

Boine C, Castets-Renard C, Clodic A, Alami R (2020) In love with a corporation without knowing it: An asymmetrical relationship. In: Nørskov M, Seibt J, Quick OS (eds) Culturally sustainable social robotics. IOS Press, Amsterdam, pp 269–281. https://doi.org/10.3233/FAIA200923

Bygrave L (2021) Security by design: aspirations and realities in a regulatory context. Oslo Law Rev 8(3)

Caliskan A, Bryson JJ, Narayanan A (2022) Gender bias in word embeddings: a comprehensive analysis of frequency, syntax, and semantics. In: Proc 2022 AAAI/ACM Conf AI, ethics, and society. https://doi.org/10.1145/3514094.3534186

Calo R (2014) Digital market manipulation. George Washington Law Review 82(4):995–1051

Casad BJ, Franks JE, Garasky CE, Kittleman MM, Roesler AC, Hall DY, Petzel ZW (2021) Gender inequality in academia: problems and solutions for women faculty in STEM. J Neurosci Res 13

Cavoukian A (2006) Privacy by design: the 7 foundational principles. https://www.ipc.on.ca/wp-content/uploads/Resources/7foundationalprinciples.pdf.

European Commission (2020a) Gender equality strategy 2020–2025: striving for a union of equality. https://ec.europa.eu/info/sites/default/files/aid_development_cooperation_fundamental_rights/gender_equality_strategy_factsheet_en.pdf.

European Commission (2020b) Opinion on artificial intelligence and gender equality. https://commission.europa.eu/document/download/2e462ba5-13b6-4d04-9f24-2615d8a0d134_en?filename=opinion_artificial_intelligence_gender_equality_2020_en.pdf.

European Data Protection Board (2022) Guidelines 3/2022 on dark patterns in social media platform interfaces: how to recognise and avoid them. https://edpb.europa.eu/our-work-tools/documents/public-consultations/2022/guidelines-32022-dark-patterns-social-media_en

European Disability Forum (2021) A disability-inclusive artificial intelligence act: a guide to monitor implementation in your country. https://www.edf-feph.org/publications/a-disability-inclusive-artificial-intelligence-act-a-guide-to-monitor-implementation-in-your-country/

Federal Trade Commission (2022) Staff report: bringing dark patterns to light. https://www.ftc.gov/system/files/ftc_gov/pdf/P214800%20Dark%20Patterns%20Report%209.14.2022%20-%20FINAL.pdf

Fedorczyk F (2023) Addressing AI-driven gender discrimination: the role of the forthcoming EU AI Act and corporate social responsibility. Riv Dir Comp 3:239

Fineman MA (2009) The vulnerable subject: anchoring equality in the human condition. Yale J Law Fem 20:1–23

Følstad A, Brandtzaeg PB (2017) Chatbots and the new world of HCI. Interactions 24(4):38–42

Forbes (2023) Analyzing the top 50 commonly searched terms on Google, over 73,000 searches each month were for AI and relationship bots. https://www.forbes.com/sites/chriswestfall/2023/09/29/as-ai-usage-increases-at-work-searches-for-ai-girlfriend-up-2400/?sh=412af8ad403b

Friedman B, Kahn PH, Borning A, Huldtgren A (2013) Value sensitive design and information systems. In: Doorn N, Schuurbiers D, van de Poel I, Gorman M (eds) Early engagement and new technologies: opening up the laboratory. Philosophy of Engineering and Technology, vol 16. Springer, Dordrecht

Friedman L (2024) Interview with Eugenia Kuyda. Lex Fridman Podcast. https://lexfridman.com/eugenia-kuyda/

Futurism (2024) Men are creating AI girlfriends and then verbally abusing them. https://futurism.com/chatbot-abuse.

Gitto S, Mancuso P (2019) Brand perceptions of airports using social networks. J Air Transp Manag 75:153–163. https://doi.org/10.1016/j.jairtraman.2019.01.010

Hagan M (2017) The state of legal design: takeaways from the Stanford law + design summit. Legal Design and Innovation. https://medium.com/legal-design-and-innovation/the-state-of-legal-design-the-big-takeaways-of-the-stanford-law-design-summit-ee363b5bf109

Hartzog W (2018) Privacy's blueprint: the battle to control the design of new technologies. Harvard University Press, Cambridge

Hartzog W (2023) Oversight on A.I.: legislating on artificial intelligence. Testimony before the US Senate Committee on the Judiciary, Subcommittee on Privacy, Technology and the Law, 12 September 2023. https://www.judiciary.senate.gov/imo/media/doc/2023-09-12_pm_-_testimony_-_hartzog.pdf

Information Commissioner's Office (2020) The UK age–Appropriate design code (Children's Code). https://ico.org.uk/for-the-public/the-children-s-code-what-is-it/

Introna LD, Nissenbaum H (2000) Shaping the Web: Why the politics of search engines matters. Inf Soc 16(3):169–185

Italian Data Protection Authority (2023a) Garante's suspension order against OpenAI's ChatGPT, 30 March 2023. https://www.garanteprivacy.it/web/guest/home/docweb/-/docweb-display/docweb/9870832

Italian Data Protection Authority (2023b) Press release on AI profiling and processing limitations. https://www.garanteprivacy.it/web/guest/home/docweb/-/docweb-display/docweb/10013893

Italian Data Protection Authority (2023c) Press release on chatbot regulation and AI bias. https://www.garanteprivacy.it/web/guest/home/docweb/-/docweb-display/docweb/9852214#english

Italian Data Protection Authority (2023d) Replika AI chatbot warning. The Garante raised concerns over user protection and transparency regarding emotional and psychological manipulation risks. https://www.garanteprivacy.it/home/docweb/-/docweb-display/docweb/9852506#english

Kılıçkaya F (2020) Using a chatbot, Replika, to practice writing through conversations in L2 English: a case study. In: Kruk M, Peterson M (eds) Advances in educational technologies and instructional design. IGI Global, Hershey, PA, pp 221–238. https://doi.org/10.4018/978-1-7998-2591-3.ch011

Kuyda E (2024) Interview with the CEO of Replika. "We don't sell your data," and "We're not therapists." In: The Verge. https://www.theverge.com/24216748/replika-ceo-eugenia-kuyda-ai-companion-chatbots-dating-friendship-decoder-podcast-interview

Leiser M, Santos C (2023) Dark patterns, enforcement, and the emerging digital design acquis: manipulation beneath the interface. https://ssrn.com/abstract=4431048

Mackenzie C, Rogers W, Dodds S (2014) Introduction: What is vulnerability and why does it matter for moral theory? In: Mackenzie C, Rogers W, Dodds S (eds) Vulnerability: new essays in ethics and feminist philosophy. Oxford University Press, Oxford, pp 1–29

Mendola D, Pera A (2021) Vulnerability of refugees: some reflections on definitions and measurement practices. Int Migr 00:1–14

Pradhan A, Mehta K, Findlater L (2018) Accessibility came by accident: use of voice-controlled intelligent personal assistants by people with disabilities. In: Proc 2018 CHI Conf Hum Factors Comput Syst, paper 459. https://doi.org/10.1145/3173574.3174033

RaiNews (2024) Florida teen suicide linked to obsessive AI relationship. The family filed a lawsuit citing the product as dangerous and privacy-invasive. https://www.rainews.it/articoli/2024/10/suicida-14enne-innamorato-di-un-chatbot-la-madre-fa-causa-allapp-a97315e5-743f-4c1d-bc70-2d8923ac71e4.html
Ramadan Z, Farah MF, El Essrawi L (2021) From Amazon.com to Amazon.love: how Alexa is redefining companionship and interdependence for people with special needs. Psychol Mark 38(4):596–609. https://doi.org/10.1002/mar.21441
Replika (2024) Homepage of the AI companion chatbot. https://www.replika.ai
Rodogno (2016) Social robots, fiction, and sentimentality. Ethics Inf Technol 18(4):257–268. https://doi.org/10.1007/s10676-015-9371-z
Rodotà S (2012) Il diritto di avere diritti. Laterza, Bologna
Schuler D, Namioka A (eds) (1993) Participatory design: principles and practices. Lawrence Erlbaum Associates, Hillsdale
Ta V, et al (2020) User experiences of social support from companion chatbots in everyday contexts: thematic analysis. J Med Internet Res 22(3):e16235. https://www.jmir.org/2020/3/e16235/
Taylor L (2023) My perfect girlfriend: are AI partners a threat to women's rights? https://www.context.news/ai/my-perfect-girlfriend-are-ai-partners-a-threat-to-womens-rights
The European Consumer Organisation (2024) The AI consumer perspective, pp 12–13
The Wire (2022) Chatbot AI nearly wrecked my marriage. https://livewire.thewire.in/livewire/chatbot-ai-nearly-wrecked-my-marriage/
UNESCO (2020) Artificial intelligence and gender equality: Global report
United Nations Regional Information Centre (UNRIC) (2024) How technology-facilitated gender-based violence impacts women and girls. https://unric.org/en/how-technology-facilitated-gender-based-violence-impacts-women-and-girls/
Wellner G, Rothman T (2020) Feminist AI: Can we expect our AI systems to become feminist? Philos Technol 33:191–210
Westfall, C. (2023). *As AI usage increases at work.* Searches for "AI girlfriend" Up 2400% online at: https://www.forbes.com/sites/chriswestfall/2023/09/29/as-ai-usage-increases-at-work-searches-for-ai-girlfriend-up-2400/#
Wischmeyer T, Rademacher T (eds) (2020) Regulating artificial intelligence. Springer, Cham
World Economic Forum (2024) Global Gender Gap Report. https://www3.weforum.org/docs/WEF_GGGR_2024.pdf
World Wide Web Foundation (2018) Artificial intelligence: open questions about gender inclusion. Policy brief W20 Argentina. http://webfoundation.org/docs/2018/06/AI-Gender.pdf
Yeung K (2008) Towards an understanding of regulation by design. In: Brownsword R, Yeung K (eds) Regulating technologies. Hart Publishing, Oxford, pp 79–94
Zang J, et al (2015) Who knows what about me? A survey of behind-the-scenes personal data sharing to third parties by mobile apps. Technology science. Published 29 Oct 2015. https://techscience.org/a/2015103001/
Zeno-Zencovich V (2024) Artificial intelligence, natural stupidity and other legal idiocies. MediaLaws 1–24. https://www.medialaws.eu/wp-content/uploads/2024/07/1-24-Zeno-Zencovich.pdf

Alessandra Pera, PhD in Comparative Law and Full Professor at Palermo University, Department of Political Science and International Relations. Research focuses on family law, ADR systems, and protection of vulnerable individuals and groups. Member of the International Society of Family Law (ISFL), Italian Association of Comparative Law (AIDC), and Juris Diversitas. Visiting scholar at IALS University of London, University of Cape Town, Rey Juan Carlos University of Madrid, and Hanoi University. Member of the editorial boards of Comparazione e Diritto Civile, Comparative Law Review, International Journal of Law and Society, and Cardozo Electronic Law Bulletin.

Sara Rigazio, PhD in Private Law, LL.M. from the University of Minnesota Law School, and Assistant Professor of Comparative Law at the University of Palermo. Visiting Fellow at the Norwegian Center for Computer and Law, University of Oslo. Author of several articles and two books on family law, child protection, legal design, and law-tech interaction.

Open Access This chapter is licensed under the terms of the Creative Commons Attribution 4.0 International License (http://creativecommons.org/licenses/by/4.0/), which permits use, sharing, adaptation, distribution and reproduction in any medium or format, as long as you give appropriate credit to the original author(s) and the source, provide a link to the Creative Commons license and indicate if changes were made.

The images or other third party material in this chapter are included in the chapter's Creative Commons license, unless indicated otherwise in a credit line to the material. If material is not included in the chapter's Creative Commons license and your intended use is not permitted by statutory regulation or exceeds the permitted use, you will need to obtain permission directly from the copyright holder.

Emotions Recognition Systems and Data Economy

Claudia Confortini

Abstract In the context of the data driven economy, the widespread deployment of emotional artificial intelligence raises serious legal issues. Should we resist to exploit emotional AI? How could privacy and autonomy be adequately protected in the face of the advancement of mind-reading technologies? Should the European Union recognise a set of neurorights? This work aims at offering a critical analysis of emotional AI current regulation and sets the stage for a discussion, identifying some loopholes in the European legislative framework and proposing how to close them in order to shape a more effective governance of emotional AI. A preliminary review suggests that current legal standards, in the European Union legal framework, may require further interpretation or amendment to ensure adequate protection against manipulative emotional profiling for business or political goals and to assure that mental data fall unambiguously within the highest standard of legal protections: i.e., under the protection of art. 9 GDPR.

Keywords Neurorights · Emotional AI · Emotion recognition systems · Mental data · Privacy

1 Introductory Remarks

In the context of the data-driven economy, the widespread deployment of computing and artificial intelligence techniques to sense, learn about, and interact with human emotional life (so-called 'emphatic media') raises serious legal issues. Both fundamental rights and civil liberties are threatened.[1]

Contemporary machine learning techniques can gain accurate information about affective states from neural data or digital footprints, predicting the course of action, sometimes subliminally. Privacy and autonomy are jeopardized. Some of the most

[1] Simoncini and Longo (2021).

C. Confortini (✉)
Tor Vergata University of Rome, Rome, Italy
e-mail: claudia.confortini@uniroma2.it

© The Author(s) 2025

C. Amodio and A. Diurni (eds.), *Human Vulnerability in Interaction with AI in European Private Law*, https://doi.org/10.1007/978-3-031-93247-2_7

serious threats to individuals' rights and democratic values are related to the possible exploitation of such technological tools for *psycho-psychological profiling*.[2] Big concerns are related to the use of emotional AI by companies, governments, and political candidates to manipulate and control economic choices, social and political behaviours.

In the first instance, this work points to analysing the major risks connected with the deployment of emotion recognition systems (*breviter*, ERSs): *i.e.*, Artificial Intelligence systems able to detect, interpret, process, and simulate human emotions. Secondly, it aims to outline the latest developments in the regulation of emotional AI within the context of the European Union, especially in light of the Artificial Intelligence Act.

Some scholars suggested we should resist to exploit emotional AI because it is based on a "reductivist approach" to 'reading'—and exerting authority over—human emotions and intentions. According to the AI Now Institute, regulators should indeed heavily restrict the deployment of emotional AI: governments should prohibit the use of affect recognition in high-stakes decision-making processes and until then, AI companies should stop employing it.[3] In the view of some civil society organizations, emotional AI represents one of the greatest threats to the European Union's desire to create an ecosystem of trust and excellence for AI and should therefore be forbidden.[4] The AI Act only partially banned emotional AI. The analysis, therefore, turns into a discussion on the extent to which the current EU legislative framework is apt to offer adequate protection to the fundamental rights enshrined in the CFREU and in the ECHR in the face of the challenges posed by emotional AI. Is there a call for the introduction of new constitutional rights or an actual need for further advancements in the EU regulation, especially concerning the protection of mental data? The work questions whether the European Union missed a chance in regulating emotional AI and investigates what could be done in the future *de lege lata* or *de lege ferenda* to strengthen the protection of the rights of European citizens from privacy and data protection to agency and non-discrimination. Efforts will focus on identifying potential loopholes. The paper will also try to suggest how to fill them in order to safeguard individuals' rights and freedoms in front of the rapid progress of mind-reading technologies in the context of a data-driven economy.

[2] Bakir and McStay (2022).

[3] AI Now Institute 2019 Report, NYU University, December 2019, p. 6.

[4] See Prohibit emotion recognition in the Artificial Intelligence Act, p. 2: paper drafted by Access Now, European Digital Rights (EDRi), Bits of Freedom, ARTICLE19 and IT-Pol, further supported by AlgorithmWatch, Fair Trials, the European Centre for non-profit Law (ECNL) and Panoptykon Foundation, following the Joint Civil Society Statement An EU Artificial Intelligence Act for Fundamental Rights, signed by 123 organisations in November 2021.

2 Emotion Recognition in the Data-Driven Economy

Emotion recognition is being widely used in many fields and has become a research milestone in several scientific areas: not only cognitive science, neuroscience, computer science, and psychology but also law. Our emotions are being detected in real-time and tracked, both in private and public spaces. Quantifying, tracking, and manipulating emotions constitute a significant part of the social media business model.[5]

It is well known that communication is a multimodal process and that emotions can be inferred based on different signals: using both non-physiological signals such as facial expressions, speech, body movements, or eye tracking[6] as well as physiological signals and images like electrical skin resistance (GSR) or heart rate (HR), electrocardiogram (ECG), functional magnetic resonance imaging (fMRI), electroencephalogram (EEG) and magnetoencephalogram (MEG). Magnetoencephalography and electroencephalography measurements of neural activity, for example, combined with generative AI models can decode human thoughts and emotions with high percentages of accuracy. However, emotion recognition does not concern uniquely neurotechnologies. The *spectrum* of applications able to infer human emotions is wider. If neurotechnologies such as brain-to-computer interfaces (BCIs) provide large sets of data to make inferences about emotional states, also non-neural contextual information like a written test can be the basis for such inferences.[7] Recent research has demonstrated that algorithms, for instance, are highly accurate in recognizing emotions from speech signals.[8]

In our online interactions we all reveal information that could be used by intelligent systems to 'read our minds'.[9]

The analysis of content shared through blogs or social media can disclose significant information about the emotional state of a person[10]: the use of certain keywords, typing patterns, likes, user tags, or emoji can provide important cues as to the emotions and intentions of an individual, being of enormous interest to businesses in the digital economy. Studies show that individuals with depression seem more likely to use an increased number of first-person singular.[11] Such information could be employed to deliver targeted messages at particular times when the person is likely to be more receptive, thereby subtly shaping (or even distorting) the thought process, emotions, and behaviours.

---

[5] Stark and Crawford (2015).

[6] Sposini (2024, 321–344).

[7] Ienca and Malgieri (2022).

[8] Singla et al. (2024).

[9] Burr and Cristianini (2019).

[10] See EDPB Guidelines 8/2020 on the targeting of social media users Version 2.0 Adopted on 13 April 2021, p. 35.

[11] Rude et al. (2004).

Technological developments allow for the grasp of emotions from various types of data: not only neural data but also behavioural and phenotypic data.[12] Privacy is threatened by various technologies which allow for mental incursion. Data protection is at risk. Neural data could illuminate and help predict personality traits,[13] addictions, mental health, and various disorders and it does not take an enormous leap of imagination to consider how this data could be misused by corporations and specific groups of interests. Information revealing personality or psychological traits could lead to discrimination; individuals with mental illnesses or psychological weakness could receive differential treatment by companies; companies might disclose information that consumers wanted (or needed) to keep private. Mental data leaks can cause harmful effects on the consumer's dignity, opportunities, and social life.

3 Potential Uses of Emotional AI: Contexts, Purposes, Challenges

Before examining more in detail the major risks associated with emotional AI—*e.g.*, privacy invasion, manipulation, unjust discrimination, etc.—and the law tools apt at mitigating them within the European Union legislative framework, is important to put in evidence that the potential uses of ERSs cover a wide range of applications: provision of personalised services; advertising and microtargeting; customer behaviour analysis; detection of diseases such as autism or prediction of psychotic disorders and depression (healthcare). In the employment sector, ERSs can help the decision-making of recruiters; can be used to identify uninterested candidates in a job interview; and monitor the moods and attention of employees. In education, ERSs can be deployed to monitor students' attention; detect emotional reactions to educative programs in order to adapt the learning path, etc. Emotional AI is being widely used in border protection and law enforcement to identify dissimulating and otherwise suspect individuals (regardless of potential harm to people and society as a whole and of substantial evidence or proof about their efficacy and accuracy). Other possible uses include the detection of political attitudes.

It is almost self-evident that ongoing advances in mind-reading technologies present both great promises and potential risks. In particular, the findings of AI in combination with neurotechnology may significantly improve the quality of life of individuals but can also seriously threaten human rights and democratic values. Devices that are capable of recording or altering the activity of the brain and the wider nervous systems have wide applications not only in settings of research and medicine, ranging from studying Alzheimer's to treating Parkinson's, but also in other contexts.

[12] Ienca and Malgieri (2022).

[13] Recently, a machine learning model has successfully inferred personality from the texts that readers consume. See Simchon et al. (2023).

As a consequence of the progress in the field of non-invasive brain-computer interfaces (BCIs), devices that can collect relevant amounts of brain data once confined to hospitals, universities, and laboratories are now increasingly user friendly, affordable, and easily available to consumers all over the world. Such products are sold mainly for entertainment and *neurogaming* or wellness and *neuroenhancement*: to deepen meditative and sleep states, reduce stress or anxiety, sharpen focus, enhance productivity, and improve cognitive states…Current wellness neurotechnology products include, for example, a headset that promises to provide home treatment for depression and anxiety using transcranial Direct Current Stimulation: the brain runs on electricity; the device sends gentle electrical impulses into the area that has slowed down. This is supposed to get cells firing again and reduce the symptoms of depression.

It is also interesting to report that in 2022, the world's largest cosmetics company, L'Oréal, launched a partnership with neurotechnology company EMOTIV to deploy EEG technology in its stores as part of personalized fragrance consultations that identify fragrance preferences through neural activity.

This is only some evidence of the growing mass commercialization of neurotechnology and of the spread use of mind-reading technologies for the purpose of *neuromarketing*. Sources report an increase of 62% in global neurotechnology investment between 2019 and 2020.[14]

There is clear evidence of the fact that neurotechnologies are proliferating far beyond medical settings into the public marketplace.

A growing number of neuro-technologies are not regulated as medical devices and can be purchased without the involvement of clinicians, researchers, or other intermediaries (without prescription). However, especially the advancement of BCIs raises profound ethical and legal issues.[15] The long-term effects of BCIs on cognitive functions and overall health are yet to be fully understood.[16] Moreover, these affordable devices, which are marketed for public consumption, allow for the collection of neural data beyond laboratory settings. The range of companies that can collect neural data from consumers today is already wide. As consumers increasingly use neurotechnology devices, companies can build bigger and bigger databases of brain scans and other neural data.

In the field of *medical research* and *health care*, the use of neural data could aid the *diagnosis* of a wide range of mental and neurological diseases, from schizophrenia to depression, bipolar disorder, anxiety, post-traumatic stress disorder, panic attacks, Alzheimer's, and Parkinson's disease.

In the area of *emotional marketing*[17] though, mental data collected through wearable neurotechnology devices could be processed for the purpose of *prediction*, (manipulative) *persuasion,* and (subliminal) *control* over human emotional states.

---

[14] Global Neurotech Industry Investment Digest (2021).

[15] Krausová (2014).

[16] See the Research Paper of the Council of the European Union From vision to reality. Promises and risks of Brain-Computer Interfaces, September 2024, p. 14 ff.

[17] Galli (2022).

Due to the fast advancements in neurotechnology and artificial intelligence-driven software, especially deep learning,[18] but also because of the commodification of brain data,[19] humans are exposed to unparalleled threats.[20]

Neural activity is the core of self and the foundation of personal identity. Manipulation of brain activity might have unprecedented consequences as regards individual identity, autonomy, and personal liability.[21] The deployment of certain types of BCIs can potentially result in manipulation or influence of decisions, undermining the very essence of free will. The use of BCIs and intelligent systems can affect a user's sense of agency.[22] Data leaks and brain hacking (of brain-computer interfaces or deep brain stimulation devices) may be a source of additional harm.[23] BCIs are potentially exposed to cybercriminality.[24]

The storage and transmission of neural data seriously challenges data security. Manipulation or theft of neural data can potentially result in identity theft. Both privacy and security breaches must be prevented.[25]

Even if it is hard to predict the pace of neurotechnology development, there is ground for arguing that the pace will be very rapid and that technologies like BCIs will be soon integrated into everyday life. It is a common view that over the coming decades, neurotechnologies will become mainstream and can potentially alter what it means to be human.[26]

In the occidental tradition, it is widely recognized that human identity is linked to consciousness, freedom of thought,[27] and the ability to self-present. Cartesio *docet*: «*cogito ergo sum*». Potential risks for humans are unrivaled.

Aside from the obvious privacy and data protection concerns, at stake are individual autonomy, equality, and human dignity.

It is well known that advertising and marketing seek to capitalize on emotions to drive financial profit.[28] Emotional AI, though, allows for the further, granular personalization of both commercial and political communications, facilitating marketing campaigns in real-time.[29]

Machine learning algorithms allow for the automated detection even from people's digital footprints of information related to emotional states, personality traits, and intents which can be used to tailor persuasive messages capable of increasing the

---

[18] LeCun et al. (2015).

[19] Farahany (2023).

[20] Ruffolo and Amidei (2024).

[21] For a critical summery of the legal implications and the main legal issues raised by modern neuroscientific acquisitions see D'Aloia (2020).

[22] Haselager (2013).

[23] Ienca (2015).

[24] Ienca and Haselager (2016).

[25] Ienca et al. (2018).

[26] Yuste et al. (2021).

[27] Alegre (2021).

[28] Clifford (2019).

[29] Burr and Cristianini (2019).

chance of a person clicking on an online advertisement and buying a product.[30] An increasingly personalised environment allows for more "nudging" potentially resulting in undue influence over (and exploitation of) individual choices, in a loop that augments the knowledge power of few actors or groups of interests. Big Data driven nudges are extremely potent due to their continuously updated, dynamic, and pervasive nature. For this reason, they have been referred to as 'hypernudges'.[31]

Emotion recognition, especially if extensively used for psychological targeting and mass persuasion, can have serious implications for democracy.

It can endanger the soundness of personal opinion formation and independent decision-making, having an impact on public opinion and altering electoral outcomes.

Through, for example, Facial Emotion Recognition technology, it is possible to infer political attitudes by looking at facial expressions and reactions of the audience during political events.

In contexts other than business-to-consumer relationships (*e.g.*, political campaigning), fine-grained, subconscious, and personalized levels of algorithmic persuasion may negatively affect the cognitive autonomy of individuals and their right to form independent opinions and make free and conscious decisions. Both democracy and the rule of law are endangered since they suppose that individuals act like independent moral agents.[32]

On social media platforms and in political campaigns, human vulnerabilities may be exploited, for example by disseminating advertisements at specific moments or in places when/where the receiver would be more sensitive to a certain kind of message.

Profiling by ERSs is highly invasive. In political communication, it could negatively affect individuals' fundamental rights and freedoms like as not being manipulated or being treated equally. It may lead to the manipulation of the electorate, producing harmful consequences on the democratic process.

The potential risks of the deployment of AI and microtargeting to craft political messages delivered to individuals based on their emotional states and personality traits are grave and probably underestimated. Recent technological advancements, involving generative AI and sentiment analysis (even personality inference from consumed text) may originate a highly scalable "manipulation machine" that targets individuals based on their vulnerabilities. This should be an area of special concern to academics and policymakers.[33]

Legal issues also concern accountability for illegal actions. Mind-reading technologies like BCIs can alter a user's mental state to the extent that a person can be no longer the same after their use, showing behavioural changes like impulsivity or

---

[30] Matz et al. (2017).

[31] Yeung (2017).

[32] See "Declaration by the Committee of Ministers on the Manipulative Capabilities of Algorithmic Processes", adopted by the Committee of Ministers on 13 February 2019 at the 1337th meeting of the Ministers' Deputies, p 2.

[33] Simchon et al. (2024).

intemperance. In such a case, it would be difficult to determine who should be held accountable for certain actions.[34]

Questions arise also about social justice and non-discrimination. The use on a large scale of neurotechnologies devices for the purpose, for example, of mental augmentation could widen social disparities and marginalise groups that do not have equal access to them.[35]

In the following pages, attention will be focused, firstly, on the main risks linked with the deployment of emotional AI in various fields; secondly, on the legal safeguards within the EU legal framework and on the shortcomings of the legislation of the European Union.

4 Main Issues Arising by ERSs: Opacity, Inaccuracy, Inconsistency, Unjust Discrimination

Some of the biggest concerns related to the deployment of ERSs are based on the fact that emotional AI, like most artificial intelligence, is often invisible to the people most affected by its decisions (*hiddenness*).

Worldwide, a growing number of AI systems (*e.g.*, vibraimage) algorithmically classify suspects/non-suspects, yet are accused of being themselves deeply suspect.[36] Data used by the system may be collected and analysed in a hidden or covert manner (for example, via CCTV at an event or in a public place) and the exact method of analysing this data is also opaque—it is not clear to its subjects how the system works or what exactly it is quantifying. The corporate value of a technology often seems to be generated through its very *opacity*.

Generally, transparency gaps are a source of vulnerability. Without knowing what Google does when it ranks sites, for instance, we cannot assess when it is acting in good faith to help users, and when it is biasing results to favour its commercial interests. The same goes for status updates on Facebook or trending topics on Twitter.[37]

Transparency alone, though, is not a sufficient condition for holding algorithmic assemblages accountable. I agree with those who criticise the idea 'that knowing is possible by seeing'.[38] Does it matter whether we can see exactly how algorithms work in this field to hold the outputs accountable? Indeed, even if we had full visibility

[34] From vision to reality. Promises and risks of Brain-Computer Interfaces, cit., p. 17.

[35] Whether and how to regulate neuroenhancement is an open question. A study of the European Parliament outlined possible strategies, identifying a reasoned pro-enhancement approach, a reasoned restrictive approach and a case-by-case approach as viable options for the EU (see European Science and Technology Options Assessment. Human Enhancement Study, 2009). For an in-depth analysis see Errigo (2020a).

[36] Wright (2021).

[37] Pasquale (2015).

[38] Ananny and Crawford (2018).

of them, how would we know whether they actually 'work' properly in interpreting emotional states?

Especially in this field, leaving algorithms without appropriate safeguards would mean opening the way towards techno-determinism, which appears to be a much more serious threat when it comes to the inner sphere of emotions and cognitive liberty.[39]

Additionally, emotional AI is likely to have algorithmic failures that lead to unfair and/or biased outcomes. There might be inference inconsistencies, *e.g.*, when the emotional AI identifies a particular facial expression but does not infer the concomitant emotion (there is undoubtedly a significant facial expression uncertainty, linked with demographic-based differences in the emotions recognized by humans and by affective AI models).[40]

Indeed, it must be noted that facial expressions and their meaning are highly dependent on social and cultural context.

When it comes to facial coding,[41] the most basic critique is that one does not necessarily smile when one is happy; common sense suggests that facial expressions do not always, or even often, map to inner feelings, that emotions are often fleeting or momentary, and that facial expressions and their meaning are highly dependent on social and cultural context.[42]

Emotion recognition systems reduce emotion to a highly reductive and simplistic model that is digitally scalable. As Barrett argues,[43] emotion isn't a simple reflex or a bodily state that's hard-wired into our DNA, and it's certainly not universally expressed.[44] Culture to culture, person to person even, it's never quite the same.

Emotion detection as well as categorising based on inferred emotions are culturally mediated processes.

There's also evidence of the fact that emotion recognition can amplify both race and gender disparities.[45] The use of machine-learning methods involved in emotion recognition systems has been harshly criticised for racial biases based on the data sets on which the algorithms are trained.

Recent studies have found that emotional analysis technology assigns more negative emotions to black men's faces than white men's faces: facial recognition programs are often biased. On average, Face++ rates black faces as twice as angry as white faces. Face API scores black faces as three times more contemptuous than white faces.[46] Black men's facial expressions are scored with emotions associated with threatening behaviours more often than white men, even when they are smiling.

---

39 McStay (2018).

40 Rhue (2019).

41 Ekman and Friesen (1978).

42 Crivelli et al. (2015).

43 Barrett et al. (2019).

44 Russell (1994).

45 Dibeklioglu et al. (2015).

46 Rhue (2019).

These studies suggest that facial recognition may perpetrate the same biases that people have, formalizing preexisting stereotypes into algorithms and automatically embedding them into everyday life.

Some argue that if emotional AI had to be evaluated in human terms, it would be judged as psychopathic.[47] ERSs are not emphatic. They do not understand our emotions: they simply process data such as biometrics and generate outputs called emotional states.[48]

It has even been argued that ER is pseudoscience. Emotions recognition systems mainly rely on the six basic emotions indicated by Ekman: *i.e.*, happiness, sadness, surprise, fear, anger, and disgust.[49] However, this classification is harshly criticized as not accurately reflecting the complex nature of an affective state.[50] It has been remarked that many more facial expressions of emotion exist and are regularly used by humans.[51]

The AI Now Institute at New York University alerts that facial recognition reactivates 'a long tradition of physiognomy and is pseudoscience since it claims facial features can reveal innate aspects of our character and personality' and emphasizes that contextual, social and cultural factors play a larger role in emotional expression than was believed by Ekman and his peers.[52]

Some argue that physiognomic AI is unjust and deceptive. Therefore, it should be banned.[53]

Leaving to one side the point that emotion detection in particular through facial expressions is a pseudoscience, it must be put in evidence that improving the accuracy of emotion detection may arguably require more invasive surveillance to gather more contextual insights and signals, paradoxically adding difficulties from a privacy perspective.[54]

---

[47] McStay (2023).

[48] Bakir and McStay (2022).

[49] Ekman and Keltner (1997).

[50] According to Barret such categories fail to capture the richness of emotional experiences. Patterns, for example, for anger or sadness are not stable among people. Barrett (2006).

[51] Du et al. (2014).

[52] AI Now Report 2018 (n. 63) 14. See also McStay (2016).

[53] Stark and Hutson (2021).

[54] Valcke et al. (2021, 65 ff).

5 ERSs Threaten Privacy, Individual Autonomy, Agency, and Dignity. Emotions Monitoring Produces Chilling Effects Encroaching on the Ability and the Freedom to "Self-Present"

In addition to technical issues about 'accuracy', these technologies pose several concerns related to the protection of fundamental rights of consumers, voters and people in general: if the scientific validity of these technologies is questionable, the potential harm from misuse is significant.

The use of emotional AI (*i.e.*, systems characterized by complexity, opacity, dependency on data, and autonomous behaviour) can adversely affect several fundamental rights enshrined in the EU Charter of Fundamental Rights as the right to respect for private and family life, and protection of personal data (Article 8 ECHR; Articles 7–8 CFREU); equality and non-discrimination (Article 14 ECHR; Articles 20–21 CFREU); freedom of thought and conscience (Art. 9 ECHR; Art. 10 CFREU).

The most serious issues raised by ERSs concern privacy,[55] which is central to this analysis, but also self-determination, individual autonomy, and human dignity.[56]

ERSs pretend to have the algorithmic authority to empower the operator to know subjects better than subjects know themselves by directly accessing and revealing their unconscious. Emotional information is often conveyed by the body through unconscious reactions to an external stimulus. Emotional AI can hence undermine the agency of the subject and his capacity to consciously and autonomously determine and communicate their own mental emotional state.

By means of ER, the right to the future tense[57] is profoundly infringed.

ERSs represent a source of power imbalance and power imbalance allows for limitless exploitation, which is a distinctive feature of digital capitalism[58] and the core of human digital vulnerability.

If consumers' vulnerability mostly depends on the imbalance in the level of knowledge between the two bargaining parties,[59] detection and exploitation of mental data can generate a new form of 'universal' vulnerability. This new shape of human digital vulnerability rests in (consciously and unconsciously) exposing sensitive parts of the self to AI technologies and to digital architectures that reside in the hands of just a few powerful actors.

It should be noted that the inference of emotions through the collection of neural data or non-physiological signals involves involuntary disclosure of information. Even if individuals consent to the collection and processing of their personal data for a narrow use, they are unlikely to be fully aware of the content or quantity of information they are sharing.

[55] Valcke et al. (2021, 67–68).

[56] Bakir and McStay (2020).

[57] Zuboff (2018).

[58] Cofone (2023).

[59] Galli (2022)

A recent study suggests that neural data holds the potential for diverse personal insights possibly beyond the current public understanding.[60]

People are not in a position to properly foresee the consequences of their inferred data. Neurotechnology users cannot decide what specific neural information they would like to disclose and they are unlikely to understand the extent to which their neural data can be decoded, currently or in the future.[61] Neurotechnologies can collect information about an individual that the individual did not even know existed.

In the digital environment, even if there is not a brute force coercing us, still individuals are under the undue influence of powerful counterparts who can nudge us to act the way that is more profitable to them.[62]

Advancements in neuroscience, combined with the use of AI in the digital realm are giving rise to a new form of 'universal' rather than 'situational' vulnerability connected to the exploitation of human emotions.[63]

Presumably, we all agree that we need to prevent and deter emotional manipulation, considering the 'ontological' vulnerability of human beings in the digital environment.[64]

The point is, as noted by Sunstein,[65] that manipulation has 'many shades' and is extremely difficult to define.

Distinguishing between (unacceptable) manipulation and (acceptable) persuasion may be problematic.[66]

Probably, we should link the concept of manipulation to the one of self-determination and individual autonomy. Therefore, we should consider a statement or action as manipulative to the extent that it does not sufficiently engage or appeal to people's capacity for reflective and deliberative choice.

Moreover, emotional surveillance may cause chilling effects on behaviour. The pervasive deployment of AI models that allow individuals and companies to take advantage of "*feeling-into*" the inner world of people, as well as the online and offline behaviour of the *civic body,* raises the spectre of perpetual surveillance.[67]

---

[60] Huang et al. (2024)

[61] House bill 24-1058 an act concerning protecting the privacy of individuals' biological data, and in connection there with, protecting the privacy of neural data and expanding the scope of the "Colorado Privacy Act" accordingly.

[62] Malgieri (2023).

[63] De Mari Casareto dal Verme (2023).

[64] In the digital environment the concept of vulnerability «is not linked to specific physical or psychological disabilities but is identified in the relationship between the physical person and the technological environment in which he/she operates'». We can therefore speak of «ontological vulnerability of human beings—in general—with respect to digital technology structures». See Gatt and Caggiano (2022). On this topic, see also Mollo (2023).

[65] Thaler and Sunstein (2008).

[66] «From a policy perspective, understanding the exact point where acceptable persuasion becomes unacceptable manipulation is one of the crucial issues for the regulation of marketing and commercial practices, especially in the digital environment». See European Commission (2023).

[67] Bakir and McStay (2022).

ERSs, in this way, encroach on our rights to freedom of expression (Art. 10 ECHR; Art. 10 CFREU), freedom of assembly and association (Art. 11 ECRH; Art. 12 CFREU), and—to the extent that our moral integrity is at stake—our right to private life and personal identity (Art. 8 ECHR; Art. 7 CFREU).[68]

There is a serious risk of chilling effects as people are becoming aware that our actions are being scrutinized and evaluated on a second-by-second basis. Such emotional monitoring can have an impact on the ability to 'self-present' individuals.[69]

We have previously referred to biases and profiling errors. Emotional AI, though, can have an impact on an individual's autonomy and capacity to self-present irrespective of its accuracy: the lack of accuracy of emotional AI, resulting in profiling errors and incorrect inferences, poses additional risks of harm.

Emotion recognition technologies add a layer of intimacy-invasion because they are capable of detecting not only expressed emotions but also underlying emotions deliberately disguised. This would constitute not merely a breach of privacy but a violation of autonomy.[70]

While privacy and autonomy are not the same, it can reasonably be argued that the right to privacy serves as a means of safeguarding autonomy.[71]

The intimate knowledge of a person is the basis of many forms of manipulation. Privacy law plays a crucial role since it helps to prevent other entities from eroding the individual autonomy of the data subject.[72]

Emotional AI challenges both (*i*) privacy as seclusion or intimacy: ER puts at risk the freedom to think without being monitored by others (*forum internum*) and (*ii*) privacy as freedom of action and self-determination.[73]

Certain rights, including the right to privacy, the right to freedom of conscience and belief, and the right to be free from discrimination are crucial for preserving human dignity.[74] Since the employment of emotional AI threatens these rights (*e.g.*, the right to respect for private and family life and the right to be free of discriminatory treatment), it poses threats to human dignity as well.[75]

It has been noted that individual autonomy and human dignity are not sufficiently protected by articles 8, 9, and 10 of the ECHR.[76] We could argue about the need for a type of 'Oviedo Convention' about (emotional) AI. However, it might be not necessary to introduce novel rights such as the right to the future tense; the right to cognitive

[68] Valcke et al. (2021, 65ff).

[69] Warner and Sloan (2014).

[70] Brown (2024).

[71] Clifford (2019).

[72] Pasquale (2024).

[73] Ziegler (2007).

[74] Feldman (1999).

[75] Valcke et al. (2021, 65ff).

[76] Council of Europe, Expert Committee on human rights dimensions of automated data processing and different forms of artificial intelligence (MSI-AUT) (2019) Responsibility and AI. A Study of the Implications of Advanced Digital Technologies (Including AI Systems) for the Concept of Responsibility within a Human Rights Framework. Rapporteur: Karen Yeung. https://rm.coe.int/responsability-and-ai-en/168097d9c5.

liberty, the right to self-determination over our brains and mental experiences[77]; the right to not be measured, analysed, or coached; the right to cognitive sovereignty; the right not to be manipulated as far as we refer to them in interpreting art. 8 of the ECHR. The introduction of novel constitutional rights may indeed have a negative effect, diluting the significance of the existing constitutional rights. Nevertheless, it is important to shape appropriate remedies, reinterpreting the existing human rights and redefining the content of art. 8 and 9 ECHR.

6 The European Legal Framework: A Multilayered Protection

Having a look at the global picture of the EU rules and principles is possible to find various positive tools to limit abusive exploitation of cognitive liberty and mental integrity.[78]

As above noted, Emotional AI challenges some of the very basic principles for a trustworthy and human-centric AI: privacy, personal autonomy, non-discrimination, human dignity, agency, and transparency. For this reason, the *Artificial Intelligence Act* of 13th of June 2024 (Reg. Eu 2024/1689) lays down several harmonised rules on ERSs. These provisions, which will be examined separately,[79] shall apply across sectors without affecting the application of existing Union law. The regulation is complementary to the existing Union law, in particular on data protection,[80] fundamental rights, and consumer protection. The text of the AI Act is clear in this respect.[81]

On the basis of the dir. 2005/29/EC, for example, unfair commercial practices leading to economic or financial harm to consumers are forbidden under all circumstances, irrespective of whether they are put in place through AI systems or otherwise (see *Recital* 29 AIA).

[77] Farahany (2023).

[78] The right to 'mental integrity' is protected in Article 3 of the Charter of Fundamental Rights of the European Union.

[79] See § 7 and § 7.1.

[80] The right to the protection of personal data is safeguarded by Reg. Eu 2016/67911, Reg. Eu 2018/172512 and by Dir. Eu 2016/680. Dir. 2002/58/EC additionally protects private life and the confidentiality of communications.

[81] According to Recital 9 of the AI Act: «The harmonised rules laid down in this Regulation should apply across sectors and, in line with the New Legislative Framework, should be without prejudice to existing Union law, in particular on data protection, consumer protection, fundamental rights, employment, protection of workers, and product safety, to which this Regulation is complementary». As envisioned in Recital 45 of the AI Act: «data protection law, non-discrimination law, consumer protection law, and competition law, should not be affected by this Regulation». Under art. 2(7-9) «This Regulation shall not affect Regulation (EU) 2016/679 or (EU) 2018/1725 [...] This Regulation is without prejudice to the rules laid down by other Union legal acts related to consumer protection and product safety».

Since AI is a data-dependent enterprise, privacy law is paramount in addressing the key emotional AI governance issues.

The intersections between the AI Act and the GDPR will be delved into further on,[82] with special regard to art. 9, 22, and art. 35 of GDPR.[83]

It is worth noting that the European legal framework counts several sets of rules that aim to protect individuals from the risk of manipulation, particularly in the digital realm.[84]

Art. 26 (3) of the *Digital Services Act*, for instance, is crucial in this respect. It prohibits to exploit people's vulnerability through advertisements based on profiling using the particular categories of personal data referred to in Art. 9 of the Reg. EU 2016/679 (*breviter*: Gdpr).[85] Other existing provisions refer to 'dark patterns'[86] and price personalization. Art. 25 of the DSA states that: «Providers of online platforms shall not design, organise or operate their online interfaces in a way that deceives or manipulates the recipients of their service or in a way that otherwise materially distorts or impairs the ability of the recipients of their service to make free and informed decisions». The main issue with this prohibition is that, according to paragraph 2, it shall not apply to practices covered by dir. 2005/29/EC or by reg. Eu 2016/679. Since is not clear whether exploiting emotions through AI emotional marketing techniques is to be considered an unfair commercial practice, is uncertain accordingly whether art. 25 DSA applies to it.[87]

In addition, dir. 2019/2161/EU introduced in dir. 2011/83/EU the letter e-*bis*) to art. 6 whereby the consumer must be informed that the price is personalised based on an automated decision-making process (one could remark that consumers

---

[82] Especially in the last paragraph.

[83] According to art. 9 GDPR «Processing of personal data revealing racial or ethnic origin, political opinions, religious or philosophical beliefs, or trade union membership, and the processing of genetic data, biometric data for the purpose of uniquely identifying a natural person, data concerning health or data concerning a natural person's sex life or sexual orientation shall be prohibited». Art. 22 GDPR provides for the data subject's right not to be subject to a decision based solely on automated processing, including profiling, which produces legal effects concerning them or similarly significantly affects them. Art. 35 GDPR states that: «where a type of processing in particular using new technologies, and taking into account the nature, scope, context and purposes of the processing, is likely to result in a high risk to the rights and freedoms of natural persons, the controller shall, prior to the processing, carry out an assessment of the impact of the envisaged processing operations on the protection of personal data» (DPIA).

[84] Parenzo (2024).

[85] Moreover, art. 26 (1) of the DSA requires providers of online platforms that present advertisements on their interfaces to take steps to ensure that the recipients of the service can understand that the information constitutes an advertisement, identify the natural or legal person on whose behalf the advertisement is presented, and the parameters used to determine the recipient of the advertisement. Under art. 26(3) of Reg. Eu 2022/2065 «Online platform providers may not present advertisements to service recipients based on profiling, as defined in Article 4(4) of Regulation (EU) 2016/679, using the special categories of personal data referred to in Article 9(1) of Regulation (EU) 2016/679)».

[86] Kollmer and Eckhardt (2023).

[87] De Mari Casareto dal Verme (2023).

should be aware of why and how the price is personalised as well as of the extent of personalization).

Like the Data Protection Impact Assessment under art. 35 of the GDPR, according to art. 34 of the DSA, very large online platforms are under a duty to assess the systemic risks arising from the design (including algorithmic systems), operation, and use of services, taking into consideration «[…]any actual or foreseeable negative effects for the exercise of fundamental rights, in particular the fundamental rights to human dignity enshrined in Article 1 of the Charter, to respect for private and family life enshrined in Article 7 of the Charter, to the protection of personal data enshrined in Article 8 of the Charter, to freedom of expression and information, including the freedom and pluralism of the media, enshrined in Article 11 of the Charter, to non-discrimination enshrined in Article 21 of the Charter, to respect for the rights of the child enshrined in Article 24 of the Charter and to a high-level of consumer protection enshrined in Article 38 of the Charter […]». Once systemic risks have been identified «Providers of very large online platforms and of very large online search engines shall put in place reasonable, proportionate and effective mitigation measures, tailored to the specific systemic risks identified pursuant to Article 34, with particular consideration to the impacts of such measures on fundamental rights» (art. 35.1 DSA).

Furthermore, in the context of online political advertising, art. 18 of the regulation EU 2024/900 prohibits targeting techniques and ad-delivery techniques involving profiling using special categories of personal data referred to in Reg. Eu 2016/679 and Reg. Eu 2018/1725. It is not possible to rely on the exceptions laid down in art. 9(2) of Regulation (EU) 2016/679 and art. 10(2) of Regulation (EU) 2018/1725 for using those techniques in the context of online political advertising. The use of targeting techniques and ad-delivery techniques involving the processing of personal data, other than special categories of personal data, is allowed only when it is based on personal data collected from the data subjects and with their explicit consent, provided separately for political advertising.

In summary, within the European legislative framework: data protection regulations impose stringent conditions on the collection and processing of personal data. European and national regulations offer robust protection to consumers, curbing manipulative practices in business-to-consumer transactions: consumer protection legislation safeguards against aggressive, unfair, and deceptive trade practices. Media and advertising laws establish clear prohibitions against false, misleading, deceptive, and covert advertising, including a specific ban on subliminal advertising (*see*, especially, the above-mentioned art. 26(3) of the DSA). Under contract law, coercion, misrepresentation, or fraud commonly constitute grounds for a contract to be annulled.

Within the European Union, the existing legislation addresses several aspects pertinent to the development and application of neurotechnologies, including regulations not only on data protection and artificial intelligence but also on medical devices safety[88] and cybersecurity.

[88] Steindl (2024).

Overall, the legislation of the EU offers multilayered protection against the potential harms of emotional AI. Still, there are shortcomings. These loopholes will be further discussed below.

7 The AI Act Provisions Regarding Emotional AI: A Brief Review

Before reviewing the substantive provisions of the AI Act concerning emotional AI is interesting to consider that the EU legislator is aware that: «There are serious concerns about the scientific basis of AI systems aiming to identify or infer emotions, particularly as expression of emotions vary considerably across cultures and situations, and even within a single individual. Among the key shortcomings of such systems are the limited reliability, the lack of specificity, and the limited generalisability. Therefore, AI systems identifying or inferring emotions or intentions of natural persons based on their biometric data may lead to discriminatory outcomes and can be intrusive to the rights and freedoms of the concerned persons [...]» (*Recital* 44).

Art. 2(6) clarifies that AI systems or AI models specifically developed and put into service for the sole purpose of scientific research and development are excluded from the scope of the AI Act (see also *Recital* 25).

The following article contains the definition of an emotion recognition system: «an AI system to identify or infer emotions or intentions of natural persons based on their biometric data» (art. 3 AIA). To properly interpret this provision, it is necessary to refer to *Recital* 18, according to which: «The notion of 'emotion recognition system' referred to in this Regulation should be defined as an AI system inferring to identify emotions or intentions of natural persons based on their biometric data. The notion refers to emotions or intentions such as happiness, sadness, anger, surprise, disgust, embarrassment, excitement, shame, contempt, satisfaction, and amusement. It does not include physical states, such as pain or fatigue, including, for example, systems used in detecting the state of fatigue of professional pilots or drivers to prevent accidents. This does also not include the mere detection of readily apparent expressions, gestures, or movements unless they are used for identifying or inferring emotions. Those expressions can be basic facial expressions, such as a frown or a smile, or gestures such as the movement of hands, arms or head, or characteristics of a person's voice, such as a raised voice or whispering».

As evident, the EU legislator only refers to emotion recognition techniques that are based on biometric data even if, as highlighted above, there are emotion scanning tools that are not based on the processing of biometric data. Not all systems capable of inferring emotions use physiological data that meet the high bar for identification required to be classified as biometric data. In such cases, providers could argue that their system is not subject to obligations under the AIA.[89] For this reason, it is open

[89] See Prohibit emotion recognition in the Artificial Intelligence Act, p. 2 ff.: paper drafted by Access Now, European Digital Rights (EDRi), Bits of Freedom, ARTICLE19 and IT-Pol, further

to debate whether, in the future, it would be useful to enlarge the definition of ERSs so as to comprise those systems that make inferences about emotions or states of mind based on physiological data or other data (*e.g.,* written tests or voice records) which are not biometric, provided that the definition (does not and) should not cover systems that detect purely physiological traits or behaviours, such as whether a bus driver is falling asleep or a man on an emergency services line is having a heart attack.

However, at the core of the regulation stands art. 5 (f), which expressly prohibits the placing on the market, the putting into service for this specific purpose, or the use of AI systems to infer emotions of a natural person in the areas of workplace and education institutions, except where the use of the AI system is intended to be put in place or into the market for medical or safety reasons.

Alongside this prohibition, the AI Act introduces, in relation to any emotion recognition system, duties to inform.

As said before, the process of monitoring and coding emotions is part of a more general paradigm of personalization of advertisements, digital services, and products offered to users. The profiling, though, this time is based on human emotions and the user does not fully know the functions and purposes of the automated process.

In this respect, art. 50, par. 3 of the AI Act plays a crucial role since it establishes «Transparency obligations for providers and deployers of certain AI systems» stating that: «Deployers of an emotion recognition system or a biometric categorisation system shall inform the natural persons exposed thereto of the operation of the system, and shall process the personal data per Regulations (EU) 2016/679 and (EU) 2018/1725 and Directive (EU) 2016/680, as applicable. This obligation shall not apply to AI systems used for biometric categorisation and emotion recognition, which are permitted by law to detect, prevent or investigate criminal offences, subject to appropriate safeguards for the rights and freedoms of third parties, and in compliance with Union law».

The transparency obligation only concerns the operation of the IA whereas it is not extended to its specific purposes or manner of use. This choice is open to doubt.

Besides, is essential to highlight that based on ANNEX III, par. 1, lett. c) AI systems intended to be used for emotion recognition are among those high-risk AI systems referred to in art. 6(2): emotion recognition systems that are not expressly prohibited under the AI Act should be classified as high-risk (*Recital* 54).

A general picture of the provisions of the AI Act related to emotional AI wouldn't be complete without mentioning Art. 27, according to which: «Prior to deploying a high-risk AI system referred to in Article 6(2) into use, with the exception of high-risk AI systems intended to be used in the area listed in point 2 of Annex III, deployers that are bodies governed by public law, or are private entities providing public services, and deployers high-risk AI systems referred to in points 5 (b) and

supported by AlgorithmWatch, Fair Trials, the European Centre for non-profit Law (ECNL) and Panoptykon Foundation, following the Joint Civil Society Statement An EU Artificial Intelligence Act for Fundamental Rights, signed by 123 organisations in November 2021.

(c) of Annex III, shall perform an assessment of the impact on fundamental rights that the use of such system may produce…».

This crucial article, which provides for a fundamental rights impact assessment for high-risk AI systems (FRIA) must be coordinated with art. 35 of GDPR, which requires a data protection impact assessment (DPIA). This AI governance solution provided for by the AI Act foresees the overlap with preexisting provisions. FRIAs, though, do not need to be conducted for aspects covered under existing legislation. As such, if a DPIA and FRIA have an overlapping aspect, that aspect arguably needs only to be covered under DPIA.[90]

8 A Critical Analysis of Emotional AI Current Regulation: Proposals

Among civil organizations there is a widespread view that European Union missed a chance in regulating emotional AI. A critical opinion asserts that "human-centric" risks becoming a buzzword when speaking of Emotional AI. Whether the AI Act is a gold standard and not primarily a concession to industry, serving police and private companies more than people is a matter of debate.[91]

Despite the criticisms, this legislative act seems to contain useful elements as it introduces some substantive prohibitions. It clearly represents a compromise, trying to establish a delicate balance that does not excessively obstruct innovation and investment.

Overall, it is important to note that art. 5 (1) lett. a) prohibits the placing on the market, the putting into service, or the use of an AI system that deploys subliminal techniques beyond a person's consciousness or purposefully manipulative or deceptive techniques, with the objective, or the effect of materially distorting the behaviour of a person or a group of persons by appreciably impairing their ability to make an informed decision, thereby causing them to take a decision that they would not have otherwise taken in a manner that causes or is reasonably likely to cause that person, another person or group of persons significant harm.

The main issue with this provision is that it reveals that the AIA follows the same (traditional) approach to vulnerability of the UCPD. It considers vulnerability as originating from the characteristics of certain groups of people rather than from the structural dimension of AI technologies and the data-driven markets in which they are deployed.[92]

To reinforce the protection of European citizens, one possible solution would be to include the deployment of emotion recognition systems for marketing or political

[90] See AI Governance in Practice Report 2024 of IAPP AI Governance Centre, June 2024, p. 31.

[91] EU's AI Act fails to set gold standard for human rights, Wednesday 3 April 2024, ARTICLE 19, Access Now, Bits of freedom Amnesty International, European Disability Forum, ProtectNot-Surveil, Algorithm Watch, European Central for Non-Profit-Law et al.

[92] Galli (2022).

micro targeting in the blacklist of unfair commercial practices contained in Annex I of the European Parliament and Council Directive 2005/29/EC. In fact, it is not clear, as noted above, whether exploiting emotions through AI emotional marketing techniques is to be considered an unfair commercial practice. The definition of aggressiveness, in particular, does not seem to involve the undue influence exercised on the irrational part of the brain.[93]

There is a need for collective answers since enforcement in individual cases risks being ineffective in mitigating the harmful effects on society of certain deployments of emotional AI.[94] The massive scale of some practices may surpass the enforcement of individual rights.[95]

Given these considerations, another option would be the introduction under Art. 5 AIA of a clear ban on emotional AI for marketing purposes.[96] The exact meaning of "subliminal techniques" and "consciousness" under art. 5 (1) lett. a) is indeed far from clear and is uncertain to what extent practices such as 'digital nudging' or 'dark patterns' would fall under the prohibition contained therein.

The AI Act has been criticised also because it introduces a blanket exemption for all the AI systems developed or used solely for the purpose of national security, regardless of whether this is done by a public or private authority.[97] Disapproval rests on the assumption that exceptions should be on a case-by-case basis; national security should not become a digital rights-free zone.[98] In this view, the partial ban of ERSs contains dangerous loopholes and entails a risk: the fact that ERSs are prohibited in the workplace and education settings but are still allowed for other purposes such as law enforcement and border control could be interpreted as a signal that EU is likely to test these intrusive AI systems against the most marginalised and vulnerable people of our society, where the risks of the deployment of these systems are potentially the gravest.[99]

A partial ban on Emotional AI, according to this opinion, may have a negative impact since it could be perceived as a sign that mind-reading is allowed in the EU and this could set a dangerous precedent in a global scenario in which the EU aims to act and be seen as a game changer.

A very large opinion, as previously noted, is in favour of a comprehensive ban against any use of AI which is held to be not compatible with fundamental human rights and freedoms. Civil society organizations like *Article 19* wish the introduction

---

[93] De Mari Casareto dal Verme (2023).

[94] Clifford (2020).

[95] Valcke et al. (2021, 65ff).

[96] Orlando (2022).

[97] According to art. 2 (3) of AI Act: «This Regulation does not apply to AI systems where and in so far they are placed on the market, put into service, or used with or without modification exclusively for military, defence or national security purposes, regardless of the type of entity carrying out those activities».

[98] EU's AI Act fails to set gold standard for human rights, Wednesday 3 April 2024, ARTICLE 19, Access Now, Bits of freedom Amnesty International, European Disability Forum, ProtectNot-Surveil, AlgorithmWatch, European Central for Non-Protfit-Law et al.

[99] EU's AI Act fails to set gold standard for human rights, cit.

of a general prohibition on emotion recognition. A study of January 2022 commissioned by the AIDA committee of the European Parliament, entitled *Identification and assessment of existing and draft EU legislation in the digital field*, stated that: «Emotion recognition systems powered by AI may have highly undesired discriminatory and dignity consequences, manipulative effects, and risk impact. Therefore, general prohibition might be an option to consider».[100]

The European Data Protection Board (EDPB) and European Data Protection Supervisor (EDPS), in their Joint Opinion on the AI Act, affirmed that the «use of AI to infer emotions of a natural person is highly undesirable and should be prohibited» further noting that exceptions should be made for «certain well-specified use-cases, namely for health or research purposes (*e.g.*, patients where emotion recognition is important), always with appropriate safeguards in place and of course, subject to all other data protection conditions and limits including purpose limitation».[101]

The main issue is that these systems are quite controversial and have been shown to be based on questionable scientific premises. For this reason, they should not be allowed in sensitive domains unless subject to rigorous clinical validation and the highest level of regulatory scrutiny.[102] Specifically, the deployment of ERSs for marketing should be prohibited. Emotional AI should be rather confined to the field of medical research and health care for diagnosis, treatment, and prevention of diseases.[103] Even if the partial ban of ERSs is important, since it makes clear that the EU is prompt to draw red lines against harmful uses of AI, we should carefully reconsider the risks and opportunities of the datafication of emotions.

[100] Available at: https://www.europarl.europa.eu/RegData/etudes/STUD/2022/703345/IPOL_STU(2022)703345_EN.pdf.

[101] EDPB-GEPD Joint Opinion 5/2021 on the proposal for a Regulation of the European Parliament and of the Council laying down harmonised rules on artificial intelligence (Artificial Intelligence Act), 18 June 2021 (35).

[102] See Prohibit emotion recognition in the Artificial Intelligence Act, p. 2: paper drafted by Access Now, European Digital Rights (EDRi), Bits of Freedom, ARTICLE19 and IT-Pol, further supported by AlgorithmWatch, Fair Trials, the European Centre for non-profit Law (ECNL) and Panoptykon Foundation, following the Joint Civil Society Statement An EU Artificial Intelligence Act for Fundamental Rights, signed by 123 organisations in November 2021.

[103] Orlando (2022).

9 Further Shortcomings of the European Legislative Framework. Should the EU Recognise a Set of Neurorights?

Further shortcomings of the EU legal framework can be identified in the lack of specific regulation concerning mental data protection and consumer neurotechnologies. These are indeed specifically regulated only through soft law tools[104] which appear unable to meaningfully address the human rights challenges posed by these advanced technologies. There are protection gaps in non-medical contexts.

Policymakers need to ensure adequate protection of mental information and to adopt a more active approach in shaping a solid governance framework for emotional AI, providing specific safeguards which can prevent the accumulation and monopolisation by a limited number of private companies of data which refer to mental features of the individuals (emotions, intentions…).[105]

Given the *vacuum* of regulation concerning (non-invasive) neurotechnology in nearly every country, some scholars claim for the advancement of neuro-rights.

The Morningside Group identified five key neuro-rights: (1) the right to mental privacy, or the ability to keep mental activity protected against disclosure; (2) the right to identity, or the ability to control one's mental integrity and sense of self; (3) the right to agency, or the freedom of thought and free will to choose one's actions; (4) the right to fair access to mental augmentation, or the ability to ensure that the benefits of improvements to sensory and mental capacity through neurotechnology are distributed justly in the population and (5) the right to protection from algorithmic bias or the ability to ensure that technologies do not insert prejudices.[106] In particular, the Morningside Group coordinated by Professor Rafael Yuste of Columbia University suggests adding clauses protecting neuro rights to International Treaties such as the 1948 Universal Declaration of Human Rights.[107]

Ienca and Andorno instead offer an alternative set of neuro rights: the right to cognitive liberty, the right to mental privacy, the right to mental integrity, and the right to psychological continuity.[108]

---

[104] See OECD (Organisation for Economic Cooperation and Development) Recommendation on Responsible Innovation in Neurotechnology, adopted in 2019; The Ethics of Neurotechnology: UNESCO appoints international expert group to prepare a new global standard, UNESCO, 22 April 2024; León Declaration on European neurotechnology: a human focused and rights' oriented approach, Spanish Presidency of the Council of the EU, 24 October 2023; Charte de développement responsable des neurotechnologies, Ministère de l'Enseignement supérieur et de la Recherche, 17 November 2022.

[105] From vision to reality. Promises and risks of Brain-Computer Interfaces, cit., p. 20.

[106] The Neurorights Foundation, 2023; available from: https://neurorightsfoundation.org/.

[107] For more insights, see Errigo (2020b).

[108] Ienca and Andorno (2017).

These proposals have attracted criticism.[109] Some argue we need new laws not new rights[110] and that neuro-specific mental privacy rights would be incompleted.[111] Information about mental states (emotions, intentions, etc.) is indeed inferable by means other than neurotechnologies.

Some advocate the creation of an independent body to monitor developments in this domain.[112]

A plausible solution would be to extensively interpret existing provisions to guide the development of European and national legal and regulatory frameworks: especially art. 8 ECHR, which provides for the "right to respect for private life"; Art. 9 ECHR, which provides "the right to freedom of thought"; art. 8 CFREU which provides for the "right to the protection of personal data"; art. 3 and art. 10 of CFREU, which respectively refer to "the right to mental integrity" and the "right to freedom of thought".

At the national level, several countries in the world have advanced or are advancing legislation and declarations aligned with the neuro rights framework. In 2021, Chile and Spain were pioneers in adopting stringent regulations for neurotechnology: Spain introduced its Charter on Digital Rights, which addresses "digital rights in the use of neurotechnologies" and emphasizes mental autonomy, privacy, and non-discrimination. Later that year, Chile amended its Constitution to safeguard brain data, mandating that such data be regulated and processed by a government agency. This amendment, which was unanimously approved by both chambers of Chile's Congress, recognizes "brain activity and the information derived from it" as a fundamental right. Additionally, the Chilean Senate passed a neuroprotection bill. In Brazil, the State of Rio Grande do Sul recently enacted legislation to protect brain activity and data. Uruguay has introduced a neuro rights bill in the Chamber of Deputies, and in the United States, Colorado, Minnesota, and California are developing state laws to protect neural data.[113]

The General Assembly of the State of Colorado has just enacted a bill that expands the definition of "sensitive data" to include "biological data" and "neural data".

The data the brain produces is indeed unlike any other data enabling unique forms of insight into the individual and reflecting mental processing associated with thoughts, moods, feelings, and personality.[114] Neural data is capable of revealing enormously sensitive information about the people from whom it was collected, including identifiable information about their mental health, physical health, and cognitive processing. Currently not specifically protected by regulation, neural data is just as sensitive as protected medical data. Neural data could afford companies unprecedented levels of insight into the cognitive states and inner worlds of

---

[109] For an overview of the criticisms see Brown (2024)

[110] Ligthart et al. (2023).

[111] Brown (2024).

[112] Wexler and Reiner (2019).

[113] Genser et al. (2024).

[114] Hallinan et al. (2014).

consumers. Such information vests commercial entities with alarming knowledge and power over intimate dimensions of user's mental and social lives.[115]

In the coming years, neural data databases will function similarly to how genetic and biometric databases function. Hence, some claim that the regulation of genetic data may serve as templates for the regulation of neurodata.[116]

As previously discussed, studies have found that when paired with generative AI, brain scans from non-invasive neurotechnologies allowed for the decoding of language, emotions, and imagery with high levels of accuracy.[117]

The human brain carries terabytes of valuable data. In the world of neuroscience, big data is truly, epically big.[118]

In the future, more investments will result in improvements to the technical capabilities of both neurotechnology and multimodal digital technologies, affording increased resolution of brain scans and larger datasets of mental data being collected, while generative artificial intelligence will accelerate the ability to accurately decode these data.

Since these developments have the aforesaid significant implications for mental privacy, we should put additional pressure on lawmakers.

Within the European Union, today, there is enormous ambiguity regarding whether neural data are to be considered a form of personal data: it is not clear whether data collected through neurotechnologies can be per se qualified as "personal data" under art. 4(1) of GDPR (even without any other identifier). In this respect, it can be reasonably assessed that neural data and brain data are personal if, in combination with other data, allow to single out a data subject.[119]

The subsequent legal issue to be addressed is obviously whether neural data, brain data, and, more in general, data concerning emotional states can or should be comprised within the special categories of personal data referred to in Art. 9 GDPR when they do not concern the health of a data subject.[120]

---

115 Kreitmair (2019).

116 Hallinan et al. (2014)

117 Minielly et al. (2020)..

118 Landhuis (2017).

119 On the concept of personal data see Gruppo di lavoro art. 29, Opinion n. 4/2007 on the concept of personal data, WP136, (20.06.2007): «in general terms, a natural person can be considered as "identified" when, within a group of persons, he or she is "distinguished" from all other members of the group». Actually, the jurisprudence of the Court of Justice of the European Union has gradually expanded the concept of personal data. For an overview of the most relevant case law on the matter see Sposini (2024, 330ff).

120 Montinaro (2024).

10 Calling for "Mental Data" Protection

A preliminary review suggests that current legal standards, in the European Union legal framework, may require further interpretation or amendment to ensure that mental data (including neural data) fall unambiguously within the highest standard of legal protections: *i.e.*, within the protection of art. 9 GDPR.[121]

To bolster human rights protection, the European legislator should consider the idea of introducing a new special category of personal data among those referred to in art. 9 GDPR: the "mental data" (*i.e.*, data referring to mental features of an individual) which should include "neural data" (*i.e.*, information concerning the activity of an individual's central nervous system or peripheral nervous systems, including the brain and spinal cord, and that can be processed by or with the assistance of a device). Mental data indeed entails all data about human brain structure, activity, and function, from neurobiological metrics, like EEG and fMRI, to non-neural data such as smartphone usage patterns.[122]

In the meantime, to regulate the process of mental data we could apply existing provisions on medical data either by analogy or extensively interpreting the concept of "mental health" which could be broadened so to include also any form of cognitive processes and affective states of the data subjects.[123] Emotions are not less "sensitive" than information about an individual's health. Mental data touches the *forum internum.* For this reason, it is probably even more "sensitive" than the data expressly mentioned in Art. 9 of GDPR.

Neural data in particular is electrical in nature and therefore is not necessarily covered by standard definitions of biometric data. It is even more difficult to qualify as sensitive data the emotion-related data inferred from written tests or voice records. For this reason, it would be valuable if the GDPR could specify that even indirect inferences affecting human emotions could be qualified as a "special category" of personal data. It could be reasonable to affirm that art. 9 (1) GDPR comes into application when the recognition of emotions based on the physical, physiological, and behavioral characteristics of the natural persons has the purpose of inferencing 'sensitive' data relating to an identifiable or identified individual.[124]

As clarified above, information about emotions can be derived from brain observation but can also be inferred by data analytics based on retrospective data mining, pattern recognition, and aggregation of various data both physiological and non-physiological.[125]

Moreover, is to be remarked that legal consent is not required to capture data about emotions that are not personal: *i.e.*, capable of (directly or indirectly) identifying or singling out a person. The GDPR does not apply to personal data that has been

---

[121] To which also the aforementioned art. 18 of the reg. EU 2024/900 on the transparency and targeting of political advertisement expressly refers.

[122] Ienca et al. (2022).

[123] Ienca and Malgieri (2022).

[124] Montinaro (2024).

[125] Ienca and Malgieri (2022).

adequately anonymized to ensure the individual can no longer be identified. But data that may be anonymous today could turn out to not be anonymous tomorrow, first of all, due to technological progress.[126] There are privacy implications even when emotional AI practices use non-personally identifying data about people to infer human emotions.[127]

In summary, there are normative gaps mostly because: (*i*) the list contained in Art. 9 GDPR is not comprehensive enough since it does not include mental data: the GDPR does not protect under the strict regime of Art. 9 personal data which are not related to the sensitive areas of health, sexuality, religious or political beliefs, etc. Emotions and moods would often be qualified as non-sensitive data, falling under the general regime set in Art. 6 of the GDPR[128]; (*ii*) the individual participation rights approach in the EU data protection law is inadequate: the concrete operation of individual rights granted by GDPR is sometimes difficult since we cannot understand which risks are involved in our privacy choices, especially with AI inferences.[129] The EU legislation does not address many of the modern data-processing initiatives involving large data sets since it either refers to personal data, which are strictly regulated, or to non-personal data, which are intentionally left unregulated. Whereas data-driven applications using Big Data, Artificial Intelligence and profiling techniques often do not rely on personal data, but make use of general data, statistical information and group profiles.[130,131] We are underestimating the risks involved in the process of anonymised personal data and still adopting an anthropocentric and individualistic approach[132].

New technologies and powerful analytics allow for the collection and analysis of large amounts of data that enable few gatekeepers of knowledge[133] to identify patterns in the behaviour of groups, communities, and even entire countries, extracting predictive inferences. The GDPR instead embraces an atomistic approach, which shows limits in the context of mass predictive analysis. It fails to take into account the collective dimension of data protection. Whereas, it would be important (*i*) to combine individual remedies with collective remedies and (*ii*) to recognise the role of entities representing collective interests since data subjects are often unable to negotiate their information and are unaware of the potential underlying prejudices.[134] Changes in

[126] Hallinan et al. (2014).

[127] McStay (2020).

[128] Ienca and Malgieri (2022).

[129] Cofone (2023).

[130] Taylor et al. (2017).

[131] Van der Sloot (2021) interestingly argues that the ECtHR "quality of life doctrine" could be used to broaden the scope of art. 8 ECHR: governments should have an obligation to inform citizens about the fact that data-driven applications might impact the quality of their lives, even when no personal data would be gathered.

[132] Floridi (2014).

[133] Control over information deriving from Big Data is not accessible to everyone, mainly because it is based on expensive technologies and specific human skills. For this reason, governments and big business are in the most favourable position to benefit from Big Data. See Mantelero (2014).

[134] Mantelero (2016).

individual-centered privacy paradigm appear to be necessary since the main issues in the Big Data era, with the expansion of the Internet of Things, transcend individuals. We need to protect nonpersonal data and grant a bigger role for representative and collective actions.[135]

In order to protect the right to privacy some called for a completely different construction of the law which shields the individual from external interference and defines boundaries to protect the *forum internum.*[136]

Notwithstanding the shortcomings, the GDPR still offers important safeguards: under EU data protection rules, according to the purpose limitation principle, the process of brain data or neural data collected for a specified, explicit, and legitimate purpose such as, for example, health self-monitoring could not be processed for commercial purposes; sensitive neural or brain data would be lawfully processed only under one of the conditions set by art. 9 (2) of the GDPR.

It could also be argued that the evaluation of the emotional state of a person for marketing purposes constitutes an automated processing pursuant to Art. 22 GDPR, when it implies a significant impact on the rights (including fundamental rights) of the data subject.[137] Moreover, under art. 35 GDPR processing of mental data that violates fundamental rights could be prevented in advance.[138] The risk assessment obligations represent a more effective tool than information requirements since they mitigate harm upstream before products and services are placed on the market. The preventive approach based on *ex ante* risk assessments appears to be more efficient than *ex post* legal actions.[139] The main issue with this tool is that it mainly relies on self-assessment.[140]

To enhance the regulatory framework, an option would be to modify Art. 5 of the AIA to include among the AI systems subject to the prohibitions envisioned therein AI profiling systems for marketing purposes that process special categories of personal data under Art. 9 (1) GDPR[141], including mental data.

In conclusion, even if the EU legislation offers safeguards against the potential harms of emotional AI, novel measures should strengthen the protection of mental privacy[142] and make sure that governments and companies properly safeguard not only neural data but any personal data that might be representative of

---

[135] Van der Sloot and van Schendel (2021).

[136] Hallinan et al. (2014).

[137] The effectiveness of this provision is a matter of debate. Indeed, is uncertain whether it establishes a right or a prohibition. Secondly, the meaning of "legal effects" and "significantly affects" is not clear. In any case, is easy for the processor to use one of the exceptions envisioned in paragraph 2. See De Mari Casareto dal Verme (2023).

[138] Montinaro (2024).

[139] Moreover, it contributes to address the risks of hidden forms of data processing. See Mantelero (2014).

[140] Fassiaux (2023).

[141] Orlando (2022).

[142] In order to protect mental freedom Bublitz and Merkel suggested to introduce a new criminal offence. See Bublitz and Merkel (2014).

mental features[143] however collected.[144] Despite the hype surrounding neuro rights, the necessity for stringent regulations governing emotional AI and neurotechnology advancements—especially their impact on agency, free will, consent, privacy, and data protection—remains crucial.[145]

In light of possible data leaks, there is a need for closer monitoring of the private sector's use of brain data.[146]

More efforts in educating the public are also necessary since there is an evident gap in consumers' understanding of their mental data. Consumers should be able to better comprehend the implications of data that neurotechnologies and other mind-reading technologies can capture.[147]

To protect the privacy of brain data, we should increase 'data literacy' in society.[148]

Moreover, public EU legislation on consumers' protection should question its premises[149] and self-determination should be secured 'per se' irrespective of situations resulting in misperceptions and/or mistakes.[150]

The current EU legal framework appears not fully capable of adequately accommodating the most recent technological developments. Neither the GDPR nor the DSA nor the AIA seem sufficient on their own. Nonetheless, the existing legislation offers several meaningful tools. Academics should therefore not only monitor the implementation of AI regulation and increase pressure on lawmakers but also promote a better coordination of existing European legislative acts[151] especially of the Artificial Intelligence Act with the Digital Services Act[152] and the GDPR. It is fundamental to recalibrate legal safeguards and to ponder the adoption of a more holistic approach.[153]

In light of the threats brought about by the deployment of emotional AI within the context of the data-driven economy, more studies are pivotal. Academics must contribute to shaping a regulatory framework that aims at preventing the targeting

143 Brown (2024).

144 Ienca (2017).

145 Gilbert and Russo (2024).

146 Huang et al (2024)

147 Huang et al. (2024).

148 Kellmeyer (2021).

149 In the classical economic model, the consumer is a rational agent. Cognitive psychology, though, has shown that most decisions are taken with the irrational part of the brain. The rational choice model is utopic. Consumers are subject to cognitive biases and emotions are one of the main factors determining economic choices. See in particular Kahneman (2011); Sunstein (2000). On the concept of "bounded rationality" see Simon (1972); Simon (1979, 65–85, 493–514); Simon (1987); Zamir and Teichman (2018).

150 De Mari Casareto dal Verme (2023).

151 Orlando (2022).

152 Tuccari (2024).

153 See Mantelero (2022), who advocates for an assessment model that overcomes the limitations of the current assessment models, considering the impact of data processing on fundamental rights and collective social and ethical values (Human Rights, Ethical and Social Impact Assessment-HRESIA).

of cognitive or emotional weakness and governs the use of emotional AI in shaping public opinion to safeguard electoral integrity and democracy.[154] We need to ensure effective protection against manipulative emotional profiling for business or political goals.

Scholars should further explore interpretative solutions to fill in the gaps of the existing legislation, without relying only on future reforms. Research shall continue to further deeper investigate how to foster a regulatory environment that, in order to boost societal and economic progress, finds a balance between the promotion of innovation and defense of cognitive liberty and human dignity, advancing a modern approach to privacy and data protection to properly deal with the ongoing Big Data revolution and the rise of new forms of human vulnerability in the era of digital capitalism.

References

Alegre S (2021) Protecting freedom of thought in the digital age. Policy Brief No. 165. Centre for International Governance Innovation. https://www.cigionline.org/publications/protecting-freedom-of-thought-in-the-digital-age

Ananny M, Crawford K (2018) Seeing without knowing: limitations of the transparency ideal and its application to algorithmic accountability. New Media Soc 20(3):973–989. https://doi.org/10.1177/1461444816676645

Bakir V, McStay A (2020) Empathic media, emotional AI, and the optimization of disinformation. In: Boler M, Davis E (eds) Affective politics of digital media, Routledge, p 263

Bakir V, McStay A (2022) Profiling, targeting and the increasing optimisation of emotional life. In: Optimising emotions, incubating falsehoods. Palgrave Macmillan, Cham. https://doi.org/10.1007/978-3-031-13551-4_6

Barrett L (2006) Are emotions natural kinds? Perspect Psychol Sci 1(1):34

Barrett LF, Adolphs R, Marsella S, Martinez AM, Pollak SD (2019) Emotional expressions reconsidered: challenges to inferring emotion from human facial movements. Psychological Science in the Public Interest 20(1):1–68

Brown CML (2024) Neurorights, mental privacy, and mind reading. Neuroethics 17 (2): 34 available at: https://doi.org/10.1007/s12152-024-09568-z

Bublitz JC, Merkel R (2014) Crimes against minds: on mental manipulations, harms and a human right to mental self-determination. Crim Law & Philos 8:51–77

Burr C, Cristianini N (2019) Can machines read our minds? Minds Mach 29:463

Clifford D (2019) The legal limits to the monetisation of online emotions. PhD thesis, KU Leuven, Faculty of Law, p 110

Clifford D (2020) Citizen-consumers in a personalised galaxy: emotion influenced decision-making, a true path to the dark side? In: Edwards L, Harbinja E, Shaffer B (eds) Future Law: Emerging Technology. Edinburgh University Press, Regulation and Ethics

Cofone I (2023) The privacy fallacy. Oxford University Press

Crivelli C, Carrera P, Fernández-Dols JM (2015) Are smiles a sign of happiness? Spontaneous expressions of judo winners. Evol Hum Behav 36:52–58

D'Aloia A (2020) Law challenged. Reasoning about neuroscience and law. In: D'Aloia A, Errigo MC (eds) Neurosciences and law: complicated crossings and new perspectives, Springer, p 1 ff

[154] Simchon et al. (2024).

Casareto DM, dal Verme T (2023) Artificial intelligence, neuroscience and emotional data. What role for private autonomy in the digital market? Erasmus Law Rev 3:83–97. https://doi.org/10.5553/ELR.000257

Dibeklioglu H, Salah AA, Gevers T (2015) Recognition of genuine smiles. IEEE Trans Multimed 17:279–294. https://doi.org/10.1109/TMM.2015.2394777

Du S, Tao Y, Martinez AM (2014) Compound facial expressions of emotion. Proc Natl Acad Sci USA 111(15):1–9

Ekman P, Friesen WV (1978) Facial action coding system: a technique for the measurement of facial movement. Consulting Psychologists Press, Palo Alto, CA. https://doi.org/10.1037/t27734-000

Ekman P, Keltner D (1997) Universal facial expressions of emotion. In: Segerstrale U, Molnar P (eds) Nonverbal communication: where nature meets culture, California Mental Health Research Digest, San Francisco, CA, pp 27–46

Errigo MC (2020a) Neuroenhancement and Law. In: D'Aloia A, Errigo MC (eds) (2020) Neurosciences and Law: complicated crossings and new perspectives, Springer, p. 208 ff. (the Author is against a total ban and in favour of a reasoned narrow approach)

Errigo MC (2020b) Neuroscienze, tecnologia e diritti: problemi nuovi e ipotesi di tutela. Dirittifondamentali.it 3:215–245

European Commission (2023) State of the art of neuromarketing and its ethical implications, 2023:27 https://op.europa.eu/en/publication-detail/-/publication/43754ac8-26aa-11eea2d3-01aa75ed71a1/language-en

Farahany N (2023) The battle for your brain: defending the right to think freely in the age of neurotechnology. St. Martin's Press

Fassiaux S (2023) Preserving consumer autonomy through European Union regulation of artificial intelligence: a long-term approach. Eur J Risk Regul 14:710–730. https://doi.org/10.1017/err.2023.58

Feldman D (1999) Human dignity as a legal value. Public Law 4:688

Floridi L (2014) Open data, data protection, and group privacy. Philos Technol 27:1–3. https://doi.org/10.1007/s13347-014-0157-8

Galli F (2022) Algorithmic marketing and EU law on unfair commercial practices. Rethinking consumer protection with AI. Springer, Cham

Gatt L, Caggiano IA (2022) Consumers and digital environments as a structural vulnerability relationship. Eur J Priv Law Technol 2:12

Genser J, Damianos S, Yuste R (2024) Safeguarding brain data: assessing the privacy practices of consumer neurotechnology companies

Gerd G (2020) What is bounded rationality? Routledge

Gilbert F, Russo I (2024) Mind-reading in AI and neurotechnology: evaluating claims, hype, and ethical implications for neurorights. AI Ethics 4:855–872. https://doi.org/10.1007/s43681-024-00514-6

Global Neurotech Industry Investment Digest (2021) Deep knowledge group for EIN News, July 14, 2021, available at https://www.einnews.com/pr_news/546252348/global-neurotech-industry-investment-digest-2021

Hallinan D, Schütz P, Friedewald M, De Hert P (2014) Neurodata and neuroprivacy: data protection outdated? Surveill Soc 12(1):55–72

Haselager P (2013) Did I do that? Brain–computer interfacing and the sense of agency. Minds Mach 23(3):405–418

Huang E et al (2024) U.S. public perceptions of the sensitivity of brain data. J Law Biosci 11(1):1–20. https://doi.org/10.1093/jlb/lsad032

Ienca M (2015) Neuroprivacy, neurosecurity and brain-hacking: emerging issues in neural engineering. Bioethica Forum 8(2):51–53

Ienca M (2017) The right to cognitive liberty. Sci Am 317(2):10

Ienca M, Andorno R (2017) Towards new human rights in the age of neuroscience and neurotechnology. Life Sci Soc Policy 13(1):5

Ienca M, Fins JJ, Jox RJ, Jotterand F, Voeneky S, Andorno R, Ball T, Castelluccia C, Chavarriaga R, Chneiweiss H, Ferretti A (2022) Towards a governance framework for brain data. Neuroethics 15:20
Ienca M, Haselager P (2016) Hacking the brain: brain–computer interfacing technology and the ethics of neurosecurity. Ethics Inf Technol 18(2):117–129
Ienca M, Haselager P, Emanuel EJ (2018) Brain leaks and consumer neurotechnology. Nat Biotechnol 36:805–810
Ienca M, Malgieri G (2022) Mental data protection and the GDPR. J Law Biosci 9(1). https://doi.org/10.1093/jlb/lsac006
Kahneman D (2011) Thinking, fast and slow, Farrar, Straus and Giroux;. In: Kahneman D, Tversky A (eds) Choices, values, and frames, Cambridge University Press, 2000
Kellmeyer P (2021) Big brain data: on the responsible use of brain data from clinical and consumer-directed neurotechnological devices. Neuroethics 14:83–98
Kollmer T, Eckhardt A (2023) Dark patterns. Bus Inf 65:201–208. https://doi.org/10.1007/s12599-022-00783-7
Krausová A (2014) Legal aspects of brain–computer interfaces. Masaryk Univ J Law Technol 8(2):199–208
Kreitmair KV (2019) Dimensions of ethical direct-to-consumer neurotechnologies. AJOB Neurosci 10(4):152–166
Landhuis E (2017) Neuroscience: big brain, big data. Nature 541(7638):559–561
LeCun Y, Bengio Y, Hinton G (2015) Deep learning. Nature 521:436–444
Ligthart S, Bublitz C, Alegre S (2023) Neurotechnology: we need new laws, not new rights. Nature 620(7976):950
Malgieri G (2023) Who is the vulnerable individual? In Vulnerability and data protection law. Oxford University Press
Mantelero A (2014) Social control, transparency, and participation in the big data world. J Internet L.: 23–29
Mantelero A (2016) Personal data for decisional purposes in the age of analytics: from an individual to a collective dimension of data protection. Comput Law Secur Rev 32(2):238–255
Mantelero A (2022) Beyond data: human rights, ethical and social impact assessment in AI Springer
Matz SC, Kosinski M, Nave G, Stillwell DJ (2017) Psychological targeting as an effective approach to digital mass persuasion. Proc Natl Acad Sci USA 114(48):12714–12719
McStay A (2016) Empathic media and advertising: industry, policy, legal and citizen perspectives (the Case for Intimacy) BD&S 3(1): 3–6
McStay A (2018) Emotional AI: the rise of empathic media. Sage, London
McStay A (2020) Emotional AI, soft biometrics and the surveillance of emotional life: an unusual consensus on privacy. Big Data Soc 7(1)
McStay A (2023) Automating empathy: decoding technologies that Gauge Intimate Life. Oxford University Press
Minielly N, Hrincu V, Illes J (2020) Privacy challenges to the democratization of brain data. iScience 23:101134. https://doi.org/10.1016/j.isci.2020.101134
Mollo AA (2023) Vulnerabilità e sostenibilità: primi spunti per uno studio dell'impatto sulle persone con disabilità e sulle future generazioni dei dispositivi [neuro]tecnologici. Eur J Priv Law and Technol: 28–49
Montinaro R (2024) Riconoscimento delle emozioni e marketing personalizzato. Persona e Mercato 3:847–894
Orlando S (2022) Regole di immissione sul mercato e «pratiche di intelligenza artificiale» vietate nella proposta di Artificial Intelligence Act. Persona e Mercato 3:346–367
Parenzo B (2024) Neuromarketing: Un inventario di (spuntati) divieti contro il pericolo di una scelta manipolata. Persona e Mercato 2:539–558
Pasquale F (2015) The black box society: the secret algorithms that control money and information. Harvard University Press

Pasquale F (2024) Enforcing and expanding legal protections for vulnerable subjects. In: Crea C, De Franceschi A (eds) The new shapes of digital vulnerability in European Private Law, Nomos, p 21 ff. https://doi.org/10.5771/9783748940913
Rhue L (2019) Affectively mistaken? How human augmentation and information transparency offset algorithmic failures in emotion recognition AI. SSRN. https://doi.org/10.2139/ssrn.3492129
Rude S, Gortner EM, Pennebaker J (2004) Language use of depressed and depression-vulnerable college students. Cogn Emot 18:1121–1133
Ruffolo U, Amidei A (2024) Diritto dell'Intelligenza Artificiale, vol. I, LUISS University Press, p 193 ff
Russell JA (1994) Is there universal recognition of emotion from facial expression? A review of the cross-cultural studies. Psychol Bull 115(1):102–141. https://doi.org/10.1037/0033-2909.115.1.102
Simchon A, Edwards M, Lewandowsky S (2024) The persuasive effects of political microtargeting in the age of generative artificial intelligence. PNAS Nexus 3(2):35. https://doi.org/10.1093/pnasnexus/pgae035
Simchon A, Sutton A, Edwards M, Lewandowsky S (2023) Online reading habits can reveal personality traits: towards detecting psychological microtargeting. PNAS Nexus. 2(6):gad191
Simon A (1972) Theories of bounded rationality. In: Decision and organization: a volume in Honor of Jacob Marschak, C.B. McGuire and Roy Radner (eds) Minneapolis, University of Minnesota Press pp 161–176
Simon HA (1979) From substantive to procedural rationality. In: Hahn F, Hollis M (eds) Philosophy and economic theory. Oxford University Press, Oxford, pp 65–85
Simon HA (1987) Bounded rationality. In: Eatwell J, Milgate M, Newman P (eds) The new palgrave—Utility and probability. Norton, New York, W.W, pp 15–18
Simoncini A, Longo E (2021) Fundamental rights and the rule of law in the algorithmic society. In: Micklitz HW (ed) Constitutional challenges in the algorithmic society, Cambridge University Press, p 35
Singla C, Singh S, Sharma P et al (2024) Emotion recognition for human–computer interaction using high-level descriptors. Sci Rep 14:12122. https://doi.org/10.1038/s41598-024-59294-y
Sposini L (2024) Neuromarketing and eye-tracking technologies under the European framework: towards the GDPR and beyond. J Consum Policy 47:321–344. https://doi.org/10.1007/s10603-023-09559-2
Stark L, Crawford K (2015) The conservatism of emoji: work, affect, and communication. Social Media+Society 1: 1–11
Stark L, Hutson J (2021) Physiognomic artificial intelligence. Fordham Intell Prop Media Entertain Law J. https://ssrn.com/abstract=3927300 or https://doi.org/10.2139/ssrn.3927300
Steindl E (2024) Consumer neuro devices within EU product safety law: are we prepared for big tech ante portas? Comput Law Secur Rev 52:105945. https://doi.org/10.1016/j.clsr.2024.105945
Sunstein CR (2000) Behavioral law and economics. Cambridge University Press
Taylor L, Floridi L, Van Der Sloot B (eds) (2017) Group privacy, Springer
Thaler RH, Sunstein CR (2008) Nudge: improving decisions about health, wealth, and happiness. Yale University Press
Tuccari E (2024) Neuromarketing: Un'asistematica disciplina... oltre il consenso? Persona e Mercato 2:511–537
Valcke P, Clifford D, Dessers VK (2021) Constitutional challenges in the emotional AI era. In: Micklitz HW, Pollicino O, Reichman A, Simoncini A, Sartor G, De Gregorio G (eds) Constitutional challenges in the algorithmic society, Cambridge University Press, p 65 ff
Van der Sloot B (2021) The quality of life: protecting non-personal interests and non-personal data in the age of big data. Eur Rev Priv Law 29(5):757–784
van der Sloot B, van Schendel S (2021) Procedural law for the data-driven society. Info Comm Tech L 30(3):304–332

Warner J, Sloan RH (2014) Self, privacy, and power: is it all over? Tulane J Technol Intellect Prop. 17:61–118. https://ssrn.com/abstract=2401165

Wexler A, Reiner PB (2019) Oversight of direct-to-consumer neurotechnologies. Science 363(6424):234–235

Wright J (2021) Suspect AI: vibraimage, emotion recognition technology and algorithmic opacity. Sci Technol Soc 1–20. https://doi.org/10.1177/09717218211003411

Yeung K (2017) 'Hypernudge': Big data as a mode of regulation by design. Inf Commun Soc 20(1):118–136. https://doi.org/10.1080/1369118X.2016.1186713

Yuste R, Genser J, Herrmann S (2021) It's time for neurorights: new human rights for the age of neurotechnology. Horizons 18:154–155

Zamir E and Teichman D (2018) Behavioral law and economics. Oxford University Press

Ziegler K (2007) Introduction: human rights and private law—Privacy as autonomy. In: Ziegler K (ed) Human rights and private law: privacy as autonomy, Hart Publishing, 1st ed

Zuboff S (2018) The age of surveillance capitalism: the fight for a human future at the new frontier of power, Public Affairs

Claudia Confortini, Teaches Private Law, Contract and Obligations Law, Media Law, and Private Law for Tourism at Tor Vergata University of Rome. Author of books and articles on Contracts and Obligations Law, Company Law, Digital Media Law, and Consumer Law. Lawyer and member of "Unione dei Privatisti." Currently working on the DiVE project.

Open Access This chapter is licensed under the terms of the Creative Commons Attribution 4.0 International License (http://creativecommons.org/licenses/by/4.0/), which permits use, sharing, adaptation, distribution and reproduction in any medium or format, as long as you give appropriate credit to the original author(s) and the source, provide a link to the Creative Commons license and indicate if changes were made.

The images or other third party material in this chapter are included in the chapter's Creative Commons license, unless indicated otherwise in a credit line to the material. If material is not included in the chapter's Creative Commons license and your intended use is not permitted by statutory regulation or exceeds the permitted use, you will need to obtain permission directly from the copyright holder.

Human Vulnerability in Interactions with Digital Health—the Need for Ethics in AI Processing of Health and Genomic Data

Maria Anastasia Arcuri

Abstract Healthcare is undergoing a digital transformation through Artificial Intelligence (AI) systems, which collect and process vast amounts of personal health and genomic data. However, the processing of such data by AI systems and human–machine interactions can generate biases and place human beings in situations of vulnerability. The primary—and even more so, the secondary—use of these types of data by AI systems can, on the one hand, contribute to scientific research and lead to advances in disease prevention and treatment. On the other hand, it risks endangering the rule of law, with the uncertainty of distorted, opaque, or harmful decisions that could result in discrimination or violations of human rights. In recent years, the need for robust international regulatory support has become increasingly clear in Europe, aiming to successfully balance the protection of personal health and genomic data with their use by AI systems. The GDPR and the AI Act stand as strong expressions of this effort. By briefly referring to the French, German, and Spanish experiences—as the main countries compared with Italy—the aim is to identify the key legal frameworks concerning the secondary use of health and genomic personal data for scientific and clinical research purposes. Legal frameworks designed to safeguard individuals from new forms of vulnerability created by digital healthcare—or from pre-existing vulnerabilities exacerbated by the technologically advanced nature of society—must be profoundly connected to ethical principles. The European legislator's primary objectives are to promote transparency in AI systems and to foster trust in their use. The more AI systems are built on principles of transparency, the better they can prevent risks related to unreliability and inspire public confidence.

Keywords Digital health · Secondary use of personal health and genetic data · Bias · Human vulnerability · Ethics and AI

M. A. Arcuri (✉)
University of Rome Tor Vergata, Rome, Italy
e-mail: mariaanastasia.arcuri@yahoo.it

© The Author(s) 2025

C. Amodio and A. Diurni (eds.), *Human Vulnerability in Interaction with AI in European Private Law*, https://doi.org/10.1007/978-3-031-93247-2_8

1 Introduction

The digitalization and telecommunication of healthcare contribute to its effectiveness by enhancing active prevention efforts, improving the retrieval and exchange of information among healthcare professionals and patients, and simplifying access to medical data.

In the healthcare sector, professionals and researchers must correlate thousands of biomedical variables with personal information (such as lifestyle and work environment) to obtain significant results for medical research. This process requires considerable effort, time, and resources, which can now be streamlined through advanced technologies.

The digital transformation of healthcare is primarily being carried out through the use of Artificial Intelligence (AI).[1] AI systems (such as language processing,[2] machine learning, and machine vision[3]) are capable of performing tasks that typically require human intelligence. Their function centers on the collection and processing of vast volumes of data (big data), enabling predictive analytics and automated decision-making, even in complex domains like healthcare.[4]

To be effectively trained and competitive in the healthcare market, AI systems require a continuous flow of healthcare and genomic data,[5] most of which is personal. These data must be robust, secure, and of high quality.[6]

The data to be processed must be collected in digital format and linked with numerous other pieces of information in order to enhance the effectiveness and quality of healthcare services. Moreover, personal health and genomic data can be used not only for direct patient care (so-called primary use of personal health and genomic data) but also, whens shared and reused, for public health interventions, scientific and historical research, and legislative or policy purposes (so-called secondary use of personal health and genomic data).

It is precisely the secondary use of personal health and genomic data by AI systems that can lead to a significant improvement in public health and, as a result, individual well-being. It also fosters advances in medicine toward personalization, prediction, prevention, and patient participation.

Among the key objectives of AI in healthcare is the identification of patterns that enable medical professionals to make more informative diagnoses, guide treatment

---

[1] Cascini et al. (2023a).

[2] Algorithms designed for language analysis and comprehension.

[3] Algorithms designed for image interpretation and recognition.

[4] AI's potential in health care is possible by improving data quality that power AI, building infrastructure to encourage efficient and trustworthy development and evaluations, sharing data for better AI, and providing incentives to accelerate the progress and impact of AI. See Silcox et al. (2024).

In particular, the digitalization of healthcare services promotes "precision healthcare," supporting the sustainability of healthcare systems. For further information on this topic see Cascini et al. (2022).

[5] Giannini (2020).

[6] High-quality data refers to data that accurately represents the reality to which it pertains and can be used in decision-making processes without introducing ambiguity or errors.

decisions, predict prognoses, and assess treatment responses over time. For instance, recognizing a clinical pattern allows physicians to determine a treatment, estimate a prognosis based on the most common progression of a condition, and evaluate treatment effectiveness by quantitatively monitoring characteristic signs and symptoms over weeks or months.

Beyond cross-referencing vast datasets, AI systems in healthcare are beginning to leverage predictive and generative capabilities, combining quantitative analysis with more advanced qualitative actions. This integration enables more efficient and timely healthcare service delivery, such as providing doctors with AI-assisted comparative analyses of patient medical records.

In practice, predictive and generative AI applications can facilitate access to remote healthcare, diagnoses, and medical consultations, allow continuous monitoring of vital parameters—sometimes imperceptibly to the patient—and enable proactive patient care by alerting healthcare providers when necessary.[7] Furthermore, these AI tools can help predict treatment outcomes, assisting doctors and pharmacists in calibrating and personalizing medical and pharmaceutical treatments based on the individual's characteristics, including genetic factors. These advances increase the accuracy of prevention measures. Additionally, AI can drive scientific research progress and improve public health planning, prevention, and crisis management.

While AI-driven healthcare offers numerous benefits, it also comes with significant risks.[8] The use of personal health and genomic data by AI tools and human-machine interactions in healthcare settings can sometimes introduce bias and place individuals in vulnerable situations.

The digital environment not only reproduces pre-existing human vulnerabilities found in other sectors,[9] but also creates new ones. Specifically, individuals may experience different types of vulnerability due to healthcare digitalization, such as: algorithmic discrimination, which can arise from the way personal health and genomic data are used or the purposes for which they are processed by AI systems; data retention and repurposing, where personal health and genomic data are stored beyond the intended period and used for purposes different from those initially agreed upon; inadequate anonymization, particularly of genetic data, which can inadvertently reveal predispositions to future diseases.

The following reflections on healthcare digitalization aim to identify some of the threats posed by AI's use of personal health and genomic data, particularly generative

---

[7] For example, through the new digital model of Italian Integrated Home Care (ADI), whose features are discussed and analyzed in terms of strengths, challenges, and future implications in the article by Cascini et al. (2023b).

[8] Interesting insights emerge from regional projects in Italy focused on the processing of health data for medical, biomedical, and epidemiological research. See, for example, Poddighe (2024).

[9] AI often relies on machine learning systems, which, due to their ability to learn and discover correlations within a given dataset, pose a certain risk of discrimination regardless of the field of application. This issue is not limited to healthcare but represents a real challenge with implications across various aspects of daily life, from healthcare to justice, as well as education and the labor market.

AI. This analysis will examine European and national regulations[10] to assess their ability—or lack thereof—to protect individuals from the vulnerabilities they may face due to AI-driven healthcare digitalization.

2 The Digitalization of Healthcare: The Emergence of Biases

The digitalization of healthcare, significantly advanced through the use of predictive and generative Artificial Intelligence (AI) tools, is demonstrating remarkable effectiveness, particularly in techno-assistance, telemedicine, and the Electronic Health Record (EHR). This transformation has led to the development of cutting-edge treatments, therapeutic innovations, and more efficient healthcare service management.

AI systems operate based on advanced algorithmic models that ingest information—initially through a pre-training phase—and then generate new insights.

Digital healthcare is built upon a healthcare ecosystem known as Connected Care, which enables patients to access their health information through integrated and interoperable digital platforms. These digital platforms facilitate the sharing of information among the various players involved in the care process, including patients, doctors, nurses, healthcare providers in the community and at home, pharmacies, insurance companies, and researchers.

The most significant expression of Connected Care and, more broadly, of digital healthcare in Italy, is the Electronic Health Record (EHR), introduced in 2012[11] to dematerialize medical reports and clinical records and to facilitate cross-border information exchange, contributing to European healthcare projects. The EHR contains various data concerning patients' medical histories and is accessible to both patients and healthcare providers, ensuring the portability of health data when care is received in regions other than a patient's residence. This tool ensures the availability of personal health data to those who need it, enabling better care. Additionally, the EHR allows citizens to access various services, acting as a centralized platform for scheduling medical tests and examinations.

Alongside the EHR, the healthcare system is becoming increasingly sustainable, remote, and interconnected, thanks to telemedicine. Telemedicine allows patients to visit hospitals only when strictly necessary, while managing all other situations remotely. It serves as a key tool for creating a healthcare system that effectively meets citizens' needs. It primarily relies on the Internet of Medical Things (IoMT),

---

[10] At the conclusion of the investigation conducted for this study, Regulation 2025/327 on the European Health Data Space (EHDS) was introduced in Europe, and the Health Data Ecosystem (EDS) was introduced in Italy. Therefore, EHDS and EDS are not analyzed for the purposes of this study, although their developments over time may give rise to future research.

[11] Decreto Legge 18 ottobre 2012 n. 179 in https://www.normattiva.it/uri-res/N2Ls?urn:nir:stato:decreto.legge:2012;179.

which enables remote access to healthcare services, specialized medical consultations (telemedicine), and constant monitoring of vital signs (telehealth), often in a way that is not perceived by the patient (teleassistance). Patients with chronic illnesses, who require continuous monitoring of certain vital parameters, benefit most from telemedicine. Continuous assistance reduces the risk of complications. Together, the Electronic Health Record and telemedicine contribute to the execution of clinical processes, service provision for users and professionals, and the collection of vast amounts of healthcare data. These data are increasingly leveraged by generative AI systems: for instance, software is being introduced into the EHR to analyze its data and provide decision support for physicians, while in telemedicine, many medical clinics are incorporating chatbots[12] that provide automated responses based on frequently asked patient questions.

The use of clinical, genomic, metabolic, laboratory, demographic, nutritional, psychological, biological, and behavioral data by AI algorithms enables predictive analytics. AI systems, by continuously monitoring patients and analyzing their data, can formulate diagnoses more quickly. They have been tested across various fields of medicine (e.g., detecting pneumonia, lung cancer, breast cancer, fractures, neoplasms, carcinoma, melanoma, retinopathy, pediatric diseases, heart attacks, and arrhythmias). Studies show that in radiology, AI tools have achieved diagnostic accuracy surpassing that of human doctors. Similarly, in pediatrics, ophthalmology, and cardiology, AI has identified pathologies with sensitivity and specificity levels comparable to those of human experts.

AI can also simulate interactions between the human body and chemical substances, contributing to the development of new drugs and pharmacological therapies. For example, AI systems have been developed to analyze tumor proteins, detect mutations, and identify enzymes capable of producing distinctive markers in malignant cells. These advances help determine the appropriate type and dosage of drugs to administer.

Additionally, AI systems serve as valuable assistants for doctors and nurses, helping schedule appointments, fill out patient questionnaires, and handle various administrative tasks. This support reduces the bureaucratic burden on healthcare institutions and mitigates the significant imbalance between the availability of healthcare professionals and the number of patients requiring services.

[12] A chatbot is a technologically advanced program or application (software) capable of simulating and processing human conversations (written or spoken), allowing users to interact with digital devices as if they were communicating with a real person.

The benefits of AI in healthcare are undeniable, both in terms of effectiveness and efficiency. However, alongside these benefits, concerns are emerging regarding algorithmic biases associated with AI use in healthcare.[13] The rapid scientific and technological advances in the sector are exposing human vulnerabilities in interactions with AI.[14]

The primary bias in healthcare is algorithmic bias, as developers select machine-learning models, feed them data, and allow the models to train autonomously to identify patterns or make predictions based on predefined goals.[15]

The data fed into AI models and the predefined objectives reflect the choices and actions of the programmer. Just as human behavior is influenced by education, experience, and culture, AI systems are shaped by the algorithms and applications designed by their developers. These systems inevitably inherit some of the biases of their creators, influencing both data selection and goal definition. Consequently, biases can infiltrate algorithms indirectly, as they already exist within those who design AI systems.

Machine-learning systems, which underpin AI, can establish correlations between data and objectives, sometimes leading to discriminatory outcomes.[16]

What happens if algorithmic processes operate on data that primarily represents the most common cases, ignoring data from underrepresented populations? This phenomenon is known as the automation of discrimination, where biased results emerge without intentional input from designers.

Certainly, given the deep connection between human beings and their discoveries and innovations, if we as humans are the first to reduce discriminatory behaviors, the algorithmic systems we use will eventually reflect and exhibit less bias as well.

Beyond biases stemming from programmers' preconceptions, biases can also arise due to poor system design. In such cases, biases may result from technical flaws in the system's structure or from the use of an AI application in unexpected situations or by an audience that was not considered during the design phase.

The processes leading to bias in AI are not yet well understood. There are too many subjective and objective factors that can influence the functioning of AI systems. Additionally, the lack of transparency in AI operations makes it difficult to detect biases.

For users to truly benefit from AI, they must be aware of the latent discrimination embedded in AI processes. Such awareness would allow for a more informed

[13] Cross (2024). The work discusses potential biases that can arise at different stages in the AI development pipeline and how they can affect AI algorithms and clinical decision-making.

[14] Hasanzadeh et al. (2025). An interesting study on the origins of bias in healthcare AI, strategies for mitigation, and responsibilities of relevant stakeholders towards achieving fair and equitable use.

[15] Panch et al. (2019).

[16] Abràmoff et al. (2023); Gianfrancesco et al. (2018). These works outlines the potential biases that may be introduced into machine learning-based clinical decision support tools that use electronic health record data and how to identify and mitigate inequities.

and effective assessment of AI's usefulness in various applications, as well as the identification of appropriate cases of use.[17]

In order to prevent biases, is it enough to educate users on how AI works? Should users be warned about potential biases? Is training on AI's advantages and disadvantages?

To answer these questions, we must delve deeper into the mechanics of AI systems so as to better understand the implications of their use.

3 The Secondary Use of Personal Health and Genomic Data: Consequences in Terms of "Vulnerability"

Healthcare can fully benefit from the potential of personal health and genomic data only if it is supported by a solid technical infrastructure that clearly enables data access (while respecting the privacy of the individuals concerned), facilitates the understanding of the mechanisms through which data is processed, ensures the security of the information systems that handle it, and implements an effective data management system. Data plays a critical role in addressing many of the challenges that the healthcare sector faces on a daily basis. Indeed, data is crucial both in healthcare planning (for example, in revising clinical, administrative, and territorial processes to improve overall efficiency) and in defining health policies (such as allocating human resources and enhancing services[18]). Additionally, data is vital for preventing and managing public health emergencies, as it enables the monitoring of health trends over time and supports preventive measures.

The information derived from data is not only vital for planning, commissioning, and improving healthcare facility services but is also—and above all—essential for advancing scientific and clinical research, which drives healthcare progress. Scientific and clinical research based on the use of personal health and genomic data can accelerate medical discoveries,[19] improve the understanding of diseases, identify significant correlations, and guide the development of more targeted therapies. To achieve meaningful results in healthcare, Artificial Intelligence (AI) systems must be fed with a large quantity of high-quality personal health and genomic data and must be pre-trained to autonomously acquire only high-quality data. After an initial pre-training phase aimed at achieving specific objectives, AI systems can autonomously acquire new data and use existing data to generate new insights.

However, storing personal health and genomic data after its original purpose has been fulfilled—and using it for new, unrelated purposes—exposes individuals to the risk of privacy violations.

---

[17] Albahri et al. (2023); Hanson et al. (2023).

[18] In operating rooms, for example, the collection and analysis of data related to surgeries and their scheduling enable better organization, including more a efficient use of operating rooms, leading to resource savings and reduced waiting times.

[19] Melchionna and Cecamore (2019).

Those who consent to the processing of their personal health and genomic data for a specific medical treatment may not agree to its subsequent use for other purposes. Therefore, data subjects have the right to withdraw their consent. The challenge lies in the fact that once data has been acquired by AI systems, it undergoes automatic processing and is mechanically reused. As a result, even though the withdrawal of consent remains legally valid, it may not prove technically effective. In order to permanently delete data from an autonomous AI system, the entire system must be reprogrammed.

Given these challenges, the secondary use of personal health and genomic data for scientific[20] and clinical research is the subject of ongoing national and international debate. The core issue lies in how the data is originally collected and for what purposes. In most cases, personal health and genomic data are gathered for healthcare purposes and only later repurposed for research purposes. This latter use constitutes a secondary purpose, distinct from the original one for which the data subject authorized processing. Hence, this is referred to as the secondary use of personal health and genomic data.[21]

Recital 50 of Regulation (EU) 2016/679 (General Data Protection Regulation—GDPR), and in Italy, Articles 110 and 110-bis of Legislative Decree No. 196 of June 30, 2003 (Privacy Code), as amended by Ministerial Decree No. 101 of August 10, 2018, permit the secondary use of personal health and genomic data without the data subject's consent if the research purpose is deemed compatible with the original intent of collection. However, issues may arise if personal health data needs to be transferred from one data controller to another for processing with a different purpose, without the data subject's consent. Issues may also emerge if the data is used for specific research sectors that were not previously identified or for investigations in unrelated fields. To address these difficulties, the GDPR states in Recital 33[22] that if it is not possible to fully determine the purpose of personal data processing for scientific research at the time of data collection, the data subject must at least be able to give consent for specific, identified research areas. The Italian Data Protection Authority, clarified in decision No. 9091942 titled "Chiarimenti sull'applicazione della disciplina per il trattamento dei dati relativi alla salute in ambito sanitario[23]", that for processing activities not strictly necessary for patient care, an additional legal basis—such as consent or another lawful justification—must be established. As a result, the use of personal health and genomic data for scientific and clinical research purposes is significantly limited in Italy, reflecting the heightened vulnerability of individuals in such contexts. The limitations imposed by the Italian Data Protection Authority reflect the heightened vulnerability individuals face in these circumstances.

---

[20] Liotta (2024).

[21] The secondary use of clinical data has great potential for scientific progress and health care improvement. At the same time, it poses relevant risks for the privacy and informational self-determination of patients whose data are used. The concept of secondary use of data, and its link to vulnerability, is well defined in literature Jungkunz et al. (2021).

[22] European Union (2016).

[23] The provision contains clarifications on the application of data processing rules for health-related data in the healthcare sector.

The debate on the secondary use of personal health and genomic data for scientific and clinical research is central in other European countries as well.

In France, under Article 44 of the Loi Informatique et Libertés (LIL), the legal basis for legitimizing the secondary use of data for scientific research can be legitimate interest, public interest, or consent, as clarified by the Commission Nationale de l'Informatique et des Libertés. However, when it comes to using genetic data for research, Article 75 LIL mandates that informed and explicit consent from the data subject is required. This implies that if the research does not involve genetic data, legal bases other than consent may be used. Furthermore, Article 74 LIL provides that data subjects have the right to object to data processing for scientific research through an opt-out mechanism, meaning that consent (opt-in) is not explicitly required. Ultimately, the data controller has the discretion to determine the appropriate legal basis based on a case-by-case assessment.

In Germany, Article 27 of the Bundesdatenschutzgesetz (BDSG, Federal Data Protection Act), which regulates the processing of special categories of data, including health data, allows processing based on consent but also on the legitimate interest of the data subject, provided that the controller's interest significantly outweighs the data subject's interest in preventing the processing. However, under Article 22(2) BDSG, the data controller must implement appropriate organizational and security measures to protect the data subject's interests. These measures must consider the state of the art, implementation costs, the nature and scope of processing, and the potential risks to data subjects' rights and freedoms.

In Spain, Ley Orgánica 3/2018 (Additional Provision Seventeen—Processing of Health Data) explicitly states that the legal basis for processing personal health data for scientific research purposes is the consent of the data subject or their legal representative. However, the law contains provisions that introduce greater flexibility. First, the provision explicitly references broad consent, meaning that consent given for a specific research purpose can also be used for related but distinct research areas. Furthermore, health authorities and public entities responsible for public health oversight can conduct studies and scientific research without the data subject's consent in cases of exceptional public health importance and severity. Additionally, Paragraph 2 of the provision establishes the legitimacy of using pseudonymized data for scientific and biomedical research. It mandates that the research team be technically and functionally separated from those who hold the decryption key for the pseudonymized data. This ensures that the research team cannot re-identify data subjects, thereby strengthening data protection. If legitimate interest is used as the legal basis for processing personal health data for research, these security measures prevent the controller's interests from overriding the rights and freedoms of data subjects.

European and national regulations appear to protect data subjects from potential privacy violations and vulnerabilities arising from the digitalization of healthcare. However, is this regulatory framework sufficient, or should additional values and principles be added?

To address this, we now turn to a closer examination of the relevant legal instruments in an effort to resolve these uncertainties.

4 The Protection of Personal Health and Genomic Data

The most urgent issue related to the digitalization of healthcare is the protection of personal health and genomic data. The collection, processing, and sharing of such data make individuals vulnerable, can negatively impact the relationship between doctors and patients, and can expose healthcare facilities to liability in case of security breaches involving sensitive patient data.

Securing personal health and genomic data affects patients' trust in digital healthcare and in the institutions and doctors practicing it. However, it also ensures that such data is used correctly and up-to-date by public and private entities involved in healthcare and scientific research.[24]

4.1 Protection Under the GDPR

The processing of personal data, including health and genomic data, by Artificial Intelligence (AI) is primarily regulated by Regulation (EU) 2016/679 ("GDPR"), which establishes a reinforced system of safeguards, regardless of the purpose for which the processing is carried out, in order to prevent violations of data subjects' rights and freedoms.

The GDPR requires that the "automated" processing of personal data through AI must be conducted for a purpose that is identified at the beginning of the project so that it is well-defined, clear, and legitimate. Further processing of such data (known as secondary use of personal health and genomic data) is allowed only if the principles of transparency, data minimization, and storage limitation are respected and if the purpose for which the data is being used is not incompatible with the original purpose.[25]

Article 25 of the GDPR clarifies that the data controller must carefully select the AI systems they intend to use, ensuring that these systems provide guarantees and comply with the principles of proportionality and data minimization. The choice of the data controller should be guided by the type of input, data, and information entered into the AI systems, as well as how these systems operate.

Specifically, the GDPR states that the processing of personal data by AI systems is allowed under Articles 13 and 14 if the data controller, in compliance with the principle of transparency, has informed the data subject of the existence of an automated decision-making process, including profiling, provided significant information about the logic used, its importance, and the possible consequences of the processing. According to Article 6, processing is lawful if the data subject has given consent, if

[24] The undeniable need to protect personal and genomic health data—both to support patient trust in physicians and to ensure the proper use of such data—has long been a subject of debate in legal scholarship. Ciacci (1991); Colapietro and Laviola(2019); Comandè (2019); Di Ciommo (2002); Fares (2017); Filippi and Melchionna (2016); Guarda (2019).

[25] Quinn et al. (2023).

it is necessary for the performance of a contract between the data controller and the data subject, if it is required to fulfill a legal obligation, if it is necessary to protect the vital interests of the data subject or another individual, if it is necessary for the execution of a task carried out in the public interest or in the exercise of official authority, or if it is necessary for the legitimate interests of the data controller or third parties.

Recognizing the significant risks associated with processing personal data through AI systems, the EU legislator has mandated that data controllers wishing to use AI must conduct a Data Protection Impact Assessment (DPIA) under Article 35 of the GDPR. This assessment identifies, evaluates, and presents a risk mitigation plan.

One of the major concerns related to the use of personal data by AI systems, which may contribute to individuals' vulnerability due to healthcare digitalization, is the potential transfer of personal data to non-European countries. Therefore, Article 3 of the GDPR defines the territorial scope of the Regulation based on two criteria: the "establishment" criterion, outlined in paragraph 1 of Article 3, states that the GDPR applies to activities conducted within the framework of a stable organization within the European Union (EU); the "targeting" criterion, regulated by paragraph 2 of Article 3, extends GDPR protection to personal data processing by non-EU entities if certain conditions related to the processing are met (Recital 23 GDPR).

The legality of transferring personal data outside the EU depends on the European Commission's recognition of the third country's adequacy or, in the absence of such recognition, on the provision of appropriate safeguards by the data controller, ensuring enforceable rights and effective legal remedies for the data subjects (Articles 45 and 46 GDPR). Consequently, if the adequacy assessment is negative, the data exporter must determine the lawfulness of the transfer based on Standard Contractual Clauses,[26] considering the circumstances of the transfer and any additional measures implemented by the data importer.

The Italian Data Protection Authority has issued a document based on the GDPR and the jurisprudence of the Italian Council of State, outlining key principles for implementing AI-based healthcare services at the national level. This document, structured as a Decalogue,[27] reiterates the principles of the GDPR and the AI Act that must be respected in the processing of personal health data by AI systems. It emphasizes that such processing, even if carried out for public health interests, is only permitted if expressly provided for by national laws, ensuring adequate safeguards for the rights, freedoms, and legitimate interests of the data subjects. These processes must be accompanied by communication campaigns informing data subjects about how AI systems operate, continuous human oversight,[28] and a prior impact assessment by the supervisory authority on their necessity and adequacy.

---

[26] European Commission (2021).

[27] Garante per la Protezione dei Dati Personali (2019).

[28] The centrality of human supervision had already been highlighted in the joint opinion of the European Data Protection Board and the European Data Protection Supervisor, n. 5/2021.

The Decalogue highlights that, from the early stages of AI system development for healthcare use, all choices must be carefully considered. The technical and organizational measures required by the GDPR must be implemented to protect data, rights, and freedoms, and the roles and responsibilities of all parties involved in the data processing must be clearly and transparently defined.

A key aspect is the indication of algorithmic logic and measures to mitigate discriminatory risks associated with using personal health and genomic data in AI systems. This ensures that individuals are less vulnerable to automated decision-making.

4.2 Protection Under the AI Act

The use of AI in healthcare is still in its early stages, and the radical changes that these technologies could bring to the sector have yet to fully materialize. For this reason, the European legislator has developed the AI Act, prioritizing the protection of citizens' privacy, data integrity, and security when processing personal health and genomic data with AI.[29] Recognizing the extreme sensitivity of such data, the AI Act establishes clear rules on their collection, use, and processing, ensuring that only the minimum necessary amount of data is used to achieve predetermined diagnostic, therapeutic, or clinical investigation objectives. According to Article 10 of the AI Act, data used for training and validating AI models must be of very high quality.

Another key element is transparency in AI use in healthcare, as outlined in Article 13 of the AI Act. Healthcare facilities using AI tools for medical purposes must ensure transparency about how these systems operate, specifying their underlying logic and decision-making criteria. Citizens must fully understand how their personal data will be processed by AI tools and must explicitly consent to the processing.

A distinctive feature of the AI Act is the emphasis on human oversight in AI systems. Article 14 explicitly requires high-risk AI systems to be supervised by human operators during their use. This means that AI operational processes must be subject to human surveillance and control, and that manufacturers must properly train healthcare personnel using these tools. The requirement for human oversight stems from the legislator's intent to foster trust in AI-based healthcare applications.

Additionally, the AI Act promotes the responsible and ethical use of AI in healthcare through relevant ethical provisions. The legislation emphasizes that healthcare institutions must not only focus on the immediate benefits of AI but also assess potential medium- and long-term risks. AI use must respect human rights and fundamental freedom, ensure transparency in AI functionality, promote equality, and eliminate discrimination.

[29] European Parliament (2024).

4.3 International Protections

The processing of personal health and genomic data by AI systems is a highly sensitive and complex area of the digital revolution, constantly evolving, yet with global implications. Therefore, the legal framework for protecting health data must also advance at the international level while fully respecting human rights.[30]

To this end, the World Health Organization (WHO) has played its role as the United Nations agency specializing in health issues. It has issued guidelines[31] identifying key principles for AI use in healthcare. These guidelines aim to promote the development of trustworthy AI systems, benefiting medical care, clinical trials, diagnostics, and treatments.

According to the WHO, privacy and data protection in AI healthcare applications are ensured if the purposes of processing, metrics, databases used, reference standards, modifications made during processing, and risk management measures are made transparent.[32]

5 Final Remarks and Ethical Considerations

As highlighted in the previous paragraphs, the undeniable value of digitalizing healthcare through the use of Artificial Intelligence (AI) systems clashes with the vulnerability it generates due to the biases it introduces.

The digitalization of healthcare has made the protection of personal health and genomic data crucial, as their collection, processing, and sharing can expose data subjects to vulnerabilities, influence the doctor-patient relationship, and increase the liability of healthcare institutions in cases of security breaches.

On the one hand, AI—both in its primary and even more so in its secondary use of personal health data—contributes to scientific research and related innovations aimed at effectively preventing and treating diseases, ultimately enhancing the efficiency of healthcare. On the other hand, it threatens the safeguarding and respect of human rights and freedoms.

The faster and more powerful technological progress becomes, the greater the need for regulatory support that can carefully balance the protection of personal health and genomic data in the use of AI systems.

The commitment to the protection of personal health and genomic data is an international goal, supported in Europe by two main regulations: the GDPR and the AI Act.

---

[30] For a critical perspective on the evolution of the European regulatory framework for the secondary use of personal health data for scientific research, see Hajduk (2023).

[31] World Health Organization (2023).

[32] WHO calls for safe and ethical AI for health. https://www.who.int/news/item/16-05-2023-who-calls-for-safe-and-ethical-ai-for-health.

The EU General Data Protection Regulation (GDPR) (Regulation 2016/679) stipulates that data processing must have a clearly defined purpose and comply with the principles of transparency, data minimization, and storage limitation. The data controller must select AI systems that adhere to the principles of proportionality and minimization and must inform the data subject about the automated processing methods, its logic, and its consequences. Furthermore, processing is lawful only if based on the data subject's consent, a legal obligation, or a public or legitimate interest. The GDPR also requires data controllers to conduct a Data Protection Impact Assessment (DPIA) to identify and mitigate the risks associated with automated processing.

The Artificial Intelligence Act (AI Act) regulates AI use in healthcare with the aim of protecting privacy, data integrity, and the security of health information. It establishes that data used to train and validate AI systems must be of high quality and that their use must be transparent. Healthcare facilities must disclose the logic and decision-making criteria underlying AI systems and obtain citizens' explicit consent. The AI Act also emphasizes an ethical approach, requiring healthcare institutions to assess potential long-term risks and ensure that AI use respects human rights, transparency, and equality, preventing discrimination.

The European regulatory framework, as a whole, aims to balance innovation with privacy protection in healthcare digitalization, ensuring that AI is used safely, transparently, and in a way that respects citizens' rights –ultimately promoting ethical conduct.

Similarly, for national legislators, protecting this type of data is essential to maintain patient trust and ensure the correct use of information in healthcare and scientific research. However, in Italy, the secondary use of this data continues to raise concerns regarding compliance with ethical and legal principles related to privacy and consent.

In Italy, there are significant limitations regarding the secondary use of personal health and genomic data. Although the Privacy Code allows secondary use of personal data for scientific or clinical research without the data subject's consent—provided that the new purposes are compatible with the original ones—the Italian Data Protection Authority imposes very strict restrictions. In the Decalogue drafted to outline the key principles for implementing AI-based healthcare services at the national level, the Italian Data Protection Authority strongly emphasizes the need for transparency, human oversight, and protective measures to safeguard the rights and freedoms of individuals and reduce discrimination risks.

From an ethical standpoint, one approach argues that ethical values and principles should be embedded in the processing of personal health and genomic data, so that regulations are inherently guided by these principles and can protect individuals effectively. As a result, both national and EU legislations share the fundamental requirement of upholding the ethical aspects of data processing, ensuring transparent conduct based on explicit and genuine actions.

The transparency of personal health and genomic data processing aims to inform data subjects about the essential aspects of data processing and any potential reuse. Furthermore, data processing transparency extends to the intended uses of the data, enabling its responsible use. This transparency allows individuals to choose how their data is used in alignment with their personal values and goals. Knowing the actual use of data enables individuals to decide whether to allow processing or not. As a result, transparency becomes a moral virtue for those handling personal health and genomic data.

Additionally, transparent operations help foster trust. Establishing trust in AI systems is necessary to overcome skepticism toward technological innovations and bridge the knowledge gap regarding AI systems, which otherwise hinder the realization of technology's benefits. The key starting point is the perception of the benefits AI applications offer—both at an individual and societal level—as they can achieve valuable advancements in evolution and social well-being. These perceptions are crucial in shaping the meaning of technology's role and in building confidence in it.

Ultimately, ethical conduct in the processing of personal health and genomic data not only seeks to avoid harming data subjects but also aims to generate positive impacts on people's lives. Protecting data subjects is a prime example of how acting transparently builds trust and produces societal benefits.

Government regulations must adopt data subject protection as a tool to transform ethics into law, giving it a strong legal standing with prescriptive and prohibitive power. In this approach, ethics is deeply embedded in legal frameworks, prescribing behaviors that ensure the protection of a technologically advanced society.

A second approach, however, argues that machines—despite technological advances—cannot attain the status of autonomous moral agents and cannot operate without direct human oversight. Moral agency belongs to humans.[33] This perspective distinguishes between the ability to complete tasks or solve problems (by setting an objective) and the awareness of a moral obligation to act ethically.

A crucial element is the consideration of consequences, meaning the impact generated by an action. It is not enough to evaluate whether a task has been completed or a problem has been solved—it is essential to assess the ethical implications of AI use beforehand.[34]

Therefore, the design of AI systems must be regulated to ensure that their use does not pose unacceptable risks to humans.[35] Ethical principles must be integrated into AI development from the outset, so that they do not require later external control.[36] The development of AI for humanity must be translated into rules and principles that protect individuals—especially the vulnerable and marginalized.

Placing ethical conduct at the core of legal systems establishes a protective framework that inherently mitigates vulnerability. This ensures not just any kind of protection but protection against all forms of discrimination and violations of individual rights.

---

[33] Moore (1903); Russ-Eft (2001).

[34] Giovanola and Tiribelli (2023).

[35] WHO outlines considerations for regulation of artificial intelligence for health. https://www.who.int/news/item/19-10-2023-who-outlines-considerations-for-regulation-of-artificial-intelligence-for-health.

[36] Veluwenkamp and van den Hoven (2023).

The ethical debate on AI represents the conflict—and reconciliation—between humans and machines. This reconciliation should be reflected in European civil law as a whole, without remaining an unresolved issue.

References

Abràmoff MD, Tarver ME, Loyo-Berrios N, Trujillo S, Char D, Obermeyer Z, et al (2023) Considerations for addressing bias in artificial intelligence for health equity. NPJ Digit Med 6(1):170. pmid:37700029

Albahri AS, Duhaim AM, Fadhel MA, Alnoor A, Baqer NS, Alzubaidi L, et al (2023) A systematic review of trustworthy and explainable artificial intelligence in healthcare: assessment of quality, bias risk, and data fusion. Inf Fusion 96:156–191

Cascini F, Gentili A, Causio FA, Altamura G, Melnyk A, Beccia F, Pappalardo C, Lontano A, Ricciardi W (2023a) Strengthening and promoting digital health practice: results from a global digital health partnership's survey. In: Al-Shorbaji N (ed) Front Public Health. eHealth Development Association of Jordan. https://www.fideliacascini.com/wp-content/uploads/2024/01/fpubh-11-1147210-GDHP-digital-Health-1-1.pdf

Cascini F, Gentili A, Melnyk A, Beccia F, Causio FA, Solimene V, Battilomo S, Paone S, Borghini A, Bartolo M, Chiarolla E, Ricciardi W (2023b) A new digital model for the Italian Integrated Home Care: strengths, barriers, and future implications. In: Denecke K (ed) Front Public Health. Bern University of Applied Sciences. https://www.fideliacascini.com/wp-content/uploads/2024/01/integrated-care-fpubh-11-1292442-1-1.pdf

Cascini F, Beccia F, Causio FA, Azzopardi Muscat N, Ricciardi W (2022) Editorial: digitalization for precision healthcare. In: Bhattacharya S (ed) Front Public Health. All India Institute of Medical Sciences (AIIMS) Deoghar. https://www.fideliacascini.com/wp-content/uploads/2024/01/fpubh-10-1078610-1-1.pdf

Ciacci G (1991) Problemi e iniziative in tema di tutela dei dati personali con particolare riguardo ai dati sanitari. Politica del diritto. Il Mulino, Bologna

Colapietro C, Laviola F (2019) I trattamenti di dati personali in ambito sanitario. Dirittifondamentali.it 2. https://dirittifondamentali.it/wp-content/uploads/2019/07/Colapietro-Laviola-I-trattamenti-di-dati-personali-in-ambito-sanitario.pdf

Comandè G (2019) Ricerca in sanità e data protection… un puzzle risolvibile. Riv Ital Med Legale

Cross JL, Choma MA, Onofrey JA (2024) Bias in medical AI: implications for clinical decision-making. PLOS Digit Health 3(11):e0000651. https://doi.org/10.1371/journal.pdig.0000651

Di Ciommo F (2002) Il trattamento dei dati sanitari tra interessi individuali e collettivi. Danno e responsabilità 2. https://www.diciommoandpartners.com/wp-content/uploads/2015/06/Trattamento-dati-senitari-Danno-e-resp.-2002.pdf

European Commission (2021) Commission Implementing Decision (EU) 2021/914 of 4 June 2021 on standard contractual clauses for the transfer of personal data to third countries pursuant to Regulation (EU) 2016/679 of the European Parliament and of the Council. https://eur-lex.europa.eu/eli/dec_impl/2021/914/oj?locale=it

European Parliament (2024) Artificial intelligence act, approved on 6 March 2024. https://www.europarl.europa.eu/doceo/document/A-9-2023-0188-AM-808-808_IT.pdf

European Union (2016). Regulation (EU) 2016/679 of the European Parliament and of the Council of 27 April 2016 on the protection of natural persons with regard to the processing of personal data and on the free movement of such data (General Data Protection Regulation—GDPR). Recital 33. https://www.privacy-regulation.eu/it/r33.htm

Fares G (2017) I dati relativi alla salute e i trattamenti in ambito sanitario. In: Califano L, Colapietro C (eds) Innovazione tecnologica e valore della persona. Il diritto alla protezione dei dati personali nel Regolamento UE 2016/679. Editoriale scientifica, Napoli

Filippi C, Melchionna S (2016) I trattamenti di dati in ambito sanitario. In: Busia G, Liguori L, Pollicino O (eds) Le nuove frontiere della privacy nelle tecnologie digitali. Bilanci e prospettive. Aracne, Roma

Garante per la Protezione dei Dati Personali (2019) Decalogue for the implementation of national healthcare services using artificial intelligence systems. https://www.garanteprivacy.it/documents/10160/0/Decalogo+per+la+realizzazione+di+servizi+sanitari+nazionali+attraverso+sistemi+di+Intelligenza+Artificiale.pdf

Gianfrancesco MA, Tamang S, Yazdany J, Schmajuk G (2018) Potential biases in machine learning algorithms using electronic health record data. JAMA Intern Med 178(11):1544. pmid:30128552

Giannini A (2020) Il trattamento dei Big Data in sanità e Intelligenza Artificiale. In: Iaselli M (ed) La tutela dei dati personali in ambito sanitario. Giuffrè Francis Lefebvre, Milano, pp 180–185

Giovanola B, Tiribelli S (2023) Beyond bias and discrimination: redefining the AI ethics principle of fairness in healthcare machine-learning algorithms. AI Soc 38(2):549–563. https://doi.org/10.1007/s00146-022-01455-6. Epub 2022. PMID: 35615443; PMCID: PMC9123626

Guarda P (2019) I dati sanitari. In: Cuffaro V, D'Orazio R, Ricciuto V (eds) I dati personali nel diritto europeo. Giappichelli, Torino

Hajduk P (2023) A walk in the labyrinth: evolving EU regulatory framework for secondary use of electronic personal health data for scientific research. https://papers.ssrn.com/sol3/papers.cfm?abstract_id=4673534

Hanson B, Stall S, Cutcher-Gershenfeld J, Vrouwenvelder K, Wirz C, Rao YD, Peng G (2023) Garbage in, garbage out: mitigating risks and maximizing benefits of AI in research. Nature 623(7985):28–31. https://doi.org/10.1038/d41586-023-03316-8. PMID: 37907636

Hasanzadeh F, Josephson CB, Waters G et al (2025) Bias recognition and mitigation strategies in artificial intelligence healthcare applications, npj Digit. Med 8:154. https://doi.org/10.1038/s41746-025-01503-7

Iaselli M (ed) (2020) La tutela dei dati personali in ambito sanitario. Giuffrè Francis Lefebvre, Milano

Jungkunz M, Köngeter A, Mehlis K, Winkler EC, Schickhardt C (2021) Secondary use of clinical data in data-gathering, non-interventional research or learning activities: definition, types, and a framework for risk assessment. J Med Internet Res 23(6):e26631. https://doi.org/10.2196/26631. PMID: 34100760; PMCID: PMC8241435

Liotta M (2024) Il favor per la ricerca scientifica e la sua effettiva applicazione nella normativa europea, nazionale e da parte dell'autorità garante. Il Diritto Dell'informazione e Dell'informatica 3:363–384

Melchionna S, Cecamore F (2019) Le nuove frontiere della sanità e della ricerca scientifica. In: Panetta R (ed) Circolazione e protezione dei dati personali, tra libertà e regole del mercato. Commentario al Regolamento UE n. 679/2016 (GDPR) e al novellato d.lgs. 101/2018 (Codice Privacy). Giuffrè Francis Lefebvre, Milano, pp 579–620

Moore GE (1903) Principia ethica. Cambridge University Press, Cambridge

Panch T, Mattie H, Atun R (2019) Artificial intelligence and algorithmic bias: implications for health systems. J Glob Health 9(2):010318. https://doi.org/10.7189/jogh.09.020318. PMID: 31788229; PMCID: PMC6875681

Poddighe E (2024) Piani epidemiologici regionali e raccolta, elaborazione e circolazione dei dati sanitari: il progetto EINS per la regione Sardegna. Il Diritto Dell'informazione e Dell'informatica 4(5):561–576

Quinn P, Ellyne E, Yao C (2023) Limits to Health data access body discretion and a need to comply with the GDPR—Enough to protect against improper sharing of health data through the EHDS? https://papers.ssrn.com/sol3/papers.cfm?abstract_id=4662816

Russ-Eft DF (2001) A case for case studies on HRD ethics and integrity. Hum Resour Dev Q 11(2):101–103

Silcox C, Zimlichmann E, Huber K, Rowen N, Saunders R, McClellan M, Kahn CN 3rd, Salzberg CA, Bates DW (2024) The potential for artificial intelligence to transform healthcare: perspectives from international health leaders. NPJ Digit Med 7(1):88. https://doi.org/10.1038/s41746-024-01097-6. PMID: 38594477; PMCID: PMC11004157

Veluwenkamp H, van den Hoven J (2023) Design for values and conceptual engineering. Ethics Inf Technol 25(1)

World Health Organization (2023) Regulatory considerations on artificial intelligence for health. https://iris.who.int/handle/10665/373421

Maria Anastasia Arcuri, Ph.D. candidate in "Theory of Contracts, Services and Markets" at the Department of Management and Law, University of Rome Tor Vergata. Member of the Editorial Committee of Teoria e Prassi del Diritto (ESI). Collaborates with the Catholic University of the Sacred Heart of Rome (Chair of Public Health and Digital Health). Published on secondary use of health-related personal data and European/national regulations in this field.

Open Access This chapter is licensed under the terms of the Creative Commons Attribution 4.0 International License (http://creativecommons.org/licenses/by/4.0/), which permits use, sharing, adaptation, distribution and reproduction in any medium or format, as long as you give appropriate credit to the original author(s) and the source, provide a link to the Creative Commons license and indicate if changes were made.

The images or other third party material in this chapter are included in the chapter's Creative Commons license, unless indicated otherwise in a credit line to the material. If material is not included in the chapter's Creative Commons license and your intended use is not permitted by statutory regulation or exceeds the permitted use, you will need to obtain permission directly from the copyright holder.

Beyond Liminality: Digital Technologies between Inclusion and Citizenship

Michele Sorice and Andrea Volterrani

Abstract This chapter explores the intricate relationship between digital technologies, citizenship and inclusion in liminal spaces—transitional areas marked by marginalisation, vulnerability and continuous change. The study is focused on how liminal communities navigate the balance between exclusion and empowerment through digital participation. The study conceptualises liminal spaces as sites of refiguration resulting from processes of poly-contextualisation, deep mediatisation and translocationalisation. Often situated in the urban peripheries, these communities experience segregated social capital and systemic marginalisation yet simultaneously develop innovative forms of resistance and democratic participation. The research reveals how 'paternalistic neoliberalism' appropriates participatory rhetoric while maintaining exclusionary practices. Through an empirical analysis of five liminal communities in Sicily, Calabria and Apulia, the authors demonstrate how digital technologies can be used for inclusion and self-empowerment. These communities develop hybrid participatory processes that combine online and offline engagement to create counter-narratives to dominant neoliberal discourse. The study identifies key factors that enable transformation, including community mobilisation, supportive local governance, openness in the third sector, and communicative ecosystems. The analysis sheds light on how active citizenship can emerge in marginal spaces, challenging traditional notions of national citizenship through participatory practices. While acknowledging digital inequalities and AI-related concerns, the research highlights the potential for technology-mediated democratic innovation in vulnerable communities. It suggests pathways towards more inclusive forms of citizenship that transcend territorial and institutional boundaries.

Keywords Citizenship · Communities · Digital technologies · Inclusion · Liminality

M. Sorice (✉)
Sapienza University of Rome, Rome, Italy
e-mail: michele.sorice@uniroma1.it

A. Volterrani
University of Rome Tor Vergata, Rome, Italy

© The Author(s) 2025

C. Amodio and A. Diurni (eds.), *Human Vulnerability in Interaction with AI in European Private Law*, https://doi.org/10.1007/978-3-031-93247-2_9

1 Two Basic Concepts: Liminality and Space

Liminality and space are strongly interconnected because, when we speak about liminality, we refer to a specific liminal space. Notably, "liminal spaces" are defined as spaces that are characterised by both (1) processes of refiguration[1] due to poly-contextualisation, deep mediatisation[2] and translocalisation[3] and (2) processes of marginalisation, vulnerabilisation,[4] gentrification[5] and defamiliarisation.[6] A "liminal space" lies "on the border of two dominant spaces, not fully part of either".[7] Thus, these spaces cannot be easily defined in terms of use and are not clearly 'owned' by a particular party. This directly contrasts with dominant spaces which are defined by main uses, have clear boundaries and contain practices that are intertwined with social expectations, routines, and norms. In liminal spaces, which are in transition, individual and collective identities remain fluid or anchored to the even sometimes deviant specificities of the territories; they belong to spaces such that they become familiar and are taken for granted in the landscape of everyday life[8] We assume that when liminal spaces are inhabited by communities and considered vital and meaningful in their everyday lives, they cease to be ambiguous spaces and become transitional dwelling places that give meaning to the activities, languages and instances that develop there.[9] Liminal communities are refigured spaces undergoing profound transformations due to both endogenous and exogenous phenomena; the first major change involves figuration. To analyse the process of the construction of social reality, Elias[10] introduced the term 'figuration' as a conceptual tool for understanding the complex problems of interdependence that the coexistence of many humans generates and how these problems are solved. Elias argues that social change is always partly a change at the figuration level. According to Elias, understanding the enduring social formations of human beings as figurations constituted by the interdependencies and interactions of the individuals involved is fundamental. They can be characterised by a certain "balance of power",[11] i.e., by power relations constituted by the interdependencies themselves. The boundaries of each figuration are defined by the shared meaning that is produced by the individuals involved through interrelated social practices, which form the basis of their mutual orientation. Liminal communities are understood as figurations of figurations (as several figurations coexist within them) in transition. In addition to traditional figurations such as families, formal

---

[1] Knoublach and Löw (2017, pp. 1–27).

[2] Hepp (2020).

[3] Hepp (2015).

[4] Castel (2014), Brown et al. (2017, pp. 497–500).

[5] Sennett (2018).

[6] Blokland (2017), Blokland et al. (2022, pp. 258–268).

[7] Dale and Burrell (2008).

[8] Blokland (2017, pp. 54–60).

[9] Casey (1993).

[10] Elias (1987).

[11] Elias (1987, p. 131).

and informal interest groups, social conformations that exist in complete illegality (e.g., organised crime) or on the borders of legality (e.g., precarious undeclared and piecework work), social actors in civil society with organisational and management peculiarities, precarious small-scale crafts and entrepreneurial paths and formations constitute liminal communities. Regardless of the value connotations we assign to the figures, they all face external pressures for change and multiple internal pressures to find a new balance in the social practices of everyday life.

The second aspect that characterises the process of the refiguration of liminal communities, poly-contextualisation, specifically refers to the multiplication of contexts and frames to which people react simultaneously, sometimes creating overlaps, conflicts, or even mutual indifference. The presence of very different cultures and subcultures within the same social space is one of the most important concepts of co-contextualisation, as it has been fuelled in the last 30 years in Western countries by numerically significant migration processes.[12]

Another relevant aspect of liminal communities is social capital. Many of these communities have very intense social relations but are more segregated than other communities, even spatially contiguous communities, are. Thus, instead of focusing on bonding or bridging social capital,[13] we should address segregated and privatised social capital.[14] In some cases, this type of social capital becomes a resource for liminal communities. Moreover, the digital ecosystem plays an important role at this level.

The second concept is spatiality, particularly in its specific meaning as referring to urban space.

Spatiality has become central to people's social and media practices,[15] transforming the way communities are formed towards greater flexibility and widespread molecularisation on the one hand and towards unprecedented forms of social innovation and resistance on the other, at least in some respects. For example, some microcommunity experiences also seem to have gained the characteristics of the workers' mutualities of the late 19th century, but with a focus on ties with the territory rather than on those born within the work context or a combination of both aspects. This was the case for the collective linked to the experience of the GKN of Campi Bisenzio near Florence, which originated from work experience and has turned into a sort of modern Workers' Mutual Aid Society, capable of also moving into the sphere of training and cultural promotion in the territory.

The concept of urban space has often been related to that of community, which constitutes a controversial theoretical dimension in both participation studies and *urban studies*. Although urban space is, in fact, a central notion, it remains vague and, above all, difficult to operationalise in empirical terms. Since the beginning of the 21st century, many studies have attempted to move away from the idea of community as a stable structure that is continuous over time and has clearly defined internal

---

[12] Ambrosini et al. (2020).

[13] Putnam (2001, pp. 41–51).

[14] Blokland and Rae (2008, pp. 23–39).

[15] Couldry (2004, pp. 115–132), Couldry and Hepp (2017), Couldry (2022).

relations. Instead, new strands of research have focused on an idea of community as an evolving structure, with relationships that do not necessarily last over time; however, the most important aspect is precisely the relationship with space (mostly declining as inhabited territory). In other words, the spatial dimension has become more prevalent than the temporal dimension. This transformation of perspective has facilitated the consideration of territorial communities starting from social practices and, in particular, urban practices in spaces of sharing, even in liminal (not necessarily marginal) spaces that are inhabited by more or less vulnerable subjects. At this level, hybrid social bodies in which the participatory dimension constitutes one of the qualifying elements of the social relationship can be studied.

Urban communities are realities connected to a territory, albeit often in a non-ascriptive way, in which relations are made possible precisely by political action. Unsurprisingly, political participation in community is the central element of the very theoretical definition of community.[16]

As aforementioned, over the last few years, many territorial realities—mostly urban—have adopted some of the early twentieth-century modalities of mutual aid societies, reversing them in a network logic with a marked political propensity. This has led to experiences that greatly differ from each other but share the need to recreate a participatory fabric capable of going beyond the exhausted forms of political organisation in common. Thus, in communicative practices (including those inherent to the adoption of digital tools), a space for facilitating inclusion, when it is not also a ground for confrontation and 'resistance', has been found for new organisational forms.

There are many 'community' experiences, often with a specific vocation for urban regeneration. The following fall into this family of experiences: (a) street associations, which are territorial communities born in the function of 'defending' a mostly circumscribed space (the neighbourhood or similar space) and in some cases connected more or less consciously to experiences of urban regeneration and/or 'shared administration'; (b) technological reappropriation groups, which are communities sharing access to the internet through open Wi-Fi connections (very fashionable in the USA but less present in Italy, where however, experiences of 'media activism' connected to struggles for access to broadcasting communication have developed in the past); (c) 'rebellion by doing' experiences, which are movement realities that have a strong sensitivity in the tactical reuse of spaces (e.g., the creation of a political sensibility through the transmission of knowledge, from home baking to the creation of shared vegetable gardens); (d) horizontal solidarity groups, including everything from solidarity purchasing groups (often in connection with proximity democracy practices) to those engaged in *cohousing* projects; and e) urban communities in the strictest sense, which are often activated by the most disparate motivations and, in many cases, also within liminal spaces and/or widespread marginality. These various experiences and organisational forms share what has often been called *creative participation.*[17]

[16] Blokland (2017).

[17] Micheletti et al. (2021).

The modality of social ties is a relevant aspect in the study of the spaces of urban practices of political participation. If the frame is, in fact, represented by the spatial dimension, traditional criteria that refer to the mere logic of network connection (friendship, family, etc.) are not sufficient to define the social ties activated within the perimeter of communities of political participation. From this perspective, Talja Blokland's (2017) proposal to study ties in terms of the modalities of social practices and orientation toward action is very convincing. Blokland's proposal refers to a kind of typology of social ties based on four variables: (a) transactions; (b) attachment; (c) interdependencies; and (d) constraints.

Communities of participatory practices are both 'diasporic'[18] (in Stuart Hall's sense, i.e., as the outcome of a conscious process and not merely the result of uprooting) and relational. These communities can also be located in liminal spaces or be the result of an action of resistance and/or resilience in such spaces. Indeed, the connection between precariousness and resilience is one of the central aspects of aggregation in border and crossing (liminal) spaces. Certainly, the notion of tactical adaptation can be applied to participatory practices in liminal spaces: in such spaces, in fact, subjects (aggregated and nonaggregated) tactically adopt participatory practices, continually redefining their relationship with the physical space.

Finally, we highlight the complex relationship between urban regeneration (especially in liminal spaces) and the emergence of so-called 'good-natured neoliberalism'[19]). Indeed, in many cases, liminal spaces are traversed by *planning* procedures, surrounded by a deep-rooted storytelling that makes them a sociopolitical construct,[20] mostly functional to the various forms of public–private partnerships. In the 'narrative' modes of good-natured neo-liberalism (which by its very nature is strongly depoliticised), planning is often narrated as the 'promotion of innovation', sometimes with references to a generic notion of inclusion, significantly placed within the framework of 'sustainable urban economic development'. In this context, expressions such as 'collaborative governance' or 'urban regeneration' are affirmed (and resemanticised), often assumed in a volatile and arbitrary manner, capable of activating forms that are only partially participatory but substantially functional to the legitimation of economic stakeholders and not necessarily to the inclusion of vulnerable subjects.

The adoption of the concept of 'governmentality' and its numerous reinterpretations, which also occur in urban regeneration practices and often in connection with the notion of 'governability',[21] is also part of this framework. It represents an important stage in both the affirmation of the new neo-liberal global rationality and in

[18] According to Stuart Hall, the diasporic intellectual maintains a critical link with their community of origin while also moving within their community of destination. They are both inside and outside of each community, not only as a result of displacement, but also by choice. In this sense, diasporic communities consciously experience their 'internal/external' relationship with space. Hall (1990).

[19] Dardot and Laval (2014), Hall and O'Shea (2015, pp. 8–24).

[20] Pizzo (2015, p. 185).

[21] Moreover, by generating a de facto hierarchy between governability and representation (in favour of the former), this tendency undermines the liberal idea of democracy itself.

the transformation of capitalism into an 'institutionalised social order', to use Nancy Fraser's (2020) effective expression[22]

These tendencies are part of the broader flow of 'naturalisation' of neoliberal capitalism, which can often include even the dimensions of protest and resistance within its dominant narrative. Thus, the logics of "appropriation" of social struggles[23] are found both in advertising campaigns[24] and in the "storytelling" that sometimes accompanies the growth (which is in itself desirable) of experiences of democratic innovation, not coincidentally often transformed into bureaucratised procedures in which vulnerable subjects are relegated to legitimising with their presence choices that have already been made[25] Not coincidentally, the most refined tendencies of 'cool capitalism'[26] find possibilities for legitimisation and affirmation precisely in the appropriation 'from above' of marginal and/or liminal spaces.

2 Towards an Inclusive Idea of Citizenship

Citizenship is substantiated by membership, which can be either ascriptive or affiliative but in any case effectively excludes those who do not belong to it by rights (Marshall had written exemplary pages on this aspect as far back as 1950); and by participatory processes as well as a true culture of participation, albeit with all the caution concerning participatory processes.

On the subject of the exclusions of citizenship, Étienne Balibar[27] has given an insightful analysis of the phenomenon. For this French scholar, citizenship constitutes a sort of compromise between the ruling and subordinate classes in the development of the modern twentieth-century state. However, this compromise has been challenged—and violently violated—by neo-liberalism, which is also among the causes (although not the only cause) of the global processes of de-democratisation. On the other hand, Balibar notes that forms of exclusion of citizenship have traversed much of human history: suffice it to think of ancient Greece where the distribution of government and administrative functions took place among subjects who had deliberative power since they were holders of a 'right of citizenship'. Thus, there was a coincidence between civil society and the State, which was only possible because some subjects were excluded and others were limited. In times closer to our own—in the age of the Enlightenment revolutions and then the industrial revolutions—citizenship is in fact superimposed on national belonging: it is the state that defines the rift between those who possess the powers to represent the will of the people and the 'mass' who are by definition incompetent.

22 Fraser (2022).

23 Boltanski and Chiapello (2005), McGuigan (2016).

24 Prodnik (2023, pp. 51–73).

25 Sorice (2021)

26 McGuigan (2009).

27 Balibar (2015).

Although the idea that there is no citizenship without democracy seems to unite many (even temporally) distant authors, the national horizon is a more critical aspect. For Balibar, for example, neo-liberalism is the breaking of the link between citizenship and democracy, an aspect that was not present in 20th century theories. If democracy is the outcome of a (very unstable) balance between the conservative dimension of institutions and the thrusts towards reconfiguring citizenship, then it is clear that it is precisely the conflictuality that questions the national dimension that is the driving force behind the new citizenships. In addition, regulated deliberation between the parties cannot suffice, which—by its very nature—tends to exclude everything that escapes the ordering logic of the nation state. The result is that the tightening of the 'territorial' dimension of citizenship can only prevent the emergence of new citizenships. In addition, it is precisely this narrowing of possibilities (or the hypostatisation of already established ones) that provokes new exclusions (from class exclusions—which have changed their name but remain—to those linked to xenophobic and racist phenomena). However, the need for a citizenship based on substantive freedom and effective equality remains an ideal project, nevertheless present in the claims and demands of contemporary social movements but also among vulnerable subjects in situations of liminality.

One of the responses to the "incorporation" of democratic innovation procedures within the framework of neoliberalism is the diverse (and thus difficult to catalogue) forms of active citizenship. In many cases, indeed, civic engagement (or civism), regardless of whether it is accompanied by digital technologies, has been a response to both a need for participation and a need to increase the quality of democracy through the implementation of *policies* consistent with citizens' demands for a higher quality of life. The demand for quality in civic processes does not necessarily imply a demand for efficiency as is often theorised only as a 'reduction of time' to implement measures. Democracy, as is well known, does not need imperfect competition that generates monopolies, nor does it need paroxysmally restricted decision-making times that cause a kind of paradox: the absolute ideal of efficiency (zero difference between the moment of planning and the moment of realisation of public policies) is theoretically realised only in dictatorial regimes with strong personalistic overtones. This may also be realised—in different and 'good-natured' forms (but no less dangerous for democracy)—in regimes with a strong efficiencyist and technocratic character, typical of the processes of social neo-liberalisation. On the other hand, an 'efficiencyist' and 'meritocratic' vision of the state does not guarantee the achievement of an acceptable standard of quality but often leads to the dissolution of democracy itself. On the other hand, the quality or *responsiveness* of democracy must grow. The various structural crises that have affected (and are affecting) advanced capitalism have paradoxically represented unprecedented opportunities for social movements, associations, groups and ordinary citizens to become aware of the democratic deficit that was (is) affecting precisely liberal-representative democracies.

However, the crisis of confidence and disaffection towards politics should not be dismissed as a simple *exit* or, worse, withdrawal into the individual and personal sphere, since there are many forms of political participation that escape the old definitions and adopt original creative modes. In liminal spaces, forms of organisation (and self-organisation) also fit into this scenario.

In the tension between potential *apathy* towards politics and the emergence of new forms of collective speech-making, however, different and apparently conflicting trends are developing; these range from the organisation of new forms of *contentious politics*[28] to the emergence of a logic of connective action thanks to digital technology and from participatory rhetoric to experiences of democratic involvement. Within this broad and not unambiguous framework, even the phenomena of abstention and the decline of trust should be redefined in a broader analysis of the transformation of the forms of democratic activity in which parties tend to lose their centrality. In other words, new forms of intermediation are emerging and seem to guarantee broader and more active participation, from pressure groups to *social forums*, from *advocacy* groups to voluntary associations and civil intervention, from social movements with general political aims to *grassroots movements,* sometimes linked to local and/or specific demands, and new urban movements. There is no lack, of course, of phenomena of anaesthetisation of political participation, caged within procedures that are as 'innovative' as they are devoid of real 'empowerment' for citizens.

The new political actors move in what Habermas called 'culturally mobilised public spheres', in which precisely the activation of new *intermediate bodies in movement* is possible. Within this framework, collective movements construct new collective identities. These new, more or less structured actors are those who adopt—in Rosanvallon's (2008) theorisation—*counterdemocratic* practices,[29] i.e., actions of vigilance, control and political denunciation. The aim of these activities, according to the French political historian, is not to achieve power but to influence and correct it, going beyond the dynamics of electoral competition (which is therefore no longer recognised as the only founding element of the democratic system). Thus, in this respect, alongside the flight into apathy, which is also present, the collective demand for new forms of social and political engagement is expanding. On the one hand, demands from the galaxy of social movements have developed; on the other hand, different and 'creative' forms of civic engagement, often labelled *active citizenship,* have asserted themselves.

Giovanni Moro very lucidly highlighted the emergence of new conceptualisations of citizenship that accompany the new 'citizenships' or at least their claims. Among these various conceptualisations, important aspects are those concerning the separation between citizenship and nationality, the centrality of participation, and the shift from the centrality of identities to the value of differences; moreover, the latter constitutes one of the objectives of xenophobic and racist neo-identitarian policies that, moreover, are perfectly in tune with the 'culture of waste' repeatedly denounced by Pope Francis. From these new conceptual perspectives, new claims for citizenship emerge; these range from urban citizenship to European citizenship (which is linked

[28] Tilly and Tarrow (2015).

[29] Rosanvallon (2008).

to a territory but not to a 'nation'), from global citizenship to digital citizenship, to gender citizenship and, of course, to active citizenship.[30]

The latter is—in Moro's beautiful and effective definition—a practice that:

> consists of a multiplicity of organisational forms and collective actions aimed at implementing rights, caring for common goods and/or supporting subjects in weakened conditions through the exercise of powers and responsibilities in policy making.[31]

Thus, active citizenship connects the nonprofit sphere, that of so-called civil society, and that of political commitment. Again, Giovanni Moro (2013) states that active citizenship does not involve political participation through political parties or through trade unions or associations operating in the world of economy and work; that is, all the so-called 'intermediate bodies' are excluded, which, while performing a representative action, do not constitute collective actions of active citizenship. Also excluded from the list of active citizenship experiences are the aggregations of civil society that carry out a relevant action of building social capital and yet are not, according to Moro, elements of active citizenship. Saying what is not active citizenship makes it possible to identify its actors. In reality, the universe of active citizenship is very broad and articulated. If political participation through parties is excluded, active citizenship includes reception centres, collective action movements, informal networks and even civic initiatives on the internet. The classification of active citizenship actors is very complex, not only because of the great variety of initiatives and organisational forms present on the ground but also because of the internet. It is certainly simpler to identify the *characteristics of active citizenship*, which Giovanni Moro classifies along six macrovariables: (a) the existence of a multiplicity of organisational forms; (b) the existence of a multiplicity of motivations on the part of 'active' citizens, from the sense of justice to the dimension of solidarity, from the desire for change to that of playing an active role in social processes, from the drive to work together to the desire to explore and experience one's own reality; (c) the existence of a multiplicity of fields of action, mostly transversal, from the environment to civil protection, from political commitment to welfare to education, from social battles for public services to consumerist ones, etc.; (d) the desire for commitment to public policy, which is considered a priority over commitment to parties and/or 'traditional politics'; (e) the development of a strong spirit of concreteness; and f) an approach to participation that is not purely symbolic but, on the contrary, a participatory spirit aimed at achieving concrete results. Some of the characteristics of active citizenship are both elements of strength (because they constitute a specific form of intervention and social relevance) and of potential weakness (the renunciation of politics in favour of 'policies' may represent, as with some forms of democratic innovation, a risk of confinement to marginal governance experiences).

Various tools and practices are adopted as part of active citizenship; Moro still calls them 'technologies' since these practices are based on tools (communicative, legal, public action) that constitute real technical–formal apparatuses.[32]

---

[30] Moro (2013).

[31] Moro (2013, p. 28).

[32] Moro (2013).

These different 'technologies' are also closely connected with the different types of active citizenship, where in-effect information or advisory activities coexist with the management of services (think of listening and guidance organisations, proximity activities, forms of reception and assistance) or even experiences of civicism (the collection of signatures or education in the critical use of the media) with mechanisms for activating institutions (from support for citizens' legal action to complaints and consumerism practices). Even when analysing the different technologies of active citizenship, one can see the breadth of a phenomenon that is difficult to classify in overly rigid interpretative grids. However, the most important aspect of this phenomenon is its capacity to activate forms of citizen participation, often outside not only the spaces of political representation through parties but also the areas of intervention and engagement traditionally occupied by nonprofits. The space of active citizenship, in fact, is located in an interstitial zone that is within civil society but is essentially informal. Moreover, it is 'a phenomenon of self-organisation that may or may not meet with institutions, but which nevertheless has as its perspective that of looking after the general interest'.[33]

The experiences of active citizenship can be placed within the framework of the third sector; at the same time, they do not completely overlap with this framework since both the active citizenship and the third sector entities contain very diverse and articulated experiences. Both in the logic of active citizenship and in that of the third sector, however, political participation constitutes both an end and a means of social and economic development, since it favours (or should favour) the increase in decision-making power of the most marginalised social groups and gives representation to the voices of these social groups. From such a perspective, the egalitarian and inclusive variables of participation are always strongly emphasised, and there is a strong sensibility aimed at recovering the 'common' dimension.[34] The perspective identified by a new 'reason for the common'[35] is almost naturally based on the development of the community as an agent of change. From this point of view, the space of participation occupied by active citizenship (and the mobilisation of the third sector) theoretically constitutes a counternarrative to neoliberal rationality. At the same time, they reverse the very logic of citizenship: it is such, in fact, only if it is inclusive and if it is capable of being founded on the idea and practices of participation. In other words, one does not participate simply because one is a citizen; in contrast, participation defines citizenship. Such an idea of citizenship—on the basis of the community dimension—cannot be inclusive.

[33] Moro (2013, p. 243).

[34] Harvey (2019).

[35] Dardot and Laval (2019).

3 Examples of Resistance

Here, we would like to mention some relevant cases of the use of digital technologies as tools for inclusion or, in other cases, as tools to support bottom-up action by vulnerable actors or as tools to connect forms of direct action.

We refer here to the case of the Belgian Citizens' Platform for Refugee Support, a genuine experience of self-representation in which the logic of 'direct representation' becomes an instrument of countervailing power.

Another case—unlike the first two—is the role of hyperlocal media, which is also increasingly central due to the significant decline in traditional journalistic models. It is precisely the possibilities offered by the internet and digital technologies that enable hyperlocal initiatives to strengthen civic engagement in territories and act as a site and resource for local deliberative processes. Many studies in this area have been conducted in the last 5–6 years in different parts of the world, especially in Northern Europe (but there are experiences spread in several areas of the world). In particular, hyperlocal media not only provide information but also contribute to community building and often act as instruments of civic mediation, sometimes even beyond their own expectations and even beyond their own projects.

In this chapter, to provide examples from empirically studied social practices, we have focused on the fifteen-year-long training course of FQTS (Formazione Quadri Dirigenti del Terzo Settore nel Sud),[36] which has enabled us to meet, train, analyse and accompany people with experiences in third sector organisations in the communities and territories of many regions in southern Italy.

Among these multiple experiences, we cite those that, owing to their peculiar characteristics and problematic nature, for the actions implemented and for the obstacles encountered, are, in our opinion, significant for the discussion of the approach we proposed in the first part of the chapter. The realities concerned are (a) the "Librino" district (in the municipality of Catania, Sicily), with a population of 15,000 inhabitants, in which the actions carried out were developed primarily in the direction of the implementation of a digital platform; (b) the "Margi" neighbourhood, in the municipality of Gela (again in Sicily), a liminal area contiguous to the now disused petrochemical pole; (c) the "Panebianco" neighbourhood, in the municipality of Cosenza (Calabria), where multiple communities coexist and in which the primary objective of the intervention was the involvement in the implementation of ecological transition objectives; (d) the "Fantasia" district, in the municipality of San Severo (in Apulia), a real "forgotten" liminal space, in which the territorial action was aimed at consolidating the links between public administration and third sector entities; and (e) the Pellaro district, in the municipality of Reggio Calabria, in which actions were developed for the implementation of hybrid processes (digital and "on site") of participation and for the social development of the community. In this district, direct action was based on a theoretical approach that referred to urban and media practices and the mediated construction of social reality. The activation

[36] FQTS is a training programme promoted by Forum del Terzo Settore Nazionale and CSV Net Coordinamento dei Centri di Servizi al Volontariato funded by 'Fondazione Con il Sud'.

of the community development process focused on the intertwining of deep mediatisation and the everyday lives of people in the neighbourhood.[37] In particular, actions that enabled the growth of social and digital/social skills among the most vulnerable people were developed. From an edu-communication perspective,[38] these people were enabled to become protagonists in the process of territorial and digital relationship development, also owing to the use of participation and community platforms, both commercial and co-constructed by citizens, and made easily accessible even to those with less basic digital skills.

Periodic meetings with third sector organisations, public administrations and citizens in these communities have made it possible to identify both the actions that have been carried out and are feasible and the main obstacles that people have faced and continue to face in their daily lives.

In general, some common elements on which to reflect can be hypothesised. The transitional liminal status of many of the selected communities is characterised by geographical, political and social characteristics. In the first case, these are peripheral and marginal territories within urban and/or regional contexts that are themselves peripheral and marginal. Sometimes the peripherality is so marked (as, for example, in the case of Gela) that it results in isolation even with respect to the mobility flows characterising the area. In terms of social aspects, all communities are characterised by deep social fractures, widespread social and digital vulnerability, a rarefaction of social relations and social capital, and difficulty in having ideas and aspirations with respect to the future, both individual and, above all, collective. In addition, there is often environmental degradation in part linked to dilapidated, obsolete and chaotic urban structures and in part linked to the infrastructural and economic development interventions carried out in the 1950s, 1960s and 1970s, which still have profound consequences for communities. An example of this is the case of the 'Liquichimica' in Saline Ioniche, just after punta Pellaro, where the beach was gutted and the company lived for only 48 hours.

The second common dimension is mistrust in the ability of local and national institutions to activate policies and actions of real transformation and change to the status quo. Isolation is not only geographical, social and political but also negatively perceived in media representations that ignore or fail to support any process of empowerment and activation of liminal communities in the South.

The third dimension is the idea that everyone must look after his or her own interests and family. This is not, of course, the amoral familism described by Banfield in the 1950s[39] but rather a deep-rootedness of neoliberal individualism that does not allow for other ways of dealing with problems and opportunities for potential social development. It is a form of de-subjectivised individualism, different from that traditionally assumed in classical theories of liberalism.[40]

[37] Hepp (2015, 2020).

[38] Barbas (2020).

[39] Banfield (1958).

[40] Sorice (2022, pp. 107–130).

Despite this general picture, individual liminal communities have tried and are trying to set up actions that attempt to address some of the issues just described. Among the actions on which we want to focus, the first is the push for the activation of groups of people, organisations, and citizens capable of mobilising themselves in relation to their own community. A thrust that often has difficulty emerging owing to the lack of awareness of the condition of liminality and marginality experienced by communities. On the other hand, the drive may arise from a problem (think of the environmental issue left by the petrochemical plant in Gela) or an opportunity (the case of participation in a Fondazione con il Sud call for proposals, as in the case of Pellaro in Reggio Calabria) experienced as coming from the outside that interacts with the assumed familiarity everyday life[41] of individuals and organisations. On other occasions, it is something that stems from a meeting on other topics (tables on social policies promoted by the municipal administration, as in the case of San Severo) that 'forces' people to discuss together for a certain period, thus having the opportunity to deepen both mutual knowledge and the density of relations, the first step towards the constitution of micronuclei of social capital. Obviously, the thrust of a group is not the only one that enables the social development of community consciousness. In fact, as a second relevant dimension, communicative processes and media ecosystems play crucial roles as both opportunities and obstacles. In the first case, social media, on the one hand, and proximity and participatory digital platforms, on the other hand, offer an informal and formal space[42] for people to come together who are not necessarily motivated by any particular endogenous or exogenous drive. To understand whether digital spaces can represent an opportunity, in Librino, the digital proximity platform has made it possible to reach those who would otherwise have been excluded from any democratic and participatory process. The virtuous circuit between digital participation and engagement in the territory has, in fact, enabled the use of 'community gardens', which have become the driving force behind a renewed push for the conscious use of spaces.[43] In Panebianco, the informal Facebook groups were able to see the activation of a portion of the community that decided to be part of the 'I am from Panebianco if...' group, recounting feelings, emotions and even ideas on the future of the neighbourhood. In other situations, on the other hand, digital spaces have been an obstacle to the development of relations because, as in Pellaro, digital platforms are either too sophisticated and difficult to understand or are still crude and, therefore, unable to keep up with what can be found in digital social media markets. The third communicative dimension is that of interpersonal, intra- and intragroup relations. In many liminal communities, one can find seamless dual presences (onsite and digital), where the intensification of relationships is the first relevant step that can anticipate the ability to imagine

[41] Blokland (2017).

[42] This is often unconscious for the former, while the latter generally have precise and delineated objectives, most of which can be located in the operating dynamics of digital capitalism (Srnicek, 2016).

[43] In this case, the role of the social centre and rugby club 'I briganti' (ASD Onlus) as a space of resistance and proposal should also be mentioned.

participatory processes. This aspect is often underestimated because it fails to be perceived as a 'concrete' aspect both by the people living in liminal communities and by those who have government roles and functions or by specific social actors (third sector organisations, trade unions). The centrality of relationships is "discovered" only when they facilitate broader and more articulated processes such as, for example, the construction of networks and partnerships that help to design projects in response to specific calls for proposals.

The immateriality of social relations and their value for social cohesion and mobility are certainly not a discovery of our reflection,[44] but what we highlight the distance between the awareness of their relevance and centrality in participatory processes and social development and in the strengthening of media ecosystems. In the first case, it is sufficient to refer to how the contrast with the hegemony of organised crime (present in many of the liminal communities examined) passes precisely fthrough the terrain of positive social relations that oppose the widespread ones oriented towards exploitation and tacit submission. In the second case, the ability to, for example, expand the storytelling coming from liminal communities depends precisely on the density and quality of the social relations present. Indeed, individual experience becomes collective in liminal communities if and how it manages to navigate through relationships. This is, for instance, the case in Gela, where young mothers were able to participate and tell their stories owing to the relationships built through their daughters and sons participating in play activities with the volunteer educators of the Margi neighbourhood. A fluidity in relational communication is activated and becomes a resource for emancipation without being imposed or prescribed from the outside.

Finally, there is no less important reflection on participatory processes. In liminal communities, it is often complicated to start or facilitate a participatory process, but once the experience has been made, the training is continuous and particularly generative of innovative paths. In Gela, after a year of discussions with a small group of activists, the creation of an 'open space' with approximately 100 citizens (10% of the inhabitants) of the Margi neighbourhood was the starting point for a possible mobilisation and practice of resistance. In Fantasia, after almost two years, it was possible to have an 'open space' and a 'fishbowl' with more than 200 people who tried to discuss together the future of the neighbourhood and the city.[45] It seems that much time is needed to learn or relearn to participate, but in reality, it means coming to terms with those processes of individualisation, disconnection and a-politics that have characterised and still characterise the current phase of neoliberalism. Here, again, the trusting relationships and industrious patience that the initial promoting

[44] Bourdieu (1979), Forsè and Tronca (2005), Putnam (2001, pp. 41–51).

[45] The open space is an articulated moment of collaborative and participatory discussion and is based on an engagement technique known as "open space technology" (also often used in school learning processes: see, among others, van Woezik et al. (2019), as well as https://openspaceworld.org/wp2/). The fishbowl is a conversation technique in the form of a dialogue that follows precise rules of organisation and architecture—also spatial—of the group/community/class that carries out this activity; the use of the discussion space in a spatial space is also a specific element of the procedure of participation and collective construction of social meanings.

groups were able to build served to avoid interrupting the mobilisation of a movement and, at the same time, to keep alive communicative and relational processes that, to have a social impact, had to be extended to a larger number of the population of the liminal community. The issue of popularity is an unavoidable element that can neither be neglected nor ignored in processes of potential transformation of liminal communities.

However, can liminal communities truly change? Our first analysis revealed that there are lights and shadows in each community. One aspect that needs to be emphasised is certainly the temporal dimension because, barring particularly violent traumas (such as a natural or man-made disaster), daily life tends to remain within the canons of familiarity rather than change. The second aspect is certainly the role of local governments. When and if they succeed in working alongside the people in the communities, they also develop possibilities for building first political and then administrative conditions for change. The case of San Severo in the province of Foggia is significant because the local administrators and the local public administration have made themselves promoters of places of confrontation on an equal footing with third sector organisations and those from liminal communities. The third aspect is the openness of third-sector organisations and intermediate bodies to communities. This is not a secondary aspect, because it is through their daily presence in the difficulties and dealing with problems that people in liminal communities feel less alone and venture into battles that seem, at first sight, almost hopeless. The fourth aspect is the role that communicative ecosystems can play in representing and narrating change. We are not referring, of course, to the old experiences of civic journalism or *citizen journalism* (which are often variously understood) but, rather, to a complex system that interacts with communities, drawing sustenance from them to be able to also change and, sometimes, survive. In Gela, journalism professionals who had left the media system because they were threatened by organised crime decided to contribute to the creation of a neighbourhood communication system that would help change the discriminating and excluding narrative. In Pellaro, on the other hand, they became an integral part of supporting the digital communication strategy and visual identity of some products (beer and bergamot marmalade) whose sale fuels the territorial mutuality born around confiscated property. A militant and resistant digital communication that, in liminality, has found new spaces for creativity, imagination and freedom that have almost disappeared in institutionalised media.[46]

[46] Experiences of 'reuse' of digital communication are of course also present elsewhere in Europe (think of the case of Bremen, Germany), although with different characteristics from those we have been able to study in the liminal spaces of southern Italy.

4 Digital Technologies Between Citizenship and Self-Empowerment

In the experiences mentioned in the previous paragraph, the importance of adopting digital technologies and, more generally, of co-constructing digital ecosystems is evident. Although limitations—in terms of ownership structures, social control, market logics, and even the risks of manipulation in digital ecosystems—are evident, they nevertheless represent instruments of potential (and sometimes real) self-empowerment of subjects living in liminal spaces and, in particular, of vulnerable subjects.[47] Thus, the inevitable adoption of digital tools constitutes an opportunity, the risks of which nevertheless seem acceptable, at least within communities in which a dialogic and inclusive participatory practice has developed.

The discourse becomes more complicated when we refer to artificial intelligence (AI). First, there is a question of sustainability (the development of AI-based tools is costly in terms of energy and the environment), and second, there is still no 'participatory' culture in the implementation of AI, even though attempts have been made.[48] Not coincidentally, over the last few years, a new focus on the reliability of AI has emerged, particularly in the development of tools that respect human rights and are fair, transparent,.safe and easily explainable—in their operating dynamics—to those who use them.[49] Then, there are economic issues: if the development of collaborative and independent digital spaces is complex but possible also owing to crowdfunding (think of the experiences of the independent browser 'Vivaldi', for instance, or of search engines such as 'Qwant' or 'SearXNG' or, again, of the many experiences of the fediverse[50]), envisioning a collaborative and horizontal development of AI is not simple at the moment. The situation of the fast transformation of the platform society[51] is not easy to analyse empirically.

Another aspect involves the short circuit between digital activism[52] and AI, which, even more than digital spaces, still seems to be strongly controlled by a few global actors. The possibilities offered by digital activism are now an important part of studies on political participation and social engagement[53]; the possibilities of using AI in implementing participatory processes and empowering citizens, especially those in vulnerable situations, certainly remain to be explored.

In the empirical cases summarised here, we have examined forms of participation that can be described as "hybrid". Along with the dynamics of democratic participation traditionally defined in international textbooks, we also consider hybrid

---

[47] Antonucci et al. (2024).

[48] Delgado et al. (2023).

[49] See, in this regard, the OECD website: https://oecd.ai/en/.

[50] Vivaldi: https://vivaldi.net; Qwant: https://www.qwant.com; SearXNG: https://searxng.devol.it. The fediverse is a set of 'federated' servers that, while remaining independent, can activate communication mechanisms, thus creating networks for publishing content on the web.

[51] Van Dijck et al. (2018).

[52] Kaun and Uldam (2018, pp. 2099–2106).

[53] Coleman and Blumler (2009), Postill (2012), Coleman (2017), Muldoon (2022).

participation processes involving online perspectives (and, potentially, in the future, applications of AI).

The first dimension lies on a continuum at the extremes of onsite and online participation. This does not mean that we will have onsite participatory processes in a certain amount and online processes in the remaining amount. However, hybridisation with a different configuration in each context also takes on singular characteristics.[54] For example, it is imaginable to activate a participatory process on how a public space should be managed for younger generations, to continue discussions on social media with those who cannot be present, and then to return to the territory with a greater number of participants and a greater awareness of the necessary actions to be taken. There is a continuity between onsite and digital knowledge that is now established in life experiences, even among non-digital natives.[55] The second dimension of hybrid participatory processes lies on the continuum between formality and informality. Examples of the first are participatory processes that can be imagined and constructed within urban regeneration paths within a public institutional framework. They often have the characteristics of a top-down process, with the sole purpose of building consensus on choices that have already been made without giving people a chance for real and effective participation.[56] Examples of the second aspect, on the other hand, are the participatory processes that arise spontaneously on the basis of different stimuli (a specific problem linked to the environment, an exceptional event, a change in the social context, etc.) and that see the use of tools that allow the opportunity to participate to be given to people who want it. We must note that in hybrid participation processes, the issue of digital inequalities does not disappear but is, at least partially, mitigated by the opportunity to be able to participate onsite without losing the thread that connects the entire participatory process for those with little digital capital. We highlight that there are no "perfect" participatory processes but rather paths that intersect the processes of refiguration of liminal communities, developing spaces and contexts, sometimes of development, often of resistance (even to the mobilising logic of populisms) and innovation.

Even if experiments with the use of AI in processes that support the empowerment of vulnerable people are still in their infancy (and, as we have said, pose numerous problems, including ethical ones), they represent a possibility that must be followed up and scientifically studied. AI represents an opportunity (not forgetting, of course, its risks), but it must be placed in a broader framework in which the various variables at play are explored and studied. In our view, it is necessary for AI—like the internet and digital ecosystems—to become spaces controlled by the "public" (not by governments and/or markets), in the logic proposed a few years ago by the "Public Service Internet Manifesto". It is in this logic, we believe, that AI should be placed, and in this way, it could become an important tool to support human vulnerability or at least a tool to support the empowerment of subjects, regardless of whether they are in liminal spaces.

---

[54] Reckwitz (2020).

[55] Boccia Artieri et al. (2017).

[56] Sorice (2021).

References

Ambrosini M, Cinalli M, Jacobson D (eds) (2020) Migration, borders and citizenship: between policy and public spheres. Palgrave Macmillan, Cham
Antonucci MC, Sorice M, Volterrani A (2024) Liminalities: social vulnerabilities between participatory processes and digital space in the neoliberal era. In: Tsatsou P (ed) (2022) Vulnerable people and digital inclusion. Palgrave Macmillan, Cham
Balibar E (2015) Citizenship. Polity, Cambridge
Banfield EC (1958) The moral basis of a backward society. The Free Press, Glencoe, IL
Barbas À (2020) Educommunication for social change. Contributions to the construction of a theory of activist media practices. In: Stephansen HC, Trerè E (eds) Citizen media and practice. Currents, connections, challenges. Routledge, London
Blokland T (2017) Community as urban practice. Polity Press, Cambridge
Blokland T, Kruger D, Vief R, Schultze H (2022) Where we turn to. Rethinking networks, urban space and research methods. In: Million A, Haid C, Ulloa IC, Baur N (eds) Spatial transformations. Kaleidoscopic perspectives on the refiguration of spaces. Routledge, New York, pp 258–268
Blokland T, Rae D (2008) The end of urbanism: how the changing spatial structure of cities affected its social capital potentials. In: Blockland T, Savage M (eds) Networked urbanism. Social capital in the city. Routledge, New York, pp 23–39
Boccia Artieri G, Gemini L, Pasquali F, Carlo S, Farci M, Pedroni M (2017) Fenomenologia dei social network. Guerini Scientifica, Milano
Boltanski L, Chiapello E (2005) The new spirit of capitalism. Verso, London
Bourdieu P (1979) La distinction: critique sociale du jugement. Editions de Minuit, Paris
Brown K, Ecclestone K, Emmel N (2017) The many faces of vulnerability. Soc Policy Soc 16(3):497–500
Casey E (1993) Getting back into place: toward a renewed understanding of the place-world. Indiana University Press, Bloomington
Castel R (2014) Les métamorphoses de la question sociale: une chronique du salariat. Fayard, Paris
Coleman S (2017) Can the internet strengthen democracy? Polity, Cambridge
Coleman S, Blumler JG (2009) The internet and democratic citizenship: theory, practice and policy. Cambridge University Press, Cambridge
Couldry N (2004) Theorising media as practice. Soc Semiotics 14(2):115–132
Couldry N (2022) The space of the world. https://www.youtube.com/watch?
Couldry N, Hepp A (2017) The mediated construction of reality. Polity, Cambridge
Dale K, Burrell G (2008) The spaces of organization and the organization of space: power, identity and materiality at work. Palgrave, London
Dardot P, Laval C (2014) The new way of the world. On neoliberal society. Verso, London
Dardot P, Laval C (2019) Common: on revolution in the 21st century. Bloomsbury, London
Delgado F, Yang S, Madaio M, Yang Q (2023) The participatory turn in AI design: theoretical foundations and the current state of practice. In: Equity and Access in Algorithms, Mechanisms, and Optimization (EAAMO '23), October 30–November 01, 2023, Boston, MA, USA. ACM. https://doi.org/10.1145/3617694.3623261
Elias N (1987) Die Gesellschaft der individuen. Suhrkamp, Frankfurt a.M.
Forsè M, Tronca L (2005) Capitale sociale e analisi dei reticoli. Franco Angeli, Milano
Fraser N (2022) Cannibal capitalism: how our system is devouring democracy, care, and the planet. And what we can do about it. Verso, London
Hall S, O'Shea A (2015) Common-sense neoliberalism. In: Hall S, Massey D, Rustin M (eds) After neoliberalism? The Kilburn manifesto. Soundings—Lawrence and Wishart, London, pp 8–24
Hall, S. (1990) Cultural identity and diaspora. In Gilroy, P., Wilson Gilmore, R. (2021) Stuart Hall. Selected writings on race and culture. Duke University Press, Durham
Harvey D (2019) Rebel cities: from the right to the city to the urban revolution. Verso, London
Hepp A (2015) Transcultural communication. Wiley, Hoboken

Hepp A (2020) Deep mediatization. Routledge, London-New York
Kaun A, Uldam J (2018) Digital activism: after the hype. New Media Soc 20(6):2099–2106. https://doi.org/10.1177/1461444817731924
Knoublach H, Löw M (2017) On the spatial refiguration of the social world. Sociologica 2:1–27. https://doi.org/10.12759/hsr.45.2020.2.263-29
McGuigan J (2009) Cool capitalism. Pluto Press, London
McGuigan J (2016) Neoliberal culture. Palgrave Macmillan, New York
Micheletti M, McFarland A (2012) Creative participation: responsibility-taking in the political world. Routledge, London
Moro G (2013) Cittadinanza attiva e qualità della democrazia. Carocci, Roma
Muldoon J (2022) Platform socialism: how to reclaim our digital future from big tech. Pluto Press, London
Pizzo B (2015) Fuoco incrociato sul planning. In: Moini G (ed) Neoliberismi e azione pubblica. Il caso italiano. Ediesse, Roma, p 185.
Postill J (2012) Digital politics and political engagement. In: Horst H, Miller D (eds) Digital anthropology. Berg, Oxford
Prodnik JA (2023) The crisis of legitimacy and the appropriation of resistance in capitalism. TripleC Commun Capital Critique 21(1):51–73
Putnam R (2001) Social capital: measurement and consequences. Can J Policy Res 2:41–51
Reckwitz A (2020) The society of singularities. Polity Press, Cambridge
Rosanvallon P (2008) Counter-democracy: politics in the age of distrust. Cambridge University Press, Cambridge
Sennett R (2018) Building and dwelling: ethics for the city. Farrar, Straus and Giroux, New York
Sorice M (2021) Partecipazione disconnessa: innovazione democratica e illusione digitale al tempo del neoliberismo. Carocci, Roma
Sorice M (2022) La razionalità neoliberista e gli ecosistemi digitali: ideologia, narrazioni, immaginari. Quaderni di Teoria Sociale 2:107–130. https://doi.org/10.57611/qts.v1i2.180
Srnicek N (2016) Platform Capitalism. Polity Press, Cambridge
Tilly C, Tarrow S (2015) Contentious politics. Oxford University Press, Oxford
Van Dijck J, Poell T, De Waal M (2018) The platform society: public values in a connective world. Oxford University Press, Oxford
van Woezik T, Reuzel R, Koksma J (2019) Exploring open space: A self-directed learning approach for higher education. Cogent Education. 6 (1)

Michele Sorice, Full Professor of Sociology of Cultural and Communicative Processes at the Department of Communication and Social Research, Sapienza University of Rome. Teaches Communication and Civic Engagement, and Theories of Communication and Digital Media.

Andrea Volterrani, Associate Professor of Sociology of Cultural and Communicative Processes at the Department of Business Engineering, University of Rome Tor Vergata. Teaches Sociology of Communication, Sociology of Political Processes, and Sociology of Cultural Processes.

Open Access This chapter is licensed under the terms of the Creative Commons Attribution 4.0 International License (http://creativecommons.org/licenses/by/4.0/), which permits use, sharing, adaptation, distribution and reproduction in any medium or format, as long as you give appropriate credit to the original author(s) and the source, provide a link to the Creative Commons license and indicate if changes were made.

The images or other third party material in this chapter are included in the chapter's Creative Commons license, unless indicated otherwise in a credit line to the material. If material is not included in the chapter's Creative Commons license and your intended use is not permitted by statutory regulation or exceeds the permitted use, you will need to obtain permission directly from the copyright holder.

The Residential Digital Divide and the 'Right to the Village'

Manlio Lisanti

Abstract Well before the Covid-19 epidemic, in 2017, the European Union set the goal of providing every member state with free Wi-Fi in the main urban centres (WiFi4EU) by 2020. This initiative stems from the awareness that Internet Access reduces inequalities caused by the digital divide. Its importance in the exercise of fundamental rights contrasts with the peppered development of infrastructural networks. This creates digital vulnerabilities for those who are left with incomplete—or even partial—access to the network. Most of these issues, at least in Italy, affect the inland areas of the Peninsula, which are home to about 13 million people and are dotted with villages at risk of depopulation. This chapter aims to investigate to what extent the digital divide may contribute to the violation of fundamental rights for residents of small towns. It also seeks to lay out a "right to the village", drawing from the right to the city. The expression represents the need, on the part of the inhabitants of villages, to claim a standard of quality of life and equal dignity of development compared to geographically more advantaged areas.

Keywords Digital divide · Access · Infrastructure · Essential service · Village

1 Introduction

The increasing reliance on digital tools and internet connectivity experienced significant acceleration due to the Covid-19 pandemic, during which normal human activities, reduced to the essentials, continued only through technology. This unforeseen circumstance caught public administrations and private entities off guard, forcing them, often reluctantly, to immediately adopt technology to fulfil their duties or to provide public services remotely, where possible.

There was an increasingly urgent need to enable and ensure internet access, a challenge that the pandemic found us only halfway prepared for, with a digitalization process that had begun but was unsatisfactory in terms of its implementation.

M. Lisanti (✉)
University of Rome Tor Vergata, Rome, Italy
e-mail: manlio.lisanti@students.uniroma2.eu

© The Author(s) 2025

C. Amodio and A. Diurni (eds.), *Human Vulnerability in Interaction with AI in European Private Law*, https://doi.org/10.1007/978-3-031-93247-2_10

This inevitably led to a slowdown in activities, services, and, ultimately, the economy on a generalized level, with even more severe issues in inland areas, so-called disadvantaged or remote areas, where internet connectivity is not guaranteed or is entirely lacking.

The situation that emerged further highlighted what had already become a reality for a significant portion of citizens: the existence of a genuine vulnerability due to the lack of adequate internet access.[1] This situation has influenced and continues to influence certain categories of individuals already identified as vulnerable, expanding the number of people facing vulnerability.[2] Indeed, there has been a disconnect between the usual categories of vulnerable individuals and those who, in themselves, would rarely be defined as such. The shortcomings of the internet network in disadvantaged areas of our country have first revealed and then exacerbated a new possible form of vulnerability—residential vulnerability.[3]

The effects resulting from the inability or limitation in accessing the internet translate into social isolation, lack of opportunities to access knowledge, greater difficulty in interacting with public administrations, and, in general, the violation of substantive equality.

The absence of infrastructure leads to the actual impossibility of accessing the internet. This becomes an obstacle to fulfilling both material needs—such as benefitting from the Internet of Things, participate in administrative procedures, or access platforms that match supply and demand for jobs—and immaterial needs related to personal development, such as accessing online knowledge, enjoying digital or digitized works of art, engaging in social interaction, or participating in political life.[4] Accessing the internet means being able to exercise one's fundamental freedoms.

These circumstances have certainly incentivized living in areas that are better connected to the network and the services that come with it, resulting in a significant contribution to the depopulation of some areas to the detriment of others, which become increasingly overcrowded. The impact of depopulation in certain

---

[1] Wessels B (2013), p. 17–28: 'One can start to assess the significance of exclusion from social networks based on digital technology when one sees that it is the use of technology within social relations that produces inequality. One can see that inclusion into digitally enabled networks is significant in terms of the opportunities people have to engage in economic life and to participate in political, social, and cultural life. The embedding of digital technology in social, economic, democratic process and cultural forms is materializing and is experienced unevenly and differently by people across the globe'.

[2] Pastore (2020, pp. 284).

[3] Human Rights Council Resolution 32/13, A/HRC/RES/32/13, 18 July 2016, para. 5. See also: Chirwa D and Ncube C (2023) p. 23–52: "Internet has a fundamental role in developing internal areas. There is a remarkable difference between rural and urban development, education, access to information, health and political participation, caused by a lack of opportunities connected to internet access. While the Geneva Principles and Plan of Action do not recognise a right of access to the internet, the Geneva Principles and its Plan of Action, Resolution 32/13 of the UNHRC emphasises the 'importance of applying a comprehensive human rights-based approach in providing and in expanding access to the internet.' Then it says that all states have to 'make efforts to bridge the many forms of digital divide.'

[4] Jones (2014, p. 4).

areas is particularly evident when compared to the growth of cities, which have been grappling for years with the opposite problem: overpopulation.

In light of these premises, the inequality is cross-cutting. It transcends the boundaries that have traditionally occupied scholars, affecting, to varying degrees[5] men and women, the elderly and the young, and the more or less impoverished.

Starting from the fact that all people are vulnerable, but some are more vulnerable than others,[6] the risk lies in the de facto exclusion of certain categories of individuals who may not fit the common conception of a vulnerable person but who nonetheless share greater difficulty in accessing the internet and exercising the rights and freedoms that it facilitates.

The lack of internet connectivity, or of a quality connection, is among the contributing factors to the depopulation of inland and rural areas, a problem that affects specific regions in every European country and beyond.[7] Particular attention must be given to the depopulation of Italy's inland areas and villages. This dynamic not only deprives territories, especially mountainous ones, of human presence, with negative consequences for the proper management and maintenance of the land, but also leads to the abandonment of villages. These villages, which serve as the embryos of cities, are part of the landscape and are part of the cultural heritage.[8]

The depopulation of villages and remote areas results in the irretrievable loss of a significant portion of the cultural, environmental, architectural identity of certain social groups. These groups, incentivized to leave their homelands, are also stripped of the traditions and memories that have accompanied them for centuries. For this reason, what was once transmitted in those areas, especially inland, along paths that were often offshoots of the ancient Roman consular roads—through merchants, itinerant artists, notaries, clerics, and pilgrims—should now be transmitted through the new channels of knowledge and wealth, whose vehicle is access to the internet. This access must be guaranteed and protected.

2 Current Data on Access

Globally, the digital divide affects about 55% of the population, effectively excluding them from the ability to exercise their rights. This phenomenon can be attributed to several causes. Some states' political agenda to prevent their populations from using the internet, seeing it as a vehicle of information and a risk to their stability; the lack of financial resources, which prevents adequate compensation and consequently makes

[5] Cole (2016, pp. 260–277, 260).

[6] Coeckelbergh (2013, p. 157).

[7] Ruiz-Martinez and Esparcia (2020, 1–17, pp. 5); Salemink et al. (2017, 555–575, pp. 558), Dyba et al. (2020, 51–59. pp. 51 ff); "Digital divide as a development issue for rural areas emerged from recent studies conducted shortly before the Covid-19 epidemic."

[8] Benvenuti (1997), p. 2: 'the historic centre is much more than a landscape or an environment: it is the landscape of man or, to use terms that might seem poetic, the environment of the soul' (author's translation).

it impossible for families to afford a computer or smartphone; and the vastness of the territory, which makes it very difficult to spread the internet network to the most remote areas with adequate infrastructure.[9]

By comparing two very different realities, one can see how territorial digital divide a common problem is in both more and less developed states. In India, for example, only 4.4% of families living outside cities own a computer, while the percentage of families that own a computer rises to 14.4% in cities.[10] The rural population, which often corresponds to ethnic minorities and tribal populations, such as the Jharkhand, Madhya Pradesh, Odisha, and Chhattisgarh, in larger states like Uttar Pradesh, West Bengal, Andhra Pradesh, Bihar, and Gujarat, has very limited access to the internet.[11] In 2019, 14.9% of rural households had internet access, compared to 42% of households in urban areas.[12]

Looking at data from the United States, the rural digital divide highlights the same network distribution problems. In 2018, about 50% of residents in rural areas of the United States had access to the internet at 250/25 megabits per second, compared to 94% of urban residents. Seven out of ten Americans living in rural areas had a broadband internet connection at home.[13] Even in 2020, over 22.3% of Americans living in rural areas did not have access to high-speed broadband, as well as 27.7% of residents in Tribal lands, compared to 1.5% of Americans living in urban areas.[14] In 2021, 85% of city residents and 75% of rural residents had internet access.[15]

The examples examined highlight how the territorial digital divide is due to a lack of infrastructure and is therefore a problem related to the insufficient capacity to offer a service that, as will be seen, must be considered essential.

The digital divide is not only an international phenomenon, between one state and another, between the more and less developed parts of the world. Its dimension is twofold. It also involves different areas within the same state, with the result that some of its inhabitants will be advantaged by residing in certain areas compared to others.

Its cross-cutting nature implies that the costs of connecting to the internet in rural areas are much higher. This happens, for example, in Australia, where internet services are much more expensive than in urban centres. In 2016, the availability of data in areas far from major Australian cities was less than 30 GB and concerned

[9] Schrubbe and Strover (2021, p. 46).

[10] National Sample Survey Organisation (NSSO). 2019. 'Key Indicators of Household Social Consumption on Education in India NSS 75th Round (July 2017–June 2018).' Ministry of Statistics and Programme Implementation. (https://pib.gov.in/Pressreleaseshare.aspx?PRID=1593251).

[11] Jeffin et al. (2023, p. 488).

[12] National Sample Survey Organisation (NSSO) (2019) Key Indicators of Household Social Consumption on Education in India NSS 75th Round (July 2017–June 2018). Ministry of Statistics and Programme Implementation. https://pib.gov.in/Pressreleaseshare.aspx?PRID=1593251.

[13] Pew Research Center (2021). See also: Jeffin et al. (2023, p. 485).

[14] Federal Communications Commission (2020).

[15] Power et al. (2020), pp. 61–67; Li and Li (2021), p. 571.

24% of the rural population. In contrast, the same availability concerned only 13% of city dwellers.[16]

Additionally, even though the service is not uniformly guaranteed, the costs of using the internet in the most remote areas of Australia are exorbitant.[17] In 2018, in Europe, just over 52.3% of rural households had access to broadband and high-speed internet.[18]

In Italy, the digital divide affects over 200 municipalities, where more than 10% of the inhabitants do not have stable access to the web. About 70 municipalities do not have access to the mobile network at all, while the latest data from the Italian Communication Authority shows that coverage with FTTH fiber, which guarantees a download speed of 1 Gb/s, benefits only 53.7% of Italian families.[19]

The main obstacle to the deployment of the infrastructure supporting the web is the morphology of the territory, characterized by internal areas that are difficult to access, affecting about 53% of the total number of Italian municipalities, well over four thousand, and covering about 60% of the national territory, representing a problem for over 13.5 million people.

3 The Nature of the Right to Internet Access

Access to the internet has increasingly become an expanding right. Even before the Covid-19 pandemic, the project of widespread digitalization in each EU member state was gaining traction through European legislation. Since 2017, the European Union set the goal of providing free Wi-Fi in the main urban gathering areas of every member state by 2020 (WiFi4EU).[20] Although the project faced several delays, it reflects the understanding that a fast and widespread internet connection is fundamental for achieving substantial equality.[21] Conversely, difficulties in accessing the internet lead to social, economic, and geographical inequalities.[22]

Legal scholars have examined the phenomenon of digitalization and internet access, not merely as a right to the internet itself but rather as a right aimed at exercising citizens' rights and prerogatives, thus as a right to access.[23] Often, the right to internet access has been identified as a fundamental or human right directly linked

[16] ACMA 2016 Australian Communications and Media Authority (2016).

[17] Malta and Wilding (2018), p. 28.

[18] European Commission (2019).

[19] AGCOM (2023).

[20] European Commission (n.d.).

[21] Pollicino et al. (2017); De Marco (2008).

[22] Norris (2001).

[23] Bassini (2019).

to freedom of speech[24]; other times, it has been seen as a common[25] or social right, based on the idea that access to the network is closely related to social public goods, which are essential for fulfilling civil and social rights, such as hospitals, public housing, and schools.[26] In this sense, these goods are classified as common, not because they are neither private nor public, but because they are the building blocks of society. Relationships of a community nature are established based on them. It is the relationship between the good and its user that qualifies it as common.[27]

However, the two perspectives tend to have many nuances, to the point of merging with each other. In fact, access to commons can be considered the logical prerequisite for enjoying fundamental rights.[28] Including internet access among the classical commons could be debatable, given that the internet does not fall into the category of scarce resources, such as a natural resource like a forest. Common goods can be either public or private, characterized by their necessity for exercising fundamental rights. If the connection between these goods and the exercise of fundamental rights is recognized, that is, if the functional relationship that binds them is highlighted, then a right of enjoyment is created, which can be protected as a personal right. The public administration is responsible for managing and organizing them, regulating how individuals may use or economically exploit them.[29]

The connection that might link web access to the category of commons concerns its functional aspect, which places the internet among those 'things that express functionalities necessary for exercising fundamental rights as well as for the free development of the person,'[30] regardless of whether a resource is scarce or not. This perspective is found in the concept of new commons,[31] among which the internet can be included, as it is a non-geographical space and represents an aberration in a property-obsessed era. It is 'a space that anyone can enter and take what they find without permission of a librarian or a promise to pay.'[32]

It should not be overlooked that internet access acts both as a tool through which freedoms and rights are exercised and as a condition for existence[33] in the 'new dimension of reality.'[34] Therefore, if the nature of internet access still needs to be thoroughly explored, what is certain is that this structure is generating new rights,[35]

---

[24] Conseil constitutionnel français, Decision no. 2009-580 DC of 10 June 2009. https://www.conseil-constitutionnel.fr/en/selection-of-dc-decisions.

[25] Gordon (1954); Hardin (1968); Ostrom (1990).

[26] Rodotà (2012); Caputi Jambrenghi (2017).

[27] Bixio (2020), p. 42.

[28] Westra (2011), p. 277; Weston and Bollier (2013).

[29] Cerulli Irelli (2022), p. 639; Cerulli Irelli and De Lucia (2014).

[30] Commissione Rodotà (2007).

[31] Hess (2013).

[32] Lessig (1999).

[33] Messinetti (2019).

[34] Brighi (2015).

[35] De Hert and Kloza (2012).

which will have to be addressed, protected, or remedies found within the legal system to prevent their misuse.

These trends have been recognized by the European Court of Human Rights, which in some cases has declared that unless there are justified and valid reasons, a public authority cannot prevent or limit an individual's access to the internet.

An emblematic case is Jankovskis v. Lithuania[36] where the European Court of Human Rights found that denying a prisoner internet access for educational purposes violated Article 10 of the Convention.

The case originated from a request made by the plaintiff to the Ministry of Education and Science, asking for information on the possibility of obtaining a second degree remotely, stating that he was temporarily in prison and could not physically attend educational institutions. The Ministry responded that all useful information could be found on the 'AIKOS' website, allowing anyone to access information about professors, courses, and programs online. The plaintiff then requested that the Correction Home provide the internet connection necessary to retrieve information from the site indicated by the Ministry.

The director of the Correction Home informed the plaintiff that his request for internet access could not be granted because no Lithuanian law allowed prisoners to use the internet or have an email account. The Kaunas Administrative Court rejected the plaintiff's request on the grounds that prisoners could still correspond with institutions via postal mail and that having internet access in prison would pose a security risk, as prisoners could continue criminal activities even while incarcerated.

The Supreme Administrative Court dismissed Jankovskis's appeal, stating that the right to use the internet was not absolute. The right of access could be restricted for certain groups, such as prisoners. This was also based on the fact that Lithuanian law did not provide any legal provisions allowing prisoners to use the internet, even for security reasons. The Court noted that the only way for the plaintiff to obtain certain information was to access the AIKOS website indicated by the Ministry and that the Lithuanian courts had focused on the ban on internet access for prisoners without considering that the plaintiff's request concerned access to the Ministry of Education's website. The Court observed that the domestic courts had not addressed the reasons behind the plaintiff's request. Based on these considerations, the Court concluded that the restrictions on internet access imposed by the Correction House and the domestic courts were unreasonable and affirmed the violation of Article 10 of the Convention.

The difficulties in connecting to the network, given technological developments and the digitalization of public administration, raise questions about the possibility of effective participation by private individuals in administrative decisions that may concern them. The repercussions of this situation could jeopardize the guarantees achieved so far. The rule of law and the principles of participation, transparency, due process, and judicial review, well-developed in most national laws, provide 'rules of the game'[37] for global procedural standards.

[36] Jankovskis v Lithuania, no. 21575/08, ECtHR judgment of 17 January 2017.

[37] Cassese (2005), p. 111.

Seeing an opportunity to increase transparency and participation, the dissemination of information via the internet was welcomed with great enthusiasm in the mid-1990s. The American Bar Association stated in a recommendation that 'agencies should adopt affirmative programs of electronic public information dissemination in order best to carry out their responsibilities to inform persons affected by their activities and generally to promote access to public information.'[38]

The importance of the link between private participation in rulemaking practices and internet use has been positively evaluated by scholars, who argue that 'while private citizens and interest groups may use the internet to mobilize support or opposition to agency decisions or changes in agency policies, the internet is a much more powerful tool for increasing genuine public participation in agency decision-making when agencies proactively use it to educate the public and solicit informed public input.'[39]

Some European states have since introduced obligations to publish administrative measures online, with the aim of increasing access to administrative acts. The right to access administrative documentation, which allows citizens to know the reasoning behind a measure or to verify whether the administration has effectively and correctly examined the documentation on which it based its decision, could be limited by the lack of stable internet access,[40] thereby violating one of the fundamental principles of procedural due process of law.

These shortcomings related to the gap in the spread of an efficient network across the territory largely contribute to creating situations of vulnerability for those groups lacking internet access; situations that affect the ability to access knowledge online. Even ancient literary works can be dematerialized and made available for the benefit of the entire world, becoming 'cornerstones of digital democracy.'[41] Similarly, works of art can be enjoyed digitally anywhere in the world, making them more easily accessible while also preserving them. Scientific results can be made available to the community through dematerialized databases, sometimes in open access.[42] Thus, it is undeniable that the internet can be seen as a driver of freedoms and rights that often cannot be exercised simply because the means, access itself, is not guaranteed.

In the Italian context, in a time when the path is toward digital normality, the lack of complete and efficient network coverage across the territory threatens the survival of villages and communities located in geographically disadvantaged areas such as inner regions. According to the 'National Strategy for Inner Areas: Definition, Objectives, Tools, and Governance 2014–2020,' within the '2014–2020 Partnership Agreement for Italy,' drafted by the Agency for Territorial Cohesion to create governance aimed at addressing demographic decline and finding solutions to imbalances in certain geographical areas, as provided by Article 174 of the Treaty on the Functioning of the European Union, inner areas represent about 53% of the total number

[38] American Bar Association, Recommendation 109C. Cited in: Johnson (1998), p. 291.

[39] Johnson (1998), p. 303.

[40] Della Cananea (2023), p. 142.

[41] Pradt Lougee (2006), p. 311 ff.

[42] Cavallo Perin (2021), p. 587; Boldrin and Levine (2012).

of Italian municipalities, over 4,000 municipalities, covering approximately 60% of the national territory, while the number of inhabitants amounts to about 23% of the national population, corresponding to over 13.5 million people. A significant number of citizens, therefore, for whom the development of territories plays a fundamental role in mitigating the disadvantages due to residential disparities. These disadvantages translate into the inability to access services guaranteed to citizens residing in urban centres.

4 'What Is a Village?' and Other Questions

If the inability to access the internet and the opportunities it offers significantly contributes to the depopulation of villages in favour of urban centres, there is also another consequence to consider: the city continues to grow, losing its original character and the ancient separation between its walls and the countryside. The digital divide, therefore, not only affects the loss of culture in small towns but also has serious repercussions in terms of environmental sustainability and land consumption.

The urgency here is that, until digital infrastructure is fully developed, it will become increasingly difficult to continue living in small peripheral towns, whose abandonment could become irreversible. Equally irreversible could be the damage caused to cities, landscapes, and the environment, considering the expansion of suburbs. This expansion indicates a trend of increasing urban sprawl that grows with the rising demand for housing.[43] The final effect corresponds to the continuous erosion of land surrounding cities, whose consumption should be brought to zero by 2050.[44]

The indiscriminate expansion of cities caused by urban sprawl has been a concern for years in some countries. This is evident in the legislation of the United Kingdom, where, starting from the 1930s, special attention was given to limiting the indiscriminate expansion of urban areas through the remedy of green belts. These are perimeters of green areas left around cities and towns where construction is still prohibited.[45]

Returning to the importance of widespread internet coverage across the national territory, it is worth asking whether this should be considered an essential service, as it is, as we have seen, the means through which constitutional rights and freedoms are exercised.

In this section of the chapter, the intention is primarily to investigate how internet access can contribute to protecting a possible right to the village, which ideally stems from the evolution of the right to the city outlined by the New Urban Agenda.

[43] Munafò (2023).

[44] European Commission (2021).

[45] Ministry of Housing, Community & Local Government of the United Kingdom (2018) Local authority green belt statistics for England: 2017 to 2018. See also: Green Belt (London and Home Counties) Act 1938 (1938 c xciii).

This right is a distillation of the need felt by citizens in internal areas to 'break free from their precarious local living conditions, demanding equal dignity with more developed areas;'[46] a need that translates into a sort of right to exist and to matter'[47] for human settlements.

To apply these principles to the dynamics concerning small towns, a preliminary question must be asked: 'What is a village?'.

In Italy, at least, there is no legal definition to answer the question. The so-called 'law to save villages'[48] in Italy does not help, as it identifies them based on the number of inhabitants. According to Italian law, villages are also small municipalities with fewer than 5,000 inhabitants.

Some Italian regional laws equate the village with the historic centre, while others place it in a rural context opposed to the urban one. Meanwhile, the National Recovery and Resilience Plan identifies villages as those historic centres at risk of depopulation.

These attempts to define the village, considered individually, are insufficient to fully capture the meaning of the word. In fact, when talking about a historic centre, one could alternatively refer to urban agglomerations that are within an urban context, to places that have been abandoned, or, on the contrary, are at the centre of the phenomenon of overtourism. However, these examples do not add anything more to a possible definition of a village.

The lack of a definition does not prevent us from understanding what is meant by a village. In fact, a village can be described based on its characteristics: it is a cluster of historic buildings, it may contain tangible or intangible cultural assets, it must be set in a natural context, and it must be affected by depopulation.

Finally, the guidelines on the implementation methods of intervention 2.1 'Attractiveness of villages,' M1C3 Tourism and Culture of the National Recovery and Resilience Plan, prepared by the Italian Ministry of Culture, aimed at identifying villages eligible for economic funds for their enhancement, can be useful for this purpose. They identify the village as a 'small historic settlement that has maintained recognizability in the historic settlement structure and the continuity of predominantly isolated historic building fabrics and/or separated from the urban centre, not coinciding with the historic centre or portions of it. Unless they are small or very small municipalities, in which case the historic centre is considered a village.' According to the Guidelines, the other elements that a village should contain for the implementation of the National Recovery and Resilience Plan must concern the maintenance and recognizability of the historic settlement structure and the continuity of the historic building fabrics. It must have significant portions of the building heritage in abandonment.

These aspects, on the one hand, are very useful because they help to better outline the profile of the village by associating it with the phenomenon of abandonment. On the other hand, they overlook the relationship of the village with the landscape,

[46] Di Mauro (2022), p. 26

[47] Di Mauro (2022), p. 26.

[48] Legge 6 October 2017, no 158.

a relationship that cannot be ignored in Italian law, given that landscape protection falls within territorial governance, an area that also includes urban planning.

4.1 Internet is a Fundamental Right and the Related Infrastructure an Essential Service

Internet access was first defined as a right by the French Constitutional Council, with its historic decision in 2009.[49] The law on the dissemination and protection of creations on the internet raised concerns about its constitutionality, particularly regarding the balance between copyright protection and internet access. Article 5 provided for the establishment of 'Hadopi,' the High Authority for the dissemination of works and the protection of rights on the internet, aimed at protecting these works online and potentially sanctioning the holder of access to communication services. If the obligation to monitor was not met, the penalties could include suspension of service access for a period of two months to a year, with the subscriber being unable to sign a new contract for public online communication services.

Following an appeal by some members of parliament, the Court found that inhibiting internet access, even after a procedure that provided for the right to be heard, would be disproportionate. This was because internet access is considered a right protected by Article 11 of the 1789 Declaration of the Rights of Man and of the Citizen: 'The free communication of ideas and opinions is one of the most precious rights of man. Every citizen may thus speak, write, and publish freely, except when such freedom is misused in cases determined by Law.'

The Court specified that: 'In the current state of communication means and given the widespread development of public online communication services and the importance of these for participation in democracy and the expression of ideas and opinions, this right implies freedom to access such services.'[50]

Furthermore, the United Nations Human Rights Council[51] has also included internet access under Article 19 of the Universal Declaration of Human Rights. The Human Rights Council affirms that 'the same rights that people have offline must also be protected online, particularly freedom of expression, which applies regardless of frontiers and through any media of one's choice.'[52]

What emerges is the importance of the right to speech, which is closely connected to the development of democratic debate. In this sense, internet access cannot be reduced to a mere tool through which this right is exercised. Similarly, if we consider

---

[49] Conseil constitutionnel français, no. 2009-580, judgment of 10 June 2009.

[50] Conseil constitutionnel français, no. 2009-580, judgment of 10 June 2009, para.12.

[51] Human Rights Council (2012a) Resolution A/HRC/20/L.13, The promotion, protection and enjoyment of human rights on the Internet, 29 June 2012.

[52] Human Rights Council (2012b) Resolution A/HRC/20/L.13, The promotion, protection and enjoyment of human rights on the Internet, Art. 19.

democratic debate itself as a means to exercise the human right of free expression, we would have to conclude that there is no right to democracy.[53]

Thus, if it is generally accepted that the right to internet access is a human right, it is unclear how this right can be effectively defined. Is it fundamental to own a computer, or to have the ability to use the web correctly, or is the infrastructure more significant?[54]

From a purely logical standpoint, it should be considered that even before being able to use the internet via a personal computer that one knows how to use, it is essential to have infrastructure that enables connection.

This particular infrastructure, then, is indispensable if it allows the exercise of a human right: it should be regarded with the same importance as a water supply system or a road.

The issue then shifts to the dynamics of building and implementing infrastructure, which are carried out through procedures characterized by administrative discretion. To define what is meant by discretion, Davis's words are useful: 'an officer has discretion whenever the effective limits on his power leave him free to make a choice among possible courses of action or inaction.'[55] This type of discretion can be divided into legal and factual discretion. The former occurs when the administration is granted the power to act at its discretion; the latter is characterized by being carried out directly by the administration, which decides how to act independently to achieve its goal, without being granted the power to act in this way and without being subject to control.[56]

The discretionary administrative decision to implement or not implement infrastructure, like that enabling internet connection, has direct consequences for the rule of law from at least two perspectives. The first is that in this way, the administration would not allow the exercise of a human right like internet access. The second is that this would violate the principles of 'fairness and transparency in the application of power.'[57] Furthermore, the implementation of such infrastructure is the responsibility of national governments, which may choose to promote service provision by private companies. This could lead to private investors' disinterest in investing in certain areas where the return on investment would not be sufficiently profitable. Conversely, equal treatment in access to essential infrastructure and services, and non-discrimination, are part of EU legislation in energy, communications, and transport. Placing such significant services outside the public sphere corresponds to a decrease in control and greater dependence on market operators.[58]

As seen, internet access has been recognized as a human right, based on Article 11 of the Declaration of the Rights of Man and of the Citizen and has found a place in Article 19 of the Universal Declaration of Human Rights. This consideration,

[53] Wang (2013).

[54] Tully (2014).

[55] Davis (1969), p. 4.

[56] Colin (2020), p. 601.

[57] McDonald (2004).

[58] Barak-Erez (2010); Colin (2020), p. 601.

when juxtaposed with the dynamics through which the administration exercises its choices, cannot be without repercussions on the procedural level. The need to protect fundamental rights has the power to guide public administrations' decision-making dynamics and to limit or increase the content of certain decisions[59] as occurs with freedom of speech.

This is so true that the European Court of Justice, in the historic case Internationale Handelsgesellschaft,[60] ruled that the protection of fundamental rights must be ensured in light of the objectives of the then European Community and must be guaranteed within the Community legal system. This principle, still valid today, combines with the principles of precaution, sustainability, equality, inclusion of diversity, and human dignity, which are of primary importance in the common constitutional traditions of the Member States[61] and which, in turn, play a decisive role in the production of regulations, overseen by the principle of legality.

4.2 *Internet Access Contributes to the Safeguard of Colletta di Castelbianco*

According to a recent study conducted by the Regional Economic Planning Institute of the Tuscany Region, the digitization of inland areas and villages represents a barrier to the depopulation of those areas.[62] The relevance of digitization of inland areas is also evident in Mission 5 of the National Recovery and Resilience Plan. The aim is to make the territories with a higher risk of depopulation more attractive, to increase job opportunities, to guarantee efficient social and health services, and to affirm the 'right to remain' for the new generations.[63]

A surprisingly positive experience concerned the small village of Colletta di Castelbianco, located in the inland of Savona, considered the first digital village.

The village was presumably established between the thirteenth and fourteenth centuries to facilitate small commercial exchanges between the local population and travellers passing from the sea to Piedmont and vice versa. When new roads were built around two centuries ago, the village lost its significance and was progressively abandoned. After the earthquake of 1887, depopulation began, reaching a point in 1971 when the village had about five residents. A few years later, it was completely abandoned. Around 1992, a businessman from Piedmont, who knew the area, decided to slowly purchase all the individual properties in the village to renovate them. His

---

[59] Auby (2017), pp. 555.

[60] European Court of Justice, Case 11-70, Internationale Handelsgesellschaft mbH v Einfuhr- und Vorratsstelle für Getreide und Futtermittel. Judgment of 17 December 1970, ECLI:EU:C:1970:114.

[61] Cassese (2017), 939 ff.

[62] IRPET (2023) Digitalizzazione – AISRe, 6–8 settembre 2023. https://www.irpet.it/wp-content/uploads/2023/08/digitalizzazione-aisre-6-8-settembre-2023.pdf.

[63] International Covenant on Civil and Political Rights, Art. 12.4, 16 Dec. 1966, T.I.A.S. 92-908, 999 U.N.T.S. 171; Lynch (2022).

intention was not to create a vacation spot but rather a place of solitude—but not isolation—for those who love a closer connection with nature but do not want to give up being connected with the rest of the world, who can organize their work remotely thanks to internet access, and who are tired of life in large cities.[64]

The case of Colletta di Castelbianco touches on an aspect of particular relevance that has been part of the legal debate in England over the last twenty years. The right to live outside urban centres, but with the same opportunities, presupposes the enhancement of human relationships with the natural environment surrounding inhabited areas. The significance of this relationship was recognized by the Countryside and Rights of Way Act of 2000 in the United Kingdom and the Land Reform Act of 2003 in Scotland. The former granted recognition in England to the 'right to roam,' allowing people to wander freely, without needing rights of way in specific 'open access land,' which includes mountains, moors, and meadows listed in specific tables contained in the law. The latter established the universal right to freely cross and access land, forests, and waters, albeit under certain conditions.

Thus, the first cyber village in Italy was created, following similar experiments that had been carried out in the United States or Scandinavia. The small village, an important example of the residential and architectural forms of the Ligurian Apennine areas, was brought back to life thanks to the wiring and fiber optics installed in the individual properties.[65]

5 Does the Right to the Village Exist?

The tools for safeguarding small villages, including through their digitalization, are already in place, as we have seen. Colletta di Castelbianco is a clear example of this. Its digitalization, combined with careful restoration and a marketing project, has led to its revival and the possibility of the village surviving for years to come. However, the case of Colletta remains isolated. For one praiseworthy and fully successful entrepreneurial experiment from thirty years ago, how many other villages have faced the same fate? How many villages are constantly at risk of being abandoned and forgotten? How much of our culture, represented by life in the village, can be sacrificed due to a lack of infrastructure? Does this dynamic only harm the individual inhabitants of the villages, or does it have broader implications?

Henri Lefebvre's idea that the inhabitants of a city can reclaim their spaces and become protagonists of a collective existence,[66] could be used to bring about a different right, that of the village. A right that would concern the inhabitants of rural areas at risk of depopulation. A right that would focus on minimum access to essential services and the possibility of democratic participation through internet

---

[64] De Carlo (2004).

[65] Bascherini (2020).

[66] Lefebvre (1991, p. 59), Liu and Wong (2020, p. 392 ff).

connectivity. A right to not see small urban centres or villages, especially those in remote and economically depressed areas, permanently abandoned.

In large metropolises, internet connectivity has become a stable element of primary urbanization and is considered a service connected to urban infrastructure.[67] The 'connected city' and urban welfare[68] have entered the landscape of city regulation, with the aim of improving the lives of its inhabitants. An opportunity that has not included the inhabitants of smaller centres and villages.

This issue becomes evident from the fact that while about half of the world's population lives in cities, the other half lives outside of them.[69]

The right to the city, theorized by Lefebvre in the late 1960s,[70] has developed legally by synthesizing an array of regulations, all united by the goal of governing various aspects of the city's legal functioning.[71] It can be broken down into three fundamental areas: the regulation of its physical spaces; how the law governs the city's economic dynamics; and the intersection between law and city governance.[72]

The method of synthesis, the ability to examine different regulations from a cross-sectional perspective rather than by categories, allows for the extraction of certain common logics and principles.[73] Among these, the principles related to the production and organization of services stand out, a field that has always seen conflict between public and private sectors, driven by the obligation to meet citizens' needs and the necessity to ensure fair profits for service providers.

Some services provided can be considered essential, as they are closely connected to the physical survival of human beings or pertain to their fundamental rights, such as the right to movement and speech. Italian law identifies them to regulate the right to strike.[74] These services must be guaranteed even when exercising this right, to meet the population's needs. Public services can include safety, access to basic household services, housing, medical care, and education. These fundamental needs of every person can be addressed locally within the legal framework of the city.[75] Therefore, if the concept of the right to the city arises from the existence of essential services that must be provided, as they pertain to the physical and moral development of people, surely among these must be included access to the internet. Its nature as a human right allows for considering the spread of the network as an essential service, on par with water supply, mobility, or educational services.

To date, there have been significant voices that have delved into the importance of conceiving the city as a work produced by its inhabitants,[76] deciphering it through

---

[67] Tillu (2021).

[68] Giusti (2021), Portaluri (2006), pp. 71 ff.

[69] Landy and Moreau (2015).

[70] Lefebvre (1968).

[71] Auby (2022), pp. 22 ff.

[72] Auby (2013).

[73] Auby (2013).

[74] Legge 12 June 1990, no. 146

[75] Auby (2013).

[76] Lefebvre (1968).

the discovery of the various regulatory connections that intertwine and enable life in the city. However, the analysis of these same regulations has been neglected from a 'beyond the city's walls' perspective, which would include rural areas and specifically the villages, which do not share the same characteristics or needs as cities. If the main problem in cities is population growth, for the village, it is the exact opposite. If housing distress is a tangible problem in cities, it is not so in villages, due to the high number of abandoned houses destined for ruin. If in the city environmental sustainability is highly valued and promoted through urban planning tools like demolition and reconstruction practices aimed at land conservation, in the village, the housing structures are likely more eco-sustainable (consider the case of Colletta di Castelbianco, where all the houses are made of local stone, extracted by farmers from the land where olive trees were cultivated as waste material). Conversely, while essential services and internet access are guaranteed in the city, this is not necessarily the case in villages.

As we have seen, the right to access the internet, when viewed through the lens of the city, takes on the characteristics of an essential public service that should also be guaranteed to the inhabitants of rural areas, as it retains its human rights character in relation to the village inhabitants.

In conclusion, the right to live in the village addresses the practical needs of its inhabitants, respects their values, and allows them the possibility of being independent from the city, using the same opportunities by adapting the same infrastructure that facilitates and improves the daily life of the urban population to its smaller scale.

The importance of internet connectivity and the success of urban experiments like those of Colletta di Castelbianco can serve as a stimulus to experiment with a new version of the right to the city. The same method of study that has allowed for the identification of a common legal framework regulating urban reality could develop in parallel, contributing to outline a right to the village, understood as a transposition and practical verification of the components of the right to the city in the rural world.

References

ACMA 2016 Australian Communications and Media Authority (2016) Regional Australias Online. Research Snapshot (https://www.infrastructure.gov.au/sites/default/files/review_of_the_acma_-_final_report_pdf_version.pdf).

AGCOM (2023) Observatory on Communications 1/2023, last update 15 June 2023

American Bar Association, Recommendation 109C. Cited in: Johnson SM (1998) The internet changes everything: revolutionizing public participation and access to government information through the Internet. Admin Law Rev 50(2):277–337

Auby JB (2013) The role of law in the legal status and power of cities. Droit de la Ville. An Introduction. Ital J Public Law, pp 302–306

Auby JB (2017) Contracting out and 'public values': a theoretical and comparative approach. In: Rose-Ackerman S, Lindseth PL, Emerson B (eds) Comparative Administrative Law, 2nd edn. Edward Elgar, Northampton-Massachusetts, p 555

Auby JB (2022) Droit à la ville et droit de la ville. Constructif 3(63):29–33. https://www.cairn.info/revue-constructif-2022-3-page-29.htm

Barak-Erez D (2010) Three questions of privatization. In: Rose-Ackerman S, Lindseth PL (eds) Comparative Administrative Law. Edward Elgar, Cheltenham, pp 533–552
Bascherini E (2020) Colletta di Castelbianco, da borgo abbandonato a borgo telematico. Un progetto di Giancarlo de Carlo. Bloom, Rivista Semestrale di Architettura 30:101–105
Bassini M (2019) Internet e libertà d'espressione. Prospettive costituzionali e sovranazionali, Aracne, Roma
Benvenuti F (1997) Introduzione. In: Caia G and Ghetti G (eds) La tutela dei centri storici. Discipline giuridiche, Giappichelli, Torino, p. 2
Bixio A (2020) Ragionamenti sulla cultura giuridica. Giappichelli, Torino
Boldrin M, Levine DK (2012) Abolire la proprietà intellettuale. Laterza, Bari
Brighi R (2015) Dati informatici e modelli dei dati. Verso 'una nuova dimensione della realtà'. In: Brighi R and Zullo S (eds) Filosofia del diritto e nuove tecnologie. Prospettive di ricerca tra teoria e pratica, Aracne, Roma, pp 281–294
Caputi Jambrenghi MTP (2017) La funzione amministrativa neutrale. Cacucci, Bari
Cassese S (2005) Global standards for National Administrative Procedure. Law Contemp Probl 68(3/4):109–126
Cassese S (2017) The «Constitutional Traditions Common to The Member States» of The European Union. Rivista Trimestrale di Diritto Pubblico (4):939 ff
Cavallo Perin R (2021) Il contributo italiano alla libertà di scienza nel sistema delle libertà costituzionali. Dir Amm (3):587–620
Cerulli Irelli V (2022) Proprietà, beni pubblici, beni comuni. Rivista Trimestrale di Diritto Pubblico 3:639
Cerulli Irelli V, De Lucia L (2014) Beni comuni e diritti collettivi. Politica del diritto 45(1):3–36
Chirwa D, Ncube C (2023) The internet, development, human rights and the Law in Africa. Routledge, London-New York
Coeckelbergh M (2013) Human being @ risk, enhancement, technology and evaluation of vulnerability transformations. Springer, Dordrecht-New York
Cole A (2016) All of us are vulnerable, but some are more vulnerable than others: the political ambiguity of vulnerability studies, an ambivalent critique. Critical Horizons 17(2):260–277 https://doi.org/10.1080/14409917.2016.1153896
Colin S (2020) Implementation: facilitating and overseeing public services at street level. In: Cane P (ed) The Oxford Handbook of Comparative Administrative Law, p 601
Commissione Rodotà (2007) Per la modifica delle norme del codice civile in materia di beni pubblici. 14 Giugno 2007
Davis K (1969) Discretionary justice: A preliminary inquiry. LSU Press, Baton Rouge
De Carlo G (2004) Colletta di Castelbianco. Places, UC Berkeley, Massachusetts, 16(2):4–12
De Hert P, Kloza D (2012) Internet access as a new fundamental right. Inflating the current rights framework? Eur J Law Technol 3(3):1–23
De Marco E (2008) Accesso alla rete e uguaglianza digitale, Giuffrè, Milano
della Cananea G (2023) The common core of European Administrative Laws. Retrospective and Prospective. Brill, Leiden
Di Mauro BG (2022) Il diritto dei borghi nel PNRR: verso una (stagione di) rigenerazione urbanisticamente orientata alla conservazione e allo sviluppo dei valori locali. Urbanistica e Appalti 4:26
Dyba M, Gernego I, Dyba O, Oliynyk (2020) Financial support and development of digital rural hubs in Europe. Manag Theory Stud Rural Bus Infrastruct Dev 42(1):51–59. https://doi.org/10.15544/mts.2020.06
European Commission (2019) Broadband Coverage in Europe 2018. Mapping Progress towards the Coverage Objectives of the Digital Agenda. https://ec.europa.eu/newsroom/dae/document.cfm?doc_id=62760
European Commission (2021) EU Soil Strategy for 2030. Reaping the benefits of healthy soil for people, food, nature and climate. COM/2021/699 final

European Commission (n.d.) WiFi4EU: Free Wi-Fi for Europeans. https://digital-strategy.ec.europa.eu/it/activities/wifi4eu-citizens
Federal Communications Commission (2020) Broadband Deployment Report. Before the Federal Communications Commission, Washington, D.C., 8 June 2020. https://www.fcc.gov/reports-research/reports/broadband-progress-reports/2020-broadband-deployment-report
Giusti A (2021) La rigenerazione urbana tra consolidamento dei paradigmi e nuove contingenze. Dir Amm 2:439–474
Gordon SH (1954) The economic theory of a common-property resource: the fishery. J Polit Econ 62(2):124–142
Hardin G (1968) The tragedy of the commons. Science 162(3859):1243–1248
Hess C (2013) Is there anything new under the sun? A discussion and survey of studies on new commons and internet. In: Constituting the Commons—the eighth biennial conference of the International Association for the Study of Common Property, Bloomington, Indiana. Available at dlc.dlib.indiana.edu.
Human Rights Council (2012a) Resolution A/HRC/20/L.13, The promotion, protection and enjoyment of human rights on the Internet, 29 June 2012
Human Rights Council (2012b) Resolution A/HRC/20/L.13, The promotion, protection and enjoyment of human rights on the Internet, Art. 19
IRPET (2023) Digitalizzazione—AISRe, 6–8 settembre 2023. https://www.irpet.it/wp-content/uploads/2023/08/digitalizzazione-aisre-6-8-settembre-2023.pdf
Jankovskis v Lithuania, no. 21575/08, ECtHR judgment of 17 January 2017
Jeffin TM, Rugmini Devi M, Girish Kumar R (2023) North–South digital divide: a comparative study of personal and positional inequalities in USA and India. Afr J Sci Technol Innov Dev 15(4):482–495 https://doi.org/10.1080/20421338.2022.2129343
Johnson SM (1998) The internet changes everything: revolutionizing public participation and access to government information through the Internet. Admin Law Rev 50(2):303
Jones BC (2014) Is social media a human right? Exploring the scope of internet rights. In: Int J Constitutional Law Blog, 2014, p 4
Landy F, Moreau S (2015) The Right to the Village. Justice Spatiale = Spatial Justice (7). https://shs.hal.science/halshs-01718604/file/intro-Droit-au-village_EN.pdf
Lefebvre H (1968) Le Droit à la ville. Anthropos, Paris
Lefebvre H (1991) The production of space. Trans: Nicholson-Smith D. Blackwell, Oxford
Lessig L (1999) Keynote address: commons and code. Fordham Intell Prop Media Ent LJ 9(2):405–420
Li S, Li E (2021) The Impact of Digital Divide on Education in USA Amid COVID-19 Pandemic. In: Stephanidis C, Antona M and Ntoa S (eds) HCI International 2021—Posters. 23rd HCI International Conference, HCII 2021 Virtual Event, July 24–29, 2021 Proceedings, Part III. Springer, Berlin, p 571
Liu R, Wong T-C (2020) 'Right to the city' versus neoliberal urbanism in globalising cities in China. In: Leary-Owhin ME, McCarthy JP (eds) The Routledge Handbook of Henri Lefebvre, The City and Urban Society, p 392 ff
Lynch TE (2022) The right to remain. Wash Int'l LJ 31(3):315–356
Malta S, Wilding R (2018) Not So Ubiquitous. digital inclusion and older adults in Australia. In: Ragnedda M, Mutsvairo B (eds) Digital inclusion. An international comparative analysis. Lexington Books, Lanham-Maryland, p 28
McDonald L (2004) The rule of law in the 'new regulatory state.' Common Law World Rev 33(3):197–221
Messinetti R (2019) Beni comuni e nuovo fondamento del diritto soggettivo. Federalismi.it (8):1–22
Ministry of Housing, Community & Local Government of the United Kingdom (2018) Local authority green belt statistics for England: 2017 to 2018. See also: Green Belt (London and Home Counties) Act 1938 (1938 c xciii)
Munafò M (2023) Consumo di suolo, dinamiche territoriali e servizi ecosistemici. Report SNPA. Available at file:///C:/Users/39320/Downloads/Rapporto_consumo_di_suolo_2023.pdf

National Sample Survey Organisation (NSSO) (2019) Key Indicators of Household Social Consumption on Education in India NSS 75th Round (July 2017–June 2018). Ministry of Statistics and Programme Implementation. https://pib.gov.in/Pressreleaseshare.aspx?PRID=1593251

National Sample Survey Organisation (NSSO). 2019. 'Key Indicators of Household Social Consumption on Education in India NSS 75th Round (July 2017–June 2018).' Ministry of Statistics and Programme Implementation. (https://pib.gov.in/Pressreleaseshare.aspx?PRID=1593251)

Norris P (2001) Digital divide: Civic engagement, information poverty, and the internet worldwide. Cambridge University Press, Cambridge

Ostrom E (1990) Governing the commons: the evolution of institutions for collective action. Cambridge University Press, Cambridge

Pastore B (2020) Vulnerabilità situata e risposte alle vulnerazioni. Etica & Politica 22(1):283–291 https://doi.org/10.13137/1825-5167/30642

Pew Research Center (2021) Internet/Broadband Fact Sheet. https://www.pewresearch.org/internet/fact-sheet/internetbroadband/

Pollicino O, Frosini TE, Apa E, Bassini M (2017) Diritti e libertà in Internet, Le Monnier, Milano

Portaluri PL (2006) Le disuguaglianze sostenibili nell'urbanistica. In: Astone A, Caldarera M, Manganaro F, Romano Tassone A, Saitta F (eds) Le disuguaglianze sostenibili nei sistemi autonomistici multilivello, Giappichelli, Torino, pp 71 ff

Power J, Musgrove AT, Nichols BH (2020) Teachers bridging the digital divide in rural schools with 1:1 computing. Rural Educ 41(1):61–67

Pradt Lougee W (2006) Scholarly communication and libraries unbound: the opportunity of the commons. In: Hess C, Ostrom E (eds) Understanding knowledge as a commons: from theory to practice. MIT Press, Cambridge-Massachusetts, p 311 ff

Rodotà S (2012) Il diritto di avere diritti, Laterza, Roma-Bari

Ruiz-Martinez I, Esparcia J (2020) Internet access in rural areas: brake or stimulus as Post-Covid-19 opportunity? Sustainability 22(12):1–17 https://doi.org/10.3390/su12229619

Salemink K, Strijker D, Bosworth G (2017) The community reclaims control? Learning experiences from rural broadband initiatives in the Netherlands. Sociologia Ruralis 57:555–575 https://doi.org/10.1111/soru.12150

Schrubbe A, Strover S (2021) Infrastructure and instance: how rural communities approach short- and long-term solutions to access. In: Hargittai E (ed) Handbook of digital inequality. Edward Elgar, Cheltenham, p 46

Tillu J (2021) The economic case for China's sustainable urban transformation. London School of Economics and Political Science. www.lse.ac.uk

Tully S (2014) A human right to access the internet. Hum Rights Law Rev 14(2):175–195. https://doi.org/10.1093/hrlr/ngu011

Wang X (2013) Time to think about human right to the internet access: a Beitz's approach. J Polit Law 6(3):67–77

Wessels B (2013) The reproduction and reconfiguration of inequality. Differentiation and class, status and power in the dynamics of digital divide. In: Ragnedda M, Muschert GW (eds) The digital divide. The internet and social inequality in international perspective. Routledge, London-New York, pp 17–28

Weston BH, Bollier D (2013) Green governance: ecological survival, human rights, and the law of the commons. Cambridge University Press, New York
Westra LS (2011) Human rights: the commons and the collective. UBC Press, Vancouver-Toronto

Manlio Lisanti, Ph.D. candidate in Administrative Law at the University of Rome Tor Vergata. His research focuses on cultural heritage protection through public contracts. Published on public–private partnerships, urban planning, and administrative litigation. Conducted research at the Bodleian Library, Oxford, and serves as Junior Executive Editor of the Italian Law Journal.

Open Access This chapter is licensed under the terms of the Creative Commons Attribution 4.0 International License (http://creativecommons.org/licenses/by/4.0/), which permits use, sharing, adaptation, distribution and reproduction in any medium or format, as long as you give appropriate credit to the original author(s) and the source, provide a link to the Creative Commons license and indicate if changes were made.

The images or other third party material in this chapter are included in the chapter's Creative Commons license, unless indicated otherwise in a credit line to the material. If material is not included in the chapter's Creative Commons license and your intended use is not permitted by statutory regulation or exceeds the permitted use, you will need to obtain permission directly from the copyright holder.

AI and the Sense of Civic Duty

Antonella Tennenini

Abstract Artificial Intelligence (AI) is a highly sophisticated tool that has been integrated into modern life. It is evolving at a rapid pace, challenging thus the skills and competencies traditionally cultivated by humans. In this paper, I outline a perspective on the subject shaped by transdisciplinary, philosophical, social, and political insights and guided by critical thinking and careful deliberations. The goal is to safeguard the human ability to choose and control, to maintain free will and self-regulation, and to preserve mental, emotional, and practical skills, to avoid being overwhelmed by technology. Humans already deeply engage with technology and benefit greatly from it, but they also have the responsibility to continue nurturing their intelligence, including emotional intelligence, as they are nevertheless sentient and intuitive beings guided by thoughts and actions. It is essential for them to remain involved and aware, able to prevent and recognize forms of technological manipulation. To center society around civic responsibility and the common good means preserving the *sapiens'* responsibility for choices and actions, especially regarding the use of AI.

Keywords Human centrality · Vulnerability · Risks · Civic duty in AI · Ethic in AI

1 Preliminary Considerations on AI

Following the recent breakthrough of generative models like ChatGPT, AI has become one of the most discussed topics across academic, professional, and institutional spheres. Incorporated into modern life, it is evolving at a rapid pace, challenging thus the skills and competencies traditionally cultivated by humans.

In this paper, I outline a perspective on the subject shaped by transdisciplinary, philosophical, social, and political insights and guided by critical thinking and careful deliberations.

A. Tennenini (✉)
University of Rome Tor Vergata, Rome, Italy
e-mail: antonellatennenini@gmail.com

© The Author(s) 2025

C. Amodio and A. Diurni (eds.), *Human Vulnerability in Interaction with AI in European Private Law*, https://doi.org/10.1007/978-3-031-93247-2_11

The thesis advocates safeguarding human agency - maintaining free will and self-regulation, and essential cognitive and emotional skills to avoid being overwhelmed by technology. While humans already deeply engage with technology, they must continue to nurture their intelligence, including emotional intelligence, as they are nevertheless sentient and intuitive beings guided by thoughts and actions.

It is crucial to carefully consider both the national and international context in which the digital transformation is taking place. Since the recent pandemic, the pace of digitalization has dramatically accelerated, raising inevitable challenges related to managing and aligning the mismatch between the old world, which is fading away, and the new one, which is struggling to emerge, leaving us trapped in a twilight zone, as Gramsci famously suggested, it is in such transitional moments that morbid phenomena emerge.[1] Commonly referred to as the Fourth Industrial Revolution, AI will lead to a transformation of the social, political, and economic structure, requiring an ongoing and comprehensive remapping of the world.[2]

This transition is taking place within this society, which is particularly complex and fraught with uncertainty for all intergenerational groups, exacerbated by ongoing crises, health emergencies, climate change, and wars.[3] These events are reshaping our anthropological existence. Despite advances in many areas of knowledge, humans are floating in a state of permanent instability, anxiety, and fluidity, as Bauman notoriously argued. Social polarization and urgent political agendas often leave little room for crucial public debates on issues of civic interest, creating fertile ground for manipulation and propaganda. Sustained, responsible civic participation is therefore indispensable amid this environment.

In the political sphere, a healthy democracy depends on well-informed citizens who are capable of engaging in thoughtful debate and making considered decisions. In this context, where solidarity, social bonds, and community strength are greatly needed, people tend to tell themselves they are connected to one another, primarily through artificial devices. But are they truly connected? How are human relationships evolving if we are more connected than ever but we are also lonelier than ever?[4] And furthermore, will we become masters or servants of AI?

Technological progress is unstoppable, but it must be counterbalanced by a strengthening of ethics, spirituality, and critical thinking, which are currently in deep crisis. Traditional society has been replaced by a consumerist one, whereby the focus is increasingly shifting onto the growth of capital at the expense of people's inner lives, resulting in the neglecting of people's souls, who easily become prey to induced needs. This context is fertile ground for the expansion of power and the weakening of criticism, and it is where the boundless potential of AI, with its many appealing aspects, comes into play.

Returning to the political sphere, data collection influences many aspects: the structure, formulation, and dissemination of messages across different segments

---

[1] Gramsci (1975, p. 311).

[2] Floridi (2014).

[3] Alvídrez et al. (2024).

[4] Turkle (2019).

of the population; the conception of misinformation campaigns to provoke social discord; and the development of algorithms to identify and tackle disinformation and other harmful uses of such data. The very notion of a free society and free will could be altered. Even if we were willing to acknowledge that these developments are advantageous or reversible, it remains a fundamental duty of global societies to understand and reconcile them with their value systems, organizational structures, and social contracts. Democracy, in particular, must retain its human characteristics by protecting deliberations, elections, and human discourse from the distortions introduced by AI. Freedom of expression must remain a prerogative of human beings and not be extended to AI.[5] AI tends to generate large volumes of subtle falsehoods, such as hallucinations[6] or deepfakes, which are increasingly difficult to distinguish from reality. It will become crucial to recognize an AI-generated, potentially distorted speech from an authentic human one, seeing that artificial falsehoods may increasingly resemble human-generated ones.

In a democratic state, the sharing of relevant information occurs through language, allowing individuals to actively participate in the political process and independently produce literature, art, and poetry.[7] Currently, major AI-producing corporations have a vested interest in promoting and encouraging widespread AI consumption to generate substantial profits. While the advantages and opportunities are undeniable, equally important are the issues surrounding its use and the management of vast amounts of data. The rapid advancement of AI, dating back to the well-known Turing test, both fascinates and raises concerns. As Eco wisely noted, it is important neither to fully embrace AI unconditionally nor to adopt an apocalyptic stance.[8] Admittedly, day by day, AI is increasingly embedded in our habits and customs, with outcomes that necessarily must be considered. Therefore, we need to approach AI with a clear framework of understanding, explanation, and handling, firmly acknowledging it as the fruit of the human mind. As AI now progressively permeates various sectors with constant intrusiveness, its scope for expansion must be clearly understood.

Consider, for a moment, just the automotive industry: beyond experimentation with fully automated driving, even a human-driven car today is equipped with numerous alert systems and sensors, far more advanced than vehicles of forty years ago.

If it is well documented that the brain is an organ that adapts extraordinarily well to new forms of thinking and cognition – such as the digital – what will be the consequences in terms of social relations, skills, and so on? Does making little to no intellectual effort to achieve results truly represent a benefit for our lives? Naturally, at this stage, more and more questions arise as we seek answers that can help us understand this phenomenon. In this light, I align with the title of Crawford's book: «AI is neither intelligent nor artificial».[9] So, what is it? How should we manage

[5] Kissinger et al. (2023).

[6] Rossi (2024).

[7] Kissinger et al. (2023).

[8] Eco (2017).

[9] Crawford (2023).

it? These are the foundational questions that will guide this thesis, highlighting the problematic aspects and various implications of its use.

By itself, AI does not think, or at least not in the way humans do. It can only function through the conscious activity of human thought, which elaborates and constructs it. Behind every thought lies an intention—an action carried out with an awareness of the purpose being pursued—a faculty that remains exclusively human. This silent intrusion of digital transition brings new tasks and new forms of interaction with the surrounding environment. As technology advances, it increasingly reinforces individual self-focus, even as it distances us from one another. This shift reshapes everyday life, contributing to greater human isolation and emotional detachment. Reliance on autonomous machines capable of providing immediate responses leads humans to depend more and more on devices that, paradoxically, themselves depend on human input. Another critical issue is the opacity of AI, the lack of transparency in its development and application, which raises doubts about the system's reliability. How algorithms work is unknown to non-experts and to the general public—will this result in rejection or assimilation? Certainly, it will be crucial to understand and explain the phenomenon, especially to safeguard the freedom of choice and democratic order.

This effort should translate into the greater promotion of essential human values, first and foremost dignity, in order to counter growing inequalities, prevent the further enrichment of the already powerful, and curb the spread of falsehoods. These falsehoods can spread through intentional or subliminal manipulation of unaware or vulnerable individuals, sowing discord. Technology is never neutral; it has the power to influence individuals, social bonds, the sense of community, and power relations within society. In this respect, AI represents an expression of social, political, and economic power.

In a highly malleable digital context, the vast array of interactions challenges the illusion that we decide freely and rationally, uninfluenced by external forces.[10] Human decision-making mechanisms are always balanced between bounded rationality, cognitive biases, and heuristics, which are mirrored in the digital environment. This environment can be designed to provide assistance (nudge) or to create traps (dark patterns, sludge) that easily lead to errors.

Faced with digital interfaces, it is essential that we continue to be regarded as fully cognitive beings, with the capacity and the proper education to be able to distinguish these dynamics.

The relationship between humans and technology is inherently hybrid and manipulated. Digital nudges applied to social norms bind and guide individuals and groups through digital influences, which may constitute cases of systematic manipulation.[11] Distortions, tampering, and manipulation of user behavior alter their very interests. Specifically, manipulation interferes with the agent's decision-making process, preventing the proper exercise of rational and reflective thought. To achieve these ends, human vulnerability is exploited. Therefore, it is essential to keep humanity

[10] Galletti and Zipoli Caiani (2024).

[11] Pozzi (2022).

at the center of attention and care, as the anthropomorphization of machines is entirely inappropriate and dehumanizing. With AI, there is a risk of dehumanization, surpassing even transhumanism. There is the danger of a turnaround, an imbalance, where humans become increasingly artificialized while machines are anthropomorphized. Hence, the true challenge is to stay human and understand how to do so.[12] No form of criticism, which by definition is questioning and reading between the lines of phenomena, can be replaced. In emphasizing the power of AI, as an autonomous machine, our faculty of choice, free will, dignity and justice are at stake. These fundamental rights, won through centuries of struggles, must not be sacrificed, and should instead be guaranteed, as the AI Act, the first regulatory attempt by the European Union, seeks to protect them. Emotions, intuitions, relationships, and instant, ever-changing solutions cannot be replicated by any machine.

Therefore, awareness, discernment, education, and training must remain central to humanity, for the development of critical and civic consciousness, especially concerning AI.

In short, this technological tsunami will profoundly affect our lives. Thus, with an attitude of openness to the innovation that is galloping to creep into our lives, let us keep in mind what Cristianini says:

> Molte mitologie marcano l'inizio della storia umana con il momento in cui noi rubiamo agli dei il segreto della conoscenza: è questo il passo che ci fa diventare Homo sapiens. E se la scoperta di questo stesso segreto, da parte delle macchine, indicasse l'inizio di un tempo diverso, quello segnato da Machina sapiens?
>
> Quando anche le macchine possono pensare, allora noi chi siamo? Siamo pronti ad incontrare un Oracolo che combina tutte le conoscenze di tutti i libri mai scritti? Questo sta diventando rapidamente possibile, e presto dovremo decidere se vogliamo continuare su questa strada o fermarci.
>
> Alla fine, credo di sapere che cosa faremo, perché so chi siamo: siamo la stessa specie di Pandora e Prometeo. Dove saremmo se non avessimo giocato col fuoco?[13]

2 Some Definitions of Intelligence

It is impossible to provide a singular definition amid a wide array of definitions; therefore, we will select a range of definitions based on their evolution over time, comparing several key concepts. In this context, it is essential to refer to classical

[12] Bertolaso (2023).

[13] Cristianini (2024), p. 146: Many mythologies mark the beginning of human history with the moment when we steal the secret of knowledge from the gods: this is the step that makes us Homo sapiens. What if the discovery of this same secret, by machines, indicates the beginning of a different time, one marked by Machina sapiens? When even machines can think, then who are we? Are we ready to meet an Oracle who combines all the knowledge of all the books ever written? This is rapidly becoming possible, and soon we will have to decide whether we want to continue on this path or stop. In the end, I think I know what we are going to do, because I know who we are: we are the same species as Pandora and Prometheus. Where would we be if we had not played with fire? (My translation).

thinkers, who provide consolidated and unequivocal references in the history of human thought.

Both Plato and Aristotle associate intelligence, or more specifically intellect, with the faculty of thinking. For these philosophers, intelligence is not merely a practical or technical capacity but is also related to the understanding of truth and moral action.

In particular, Aristotle, in the sixth book of the Nicomachean Ethics, outlines five dianoetic virtues, which we will consider in our discussion, revisiting them later. Among these, he includes intelligence as an integral component. The intellectual virtues are scientific knowledge, art, practical wisdom, intellect, and theoretical wisdom. The intellect is a rational habit that has the faculty of intuiting the first principles of knowledge, as well as the 'ultimate terms', that is, the ends to which the action must be directed; together with science constitutes wisdom, which is the highest and most universal form of knowledge.[14]

It can be concluded, therefore, that for Aristotle, intelligence, in addition to being generally defined as the faculty "through which the soul reasons and understands", is also a specific dianoetic virtue, that is, a rational habit that enables one to comprehend the principles of demonstrations.[15]

Jumping ahead to contemporary philosophy, we can refer to Bergson's analysis, in which intelligence is «la facoltà di fabbricare oggetti artificiali e in particolare utensili atti a produrre altri utensili, e di variarne indefinitamente la fabbricazione».[16]

Therefore, it represents a pragmatic or constructive rationality, capable of solving problems through the use of tools and understanding the relationships between things. Its adaptability is driven by practical aims and oriented toward action, lacking the distinctive features of pure contemplation. In *Creative Evolution*, Bergson argues for a continuity between technique and life: just as an organism gives rise to a vital impetus, so human intelligence converts inorganic matter into tools: «se i nostri organi sono strumenti naturali, i nostri strumenti sono organi artificiali. Lo strumento dell'operaio continua il suo braccio; l'attrezzatura dell'umanità è dunque un prolungamento del suo corpo».[17]

Thus, from the perspective of the French philosopher, any distinction between the natural and the artificial disappears, as tools become an extension of the organism through other means. Hence, *Homo faber*, because they live and operate within the surrounding environment through their intelligence. For Bergson, it is in this perspective that the intellectual dimension has no contemplative connotation.

Considering these two fundamental conceptions, if we extend the definition of intelligence to its physical aspect, we can assert that human intelligence (and also animal intelligence) is the capacity to adapt to the context, providing coherent

[14] See Aristotle (1999), Etica Nicomachea, Italian translation and notes by C. Natali, Milan, VI, pp. 222–255.

[15] Abbagnano (1971).

[16] Bergson (2002), p. 117: the power to manufacture artificial objects and in particular tools suitable for producing other tools, and to vary their manufacture indefinitely (My translation).

[17] Bergson (2006), p. 237: If our organs are natural tools, our tools are artificial organs. The worker is tool continues his arm; humanity is equipment is thus an extension of his body (My translation).

responses to the stimuli they perceive and the emerging issues. In this case, intelligence can be attributed to the behavior of an agent capable of acting and interacting with the environment. This implies that the subject must possess a real body.[18]

What, then, is meant by the so-called artificial intelligence? It refers to infrastructural and computational systems, designed and built by Homo sapiens, in the form of hardware, software, chips, neural networks, energy supplies, and other specific materials, that operate within the environment, interpreting the quantity and quality of data fed into them and trained to achieve a purpose. Often, they utilize rational systems that can be adaptive and predictive based on the outcomes of their previous actions in the environment, employing high-level statistical language.

Until now, the central decision-maker of the cosmos has been *Homo sapiens*, with his intelligence, but from now on, the evolution of these technological systems could change the course of history, as Cristianini suggests:

> Nell'abbandonare una visione antropocentrica dell'intelligenza, non dovremmo aspettarci cose come senzienza o autocoscienza, l'emergenza di un linguaggio delle macchine che sia traducibile nel nostro, e tratti emotivi come l'invidia e la paura che possono influenzare la nostra relazione con questi agenti. Tutte queste sono solo proiezioni della nostra incapacità di immaginare intelligenze veramente aliene. È più probabile che incontriamo completa indifferenza o una 'ribellione prometeica' in una lumaca del giardino o nel filtro antispam?[19]

Thus, AI is something different, and humans must find ways to use it.

Despite the numerous definitions and concepts that could be enumerated—pertaining to philosophical, psychological, and physical domains—a methodological choice has been made here to focus on the explainability of current developments through a comparison of past and present perspectives, ensuring continuity and a transition that respects evolution.

Therefore, human intelligence—generally understood as comprehension, explanation of phenomena, capacity for connections, and problem-solving abilities—stems from the brain, which remains one of the greatest mysteries, still largely unexplored in its intricacies. Additionally, other forms of intelligence are emerging that are not competitive, although they may increasingly exhibit characteristics that could make them so; in particular, AI, as a human invention, is based on the simulation and duplication of human actions (it speaks, writes, sings, plays…), often with high levels of autonomy and superhuman performance. However, it can also reproduce the same errors and difficulties. To date, human intelligence—originating within and shaped by the natural world—remains the sole known form of intelligence, serving as the foundation for daily life and societal organization.

We still identify ourselves as humans because we are not only made up of bland materialism, but also of feelings—above all the ineffable one, love—creativity,

---

[18] For this entire section on intelligence in Bergson, see the extensive article by Scotti (2024).

[19] Cristianini (2023), p. 23: In abstaining from an anthropocentric view of intelligence, we should not expect things like sentience or self-awareness, the emergence of a machine language that is translatable into our own, and emotional traits such as envy and fear that can affect our relationship with these agents. All of these are merely projections of our inability to imagine truly alien intelligences. We are more likely to encounter complete indifference or a 'promoteic rebellion' in a garden slug or spam filter? (My translation).

wounds, care, talents, and interactive communication, characterized by glances, laughter, and tears, and tactile experiences without the need for microchipped screens. All of these factors are, of course, irreplaceable.

3 The Problematic Nodes of AI and Civic Sense

The Nobel Prize in Physics 2024 was awarded to John Hopfield and Geoffrey Hinton, pioneers in the study of artificial neural networks and self-learning computers.

Professor Geoffrey Hinton from the University of Toronto predicts that artificial intelligence:

> I think it will have a huge influence. It will be comparable with the Industrial Revolution, but instead of exceeding people in physical strength, it will exceed people in intellectual ability. We have no experience of what it is like to have things smarter than us. It's going to be wonderful in many respects. In areas like healthcare it's going to give us much better healthcare. In almost all industries it's going to make them more efficient. People are going to be able to do the same amount of work with an AI assistant in much less time. It'll mean huge improvements in productivity. We also have to worry about a number of possible bad consequences, particularly the threat of these things getting out of control.[20]

As highlighted by the Nobel Prize winner, there are numerous concerns regarding the dangers of AI development. It is part of the realm of technology, which is often compartmentalized and largely unknown in its functioning to the general public. It is introduced by a small number of mostly cynical and amoral individuals, who are more interested in profit, as previously mentioned, than in the genuine necessity for social good, aside from the advantages that may ensue. The creators of AI are guided by their minds and feelings, through which they make choices about the application of algorithms that affect living beings. AI management raises significant questions of a financial, political, anthropological, and religious nature. Concerning the latter, for example, if the most extreme form of nihilism has proclaimed that God is dead, the question becomes increasingly important: where does *Homo sapiens* go from here? Therefore, now more than ever, philosophy must expand and work synergistically with all other disciplines of human knowledge to face the current revolutionary process impacting human life, which must not become an illusion but, rather, requires a reinforcement of the sense of humanity. Machines can undoubtedly arrive where human action gets tired, stops, limits itself, but without allowing human action itself to be overpowered or lose control.

[20] Hinton's comment is at article 'Godfather of AI' Geoffrey Hinton wins Nobel prize and warns humanity, in «The Times», 08.10.2024, available online: https://www.thetimes.com/uk/science/article/godfather-of-ai-wins-nobel-prize-and-issues-warning-to-humanity-svvw0vfzr.

Moreover, Heidegger warned: «Quanto più ci avviciniamo al pericolo, tanto più chiaramente iniziano ad illuminarsi le vie verso ciò che salva, e tanto più noi domandiamo. Perché il domandare è la pietà del pensiero».[21]

Reconsidering, therefore, the dianoetic virtues that should guide education allow us to reassure minds regarding the significant risks upon which the ongoing debate is primarily based. The dangers concerning inequalities and discrimination must be framed not only within a regulatory framework but, more importantly, from an ethical, social, and economic-financial perspective. Consider, for example, what unbalanced algorithm training can cause, due to biases and prejudices, to some more sensitive characteristics of individuals.

Furthermore, segments of the population in various parts of the world will have widespread access to AI and will be privileged in every respect compared to others who, lacking the necessary cultural and economic tools, will be irreparably marginalized. This discussion must find space in forums dedicated to analyzing and addressing the narrowing of disparities, such as institutional and political bodies.

The debate concerning the Digital Age should be transferred as soon as possible into the public sphere, with detailed informational clarity from institutions to all citizens, ensuring that transparent participation in changes is democratically guaranteed. Citizens, who are required to possess considerable flexibility and adaptability to the new, cannot be alienated from socio-economic-political decisions, which are increasingly mediated by technology. As much as possible, they must understand and be aware of the opportunities and pitfalls of AI, especially given its rapid and pervasive spread. For this reason, human intelligence—understood as comprehension of things and situations—must remain a constantly lit beacon, cultivated more than ever in both thought and emotion, in an increasingly multipolar world. This is particularly crucial because machine learning involves the use of vast amounts of data constructed and continuously fed by the digital traces left by online actions, which impact privacy protection as well as the respect and safeguarding of justice, legality, and rights. This must be subject to even greater consideration if decisions are made by algorithms.

Transparency is essential for tracing the elements, data, and information that inform a given decision. However, this principle is not always upheld by humans—as evidenced in cases of corruption—and its absence in machine learning systems may give rise to new challenges. Unlike human decision-making, algorithmic processes operate through classification patterns that typically lack explanatory reasoning. This raises significant concerns regarding accountability, particularly when algorithmic outcomes are unfavorable or erroneous.

Moreover, one should not underestimate user profiling, whereby algorithms suggest and recommend what is of most interest to the user, effectively transforming into a form of manipulation. The user may become susceptible to conditioning and

---

[21] See Heidegger (1976), p. 27: The closer we come to danger, the more clearly the paths to what saves us begin to illuminate, and the more we question. Questioning is the piety of thought (My translation).

lose autonomous decision-making capacity, developing a sense of trust and dependence on an algorithmic system that seemingly thinks on their behalf. Historically, the human decision-making process has always prompted thinkers to question its correctness and fairness from an anthropological and moral perspective.

Focusing solely on fears, hopes, and unrealistic expectations does little to clarify how we might be assisted or complemented by AI, but never replaced by it.

In social spheres, AI is raising numerous concerns regarding its management and controllability. There is a particularly pressing inquiry into whether humans will continue to govern or be governed—not only by AI itself but also by those who produce and train it. In this context, the term algocracy,[22] referring to the dominance of algorithms, was first used in 2013. One potential risk is the transformation of our democracies into societies under the surveillance of algorithms themselves.

Thus, humans have developed the capacity to anthropomorphize some of their abilities, to crudely simulate them, only to subsequently fear them. In particular, the collective imagination can be manipulated by powerful, few entrepreneurs who have a vested interest in doing so, potentially leading to age-old visions through the most potent tools invented by science. As Bauman asserts: «[…] i congegni tecnologici non fanno altro che rendere più o meno realistici i nostri desideri, e più o meno rapida ed efficace la nostra ricerca…».[23]

AI, in fact, is neither autonomous nor rational; it is supported by political and social structures and makes decisions based on human instructions, contingent upon what humans do and how they do it.

For this reason, it is crucial to consider ethics—or more specifically, "algorethics"[24]—in both the ends and the means employed in its application.

Generative AI, aside from presenting numerous challenges, particularly concerning the distinction between what is true and false in texts, images, videos, and music, could have a massive impact on interpersonal relationships and emotional connections. These connections already exhibit degrees of vulnerability and, at times, can be further compromised by excessive use of social media, which may lead to isolation, dependency, disconnection from reality, anxiety, and feelings of inclusion or exclusion, depending on accessibility and acceptance, among other factors. For instance, consider the effects of image distortion that surpass even imagination itself.

AI undoubtedly represents an evolution in social relationships. The increasing tendency of users to perceive interactions with artificial systems as authentic human exchanges raises concerns about psychological vulnerability. This phenomenon is driven both by individual predispositions and by the intentional design of technologies that mimic empathy and respond to users' emotional states. As a result, users may be exposed to heightened risks of manipulation, emotional dependency, and

[22] The etymology of both the term algoretic and algocracy can be found online: https://accademiadellacrusca.it/it/parole-nuove/algoretica/18479.

[23] Bauman (2012), p. 169: […] Technological devices do nothing but make our desires more or less realistic, and our search more or less swift and effective… (My translation).

[24] Benanti (2018).

addictive behaviors.[25] So, how does AI fit into the human and spiritual realm? The so-called "Socratic" dialogue, characterized by moments of listening, pauses, silence, understanding, agreement, and disagreement, cannot be fully realized with machine learning. In fact, the human mind is not naturally comparable to ChatGPT (or similar systems), which ingests vast amounts of data and extrapolates the most plausible (or acceptable) response to a question. Instead, the human mind operates with a limited amount of information to seek explanations, recognize errors, and make improvements. In summary, without resorting to exaggeration or demonization, AI serves as a tool of great opportunity due to its computational potential—consider, for instance, its capacity to process vast bodies of knowledge, such as entire libraries,—yet it also poses risks, such as errors in facial recognition, which underscore the need to reinforce human intellect and relationships to ensure its proper functionality, reliability, and fairness.

To accompany this transformation, humans have civic duties: to defend the value of life through education, artistic, technical, and spiritual training in an anthropological sense; to recognize and establish human dignity as the foundation for coexistence between humans and machines; to perform and promote democratic functions, rather than being governed or subjected to the power of technology; to avoid creating, designing, or distributing technologies primarily intended to foster dependency, and above all, not to ascribe excessive power to them solely for the sake of economic gain. In the digital context, the primary objectives must be the respect for human rights and individual freedoms, as recognized over the centuries; the analysis of sources to understand their reliability or manipulation; and the protection of privacy, online security, mental and physical health, and interpersonal relationships.

All actors involved in the design and use of AI must, therefore, commit to ensuring equity, alleviating social inequalities, and lightening the burden of surveillance capitalism.[26] How can this be achieved? It is essential to always reason with a critical sense. Thus, from the early years of schooling, it is necessary to educate individuals critically and raise awareness about reflective use of the technology they interface with, to develop a decentralized and pluralistic thought through an interdisciplinary approach. The role of education and instruction is fundamental in understanding the functioning of digital technology and for developing the skills necessary for its conscious and responsible use. Instructions for thinking, preventing, judging, and confronting complexity can help recognize the potential consequences of one's own and others' actions in the digital realm.

In the academic field, research must facilitate the evaluation of the risks alongside the opportunities presented by these algorithmic tools. This should be achieved through information and communication campaigns directed at users, allowing them to choose whether to adopt these tools, for what purposes, and in which contexts. AI

[25] See the article available online: https://www.clioedu.it/documenti/eventi-live-ondemand/rivista-elettronica/Rivista-elettronica-4_2023.pdf, p. 82.

[26] Zuboff (2019).

systems are often designed to serve dominant interests; they are actors in the formation of knowledge itself, communication, and power. There is a need for reconfigurations at the level of epistemology, principles of justice, social organization, political expression, culture, concepts of the human body, subjectivity, and identity to effectively benefit from the opportunities offered by AI.

The following section will relate AI to some important—delicate and vulnerable—sectors of human life, such as memory, work, and education to understand how to keep the civic sense alive.

4 The Relationship Between AI and Memory

For the purposes of our discussion, in order to better understand the distinction between what has been and what will be, it is important to also consider the relationship between intelligence and memory. The concept of memory immediately brings to mind an iconic accumulation of corporeal and non-corporeal images, thoughts, facts, and objects—more generally, a set of elements linked to the human mind that resurface as a retrieval of positions or mental sedimentations, with a varying degree of authenticity. We are basically inclined to give historical and cultural value to memory, which is more appropriately, though not exclusively, linked to the emotional sphere, to remembrance. Memory, in fact, situates itself within the context of a lived past that the present is still processing. This understanding relates to the literal meaning of the Latin term *cogitare* (derived from *cogo*, meaning "to gather" or "to compel"), which is inherently linked to the act of thinking. Memory is thus closely connected to learning, whether individual or guided, as it facilitates the acquisition of new knowledge, behaviors, skills, values, or preferences through interaction with the environment and intelligence. It also encompasses the efforts humans undertake for self-fulfillment, allowing us to process and manage information within the time frames of specific tasks we are performing. Memory also evokes the sense of eternity that humankind has always pursued, like an asymptote, digging deep and leaving traces of itself.

This topic has been extensively studied in the fields of philosophy, psychology, and history. Today it is also being studied by neuroscience, which examines memory acquisition through the modulation of synapses—contacts between aggregations of neurons that represent distinct aspects of the environment or the internal state of the organism, via a process of association.

Memory may involve the act of recalling something or simply remembering it. In either case, the act of retrieving something from the mental repertoire precedes that of recollection, of finding the words, of expressing the memorial data. Therefore, memory is a specific function of the brain, which encodes, stores, and retrieves information, but it is also a representation. For instance, we refer to "memory" when talking about a legal document that summarizes the data of a legal proceeding. Memory exists in two dimensions: individual and social. It serves as an archive, but it always requires a subject to act as a witness. More broadly, memory is a cultural mechanism and can hold significant political value. The concept of *damnatio memoriae*, for instance, refers to the condemnation, whether immediate or deferred, of a name or event to be erased from records, books, and history.[27]

Up to this point, we have briefly and concisely outlined how memory functions and its capabilities.

Today we are aware that in addition to the natural intelligence of the animal and plant worlds, there is so-called artificial intelligence, with its associated memory, neural networks, and predictive systems.

Thus, how can natural memory be distinguished from artificial memory?

Natural memory is a complex system that processes and stores acquired information.[28]

However, with various technological advancements, from writing, to printing, and to personal computers, memory has become increasingly connected to tools, which may contribute to the reduction of mental and memory training. In this regard, Ferraris defines humans as *polytechnicians*, precisely because we are increasingly immersed in and surrounded by technological tools.[29]

On the other hand, artificial memory is based on natural memory, which is an existential dimension. Artificial intelligence is nurtured, expanded, and trained by human intelligence to such an extent that well-known AI models, like ChatGPT, are generative, meaning they can produce new content and ideas—such as conversations, stories, images, videos, and music—by attempting to imitate human creativity.

If memory is understood as the succession of events, derived from the recollection of occurrences, human sleep (which machines do not experience, despite having a standby mode) serves the function of repositioning episodic memory, which is reprocessed and becomes semantic memory—in other words, it becomes part of our knowledge.

Natural memory is dynamic and encompasses, preserves, and greatly utilizes artificial intelligence. We can think of things we have learned without truly understanding them (such as multiplication tables), or the automatic processes involved in using tools without knowing their manufacturing or configuration (e.g., the television). These processes are, in fact, artificial or part of artificial systems. Moreover, artificial memory has no physical body; it does not possess natural memory.[30] Consider the personal computer: it has no body, unlike human nature, which is understood as an organism capable of developing and expanding through what we learn from the outside world and internalize in our lives.

Both human intelligences, represented by the brain, and artificial intelligence, represented by machines, consume energy to perform their functions, but they do so

---

[27] See the article by Caprettini (2021), Memoria e ricordo, la mente e il cuore, available online: https://www.lindipendente.online/2021/12/11/memoria-e-ricordo-la-mente-e-il-cuore/

[28] See online: https://www.treccani.it/enciclopedia/memoria_(Enciclopedia-delle-scienze-sociali)/

[29] In his works, Ferraris (2021) allocates substantial consideration to artificial intelligence, a subject examined in the present paragraph. The term polytechnician was used by him in seminars and conferences.

[30] See Ferraris (2021).

in different ways. The human organism undergoes metabolism, which changes with age, while mechanical systems are subject to deterioration.[31]

Assuming that humans are thinking beings, the lingering question is: do machines not think? Algorithmic sequences, with their capacity to process infinite data and their increasing ability to influence our thoughts and decisions, raise critical concerns about agency, privacy, and transparency.

At present, the key differences lie in how our brain functions. Additionally, humans design their lives because we are aware of our finitude, which provokes a range of emotions, visions, and perspectives. In contrast, machines turn on, turn off, and turn back on again. A human, however, cannot simply "turn back on"; therefore, we preserve memory—whether oral, written, or artificial—as long as our existence endures (consider Aristotle's *to tí ên eînai*, or "substance"). This illustrates the difference between natural and artificial intelligence: humanity remains fundamentally the same, whereas artificial intelligence can reach superhuman capabilities.

Our minds are equipped to face situations and solve problems, even though we rely on other humans and technical systems, using our hands to manipulate tools and language to comprehend them. Our bodies are connected to tools, which we have to learn to use and manage. Humans, positioned between their animal nature and machines, are distinct from these two, which are either purely soulful or purely technical. Therefore, humans are always in motion and equipped to deal with an array of mechanisms.

Artificial intelligence can substitute natural intelligence, but not the other way around. Although both humans and machines consume energy, they do so through fundamentally different processes—biological in the former, mechanical in the latter.

In short, to restate the pressing question already posed: are we slaves to technology? There is a very high level of concern about the risks of technology's domination over humans, of its imposition, and of acting under its impulse. It is precisely the power of human memory that has shown how technology, when combined with strategic and relentless propaganda rooted in a single culture, can transform humans into mere order-followers, as seen during the Holocaust.

Today, thoughts turn to the extreme danger posed by contemporary technology, specifically the atomic bomb, whose destructive power, once initiated, cannot be halted—raising daily questions about whether its use is truly under control.

Therefore, what might be the most imminent risk associated with artificial intelligence? Rather than AI dominating us, the greater concern is that it is too readily available to humans, making it possible to create an algorithm with devastating consequences. Thus, it is crucial to develop a reflection on the influence and effects that new technologies and artificial intelligence have on people's mental lives, from the perspectives of both cognitive processes and emotions.[32]

---

[31] For the purpose of this work, see online by Ferraris M., L'intelligenza è corporale, in «Il Corriere della Sera», 01.08.2024: https://www.pressreader.com/italy/corriere-della-sera/20240801/282527253704307?srsltid=AfmBOopZ8Td-RM84f_4LEs0Y9-Zgqc3I-KE9_pUPNxpBJsYwTcp8zkFy

[32] See Jacomuzzi (2023).

5 AI and Work

For human beings, work represents not only a means of sustenance—nourishing life—but also a path to self-realization and a reciprocal civic contribution to the proper functioning of the social structure. With the rise of AI, there is growing alarm about the potential loss of numerous jobs, particularly in skilled and intellectual professions, which could be replaced by AI. Human beings are increasingly operating within algorithmic mechanisms and standardized procedures, which can, in fact, act in their place.

However, this fear contains a fundamental misunderstanding. Thinking that the threat comes solely from AI is not entirely correct, as it is necessary to trace back who organizes work and how it is organized. Indeed, if AI inevitably replaces certain trades, professions, and jobs, the discussion must always focus on safeguarding and guaranteeing existing labor rights, as applied to emerging new professions. Technological applications require new knowledge, skills, abilities, and competencies to be used and maintained.

It is quite plausible that, in the near future, professions such as lawyers, public officials, translators, doctors, or teachers could be replaced by automated systems—just as during the first industrial revolution, human labor was progressively integrated with machines. The idea that even traditional elite professions could be replaced has raised an alarm. However, this is merely the latest stage in the same process that saw artisanal and agricultural production—which was less homogeneous and more limited in quantity compared to serial production—mechanized. Just think of fields such as carpentry, metalworking, construction, and tailoring. The uniqueness of craftsmanship made it possible to achieve high levels of excellence, which are currently unattainable, but it did not ensure a uniform model. Therefore, the ability to distinguish well-crafted work from mediocre products relied on the discernment of the user.

Automated production systematically reduces experimental innovation, levels out peaks of excellence, and diminishes the consumer's capacity to choose, as they are offered serial products without exclusive characteristics. At the same time, of course, standardized production makes it possible to obtain enormously larger quantities of a product than were available in the past, lowering prices and increasing accessibility. To achieve this result, the experience of master artisans was needed. Their contribution allowed for the construction of serial production systems that could employ individuals who would never have worked in a craft workshop. As a result, higher and more specialized skills have gradually diminished. In the shift from artisan to factory worker on the assembly line, humans have become increasingly assimilated into machines, allowing mechanical processes— anonymous and infinitely repeatable in nature—to proliferate. The mechanization of production has delivered unprecedented quantitative power, but at the cost of compromising qualitatively unique aspects.[33]

[33] See, for the discussion of the entire part of this paragraph so far, the article by Zhok (2024).

In this context of social transformation, the labor market finds itself undergoing significant losses due to both crises and change, yet it is also being reshaped by new modes of work, among which particular attention should be given to *agile work* (remote or flexible work).[34]

This new form of work has accelerated the adoption of digitalization and AI, deserving a brief discussion in terms of opportunities and limitations from a relational point of view. In Italy, agile work is governed by Law No. 81/2017. The innovation of agile work lies in its detachment from specific time and space constraints, as it is based on achieving predefined goals. Until the onset of the pandemic, this work modality faced considerable difficulties in gaining traction and acceptance in both the public and private sectors. Only rare experimental implementations existed, largely obstructed by a managerial class not yet culturally ready and open. However, with the COVID-19 emergency, approximately 8 million Italians, across all levels, found themselves suddenly working from home in March 2020, without any prior training or preparation.

Thus, while agile work served as an immediate solution during the emergency when travel between workplaces was impossible, its advantages for continuing this mode of work in the post-pandemic routine have become evident, along with its limitations: feelings of isolation, exclusion from processes, discrimination, and unequal treatment—such as cases within the same organization where only certain workers are granted remote work or where there is an imbalanced distribution of workdays. In short, while agile work offers numerous benefits for both quality of life and the environment—although this is not always fully understood, primarily due to managerial resistance—it is crucial to ensure that it is not proposed as fully digitalized and home-based. While remote work was functional during the peak of the health crisis, it cannot now be projected in the same terms (solely remote) in the future, because the risk is distancing people from the workplace and the relational dynamics associated with it, particularly for women. Agile work, indeed, is a tool that, when used for the entire duration of the workday, does not *reconcile* with private life. Instead, it shifts the entire family burden onto women, turning it into a "trap", as Branchetti asserts.[35]

6 AI in Education

Another sector that requires special consideration for civic formation and personal development is education, where AI is quickly making its mark. For the current 2024/25 academic year, the Ministry of Education[36] has banned the use of smartphones and similar electronic devices during educational activities from early childhood through middle school, where their use is less common. However, this ban does not apply

[34] See, among his many articles, speeches, books on agile work, De Masi (2020).

[35] Branchetti (2020).

[36] The circular can be found online: https://www.orizzontescuola.it/wp-content/uploads/2024/07/m_pi.AOODPIT.REGISTRO-UFFICIALEU.0005274.11-07-2024.pdf.

to high schools, where digital devices have become a widespread practice. At the same time, the introduction of AI experimentation in schools has begun,[37] potentially aiming to familiarize students with AI usage. It would seem a contradiction, as experimentation is only possible through access to digital devices. Referring to school, the first thought goes to the delicate learning process, which requires commitment, dedication, concentration and memory.

We know that the internet willingly exempts us from the need to memorize because we can simply search for information online. Consequently, there is a serious risk that AI will do the thinking for young minds in the process of formation, as they can simply consult the 'generative oracle'. Offering the support of AI to a young person who is still learning to reason is potentially dangerous. Encouraging AI use might reduce the capacity to learn to think independently.[38]

The introduction into schools of AI, which can perform tasks and exercises essential for training the mind and developing a sense of responsibility, highlights the need for careful attention to the importance of nourishing the human brain from early childhood.

Digital education, which was massively tested during the COVID-19 pandemic, certainly represents an alternative—especially for older students—but has shown significant management challenges. Issues such as unstable connectivity, frequent distractions, and reduced social interaction can undermine its effectiveness and efficiency.

Technology is seductive when it satisfies human vulnerability, sometimes with illusions or deceptions.[39] This is particularly concerning for younger generations, who require constant protection. It is vital to monitor whether these tools are manipulating young minds in any way, potentially compromising their sense of freedom as they grow up.

That said, digitalization and AI are now an integral part of our world, and young people urgently need education and training that allows them to use these technologies to their advantage, rather than to their detriment. It remains critically important that education, training, and culture as a whole do not become subservient to the demands of large financial groups or digital multinationals.

Special attention must be paid to preserving the development of "human culture", ensuring that the process of cultural production does not become overly standardized or mechanized at any level. A cultural renaissance must be grounded in educating young people and promoting lifelong learning for adults.

This approach can empower future generations to engage with technology critically and thoughtfully, ensuring that human values, creativity, and independent thinking remain central to the educational experience.

---

[37] The information is available online: https://miur.gov.it/web/guest/-/intelligenza-artificiale-al-via-la-sperimentazione-nelle-scuole.

[38] See the article by Prandel (2024).

[39] See Natale (2022).

7 Ethics for AI or in AI?

To introduce this final section on AI and its ethical implications, it is important to recall a passage from a speech given by Rodotà, the Italian Privacy Commissioner, in 2003:

> [...] non tutto ciò che è tecnologicamente possibile è anche socialmente desiderabile, eticamente accettabile, giuridicamente legittimo. Oggi dobbiamo aggiungere che le derive tecnologiche possono produrre gravi effetti distorsivi. Distorsioni nell'uso delle risorse quando, ad esempio, queste vengono investite in impianti di videosorveglianza privi di vera utilità per la sicurezza.
>
> Distorsioni nell'organizzazione degli interventi quando, ad esempio, ci si affida a grandi banche dati centralizzate, tecnicamente difficili da gestire, vulnerabili agli attacchi, accompagnate da affidamenti in outsourcing spesso inadeguati, soprattutto tali da distogliere l'attenzione dalla necessità di raccolte e di indagini mirate. Distorsioni nella percezione e nell'analisi della realtà quando, ad esempio, le raccolte di informazioni vengono adoperate per frettolose traduzioni di un fenomeno in termini di ordine pubblico, invece di indagarne le ragioni sociali e di avviare, quindi, politiche più adeguate.[40]

One of the most heated debates concerns whether it is appropriate to embed ethics (the question, however, is *which* ethics?) into algorithms, or whether we should focus on the ethics of people themselves, which seems increasingly fragile or non-existent. Any progress must come with a call to responsibility. There is a concern that life could become completely replaced by computation, turning humans into holographic figures, especially as elites increasingly see AI as a means of exercising control.

The central question is: can ethics be translated into computable terms? The answer is relatively straightforward—ethics is inherently human, while technology lacks it. Technocratic ethics is inherently limited and circumscribed. AI can simulate human thought, but it lacks memory in the deeper sense—memory as a historical testimony of lived experience. AI consumes information through data, but not knowledge, which involves a deeper process of both external and internal inquiry.

We are witnessing an evolution of power that seeks to dominate nature, which now threatens the future of the human species. Artificial agents are becoming capable of assisting humans in tasks that can be delegated to machines. The ongoing debate around AI often overstates what it can deliver. Automation feeds into a process of massification, conformism, and homogenization, relying on standardized procedures

[40] See online this speech of Rodotà S. at the presentation of the 2003 Report, p. 6: https://www.garanteprivacy.it/web/guest/home/docweb/-/docweb-display/docweb/1314441: [...] not everything that is technologically possible is also socially desirable, ethically acceptable, legally legitimate. Today we must add that technological drifts can produce serious distorting effects. Distortions in the use of resources when, for example, these are invested in video surveillance systems with no real security utility. Distortions in the organization of interventions when, for example, reliance is placed on large, centralized databases that are technically difficult to manage, vulnerable to attack, and accompanied by outsourcing that is often inadequate, especially such as to divert attention from the need for targeted collections and investigations. Distortions in the perception and analysis of reality when, for example, information collections are used for hasty translations of a phenomenon in terms of public order, instead of investigating its social reasons and thus initiating more appropriate policies (My translation).

and statistical models. This is currently monopolized by Silicon Valley's imperialistic grip on technology. Furthermore, the "capitalism of information" threatens both the truth and our freedom through increased surveillance. Is AI simply a tool of power, or has it become the very center of power?

Algorithms are opaque; we do not know how they work or how they are structured, and hegemonic classes decide where and how they should be applied. This jeopardizes human rights, highlighting the need for decisions to be made with respect for human life. The very existence of democracy, already precarious, is at stake. Whoever enters data into AI performs an action of collective interest, as did the medieval scribes. This is why it is essential to understand whether the actions we are taking will have a positive or negative impact on human life. The purpose and direction of technological development must be made clear—not only to those in power, but to society as a whole.

The increasing demand to be constantly connected digitally clashes with our freedom of choice and free will. However, humans are very seduced by AI because they see it as a perfect system, overcoming their imperfection and mortality, even at the cost of reducing themselves to the level of a machine.[41]

Moving beyond anthropocentrism, and appealing to humans' sense of responsibility, an ethical theory needs to be developed, based on equity and social justice,[42] smoothing out inequalities in access to and use of AI. Humans do not have a predetermined nature; we construct it day by day, alongside our system of values. The ethical moment is what allows us to transcend animality and reach humanity through rationality and argumentation.

Ethics also involves resisting the process of passive compliance, profiling, and the erosion of our capacity to think independently. It is about remembering who we are and how we arrived at the twenty-first century, though much has been contaminated along the way. Ethics can be linked to wisdom and logic as human traits, not necessarily tied to pure reason, in order to preserve the capacity to judge and choose.[43] Ethics is historical, temporal, and contextual—it is built through knowledge and by listening to the opinions of others.

Therefore, it becomes essential to restore faith in human responsibility regarding AI actions. Hans Jonas reminds us that ethics must be treated differently today than in the past, because human actions have changed in their scope and impact.[44] We must recognize that the choices we make about AI are, in fact, choices about humanity's future.

AI challenges our concept of anthropocentrism, yet it simultaneously offers individuals the opportunity to form an ethical community that can develop a common language and agree on policies and social goals. However, the meaning and significance of AI vary for each person, and its impact on social relationships, both in time and space, is profound.

---

[41] Kissinger et al. (2023).

[42] Fabris and Belardinelli (2024).

[43] Varanini (2024).

[44] Jonas (2009).

As machines acquire the capacity for autonomous learning, they may begin to operate according to a logic that exceeds the current boundaries of human reasoning. In response, society must engage collectively to both comprehend and navigate this transformation. While the advancement of artificial intelligence may be inevitable, its trajectory is not. It is therefore imperative that humans retain the ability to guide and shape this evolution in alignment with their fundamental values.

Thus, the need for an ethics that understands and guides AI is fundamental. Everyone must participate in an open exchange of opinions, free from bias. Humans will manage algorithms that process vast amounts of data, but AI cannot be reduced to mere time and computational power. It is porous, learning from humans, but the spontaneous experience of reality, with all its contradictions and complexities, remains a crucial aspect of the human condition, even when it leads to inefficiency or error.

Modern humans have built AI with their own minds and hands, but throughout the twentieth century, they have increasingly become passive, alienated consumers. Society needs individuals who collaborate with each other, but instead, humans appear to be dominated by their own technological creations and by self-serving interests. This alienation renders individuals less capable of empathy and love. The growing discrepancy between technical intelligence and reason without limits could lead to catastrophic consequences. As Fromm observes:

Gli uomini sono sempre più automi, costruttori di macchine che agiscono come uomini e producono uomini che si comportano come macchine; la loro ragione si deteriora mentre la loro intelligenza aumenta, creando così una pericolosa situazione in cui l'uomo è fornito di enorme potenza materiale senza possedere la saggezza e la prudenza necessarie per usarla.[45]

In this context, how can we maintain a sense of identity and continue to live a meaningful life? The answer lies in the ability of humans to love and to make their work meaningful. Love, truth, and justice must remain the principal pillars of human existence.

Therefore, ethical education and the development of personal virtues are crucial to addressing contemporary problems. It is more feasible to pursue this goal than to undertake a vague attempt to "moralize" algorithms. Strengthening fundamental human rights, especially those related to life and freedom, is far more important than regulating machine rights. Unjust biases will not be rectified by merely reprogramming algorithms but by cultivating virtuous individuals through creativity, hard work, and prudence.

Traditional ethics, once anthropocentric, have now shifted toward a biospheric perspective.[46] It is crucial to preserve the concept of humanity with its emotional and organic roots. We must urgently develop a new form of ethics to prevent technology

[45] Fromm E. (1975), p. 107: Men are more and more automatons, builders of machines that act like men and produce men who behave like machines; their reason deteriorates as their intelligence increases, thus creating a dangerous situation in which man is endowed with enormous material power without possessing the wisdom and prudence necessary to use it (My translation).

[46] Floridi L. (2022).

from becoming a threat or a disaster for humanity.[47] Modern humans are powerless when facing the social forces they have created and must face contradictions that they are unable to resolve. Technologies must become their servants, not their idols.

So, should we be Promethean, daring to defy fate, or Epimethean, reflecting on the consequences of our actions? In the contemporary labyrinth, humans must possess an adventurous spirit, courage, imagination, and sensitivity to live in the most human world possible. Using technology for the common good, without idolizing it, can be highly beneficial, while preserving the sense of vulnerability and finitude that defines our humanity.

8 Conclusions

At the heart of this epochal change, situated within a national and international context of widespread uncertainty and instability, remains the vulnerability of human beings, along with their value systems and existential meanings—multifaceted and imperfect, along with their aspirations and needs for freedom of choice—dimensions that become significantly constrained with the advent of new digital technologies.

The regulation of the digital sphere and the protection of inalienablee human dignity are foundational to the human-centric vision[48] or the emerging paradigm of cyberhumanism.[49] These currents of thought aim to safeguard individuals from automated mechanisms. Digital humanism, alongside other disciplines, is tasked with analyzing the impact of technological innovation and its possible criticalities on individuals who act, interact, and relate to others within the society of which they are a part. As digital machines increasingly replicate aspects of human experience, placing the individual at the center of a technology-shaped environment becomes essential to safeguarding quality of life, social heritage, and collective memory. Certainly, genius, talent, intuition, and orality—viewed as an unparalleled ancestral matrix compared to any other form of expression—will never be subject to simulation by AI.

Thus, the anthropological and cultural consequences of AI must be appropriately assessed by human beings regarding responsibility for ethical and legal aspects, to address this social revolution using tools and good practices that respect what AI will never possess: the aforementioned civic sense, which aims to safeguard the irreplaceable human life that is performative, value-laden, and conflictual.

The complex interaction between the human and non-human cannot be left solely in the minds and affairs of large corporations. This issue needs to be addressed promptly, for instance, through the establishment of specific and permanent ethical committees alongside the technicians, so that innovative impacts can take place within a democratic context—imperfect, unfinished, and challenging in itself—that needs to be considered in a hybrid of humans and so-called intelligent machines.

[47] Fossa et al. (2021).

[48] Messina (2023).

[49] Camisani Calzolari (2024).

References

Abbagnano N (1971) Dizionario di filosofia, Turin, under the word "Intellect"

Alvídrez S, Chomsky N, Mujica P (2024) Sopravvivere al ventunesimo secolo, Italian translation by V. Nicolì, Milan

Aristotle (1999) Etica Nicomachea, Italian translation and notes by C. Natali, Milan, pp 222–255

Bauman Z (2012) Un mondo fuori asse, Italian translation by M. Cupellaro, Bari-Rome, p 169

Benanti P (2018) Oracoli. Tra algoretica e algocrazia, Rome

Bergson H (2002) L'evoluzione creatrice, Italian edition F. Polidori, Milan, p 117

Bergson H (2006) Le due fonti della morale e della religione, Italian translation by M. Vinciguerra, Milan, p 237

Bertolaso M (2023) Umanesimo tecnologico. Una riflessione filosofica sull'intelligenza artificiale, Rome

Branchetti S (2020) Donne!!! È arrivato lo smart working: opportunità o trappola?, Palermo

Camisani Calzolari M (2024) Cyberumanesimo, Milan

Caprettini GP (2021) Memoria e ricordo, la mente e il cuore, available online: https://www.lindipendente.online/2021/12/11/memoria-e-ricordo-la-mente-e-il-cuore/

Cristianini N (2023) La scorciatoia. Come le macchine sono diventate intelligenti senza pensare in modo umano, Bologna, p 23

Cristianini N (2024) Machina sapiens. L'algoritmo che ci ha rubato il segreto della conoscenza, Bologna, p 146

Crawford K (2023) Né intelligente né artificiale. Il lato oscuro dell'IA, Milan

De Masi D (2020) Smart working. La rivoluzione del lavoro intelligente, Venice

Eco U (2017) Apocalittici e integrati, Milan

Fabris A, Belardinelli S (2024) Digital environments and human relations: ethical perspectives on AI issues. https://doi.org/10.1007/978-3-031-76961-0

Ferraris M (2021) Documanità. Filosofia del mondo nuovo, Bari-Roma

Floridi L (2014) La quarta rivoluzione. Come l'infosfera sta trasformando il mondo, Milan

Floridi L (2022) Etica dell'intelligenza artificiale. Sviluppi, opportunità, sfide, Italian edition by M. Durante, Milan

Fossa F, Tamburrini G, Schiaffonati V (2021) Automi e persone. Introduzione all'etica dell'intelligenza artificiale e della robotica, Rome

Fromm E (1975) Dogmi, gregari e rivoluzionari, Milano, p 107

Galletti M, Zipoli Caiani S (2024) Filosofia dell'intelligenza artificiale: sfide etiche e teoriche, Bologna

Gramsci A (1975) Quaderni del carcere, ed. by V. Gerratana, Turin, Vol. 1, Notebook 3 (XX), § 24, p 311

Heidegger M (1976) La questione della tecnica, in G Vattimo (ed) Saggi e discorsi, Milan, p 27

Jacomuzzi A (2023) Introduzione alle scienze cognitive, Bologna

Jonas H (2009) Il principio responsabilità. Un'etica per la civiltà tecnologica, Turin

Kissinger HA, Schmidt E, Huttenlocher D (2023) L'era dell'intelligenza artificiale. Il futuro dell'identità umana, Italian translation by A. Piccato, Milan, ch. I, VI

Messina D (2023) La tutela della dignità nell'era digitale. Prospettive e insidie, tra protezione dei dati, diritto all'oblio e intelligenza artificiale, Naples

Natale S (2022) Macchine ingannevoli. Comunicazione, tecnologia, intelligenza artificiale, Turin

Pozzi F (2022) Digital nudge. L'architettura delle scelte nei contesti digitali, Milan

Prandel F (2024) Se questa è una scuola, available online: https://www.lafionda.org/2024/09/17/se-questa-e-una-scuola/

Rossi F (2024) Intelligenza artificiale. Come funziona e dove ci porta la tecnologia che sta trasformando il mondo, Bari-Rome

Scotti A (2024) Henri Bergson and the intelligence in things, available online: https://www.scienzaefilosofia.com/2024/01/06/henri-bergson-e-lintelligenza-nelle-cose/

Turkle S (2019) Insieme ma soli. Perché ci aspettiamo sempre più dalla tecnologia e sempre meno dagli altri, Turin
Varanini F (2024) Splendori e miserie delle intelligenze artificiali: alla luce dell'umana esperienza, Milan
Zhok A (2024) Intelligenza Artigianale, available online: https://www.ariannaeditrice.it/articoli/intelligenza-artigianale
Zuboff S (2019) Il capitalismo della sorveglianza. Il futuro dell'umanità nell'era dei nuovi poteri, Italian translation by P. Bassotti, Rome

Antonella Tennenini, Ph.D. Candidate in History and Philosophical Social Sciences at the University of Rome Tor Vergata. The first part of her interdisciplinary research focuses on the theoretical aspects of the formation of public opinion and its transformations in the Digital Age, with a focus on the ethical implications of artificial intelligence. The empirical part examines the reception of public debate by the Public Administration, with particular regard to the infrastructure sector.

Open Access This chapter is licensed under the terms of the Creative Commons Attribution 4.0 International License (http://creativecommons.org/licenses/by/4.0/), which permits use, sharing, adaptation, distribution and reproduction in any medium or format, as long as you give appropriate credit to the original author(s) and the source, provide a link to the Creative Commons license and indicate if changes were made.

The images or other third party material in this chapter are included in the chapter's Creative Commons license, unless indicated otherwise in a credit line to the material. If material is not included in the chapter's Creative Commons license and your intended use is not permitted by statutory regulation or exceeds the permitted use, you will need to obtain permission directly from the copyright holder.

Human-Machine Interaction and Policy Strategies Between Anticipatory Governance and Sustainability of Risks

Human Vulnerability and AI: The Risk of Risk Regulation

Guido Smorto

Abstract The new EU Regulation 2024/1689 on Artificial Intelligence has been subject to many criticisms, especially from those who believe it is not fully adequate to tackle the needs arising from the growing use of AI systems: a limited number of prohibitions, basic transparency obligations for AI systems that present specific risks of impersonation or deception, a risk management system based on documents and conducted by the same provider of the system. Less attention has been paid to the preliminary option made by the EU legislature to adopt a so-called risk-based approach. This article aims to focus on the choice to regulate AI systems through so-called risk regulation and also ponder the consequences of this choice on the distribution of costs and benefits originating from the use of AI systems and the protection of individual rights. In its final part, the article formulates some proposals that support an interpretation of the Regulation more oriented toward risk distribution and protection of rights.

Keywords Artificial Intelligence · EU Artificial Intelligence Act · Risk · Distribution · Liability

1 The European Regulation on Artificial Intelligence

After a long and complex negotiation, in 2024, the European Union finally adopted the European Regulation on Artificial Intelligence (henceforth, Regulation).[1] The leading representatives of the European institutions agreed to call this result a historical one, stressing how this Regulation is a true "first" across the world: the first law

G. Smorto (✉)
University of Palermo, Palermo, Italy
e-mail: guido.smorto@unipa.it

[1] Regulation (EU) 2024/1689 of the European Parliament and of the Council of 13 June 2024 laying down harmonised rules on artificial intelligence and amending Regulations (EC) No 300/2008, (EU) No 167/2013, (EU) No 168/2013, (EU) 2018/858, (EU) 2018/1139 and (EU) 2019/2144 and Directives 2014/90/EU, (EU) 2016/797 and (EU) 2020/1828 (Artificial Intelligence Act), OJ L, 2024/1689, 12.7.2024.

© The Author(s) 2025

C. Amodio and A. Diurni (eds.), *Human Vulnerability in Interaction with AI in European Private Law*, https://doi.org/10.1007/978-3-031-93247-2_12

ever on artificial intelligence meant to become a global standard for the development of reliable artificial intelligence, which guarantees security and fundamental rights.

To achieve these ambitious goals, the Regulation adopts a risk-based approach. It categorises AI systems according to whether they generate unacceptable, high, specific, limited, or minimal risks.

To provide rules that are "proportionate" to the interests to be protected and the associated risks, for each of these types of risks it sets prohibitions, mandatory minimum requirements under which to design and develop AI systems, transparency obligations, or simple measures to promote self-regulation.[2]

Within this typological categorisation, at the heart of the Regulation are "high-risk" AI systems, i.e., those that "have a significant harmful impact on the health, safety and fundamental rights of persons".[3] The definition of an AI system as "high-risk" entails the provider's obligation to establish, implement, document and maintain a quality management system, i.e., a set of policies, procedures and instructions for the development, control and quality assurance of AI systems, to be applied at the various life stages of the systems in question: design, development, marketing, use, and post-market monitoring.[4]

The risk management system lies at the heart of the quality management system.[5] In detail, the Regulation requires the provider to adopt a risk management system "proportionate" to the size of its organization,[6] to draw up the EU declaration of conformity,[7] to affix the CE marking to the system,[8] and to implement post-market monitoring to evaluate the continuous compliance of AI systems with the requirements set out in the Regulation.[9] Wherever an AI system meets these requirements, or namely in other words, where risk mitigation measures are "appropriate" under

[2] In its final version, the Regulation (EU) 2024/1689, includes general-purpose AI models, with obligations modelled on those set for high-risk AI systems. Cf. Chapter 5.

[3] Regulation (EU) 2024/1689, Rec. 46 ("AI systems identified as high-risk should be limited to those that have a significant harmful impact on the health, safety and fundamental rights of persons in the Union and such limitation should minimise any potential restriction to international trade."); art. 6 (Classification rules for high-risk AI systems) considers an AI system to be high-risk if it is intended to be used as a safety component of a product or if the AI system is itself a product covered by the Union harmonisation legislation. In addition, an AI system is deemed as high-risk if employed in those sectors listed in Annex III (High-risk AI systems referred to in Article 6(2)): biometrics; critical infrastructure; educational and vocational training; employment, workers management and access to self-employment; access to and enjoyment of essential private services and essential public services and benefits; law enforcement; Migration, asylum and border control management.

[4] Regulation (EU) 2024/1689, Article 17.

[5] Regulation (EU) 2024/1689, Article 9.

[6] Regulation (EU) 2024/1689, Article 17, para. 2: "The implementation of the aspects referred to in paragraph 1 shall be proportionate to the size of the provider's organisation."

[7] Regulation (EU) 2024/1689, Article 47.

[8] Regulation (EU) 2024/1689, Article 48.

[9] Regulation (EU) 2024/1689, Article 72.

the Regulation, the relevant residual risk associated with each hazard and the overall residual risk of the high-risk AI systems is deemed "acceptable."[10]

Following the approach known as the "New Legislative Framework",[11] the Regulation gives the so-called European standardisation organisations the task of developing - at the request of the Commission - special "harmonised standards", which translate legal requirements prescribed by the Regulation into detailed technical rules, setting the conditions for the marketing and use of AI systems. High-risk AI systems that comply with such harmonised standards enjoy a presumption of conformity with the Regulation.[12]

2 Critical Reflections on the Regulation

The Regulation has been the subject of much criticism, especially from those who believe it is not fully adequate to handle the dangers associated with the use of artificial intelligence.[13]

With regard to those AI practices that are prohibited as they generate unacceptable risks, the list of prohibitions has been criticised for being extremely limited, due to the combination of different provisions that, on the one hand, establish in detail what is prohibited and, on the other hand, are constructed around a series of explicit or sometimes implicit exceptions that end up broadening the permitted uses of artificial intelligence, including those that are potentially at odds with European values.[14] Regarding the risks of impersonation or deception of those who interact with the AI

---

[10] Regulation (EU) 2024/1689, Art. 9, par. 5 ("The risk management measures referred to in paragraph 2, point (d), shall be such that the relevant residual risk associated with each hazard, as well as the overall residual risk of the high-risk AI systems is judged to be acceptable."). Neither the text of the Regulation nor the Explanatory Memorandum offer clarification as to what an acceptable residual risk is. Clause 3.8 of Safety Aspects - Guidelines for Their Inclusion in Standards defines it as "any risk remaining after risk reduction measures have been implemented"; and "acceptable" the level of risk "that is accepted in a given context based on the current values of society" (Clause 3.15). In literature, residual risk is commonly deemed to be the risk which remains after appropriate risk management measures have been implemented, and can be expressed by the formula: residual risk equals risk proper to a certain activity minus risk control. On this point, see, e.g., Tamboli A (2019, p. 103) (Residual Risk = Inherent Risk – Risk Control). Cost-benefit analysis is a central element of risk acceptability assessment. On this point, see Schuett J (2023, p. 13), Fraser and Bello Y Villarino (2022, p. 5): "We find that the greater the emphasis on safety and precaution, the more the cost of residual risks is borne by AI providers (and the higher the barriers to market entry for high-risk AI systems); the greater the emphasis on the social utility of the system, the more likely it is that individuals will carry the residual risks of AI systems –jeopardizing their rights and safety".

[11] European Council (2008) New Legislative Framework adopted on July 9, 2008, as referenced in Annex II of Regulation (EU) 2024/1689.

[12] Regulation (EU) 2024/1689, Article 40.

[13] Veale and Zuiderveen Borgesius (2021, p. 97), Malgieri and Pasquale (2022, p. 1), Kaminski (2019, p. 1529).

[14] Regulation (EU) 2024/1689, Article 5. For a review, see Ruschemeier (2023, p. 372), Veale and Zuiderveen Borgesius (2021, p. 98).

systems, the absence of substantive limitations on using such systems has also been criticised, as the Regulation prescribes mere transparency requirements.[15]

Yet, the most significant reproach is focused on high-risk AI systems. The Regulation has been criticised for using relatively mild risk regulation techniques.[16] It does not provide for a system of licences, time permits, and "resilience" tools, which both literature and practice have identified as characteristic of this regulation.[17] It only resorts to strong precautionary measures - emergency protocols, risk thresholds whose attainment automatically results in the system's withdrawal from the market, or conditional licences – to a limited extent. It forgoes applying the precautionary principle in favour of a cost–benefit analysis.[18] It places a conformity assessment at the centre, primarily made up of duties to comply with documentary and monitoring obligations. The conformity assessment procedure and the confirmation of compliance with risk mitigation measures must be conducted by the very same providers rather than by third-party, independent bodies.[19] In employing proportionality between risks and benefits as its main principle, it resorts to open standards – adequacy, acceptability, appropriateness – which are left to the interpretation of those directly involved. It chooses a governance model centred on European standardisation organisations.

While critical comments on the Regulation have focused mainly on the limitations of the legal measures adopted for risk mitigation purposes, far less attention has been paid to the preliminary choice of looking at the uses of artificial intelligence through the technical toolkit of risk regulation and to the consequences that such a choice entails.[20]

---

[15] Regulation (EU) 2024/1689, Article 50.

[16] Kaminski (2023b, p.1381) defines the system adopted by the Regulation as "ultra-lite licensing".

[17] Kaminski (2023b, p. 1370), Marchant and Stevens (2017, p. 236 ff).

[18] On the different parameters used in risk assessment, see Coglianese (2020) 1, at 9: "In making these value judgments about risk, decision-makers can adhere to one of four basic normative principles or approaches: (1) Eliminate all risk – or at least all man-made risk (the zero-risk approach); (2) Reduce risk to an acceptable level (the acceptable risk approach); (3) Reduce risk until the cost of doing so reaches an unacceptable level (the feasibility approach); and (4) Balance the benefits of risk reduction with the costs (the efficiency approach)". On the contrast between the precautionary principle and cost-benefit analysis in risk regulation, see Posner (2004, p. 140), Sunstein (2005); Sunstein (2000, p. 1059). In a comparative perspective, for a comparison between the North American and European models, see Marchant and Stevens (2017, p. 240 ff.), Kysar (2006, p. 1), Wiener (2003, p. 207), who affirms that the conventional between Europe (in favour of the precautionary principle) and the United States of America (which instead adopts cost-benefit analysis) in many cases amounts to an excess of simplification.

[19] The Regulation departs from other harmonised rules that confer the power of conformity assessments on independent authorities, such as the pharmaceutical sector, where the European Medicines Agency (EMA) approves the introduction of new products onto the market and monitors their safety throughout their life span in order to protect public health and ensure the availability of high quality, safe and effective medicines. The point is well argued by Veale and Zuiderveen Borgesius (2021, p. 102). Under the Regulation, only limited biometric systems undergo a conformity assessment by so-called "notified bodies."

[20] De Gregorio and Dunn (2022, p. 473), Chamberlain (2023, p. 1), Schuett (2023, p. 1).

Against this backdrop, the purpose of this article is to focus on the choice that informs the overall logic of the entire regulatory framework of the Regulation and the detailed rules that comprise it: namely, that of regulating AI systems from an ex-ante perspective, based on the model of EU product safety regimes. To this end, after assessing the potential benefits of risk regulation in an area such as artificial intelligence, the article ponders the consequences of adopting such a regulatory model in this field, in order to focus attention on the implications of this choice on the distribution of costs and benefits resulting from the use of AI systems, and also the consequences in terms of protection of fundamental rights and the respect for EU values. In the final part, it formulates some initial interpretive proposals aimed at enhancing the individualised and contextual dimension of the risks generated by artificial intelligence under the Regulation.

3 The Reason Behind the Use of Risk Regulation for Artificial Intelligence

The relatively minor attention paid to the fundamental choice made by the European legislature to adopt risk regulation in the field of AI systems is probably due to the confluence of several different factors. On the one hand, the option chosen by the EU legislature to regulate potential harms from AI systems as risks to be managed is entirely in line with what is happening in the rest of the world. We are, in fact, witnessing a remarkable convergence at the global level of the use of risk regulation as the most appropriate way to govern artificial intelligence, complemented by studies that emphasise the many advantages such an approach would provide in contexts such as those related to the regulation of new technologies and, in particular, artificial intelligence.[21]

Firstly, based on an ex-ante, prognostic, and future-oriented view, risk regulation is deemed particularly well suited to establish flexible rules for a constantly changing field with blurred boundaries. On the one hand, risk regulation would allow for adequate protection of those values and interests that only sometimes translate into vested rights recognised by the legal system, as may often be the case in the digital realm. In a similar vein, this regulatory technique would prove to be particularly suitable for governing potentially harmful consequences that are difficult to predict and quantify accurately, such as those arising from dangers that are not fully known (e.g., those of so-called virtual harms).[22]

Similar reasoning applies to the ascertainment of the occurrence of damage, causation and identification of the liable party: something which could prove particularly

[21] See, e.g., the proposals developed by the National Institute of Standards and Technology (2023) in the USA. Cf AI Risk Management Framework (AI RMF 1.0), p. 13. In literature, see, among others: Guihot et al. (2017, p. 446), Marchant and Stevens (2017, p. 236), Scherer (2016, p. 356), Solow-Niederman (2020, p. 691).

[22] Wolfendale (2007, p. 111), Young (2023, p. 1), Carter and Palermos (2016, p. 542).

complex in the event of the development and use of increasingly sophisticated forms of artificial intelligence, also given the opacity of AI systems that is further intensified by the protection of industrial secrets of these systems, famously termed as black boxes.[23] In this context, the decision to adopt the New Legislative Framework, with the resulting involvement of specialised technical bodies in the definition of risk mitigation measures, is also considered the most appropriate for addressing issues of considerable technical complexity, such as those related to the use of artificial intelligence.

4 Civil Liability and Risk Regulation

The line of reasoning that highlights the many benefits of ex-ante regulation is often conducted in a comparison, whether implicit or explicit, with ex-post remedies and, in particular, with torts and insurance law. Drawing on studies in the economic analysis of law,[24] it is commonly believed that ex-ante regulation is preferable to a system based on ex-post remedies and compensation in contexts such as the one under consideration.

Following a similar path to that taken in the context of environmental damage,[25] many affirm that the technical complexity of AI systems may amount to an insurmountable obstacle to individual access to ex-post forms of compensation, significantly raising the costs that the injured party wishing to take legal action would have to bear, and thus discouraging them from taking any course of action.[26] This risk would be even more significant in legal systems that do not offer full recognition of class actions and leave the compensatory remedies to individual plaintiffs.[27]

The same holds true for damages that are negligible at the individual level but significant at the aggregate level. In such cases, the incentive for individual action is inevitably diluted, and the tort system does not result in an optimal level of deterrence for reasons of collective action.

In light of these limitations, the tort system would end up being merely conjectural and, as a result, would not bring about the deterrent effect and internalisation of risks that typically result from the fear of incurring tortious liability. The many obstacles to a comprehensive and adequate ex-post compensatory type of protection, highlighted in the literature, would produce an overall reduction in tort liability's regulatory (as well as compensatory) function, with the consequence of diluting the deterrent

---

[23] Pasquale (2015).

[24] On the relationship between risk regulation and liability, see, among others, Calabresi (1970), Shavell (1984a, p. 271, 1984b, p. 357), Shavell (1987), Stapleton (1986, 1995, p. 820), Sugarman (1989, p. 555), Schuck (1991, p. 1345), Atiyah (1997); Cane (1997, 2018), Harlow (2004).

[25] On the relationship between risk regulation and environmental damages, see Abraham (2002, p. 379), Hylton (2002, p. 515), Schroeder (2002, p. 583), McGarity (2005, p. 371), Abelkop (2014, p. 381), Kysar (2018, p. 48).

[26] Froomkin (2015, p. 1713), Hirsch (2006, p. 1), Ben-Shahar (2019, p. 104).

[27] Edwards and Veale (2017). In Italian literature, see Comandé (1999).

effect from what is socially desirable.[28] It is also from this widespread recognition of the difficulties in the tort system that ex-ante risk-reducing regulation has come to dominate as the preferred model for regulating AI systems.[29]

5 The Consequences of Risk Regulation

The European discipline on artificial intelligence is often presented by appealing to common sense: the more significant the risk, the stricter the rules, using a basic approach symbolised by the famous pyramid of risks adopted by European institutions to epitomise and disseminate the European approach to artificial intelligence.[30]

However, far from being a neutral or even obligatory choice, framing the potential harms of AI systems as risks and prescribing measures for their mitigation brings with it a specific technical toolkit and a distinct way of handling the consequences of using artificial intelligence, which amounts to value-laden regulatory decisions.[31]

Firstly, considering the potential harms caused by artificial intelligence as risks to be mitigated, and demanding the adoption of ex-ante technical measures aimed at reducing the risks within acceptable levels implies that the technology in question is permitted despite the harm it may cause.[32] As an example, in qualifying as high-risk AI systems, those systems used in several key sectors of society (biometrics; critical infrastructure necessary for the provision of an essential service; education and vocational training; labour; essential private services and essential public services and benefits; law enforcement; migration, asylum and border control; administration of justice and democratic processes),[33] the Regulation permits the use of AI systems in all of these areas, once such systems have appropriate risk mitigation measures in place.[34]

Secondly, regulating the uses of artificial intelligence according to the tools and the logic of risk regulation implies that problems arising from their use are considered to be such that they can be solved through technical solutions. Risks are identified, their

[28] Coglianese (2020, 1).

[29] Spindler (1998, p. 316).

[30] https://digital-strategy.ec.europa.eu/en/policies/regulatory-framework-ai

[31] Kaminski (2023b, p. 1351), Kaminski (2023a, p. 70), Boyd (2012, p. 897) ("As understood here, risk thinking is intended as shorthand for the various concepts, tools, and practices that underwrite the formal understanding and assessment of risk").

[32] Risk is commonly defined as the combination of the probability of the occurrence of an injury and the severity of that injury. Cf. ISO/IEC, Guide 51:2014, Safety aspects – Guidelines for their inclusion in standards. §3.9 defines risk as the combination of the probability of the occurrence of an injury and the severity of that injury. Available at: https://www.iso.org/standard/53940.html.

[33] Regulation (EU) 2024/1689, Annex III.

[34] Pardolesi and Davola (2020, p. 104), Busch and De Franceschi (2018, p. 408), Casey and Niblett (2017, p. 1401).

probability of occurrence is estimated, a tolerable level of risk is established ("acceptable", according to the Regulation),[35] and appropriate measures to achieve this goal are implemented. The view is "to improve" a specific technology through quantitative solutions rather than critically assessing the suitability of its use in a particular context or field, following a trend described critically as "techno-correctionist".[36] Such an approach, it is noted, fails to consider how artificial intelligence changes the features of the field of activity in which it is employed and, especially, the distribution of costs and benefits.[37]

Also, in assessing the specific case and identifying appropriate technical solutions, the technical bodies issuing harmonised standards make mathematical and statistical evaluations, adopting an ex-ante prognostic logic, which often encapsulates normative assessments: for example, they may assessthe acceptability of the probability of harm to individual rights or groups, or on the appropriate level of risk with which members of a society may be confronted when faced with using a specific AI system. In other words, by employing risk regulation tools, crucial normative judgements are translated into mere technical measures made up of quantitative standards.[38]

In such cases, risk regulation raises the greatest perplexity. The standardised procedural remedy-based technical and quantitative approach, typical of risk regulation, ends up transforming even non-economic values and interests, from human life to respect for fundamental rights, into monetary standards, making vital choices for society through the use of metrics, technical and documentary obligations and statistical surveys, or rather, through the typical tools of risk regulation.[39]

Such an approach leaves several interpretive questions open. How can we determine when residual risk is acceptable when fundamental rights are at stake? How do

---

[35] On the difficulties of defining acceptable residual risk, see Fraser and Bello Y Villarino (2022, p. 23).

[36] Eaglin (2021, p. 151) ("The challenge, then, is not simply to regulate the tools through law, but to see how law creates the dilemmas that the tools present"). A number of questions arise from this observation: "How has law socially constructed the discourse around technology? How does law facilitate the material conditions that produce the demand for certain technologies? How do technologies reproduce or alter our understanding of race in society, and what is the role of law in perpetuating that meaning?" Hellman (2020, p. 814), Starr (2014, p. 806).

[37] Gabriel (2022, p. 218) ("AI is not simply an additional ingredient that supervenes onto a stable practice leaving the fundamental elements of that practice untouched. Rather, AI interacts with the behavior of human decision-makers to shape the character of these practices, including how they distribute benefits and burdens across the population").

[38] Fraser and Bello Y Villarino (2022, p. 12) ("Impact assessment tools, and risk assessment and management standards will help in identifying, quantifying, comparing, prioritising and planning the management of residual risks. But they cannot tell a duty-holder whether in all the circumstances, a risk posed by a specific system deployed in a specific context for a specific purpose is acceptable").

[39] Coglianese (2020, p. 8) ("Put simply, the issue has often been characterized by the question: How safe is safe? Answering this question requires making a normative decision about how much risk members of the public should confront in their lives"), Wagner (1995, p. 1613). With specific reference to AI Regulation see: Schuett (2023, p. 1), Kaminski (2023a), Kim (2017, p. 202), Hellman (2020, p. 834), Ajunwa (2020, p. 1679), Ackerman and Heinzerling (2004), Kelman (1981, p. 33). With specific regard to data, see Barocas and Selbst (2016, p. 671), Kim (2017, p. 202).

we decide, for example, when a risk of discrimination is acceptable if the expenditure of one hundred allows for a fifty per cent reduction in risk, while achieving a seventy per cent reduction requires spending three hundred (assuming that such an assessment is possible)? In such a case, is it acceptable to limit risk reduction to only fifty percent, given the costs to be incurred?[40] The extensive use of open standards throughout the entire Regulation amplifies the issue, deferring subtle balancing acts to technical bodies that translate them into technical prescriptions.[41] In conclusion, the actuarial and technocratic logic of risk regulation systems encapsulates fundamental policy choices that must be rendered explicit.

Risk regulation is an appropriate regulatory technique for managing easily identifiable and quantifiable risks. However, resorting to standardised technical measures aimed at rationalising and quantifying risks through statistical, actuarial, and insurance tools according to mathematical calculations may not be entirely appropriate for fundamental rights and values that do not lend themselves easily to quantification. In other words, risk regulation is more suitable for estimating quantifiable risks and much less so for those more challenging to domesticate in terms of numbers.

Despite using the language of scientific certainty and hard science, this type of cost–benefit analysis involves making complex normative judgments, such as the ones typically arising from the violation of rights, where it is far more problematic to use technical tools for evaluating and measuring activities.[42]

The danger is to overlook the risks of violating fundamental rights or key societal values, making these risks less visible. Correspondingly, by framing delicate policy issues as neutral technical choices, the Regulation leaves the definition of broad and indefinite notions – such as fairness, diversity or non-discrimination, among others – to technical standards set by private entities.[43]

Moreover, the characteristic standardisation of risk regulation, and the resulting formulation of complex normative judgments on how to assess benefits and risks, is even more problematic in an area, such as that of the use of artificial intelligence, where the development of shared ethical standards is far from being reached,[44] and the risks are not yet entirely known due to the absence of an established case history.[45] These difficulties are further exacerbated by empirical uncertainties that often affect

[40] In recalling the proportionality between risks and measures to be taken, under the Regulation, one of the central elements of said proportionality judgment is the costs incurred. See, e.g., Regulation (EU) 2024/1689, Recital 146

[41] Ebers et al. (2021, p. 592), Solow-Niederman (2023, p. 2), Laux et al. (2024).

[42] Kaminski (2023b, p. 1378) ("This, then, is one of the core challenges for AI risk regulation: it deploys a largely ex ante regulatory tool best suited for readily quantifiable harms to address big, often-unquantifiable, often-contested, often-contextual, and often-individualized 'risks'").

[43] Veale and Zuiderveen Borgesius (2021).

[44] Schuett (2023, p. 13).

[45] Fraser and Bello Y Villarino (2022, p. 12) ("Developing standards is complicated in the context of AI. Standardisation works well in contexts where risks are known and there is good evidence from past events, less well when data from previous experience is missing, and potentially terribly when a system has not been tested in real life or can change its expected behaviour through a process of learning."). See also Kleindorfer and Kunreuther (1999, p. 149–155), Turner (2019, p. 75).

risk regulation, as testified by the considerable diversity in results obtained from using this regulatory technique in different fields.[46]

6 Risk Distribution

Having considered the many reasons why the seemingly neutrality of risk management through standardised technical norms is contradicted by the need for normative judgments embedded in technical choices, as well as by frequent empirical difficulties, we can now focus on the distributional effects of this normative technique when fundamental rights and values are at stake.

The importance of in-depth reflection on the distribution of risks and benefits associated with artificial intelligence and the problematic issues involved in using risk regulation stem from the fact that the potential risks and benefits resulting from the use of a particular AI system rarely fall on the same individuals or groups.

As made explicit in the recitals of the Regulation, society takes certain risks in the name of the benefits that a specific choice may bring. This assessment is performed in aggregate, looking at the overall balance between costs and benefits, leaving considerations of whether these are distributed to different degrees over distinct segments of the population in the background.

In the aggregate, adopting technologies that carry high risks for individuals or groups is perfectly rational if more significant societal benefits offset these risks. Indeed, the standardisation of ex-ante risk regulation systems does not consider the individualised and contextual nature of some types of risks and the biases that AI systems may bring.[47] The use of artificial intelligence, for example, to manage state welfare, select job applicants or grant a mortgage, can have overall positive effects for the state, the employer or the bank that adopts such systems, with undeniable benefits, for example, in terms of efficiency. At the same time, adopting these AI systems may produce detrimental effects and risks of discrimination for specific individuals or groups who are particularly disadvantaged by such systems.[48]

In addition, treating potential harms as risks to be managed not only means adopting an aggregate view that looks at the overall impact of a given risk on society, to the detriment of specific individuals or groups. In most cases, the most vulnerable individuals or groups are those most exposed to the detrimental consequences of choices based on the overall impact of these systems.[49] This may occur mainly due to the fact that the standards and thresholds used to make this risk assessment often

---

[46] Coglianese (2020, p. 12) ("Currently, the estimated net benefits of risk regulation vary markedly across, and within, policy areas. Some regulations have been estimated to cost only in the tens of thousands of dollars per life saved; others have been estimated to cost billions of dollars for each life saved"). See also Breyer (1993).

[47] Chamberlain (2023, p. 7).

[48] Eubanks (2018), Umoja Noble (2018), Benjamin (2019).

[49] Barocas and Selbst (2016, p. 684).

refer to an average standard, such as the archetypical "reasonable person", to the detriment of a more nuanced and subtle view of society, which takes into account the differences and diversities between individuals and between groups.[50]

7 Risk Regulation and Ex-Post Liability

The flaws of a strategy solely based on risk mitigation are further exacerbated by the fact that the Regulation does not expressly provide for ex-post compensatory remedies (thus, marking a departure from choices made in the past, as in the case of the GDPR). The risk is to leave those who suffer the harm without remedies or with insufficient remedies, undermining the possibility of obtaining protection once the harm has occurred.

With specific regard to the Regulation, the crucial question is the compensation of so-called "residual risk", i.e., the risk that remains even after appropriate mitigation measures have been taken; namely, whether it is possible to get compensation in the case of AI systems that have an "acceptable" level of risk, based on the ex-ante assessment made in compliance with the Regulation.

In this regard, a preliminary aspect of the relationship between ex-ante risk regulation and ex-post liability must be clarified. In principle, the Regulation merely dictates the conditions under which AI systems can be placed on the market. At the same time, the consequences arising from using AI systems, once placed on the market, are still subject to the ordinary rules governing the area they operate in. For example, the actions of an employer who uses an AI system to fire, promote or hire a person are, per se, susceptible to judicial review in the same way that decisions made by the same employer without using AI systems would be.

In principle, we can limit our analysis to recognising the formal autonomy of the two systems – ex-ante risk regulation and ex-post tortious liability - and conclude for the autonomy of the regulation of the conditions for placing AI systems on the market and the liability regimes for damages resulting from the use of these systems. However, such a conclusion neglects to evaluate the overall effects of ex-ante regulation on the enforceability of ex-post remedies to protect individual rights. While not excluding liability for damages arising from AI systems, the peril is that compliance with legally prescribed risk mitigation measures may, in many cases, result in a considerable obstacle to the affirmation of individual, ex-post liability.

Such a danger is indisputably more severe in the case of fault-based liability. The many similarities between risk assessment criteria and the factors commonly considered for assessing fault in tortious liability reveal this potential overlap. The similarity of the elements involved in risk management and liability regimes heightens the possibility that compliance with technical standards may be considered sufficient

[50] Boyd (2012, pp. 912 and 927).

to exclude fault, with an exchange of doctrines and evaluations that the role of expert witnesses in litigation may foster.[51]

In principle, more room should still be allowed for compensatory damages under a strict liability regime. However, even in this case, it is easy to imagine numerous obstacles to compensation for damages arising from AI systems that comply with the Regulation.[52] What makes individual liability marginal, even in the case of strict liability, is not only the limited scope of the strict liability regime in most Member States. Also, many doctrines applicable to strict liability may end up significantly limiting compensatory claims related to AI systems, even when a strict liability regime applies: as an example, for risks that cannot be reasonably mitigated or eliminated through the development or design of the AI system or by providing adequate technical information (so-called, unavoidably unsafe products doctrine)[53]; or for those unknown risk and harms, in light of the state of scientific and technical knowledge.[54]

In the past, the European Parliament suggested extending the area of strict liability to damages caused by high-risk AI systems and applying a special fault-based liability regime to other AI systems, also providing for a presumption of fault.[55] In this way,

---

[51] Cafaggi (2006, p. 199) ("To the extent that regulation has increasingly provided new standards for examining the conduct of potential injurers, the corresponding modifications in civil liability have proved significant for the definition of standards in negligence and strict liability"); Kysar (2018, p. 51).

[52] Chamberlain (2023, p. 8) draws a parallel between the regulation of high-risk AI systems and the imposition of strict liability regimes.

[53] Cf. art. 9, para. 3 (The risks referred to in this Article shall concern only those which may be reasonably mitigated or eliminated through the development or design of the high-risk AI system, or the provision of adequate technical information."). In literature, see, e.g., Page (1996, p. 87).

[54] See Recital 64 AI Act ("The measures adopted by the providers to comply with the mandatory requirements of this Regulation should take into account the generally acknowledged state of the art on AI"); Recital 121 ("Standardisation should play a key role to provide technical solutions to providers to ensure compliance with this Regulation, in line with the state of the art"); art. 8 ("High-risk AI systems shall comply with the requirements laid down in this Section, taking into account their intended purpose as well as the generally acknowledged state of the art on AI and AI-related technologies."); art. 25 para. 4 ("The provider of a high-risk AI system and the third party that supplies an AI system, tools, services, components, or processes that are used or integrated in a high-risk AI system shall, by written agreement, specify the necessary information, capabilities, technical access and other assistance based on the generally acknowledged state of the art"); art. 50 para. 2 ("Providers shall ensure their technical solutions are effective, interoperable, robust and reliable as far as this is technically feasible, taking into account the specificities and limitations of various types of content, the costs of implementation and the generally acknowledged state of the art, as may be reflected in relevant technical standards."); art. 51 para. 3 ("The Commission shall adopt delegated acts in accordance with Article 97 to amend the thresholds listed in paragraphs 1 and 2 of this Article, as well as to supplement benchmarks and indicators in light of evolving technological developments); art. 96 para. 1 ("The guidelines referred to in the first subparagraph of this paragraph shall take due account of the generally acknowledged state of the art on AI").

[55] European Parliament Resolution (2020) On a liability regime for artificial intelligence (2020/2014(INL)), OJ C 404/05 (2021). In 2022, the EU Commission had also submitted a Proposal for a Directive on adapting non-contractual civil liability rules to artificial intelligence (AI Liability Directive), COM(2022) 496 final, which was not followed up.

high-risk AI systems would have been equated to dangerous activities, such as those that typically warrant the application of a strict liability regime. However, the proposal remained a dead letter, and, in any case, would have charted a course that would have been difficult to follow, given the diversity - within the European Union - of areas subject to strict liability in national legal regimes and the considerable difficulties of applying a special liability regime to a category - that of high-risk AI systems - that has blurred boundaries.

8 Concluding Remarks

So far, we have highlighted the various reasons why a system of risk regulation adopts an overall, aggregated and standardised view of the risks arising from the use of AI systems, at the expense of an assessment more focused on the individualised and contextual dimension of the consequences stemming from the use of these systems, which pays closer attention to the individuals and groups on whom these risks fall. Moreover, we have pointed out how this disregard for risk distribution and protection of individual rights mainly affects the most vulnerable.

In the conclusion, we provide some interpretive suggestions aimed at fostering an understanding of the Regulation that is more oriented toward distributional considerations and leaves more space for those needs that the Regulation recognises to a limited extent only.

To complement the aggregate and standardised assessment of risks with a consideration of the distribution of these risks, a first group of provisions concerns how the powers reserved by the Regulation for the EU Commission are to be exercised. The first is the procedure the Regulation prescribes for qualifying AI systems as high-risk under art. 7 of the Regulation, which confers the power to identify these systems upon the Commission. In exercising its power to define AI systems as high-risk, the Commission should not only consider the potential extent of harm or negative impact in terms of intensity and capacity to affect more than one person but also give special consideration to the capacity to disproportionately affect a particular group, a feature added only in the latest version of Regulation, which was then adopted.[56]

In a complementary manner, the common specifications, adopted by the Commission in all cases where harmonised standards do not sufficiently consider fundamental rights concerns,[57] should play a central role, despite the express reference to their exceptional nature in the Regulation.[58]

[56] Regulation (EU) 2024/1689, art. 7, para. 2(f) ("When assessing the condition under paragraph 1, point (b), the Commission shall take into account the following criteria: (…) 'the potential extent of such harm or such adverse impact, in particular in terms of its intensity and its ability to affect multiple persons or to disproportionately affect a particular group of persons'").

[57] Regulation (EU) 2024/1689, art. 41.

[58] Regulation (EU) 2024/1689, Recital 121 defines common specifications as an "exceptional" solution ("The common specification should be an exceptional fall back solution to facilitate the provider's obligation to comply with the requirements of this Regulation, when the standardisation

Also, in formulating requests to draft a harmonised standard to the relevant European organisations under Article 40, the Commission should emphasise those normative questions that stem from developing those technical solutions that European organisations are called upon to lay down.

Finally, when establishing a post-market monitoring plan under article 72(3), and in determining the obligations of providers related to post-market monitoring of an AI system, the Commission should consider any unfavourable effects of an AI system on specific individuals or segments of the population, and take this assessment into account when determining appropriate corrective measures, especially where the most vulnerable are affected.[59]

As is evident, the way the EU Commission will exercise the prerogatives granted by the Regulation will be a decisive factor in giving greater or lesser relevance to distributional considerations in assessing the impact of AI systems. At the same time, other norms of the Regulation are of the utmost importance for our analysis.

The fundamental rights impact assessment for high-risk AI systems also plays a vital role.[60] While not applicable across the board, but only to "deployers that are bodies governed by public law, or are private entities providing public services", as well as to specific high-risk AI systems, the individual and contextual dimensions of the impact of AI may be attained by putting a particular emphasis on some of those aspects listed in art. 27: primarily, the categories of natural persons and groups likely to be affected by its use and the specific risks of harm likely to impact the categories of natural persons or groups of persons.[61]

Lastly, the many limitations underscored in these pages are further exacerbated by the possible obstacles to ex-post liability regimes. Hence, it is crucial to avoid the Regulation from weakening liability regimes for AI systems, as this would undermine the effectiveness of risk regulation by depriving it of ex-post feedback that may complement, rather than replace, ex-ante risk determination and mitigation. This is even more pressing where risk homogeneity is low, i.e., where the differentiation in the degree of risk is high due to the different actors involved. When this is the case, i.e. whenever the risk is highly contextual and individualised, the ex-post liability system may be more efficient than an ex-ante system of risk regulation.[62] In such a context, civil liability may play a critical role, not only as a way to provide compensation but also as an incentive for an efficient level of activities, thus taking a strategic

---

request has not been accepted by any of the European standardisation organisations, or when the relevant harmonised standards insufficiently address fundamental rights concerns, or when the harmonised standards do not comply with the request, or when there are delays in the adoption of an appropriate harmonised standard.").

59 Gabriel (2022, p. 225) applies a Rawlsian approach to technology ("When AI is integrated into a key social practice, in a way that affects the overall distribution of benefits and burdens, it is pertinent to ask whether it does the most it possibly can do to improve the position of the least advantaged member of that system.").

60 Regulation (EU) 2024/1689, art. 27.

61 Regulation (EU) 2024/1689, art. 27, para. 1(c–d).

62 Chamberlain (2023, p. 7), Cafaggi (2006, p. 191 ff.), Kysar (2018, p. 52). On the relationship between tort liability and distributive justice, see Gardner (2019).

regulatory function that is imperative in the legal challenge of governing artificial intelligence by protecting the fundamental rights and values of the European Union.

References

Abelkop ADK (2014) Tort Law as an Environmental Policy Instrument. Or. L. Rev. 92(2): 381–469

Abraham KS (2002) The relation between civil liability and environmental regulation: An analytical overview. Washburn Law J. 41: 379–398

Ackerman F, Heinzerling L (2004) Priceless: on knowing the price of everything and the value of nothing. The New Press

Ajunwa I (2020) The paradox of automation as anti-bias intervention. Cardozo Law Rev 41:1671

Atiyah P (1997) The damages lottery. Hart Publishing

Barocas S, Selbst AD (2016) Big data's disparate impact. Calif Law Rev 104:671

Benjamin R (2019) Race after technology: Abolitionist tools for the new Jim Code. Polity, Cambridge

Ben-Shahar O (2019) Data pollution. J. Legal Analysis 11: 104–159

Boyd W (2012) Genealogies of risk: Searching for safety, 1930s-1970s. Ecology L.Q. 39: 895–987

Breyer SG (1993) Breaking the vicious circle: Toward effective risk regulation. Harvard University Press

Busch C, De Franceschi A (2018) Granular legal norms: Big data and the personalization of private law. In: V. Mak, E. Tjong Tjin Taj, A. Berlee (eds) Research handbook on data science and law. Edward Elgar Publishing Limited, pp 408–424

Cafaggi F (2006) The legitimacy of private regulators vis-à-vis third parties: Rights, duties, and liability. EUI Working Paper LAW 2006/32, p 191

Calabresi G (1970) The costs of accidents: A legal and economic analysis. Yale University Press

Cane P (1997) The anatomy of tort law. Hart Publishing

Cane P (2018) Atiyah's accidents, compensation and the law, 9th edn. Cambridge University Press

Carter JA, Palermos SO (2016) Is having your computer compromised a personal assault? The ethics of extended cognition. J. Am. Philos. Assoc. 2(4): 542–560

Casey AJ, Niblett A (2017) The death of rules and standards. Indiana Law Journal 92(4):1401–1447

Chamberlain J (2023) The risk-based approach of the European Union's proposed artificial intelligence regulation: Some comments from a tort law perspective. Eur J Risk Reg 14(1):1–13

Coglianese C (2020) The law and economics of risk regulation, in Penn Carey Law: Legal Scholarship Repository. All Faculty Scholarship. 2157. https://ssrn.com/abstract=3552703

Comandè G (1999) Risarcimento del danno alla persona e alternative istituzionali. Giappichelli

De Gregorio G, Dunn P (2022) The European risk-based approaches: Connecting constitutional dots in the digital age. Common Market Law Review 59(2): 473–500

Eaglin JM (2021) When critical race theory enters the law & technology frame. Mich. J. Race & L. 26: 151–168

Ebers M, Hoch VRS, Rosenkranz F, Ruschemeier H, Steinrötter B (2021) The European commission's proposal for an artificial intelligence act - A critical assessment by members of the Robotics and AI Law Society (RAILS). J. 4: 589–603

Edwards L, Veale M (2017) Slave to the algorithm? Why a 'right to an explanation' is probably not the remedy you are looking for. Duke Law Technol Rev 16:18

Eubanks V (2018) Automating inequality: How high-tech tools profile, police, and punish the poor. St Martin's Press, New York

European Commission (2021) Regulatory framework on AI. Available at: https://digital-strategy.ec.europa.eu/en/policies/regulatory-framework-ai

Fraser H, Bello Y Villarino JM (2022) Where residual risks reside: a comparative approach to art 9(4) of the European Union's proposed AI Regulation. https://ssrn.com/abstract=3960461

Froomkin AM (2015) Regulating mass surveillance as privacy pollution: Learning from environmental impact statements. U. Ill. L. Rev. 2015(5): 1713–1790
Gabriel I (2022) Toward a theory of justice for artificial intelligence. Daedalus 151(2): 218–231
Gardner J (2019) Torts and other wrongs. Oxford University Press
Guihot M, Matthew AF, Suzor NP (2017) Nudging robots: innovative solutions to regulate artificial intelligence. Vand. J. Ent. & Tech. L. 20(2): 385–456
Harlow C (2004) State liability, tort and beyond. Oxford University Press
Hellman D (2020) Measuring algorithmic fairness. Va. L. Rev. 106(4): 811–866
Hirsch DD (2006) Protecting the inner environment: What privacy regulation can learn from environmental law. Ga Law Rev 41:1
Hylton KN (2002) When should we prefer tort law to environmental regulation? Washburn Law J. 41: 515–534
Kaminski ME (2019) Binary governance: Lessons from the GDPR's approach to algorithmic accountability. S. Cal. L. Rev. 92: 1529–1616
Kaminski ME (2023a) The developing law of AI: A turn to risk regulation. The Digital Social Contract: A Lawfare Paper Series. U of Colorado Law Legal Studies Research Paper No. 24-5, pp 1–26
Kaminski ME (2023b) Regulating the risks of AI. B.U. L. Rev. 103: 1347–1411
Kelman S (1981) Cost-benefit analysis: an ethical critique. Reg Policy 5:33
Kim PT (2017) Auditing algorithms for discrimination. U. Pa. L. Rev. Online 166: 189–203
Kleindorfer PR, Kunreuther HC (1999) Challenges facing the insurance industry in managing catastrophic risks. In: K.A Froot (ed.) The financing of catastrophe risk. University of Chicago Press, pp 149–194
Kysar DA (2006) It might have been: Risk, precaution and opportunity cost. J. Land Use & Env't L. 22: 1–58
Kysar DA (2018) The public life of private law: Tort law as a risk regulation mechanism. Eur. J. Risk Reg. 9: 48–65
Laux J, Wachter S, Mittelstadt B (2024) Three pathways for standardisation and ethical disclosure by default under the European Union Artificial Intelligence Act. Comput Law Secur Rev 53:105957
Malgieri G, Pasquale F (2022) From transparency to justification: Toward ex ante accountability for AI. Brooklyn L. School. Legal Studies Paper No. 712: 1–27 https://ssrn.com/abstract=4099657
Marchant GE, Stevens YA (2017) Resilience: A new tool in the risk governance toolbox for emerging technologies. U.C. DAVIS L. REV. 51: 233–271
McGarity TO (2005) Regulation and litigation: Complementary tools for environmental protection. Colum. J. Envtl. L. 30: 371
Page JA (1996) Liability for unreasonably and unavoidably unsafe products: Does negligence doctrine have a role to play. Chi.-Kent L. Rev. 72: 87–128
Pardolesi R, Davola A (2020) Algorithmic legal decision making: la fine del mondo (del diritto) o il paese delle meraviglie? Questione Giustizia 1: 104–111
Pasquale F (2015) The Black Box Society: the secret algorithms that control money and information. Harvard University Press
Posner R A (2004) Catastrophe: Risk and response. Oxford University Press, Oxford
Ruschemeier H (2023) AI as a challenge for legal regulation. The scope of application of the Artificial Intelligence Act proposal. ERA Forum 23: 361–376
Scherer MU (2016) Regulating artificial intelligence systems: Risks, challenges, competencies, and strategies. Harv J Law Technol 29:353
Schroeder CH (2002) Lost in the translation: What environmental regulation does that tort cannot duplicate. Washburn Law J. 41: 583–606
Schuck P (1991) Tort law and the public interest: Competition, innovation, and consumer welfare. Norton
Schuett J (2023) Risk management in the Artificial Intelligence Act. Eur. J. Risk Reg. 1–19

Shavell S (1984a) A model of the optimal use of liability and safety regulation. RAND J Econ 15:271–280
Shavell S (1984b) Liability for harm versus regulation of safety. J Legal Stud 13:357–374
Shavell S (1987) Economic analysis of accident law. Harvard University Press
Solow-Niederman A (2020) Administering Artificial Intelligence. S. Cal. L. Rev. 93: 633–695
Solow-Niederman A (2023) Can AI standards have politics? UCLA L. Rev. Disc. 71: 2–17
Spindler G (1998) Market Processes, Standardization, and Tort Law. European Law Journal 4: 316–336
Stapleton J (1986) Disease and the compensation debate. Oxford University Press
Stapleton J (1995) Tort, insurance and ideology. Modern Law Review 60: 820–845
Starr SB (2014) Evidence-based sentencing and the scientific rationalization of discrimination. Stanford Law Rev 66:803–872
Sugarman D (1989) Doing away with personal injury law. Bloomsbury Academic
Sunstein C R (2000) Behaviorallawandeconomics.CambridgeUniversityPress
Sunstein C R (2005) Laws of fear: Beyond the precautionary principle. Cambridge University Press
Tamboli A (2019) Keeping Your AI Under Control: A Pragmatic Guide to Identifying, Evaluating, and Quantifying Risks. Apress Berkeley, New York
Turner J (2019) Robot rules: Regulating artificial intelligence. Palgrave Macmillan
Umoja Noble S (2018) Algorithms of oppression: How search engines reinforce racism. NYU Press, New York
Veale M, Zuiderveen Borgesius F (2021) Demystifying the draft EU Artificial Intelligence Act – analysing the good, the bad, and the unclear elements of the proposed approach. Comput Law Rev Int 4:97–112
Wagner WE (1995) The science charade in toxic risk regulation. Columbia Law Rev 95:1613–1723
Wiener J B (2003) Whose Precaution After All? A Comment on the Comparison and Evolution of Risk Regulatory System. Duke J. Compar. & Int'l L. 13: 207–262
Wolfendale J (2007) My avatar, my self: Virtual harm and attachment. Ethics Inf Technol 9:111–119
Young G (2023) What would strong AI understand consent to mean, and what are the implications for sexbot rape? AI and Ethics 5:579–590

Guido Smorto, Full Professor of Comparative Law at the University of Palermo and EU Jean Monnet Chair in "Comparative and European Digital Law." Expert advisor for the EU Commission and Parliament on digital law. Co-author of Comparative Law. A Very Short Introduction (OUP, 2023) and Diritto privato dei mercati digitali (Mondadori, 2024, 2nd ed.).

Open Access This chapter is licensed under the terms of the Creative Commons Attribution 4.0 International License (http://creativecommons.org/licenses/by/4.0/), which permits use, sharing, adaptation, distribution and reproduction in any medium or format, as long as you give appropriate credit to the original author(s) and the source, provide a link to the Creative Commons license and indicate if changes were made.

The images or other third party material in this chapter are included in the chapter's Creative Commons license, unless indicated otherwise in a credit line to the material. If material is not included in the chapter's Creative Commons license and your intended use is not permitted by statutory regulation or exceeds the permitted use, you will need to obtain permission directly from the copyright holder.

EU Institutions and Competent Authorities Dealing with the Revolution of Artificial Intelligence for Health

Fidelia Cascini

Abstract The rapid evolution of Artificial Intelligence is transforming healthcare, presenting both significant opportunities and considerable challenges. The European Union has adopted a risk-based regulatory approach with the AI Act (Regulation (EU) 2024/1689) to balance innovation with fundamental rights protection. This law classifies AI systems into four risk levels where high-risk systems, such as those used in medical diagnostics and robotic surgery, are subject to stringent compliance and ex-ante assessments. Despite AI promises improvements in several areas of Medicine (e. g. drug discovery, medical imaging, early diagnosis, disease prevention) potentially enhancing efficiency and reducing medical errors, current critical concerns include automation bias, the lack of long-term prediction accuracy, potential inequalities in technology access, and algorithmic opacity. For these reasons, AI systems can also exacerbate existing forms of human vulnerability and introduce new ones through the interaction between inferences, predictions, and AI-generated content. Competent authorities play a crucial role in ensuring that AI systems for health are governed and implemented effectively, and are prepared with adequate resources to meet market demand for testing and evaluation. Controlled environments (i.e. regulatory sandboxes) facilitate the testing and verification of AI systems through collaboration among developers, healthcare providers, regulators, and patients. These ensure that new technologies are safe, effective, and ethical before widespread clinical adoption, mitigating risks and protecting human vulnerability. The role of Competent Authorities is crucial to guarantee the protection of fundamental rights, health, and safety.

Keywords Artificial intelligence · Regulatory sandboxes · Competent authorities · Healthcare · AI Act

---

F. Cascini (✉)
University S. Raffaele, Rome, Italy
e-mail: fidelia.cascini@uniroma5.it

© The Author(s) 2025

C. Amodio and A. Diurni (eds.), *Human Vulnerability in Interaction with AI in European Private Law*, https://doi.org/10.1007/978-3-031-93247-2_13

1 The EU Approach Towards Artificial Intelligence for Health

Human vulnerability, while not a consolidated legal concept, is embraced in recent EU regulations and political interventions mainly to protect vulnerable groups or minorities. This means a group-based understanding of vulnerability, i.e. by prohibiting AI systems that aim to exploit individual vulnerabilities due to their age, disability, social or economic conditions. From a broader perspective, AI systems bring the concrete risk to negatively impact on natural person's rights such as those related to privacy protection, freedom of expression and information, health. Consequently, AI systems can exacerbate existing forms of human vulnerability and introduce new ones through the interaction between inferences, predictions, and AI-generated content. This scenario brings additional challenges in the healthcare sector, where the management of potential harm related to AI is characterized by unconsolidated attempts of governance, despite the EU's effort to be the first in the world regulating AI using a risk-based approach and considering vulnerabilities.

On 1 August 2024, Regulation (EU) 2024/1689 (AI Act)[1] came into force, establishing harmonized rules on the use of artificial intelligence systems in the EU territory to protect European citizens from potential negative consequences. The legislator considered it relevant to explore artificial intelligence-based innovations introduced globally, preparing to address their potential risks. Promoting the development of artificial intelligence by strengthening investments and, at the same time, protecting the fundamental rights of individuals and businesses by developing new rules was the strategic approach followed by the European Commission. Regulatory action appeared essential in high-impact sectors, including the environment, the public sector, finance, mobility, home affairs, agriculture and, in our case, healthcare. Through the AI Act, the European Commission proposed a regulatory framework aimed at ensuring that the artificial intelligence systems used are safe, transparent, ethical, impartial and under human control. The scope of the admissibility of artificial intelligence practices has been defined based on four levels of risk: unacceptable, high, limited, and minimal.

Unacceptable risk is that linked to the practice of artificial intelligence for purposes and/or in ways that are contrary to the values of the European Union, for example, because they violate the fundamental rights of natural persons. The prohibitions therefore concern practices that have high potential in terms of manipulating people through subliminal techniques without their awareness or exploiting the vulnerabilities of specific vulnerable groups, such as minors or people with disabilities, to materially distort their behavior to cause psychological or physical harm. The attribution of a social score based on artificial intelligence for general purposes by public

[1] Regulation (EU) 2024/1689 of the European Parliament and of the Council of 13 June 2024 laying down harmonized rules on artificial intelligence and amending Regulations (EC) No 300/2008, (EU) No 167/2013, (EU) No 168/2013, (EU) 2018/858, (EU) 2018/1139 and (EU) 2019/2144 and Directives 2014/90/EU, (EU) 2016/797 and (EU) 2020/1828 (Artificial Intelligence Act) (Text with EEA relevance). https://eur-lex.europa.eu/eli/reg/2024/1689/oj/eng.

authorities is also prohibited, as is the use of 'real-time' remote biometric identification systems in spaces accessible to the public for law enforcement purposes, without prejudice to the application of certain limited exceptions.

High-risk artificial intelligence systems are permitted in the European market and are subject to compliance with certain mandatory requirements and an ex-ante conformity assessment. The classification of a system as high risk is based on its intended purpose in line with the current EU legislation on product safety, which, with respect to medical devices, refers, for example, to the Medical Device Regulation (EU Regulation 2017/745)[2] and Regulation (EU) 2017/746[3]on in vitro diagnostic medical devices. The classification of a product as high risk depends not only on the function performed by the system but also on the specific purposes and ways in which the system is used. In the medical field, for example, artificial intelligence-based medical diagnostic devices and applications in robotic surgery are included, since they represent safety components of products (or even products themselves), which must be carefully assessed by a third-party body that expresses its opinion on the conformity of the product component within the scope of application of a given Union harmonization regulation, both before it is placed on the market and throughout its life cycle.

The extent of the negative impact of artificial intelligence systems on the rights protected by the Charter of Fundamental Rights of the European Union is relevant for classifying a system as high risk. These rights include the right to human dignity, respect for private and family life, and the protection of personal data (Official Journal 2000/C 364/01)[4] In line with the objectives of EU legislation to facilitate the free movement of products in the internal market by ensuring that only safe and compliant products can be placed on the market, it is important that risks that a product may generate because of its digital components (including artificial intelligence) are duly prevented and mitigated. For example, increasingly autonomous robots, both in the context of caring for and assisting people, should be able to operate and perform their functions safely in complex environments. Similarly, increasingly sophisticated artificial intelligence-based systems for diagnostics and for supporting human decisions in healthcare should be reliable and accurate.

Regarding digital components, including artificial intelligent systems and their relationships with medical devices, the Court of Justice of the EU pronounced an interesting decision in 2017[5] as the first instance ruling on standalone software

---

[2] Regulation (EU) 2017/745 of the European Parliament and of the Council of 5 April 2017 on medical devices, amending Directive 2001/83/EC, Regulation (EC) No 178/2002 and Regulation (EC) No 1223/2009 and repealing Council Directives 90/385/EEC and 93/42/EEC. https://eur-lex.europa.eu/eli/reg/2017/745/oj/eng.

[3] Regulation (EU) 2017/746 of the European Parliament and of the Council of 5 April 2017 on in vitro diagnostic medical devices and repealing Directive 98/79/EC and Commission Decision 2010/227/EU. https://eur-lex.europa.eu/eli/reg/2017/746/oj/eng.

[4] Charter of Fundamental Rights of the European Union (2000/C 364/01). https://www.europarl.europa.eu/charter/pdf/text_en.pdf.

[5] Case C-329/16, Syndicat national de l'industrie des technologies médicales (Snitem) and Philips France v Premier ministre and Ministre des Affaires sociales et de la Santé, Judgment of the

within the medical device context. The French Conseil d'État asked whether prescription support software enabling healthcare practitioners to obtain patients' relevant information (e.g., drug interactions, dosage limits) may constitute a medical device according to Article 1(2)(a) of the Medical Device Directive.[6] The Court, agreeing with Advocate-General's Opinion, held that this software can be a medical device notwithstanding the fact that the software does not itself act in or on the human body. A key factor considered by the Court in reaching its decision was that the software in question (IntelliSpace Critical Care Anaesthesia) facilitated the calculation of medication dosage and the proper design of the treatment by providing relevant information to healthcare professionals, therefore suggesting a "medical purpose", i.e., assisting in the prevention, monitoring, treatment or alleviation of the disease. Indeed, the intended purpose of software, alongside the action it performs on data, is central in determining whether the software might be qualified as a medical device.

The AI Act is supported by the work being done on the Data Governance Act, the Open Data Directive and the initiatives under the European strategy of data. In the European strategy of data[7] focused on the relevant deployment of data infrastructures, tools and computing for the European Health Data Space, which will determine the availability of high-quality data essential for training and further developing artificial intelligence systems. This specific space facilitates non-discriminatory access to health data and the training of artificial intelligence algorithms on those datasets in a privacy-preserving, secure, timely, transparent and trustworthy manner supported by institutional governance. In fact, through this regulatory framework, the European Commission is seeking to ensure common normative standards for all high-risk artificial intelligence systems. The health sector's involvement in high-stakes situations, which require the use of sophisticated diagnostic systems and systems supporting human decisions, needs to be reliable and accurate. Building on this aspect is the important element of "human oversight" outlined in Article 14 of the Act, where human oversight will play an important role in preventing or minimizing the risks to health that may emerge because of the implementation of a high-risk system.

For the development of high-risk artificial intelligence systems such as those for health purposes, the EU considers it appropriate to grant entities responsible for digital innovation (such as suppliers, notified bodies and other relevant entities), as well as testing and experimentation facilities and researchers involved in such trials, to access and use high-quality datasets. Common European data spaces available in the EU and facilitating data sharing between companies and with governments and institutions in the public interest are therefore essential to provide reliable, responsible and non-discriminatory access to high-quality data for the training, validation and testing of artificial intelligent systems. The European Health Data Space, for example, will facilitate access to health data and the training of algorithms on

---

Court (Fourth Chamber) of 7 December 2017. https://eur-lex.europa.eu/legal-content/EN/TXT/?uri=celex:62016CJ0329.

[6] Council Directive 93/42/EEC of 14 June 1993 concerning medical devices. https://eur-lex.europa.eu/eli/dir/1993/42/oj/eng.

[7] European Commission (2020a).

such datasets in a secure, timely, transparent, trustworthy, and privacy-preserving manner, as well as with adequate institutional governance. In fact, personal data legally collected for other purposes may be processed for the purposes of developing innovative artificial intelligence systems and carrying out trial tests of these algorithms in the experimental phase.

Such systems should be developed to safeguard the public interest, such as for public health purposes, including disease prevention and control. As part of the EU Digital Strategy,[8] the creation of testing and experimentation facilities (TEFs)[9] for the verification and experimentation of artificial intelligence-based technologies and systems started in the EU, providing a common EU platform for the design and manufacturing of artificial intelligence components and systems and reference sites for applications in sectors such as healthcare. TEFs are test beds that have emerged as a remarkably interesting option for testing artificial intelligence in real conditions, implying strong collaboration between startups or companies creating the systems and healthcare facilities.

According to EU legislation, once the artificial intelligence system is on the market, authorities are responsible for market surveillance, and users ensure surveillance and monitoring related to the human use of tools, while providers have a postmarket monitoring system. Providers and users also report serious incidents and malfunctions. Low-risk systems such as chatbots are subject to minimum transparency requirements designed to allow people to make informed decisions (e.g., the user of the chatbot can decide to continue or stop using the application). The vast majority of artificial intelligence systems fall into the low-risk category, except those for health applications, which are not covered by the new rules because they pose only minimal or no risk to the rights or safety of citizens. Artificial intelligence technologies are designed by companies or through public–private partnerships. To strengthen

[8] The EU Digital Strategy (https://commission.europa.eu/strategy-and-policy/priorities-2019-2024/europe-fit-digital-age_en) is part of the European Commission political priorities form several years. TheEU's Digital Single Market strategy, launched in 2015, paved the way for closer digital harmonization between the EU Member States with the aim to contribute to economic growth, boosting jobs, competition, investment and innovation in the EU. In March 2021 the Commission proposed a path to the Digital Decade. This policy programme is guided by the 2030 Digital Compass—a plan to achieve digital transformation of the EU economy and society. The Digital Compass (https://eufordigital.eu/discover-eu/eu-digital-strategy/) aims towards a secure human-centred digital ecosystem, where citizens are empowered, and businesses prosper from the digital potential. The Compass indicates four cardinal points for this trajectory: digital skills, secure and performant digital infrastructure, digital transformation of businesses and the digitalization of public services. This EU political agenda aligns with EU norms and standards to strengthen the EU's digital sovereignty. A number of budgetary instruments will support the investments necessary to build Europe's Digital Decade on solid foundations.

[9] TEFs are a combination of physical and virtual facilities, in which technology providers can get primarily technical support to test their latest AI-based software and hardware technologies (including AI-powered robotics) in real-world environments. Thus, they are specialized large-scale reference sites open to all technology providers across Europe to test and experiment at scale state-of-the art AI solutions, including both soft-and hardware products and services, e.g. robots, in real-world environments. More information are available at: https://digital-strategy.ec.europa.eu/en/faqs/testing-and-experimentation-facilities-tefs-questions-and-answers.

EU competitiveness through these partnerships[10] and to engage various stakeholders and investors in the artificial intelligence development market in the EU, the European Commission has invested much money in recent years, with an overall 1.1 billion € spent under the Horizon 2020 research and innovation program, including healthcare. Some of the world's largest technology companies are developing new applications and services, which they either own or invest in.

2 Artificial Intelligence for Healthcare Purposes[11]

Artificial intelligence-based algorithms are transforming medicine, medical research, and public health. The United Nations Secretary-General has stated that safe deployment of new technologies, including artificial intelligence, can help the world achieve health-related objectives under Sustainable Development Goal #3. Artificial intelligence could also be the key to improving global commitments to achieving universal health coverage.[12] On the other hand, a coordinated strategic and regulatory approach from the EU addressing opportunities and challenges of artificial intelligence tools (see paragraph 1) is creating an environment for growth without leaving single Member States lagging. Since 2020, the European Commission has described the characteristics of the policy framework necessary to develop trustworthy and secure artificial intelligence applications for all areas, including healthcare, in the white paper on artificial intelligence.[13] EU willingness is to become an ecosystem of excellence in research and innovation, accelerating the adoption of artificial intelligence-based solutions with the involvement of SMEs and, at the same time, an ecosystem of trust that is compliant with EU rules and regulations, including those protecting fundamental rights and consumer rights, particularly regarding high-risk artificial intelligence systems.

The use of artificial intelligence to improve healthcare systems holds a promising future, with progress already being made in various health-related fields, such as drug discovery, medical imaging, screening, diagnosis, and prevention of diseases. Artificial intelligence could help healthcare providers increase their performance and avoid medical errors. It can allow clinicians to be more focused on providing care to patients and solving complex cases while saving time while achieving better clinical outcomes. One of the main focuses is creating a support system to improve the early diagnosis of various diseases. This is particularly explored in the field of oncology, where artificial intelligence is being evaluated for use in radiological diagnoses, such as in whole-body imaging, colonoscopies, and mammograms. Artificial

---

[10] Public–Private Partnership on AI, Data and Robotics. https://stip.oecd.org/stip/policy-initiatives/2019%2Fdata%2FpolicyInitiatives%2F26437.

[11] This paragraph is an extract of Cascini et al. (2023).

[12] Dept. of Economic and Social Affairs Sustainable Development, Developmental Goal 3. https://sdgs.un.org/goals/goal3.

[13] European Commission (2020b, 2021).

intelligence can also aid in optimizing radiological treatment dosing, recognizing malignant disease in dermatology or clinical pathology, and guiding RNA and DNA sequencing for immunotherapy.[14] In general, artificial intelligence developments in early diagnosis are being studied in most health-related fields, such as in the early diagnosis of diabetic retinopathy, cardiovascular disease, liver disease and neurological disorders[15] Currently, there are only a handful of prospective clinical trials on the effectiveness of artificial intelligence in early diagnosis, with some showing promise of equivalent detection ability to that of human professionals in specific tasks, with even fewer focusing on the potential benefits of human–machine partnerships. One of the risks of relying excessively on artificial intelligence is the development of automation bias, where medical practitioners might not consider other important aspects of patient care and may overlook errors that should have been spotted by human-guided decision making.

Artificial intelligence can also be used to digitalize and store traditional paper medical records and process large amounts of data from images and other types of inputs or signals (such as motion data or sound data). Steps in image and signal processing algorithms typically include signal feature analysis and data classification via tools such as artificial neural networks, which work via complex layers of decision nodes[16] Medical imaging is one of the most rapidly developing areas of artificial intelligence application in healthcare. While improving automated image interpretation and analysis are a priority, other important aspects of AI application to medical imaging are being explored, such as data security and user privacy solutions for medical image analysis, deep learning algorithms for the restoration/reconstruction and segmentation of complex images and the creation of fuzzy sets or rough sets in medical image analysis.[17]

Furthermore, with health systems, in general, becoming increasingly complex every year, the administration and management of care are becoming increasingly laborious. Artificial intelligence can be used to assist personnel in complex logistical tasks, such as optimization of the medical supply chain, to assume mundane, repetitive tasks or to support complex decision-making[18] This is made possible by a combination of artificial intelligence advancements in the fields of natural language processing, automated scheduling and planning, and expert systems. Many artificial intelligence tools can also be used in specific public health programs or in wide public health approaches to improve wellbeing. Artificial intelligence can be used for health promotion or to identify target populations or locations with "high-risk" behaviour concerning communicable and noncommunicable diseases. Artificial intelligence can improve the effectiveness of communication and messaging specifically directed at certain subpopulations, both in terms of its ability to recognize priority groups and

[14] Bi et al. (2019).

[15] Kamdar et al. (2020).

[16] Wahl et al. (2018).

[17] Artificial Intelligence for Medical Image Analysis, Special Issue. https://www.hindawi.com/journals/bmri/si/617603/.

[18] Schwalbe and Wahl (2020).

its adaptiveness in creating tailored messages to benefit population health (micro-targeting).[19] One example of such an application is microtargeting individuals or communities with technological, linguistic, or cultural barriers to better communicate the importance and safety of vaccinations, such as the COVID-19 vaccination[20] AI tools could therefore be adapted to improve access and equity of care, furthering the development of truly personalized medicine. AI can also play a leading role in performing analyses of patterns of data for health surveillance and disease detection[21] AI tools can be used to identify bacterial contamination in water treatment plants, identify foodborne illnesses in restaurants or hospitals, simplify detection and lower costs. Sensors can also be used to improve environmental health, such as by analysing air pollution patterns or using machine learning to make inferences between the physical environment and healthy behaviour.[22]

Another application of AI in public health surveillance is evidence collection and its use to create mathematical models to make decisions. Although many public health institutions are not yet making full use of all possible sources of data, some fields, such as real-time health surveillance, are steadily improving. This has improved the public health outlook on pandemic preparedness and response, although the long-term ramification of such important changes will only be evident in the future[23] The development of public health policy also proves to be fertile ground for artificial intelligence, where attempts at analysing argumentation on food quality in a public health policy were attempted. This action resulted in the creation of models that output new recommendations on the basis of stakeholders' arguments by targeting specific audiences[24] Healthcare has always depended in part on predictions, prognoses, and the use of predictive analytics. AI is just one of the more recent tools for this purpose, and many possible benefits of prediction-based health care rely on the use of this technology. For example, AI can be used to assess an individual's risk of disease, which could be used for the prevention of diseases and major health events. Various studies suggest that artificial intelligence may improve several pathologies, such as heart failure, by utilizing predictive models and telemonitoring systems for clinical support and patient empowerment. For example, given the expected increase in the number of heart failure patients in the future due to the aging of the population, predicting the risk of a patient having heart failure could prevent hospitalizations and readmissions, improving both patient care and hospital management, which would have a high impact on costs and time.[25]

Machine learning is also increasingly being applied to make predictions related to population health: the use of novel big data resources, which are ripe with different data types, may allow for improvements in the prediction algorithms necessary to

[19] Privacy International (2021).

[20] Harris (2021).

[21] Morgenstern et al. (2021).

[22] Roski et al. (2019).

[23] Whitelaw et al. (2020).

[24] Bourguet et al. (2013).

[25] Larburu et al. (2018).

navigate complex health data ecosystems successfully. A good example of this is the integration of data types to better understand complex associations between genetics, the environment, and disease. The Harvard group has used large administrative datasets to untangle the relationship between genetics and the environment in all diseases recorded in health insurance claims data[26] Use of biobanks and their massive datasets allows scientists around the world to discover new genetic variants (e.g., through genome-wide association studies) and novel risk factors associated with disease more efficiently and with higher sensitivity and specificity compared to traditional "one-at-a-time" methods[27] Using electronic medical record data, machine- and deep-learning algorithms have been able to predict many important clinical parameters, including suicide, Alzheimer's disease, dementia, severe sepsis, septic shock, hospital readmission, all-cause mortality, in-hospital mortality, unplanned readmission, prolonged length of stay and final discharge diagnosis.[28]

Overall, predictive models have been used much more widely by clinicians than by public health professionals. However, on closer inspection, any application that improves patient care at any level can be considered relevant to the field of public health. The ability of clinicians and healthcare providers to make better informed decisions on patient health can be improved by context-specific algorithms, which use massive quantities of clinical, physiological, epidemiological, and genetic data. Precision medicine will further benefit from these advanced algorithms, as their accuracy, timeliness and appropriateness in clinical care improve over time, decompressing our reliance on human resources. This advancement, however, still necessitates computer-literate physicians, who are up-to-date with new generation data-driven approaches. The key to the complete incorporation of AI into clinical care will therefore be the integration of human clinical judgement with advanced clinical machine learning algorithms.[29]

To maximize these benefits, however, legal, ethical, economic, and social constraints of artificial intelligence must be addressed first. The potential benefits of these technologies and the economic and commercial potential of artificial intelligence for healthcare warrant ever-greater use worldwide[30] Different organizations throughout the world are building on this important discussion. The Pan American Health Organization, for example, offers its own guiding principles for all applications in healthcare or public health[31]:

1. People-centred: artificial intelligence technologies must respect the rights of the individual.
2. Ethically grounded, progress and discussion must be made in compliance with the principles of human dignity, nonmaleficence, and justice.

---

26 Lakhani et al. (2019).

27 Centers for Disease Control and Prevention (2019).

28 Topol (2019).

29 Khemasuwan et al. (2020).

30 World Health Organization (2021).

31 Pan American Health Organization (2021).

3. Transparent: When developing artificial intelligence algorithms, having clear objectives and goals is mandatory.
4. Data protection: Data privacy and security are paramount in artificial intelligence development.
5. Scientific integrity: artificial intelligence applications must be reliable, reproducible, fair, honest, and accountable, according to best practices.
6. Open and shareable: Openness and shareability must be the founding principles of every artificial intelligence development process.
7. Nondiscriminatory: artificial intelligence for public health must be based on fairness, equality, and inclusiveness.
8. Human-controlled: All automated decisions must be reviewed by human beings.

These guiding principles are fundamental in developing global cooperation initiatives centred on artificial intelligence use for health while navigating the different regulatory and policy environments worldwide.

3 Critical Aspects of Artificial Intelligence for Healthcare Provision

The application of artificial intelligence for health is very promising. Nevertheless, the current scientific landscape still lacks clinical trials highlighting the impact of artificial intelligence tools in delivering healthcare (in terms of safety, effectiveness, patient outcomes) compared with traditional approaches and their sustainability in terms of economic and ethical aspects. The development of evidence-based guidelines and the implementation of best practices are fundamental to promote the use of artificial intelligence in routine clinical practice, fostering a significant positive transformation in the health sector. Furthermore, artificial intelligence currently poses major technological, ethical, and social challenges, which need competent professionals to address. Critical issues slow the adoption of innovative artificial intelligence-based applications. For example, regarding public health interventions, it is still unknown whether the introduction of artificial intelligence in clinical practice might either improve or worsen health inequities on a large scale.[32] Although the promotion of artificial intelligence addresses personalized recommendations and individual action, this should not threaten the importance of collective action to take care of social and structural determinants of health[33] Moreover, similar to all public health interventions, the use of artificial intelligence to create enduring benefits requires not only a broad coalition of support and partnerships between the public and private sectors but also the trust and enduring support of patients.

In addition, despite their wide testing, artificial intelligence-based algorithms affecting patient care have not yet reached the sufficient level of accuracy needed for

[32] Weiss et al. (2018).

[33] Panch et al. (2019).

precise long-term predictions. This poses a serious challenge for healthcare workers, as long-term predictions of limited reliability could impact an individual's life for years in the future (e.g., both false-positive/negative predictions on an essential diagnosis could affect the level of risk that clinicians are willing to undertake to treat a disease, thus heavily impacting patient health outcomes). Prediction algorithms could also be biased towards or against certain population subgroups (e.g., ethnic groups, religious groups), both in terms of potentially discriminatory health practices suggested and issues related to individual autonomy in personal data use and informed consent. These potential pitfalls of artificial intelligence and its long-term health implications raise essential ethical concerns that must be addressed by all the stakeholders involved (i.e., governmental institutions, healthcare authorities, medical and patient associations, healthcare providers and industries).[34] From a public health perspective, one of the main and most obvious implications of artificial intelligence use for healthcare is the risk of inequalities in accessing technologies and in the financial burdens that they can generate.[35] This gap could emerge among patients population subgroups and between researchers and clinicians operating in different contexts or areas and between the public and private sectors as well as in the health systems of different regions and countries.[36]

As another issue, artificial intelligence systems might be programmed according to certain values and judgments that could create or worsen health inequities, such as those related to gender, race or belonging to minority groups. Moreover, there could be disagreement about the system of values that informs artificial intelligence systems.[37] At the research stage, proper development of a precautionary supervised system of artificial intelligence trials would ensure that they are ethical, legal, and inclusive in scope. The greatest challenge related to artificial intelligence tools for health remains their adoption in everyday clinical practice following the consensus of the scientific community in different medical areas. In fact, for widespread adoption to take place, artificial intelligence systems must be approved by scientists and regulators, integrated with digital health platforms through health data pipelines, standardized at a level such that similar products perform similarly, taught to clinicians, accepted by patients, paid for by public or private payer organizations, and updated over time. The dysregulated use of artificial intelligence can, in fact, negatively affect patients, professional and health systems because of some characteristics of this family of technologies, possibly generating critical issues regarding the absence of transparency and comprehensibility of their way of functioning, the generation of biases related to the programming and/or training of machine learning systems, the lack of robust data protection and cybersecurity requirements, the difficult definition of responsibility and accountability concerning their use and the reliability of their performance. Biased algorithms are, for example, those trained mainly on healthy men but are also used in clinical practice with women and children. If errors in

[34] World Health Organization (2019).

[35] IEEE (2017).

[36] Smith et al. (2020).

[37] Caliskan et al. (2017).

an algorithm used for the diagnosis of serious and potentially fatal diseases such as cancer are undetectable by the physician, the physician can make incorrect diagnoses with serious consequences for the patient's outcome. Furthermore, the standards of care in the artificial intelligence-based decision support system medicine era and who will assume risks and liability for medical malpractice caused by errors in AI systems are still unknown. Common issues related to the uncontrolled use of artificial intelligence tools include transparency and explainability,[38] bias and discrimination,[39] responsibility and accountability,[40] data privacy and security,[41] reliability and performance.[42]

4 Regulatory Sandboxes in Healthcare Are Needed to Solve Some Critical Problems

Article 57 (1) of the EU AI Act requires that Member States ensure that their competent authorities establish at least one AI regulatory sandbox at the national level to facilitate the development and testing of innovative AI systems under strict regulatory oversight before these systems are placed on the market. Regulatory sandboxes can be considered controlled environments to foster innovation through the cooperation of multiple stakeholders (producers and innovators, providers, end-users, and authorities). The sandbox participants collaborate to design and drive innovation without the associated risks. Competent authorities provide, as appropriate, guidance, supervision and support with a view to identifying risks, particularly fundamental rights, health and safety.

Stakeholders' ability to collaborate effectively is one of the key measures identified for the success of sandboxes in general. This collaboration can be assisted via directed consortia, a partnership framework that provides collaborative environments

[38] The lack of transparency and explainability means that the healthcare professional may not understand the machine's decision-making process, with impact on trust (risk of both excessive distrust and unjustified trust), impacting on patient's outcome.

[39] The artificial intelligence system can perpetuate or amplify existing biases in the health dataset used for its design and training. This can lead to wrong decisions of the professional in providing the right healthcare services or treatments to the right patients.

[40] The question of responsibility is crucial: it is not clear who should take responsibility for the wrong decisions made by artificial intelligence systems. This raises ethical and legal questions, especially when such decisions have significant impacts on people's health and lives.

[41] The use of artificial intelligence tools in the healthcare sector involves the collection and analysis of large amounts of personal health data, raising concerns about privacy. In all the cases where rigorous measures to protect patient's data and ensure their ethical use are not implemented, there is a concrete risk of violations of natural persons rights.

[42] When artificial intelligence systems are not properly tested and evaluated through clinical trials, the risk they generate confusing or inaccurate results in clinical practice is high. Additionally, the reliability of artificial intelligence systems for healthcare applications requires constant monitoring of their performance allowing professionals to be aware about their limitations.

for multiple organisations with differing priorities. The use of clear mission statements, targeted deliverables and timeframes, workstreams defined by the participants involved, and expected milestones are key success factors.[43] In the healthcare sector, the engagement of clinicians and patients and public and private healthcare providers working closely with regulators, technology developers, and academics is essential in developing artificial intelligence products for health and ensuring the uptake and diffusion of innovation within the healthcare system.

The sandboxes allow innovators to trial products, services, and business models in a safe space to confirm their compliance with existing regulations before wide implementation in the sector. Within these spaces, it is possible to test new technologies in real conditions without immediately incurring all the normal regulatory consequences.[44] Artificial intelligence-based technologies and advanced therapy medicinal products can be, for instance, valuably assessed in these environments before their adoption and implementation for health. In fact, regulatory sandboxes enable the testing of late-stage products, the verification of compliance with existing regulations, and the exploration of models that may violate current regulations while providing substantial benefits if implemented. They can be seen as *ex ante* instruments to certify the safety and quality of artificial intelligence-based products and services in an efficient manner: testing an artificial intelligence product in a regulatory sandbox helps an agency or authority decide to certify its quality or safety.[45] Using an anticipatory sandbox approach such as facilitating the development of appraisal methods, policies, and processes and adapting to the unique features of disruptive innovations would enable all stakeholders involved to have a constructive discussion that would facilitate faster uptake and patient access to these technologies.

Healthcare regulatory sandboxes have been classified as outcome-focused sandboxes or data-focused sandboxes according to their aims and outputs.[46] The outcome-focused methods are designed to improve clinical outcomes through the adoption of new technologies such as digital triage tools, the use of machine learning applications within diagnostics, interventions related to telemedicine and mobile health, and the use of blockchain technology. Other uses include testing service models such as those focused on restructuring social care services and determining the appropriate staff skill mix to support care home services. The data-focused sandboxes are designed to use electronic health data to facilitate the testing of new technologies. The access to and use of health data, such as electronic health records, is thus facilitated for innovative product testing.

There are consistent benefits related to regulatory sandboxes that concern the producer of new technologies, the user (as in the healthcare sector patients, clinicians, providers), and the policymaker. The benefits for artificial intelligence producers

[43] Lim (2014).

[44] The sandbox approach is an example of anticipatory regulation where regulation is seen as a support tool rather than a barrier to innovation. Anticipatory regulation is designed to anticipate future challenges, and support innovators when faced with them.

[45] Buocz et al. (2023).

[46] Leckenby et al. (2021).

include less time to market (shorter authorization process), less regulatory uncertainty (e.g., the prohibition of new technologies), and more feedback on regulatory requirements and risks. With respect to the user, the most relevant benefit is the greater ability to choose new safer AI-based products and services for health. For policy makers, benefits include the opportunity to be informed through learning and experimentation, being supported to update regulations, and being connected and engaged with market stakeholders. Despite all these benefits, stakeholders' engagement can be characterized by some issues related to cultural and organizational resistance that can limit the adoption of innovations. On the other hand, competent authorities are asked to be prepared (with adequate implementation resources) to meet the increasing market demand regarding artificial intelligence system testing and evaluation through regulatory sandboxes, especially in the healthcare sector, and to meet the need for the integration of the EU and national regulations involving artificial intelligence for health and health data (governance, use, protection, security) used to train artificial intelligence algorithms. Standardized approaches and methods to validate artificial intelligence algorithms before marketing should also be prepared, taking into account scientific and legal principles concerning biomedical research for clinical practice.

References

Bi WL, Hosny A, Schabath MB, Giger ML, Birkbak NJ, Mehrtash A et al (2019) Artificial intelligence in cancer imaging: clinical challenges and applications. CA Cancer J Clin 69(2):127–157

Bourguet JR, Thomopoulos R, Mugnier ML, Abécassis J (2013) An artificial intelligence-based approach to deal with argumentation applied to food quality in a public health policy. Expert Syst Appl 40(11):4539–4546

Buocz T, Pfotenhauer S, Eisenberger I (2023) Regulatory sandboxes in the AI Act: reconciling innovation and safety? Law Innov Technol 15(2):357–389

Caliskan A, Bryson JJ, Narayanan A (2017) Semantics derived automatically from language corpora contain human-like biases. Science 356:183–186

Cascini F, Buttigieg S, Pastorino R, Ricciardi W, Boccia S (2023) Personalized medicine through artificial intelligence: a public health perspective. In: Cesario A, D'Oria M, Auffray C, Scambia G (eds) Personalized medicine meets artificial intelligence. Springer, Cham. https://doi.org/10.1007/978-3-031-32614-1_1

Centers for Disease Control and Prevention (2019) Data science and machine learning in public health: promises and challenges. https://blogs.cdc.gov/genomics/2019/09/20/data-science/

European Commission (2020a) A European strategy for data. https://eur-lex.europa.eu/legal-content/EN/TXT/PDF/?uri=CELEX:52020DC0066&from=EN

European Commission (2020b) White Paper on Artificial Intelligence—a European approach to excellence and trust. https://commission.europa.eu/publications/white-paper-artificial-intelligence-european-approach-excellence-and-trust_en

European Commission (2021) Regulatory framework on AI. https://digital-strategy.ec.europa.eu/en/policies/regulatory-framework-ai

Harris B (2021) As vaccine demand slows, doctors shift to 'microtargeting' vulnerable communities. NBC News, 1 May 2021

IEEE (2017) Ethically aligned design, version 2: ethics in action for the development of autonomous and intelligent systems. https://standards.ieee.org/news/2017/ead_v2.html
Kamdar JH, Jeba Praba J, Georrge JJ (2020) Artificial intelligence in medical diagnosis: methods, algorithms and applications. In: Jain V, Chatterjee J (eds) Machine learning with health care perspective. Learning and Analytics in Intelligent Systems, vol 13. Springer, Cham
Khemasuwan D, Sorensen JS, Colt HG (2020) Artificial intelligence in pulmonary medicine: computer vision, predictive model and COVID-19. Eur Respir Rev 29(157):200181
Lakhani CM, Tierney BT, Manrai AK, Yang J, Visscher PM, Patel CJ (2019) Repurposing large health insurance claims data to estimate genetic and environmental contributions in 560 phenotypes. Nat Genet 51(2):327–334
Larburu N, Artetxe A, Escolar V, Lozano A, Kerexeta J (2018) Artificial intelligence to prevent mobile heart failure patients decompensation in real time: monitoring-based predictive model. Mob Inf Syst, Article ID 1546210
Leckenby E, Dawoud D, Bouvy J, Jónsson P (2021) The sandbox approach and its potential for use in health technology assessment: a literature review. Appl Health Econ Health Policy 19(6):857–869
Lim MD (2014) Consortium sandbox: building and sharing resources. Sci Transl Med 6:242cm6
Morgenstern JD, Rosella LC, Daley MJ, Goel V, Schünemann HJ, Piggott T (2021) "AI's gonna have an impact on everything in society, so it has to have an impact on public health": a fundamental qualitative descriptive study of the implications of artificial intelligence for public health. BMC Public Health 21
Pan American Health Organization (2021) Artificial intelligence in public health. Digital transformation knowledge capsules. https://www.paho.org/en/documents/digital-transformation-knowledge-capsules-artificial-intelligence-public-health
Panch T, Pearson-Stuttard J, Greaves F, Atun R (2019) Artificial intelligence: opportunities and risks for public health. Lancet Digit Health 1:e13–e14
Privacy International (2021) Microtargeting. https://privacyinternational.org/learn/microtargeting
Roski J, Chapman W, Heffner J, Trivedi R, Del Fiol G, Kukafka R et al (2019) How artificial intelligence is changing health and health care. In: Matheny M, Thadaney Israni S, Ahmed M, Whicher D (eds) Artificial intelligence in health care: hope, hype, promise, and peril. National Academy of Medicine, Washington DC. https://nam.edu/artificial-intelligence-special-publication/
Schwalbe N, Wahl B (2020) Artificial intelligence and the future of global health. Lancet 395:1579–1586
Smith MJ, Axler R, Bean S, Rudzicz F, Shaw J (2020) Four equity considerations for the use of artificial intelligence in public health. Bull World Health Organ 98:290–292
Topol EJ (2019) High-performance medicine: the convergence of human and artificial intelligence. Nat Med 25:44–56
Wahl B, Cossy-Gantner A, Germann S et al (2018) Artificial intelligence (AI) and global health: how can AI contribute to health in resource-poor settings? BMJ Glob Health 3:e000798
Weiss D, Rydland HT, Øversveen E, Jensen MR, Solhaug S, Krokstad S (2018) Innovative technologies and social inequalities in health: a scoping review of the literature. PLoS ONE 13:e019544
Whitelaw S, Mamas MA, Topol E, Van Spall GC (2020) Applications of digital technology in COVID-19 planning and response. Lancet Digit Health 2:e435–e440
World Health Organization (2019) WHO consultation towards the development of guidance on ethics and governance of artificial intelligence for health: meeting report, Geneva, Switzerland, 2–4 October 2019. https://iris.who.int/handle/10665/340089
World Health Organization (2021) Ethics and governance of artificial intelligence for health. https://www.who.int/publications/i/item/9789240029200

Fidelia Cascini, M.D., Ph.D., Associate Professor of Hygiene and Public Health at University S. Raffaele, Rome, Italy. Head of the Scientific Secretariat of the Presidency, National Institute of Health. Digital health advisor, Ministry of Health. Italian representative at the Committee on the European Health Data Space, European Commission, and Co-Chair at the Global Digital Health Partnership. Author of over 90 papers and 4 monographs.

Open Access This chapter is licensed under the terms of the Creative Commons Attribution 4.0 International License (http://creativecommons.org/licenses/by/4.0/), which permits use, sharing, adaptation, distribution and reproduction in any medium or format, as long as you give appropriate credit to the original author(s) and the source, provide a link to the Creative Commons license and indicate if changes were made.

The images or other third party material in this chapter are included in the chapter's Creative Commons license, unless indicated otherwise in a credit line to the material. If material is not included in the chapter's Creative Commons license and your intended use is not permitted by statutory regulation or exceeds the permitted use, you will need to obtain permission directly from the copyright holder.

Private International Law and Developments in Artificial Intelligence

Gérardine Goh Escolar

Abstract As a transformative technology that is constantly evolving, online and inhabiting a space beyond jurisdictional borders, AI pushes the boundaries of the private international law (PIL) frameworks that are in place today. The cross-border nature of artificial intelligence-related applications, transactions and disputes, compounded by challenges of decentralisation, online operation, and digital transformation, raise fascinating questions about the future-readiness of PIL. Yet AI itself may be the crucial tool in assisting humans in the progressive unification of PIL. This chapter critically discusses the significance and impact of AI on PIL and considers the challenges to the basic tenets of PIL posed by AI applications and uses. It postulates some ideas on how the discipline of PIL can evolve in response to these challenges, while acknowledging the myriad public policy considerations that should be considered in relation to AI in the context of PIL. The chapter then turns to consider the impact of AI on the application of the current PIL frameworks established under the auspices of the Hague Conference on Private International Law (HCCH). It assesses how AI may contribute to the development and unification of PIL rules, before concluding with some final thoughts on the future of PIL in an increasingly AI-enabled world.

Keywords Private international law · Party autonomy · Hague Conference on Private International Law (HCCH) · Digital transformation

1 Introduction

Likely one of the most oft-quoted people in artificial intelligence (AI) is Nick Bostrum, who famously stated in his seminal TED Talk, "Machine intelligence is the last invention that humanity will ever need to make".[1] The potential benefits

[1] Bostrum (2015).

G. G. Escolar (✉)
Hague Conference on Private International Law (HCCH), The Hague, The Netherlands
e-mail: gge@hcch.net

© The Author(s) 2025

C. Amodio and A. Diurni (eds.), *Human Vulnerability in Interaction with AI in European Private Law*, https://doi.org/10.1007/978-3-031-93247-2_14

and existential risks raised by AI technologies and applications were explored by James Barrat in his book, *Our Final Invention: Artificial Intelligence and the End of the Human Era*, in which he confessed that he wrote the book "to warn you that artificial intelligence could drive mankind into extinction, and to explain how that catastrophic outcome is not just possible, but likely if we do not begin preparing very carefully now".[2] These perspectives highlight concerns as to the vulnerabilities posed to humans by AI, including that AI could and would surpass human control and protective frameworks, making it potentially the final invention humans need to develop, and creating a need for novel ways of crafting legal frameworks to protect ourselves from—potentially—our greatest and last invention.

What is clear is the role of AI in enabling machines to emulate aspects of human intelligence. As a transformative technology that is constantly evolving, online and inhabiting a space beyond jurisdictional borders, AI pushes the boundaries of the private international law (PIL) frameworks that are in place today. The cross-border nature of AI-related applications, transactions and disputes, compounded by challenges of decentralisation, online operation, and digital transformation, raise fascinating questions about the future-readiness of PIL.

Yet AI itself may be the crucial tool in assisting humans in the progressive unification of our legal norms, in particular in PIL. As a platform for research across languages and cultures, a means for large dataset comparisons, and a large-scale reasoning and problem-solving device, AI can produce solutions that may prove to be the answer to the age-old questions raised in PIL.

This chapter will first discuss what AI is, and analyse the significance and impact of AI applications on PIL, including the types of harms that AI systems can cause. It then considers the challenges to the basic tenets of PIL posed by AI applications and uses, and suggests some ideas on how the discipline of PIL can evolve in response to these challenges. The chapter will then discuss, within the context of PIL, the public policy considerations and overriding mandatory regulations that should be considered in relation to AI. The chapter will then turn to consider the impact of AI on the application of the current PIL frameworks established under the auspices of the Hague Conference on Private International Law (HCCH). It assesses how AI may contribute to the development and unification of PIL rules. This chapter aims to provide a grounded yet forward-looking overview of the intersection between AI and PIL. It raises many more questions than answers, but perhaps asking the questions at the right time and with the right context is the first step to addressing the challenges to PIL raised by AI.

---

[2] Barrat (2013).

2 What Is AI?

What is AI? AI is commonly taken to refer to computer systems designed to perform tasks that traditionally require human intelligence. These tasks include learning, reasoning, problem-solving, and decision-making. AI systems operate through algorithms and machine learning techniques that enable them to analyse data, recognise patterns, and make decisions with varying degrees of autonomy.[3]

AI is thus the generic term applied in industry to computing systems capable of performing tasks that typically require human intelligence, such as reasoning, learning, problem-solving, perception, and language understanding. For example, Google states that, "on an operational level for business use, AI is a set of technologies that are based primarily on machine learning and deep learning, used for data analytics, predictions and forecasting, object categorization, natural language processing, recommendations, intelligent data retrieval, and more".[4] IBM defines AI as "technology that enables computers and machines to simulate human learning, comprehension, problem-solving, decision-making, creativity and autonomy".[5] McKinsey & Company describes AI as "a machine's ability to perform cognitive functions we associate with human minds, such as perceiving, reasoning, learning, interacting with the environment, problem-solving, and even exercising creativity".[6] Amazon Web Services offers a broader description, noting that it "is a technology with human-like problem-solving capabilities. AI in action appears to simulate human intelligence—it can recognize images, write poems, and make data-based predictions".[7]

The use of AI on digital platforms is rapidly increasing and touches on multiple facets of the consumer's experience of a platform. In one survey on business uses of AI, the most popular applications included customer service (56% of respondents) and cybersecurity and fraud management (51% of respondents)[8]; conversely, in a survey of consumers with respect to the use of AI by businesses, respondents expressed the highest concern about AI affecting product descriptions (70% "concerned") and personalised advertising (64% "concerned").[9]

[3] Haenlein and Kaplan (2019).

[4] Google (2024b).

[5] IBM (2024).

[6] McKinsey and Company (2024).

[7] Amazon Web Services (2024).

[8] Forbes.com (2024b).

[9] Forbes.com (2024a).

2.1 Definitions of AI in Global and Regional Legal Frameworks

While AI is a technological concept, its legal implications have gained global attention, leading to efforts to define and regulate it in various international and regional legal frameworks.

The United Nations (UN) Principles for the ethical use of AI in the UN system note that AI systems "are understood to be systems that have the capacity to automatically process data and information in a way that resembles intelligent human behaviour, and they typically include aspects of reasoning, learning, perception, prediction, planning or control".[10] These Principles are based on the AI Ethics Recommendation promulgated by the United Nations Educational, Scientific and Cultural Organization (UNESCO).[11]

The European Union (EU)'s Artificial Intelligence Act, which entered into force on 1 August 2024, establishes a common regulatory and legal framework for AI within the EU. According to the EU's AI Act, an "AI system" means "a machine-based system that is designed to operate with varying levels of autonomy and that may exhibit adaptiveness after deployment, and that, for explicit or implicit objectives, infers, from the input it receives, how to generate outputs such as predictions, content, recommendations, or decisions that can influence physical or virtual environments".[12]

This definition recognises that AI can operate autonomously to influence human decision-making and interact with the real world. Along the same lines, the Organisation for Economic Co-operation and Development (OECD) defines an AI system as "a machine-based system that, for explicit or implicit objectives, infers, from the input it receives, how to generate outputs such as predictions, content, recommendations, or decisions that can influence physical or virtual environments. Different AI systems vary in their levels of autonomy and adaptiveness after deployment".[13]

The Guide on AI Governance and Ethics issued by the Association of Southeast Asian Nations (ASEAN) defines AI as "an engineered or machine-based system that can, for a given set of objectives, generate outputs such as predictions, recommendations, or decisions influencing real or virtual environments".[14] An AI system,

[10] UN (2022, at para. 3).

[11] UNESCO (2024).

[12] Article 3(1), Regulation (EU) 2024/1689 of the European Parliament and of the Council of 13 June 2024 laying down harmonised rules on artificial intelligence and amending Regulations (EC) No 300/2008, (EU) No 167/2013, (EU) No 168/2013, (EU) 2018/858, (EU) 2018/1139 and (EU) 2019/2144 and Directives 2014/90/EU, (EU) 2016/797 and (EU) 2020/1828 (Artificial Intelligence Act), 13 June 2024, https://eur-lex.europa.eu/legal-content/EN/TXT/?uri=CELEX:32024R1689#art_3. Note Recital 12 of the Preamble, which notes that notion of "AI system" in this Regulation should be clearly defined and should be closely aligned with the work of international organisations working on AI to ensure legal certainty, facilitate international convergence and wide acceptance, while providing the flexibility to accommodate the rapid technological developments in this field.

[13] OECD (2024).

[14] ASEAN (2024).

according to the ASEAN Guide, is "a machine-based system that is capable of influencing the environment by producing an output (predictions, recommendations or decisions) for a given set of objectives. It uses machine and/or human-based data and inputs to (i) perceive real and/or virtual environments; (ii) abstract these perceptions into models through analysis in an automated manner (e.g., with machine learning), or manually; and (iii) use model inference to formulate options for outcomes. AI systems are designed to operate with varying levels of autonomy".[15]

2.2 *Types of AI and Their Relevance to PIL*

AI systems vary in complexity and functionality. Researchers and industry actors typically classify AI into different types based on their capabilities: reactive, limited memory, generative, theory of mind, and self-aware.[16]

2.2.1 Reactive AI

Reactive AI is the simplest form of AI.[17] It responds to stimuli in real-time but does not learn from past experiences or store data for future decisions. Reactive AI is a common application in gaming and early robotics. These applications excel at specific tasks but cannot adapt beyond their programming. An example of reactive AI's real-world applications is a gaming application such as Deep Blue by IBM,[18] a system that calculates all possible moves and selects the best response but does not adapt beyond its programmed logic.[19] Another example is AI-based spam filters in email systems, which react to rule-based filters built with predefined keywords and block spam messages but do not analyse past user interactions. The "Sentinels" in the 1999 movie, *The Matrix*, constitute one extreme example of the use of reactive AI.[20] These machine enforcers of the Matrix world follow strict programming to hunt and destroy humans.[21] They do not learn or adapt but instead react to their environment based on their directives.

In terms of the PIL implications of reactive AI, these are limited, as these systems are primarily task-driven and lack decision-making autonomy. They also generally do not process data across borders or make autonomous contractual decisions.

[15] Id.

[16] For an excellent summary, see Papajorji and Moskowitz (2024). See also Crevier (1993).

[17] Brooks (1991).

[18] Murray et al. (2002). See also Kasparov (2022).

[19] Hsu et al. (1990).

[20] Wachowski and Wachowski (1999).

[21] The Sentinels would, of course, be in violation of Isaac Asimov's First Law of Robotics: "A robot may not injure a human being or, through inaction, allow a human being to come to harm." See Asimov (1968, pp. 183–206).

However, AI-powered spam filters operated by multinational companies may raise jurisdictional questions in data protection disputes.

2.2.2 Limited Memory AI

Limited memory AI can learn from past experiences and improve its decision-making based on historical data. Limited memory AI is the technology that powers most of machine learning applications as of 2025.[22] Real-world applications include autonomous vehicles such as Tesla's Autopilot, which uses sensors in combination with historical and programmed data to navigate roads and avoid obstacles. Other applications include some facial recognition technologies such as Apple Face ID, which rely on stored biometric data to recognise users over time, and predictive algorithms in finance, such as AI-powered stock trading systems, which analyse past market data to make real-time trading decisions. Perhaps most evocatively, the R2-D2 droid in the *Star Wars* franchise is a good example of limited memory AI.[23] These droids can remember past interactions and make decisions based on previous experiences, learning how to navigate different terrains and provide unique responses to commands.

Limited memory AI may have some PIL implications. For example, which forum would have jurisdiction where an autonomous vehicle causes an accident in a foreign State? Would AI facial recognition used in airports raise conflicts between data protection laws in different jurisdictions?

2.2.3 Generative AI

Generative AI can create new content, such as text, images, and music, based on existing data.[24] These models use deep learning techniques such as Generative Adversarial Networks (GANs) and transformer models. At the time of writing (in 2025), perhaps the most well-known generative AI application is ChatGPT from OpenAI.[25] Together with other generative AI applications, such as Gemini from Google,[26] these models generate human-like text and assist in customer service and legal research.[27] Another form of generative AI is deepfake technology, which can manipulate video and audio, creating realistic but fake media. Increasingly finding traction in broad public use are applications that allow AI-generated art and music, such as DALL·E[28]

---

[22] Naveed et al. (2023).

[23] Lucasfilm Ltd.; 20th Century Fox. (2013). Star Wars original trilogy.

[24] McCorduck (2004).

[25] OpenAI (2023).

[26] Google (2024a).

[27] Zhao et al. (2023).

[28] OpenAI (2024) https://openart.ai.

and Jukebox[29] by OpenAI, which can generate paintings, music, and designs based on text-prompt inputs by human users. Popular culture anticipated forms of conversational and generative AI as early as 1968 with HAL 9000 in the movie *2001: A Space Odyssey*.[30] In the movie, HAL generates human-like conversation and makes independent decisions but ultimately malfunctions, leading to a life-or-death conflict with the astronauts. Another example is Ava in the 2014 movie *Ex Machina*,[31] which can engage in deep conversations, generating responses that mimic human emotions and creativity, much like ChatGPT or DALL·E.

Several PIL questions arise in relation to the use of such generative AI. For example, since generative AI can create new content, including text, images, and even human-like speech, and is capable of writing, designing, or generating artistic works, which State's law is applicable when AI-generated content is used commercially? In relation to the use of deepfakes, if an AI application creates fake content about a person across borders, which defamation laws would apply? Can an AI-generated judgment be refused recognition and enforcement abroad on the grounds of public policy, and what implications does that have for the HCCH 2019 Judgments Convention?[32] If an AI application generates a contract on behalf of contracting parties, are there choice of law and party autonomy issues?

2.2.4 Theory of Mind AI

Theory of mind AI is, at the time of writing, a theoretical next step in AI technology, and would be capable of understanding human emotions, beliefs, and social contexts, allowing it to interact with people in an empathetic and intuitive manner.[33] There is some concern that certain generative AI applications, such as ChatGPT, may appear to exhibit theory of mind-like capabilities, but such responses from current generative AI applications are still based on inferences from "user intent" as opposed to responding from embedded capability.[34]

Potential real-world applications of theory of mind AI include AI-powered therapists and mental health chatbots, which could offer personalised mental health advice, and advanced negotiation AI, which could participate in diplomatic negotiations or contract discussions. Pop culture references to theory of mind AI applications include the figure of Sonny in the 2004 movie *I, Robot* where, unlike other robots in the film, Sonny understands emotions and motives, engaging in complex reasoning beyond programmed responses.[35] The character Data in the *Star Trek: The Next Generation* series (1987–1994) is an example of an advanced theory of mind AI in a cybernetic

[29] OpenAI (2024) https://openai.com/index/jukebox/.

[30] Dullea et al. (1968).

[31] Garland (2014).

[32] Taherdoost (2023).

[33] Nebreda et al. (2023).

[34] Khan et al. (2025).

[35] Proyas A (2004) I, Robot. Twentieth Century Fox.

android body.[36] Throughout the series, Data actively seeks to understand human emotions and resolve ethical dilemmas.[37]

Multiple PIL challenges would arise with the use of theory of mind AI. For example, if AI systems negotiate a contract on behalf of the parties, is the contract legally binding? What choice of law issues would arise?[38] In relation to consumer protection, if AI misinterprets human emotions and provides harmful advice in the context of medical or therapeutic procedures, who is liable? If a theory of mind AI application is used as an emotional support tool (including in social contexts such as semi-autonomous companions in AI-powered dating), and that AI application causes emotional distress or other harm resulting from that emotional distress, which law would be applicable? Which forum would have jurisdiction? How would cross-border accountability and liability be dealt with in relation to theory of mind AI?

2.2.5 Self-Aware AI

Self-aware AI remains theoretical and, at the time of writing, technologically unrealised. It would refer to AI, which theoretically would possess consciousness, self-awareness, and independent reasoning capabilities. Self-aware AI would include, potentially, fully autonomous robots with independent thought, or autonomous decision-makers in international disputes. Such self-aware AI has been the subject of fictional works, memorably including Skynet in the 1984–2019 *The Terminator* series of movies,[39] which becomes self-aware and decides to exterminate humanity to ensure its survival, Ultron in the 2015 movie *Avengers: Age of Ultron*,[40] in which Ultron gains self-awareness and determines that human extinction is the key to peace, and the Hosts in the 2016–2022 *Westworld* series,[41] in which AI robots become self-aware and demand rights and autonomy.

PIL questions as to legal personality, similar to those arising in relation to corporations, would certainly arise.[42] Should such self-aware AI applications be treated as legal entities, capable of being sued? If so, where would an AI entity be domiciled or "habitually resident" for jurisdictional purposes? Could a self-aware AI judge issue binding decisions in cross-border disputes? Could a judgment written or generated by a self-aware AI judge be recognised and enforced in a foreign jurisdiction?

[36] Paramount Pictures (1987–1994) Star Trek: The Next Generation.

[37] See, in particular, Snodgrass MM & Scheerer R (1989) The measure of a man (Season 2, Episode 9) [TV series episode]. In Star Trek: The Next Generation, id.

[38] On the matter of party autonomy in PIL in relation to contracts, see Ruhl (2007).

[39] Cameron J (1984–2019) The Terminator series. Orion Pictures.

[40] Whedon J (2015) Avengers: Age of Ultron. Walt Disney Studios Motion Pictures.

[41] Nolan J, Joy L (2016–2022) Westworld. HBO Entertainment.

[42] Chesterman (2020). See also Novelli et al. (2021).

2.2.6 Conclusion: Categories of AI and Their PIL Implications

The evolution of AI presents significant legal challenges, particularly in PIL. While reactive AI and limited memory AI already raise jurisdictional questions, the rise of generative AI and future theory of mind AI could profoundly impact PIL considerations in relation to contract law, intellectual property, legal personality, and tortious liability across borders. As AI systems become more autonomous, PIL frameworks must evolve to address issues of the determination of applicable law, jurisdiction, and the recognition and enforcement of judgments in an AI-driven world. As AI technology advances, PIL frameworks must address questions once confined to science fiction, but which are increasingly relevant in today's world.[43]

2.3 Types of AI-Related Harms and Their Challenges to PIL

These PIL challenges arise in different permutations on the basis of the different types of harm that may be caused by AI.[44] Types of AI-related harm range from economic harm arising from breach of contract, to personal harm caused by tortious actions, and to physical harm caused to persons and property.[45] Such AI-related harms have already arisen.

In relation to economic harm that may be caused by AI applications, one example arises from AI-driven financial trading algorithms that can cause economic harm through mispricing and market manipulation. A clear PIL framework will be necessary to address which forum has jurisdiction, or which law would be applicable to govern such harms. Where there are AI-generated errors in contract formation, do choice-of-law provisions within that same (erroneous) contract apply?[46] Where AI-powered self-executing smart contracts on distributed ledger technology cause unintended economic harm due to a faulty algorithm, how will the rules of PIL determine which law would apply?

Another real-world example that has already seen multiple instances relates to AI-powered deepfakes and automated content moderation, which can respectively create fake news or cause reputational harm through defamation, misclassification, amplification or suppression.[47] In such cases, should new rules on cross-border AI-related tortious claims in relation to digital reputation damage be developed?[48]

AI-caused physical harm, whether to persons or to property, raises another plethora of PIL questions.[49] For example, when an AI-driven autonomous vehicle causes a

[43] See, for an excellent exposition, Kaplan (2022).

[44] Li et al. (2022).

[45] Fraser and Suzor (2024).

[46] Hoffman and Arbel (2024).

[47] Sunkari and Srinagesh (2024).

[48] Shirish and Komal (2024).

[49] Araromi et al. (2024).

crash in a foreign State, which jurisdiction is appropriate and which law applies?[50] Where an AI-powered medical diagnosis programme provides an erroneous diagnosis that causes harm to the patient, how would that patient overcome jurisdictional challenges in their claim for compensation? Some commentators have argued that a technology-sensitive application of the doctrine that allows "piercing the digital veil" could be developed to hold AI developers or operators accountable.[51]

Certain sectors may be more susceptible to harms arising from AI-powered applications. One such example relates to the question of AI-generated content, such as music, graphics and text, and the PIL framework to determine which intellectual property laws would apply.[52] How would the appropriate jurisdiction be established over disputes relating to AI-generated content that may involve AI systems that scrape data in several jurisdictions, process and analyse the data in others, and generate content online (thereby lacking a clear and obvious connecting factor to determine applicable law or grounds for jurisdiction)?

The various harms that may be caused by AI, in particular the breadth of such possible harms, expose the inherent vulnerabilities in our contemporary application of PIL frameworks. They also raise questions as to whether the basic tenets of PIL, which have served the discipline so well for so long, can adequately address the challenges posed by AI. The next section considers the challenges posed by AI to the basic tenets of PIL, and considers how PIL as a discipline may need to evolve in order to address these challenges.

3 Challenges Posed by AI to the Basic Tenets of PIL

The origins of PIL as the discipline we know today can be traced back to the Renaissance, as new questions on the interaction between different legal systems arose with the expansion of trade between the Northern Italian city-states.[53] However, as prominent PIL scholars have sought to show, the history of PIL may also be traced through several longer chains of historical evolution—from ancient Greek cities to today in the European context[54]; throughthe interaction between Islamic traditional law and imperial China in the ninth century,[55] and through precolonial Africa in the

[50] Irwan and Mursyid (2024).

[51] For an analogous application most recently used in finding connecting factors in relation to activities carried out by decentralised autonomous organisations, see Schuppli and Jafari (2021).

[52] Chesterman (2024).

[53] See Siehr (2017). An excellent overview of the history of the theory of PIL is provided by Mills (2006).

[54] See Gautier (1972).

[55] Paul (1991) and Depping (1830); but noting that much of modern PIL in contemporary practice in China reflects the European tradition, see Kong and Hu (2002).

fifteenth century.[56] Naturally, whatever imaginative possiblitites the great philosophers of these varied traditions may have contemplated, many of the basic tenets and concepts of PIL were not developed with AI in mind.

Nor was the future impact of AI evident by the time PIL became an undertaking by international organisations working on the progressive unification of PIL.[57] This may be evident in the formulation and foundations of many of the basic tenets and concepts of modern PIL: party autonomy, objective connecting factors, grounds for jurisdiction, technology neutrality, functional equivalence, and characterisation, among others. This section will consider the challenges posed by AI to the basic tenets and concepts used in the PIL discipline, and how some of these challenges may be met by taking a novel approach to traditional questions.

3.1 Party Autonomy

Party autonomy has been described as "arguably the most enigmatic principle" in PIL.[58] While many other PIL rules are rooted in objectively searching for the appropriate connecting factor, party autonomy is grounded in the parties' intent to determine the applicable law. As Yuko Nishitani explains,

> The parties are entitled to select the law which governs the legal relationship concerned, including the mandatory rules of the chosen law. As a corollary, mandatory rules of the lex fori, the law which would otherwise govern the legal relationship or any other law, are excluded by the parties' simple designation of the applicable law in principle.[59]

It is beyond the scope of this chapter to trace the development of what has become a foundational principle in PIL, which allows parties in cross-border transactions to select the applicable law and jurisdiction governing their legal relationships.[60] It is now broadly considered that the party autonomy principle promotes legal certainty, contractual freedom, and predictability, particularly in international contracts, arbitration agreements, and dispute resolution mechanisms.[61]

However, the rise of AI, with its capacity for autonomous decision-making, algorithmic negotiation, and self-executing smart contracts, raises fundamental challenges to the assumption that parties to an agreement formed through AI-enabled processes possess meaningful autonomy. AI introduces new complexities regarding consent, intention, liability, and contractual fairness, which raise questions as to whether traditional party autonomy doctrines remain viable or need reform. Various

[56] See Diop (1987). See also Oppong (2007).

[57] See Steiner (1965); see also Josephus Jitta (1920).

[58] Nishitani (2016).

[59] Id.

[60] Von Savigny (1849); Gamillscheg (1955); also Symeonides (2014); Nishitani (2000).

[61] Commentary on the Hague Principles on Choice of Law in International Commercial Contracts, online at https://www.hcch.net/en/instruments/conventions/full-text/?cid=135. See also Vogenauer (2013). Also Neuhaus (1976).

questions arise that relate to the autonomy of an AI-driven system. For example, can an AI application contract autonomously, and how does this affect contractual PIL rules? Do self-executing smart contracts or AI-enabled blockchain transactions challenge the basic assumptions of party autonomy? While PIL has strongly favoured party autonomy, viewing it as an enabler of efficient and predictable dispute resolution, AI complicates this perspective by introducing non-human decision-making, automated negotiations, and opaque algorithmic choices.

How exactly does AI challenge party autonomy in PIL? Arguably, through the introduction of contradictions to the basic assumptions that underlie the principle of party autonomy itself: the concept of party intention, the role of the negotiator in contractual relationships and the automation of contract negotiation and formation, imbalances in bargaining power, and the complexities involved in multi-jurisdictional operations.[62]

Turning first to the concept of party intention: a core assumption behind party autonomy is that contracting parties possess rational intent and understanding of the legal consequences of their choices.[63] AI-powered contract formation challenges this assumption in multiple ways. Where an AI application is used to perform functions analogous to those of a contracting agent, the application may autonomously negotiates and executes contracts without direct human intervention. For example, smart contracts on blockchain platforms, such as Ethereum-based supply chain contracts, may execute self-programmed agreements without user intervention. The question that arises here is a foundational one: Can AI-generated agreements be considered contracts under rules of PIL if no human consciously selected the applicable law?

Two further assumptions are that party intention is rational and clearly expressed.[64] However, AI applications optimise contract terms dynamically, sometimes in ways that commercial or individual parties may not fully understand or be privy to. For example, online platforms may use AI-driven price discrimination. An example is an AI-enabled airline ticket pricing algorithm that adjusts prices in real time. With such algorithmic decision-making, the question arises as to whether the parties have meaningfully exercised autonomy.

Second, we turn to the role of the negotiator in contractual relationships and the automation of contract negotiation and formation.[65] In scenarios where AI systems are not merely tools but act as negotiators on behalf of one or both parties, determining whether the choices (including the selection of applicable law) reflect genuine autonomous consent may become problematic. If an AI system is tasked with negotiating the terms, including the clauses relating to the determination of applicable law and jurisdiction, questions arise regarding accountability, autonomy and the adequacy of the consent provided. In these situations, there may arise a need to clarify the legal status of AI systems in contractual negotiations for the purposes of PIL considerations, with guidelines to define the limits of the AI application's autonomy, ensuring

---

[62] On the scope and limits to party autonomy in contracts, see Symeonides (2019).

[63] Mansel (2016).

[64] Jayme (1991, 1995).

[65] Mik (2023).

that its actions are subject to human confirmation. Clear rules for such decisions made by AI systems can help ensure that parties continue to exercise meaningful autonomy over the final contractual terms, thereby safeguarding the integrity of the party autonomy principle.[66]

Another interesting challenge that arises out of the automation of contract negotiation and formation is the increasingly common use case of online platforms and smart contracts using AI to draft, negotiate, and finalise contract terms automatically and without human intervention. When algorithms generate contractual provisions without human intervention, the human parties may have less direct control over the substantive and procedural choices made in those contracts, including the selection of governing law.[67] This undermines the precepts that underpin party autonomy because the decision-making process becomes opaque and can favour pre-set defaults embedded within the AI system. One possible way to address this is to require that AI systems used in contract formation clearly disclose how default clauses, including choice of law and choice of forum provisions, are arrived at. Ensuring human oversight in the final approval process can also help preserve party autonomy. For certain contracts, such as consumer or labour-related contracts, updating PIL frameworks to explicitly incorporate mandatory rules or override provisions when AI-generated contracts conflict with essential protections may become necessary.

Third, party autonomy assumes that parties are equally positioned to negotiate terms, but AI disrupts this balance, particularly when one party has superior algorithmic capabilities.[68] AI-driven contract platforms often favour the interests of larger, technologically advanced entities that control the algorithms. Small businesses or individual consumers might unknowingly accept jurisdictional clauses or choice of law provisions pre-determined by the platform, limiting their ability to negotiate terms. For example, some digital platforms may use data-driven systems to personalise user experiences or risk assessments, raising the question of whether legal terms, dispute resolution mechanisms, or default choices could be shaped by algorithmic design.[69] For example, terms of service of some social media platforms may use AI to customise legal terms, which may include the automatic selection of dispute resolution fora. Large tech companies (including AI-powered e-commerce platforms) also increasingly use AI to dynamically customise contract terms in real time, tailoring choice of law and jurisdictional provisions based on user data and in response to algorithmic risk assessments. Such AI-curated choice-of-law provisions may not align with genuine party autonomy, instead reinforcing information asymmetries. This imbalance of bargaining power weakens the practical application of party autonomy, as one party's choice, often driven by algorithmic design, dominates the contractual framework. In such cases, it may be necessary to enhance legal review requirements, encouraging or mandating human review of AI-generated contracts, especially in

[66] Conrad et al. (2023)

[67] Oliver (2001).

[68] Scholz (2017).

[69] Zafar (2024).

consumer or small business contexts, to ensure that the selection of governing law and forum is fair and informed.

Another interesting question that arises in relation to the imbalance of bargaining power relates to the use of AI for automated dispute resolution in cross-border e-commerce (e.g., PayPal's AI-driven dispute resolution mechanisms). On many e-commerce and e-payment platforms, AI-drive dispute resolution mechanisms automatically resolve disputes, sometimes without human review. Questions arise as to whether parties exercise autonomy in accepting AI-driven dispute resolution clauses, or whether they are effectively coerced into pre-programmed legal outcomes.

Fourth, the complexity of multi-jurisdictional operations raises multiple PIL challenges since AI applications, such as those used in global e-commerce or financial trading, often operate across multiple jurisdictions simultaneously. When disputes arise, the default choice of law clause embedded in an AI-generated contract might not account for the nuanced legal differences across borders. This leads to questions about which law is applicable, which forum should hear the dispute, and whether the parties' autonomy was fully respected in such a multifaceted environment.[70] In such cases, one way forward may be for courts and arbitrators to adopt more flexible conflict-of-law analyses that consider both the algorithm's default selections and the objectively-ascertainable intentions of the parties involved. Another possible way forward is for jurisdictions around the world to update existing international legal frameworks or to conclude modern fit-for-purpose frameworks to better accommodate the transnational nature of AI-driven transactions.

AI's unique features may necessitate a recalibrated approach that balances autonomy with safeguards against AI-driven asymmetries and algorithmic unpredictability. While party autonomy remains a fundamental principle in PIL, the increasing use of AI in contract formation, negotiation, and dispute resolution challenges this tenet. The opacity of algorithmic decision-making, imbalances in bargaining power, and the cross-border nature of AI applications all contribute to the potential erosion of genuine party autonomy. Addressing these challenges requires a multipronged approach, ranging from enhanced transparency and human oversight to the development of new legal frameworks and international harmonisation efforts, in order to ensure that the parties' intentions are fully respected.[71]

Three initiatives may be necessary for PIL as a discipline to address the obstacles to party autonomy posed by AI:

- AI-specific autonomy safeguards may need to be put in place to ensure contracts reflect genuine consent;
- Frameworks for AI-driven legal agreements may need to ensure transparency and human oversight to mitigate algorithmic bias;
- AI-sensitive public policy considerations and mandatory rules may need to be explicitly put in place to qualify party autonomy where a blind application of the party autonomy principle could lead to significant harm.

---

[70] Wang (2010).

[71] See Ebers (2022).

In short, PIL should adopt a technology-sensitive approach, ensuring that AI remains an enabler of cross-border legal certainty without compromising fairness and accountability.

3.2 Objective Connecting Factors

Another of the core principles of PIL under strain is the reliance on traditional objective connecting factors, which have long served to establish links for the purpose of determining applicable law.[72] Objective connecting factors, such as domicile, habitual residence, place of performance, location of the harm, or nationality, assume physical presence or a clear geographic nexus.[73] However, many AI applications operate in virtual, decentralised, or cloud-based environments. Data can be collected across several locations, and may be processed in one State, stored in another, and ultimately affect individuals in other locations. This dispersion, decentralisation and virtual nature of AI applications render conventional connecting factors less effective in pinpointing the appropriate applicable law.[74]

There are several real-world examples today of how traditional objective connecting factors may not work in AI-enabled applications.[75] For example, an accident involving an AI-driven vehicle may occur on the road in one State while the vehicle's software, its development team, and data centres are located in different countries. This raises difficult questions about whether the applicable law should be based on the location of the accident (*lex loci delicti*) or the domicile of the manufacturer, or even the place where the software was developed.

Another example relates to online platforms with data-driven services such as social media networks and e-commerce sites which use AI to curate content or manage transactions. When a dispute arises as a result of AI-generated content, for example, defamation due to deepfakes generated or disseminated through an online, AI-driven platform, the fact that the platform operates from one location, hosts data in another, and reaches a global audience challenges the traditional notion of a single connecting factor.[76]

Yet another example relates to AI-driven trading systems that may execute transactions across multiple exchanges worldwide. An algorithmic error causing market disruption could involve parties and assets in several jurisdictions, making it unclear the law of which jurisdiction should apply.[77]

In many AI-enabled transactions or interactions, the place where performance occurs or where harm is suffered may not be physically locatable. AI applications can

---

[72] Ungerer (2022).

[73] O'Hara and Ribstein (2000).

[74] Svantesson (2020).

[75] Huang (2020).

[76] Sakolciova (2021).

[77] Zetzsche et al. (2020).

deliver services, generate content, or execute decisions in a manner that transcends borders, complicating the determination of a clear "place" that anchors the legal analysis. For example, an AI-enabled service used for data analytics might be accessed online by users from around the world. If an error in the algorithm leads to financial losses for a multinational corporation, the "place of performance" is ambiguous since the service was rendered virtually rather than at a fixed location. Similarly, an AI system that automates contract formation or dispute resolution on a global e-commerce platform blurs the line between where the contract is concluded and where the service is performed. This creates challenges in identifying the connecting factors to determine the governing law that should apply.

3.3 *Grounds for Jurisdiction*

The global nature of AI-powered applications further complicates the traditional grounds for the determination of jurisdiction.[78] Since AI systems often operate across borders, the exercise of determining jurisdiction becomes a multi-layered problem where conventional criteria (such as the defendant's domicile or the location of the event) may yield conflicting results. This fragmentation can lead to forum shopping or jurisdictional gaps where no single jurisdiction is clearly competent to adjudicate the dispute.

For example, when AI systems are used to process personal data, a breach could affect users in multiple countries. The affected parties might face challenges in determining which State's courts have jurisdiction, particularly when the service provider is established in one State, its servers located in others, the users located, domiciled or habitually resident elsewhere, and the damage occurs online.[79]

3.4 *Technology Neutrality*

Technology neutrality has long been an assumed principle in the development and application of PIL. Technology neutrality in PIL is based on the premise that legal frameworks should not be designed around specific technologies but should instead remain adaptable to different innovations, ensuring the continuing and consistent application of PIL rules regardless of the technology involved. This, in turn, ensures that the legal framework remains stable and adaptable in the face of innovation, enhancing legal certainty.[80]

---

[78] See Yokomizo (2021).

[79] See for an exposition of jurisdictional issues relating to AI, Chandra (2021).

[80] See Rodríguez de las Heras Ballell (2019).

However, the rapid evolution of AI raises questions about the viability and desirability of this principle. The relevant question is whether PIL can remain technologically neutral in the face of AI-driven legal challenges, including jurisdictional uncertainty, evolving connecting factors, AI-generated contractual and tortious liability, and the enforceability of AI-driven dispute resolution mechanisms. While the aspiration of technology neutrality in PIL has merit, an AI-specific legal response may be necessary to address AI's unique characteristics and transnational implications.[81]

The justifications for technology neutrality in the development of PIL are threefold:

a. Stability and predictability: PIL principles (e.g., jurisdiction, choice of law, recognition, and enforcement of foreign judgments) should not be dependent on specific technological developments.
b. Legal consistency and certainty: A principles-based approach avoids the need for constant legal reform each time new technology emerges.
c. Innovation-friendliness: Neutral legal frameworks encourage technological progress by providing legal certainty without creating unnecessary legal and regulatory burdens.

However, PIL frameworks have traditionally been shaped by human-driven transactions and legal relationships. AI disrupts these assumptions by introducing non-human decision-making, decentralisation, and automated legal interactions that challenge established conflict-of-law principles.

AI-driven applications have, through the removal of a human-centred initiation and approach to transactions and activities, arguably had a disruptive impact on the technologically neutral approach to PIL.[82] As described above, while PIL relies on objective connecting factors, such as domicile, habitual residence, place of performance, or place of harm, to determine jurisdiction and applicable law, AI disrupts these factors in several ways. AI systems that execute contractual steps without direct human intervention complicate the determination of where a contract is formed or performed. Algorithmic decision-making also raises PIL questions in cross-border torts, where AI-generated defamation, AI-driven financial fraud, or accidents caused by AI-operated vehicles challenge traditional notions of where harm occurs and who is responsible. Moreover, while traditional PIL grounds for jurisdiction assume identifiable parties responsible for legal disputes, AI-enabled automated decision-making, including AI-generated contractual terms, automated settlements, and AI-led negotiations, may not fit within the existing legal framework that assumes human intent and responsibility. In addition, courts may struggle to attribute legal responsibility to an AI entity, a company deploying AI, or an end-user.[83]

---

[81] See Allen (2021).

[82] Svantesson (2019).

[83] See also the discussion about recent developments and trends in the digital economy, including distributed ledged technology (DLT) systems and applications, in HCCH, Developments with respect to PIL Implications of the Digital Economy, Prel. Doc. No 4 REV of January 2022, https://assets.hcch.net/docs/b06c28c5-d183-4d81-a663-f7bdb8f32dac.pdf, paras 9–35.

These issues, uniquely raised by the technology that powers AI, test the limits of the principle of technology neutrality where AI is involved. While maintaining a general principle of technology neutrality in the development and application of PIL rules can provide consistency, AI presents unique characteristics that challenge traditional legal assumptions:

a. Autonomy and non-human decision-making: Unlike prior technologies, AI operates with degrees of independence that PIL was not designed to regulate.
b. Opacity: The inability to fully explain AI-generated decisions ("black box" AI)[84] challenges legal principles of accountability and due process.
c. Decentralisation and distributed localisation: AI applications deployed across multiple jurisdictions weaken the effectiveness of traditional geographically-based PIL frameworks.

Given these challenges, it may be argued that absolute adherence to the principle of technology neutrality in PIL is increasingly unfeasible, and that AI's unique legal implications instead necessitate tailored solutions.

A secondary, but no less important, question, is whether the principle of technology neutrality remains desirable in the face of AI-enabled applications. Absolute commitment to technology neutrality may hinder effective legal responses to AI-related disputes. However, a technology-sensitive approach could ensure that PIL remains adaptable while addressing AI's distinct legal implications. Such a technology-responsive approach may be undertaken through three initiatives:

a. Sector-specific adaptations: Rather than abandoning the principle of technology neutrality or rewriting PIL frameworks entirely, AI-specific guidelines could be monitored and, where relevant, integrated into existing frameworks. One example of such work is the monitoring of developments undertaken by the HCCH in its Digital Economy Project.[85]
b. Harmonisation efforts: Multilateral consultations through international organisations could update existing frameworks and also lead to AI-focused instruments to fill existing gaps.
c. New AI-specific connecting factors: Developing AI-adapted PIL rules where necessary, such as linking jurisdiction to the AI system's governing algorithm, its point of decision-making, or its primary data sources, may be helpful to ensure that PIL frameworks remain fit for purpose. Studying the use of novel AI-specific connecting factors, for example, considering whether an "algorithmic domicile", such as the place where an AI system is trained, maintained, or substantially controlled, could operate as a new connecting factor for PIL disputes, may be one way to ensure legal certainty in the determination of applicable law for AI-related transactions and disputes.[86]

[84] Von Eschenbach (2021).

[85] For more on the HCCH's Digital Economy Project, see HCCH, "Digital Economy Project", online at https://www.hcch.net/en/projects/legislative-projects/digital-economy.

[86] HCCH, Private International Law Aspects of the Digital Economy: Report, Prel. Doc. No 5A of February 2024, https://assets.hcch.net/docs/b74f3bfe-51dd-4d0e-8d4b-59e5e32367da.pdf.

These three approaches allow PIL to evolve towards a more technology-responsive framework that retains legal certainty while adapting to AI's specific challenges. Taking a technology-responsive approach enables the formulation of a forward-looking PIL framework that moves beyond a rigid understanding of technology neutrality by incorporating AI-specific PIL rules. As AI continues to shape global commerce, dispute resolution and liability allocation, PIL must remain adaptable. The goal should not be blind and absolute adherence to the principle of technology neutrality, but rather legal adaptation and technology-sensitivity to allow for a principled approach to meeting the challenges that AI raises for PIL.

3.5 Functional Equivalence

Functional equivalence is a key principle in PIL that operates on the premise that new technological developments do not require the reinvention of legal principles but can instead be mapped onto existing legal categories by identifying their functional counterparts rather than requiring exact technological conformity.[87]

This principle has historically allowed PIL to adapt to past technological developments without requiring fundamental changes to its core doctrines.[88] Examples include:

a. Electronic contracts and signatures: Recognised as functionally equivalent to traditional contracts and handwritten signatures under instruments like the 1996 UNCITRAL Model Law on Electronic Commerce[89];
b. Online dispute resolution (ODR): Treated as functionally equivalent to offline dispute resolution processes when assessing jurisdiction and enforcement of judgments; and
c. E-commerce and traditional sales law: Online transactions are often assimilated into existing contractual frameworks under instruments like the United Nations Convention on Contracts for the International Sale of Goods (CISG).[90]

This principle has been useful in avoiding unnecessary legal fragmentation, promoting legal certainty, and ensuring the continued enforceability of rights across borders. However, functional equivalence assumes that new technologies perform the same legal function as their predecessors, albeit in a different form.[91] The advent of AI raises fundamental questions about whether functional equivalence can adequately address AI-specific PIL challenges, given that AI may introduce non-human agency,

[87] Paredes Pérez (2012).

[88] Estrella Faria (2004).

[89] United Nations Commission on International Trade Law. (1999). UNCITRAL model law on electronic commerce, with guide to enactment, 1996: with additional article 5 bis as adopted in 1998. United Nations: New York.

[90] United Nations Convention on Contracts for the International Sale of Goods, Apr. 11, 1980, S. Treaty Doc. No. 98–9, 1489 U.N.T.S. 3. (1983).

[91] Michaels (2019).

decision-making opacity, autonomous legal interactions, and decentralised systems that may not have clear functional analogues in traditional legal frameworks. Three concrete questions arise in relation to the continued relevance of the principle of functional equivalence in the face of AI-driven applications.

First, is an AI-generated agreement functionally equivalent to a human-made contract? AI systems are increasingly being used to negotiate terms and execute contractual steps without direct human intervention. These systems raise questions about whether contractual intent, capacity, and mutual consent, which constitute fundamental legal components of contract formation, can be meaningfully attributed to AI-driven agreements. One difficulty that could complicate the application of the functional equivalence principle is when an AI system acts outside its programmed scope or generates contractual terms that neither party fully understands, or is cognisant of. One example is the use of AI-enabled dynamic pricing algorithms in many e-commerce platforms today that lead to contractual terms that may be less transparent or comprehensible. Another example is the case of an AI-powered trading bot executing a financial contract at extreme speed. Can the automated process be treated as functionally equivalent to human negotiation and agreement? If a dispute arises over the bot's actions, traditional PIL doctrines governing choice of law, jurisdiction, and party autonomy may no longer neatly apply.

Second, are AI-generated cross-border harms functionally equivalent to human-caused harms, and how would liability be apportioned? The application of liability laws assumes that manufacturers, designers, or users are responsible for defects. However, AI systems that modify their own behaviour over time introduce system-generated actions that do not have a clear human counterpart. For example, if an autonomous vehicle causes an accident in a foreign jurisdiction, PIL frameworks traditionally determine liability based on where the harm occurred or where the product was manufactured. But if the AI system continuously updates itself via cloud-based learning, what functionally equivalent rule should apply?[92]

Third, are AI-generated decisions functionally equivalent to decisions made by humans in transnational litigation or arbitral proceedings? With AI increasingly used in automated dispute resolution, including in transnational litigation, is such AI-powered automated dispute resolution functionally equivalent to traditional decision-making by courts or arbitral tribunals? Moreover, concerns may arise about the lack of human reasoning and legal interpretation, as well as the possible lack of accountability if an AI-generated decision contains errors or bias. For example, if a judgment is produced through substantial reliance on an AI-powered application, will it be recognised and enforceable outside the borders of the jurisdiction that rendered the decision? Can AI-generated reasoning meet the requirements of due process and public policy considerations under PIL frameworks?[93]

---

[92] See infra Sect. 5.3 on the HCCH 1971 Convention on Traffic Accidents.

[93] See infra Sect. 5.1 on the HCCH 2019 Judgments Convention.

Given these questions, is the principle of functional equivalence still relevant and desirable when considering PIL issues relating to AI-powered transactions and applications, and what are the limits to functional equivalence in this context?[94] Much like the principle of technology neutrality, the unique features of autonomy, opacity and unpredictability that AI applications possess may suggest that strict adherence to the principle of functional equivalence may be increasingly difficult. In this regard, PIL frameworks may have to evolve new legal categories for AI-created rights and obligations that distinguish between human-initiated and AI-autonomous agreements. Novel connecting factors and grounds for jurisdiction, such as algorithmic jurisdiction rules to determine the appropriate forum on the basis of where an AI system is trained, deployed, or substantially controlled, may need to be studied and considered.

Certain transparency and accountability safeguards may need to qualify the application of the principle of functional equivalence to AI-powered applications. For example, the application of the principle of functional equivalence may be made subject to carve outs when AI's lack of explainability (the "black box" AI problem)[95] makes it impossible to assess legal responsibility under existing doctrines.

Much as for the principle of technology neutrality, a rigid adherence to functional equivalence may obscure fundamental legal differences introduced by AI. To counter this, PIL may benefit from pursuing a modified functional approach, where functional equivalence is a rebuttable presumption and where decision-makers and lawmakers should assess whether AI applications perform sufficiently similar legal functions before treating them as equivalent. In this respect, instead of imposing a one-size-fits-all model, it may be best to allow for characterisation-specific adaptations, such that different AI applications, for example, AI-generated contractual harms as opposed to AI-generated tortious harms, may be assessed under tailored legal frameworks. Again, international coordination on this topic may allow PIL to evolve to meet the challenges posed by AI to the functional equivalence principle without abandoning the principle entirely.

AI challenges the assumption that all new technologies can be easily assimilated into PIL through functional equivalence. While functional equivalence remains a valuable tool, a strict application of the principle risks legal uncertainty and potential gaps in responsibility. Rather than posing a binary question of whether functional equivalence is possible, the real challenge is how PIL can balance continuity with innovation, ensuring that AI is regulated effectively while preserving the core objectives of PIL.

3.6 Characterisation

Characterisation is a foundational concept in PIL that determines the legal category under which a dispute falls, thereby identifying the applicable conflict-of-laws

[94] See supra note 88.

[95] See supra note 84.

rules.[96] This process allows courts to classify legal issues (e.g., contract, tort, property, or procedural law) before applying the relevant jurisdictional and choice-of-law rules. Traditionally, characterisation has been based on human-driven transactions and well-established legal categories. However, AI challenges these traditional methodologies and may require a rethinking of categorisation approaches to ensure legal certainty and fairness.

One of the fundamental assumptions of characterisation is that legal disputes can be clearly classified into established categories. However, AI blurs traditional distinctions between contracts, torts, property, and regulatory issues. For example:

a. In AI-generated contracts: Can an agreement formed through substantial reliance on AI-enabled processes (e.g., dynamic pricing algorithms, or automated trading bots) be classified under traditional contract law, or does it require a new legal category?
b. In AI-caused harm: If an AI system causes financial losses or reputational damage, should it be treated as a tort (e.g., negligence) or as a product liability issue?
c. AI as property vs. AI as an actor: Some AI applications function as tools, while others perform decision-making functions with varying degrees of autonomy. Should AI be treated as an asset, a service, or a decision-making system?

Characterisation also determines who bears legal responsibility in AI-related disputes. However, AI's ability to act autonomously or semi-autonomously raises the question of whether traditional liability frameworks apply. For example, if an AI-enabled autonomous vehicle causes an accident, is the case one of simple tortious harm and, if so, is it a case of driver liability, manufacturer liability, or AI-specific liability? If an AI-driven chatbot defames a person, should it be classified as a tort claim (and if so, against whom) or as a data protection issue? These uncertainties suggest that existing characterisation methods may struggle to classify AI-related disputes within traditional PIL categories.

Despite these challenges, characterisation remains a necessary function in PIL. Characterisation provides decision-makers with a structured, familiar and well-accepted method for resolving cross-border AI disputes. Consistent application of characterisation rules also prevents legal fragmentation, ensuring AI-related cases are treated similarly in different jurisdictions.[97] It is also arguable that many AI disputes can still be resolved under existing characterisation categories, provided adaptive interpretation techniques are adopted. However, attempting to fit AI into outdated characterisation methodologies could lead to incorrect or unfair legal outcomes. There is also the risk that, without AI-specific classification frameworks, the inconsistent characterisation of AI-related disputes may lead to legal uncertainty.

One possible way forward is for PIL to adopt new approaches and methodologies for characterising AI-related disputes. Three possible suggestions may be considered in this regard. First, functional characterisation may be helpful to ensure accurate

[96] Unger (1937).
[97] Schulze (2006).

characterisation of AI-related disputes. This entails, instead of forcing AI disputes into rigid categories, the assessment by courts and decision-makers of the function performed by the AI system, for example, decision-making, content creation, or autonomous transactions, and classifying disputes accordingly. Second, novel algorithmic connecting factors specific to AI may need to be studied. These include the location of the AI's training data or model development in the case of algorithmic decision-making, the jurisdiction where the AI's decisions take effect in liability cases, and the governing jurisdiction of the AI's developer where regulatory oversight is relevant. Third, AI-specific characterisation methodologies and frameworks may need to be developed, harmonised and codified where necessary and relevant, especially at the global level. The goal would be to modernise the approaches and methodologies used in characterisation to ensure that AI-related disputes can be effectively resolved within existing PIL structures while adapting to the realities of autonomous decision-making and digital transformation.

3.7 Conclusion: Modernising Approaches to the Basic Tenets of PIL

This section has sought to discuss the challenges posed by AI to the traditional approaches taken to the basic tenets of PIL. These basic tenets of PIL—party autonomy, objective connecting factors, grounds for jurisdiction, technology neutrality, functional equivalence, and characterisation—affect the three pillars of PIL, as they are determinative of questions relating to jurisdiction, applicable law, and the recognition and enforcement of foreign decisions. Agreement at the global level on the contemporary interpretation and application of the basic tenets of PIL has allowed the international community to build international cooperation mechanisms and agreements that aim at the progressive unification of the rules of PIL. The advent of AI-enabled and AI-powered applications risks disrupting the long legacy of PIL in providing legal certainty for individuals, businesses and other operators in cross-border situations.

To mitigate these issues, this section has discussed several approaches to modernise approaches to PIL rules. Updating traditional approaches to foundational tenets of PIL to incorporate digital elements such as data origin, server location, or the place of establishment or substantial control of the algorithm's developers can help provide a more accurate reflection of the AI ecosystem and ensure the continued relevance of foundational approaches to PIL. Moreover, harmonisation and progressive legislation at the global level remain key to ensuring that PIL frameworks remain fit for purpose in the face of challenges posed by AI. Developing new international frameworks or updating existing ones, including those under the auspices of the HCCH, to specifically address the unique challenges posed by AI can enhance predictability and uniformity in cross-border disputes. In this regard, cross-border cooperation mechanisms, including the exchange of technical expertise and judicial experience regarding AI systems, can help overcome the hurdles posed by AI. A more flexible, technology-aware approach may also benefit decision-makers and lawmakers, ensuring that both traditional and digital connecting factors are considered in tandem so as to accurately reflect the complex nature of AI-driven disputes.

AI applications may challenge traditional approaches to and tenets of PIL by undermining the efficacy of established connecting factors, complicating the determination of the applicable law, and raising uncertainties in jurisdictional and enforcement matters. Real-world examples, from autonomous vehicles to smart contracts, illustrate that the borderless nature of AI demands an evolution of PIL approaches and methodologies to ensure that disputes can be resolved fairly and predictably in a globalised digital environment.

4 Public Policy and Overriding Mandatory Rules

AI applications intersect with PIL in ways that may necessitate the application of public policy considerations and overriding mandatory rules.[98] These rules ensure that certain fundamental legal and ethical standards are maintained, regardless of the parties' contractual choices or the chosen PIL framework. As such, public policy considerations and overriding mandatory rules generally qualify party autonomy. In some cases, public policy and mandatory rules may also limit the usual application of PIL rules, subjecting the traditional PIL framework to the relevant regulatory regime that may apply.[99]

Key public policy and mandatory rules that may be particularly relevant in considering PIL issues arising from AI applications include cybersecurity and other security regulations, digital sovereignty considerations, the ethical and human rights standards in domestic law, frameworks in domestic law for certain regulated markets, data protection regulations, public safety, consumer protection, product liability and safety standards, employment and labour law, and the application of international agreements and frameworks in domestic jurisdictions. This section will look at each of these in turn.

Cybersecurity and other security regulations: AI systems that interact with critical infrastructure or manage sensitive data may be subject to rigorous cybersecurity regulations. These laws apply regardless of any international contractual framework and are designed to prevent breaches that could have widespread ramifications. Moreover, AI applications that impact national security, such as those used in defence, surveillance, or critical public services, must adhere to strict regulatory controls. Such regulatory controls may constitute or operate as overriding mandatory rules,

[98] See generally Lehmann (2020).

[99] Mills (2008).

ensuring that national interests take precedence over private contractual autonomy in cross-border disputes.[100]

Digital sovereignty: Digital sovereignty refers to a State's ability to regulate and control digital technologies, data flows, and AI operations within its territorial jurisdiction. Digital sovereignty has emerged as a significant public policy concern that may override or limit the principle of party autonomy in PIL.[101] Different jurisdictions assert control over AI operations in various ways, creating diverse public policy considerations that qualify PIL rules. For example, some States have data localisation laws that require AI-driven data processing to occur within national borders. Contracts allowing data to be processed in third States may be adjudged unenforceable under public policy rules. Other controls include regulations that require explainability and fairness in AI decision-making, as well as export controls on AI technologies.[102] A contractual choice of law that contravenes these digital sovereignty considerations may be challenged on public policy grounds.

Protection of human rights: There is growing recognition that AI applications must operate in line with fundamental human rights standards. This includes ensuring that algorithms do not perpetuate discrimination or violate human rights protections, including privacy. Mandatory human rights laws can override contractual choices if an AI-driven decision adversely affects an individual's fundamental rights. In some jurisdictions, emerging frameworks or guidelines on ethical AI require that AI systems maintain transparency, accountability, and fairness. These frameworks on ethics in the use of AI may eventually acquire mandatory status, given the grave concerns relating to inherent programmed and algorithmic bias, as well as the growing realisation of the importance of regulatory oversight to ensure anti-discrimination and human rights protections in the use of AI.[103]

Regulated markets: As AI-driven technologies increasingly shape financial markets, securities trading, and investment decision-making, regulators worldwide have taken steps to assert control over AI operations that transcend borders. The use of AI in regulated markets, such as securities trading, algorithmic trading, robo-advisory services, and fraud detection, raises systemic risk concerns, prompting jurisdictions to impose mandatory regulatory controls that override party autonomy in PIL.[104]

Data protection regulations: Many jurisdictions enforce data protection and privacy regulations that apply to AI systems processing personal data. These rules are non-negotiable, meaning that even if parties opt for a foreign law through contractual clauses, the local mandatory data protection provisions will still govern the

---

[100] For example, see the perspective of the United States of America, as described in Coyle (2019).

[101] Dimitropoulos (2022–2023).

[102] See generally De Gregorio (2021).

[103] For an excellent exposition of the role of PIL in global governance, and its need to take human rights considerations into account, see Watt (2011).

[104] For an analysis of how PIL frameworks may be subject to the regulatory framework in certain regulated markets, see generally Bradley (2005–2006). See also Watt (2015), Wittmann (2023). Lehmann (2018).

processing of personal data. One example is the EU's General Data Protection Regulation (GDPR), which may have certain extraterritorial effects, applying not only to business entities established in the EU, but also to non-EU companies operating within the EU market on the basis of the market location principle.[105]

Public safety: In many jurisdictions, mandatory liability rules dictate how responsibility is allocated in cases of harm caused by AI-related errors. These rules are designed to protect public welfare and cannot be circumvented by contractual provisions, ensuring that manufacturers and operators remain accountable.[106]

Consumer protection: AI-driven products and services, such as autonomous vehicles or smart consumer devices, are subject to national consumer protection standards.[107] These mandatory rules protect consumers from unfair contract terms or unsafe products,[108] ensuring that the law of the consumer's domicile may override contractual choices made via AI platforms.

Product liability and safety standards: Autonomous vehicles, medical devices, and other AI-driven products must comply with local safety and product liability regulations. Even when parties agree to foreign law governing their contractual relationship, mandatory safety standards remain binding to protect public safety.[109] For example, if an AI-enabled car causes an accident abroad, the applicable product liability rules of the affected jurisdiction may still apply.

Employment and labour law: AI applications used in recruitment, performance evaluation, or workforce management are increasingly subject to local labour laws that safeguard employee rights.[110] These laws, which include non-derogable labour standards and are often viewed as overriding mandatory provisions, ensure that even if an employer uses AI to automate employment decisions, the employer must comply with local minimum standards and anti-discrimination provisions. Regulations may require transparency and fairness in AI-driven employment decisions to protect employees or job candidates against algorithmic bias, overriding any choice of law that might otherwise favour an employer's discretion. This ensures that workers are not adversely impacted by opaque AI processes.

International agreements and frameworks: As the use of AI becomes increasingly pervasive, there is growing discussion around establishing international standards or conventions that specifically address AI-related disputes. These new norms

---

[105] See for an overview of the application of the GDPR to AI applications, European Parliamentary Research Service, Scientific Foresight Unit, The impact of the General Data Protection Regulation (GDPR) on artificial intelligence (June 2020), online at https://www.europarl.europa.eu/RegData/etudes/STUD/2020/641530/EPRS_STU(2020)641530_EN.pdf.

[106] Akkermans (2020).

[107] Schu (1996).

[108] Tang (2010).

[109] Dutson (1999). For a historical overview of global PIL frameworks for product liability, see Saunders (1972). A more recent European perspective is provided by Illmer (2009).

[110] Employment law and labour law have traditionally been specific exceptions to party autonomy in PIL frameworks, see for a European perspective Grušić (2015). Another excellent overview is Carballo Piñeiro and Piñeiro (2015).

could impose mandatory rules, including minimum safety standards or accountability measures, that would override private contractual agreements in cross-border disputes.

In summary, a range of public policy considerations and overriding mandatory rules must be observed when AI applications are involved. These public policy considerations and overriding mandatory rules qualify party autonomy to ensure that AI applications operate in a manner that protects public welfare and individual rights. As AI continues to evolve, both domestic and international legal frameworks will likely see further development of these mandatory rules to address the unique challenges posed by emerging technologies.

5 Current International PIL Framework and AI: The Impact of AI on the Conventions and Normative Work of the HCCH

The HCCH is an intergovernmental organisation the mandate of which is "the progressive unification of the rules of private international law".[111] The HCCH's mission is to provide a forum for its Members for the development and implementation of common rules of PIL to co-ordinate the relationships between different private law systems in international situations, and to promote international judicial and administrative co-operation in the fields of protection of the family and children, civil procedure and commercial law. The work of the HCCH focuses on global PIL frameworks that provide certainty as to which authority has jurisdiction, which law is applicable, how decisions are recognised and enforced, and what co-operation mechanisms are available to overcome challenges arising from cross-border judicial or administrative procedures.[112]

The normative work of the HCCH consists of the negotiation and adoption of Conventions and other legal instruments that respond to global needs. Since its inception, over 40 Conventions and instruments have been adopted under the auspices of the HCCH. By way of case studies, this section takes a look at how AI impacts five of these 40 Conventions and instruments:

a. HCCH 2019 Judgments Convention[113];
b. HCCH 2005 Choice of Court Convention[114];

[111] Art. 1, Statute of the Hague Conference on Private International Law, entered into force 15 Jul 1955. https://assets.hcch.net/docs/d7d051ae-6dd1-4881-a3b5-f7dbcaad02ea.pdf.

[112] HCCH, "About the HCCH", online at https://www.hcch.net/en/about.

[113] Convention of 2 July 2019 on the Recognition and Enforcement of Foreign Judgments in Civil or Commercial Matters. https://assets.hcch.net/docs/806e290e-bbd8-413d-b15e-8e3e1bf1496d.pdf.

[114] Convention of 30 June 2005 on Choice of Court Agreements. https://assets.hcch.net/docs/510bc238-7318-47ed-9ed5-e0972510d98b.pdf.

c. HCCH 1971 Traffic Accidents Convention[115];
d. HCCH 1970 Evidence Convention[116]; and
e. HCCH 1965 Service Convention.[117]

5.1 HCCH 2019 Judgments Convention

The HCCH 2019 Judgments Convention[118] facilitates the circulation of judgments among its Contracting Parties.[119] By establishing conditions for recognition and enforcement, and possible grounds for their refusal, the Convention provides certainty and predictability for those operating in transnational civil or commercial situations. This ensures that a successful party will have a meaningful judgment, enhancing their access to justice by reducing timeframes, costs, and risks. It also allows a plaintiff to make an informed decision as to where to initiate proceedings, taking into account where a judgment will be recognised and enforced.

The Convention applies to the recognition and enforcement of judgments in civil or commercial matters (Art. 1), including consumer and individual employment contracts. The Convention excludes certain matters from its scope, such as the status and legal capacity of natural persons, family law matters, insolvency, privacy, intellectual property, and certain anti-trust matters (Art. 2(1)). In addition, it applies neither to arbitration and related proceedings (Art. 2(3)), nor to interim measures of protection (Art. 3(1)(b)). Contracting Parties may also declare that the Convention does not apply to other specific matters (Art. 18(1)).

The Convention establishes a common framework under which judgments from one Contracting Party will be recognised and / or enforced in another if they are eligible for circulation and the grounds for refusal do not apply. The Convention provides a list of criteria to be used by the court addressed to ascertain whether the judgment is eligible for recognition and enforcement. A judgment will be eligible for circulation under the Convention if any of the criteria listed in Article 5(1) are satisfied. An exclusive basis is provided in Article 6 for judgments ruling on rights *in rem* in immovable property, which would be eligible for circulation if, and only if, the immovable property is situated in the State of origin.

These are minimum requirements for recognition and enforcement; that is, the Convention does not prevent or limit the recognition and enforcement of judgments

[115] Convention of 4 May 1971 on the Law Applicable to Traffic Accidents. https://assets.hcch.net/docs/abcf969d-bac2-4ad5-bf52-f1aabc0939ad.pdf.

[116] Convention of 18 March 1970 on the Taking of Evidence Abroad in Civil or Commercial Matters. https://assets.hcch.net/docs/dfed98c0-6749-42d2-a9be-3d41597734f1.pdf.

[117] Convention of 15 November 1965 on the Service Abroad of Judicial and Extrajudicial Documents in Civil or Commercial Matters. https://assets.hcch.net/docs/f4520725-8cbd-4c71-b402-5aae1994d14c.pdf.

[118] Concluded 2 Jul 2019, entered into force 1 Sep 2023. Article numbers in this section refer to the HCCH 2019 Judgments Convention.

[119] HCCH, Outline: HCCH 2019 Judgments Convention, https://assets.hcch.net/docs/36b240ac-8228-481d-a33b-3716baf4c656.pdf.

under national law, bilateral, regional or other international instruments (Arts 15 and 23), with the exception of Article 6. In this sense, the Convention provides a "floor" rather than a "ceiling" for the recognition and enforcement of foreign judgments.

AI applications in international disputes could impact the enforcement of foreign judgments under the HCCH 2019 Judgments Convention. Questions arise about whether decisions produced with substantial reliance on AI systems satisfy the requirements applicable to court judgments for the purposes of recognition and enforcement.[120] Moreover, when decisions are rendered in disputes involving AI, especially those arising from novel contractual or tort scenarios, the process of obtaining reciprocal recognition and enforcement of judgments may be complicated. Courts in different jurisdictions may be reluctant to enforce decisions that rest on ambiguous jurisdictional links.

Consider a dispute in which an AI system is substantially relied upon in rendering a decision in a commercial matter involving an AI-generated contract. If one party would like to enforce that decision in another State, and if both countries are Contracting Parties to the Convention, the Convention's framework would be invoked. However, questions arise regarding transparency and accountability when the judgment is generated by, or is heavily reliant on, a "black box" algorithm.[121] Key considerations may include transparency requirements that AI-generated or AI-assisted judgments must meet, or enforcement may be denied on public policy grounds. Explicit AI-specific criteria may thus be necessary to ensure that AI-influenced judicial decisions meet due process standards before being enforced across borders.

5.2 *HCCH 2005 Choice of Court Convention*

The HCCH 2005 Choice of Court Convention[122] is aimed at ensuring the effectiveness of choice of court agreements (also known as "forum selection clauses") between parties to international commercial transactions.[123] It does so by ensuring that parties' choice of forum is upheld by courts, thereby enhancing access to justice and creating a climate more favourable to international trade and investment.

The Convention applies in international cases to exclusive choice of court agreements concluded in civil or commercial matters (Art. 1). It may apply to non-exclusive choice of court agreements, in accordance with reciprocal declarations made by Contracting Parties (Art. 22). A case is "international" where the parties are not

[120] Said et al. (2023).

[121] For similar considerations in the context of arbitration, see Kasap (2021).

[122] Concluded 30 Jun 2005, entered into force 1 Oct 2015. Article numbers in this section refer to the HCCH 2005 Choice of Court Convention.

[123] HCCH, Outline: HCCH 2005 Choice of Court Convention. https://assets.hcch.net/docs/89be0bce-36c7-4701-af9a-1f27be046125.pdf.

resident in the same Contracting Party and their relationship and all other elements relevant to the dispute are not connected only with that Contracting Party.

The agreement must be concluded in writing or in another form of communication that renders the information accessible (Art. 3). The Convention does not apply to consumer and employment contracts, nor to other specified "excluded matters" (Art. 2). Contracting Parties may also choose to exclude other specific matters (Art. 21).

Subject to some exceptions, the Convention contains three key obligations:

a. The chosen court must hear the dispute (Art. 5), ensuring predictability of the forum, as chosen by the parties.
b. Any non-chosen court must suspend / dismiss proceedings, in favour of the chosen court (Art. 6), preventing parallel proceedings.
c. Judgments given by the chosen court must be recognised and enforced in other Contracting Parties (Art. 8), ensuring their global circulation.

In many commercial digital environments, AI systems (or smart contracts on blockchain platforms) may automatically incorporate forum selection clauses. When a dispute arises, for example, regarding a defective AI-powered product, these pre-set clauses may purport to determine which court should hear the case. AI may generate standardised clauses that favour the platform's home jurisdiction, potentially disadvantaging the counter-party. Even though the parties appear to have chosen a forum, questions of fairness and consent arise, particularly if the clause was imposed algorithmically.

Should a judgment be rendered by a court chosen via an AI-selected or AI-inserted clause, disputes that may arise in relation to the Convention's mechanisms may focus on whether the automated process provided a real choice to the parties to the agreement. Moreover, recognition and enforcement of the judgment may be refused if it "would be manifestly incompatible with the public policy of the requested State, including situations where the specific proceedings leading to the judgment were incompatible with fundamental principles of procedural fairness of that State" (Art. 9(e)).

5.3 HCCH 1971 Traffic Accidents Convention

Traffic accidents constitute one of the most voluminous sources of non-contractual obligations worldwide. Increasing cross-border traffic and transport lead to growing numbers of traffic accidents that include international elements. In order to determine questions of liability, the existence, kinds and extent of damages, and the applicability of rules of prescription and limitation, it is crucial to be able to determine *ex ante* and with certainty what law applies to these questions. The HCCH 1971 Traffic Accidents

Convention's[124] primary aim is to provide clear, precise and easily applicable rules to determine what law applies to a traffic accident.

The main rule of the Convention is that the applicable law is the internal law of the State where the accident occurred (Art. 3).[125] The Convention also provides for subcategories of rules based on the registration of the vehicle and the habitual residence of the person(s) involved, for a certain number of specific groups of situations where these are more connected with a different legal environment than that of the place of the accident. The Convention allows the law of the place of the accident to be set aside according to two criteria: (1) whether one or more vehicles are involved, and (2) whether the person(s) involved is / are (a) the owner, person in control of the vehicle or the driver, (b) a passenger, or (c) a person outside the vehicle (Art. 4). Where there is damage to goods, goods belonging to the passenger follow the regime that applies to the passenger under Articles 3 and 4. Liability for goods outside the vehicle is, in principle, determined by the law of the place of the accident (Art. 5).

AI-powered autonomous vehicles operating across borders challenge the application of existing liability frameworks. Where an autonomous vehicle operated by a sophisticated AI system causes an accident in a State different from where the vehicle is manufactured or where the AI system was developed, in principle the HCCH 1971 Traffic Accidents Convention could be applied to determine which law is applicable to the incident.

However, with AI, the "place of the accident", may remain physically identifiable while failing to capture all relevant elements of causation where the accident is linked to algorithmic decision-making, remote software updates, or other AI-related malfunctions involving online or decentralised data processing. Moreover, if an accident involves elements from multiple jurisdictions, for example, hardware from one State, software from another, and an accident occurring in a third, applying the framework of the HCCH 1971 Traffic Accidents Convention may become complex. Courts may have to consider whether, in the case of accidents involving AI-powered autonomous vehicles, the notion of "place of the accident" adequately captures the connecting factor to determine the law applicable to such incidents.

5.4 HCCH 1970 Evidence Convention

In international judicial proceedings, the process of obtaining evidence across borders is often complicated by differences between legal systems, including those based on the civil and common law traditions. The HCCH 1970 Evidence Convention[126]

[124] Concluded 4 May 1971, entered into force 3 Jun 1975. Article numbers in this section refer to the HCCH 1971 Traffic Accidents Convention.

[125] HCCH. Outline: HCCH 1971 Traffic Accidents Convention. https://assets.hcch.net/docs/545975a7-8a1b-48cd-85d5-150e0d980640.pdf.

[126] Concluded 18 Mar 1970, entered into force 7 Oct 1972. Article numbers in this section refer to the HCCH 1970 Evidence Convention.

seeks to overcome these differences by establishing a uniform framework of cooperation mechanisms to facilitate and streamline the taking of evidence abroad. The Convention achieves this with two separate and independent systems: (a) Chapter I: Letters of Request and (b) Chapter II: diplomatic officers, consular agents, and commissioners.[127]

Under Chapter I, a judicial authority of one Contracting Party may request another Contracting Party to obtain evidence, or perform some other judicial act, using a Letter of Request sent to the Central Authority of the other Contracting Party. The request must relate to evidence for use in judicial proceedings that are commenced or contemplated (Art. 1). The judicial authority that executes a Letter of Request shall apply its own law to the methods and procedures to be followed (Art. 9), including in relation to the use of any appropriate measures of compulsion (Art. 10). However, the requesting authority may ask that a special method or procedure be followed (Art. 9). This method of taking of evidence is available to all Contracting Parties to the Convention.

Under Chapter II, a diplomatic officer or consular agent of a Contracting Party may, without compulsion, take evidence of nationals of the State that officer or agent represents (Art. 15). This may be subject to permission from the appropriate authority in the State where the evidence is taken. A diplomatic officer, consular agent, or commissioner may also, without compulsion, take evidence of other nationals if permission to do so has been granted by the competent authority of the Contracting Party in which evidence is to be taken (Arts 16 and 17). The Convention also provides a mechanism to obtain evidence by compulsion (Art. 18). The diplomatic officer, consular agent, or commissioner shall apply the law of the court before which the action is pending, unless incompatible with the law of the Contracting Party where the evidence is taken or contrary to permission granted (Art. 21). Contracting Parties may exclude, in whole or in part, application of this Chapter of the Convention (Art. 33).

The technology-neutral language of the Convention allows Contracting Parties to use modern technology in the transmission and execution of requests. This includes the use of videolinks to assist in the taking of evidence under both Chapter I and Chapter II of the Convention, with approaches varying between Contracting Parties.[128]

AI presents several challenges to the taking of evidence under the HCCH 1970 Evidence Convention, particularly concerning the authenticity, reliability, and processing of evidence, including in remote evidence-gathering methods such as video links. First, the potential use of AI-generated evidence such as deepfake videos, synthetic voices, and AI-assisted document generation, may raise questions about

[127] HCCH. Outline of the HCCH 1970 Evidence Convention. https://assets.hcch.net/docs/ec1fc148-c2b1-49dc-ba2f-65f45cb2b2d3.pdf.

[128] HCCH. 1970 Evidence Convention Guide to Good Practice: The Use of Video-Link. https://assets.hcch.net/docs/569cfb46-9bb2-45e0-b240-ec02645ac20d.pdf. An updated Practical Handbook for the Convention, incorporating an updated version of this Guide to Good Practice, is forthcoming in mid-2025.

authenticity. AI-powered deepfake technology can be used to manipulate video testimony, making it difficult to ensure witness identity and credibility. AI-powered real-time voice alteration tools can allow a third party to impersonate a witness, complicating authentication. Courts may also struggle to determine whether AI-altered evidence has been manipulated. Moreover, AI-assisted transcription, translation, or analysis tools may introduce bias or errors that affect the integrity of evidence. There may also be legal and procedural challenges relating to AI-generated summaries of depositions, where some AI systems may automatically summarise or filter testimony, affecting its completeness and accuracy.

As AI technology advances, the HCCH 1970 Evidence Convention may need amendments or interpretative guidance to ensure its continued effectiveness in an era of AI-driven litigation. Protocols for AI-assisted evidence-taking may need to be developed, ensuring uniformity in cross-border litigation.

5.5 *HCCH 1965 Service Convention*

Service is an essential part of any legal proceeding, but one that can be costly and time-consuming in cross-border cases. The HCCH 1965 Service Convention[129] seeks to simplify this process, establishing a uniform framework designed to facilitate and streamline the channels of transmission for judicial or extrajudicial documents to be served abroad.[130] The Convention provides for one main channel of transmission between Contracting Parties, while preserving flexibility to use alternative channels. The Convention deals primarily with the transmission of documents and does not address or comprise substantive rules relating to the actual service of process.

The Convention applies where: (i) there is a judicial or extrajudicial document, (ii) that is to be transmitted for service from one Contracting Party to another, (iii) the address of the person to be served is known, and (iv) the document to be served relates to a civil or commercial matter (Art. 1). The Convention is exclusive, which means that, if these requirements are met, the transmission channels provided for under the Convention must be applied. In relation to the requirement of transmission to another Contracting Party, it is important to note that it remains for the law of the forum to determine whether transmission abroad is necessary.

The main channel of transmission under the Convention is where an authority or judicial officer competent under the law of one Contracting Party transmits a request for service to the Central Authority of the Contracting Party in which service is to be effected (Art. 5). The request must conform to the Model Form annexed to the Convention. The Central Authority of the requested Contracting Party shall, under its own law, serve the document or arrange for its service by a competent authority

[129] Concluded 15 Nov 1965, entered into force 10 Feb 1969. Article numbers in this section refer to the HCCH 1965 Service Convention.

[130] HCCH. Outline: HCCH 1965 Service Convention. https://assets.hcch.net/docs/f4ccc07b-55ed-4ea7-8fb9-8a2b28549e1d.pdf.

(Art. 5). However, the applicant (i.e., the forwarding authority in the requesting Contracting Party) may request that a particular method or procedure be used, to the extent that it is not incompatible with the law of the requested Contracting Party. Finally, the authority executing the request must complete the certificate annexed to the Convention, stating that service was effected, or if not, the reasons that prevented service (Art. 6).

The Convention preserves the freedom of Contracting Parties to use alternative channels of transmission, including through:

- diplomatic or consular channels (Arts 8 and 9);
- postal channels (Art. 10(a));
- direct communication between judicial officers, officials or other competent persons (Art. 10(b)); and
- direct communication between an interested party and judicial officers, officials or other competent persons (Art. 10(c)).

The technology-neutral language of the Convention allows Contracting Parties to use modern technology in the transmission and execution of requests. In practice, this is generally subject to the law of the requested Contracting Party.

AI may present challenges to the practical operation of the HCCH 1965 Service Convention. These challenges primarily relate to the authenticity, reliability, and legality of AI-assisted methods of transmission or service, where permitted by the applicable law, as well as the potential implications for due process.

AI-powered process servers and automated legal bots may be used, or proposed for use, to identify recipients, assist with address verification, or facilitate digital transmission where such methods are permitted. AI-based email tracking or chatbots might simulate acknowledgment of receipt, raising questions of consent and due process. For example, an AI-generated email notification may not guarantee that the recipient actually received or understood the legal documents, raising issues under domestic rules on proper notice and, where relevant, the Convention's requirement of proper notice in its framework for transmission abroad.

Moreover, there may be challenges to the validity of AI-generated proofs of service. AI-generated confirmation of service, such as digital certificates and blockchain-based proof, may not be recognised as equivalent to traditional service under the Convention. Additionally, AI-generated deepfake emails, fake domain names, or impersonation software may be used to simulate service of process, making it harder to verify authenticity and raising risks of fraudulent or manipulated service. For example, a party might claim that an AI-generated fake email confirmation acknowledged receipt of legal documents, when in reality, no valid service occurred.

5.6 AI and the Current Normative Work of the HCCH

The evolution of AI is forcing a re-examination of how established international legal instruments apply to new technological realities. As the uses and applications of AI become more prevalent, the PIL frameworks enshrined in the HCCH Conventions must adapt to ensure that international legal cooperation remains robust in the face of AI's rapid expansion.

Since 2020, following on the mandate of its governing body, the Council on General Affairs and Policy of the HCCH (CGAP), the Permanent Bureau (PB) of the HCCH has studied the impact of recent developments in the digital economy, with the aim of identifying PIL issues for potential future work. The mandate includes monitoring of developments with respect to digital platforms, AI and automated contracting, immersive technologies, and decentralised autonomous organisations (DAOs).

The PB has continued to monitor PIL developments in relation to AI and automated contracting, including developments in legislation and jurisprudence in the field. While automated contracting is not a new concept, having been the basis of applications such as point-of-sale systems and electronic data interchange (EDI) for many decades, the use of automated contracting has dramatically expanded with the growth of the digital economy.[131] Today, the use of automated contracting in smart contracts, computable contracts, and algorithmic contracts has meant an increased reliance on AI in both commercial and end-user contracts.[132] In particular, transactions conducted on online platforms and smart devices (including high-frequency trading transactions) can involve interactions between a human and an automated system, or interactions between automated systems (referred to as "M2M contracting"). Automation at the different stages of the contract life cycle, together with legal tech software that automate applications in the contract life cycle from drafting to negotiation and management to analysis,[133] allows for the streamlining and systematising of cross-border contracting on digital platforms.

The monitoring conducted by the PB has validated many of the PIL questions that developments in AI and automated contracting have raised[134]:

a. Determination of applicable law: When AI-driven technologies perform acts or take part in transactions, the online nature of most AI-driven systems may make traditional connecting factors difficult to apply.
b. Jurisdiction: The use of AI-driven systems may make determining jurisdiction difficult due to the challenges in determining location on online platforms. These challenges may also include the application of the *forum non conveniens* doctrine, where relevant. Another challenge relates to the identification of the type of harm that an AI-driven system may cause, and to the localisation of such harm, since, traditionally, *situs*-based PIL connecting factors may not be useful in linking the occurrence of the damage with a certain jurisdiction. For example, a generative AI-driven online or networked system that is not localised to a particular *situs*

[131] Martin-Bariteau and Pavlović (2021 pp. 4ff).

[132] Id.

[133] See Ebers (2022).

[134] HCCH, "Private International Law Aspects of the Digital Economy: Report", Prel. Doc. No 5A of February 2024, online at https://assets.hcch.net/docs/b74f3bfe-51dd-4d0e-8d4b-59e5e32367da.pdf, paras 10–11.

may scrape data from one website in a particular jurisdiction to generate new content on another website sited elsewhere.[135]

c. Recognition and enforcement: The enforcement of foreign judgments may be challenging as a result of various jurisdictions' approaches to AI-driven systems, with public policy and other concerns potentially presenting obstacles to the recognition and enforcement of decisions and judgments both in situations where AI-driven algorithms and tools are partially involved, and where they are empowered to render final decisions.

At the time of writing, the HCCH continues with its work of monitoring these developments at the Secretariat level under its Digital Economy Project.[136]

6 AI and the Future Development of PIL

Before closing the chapter, a look at the potential of AI to contribute positively to the future development of PIL seems warranted. Can AI be beneficial to the discipline as a whole, and can its capabilities, such as enhancing efficiency, consistency, and predictive power in legal processes, be of assistance to the future development of PIL? As Melvin Kranzberg's First Law of Technology states, "Technology is neither good nor bad; nor is it neutral."[137] It is in our use of the relevant technology that its impact is determined. So, what role can AI play in the progressive unification of PIL?

AI can streamline legal research and comparative analysis, a capacity that is of particular utility in a field that requires an across-the-board review of vast amounts of case law, treaties, and statutes across multiple jurisdictions.[138] By leveraging natural language processing and machine learning, AI tools can identify patterns, similarities, and discrepancies in how laws are applied in different countries.[139] This can contribute to a more consistent application of legal principles by comparing judicial decisions across jurisdictions. It can help identify trends where different legal systems converge or diverge, thereby informing efforts to harmonise conflict-of-law rules.[140]

AI can also enhance legal certainty through predictive analysis.[141] Machine learning models can be trained on past cross-border disputes to estimate the likely outcomes of similar cases. For instance, if an autonomous vehicle accident involves parties from several countries, AI can analyse previous judgments to offer guidance

135 Ho-Dac and Pellegrini (2023).

136 See supra note 85.

137 Kranzberg (1986).

138 For an analogy to other fields of research, see Meyer et al. (2023).

139 Mok and Mok (2019).

140 See generally Miganelli (2020).

141 Eboigbe (2024).

on which law courts would be likely to find applicable. This data-driven insight may aid parties and policymakers in making more informed decisions.

Additionally, AI can streamline dispute resolution by automating routine aspects of litigation processes. This not only accelerates the process but also reduces costs and increases access to justice for parties involved in cross-border disputes. For example, AI-driven ODR platforms can manage documentation, translate materials, and even propose settlement options based on historical data. In disputes arising from online transactions or AI-generated contracts, such case management platforms can provide preliminary assessments or recommendations that, while subject to human oversight, help narrow down the contentious issues quickly.[142]

By aggregating and analysing data from diverse sources, AI can offer insights into the evolving landscape of cross-border legal disputes. This information can be crucial for policymakers aiming to reform existing PIL frameworks to address the challenges posed by digital and AI-driven transactions. Governments and international bodies can use AI to monitor trends in disputes and adjust PIL reform efforts accordingly. AI may aid in the identification of which traditional connecting factors are increasingly less relevant and support consideration of new criteria, for example data origin or the place of model development, deployment, or substantial control, that better reflect modern realities.

AI is therefore not only a source of challenges for PIL but may also be a powerful tool for its evolution. By improving legal research, promoting consistency in judicial decisions, facilitating progressive development, streamlining dispute resolution, and informing policy reform, AI can help create a more dynamic, efficient, and harmonised PIL framework that better accommodates the complexities of a globalised, digital environment, provided that its use remains subject to human judgment, institutional accountability, and legal safeguards.

7 Conclusion: Some Final Thoughts

AI is reshaping the legal landscape, and PIL must evolve to meet the challenges posed by AI. Effective legal frameworks will ensure AI remains a tool for progress rather than a source of legal uncertainty. This chapter has sought to provide a structured analysis of AI's impact on PIL, offering insights into its challenges, opportunities, and the necessary legal adaptations required in an increasingly AI-driven world.

Isaac Asimov, one of the greatest minds in futurism, once wrote: "There is a single light of science, and to brighten it anywhere is to brighten it everywhere."[143] This sentiment applies to AI's role in PIL. It is a tool that, when properly guided, can illuminate the complexities of cross-border legal frameworks, making them more efficient, consistent, and just.

---

[142] Alessa (2022).

[143] Asimov I. Reprinted in Gruwell and McCourt (2007).

The future of PIL in the AI era must be one of adaptability, cooperation, and ethical responsibility. As global stakeholders, including lawmakers, judges, arbitrators, and technologists, work together to address the legal implications of AI, the guiding principles of justice, fairness, and transparency must remain at the core of such work. AI does not replace the need for human judgment; instead, it may augments human capacity to make better, more informed decisions in an increasingly interconnected world.

By embracing AI's potential while establishing clear guardrails, we can build a PIL framework that is not only resilient but also future-ready. In doing so, we ensure that AI serves as a force for legal certainty, fairness, and progress in a world that continues to leverage technology and law to support the human condition and address our, quintessentially human, vulnerabilities.

References

Akkermans B (2020) Public policy (orde public) a comparative analysis of national, private international law, and EU public policy. Eur Prop Law J 8(3):260

Alessa H (2022) The role of Artificial intelligence in online dispute resolution: a brief and critical overview. Inf & Commun Technol Law 31(3):319–342. https://doi.org/10.1080/13600834.2022.2088060

Allen JG (2021) Cryptoassets in private law. In Chiu I, Deipenbrock G (eds) Routledge handbook of financial technology and law, 1st edn. Routledge. https://doi.org/10.4324/9780429325670

Amazon Web Services (2024) What is AI? https://aws.amazon.com/what-is/artificial-intelligence/

Araromi MA, Oluwabiyi AA, Olaleke AM (2024) Determination of Tort Liability in the Deployment of Artificial Intelligence Technology. JL Pol'y & Globalization 141:29

ASEAN (2024, Feb) Guide on AI Governance and Ethics, p 9. https://asean.org/wp-content/uploads/2024/02/ASEAN-Guide-on-AI-Governance-and-Ethics_beautified_201223_v2.pdf

Asimov I (1968). I, Robot. Grafton Books, New York

Barrat J (2013) Our final invention: artificial intelligence and the end of the human era. Thomas Dunne, New York

Bostrum N (2015) What happens when our computers get smarter than we are? TED2015. https://www.ted.com/talks/nick_bostrom_what_happens_when_our_computers_get_smarter_than_we_are

Bradley C (2005–2006) Private international law-making for the financial markets. Fordham Int'l LJ 29:127

Brooks RA (1991) Intelligence without representation. Artif Intell 47(1–3):139–159. https://doi.org/10.1016/0004-3702(91)90053-M

Carballo Piñeiro L Piñeiro LC (2015) Collective labour relations and private international law. Int Marit Labour Law, 229–311

Chandra S (2021) Private international law and Artificial Intelligence: a critical analysis of jurisdictional claims and governance. Indian J Artificial Intelligence and Law 2(1):31

Chesterman S (2020) Artificial intelligence and the limits of legal personality. Int Comp Law Q69(4):819–844. https://doi.org/10.1017/S0020589320000366

Chesterman S (2024) Good models borrow, great models steal: intellectual property rights and generative AI, Policy and Society. puae006. https://doi.org/10.1093/polsoc/puae006

Conrad JG, Chaudhuri SR, Paul S, Ghosh S (2023). AI & Law: Formative Developments, State-of-the-Art Approaches, Challenges & Opportunities. In Proceedings of the 6th Joint International Conference on Data Science & Management of Data (10th ACM IKDD CODS and

28th COMAD) (CODS-COMAD '23). Association for Computing Machinery, New York, pp. 320–323. https://doi.org/10.1145/3570991.3571050
Coyle JF (2019) The role of public policy in U.S. private international law. unc legal studies research paper. https://doi.org/10.2139/ssrn.3485580
Crevier D (1993) AI: the tumultuous history of the search for artificial intelligence
De Gregorio G (2021) Digital sovereignty and platform governance: a european constitutional laboratory. https://www.giga-net.org/2021SymposiumPapers/Digital%20Sovereignty%20and%20Platform%20Governance.pdf
Depping GB (1830) Histoire du commerce entre le Levant et l'Europe – Tome I, pp 22–23
Dimitropoulos G (2022–2023) Law and digital globalization. U Pa J Int'l L 44:41
Diop CA (1987) Precolonial Black Africa. Laurence Hill Books, Chicago, p 125
Dullea K, Lockwood G, Kubrick S, Clarke AC (1968) 2001: A Space Odyssey
Dutson S (1999) Product liability and private international law: choice of law in tort in England. Am J Comp L 47:129
Ebers M (2022) Artificial intelligence, contracting and contract law. In: Ebers M, Poncibò C, Zou M (eds) Contracting and contract law in the age of artificial intelligence. Bloomsbury, London, p 102
Eboigbe EO (2024) AI in legal analytics: balancing efficiency, accuracy, and ethics in contract and predictive analysis. https://doi.org/10.2139/ssrn.4997519
Estrella Faria JA (2004) E-commerce and international legal harmonization: time to go beyond functional equivalence? SA Mercantile L J 16(4):529
Forbes.com (2024a) 22 top AI statistics and trends in 2024. https://www.forbes.com/advisor/business/ai-statistics/
Forbes.com (2024b) How businesses are using artificial intelligence in 2024. https://www.forbes.com/advisor/business/software/ai-in-business/
Fraser H, Suzor N (2025) Locating fault and responsibility for AI harms: a systems theory of foreseeability, reasonable care and causal responsibility in the AI value chain. Law, Innov Technol 17(2)
Gamillscheg F (1955) Der Einfluss Dumoulins auf die Entwicklung des Kollisionsrechts, De Gruyter, Berlin, Boston
Garland A (2014) Ex machina. A24
Gautier P (1972) Symbola: Les étrangers et la justice dans les cites grecques
Google (2024a) https://gemini.google.com
Google (2024b) What is artificial intelligence (AI)? https://cloud.google.com/learn/what-is-artificial-intelligence
Grušić U (2015) The European private international law of employment. Cambridge University Press.
Gruwell E, McCourt F (2007) The gigantic book of teachers' wisdom. NY: Skyhorse Pub, New York
Haenlein M, Kaplan A (2019) A brief history of artificial intelligence: on the past, present, and future of artificial intelligence. Calif Manag Rev. https://doi.org/10.1177/0008125619864925
Ho-Dac M, Pellegrini C (2023) Governance of artificial intelligence in the European Union: what place for consumer protection? Bruylant, Bruxelles
Hoffman DA, Arbel Y (2024) Generative interpretation. NYU Law Review 99:451
Hsu FH, Anantharaman TS, Campbell MS, Nowatzyk A (1990) Deep thought. In Computers, chess, and cognition. Springer, New York, pp 55–78. https://doi.org/10.1007/978-1-4613-9080-0_5
Huang J (2020) Applicable law to transnational personal data: trends and dynamics. Ger Law J, p 1285
IBM (2024) What is AI? https://www.ibm.com/think/topics/artificial-intelligence
Illmer M (2009) The new European private international law of product liability–steering through troubled waters. Rabels Zeitschrift für ausländisches und internationales Privatrecht/The Rabel Journal of Comparative and International Private Law (H. 2):269–313

Irwan M and Mursyid M (2024) AI-driven traffic accidents: a comparative legal study. Artes Libr Law Soc J 1(1):1–20. https://doi.org/10.12345/jxt3j717
Jayme E (1991) L'autonomie de la volonté des parties dans les contrats internationaux entre personnes privées. Annuaire de l'Institut de Droit International, vol 64 (1), Session de Bâle, pp. 65 f
Jayme E (1995) Identité culturelle et intégration: Le droit international privé postmoderne. Recueil des Cours, vol 251
Josephus Jitta D (1920) The development of private international law through conventions. Yale LJ 29(5):497
Kaplan A (2022) Artificial intelligence, business and civilization. Our fate made in machines. Routledge, London
Kasap GH (2021) Can artificial intelligence ("AI") replace human arbitrators? Technological concerns and legal implications. J Disput Resolut. https://scholarship.law.missouri.edu/jdr/vol2021/iss2/5
Kasparov G (2022). Garry Kasparov on chess, technology and democracy. The TED Interview
Khan ND, Khan JA, Li J, Ullah T, Zhao Q (2025) Leveraging large language model ChatGPT for enhanced understanding of end-user emotions in social media feedbacks. Expert Systems with Applications, Elsevier. https://doi.org/10.1016/j.eswa.2024.125524
Kong Q, Hu M (2002) The Chinese practice of private international law. Melbourne J Intl L 3:414
Kranzberg M (1986) Technology and history: Kranzberg's laws. Technol Cult 27(3):544–560. https://doi.org/10.2307/3105385
Lehmann M (2018) Private international law and finance: nothing special? Nederlands international privaatrecht, Special Issue, 3-25https://www.nipr-online.eu/pdf/2018-114.pdf
Lehmann M (2020) Regulation, global governance and private international law: squaring the triangle. J PrivE Int Law 16(1):1–30. https://doi.org/10.1080/17441048.2020.1744255
Li S, Faure M, Havu K (2022) Liability rules for AI-related harm: law and economics lessons for a European approach. Eur J Risk Regul 13(4):618–634. https://doi.org/10.1017/err.2022.26
Mansel HP (2016) Party autonomy, legal doctrine on choice of law, and the general section of the european conflict of laws. In: Leible S (ed) General principles of European private international law. Nijhoff, Alphen aan den Rijn, p 145
Martin-Bariteau F, Pavlović M (2021) AI and Contract Law. In: Martin-Bariteau F, Scassa T (eds.), Artificial Intelligence and the Law in Canada, Toronto. LexisNexis, Canada
McCorduck P (2004) Machines who think (2nd ed.). A K Peters/CRC Press, Boca Raton
McKinsey & Company (2024, 3 Apr) What is AI (artificial intelligence)? https://www.mckinsey.com/featured-insights/mckinsey-explainers/what-is-ai
Meyer JG, Urbanowicz RJ, Martin PCN, O'Connor K, Li R, Peng P-C, Bright TJ, Tatonetti N, Won KJ, Gonzalez-Hernandez G, Moore JH (2023) ChatGPT and large language models in academia: opportunities and challenges. BioData Mining 16(1):20. https://doi.org/10.1186/s13040-023-00339-9
Michaels R (2019) Beyond universalism and particularism in international law—Insights from comparative law and private international law. BU L Rev 99:18
Miganelli N (2020) Critical legal research: who needs it? Law Libr J 112:327
Mik E (2023) Much ado about artificial intelligence or: the automation of contract formation. Intl J Law and Information Technology 30(4):484–506
Mills A (2006) The private history of international law. ICLQ 55(1):1
Mills A (2008) The dimensions of public policy in private international law. J. Private Intl L 4(2):201–236. https://doi.org/10.1080/17536235.2008.11424339
Mok WY, Mok JR (2019) Legal machine-learning analysis: first steps towards A.I. assisted legal research. In: Proceedings of the seventeenth international conference on artificial intelligence and law (ICAIL '19). Association for Computing Machinery, New York, NY, USA, pp 266–267. https://doi.org/10.1145/3322640.3326737
Murray CA, Joseph Hoane J, Hsu F (2002) Deep blue. Artif Intell 134:57–83

Naveed H, Khan AU, Qiu S, Saqib M, Anwar S, Usman M, Akhtar N, Barnes N, Mian A (2023) A comprehensive overview of large language models. https://github.com/humza909/LLM_Survey.git

Nebreda A, Shpakivska-Bilan D, Camara C, Susi G (2023) The social machine: artificial intelligence (AI) approaches to theory of mind. In: Lopez-Soto T, Garcia-Lopez A, Salguero-Lamillar FJ (eds) The theory of mind under scrutiny. Logic, Argumentation & Reasoning, vol 34. Springer, Cham. https://doi.org/10.1007/978-3-031-46742-4_22

Neuhaus PH (1976) Die Grundbegriffe des internationalen Privatrechts, 2nd ed. Tübingen, Mohr Siebeck

Nishitani Y (2000) Mancini und die Parteiautonomie im Internationalen Privatrecht – Eine Untersuchung auf der Grundlage der neu zutage gekommenen kollisionsrechtlichen Vorlesungen Mancinis. Carl Winter Universitätsverlag, Heidelberg

Nishitani Y (2016) Party autonomy in contemporary private international law: The hague principles on choice of law and East Asia. Japanese Yb Intl L 59:300 at 306. https://assets.hcch.net/docs/09654ddf-b26f-4751-9dd2-bdc517086366.pdf

Novelli C, Bongiovanni G Sartor G (2021) A conceptual framework for legal personality and its application to AI. Jurisprudence 13(2):194–219. https://doi.org/10.1080/20403313.2021.2010936

OECD (2024, May 3), Recommendation of the council on artificial intelligence. https://legalinstruments.oecd.org/en/instruments/OECD-LEGAL-0449

O'Hara EA, Ribstein LE (2000) From politics to efficiency in choice of law. University of Chicago L Rev 67:1151

Oliver M (2001) Contracting by artificial intelligence: open offers, unilateral mistakes, and why algorithms are not agents. ANU J of Law and Tech 2(1):45

OpenAI (2023) https://chat.openai.com

Oppong RF (2007) Private international law in Africa: The past, present and future. Am J Intl L 55(4):677

Papajorji P, Moskowitz H (2024) Introduction to artificial intelligence. In: Papajorji P, Moskowitz H (eds) The mind of everyday: combining individual and artificial intelligence. Springer, New York, pp 67–89

Paredes Pérez JI (2012) Alcance y Contenido de la Noción de Equivalencia en el Derecho Internacional Privado. Anuario Espanol Derecho Int'l Priv 12:91

Paul JR (1991) Comity in international law. Harv Intl LJ 32:35

Rodríguez de las Heras Ballell T (2019) Legal challenges of artificial intelligence: modelling the disruptive features of emerging technologies and assessing their possible legal impact. Unif Law Rev 24(2):302–314. https://doi.org/10.1093/ulr/unz018

Ruhl G (2007) Party autonomy in the private international law of contracts: transatlantic convergence and economic efficiency. Comparative research in law & political economy. Research Paper No 4/2007. https://digitalcommons.osgoode.yorku.ca/cgi/viewcontent.cgi?referer=&httpsredir=1&article=1227&context=clpe

Said G, Azamat K, Ravshan S, Bokhadir A (2023) Adapting legal systems to the development of artificial intelligence: solving the global problem of AI in judicial processes. Int J Cyber Law. https://doi.org/10.59022/ijcl.49

Sakolciova S (2021) Defamation on social media: Challenges of private international law. Bratislava L Rev 5(1):121

Saunders ML (1972) An innovative approach to international products liability: the work of the hague conference on private international law. Law Pol'y Int'l Bus 4:187

Scholz LH (2017) Algorithmic Contracts. Stan Tech L Rev 20:128

Schu R (1996) Consumer protection and private international law in internet contracts. Arelano Law Policy Rev 8(2):31

Schulze C (2006) Formalistic and discretionary approaches to characterization in private international law. South African L J 123(1)

Schuppli B, Jafari GA (2021) Piercing the digital veil: a case study for a DAO legal framework under swiss law. JIPITEC 12:331 para 1
Shirish A and Komal S (2024). A socio-legal inquiry on Deepfakes. Calif West Int Law J 54(2). https://scholarlycommons.law.cwsl.edu/cgi/viewcontent.cgi?article=2066&context=cwilj
Siehr K (2017) History of private international law. In Basedow J et al (eds) Encyclopaedia of private international law. Elgar, p 1391
Steiner HJ (1965) The development of private international law by international organizations. Proc Am Soc Intl L 39:38
Sunkari V, Srinagesh A (2024) System architecture for AI-driven DeepFake detection and moderation on social media platforms 3rd international conference on optimization techniques in the field of engineering (ICOFE-2024). https://doi.org/10.2139/ssrn.5065478
Svantesson D (2020) The (uneasy) relationship between the HCCH and information technology. In: John T, Gulati R, Koehler B (eds) The Elgar companion to the Hague conference on private international law. Elgar, London, p 462
Svantesson DJB (2019) A vision for the future of private international law and the Internet—Can artificial intelligence succeed where humans have failed? Harvard Intl L J. https://journals.law.harvard.edu/ilj/2019/08/a-vision-for-the-future-of-private-international-law-and-the-internet-can-artificial-intelligence-succeed-where-humans-have-failed/
Symeonides S (2019) The scope and limits of party autonomy in international contracts: a comparative analysis. In: Ferrari F, Fernández Arroyo DP (eds) The continuing relevance of private international law and new challenges. https://doi.org/10.2139/ssrn.3359988
Symeonides SC (2014) Codifying choice of law around the world: an international comparative analysis. Oxford University Press, Oxford
Taherdoost H (2023) Deep learning and neural networks: decision-making implications. Symmetry 15(9):1723. https://doi.org/10.3390/sym15091723
Tang ZS (2010) Private international law in consumer contracts: a European perspective. 6(1) J of Private Int'l L 225
UN (2022, 27 Oct) Principles for the ethical use of artificial intelligence in the United Nations System. https://unsceb.org/sites/default/files/2023-03/CEB_2022_2_Add.1%20%28AI%20ethics%20principles%29.pdf
UNESCO (2024) Principles for the ethical use of artificial intelligence in the United Nations System. https://unsceb.org/principles-ethical-use-artificial-intelligence-united-nations-system.
Unger J (1937) The place of classification in private international law. Bell Yard JL Soc'y Sch L 19:3
Ungerer J (2022) Nudging in private international law: the design of connecting factors in light of behavioural economics. Rabels Zeitschrift Für Ausländisches Und Internationales Privatrecht / The Rabel Journal of Comparative and International Private Law 86(1):1–31. http://www.jstor.org/stable/45419016
Vogenauer S (2013) Regulatory competition through choice of contract law and choice of forum in Europe: Theory and Evidence. European Review of Private Law. 21, 13-78
von Eschenbach WJ (2021) Transparency and the black box problem: why we do not trust AI. Philos Technol 34:1607–1622. https://doi.org/10.1007/s13347-021-00477-0
von Savigny FK (1849) System des heutigen römischen Rechts, Vol 8. Veit, Berlin
Wachowski L, Wachowski L (1999) The matrix. Warner Bros
Wang FF (2010) Internet jurisdiction and choice of law: legal practices in the EU, US and China. Cambridge University Press, Cambridge
Watt HM (2011) Private international law beyond the schism. Transnatl Leg Theory 2(3):347–428. https://doi.org/10.5235/204140011800664120
Watt HM (2015) Governing networks: a global challenge for private international law. Maastricht J Eur Comp Law 22(3):352–369. https://doi.org/10.1177/1023263X1502200303.(Originalwork published2015)
Wittmann J (2023) Financial market regulation and private law: a new frontier of transnational commercial law. Uniform Law Review 28(3):349. https://doi.org/10.1093/ulr/unae003

Yokomizo D (2021) Digital platforms and conflict of laws. Japanese Yb of Int'l Law 64:202
Zafar A (2024) Balancing the scale: navigating ethical and practical challenges of artificial intelligence (AI) integration in legal practices. Discov Artif Intell 4:27. https://doi.org/10.1007/s44163-024-00121-8
Zetzsche DA, Arner DW, Buckley RP (2020). Decentralized Finance. J Financial Regulation 6(2):172
Zhao WX, Zhou K, Li J, Tang T, Wang X, Hou Y, Min Y, Zhang B, Zhang J, Dong Z, Du Y, Yang C, Chen Y, Chen Z, Jiang J, Ren R, Li Y, Tang X, Liu Z, Wen J-R (2023) A survey of large language models. https://doi.org/10.48550/arXiv.2303.18223

Gérardine Goh Escolar, Deputy Secretary General of the Hague Conference on Private International Law (HCCH) and Head of its International Commercial, Digital, and Financial Law Division. Full Professor (Adj.) and Academic Fellow at the Centre for Technology, Robotics, AI, and the Law at the National University of Singapore.

Open Access This chapter is licensed under the terms of the Creative Commons Attribution 4.0 International License (http://creativecommons.org/licenses/by/4.0/), which permits use, sharing, adaptation, distribution and reproduction in any medium or format, as long as you give appropriate credit to the original author(s) and the source, provide a link to the Creative Commons license and indicate if changes were made.

The images or other third party material in this chapter are included in the chapter's Creative Commons license, unless indicated otherwise in a credit line to the material. If material is not included in the chapter's Creative Commons license and your intended use is not permitted by statutory regulation or exceeds the permitted use, you will need to obtain permission directly from the copyright holder.

Freedom to Tinker with Algorithmic Recommender Systems, a Faustian Bargain in the Current European Context and Some Chinese Insights

Giulio Santoni

Abstract For the purposes of this article, tinkering is understood as the technical possibility, or the right, to understand, discuss, repair and modify a technological device. In the perspective of an individual user, a right to tinker with the recommender system of an online platform can be understood as a tool to overcome the limits in the GDPR's lack of a right to explanation. Nevertheless, the new Digital Services Act has a limited approach to this right. While it enables the user to acquire more information on the algorithm, for example on the parameters and the ranking criteria, it does not provide for a right to intervene directly on such criteria. On the other hand, recent secondary regulations issued by the Cyberspace Administration of China show the promises and perils of a more wide-ranging right to tinker. Here, users of platform services are provided a broad degree of freedom to tinker. This, however, far from empowering users with a right to self-determination, exists in a digital environment that the law requires to be manipulative.

Keywords Digital Services Act · Tinkering · User rights · China · Comparative law

1 Definitions and Methodology

Freedom to tinker has been defined as the freedom to understand, discuss, repair, and modify the technological devices you own.[1] Such freedom is, among other things, a fundamental prerequisite to innovation[2] The tension between the freedom to tinker and the shift of human activities from an analogical to an informational environment is evident from at least two different perspectives. Firstly, informational architectures,

[1] Felten (2013).

[2] Cohen (2013).

G. Santoni (✉)
Giulio Santoni, Rome, Italy
e-mail: giuliosantoni14@gmail.com

© The Author(s) 2025

C. Amodio and A. Diurni (eds.), *Human Vulnerability in Interaction with AI in European Private Law*, https://doi.org/10.1007/978-3-031-93247-2_15

or code, embed a normative quality.[3] Software, particularly, can operate as a set of patterns that limits human activities within a set of predetermined functions or patterns. This may prevent the serendipitous encounters that are a prerequisite to discoveries and limit innovation within the variables taken into consideration in the predetermined patterns that compose the software.[4] Secondly, software is a creative work protected through copyright and sui generis rights, preventing third parties from adapting the software to better suit the needs of a person or to develop a new software.

Platform algorithmic recommender systems (RS) are a specific type of software that play a fundamental role in distributing content and data through information societies.[5] By tailoring their offer to the perceived interests of their data subjects, RSs play a central role in determining the information that individuals encounter.[6] RSs can also impact content creation, as both individual and commercial users inevitably tailor their content to fit into the patterns that RSs tend to favor. As RSs influence both the input and output of information, thus determining individual and societal decision-making processes, it is widely discussed that they do not only affect the individuals and businesses, but also produce a systemic impact.[7]

Framing the issues arising from the usage of RSs on the problem of tinkering with software, the right to tinker with algorithms can be conceived in two different ways. In the first sense, it refers to tweaking an existing algorithm deployed by a platform for the purpose of adapting its functioning to the conscious needs of a user-consumer, in opposition to the user's needs that the platform infers through data analysis. In the second sense, it refers to modifying an algorithm that is owned by a third party, to create a new one. As hinted above, this latter matter is regulated by copyright and *sui generis* rights tailored the peculiar nature of software, which, paired with contractual and criminal law provisions[8] can inhibit a creators' ability to effectively tinker with creations belonging to others,[9] more in general for a critical outlook on the relation between copyright and creativity.[10] However, legal protections notwithstanding, for an average user it is not feasible or cost effective to re-program a software to match its results to his specific needs and therefore he is stuck with the options that he is given by the software developer. When analyzing how the relation between software developers and users can affect the latter's freedom of speech, traditional U.S. doctrine relies on the idea of free market of information, to claim that users have the option to switch to a different software provider and therefore have the power to influence the programming of software.[11] However, the idea that

[3] Lessig (1999).

[4] Reviglio (2019).

[5] Helberger et al. (2015) and Milano et al. (2020).

[6] Pasquale (2015).

[7] Pasquale (2015) and Milano et al. (2020, p. 958).

[8] Kilovaty (2019).

[9] Gervais et al. (2021) and Samuelson (2016).

[10] Geiger and Izyumenko (2022).

[11] Klonick (2018).

users can switch between different recommender systems by choosing a different provider of online services clashes against the reality that most of these services are indeed natural monopolies.[12] A wide array of legal remedies has been developed with the purpose of enabling individuals, as well as societies, to maintain a degree of agency over the information they encounter, create and distribute, when accessing one of such monopolists.

In analyzing such remedies, a further premise ought to be made. Legal remedies can be categorized as public law or private law remedies, depending on whether they are actionable by public bodies or by individuals.[13] This essay aims to contribute to the debate by focusing on remedies that leverage intervention on RSs on an individual level. A research methodology centered on public law remedies would need to focus on the criticism that the exercise of a primarily individual freedom, as is after all the right to tinker, cannot be solely entrusted to public bodies. In democratic countries, privacy has been after all originally developed as a tool to shield the autonomous individual that liberal ideology assumes from governmental intrusion[14] Such criticism is incorporated in the parts of this short essay that delve into the analysis of a European piece of legislation, Regulation 2022/2065 or Digital Services Act (hereinafter DSA). Centering the discussion on private law remedies, under the premise that the protection of individual rights should be, at least partly, entrusted to individuals themselves, on the other hand, paradoxically enables us to highlight the importance of a system of legal protections that combines private and public law remedies for the creation of a digital environment that protects individual decision making from algorithmic manipulation. Indeed, on a methodological note, it should also be noted that since private law remedies enabling a right to tinker are fewer in number they are also better suited to the format of this short essay.

More specifically, the following paragraphs focus on the rise of a right to algorithmic explanation in the DSA and how it interacts with the loopholes that affect the exercise of GDPR rights. Subsequently, the analysis will shift to some technical rules on algorithms, issued by the Cyberspace Administration of China (CAC). These provide users with a scalable tool to control algorithmic recommendation in the lack of clear criteria for algorithmic explainability, in contrast with the mere right to opt out provided for by the DSA.

Finally, it should also be added that certain provisions on algorithmic transparency are also provided in another European piece of EU legislation, Regulation 2019/1150, also known as Platform-to-Business or P2B. This Regulation applies to e-commerce platforms and search engines and aims at reducing self-favoring by these entities, thus potentially enabling commercial users of such services to tinker with the parameters of their offer. Nevertheless, this Regulation is not taken into account in this essay, partly because it would fall outside of its scope, partly because it falls under the same shortcomings that affect the DSA.

---

[12] Pasquale (2015) and Milano et al. (2020, p. 141).

[13] Djeffal et al. (2021).

[14] For comparison with the evolution of the idea of privacy in the Chinese legal system, see: Santoni (2023).

2 Methodological Contribution Through the GDPR Perspective

Before approaching positive attempts to establish a right to tinker with algorithms, it is useful to look at GDPR rights actionable by individuals, to clarify how they not only fail to clearly provide a right to explanation but also take a stance that is compatible with the protection of tinkering. The GDPR contains provisions of various kinds, aimed at ensuring that the economic exploitation of personal data takes place with respect for personality rights, and in particular privacy. To this end, two macroscopic categories of remedies converge in the system envisaged by the GDPR: remedies aimed at favoring public objectives and individual remedies. The latter aim to enable individuals to control the processing of their personal data, to exercise what is referred to by some as sovereignty,[15] by others as autonomy[16] or even self-management.[17] Information that identifies an individual can be legally processed and exchanged in the data economy, thus fueling algorithmic recommender systems, provided there is a legal basis, such as the consent of the person identified by the data (GDPR, Art. 6(1)). Having identified the boundary beyond which the processing of personal data, however legitimate, overlaps with the individual's right to privacy, the Regulation provides for both individual rights aimed at ensuring the persistence of that boundary, including the revocation of consent (Art. 7), and individual rights that allow the individual to exercise a certain degree of agency over the personal data being processed. The rights set out in Articles 15–22 of the GDPR include individual rights to access, rectification and erasure, restriction of processing, erasure, portability, object and to prevent automated decision making.

These rights fundamentally operate according to a binary scheme, that aims at preserving individual autonomy, intended as an extension of an inherently autonomous self[18] This systematic approach constrains the individual to either accept the processing of data as unilaterally determined by the data controller, or to oppose it by restricting, or erasing it.[19] They do not, on the other hand enable individuals to take a modular approach, one that allows the data subject to adjust the processing of data to their needs.[20]

The GDPR pairs remedies that aim at achieving individual sovereignty over personal data with organizational measures that the data controller is required to comply with, aimed at ensuring that the data processing is carried out in accordance with the principles set out by the GDPR itself. These include principles relating to the design of the processing mechanism (Articles 25, 32); transparency obligations that require the data controller to clarify the risks to individual rights that the

---

[15] Reviglio and Agosti (2020).

[16] Djeffal et al. (2021).

[17] Solove (2013).

[18] Cohen (2013).

[19] Pasquale (2015).

[20] Cohen (2013).

processing entails (Articles 35, 36 and 40 et seq.); and finally measures relating to the allocation of responsibility for the processing within the corporate structure of the data controller. The implementation of such provisions, however, falls under the supervision of national authorities.[21] The only tool that individuals are given to influence the liaison between national authorities and data controllers is the right to lodge complaints under Article 77. Although a procedure started under such provision can lead to a jurisdictional recourse, where the data subject can claim their rights against the controller, this does not equate to a widespread ability to influence the modular processes of data processing.[22]

3 Algorithmic Explainability and Its Relation to the Right to Tinker

Whether the GDPR includes a right for data subjects to obtain explanations regarding the data processing has been a debated topic.[23] A principle of recommender system transparency is also laid out in the DSA, where Article 27 provides that recommender systems must explain why certain information is suggested to the user, including information on the main parameters and on their relative importance. Online advertisement has some specific rules laid out in Article 26, as platforms are required to disclose whether the information is an advertisement, the entity on whose behalf the advertisement is shown and, most importantly, the parameters that lead a certain advertisement to be shown to the user. If the option of intervening on those parameters is given, it should be communicated to the user.

Going back to general provisions on algorithm transparency, additional information is required under Article 34 from entities designated as VLOPs, that is to say, platforms that have more than 45 million users in the EU. It ought to be noted that this numerical parameter to identify VLOPs fails to include recommender systems that pose a high risk for the sole reason that such risk affects a number of users fewer than 45 million.[24]

Similarly to what Article 26 establishes for online advertisements, the functionality to customize or personalize (i.e. to tinker with) parameters that affect recommender systems, however, is not mandated by the DSA. Par. 3 of Article 27 simply provides that in case such option is provided it should be easily accessible and modifiable. It is however not clearly stated that such a tool should be implemented in good faith. To prevent personalization tools from being used to manipulate users (for example to extract more data about their conscious preferences), the DSA relies on a general provision contained in Article 25. Here platforms are prohibited, albeit in very general terms, from implementing dark patterns, i.e. to design, organize or

[21] Mantelero (2022).

[22] Veale et al. (2018).

[23] Wachter et al. (2017).

[24] Laux et al. (2021).

operate their online interfaces in a way that impairs or distorts the ability of online recipients to make free and informed decisions, the scope of which is further clarified by Recital 67. The Recital (a non-binding provision) describes unfair practices that platforms often engage in, "deceiving or nudging recipients of the service and from distorting or impairing the autonomy, decision-making, or choice of the recipients of the service via the structure, design or functionalities of an online interface or a part thereof". which may affect users' decision-making processes or final choices. It is noteworthy that the provision distinguishes between decision making and choice, therefore including also processes that are internal to the user and not only referring to the final choice,[25] 10). Recital 67 states as an example that a dark pattern would be "making the process of unsubscribing from a service significantly more onerous than subscribing to it".

It is therefore clear that, albeit through provisions that are not fully binding, the DSA prohibits dark patterns, which could in theory also be deemed to be prohibited under EU consumer protection laws.[26] However, the legal remedies that users are given when they do encounter practices or architectures that are deceiving or nudging are, however, limited. Under Article 53 of the DSA, users have the right to lodge a complaint with the Digital Services Coordinator of the Member State where they are located. Digital Services Coordinators are the public authorities entrusted with the enforcement of the DSA. Their powers, which include requiring information from platforms, carrying out inspections and interrogating the staff are described in Articles 51 and 52 of the DSA. However, individuals who are affected by manipulatory or deceiving practices have no right to participate in the proceedings or to be heard. Article 54 states that they have the right to obtain compensation if damages are caused. Such provision is both redundant and ineffective. It is redundant at least in those EU Member States that provide a general provision for tort liability, such as Article 2043 of the Italian Civil Code, that states that any damage caused by an unlawful act should be compensated. More importantly, it is also ineffective, if we again frame the rule against Italian Tort Law, which provides for a limited number of cases in which "nonpecuniary" damages (danni non patrimoniali) can be compensated. Leaving Italian Tory Law aside, it is undeniable that damages arising from algorithmic manipulation are hardly quantifiable, especially when the target of the manipulatory practice is the individual's ability to self-determine his informational choices.

Going back to the core issues of algorithmic explainability, procedural uncertainties do not only affect the enforcement of provisions against user manipulation, but also their ability to detect it. The fact that the DSA pursues the policy objective of enabling users to take informed decisions leads back to a core question of RSs, that is the explanation of algorithms. Is the mere explanation provided by the platform under Article 27 sufficient to detect manipulatory practices?

In terms of algorithmic explainability, a central question is the problem of counterfactual analysis. It questions how to measure discrimination against a commercial

---

[25] Brenncke (2024).

[26] Brenncke (2024, p. 8).

user when there is no minimum standard of guaranteed visibility to the individual information or, in the case of information services, to the individual commercial offer.[27] It should be clear that this is not merely a theoretical problem. In the well-known Google Shopping case, Google defended itself against the accusation that it had favored vertically integrated services to the detriment of competitors by objecting that the Commission had failed to identify a minimum standard of visibility that Google should have guaranteed to its competitors (CJEU (2024), par. 233, also see the General Court's earlier judgement at par. 359, 374).

Objective criteria of visibility of information on the web facilitate but are not indispensable to the counterfactual analysis necessary to assess ranking violations, can be derived by breaking down the algorithm that determines the results of searches made through intermediary services into its different elements. It should be possible to identify elements that assign a basic score to information to favor information that is more likely to attract a user's attention.[28] Other elements are added onto that basic score at a later stage, awarding *bonuses* and *maluses* that can further adjust the ranking to the criteria preset by the service provider.

The issue of counterfactual analysis in the perspective adopted in this essay is, however, that it cannot be used by individuals. Indeed, counterfactual analysis relies on large statistical analysis, to infer which parameters an RSs is using[29] or whether the RSs is deviating from its own parameters.[30] Users have, in other words, no tool to verify that the information a platform provides under Article 27 of the DSA is accurate or truthful.

Going back to Article 25 of the DSA, it ought to be noted that it does not provide a right to tinker to users, besides the right to switch off the RSs and to therefore use a "plain" version of the online platform's service. On the contrary, it gives platforms the option to enable users to intervene on the parameters of the RSs, in a legal framework where legal protection from manipulatory practices is still weak. The risk that platforms use this option as a tool to manipulate users is strong, but contextually users have no right to intervene on those parameters and therefore empirically adjust the platform to their preferences.

4 Platform Manipulation in the Chinese Context

Before discussing platform regulation in China, it might be useful to briefly introduce the main regulatory authority in this framework, the Cyberspace Administration of China, or CAC. Chinese scholars divide the path of regulation of digital platforms in China into two phases, characterized by different macro trends.[31] The first runs from

[27] Gillespie (2022).

[28] Leersen (2020).

[29] Wachter et al. (2017, pp. 854–856).

[30] Leersen (2020, pp. 8–9).

[31] Miao et al. (2021).

1994 to 2012 and the second from 2012 to the present. Online content regulation initially focused on the censorship of politically controversial material. This allegedly led to the exclusion of most foreign companies, resulting in a form of protectionism that allowed Chinese network operators to thrive in a market that was closed to the outside world but highly deregulated at home. Against this background of encouraging the creation of a domestic digital industry, personal data were only specifically regulated in 2012. While the second phase was characterized by an increased use of legislation, in the years prior to 2012 regulation of networks was often contained in directives, decisions, decrees, administrative measures and even 'opinions'. As if this were not enough, this wide array of administrative acts came from a large number of ministries and agencies. They were formally coordinated by the Ministry of Industry and Information Technology (MIIT), but in reality responded to conflicting interests brought in by the different articulations of the Chinese state.[32]

The dispersion of regulatory powers described led to the creation of a centralized authority, the CAC. Aside from being the central regulatory authority for issues related to the dissemination of content online, the CAC is given the power to perform a graduated response, which is the basis of the "graded and categorized classification mechanism" (行分类分级). In essence, the CAC has broad discretion and is allowed to modulate its interventions and response to the specific characteristics of any platform. Indeed, it has a higher formal ranking than a Chinese Ministry, as it is placed under the direct control of the Chinese Communist Party's Politburo Standing Committee. Since the creation of the cAC, secondary legislation has become more rational and coherent, partly through the establishment of a centralized Internet governing body. Yet, as noted by Creemers, one of the main public policy goals of the CAC is to spread positive energy online.[33]

This is to say that an intellectually honest comparison between the European and Chinese approach to user tinkering must begin with a clarification of the broadly different goals that characterize these two legislations. The EU treats a user's decision-making processes and ability to independently choose as a right worthy of legal protection. China's legislation, on the other hand, openly targets user decision making processes, as its main goal is to nudge users into content that is comforting and "positive".[34] Nevertheless, some authors have noted how Western private online platforms, just like the Chinese Communist Party, sometimes tend to push aside ideas that might be unsettling for large chunks of their audience.[35] In this sense, the lack of tools that allow individual users to tinker with algorithms also affects EU law, might in the end also produce an online environment that fails to respect users' right to engage with algorithms on their own terms.

The two main CAC Regulations that focus on algorithmic recommender systems in China are the Regulation No. 5 of 2020, titled "Regulations on environmental

[32] Miao et al. (2021).

[33] Creemers et al. (2024).

[34] Shen et al. (2024, p. 10).

[35] Shen et al. (2024, p. 4).

governance of the content of online information"[36] and Regulation No. 9 of 2022, titled "Internet Information Service Algorithmic Recommender Management Regulation" (hereinafter IISARM).[37] Both Regulations require platforms to actively nudge users into certain political ideas and, more in general to provide a comforting online space. Article 6 of IISARM requires RS platform operators to adhere to "*mainstream* value orientations" and "vigorously spread positive energy," while Regulation No. 5 of 2020 provides a detailed grid of what content should be elevated (Art. 5), deleted (Art. 6) or demoted (Art. 7). Art. 5 of the 2020 Regulations stipulates that online service providers must not only propagate Xi Jinping's thoughts on socialism with Chinese characteristics in the new era, but also that they help the masses "resolve doubts" and "form consensus". Conversely, by Art. 6 of the 2020 Provisions provides a list of content that is openly prohibited, such as content "against the Constitution", "leaking State secrets", "damaging national honor", "pornography", etc. In China's political system, based on the dominance of a single political party, this kind of predicament is unavoidable. However, it highlights a more general risk related to the provisions that dictate the design of platforms, namely, the inscription of legislators' political biases and opinions within the very architecture that is supposed to protect users. Article 7 lists content that is not prohibited but is against network ecology and should therefore be demoted, meaning that users should be nudged away from such content. It includes content with misleading titles; gossip; "inappropriate"; sexually titillating, that shows blood to a discomforting level, that incites to religious discrimination, that is vulgar or "kitch"; that may cause minors to imitate unsafe behavior. All the content listed in Article 7 should be, as mentioned above, demoted and records of it sent to the CAC (Article 10 of CAC Regulation 5/2020). Furthermore, under Article 11 of the same Regulation, content listed in Article 7 cannot appear in prominent positions, such as the homepage of a webpage or the main page of an app, or otherwise highlighted (such as being listed as a popular item or a hot search in a search engine).

In the CAC regulations, rules aimed at preventing platforms from manipulating users openly coexist with the aim of imprinting political views favorable to the CCP and its policies on the same users. Article 8 of IISARM prohibits the deployment of algorithmic techniques aimed at creating addiction or further consumption in users, without providing further details and definitions. While provisions on the protection of adult users are scant, preventing children from compulsive use of the Internet, and more specifically online video games, seems to be a major concern of the Chinese legislature.[38] The Child Protection Law (未成年人保护法) provides a rigid online environment, also relying on the cooperation of parents relatives and schools, as minors are not allowed to bring smartphones into schools, play online video

[36] The term used in the title of the Regulation is 生态治, literally meaning ecological or environmental governance. Here, I chose the term environmental, which in my opinion better gives the idea of a holistic approach to Internet governance, which the title probably refers to.

[37] A full translation of the Regulation is available at https://digichina.stanford.edu/work/translation-internet-information-service-algorithmic-recommendation-management-provisions-effective-march-1-2022/.

[38] Xie (2022).

games after 10 p.m. (Art. 75) and can only spend 4 h per week playing videogames. Other tools aimed at controlling minors rely on the cooperation of ISPs and online platforms. For example, online streaming services must create separate rooms, where minors can interact more safely. Other provisions aim at protecting other categories of vulnerable users. Article 19 of IISARM requires online platforms to pay special attention to the needs of older users, with particular reference to, but not limited to, fraud prevention.

The lack of explicit provisions regarding addiction or, more generally, the vulnerability of adult Internet users raises questions about the applicability of Article 8 of IISARM. After all, the limited Chinese scholarship available on the subject refers to Article 8 only with regard to minors, just as the official interpretation of the CAC of IISARM does not mention the vulnerability of adult users (Yang, 2022). On the other hand Article 8, in prohibiting "algorithms that violate laws and regulations or ethics and morals, for example by inducing their users to addiction," makes no distinction between minors and other users. A possible interpretive solution could be reached by combining Article 7 of CAC Regulations No. 5 of 2020, imposing the demotion of certain content, to Article 8 of the IISARM. While not overtly mentioning Internet addiction or user manipulation, Article 7 of Regulation 5/2020 applies to content that does not openly violate the law, otherwise it would be prohibited under Article 6, but is contrary to ethics and morals and should therefore be demoted. Furthermore, Article 7 applies to content that is grotesque, exaggerated, vulgar, and sexually allusive content, all types of content that exploit human attention. Taking a closer look to the list of content that should be demoted under Article 7 more in detail highlights further aspects. For example, n. 1 of Article 7 mentions content with a serious discrepancy between the content and the exaggerated title. Again, n. 4 talks about content that is sexually suggestive or titillating and is likely to make people think sexually, or, in other words content that is not pornographic (pornography falls under the prohibitions of Article 6), but that uses sexuality to capture the attention or otherwise manipulate the user.

All this leads to the conclusion that in the view of the Chinese legislator, it seems that manipulation can be prevented incidentally, because certain types of content that tend to be particularly addictive are also contrary to the principle of network ecology that the CAC promotes. The result is paradoxical. Under the concept of network ecology, platforms are required to combine tools to protect users from algorithmic manipulation with others that require platforms to nudge users towards content that promotes core socialist values. Examining China's legal framework on algorithmic governance might help highlight a possible clash between said principle of autonomy and the prohibition (or demotion) of certain categories of content as they appeal to man's innate curiosity for grotesque, lewd, and violent content.

5 Tinkering with Chinese Algorithms

Article 17, par. 3 of IISARM swiftly addresses the issue of algorithm explainability, as it requires platforms to disclose the parameters used to calibrate the algorithm in simple, understandable language. Users who wish to acquire additional information on algorithmic recommender systems might, on the other hand, find little relief in provisions stating that some additional information can be extrapolated from the information about the platforms' algorithms disclosed on the CAC webpage, as required by Article 24 of the IISARM. A basic search on the CAC webpage highlights how the information provided under this norm are scarce. Douyin, for example, claims that it uses "activity information" related to users' historical clicks, duration (of interaction), likes, comments, shares and *retweets*, dislikes, and other behavioral data to recommend content, and through deep learning technology, activities that, when anonymized, are not personal data, but likely fall under the definition of "*tags* that identify personal characteristics." The goal of these transparency-based provisions does not seem to be to enable a user to fully understand how his or her actions are shaping the content being recommended to him or her. Assuming that the decisions made by algorithms can be fully understood by people, Articles 17 and 24 of the IISARM do not openly state a right to algorithmic explanation.

On the other hand, Article 17 of the IISARM also includes a personalization tool, as it states that platforms must allow users to select or deselect *tags* that identify their personal characteristics. In addition to the power to switch off the RSs, similarly to what Article 25 of the DSA requires, Article 17 of the IISARM also enables users to tweak the algorithm according to their needs. Accessing a Chinese platform, in this case Douyin, shows that the RSs can be tweaked by intervening on the tags that identify the users' preferences. Users are presented with a grid in which they can manually set which types of content they want to be recommended and which content they would not like to be recommended. Personal tags are divided into macro-categories, such as "food delicacies", "humanistic sciences" and "travel", which are in turn divided in subcategories. For instance, the category "food delicacies" is divided into: "scouting restaurants", "enjoying delicacies", "traditional snacks" and "purchasing ingredients". Once they choose a category or subcategory of content, users are also given the option to select the intensity with which they wish the content to be recommended, or, in other words, how much they are interested in it. In its simplicity, and without the aim of enabling users to fully understand the scope of their interventions, the IISARM scheme offers a clear right to intervene on platform RSs.

Such right is relevant at least under three perspectives. The first is the importance of tinkering per se. As mentioned in the introduction, tinkering can be a useful tool to enable individuals to come in contact with new or unexpected ideas, and therefore to innovate. Second, the tool provided for by Article 17 of the IISARM is useful in explaining algorithms. Rules on RS explanation in Europe have been criticized for being too focused on algorithmic logic rather than user experience, thus falling into the fallacy of "algorithmic centrism".[39] In its simplicity, and without the goal of allowing users to fully understand the extent of their interventions, the IISARM scheme offers a clear right to intervene on the platform's RSs and empirically evaluate the results. Related to this issue is the third point, which we will further discuss in the next paragraph. As the Chinese Civil Code provides a right of compensation for algorithmicdamages, which enables a user to be compensated for the damages caused by a recommender system, the IISARM provision can be a useful tool to detect an algorithmic harm.

6 Conclusion: The Practical Effects of the Freedom to Tinker in the Chinese Regulations

This final section, in conclusion, analyzes the practical effects of a user centric tool to enable tinkering, besides the value that is inherent in a tool that enables users to tweak the RSs to their liking. As a tool that makes some degree of empirical analysis on the effect of the recommender system possible, the IISARM enables the possible tort liability of algorithmic damages.[40] Chinese scholars distinguish between generic or abstract algorithmic harm types and specific algorithmic harm types. The former defines generic infringements of freedom of information, expression, and health harms that manipulative techniques implemented through algorithms generically cause to the individuals. Specific algorithmic harm, on the other hand, refers to the rights infringements caused through an algorithmic decision-making process. This decision-making process can obviously be challenged, from the standpoint of methodological correctness, the data fed into the system, or other grounds that lead to a decision that injures an individual right. This distinction serves to highlight the difference between algorithmic decision-making, which is at best regulated through ex ante regulatory schemes, whether entrusted to authorities or individuals, and the result of that process, which may instead result in the occurrence of compensable harm. At the systemic level, algorithmic harm liability is considered as a response mechanism that enriches the roster of *ex post* remedies, which are characterized by a certain weakness. Indeed, as noted above, IISARM gives the individual a right to *tinker*, a right for the individual to play with the algorithm to the point of finding an optimal outcome. This right, as opposed to the right to explanation that is struggling to emerge in the European experience, may have the practical effect of providing the individual with a tool to shape his or her confrontation with algorithmic decision making to his or her advantage.

On a separate note, it should also be added that the existence of a right to tinker with RSs in the context of China's "ecological" Internet environment highlights that such right can exist in a manipulative environment. As mentioned in the previous paragraphs, CAC regulations require RSs to nudge users into content that is favorable

[39] Leersen (2020, 2022).

[40] Wang (2022).

to the CCP and it seems unlikely that such provision can be disregarded if the user tinkers with the algorithm to enable it to suggest other types of content. The freedom to tinker comes at a risk that is to give the user a mere impression of enhanced control, while it simply introduces a variable in a complex set of patterns at the cost of the disclosure of a users' conscious preferences. In this sense, while still a useful tool in breaking the monotony of platform recommended content, the freedom to tinker comes at a cost. In this sense, the obligations that the DSA lays out with regard tothe option to tinker under Article 27, and their relation to the norms on dark patterns should be treated as a Faustian bargain.

References

Brenncke M (2024) Regulating dark patterns. Notre Dame Journal of International & Comparative Law. 14:1, Article 5

Cohen J (2013) What privacy is for. Harvard Law Review. 126:1904-1933

Creemers R, Papagianneas S, Knight A (eds.) (2024) The emergence of China's smart state. Rowman & Littlefield Publishers

Djeffal C, Magrani E, Hitrova C (2021) Recommender systems and autonomy: a role for regulation of design, rights, and transparency. Indian J Law Technol 17(1):1–52. https://doi.org/10.55496/JFSP9105

Felten E (2013) The new freedom to tinker movement. https://blog.citp.princeton.edu/2013/03/21/the-new-freedom-to-tinker-movement/

Geiger C, Izyumenko E (2022) From internal to external balancing, and back? Copyright limitations and fundamental rights in the digital environment. In: López J, Saiz García C (eds) Digitalización, acceso a contenidos y propiedad intelectual. Dykinson, Madrid, pp 103–135. https://doi.org/10.2139/ssrn.3976407

Gervais J, Lemercier C, Pelletier W (2021) La valeur du service public. La Découverte, Paris

Gillespie T (2022) Do not recommend? Reduction as a form of content moderation. Social Media + Society, 8:3 https://doi.org/10.1177/20563051221117552

Helberger N, Kleinen von Königslöw K, Van Der Noll R (2015) Regulating the new information intermediaries as gatekeepers of information diversity. Comput Sci: 53

Kilovaty I (2019) Freedom to hack. Ohio State Law J: 490

Klonick K (2018) The new governors: the people, rules, and processes governing online speech. Harv Law Rev 131(6):1598–1670

Laux J, Mittelstadt B, Wachter S (2021) Taming the few: platform regulation, independent audits and the risks of capture created by the DMA and DSA. Computer Law and Security Review. 43(105613): 1-12

Leersen P (2020) The soap box as a black box: regulating transparency in social media recommender systems. European Journal of Law and Technology, 11(2): 1-51

Leersen P (2022) Algorithm centrism in the DSA's regulation of recommender systems. Verfassungsblog. 29 March

Lessig L (1999) Code and other laws of cyberspace. Basic Books, New York

Mantelero A (2022) Beyond data: human rights, ethical and social impact assessment in AI. T.M.C. Asser Press, The Hague. https://doi.org/10.1007/978-94-6265-531-7

Miao W, Jiang M, Pang Y (2021) Historicizing internet regulation in China: a meta-analysis of Chinese internet policies. International Journal of Communication. 15: 1-24

Milano S, Taddeo M, Floridi L (2020) Recommender systems and their ethical challenges. AI & Soc 35, 957–967

Pasquale F (2015) The Black Box society: The secret algorithms that control money and information. Harvard University Press
Reviglio U (2019) Serendipity as an emerging design principle of the infosphere: challenges and opportunities. Ethics Inf Technol 21, 151–166
Reviglio U, Agosti C (2020) Thinking outside the black box: the case for "algorithmic sovereignty" in social media. Social Media + Society, 6(2)
Samuelson P (2016) Freedom to tinker. Theor Inq Law 17(2):562–600. https://doi.org/10.1515/til-2016-0021
Santoni G (2023) Personal data as a market commodity: legal irritants from China's experience. European Journal of Privacy Law and Technologies. 1: 128-146.
Shen S, Andrejevic M, Fordyce R (2024) Banning "braingasm": an investigation of misogynistic politics in 8Chan's, U.S. platforms' and CCP's regulation of ASMR. Feminist Media Studies, 25(4), 969–983.
Solove DJ (2013) Privacy self-management and the consent dilemma. Harvard Law Rev 126:1880–1903
Veale M, Binns R, Ausloos J (2018) When data protection by design and data subject rights clash. International Data Privacy Law, 8(2):105–123
Wachter S, Mittelstadt B, Floridi L (2017) Why a right to explanation of automated decision-making does not exist in the General Data Protection Regulation. International Data Privacy Law, 7(2): 76–99
Wang Y (王莹) (2022) 算法侵害责任框架刍议. 中国法
Xie Y (谢英豪) (2022) 未成年人保护视域下网络游戏监管政策探析. 娱乐法内参

Giulio Santoni, Adjunct Professor in Comparative Law at the University of Ferrara, Ph.D. in Comparative Law from the University of Rome Tor Vergata (2022). Specializes in regulation of online activities and Chinese law. Published a 2024 monograph comparing US, EU, and Chinese legislation on online service provider liability. Holds an LL.M. in Chinese Law from China University of Political Science and Law, Beijing. Admitted to the Rome Bar since 2018.

Open Access This chapter is licensed under the terms of the Creative Commons Attribution 4.0 International License (http://creativecommons.org/licenses/by/4.0/), which permits use, sharing, adaptation, distribution and reproduction in any medium or format, as long as you give appropriate credit to the original author(s) and the source, provide a link to the Creative Commons license and indicate if changes were made.

The images or other third party material in this chapter are included in the chapter's Creative Commons license, unless indicated otherwise in a credit line to the material. If material is not included in the chapter's Creative Commons license and your intended use is not permitted by statutory regulation or exceeds the permitted use, you will need to obtain permission directly from the copyright holder.

Hybridization of Man and Machine: Article 30 of the New Italian Public Procurements Code and Comparison with the AI Act—A Challenge for the Future

Giuseppe Sferrazzo

Abstract This article investigates the integration of automated decision-making within the Italian Public Administration, with a specific focus on Article 30 of the new Public Procurement Code (Legislative Decree No. 36/2023) and its alignment with the European Union's Artificial Intelligence Act (AI Act). The analysis explores the growing application of algorithmic systems and machine learning technologies—including Large Language Models (LLMs)—in administrative procedures, highlighting their potential to enhance efficiency, impartiality, and consistency. At the same time, the paper critically examines the legal challenges posed by algorithmic opacity, the traceability of decision-making processes, and compliance with fundamental constitutional principles such as legality, transparency, non-discrimination, and accountability. The study addresses the safeguards introduced by Article 30, including the mandatory presence of human oversight, access to source code, and the implementation of technical and organizational measures aimed at minimizing errors and ensuring fairness. Particular attention is given to the classification of public procurement as a "high-risk" sector under the AI Act, emphasizing that risk derives not from the sector itself but from the specific modalities of technological deployment. Ultimately, the article underscores the need for a robust and coherent governance framework capable of ensuring the responsible adoption of artificial intelligence within the public sector. Such a framework must protect citizens' fundamental rights—foremost among them the right to explanation—when faced with decisions generated by opaque or non-interpretable AI systems.

Keywords Article 30 of the Public Procurement Code · AI systems · Large language models · AI Act · Fundamental rights

G. Sferrazzo (✉)
University of Rome Tor Vergata, Rome, Italy
e-mail: giuseppesferrazzo01@gmail.com

© The Author(s) 2025

C. Amodio and A. Diurni (eds.), *Human Vulnerability in Interaction with AI in European Private Law*, https://doi.org/10.1007/978-3-031-93247-2_16

1 The Introduction of Digitalization and the Automation of Administrative Decision-Making

The Italian Public Administration has been under reform since 1970, culminating in the Digital Administration Code (Legislative Decree No. 82 of March 7, 2005). The Digital Administration Code aimed at promoting the "use of information and communication technologies within Public Administrations, coupled with organizational changes and the acquisition of new skills in order to improve public services, democratic processes, and strengthen the support of public policies".

In the initial stages, the use of information technology was limited to documenting, preserving, and communicating administrative acts. The goals were, on the one hand, to simplify interactions between citizens and the Public Administration and, on the other, of making the Public Administration's actions more efficient and effective by leveraging on ICT (Information and Communications Technology) tools.[1]

Recent advances in digital technology expanded the range of available data and tools. This enabled the processing information through models and systems referred to as "algorithmic".[2] Algorithmic systems can make evaluations or predictions, and thus take decisions based on the data from which they "learn". The use of algorithms has enabled a shift in the digitalization of administrative activity. It is no longer merely understood as the collection and preservation of administrative acts and documents in digital format. Algorithmic administration can produce an administrative decision through software programmed to generate an output based on the input provided.[3]

A copious jurisprudence suggests that the use of computerized and automated procedures in administrative actions must certainly be encouraged,[4] as it allows for the full realization of the general principles of efficiency and cost-effectiveness, as well as the constitutional principles enshrined in Article 97 of the Italian Constitution.[5]

---

[1] Simoncini (2020).

[2] For further information, Carloni (2008).

[3] Avanzini (2019), Auby (2019), Carloni (2020), Cavallo Perin (2020), Costantino (2017), D'Orlando and Orsoni (2019), Delgado (2016, 2019), Falcone (2023), Fanti (2022), Forte (2020), Galetta and Corvalan (2019), Gallone (2023), Marongiu (2020), Masucci (2020, 2022), Sterpa (2024), and Torchia (2023).

[4] Consiglio di Stato, case law 8 April 2019, n.° 2770; 3 December 2019, nn. 8472, 8473, 8474; 4 February 2020, n.° 881.

[5] Patroni Griffi (2018). In particular, as has been authoritatively noted that "the advantages of automating administrative decision-making processes are evident with regard to serial or standardized procedures, characterized by a high degree of constraint or based on presumptions that are probabilistically indicative of a certain fact. Consider, for example, procedures for simultaneous transfers or initial assignments of teaching positions, as well as the distribution of welfare benefits to eligible recipients based on predetermined criteria. Moreover, consider adverse decisions, such as tax assessments based on presumptive data compiled by a machine, or administrative sanctions (such as for speeding violations) that are processed automatically, both in terms of detecting the infraction and determining the corresponding penalty, as well as the very 'formation' of the administrative measure."

Using such tools, on the one hand, accelerates administrative procedures, ensuring greater impartiality, and, on the other hand, benefits public officials by relieving them from repetitive tasks.[6]

It is necessary to define a notion of the algorithmic decision, understood as a general administrative norm or a legal rule expressed in the form of an algorithm, with several fundamental consequences.[7] Firstly, the algorithmic decision has legal nature and, as such, must comply with the principles of publicity, transparency, reasonableness, and proportionality.[8] Secondly, it cannot leave discretionary margins in its application and must, therefore, provide specific solutions for every possible case. Thirdly, the algorithmic decision must respond to interests identified *ex ante* by law or by the Administration itself. This implies that the Administration is required to continuously monitor the algorithm's alignment with these interests. Finally, it must foresee the possibility for the judiciary to assess and verify the correctness of the automated process that led to the decision.

On this point, the digital revolution seems to proceed with new procedures as machine learning and, in particular, deep learning techniques.

These more advanced mechanisms have been developed specifically to overcome the inherent limitations of traditional algorithms.[9] In deep learning systems, the information required to take a particular decision is autonomously extracted by the machine through the analysis of large datasets.[10] Such data is processed to infer patterns and parameters, thereby enabling the system to make informed decisions. It is important to underscore that the output, or "decision", generated by a deep learning algorithm may appear in various forms. These include—but are not limited to—a Boolean value (true or false), a narrative text, or any other data representation contingent upon the specific requirements of the case at hand.[11]

Deep learning systems consist of two main components. The first component is the source code, a text written in a particular programming language that can be understood by an individual with the necessary expertise. The second key component is the "model", which refers to a set of parameters that provide the algorithm with the capacity to make informed decisions.[12] It should be noted, however, that this latter component is generally not directly interpretable by humans.[13] This is, however, in

[6] Corbino (2024).

[7] Simoncini (2020).

[8] Resta (2019). The author notes that "great importance is attributed to the principle of transparency, which is articulated in various and often converging forms: the right to be informed ex ante of the existence of automated processing; the right to know the logic upon which such processing is based; the right to understand the manner and extent to which algorithmic processing has influenced the outcome of a decision affecting the individual; and the right to access the algorithm as an integral part of an administrative procedure."

[9] Chollet (2021).

[10] Mohri et al. (2012).

[11] Carullo (2023).

[12] Goodfellow et al. (2016).

[13] Slosser (2022).

stark contrast with the abovementioned principles, which regulate how the Public Administration operates.

Thus, the algorithmic decision should be interpreted as general administrative rule of the Public Administration, with the aim of guaranteeing citizens—the end users of the service—and implementing an efficient, effective, and transparent administrative action.[14]

The introduction of public algorithmic decision making has led to the need to define the scope of application of this new "power". It aims at ensuring respect for constitutional principles that, on the one hand, pertain to the proper functioning of administrative action and, on the other, to the transparency and knowability of the procedures used to reach an administrative decision.

In Italy, one of the sectors where the Public Administration is not only digitalized but also algorithmic is public procurement. In this context, the analysis will focus on the recent public procurement code, issued by Legislative Decree No. 36/2023. Case law has played a crucial contribution, as well, defining fundamental principles and criteria to ensure that the use of algorithms remains within the strict bounds of constitutional principles, enabling human supervision on the use of these tools.

2 Article 30 of the New Public Procurement Code

Article 30 of the new Public Procurement Code represents a groundbreaking development in the national regulatory landscape. It has introduced and promoted the automation of administrative activities throughout the public procurement life cycle, from planning to execution. At the same time, the legislature has sought to introduce safeguards. The primary goal is to ensure that the operational logic of the chosen technological solutions is not only adequately understood and accessible but also not entirely dependent on the machine. It mandates that the algorithmic decision within the decision-making process must be capable of being monitored, validated, and, eventually, overridden by a human supervisor. This is further supported by the requirement to adopt "any technical and organizational measures necessary to ensure that inaccuracies in the data are corrected, and the risk of errors is minimized."

Indeed, Paragraph 1 of the Article 30 of the new Code states that, to improve efficiency, contracting authorities and their contractors shall, wherever possible, automate their activities by utilizing technological solutions, including artificial intelligence and distributed ledger technologies, in compliance with applicable regulations. When purchasing or developing such solutions, contracting authorities and concessionary entities must: (a) ensure the availability of the source code, related documentation, and any other element necessary to understand their operational logic; (b) introduce clauses in the tender documents to ensure the provision of assistance

[14] On this point, on the inherent difficulties involved in explaining the operational logic of the most complex software to individuals who do not possess expertise in information technology: Borgesius (2018) and Crawford (2016).

and maintenance services necessary to correct errors and undesired effects resulting from automation.

Article 30 further requires that decisions made through automation comply with the following principles: (i) Knowability and comprehensibility—every economic operator has the right to be informed of the existence of automated decision-making processes that affect him and, in such cases, to receive significant information about the logic used; (ii) Non-exclusivity of algorithmic decision-making—a human supervisor enabled to monitor, validate, or overturn the automated decision must be involved[15]; (iii) Non-discrimination in algorithms[16]—the responsible party must implement appropriate technical and organizational measures to prevent discriminatory effects against economic operators.[17]

3 The Use of Artificial Intelligence in the Public Procurement Code

Within what scope can automated artificial intelligence be used under the new Code? The answer is not straightforward and is subject to various interpretations.

Undoubtedly, it can be used in the initial phase of the procurement life cycle. This includes preparatory and investigative activities, such as the location of a public work.[18] Indeed, an algorithm can analyze the feasibility and quality of the public work, examining various aspects such as those related to environment and sustainability. This also allows the official to monitor its progress and the results produced by the algorithm.

Another area where AI can be utilized is the evaluation of the design of the work. In this case, the algorithm, based on the data it possesses and the data provided by the relevant public administration, can make informed choices compliant with

[15] Contracting authorities, when purchasing or developing technological solutions, must ensure the availability of the source code and any other elements necessary to understand the logic of its operation. Moreover, the decision resulting from an automated process must be attributed to the contracting authority. The principles are also acknowledged that the decision-making process must not be left entirely to the machine; human input is required to monitor, validate, or overturn the automated decision. Additionally, the algorithmic decision must not result in any form of discrimination.

[16] To this end, contracting authorities and concessionary entities shall adopt all necessary technical and organizational measures to ensure that any factors leading to data inaccuracies are corrected and the risk of errors is minimized, as well as to prevent discriminatory effects against individuals based on nationality, ethnic origin, political opinions, religion, personal beliefs, trade union membership, physical characteristics, genetic status, health condition, gender, or sexual orientation.

[17] Art. 30, co. 5, D.lgs. n.° 36/2023: Le pubbliche amministrazioni pubblicano sul sito istituzionale, nella sezione «Amministrazione trasparente», l'elenco delle soluzioni tecnologiche di cui al comma 1 utilizzate ai fini dello svolgimento della propria attività.

[18] Colletti (2024).

sector regulations. In this scenario, a bundle of rules known as Design Information Package (DIP[19]), may apply. These include all requirements necessary for the construction of the work (e.g., required architectural quality, morphology, distances between buildings, etc.).

In addition to the preparatory aspects of the work, authomated artificial intelligence can be deployed during the preparatory phase, in particular in the evaluation of bids, specifically the technical ones.

In this perspective, economic bid evaluations are already performed according to mechanical calculations that do not require machine learning, as they involve simple mathematical calculations. Technical evaluations are subject to discretionary decisions by the Public Administration and therefore involve choices and assessments that cannot be left to the machine, especially if the reasoning behind those choices is not transparent.

The evaluation parameters in question are very broad and making a choice can lead to a positive assessment of a bid, to the detriment of others. Such evaluations involve difficult choices regarding complex and non-simplistic parameters, and the machine might err in its reasoning. Many parameters need to be considered—from improvements, sustainability, and energy savings to architectural quality, cost savings, and project completion times, ending with the choice of materials used, which involves subtle and complex evaluations. These possibilities can be pursued through artificial intelligence. They cannot, however, be based on simplistic data, but rather on the big data that the public administration possesses, which should be clear.

Once the evaluative-decision-making phases are defined, it is necessary to ask which type of AI can be utilized by contracting authorities in their discretionary activities. In this regard, the best and most used artificial tools are Large Language Models (LLMs). These systems are based on source inputs (prompts) that generate and return a sequence of words, codes, or data (outputs). Recent LLMs include GPT-3, PaLM, LaMDA, Gopher, and OPT.[20]

These models provide clear, immediate, and effective responses and can be used by public administrations for their functionality. However, these tools require two prerequisites to ensure the validity of outputs or to allow for their rejection through a review process that may lead to their refutation according to Article 30 of Legislative Decree No. 36/2023.[21]

The first prerequisite is a training system appropriate for the activity that the LLM is destined to carriy out. It is essential for the machine learning system to be developed through training processes, including deep learning via neutral networks.

---

[19] The Design Information Package (DIP) is a document to be prepared in alignment with the needs framework and the solution identified in the Feasibility Document for Design Alternatives (DOCFAP). The DIP is a strategic document that specifies the characteristics, requirements, and design documents necessary for defining each level of the design, in relation to the size, specific type, and category of the intervention to be implemented.

[20] Mokander et al. (2023) and Floridi and Chiriatti (2020).

[21] Art. 30 co 3 lett. b) "non esclusività della decisione algoritmica, per cui comunque esiste nel processo decisionale un contributo umano capace di controllare, validare ovvero smentire la decisione automatizzata".

On the other hand, it will be necessary to establish and ensure a rigorous system of controls and governance both before and after to monitor, verify, and, if necessary, refute the automated decision.[22]

This implies that, when deep learning models are trained on human discretionary administrative decisions, they can learn to generate texts that closely emulate the language and structure of such acts.[23] Consequently, upon the completion of the training phase, during execution, the algorithm can generate a well-structured decision that mirrors the terminology used during training yet incorporates new content that is consistent with the updated input data.[24]

4 Article 30 and the New A.I. Act

It is essential to understand the relationship between Article 30 of Legislative Decree No. 36/2023 and the new EU regulation, the AI Act.[25]

AI systems must be trained with secure, clear, and optimized data to ensure that AI tools can achieve optimal and safe results. Indeed, the initial effects and results that will emerge are entirely dependent on the environment in which the system was developed and trained. From this perspective, the Public Administration must focus on creating a governance system that allows for the training of AI systems in a way that aligns with the expected results, also from a qualitative standpoint. In this sense, biases, errors, and incorrect results depend primarily, as previously highlighted, on the data fed into the LLM. Since the training mechanism is autonomously executed by the system, it is no longer possible to control this process. In the absence of correct and appropriate data, both in quality and quantity, the results produced by the machine will be partial, limited, incorrect, or insufficient.[26]

The EU addresses this issue in Articles 10 and 11 of the AI Act. It mandates that high-risk AI systems utilizing techniques that involve training models with data must be developed based on training, validation, and testing datasets that meet the quality criteria outlined in Paragraphs 2 through 5.

Training, validation, and testing datasets must be governed by policies implemented through appropriate governance and data management measures suited to the intended purpose of the AI system, particularly for high-risk systems. These

[22] Barbiero (2024).

[23] Carullo (2023): "Given the necessity to comprehend the rationale behind an automated decision, we can thus now rely on AI systems that produce intelligible decisions articulated in textual format. As such, these decisions are comprehensible to humans. This may also be supported by additional output information, to provide clearer and more comprehensible explanations of the algorithm's decision-making process".

[24] Schweighofer (2004).

[25] Artificial Intelligence Act (Regolamento (UE) 2024/1689).

[26] Delle Cave (2024).

datasets must also undergo annotation, cleaning, continuous updating, implementation, and integration with similar data to ensure they accurately represent the aspects they are meant to convey.

Furthermore, especially for systems affecting individuals' health and safety, they must be subjected to strict rules to avoid any negative impact on fundamental human rights, preventing any form of discrimination prohibited by the European Union.

In addition, the datasets must consider, to the extent required by the intended purpose, the specific characteristics or elements of the geographical, contextual, behavioral, or functional environment in which the high-risk AI system is intended to be used.

Moreover, in accordance with the provisions of Annex IV, specific technical documentation for the data and tools required by Article 11 must be provided to the relevant supervisory authority if the AI system is to be used.

A detailed description of the elements of the AI system and the process for its development, including:

> (a) the methods and steps undertaken in the development of the AI system, including, where applicable, the use of pre-trained systems or tools provided by third parties and how they were used, integrated, or modified by the provider; (b) the system's design specifications, namely the overall logic of the AI system and algorithms; the key design choices, including the rationale and assumptions made regarding the individuals or groups of individuals for whom the system is intended to be used; the main classification choices; what the system is designed to optimize for, and the relevance of the various parameters; a description of the system's expected output and output quality; the decisions regarding trade-offs made when adopting technical solutions to comply with the requirements in Chapter III, Section 2; (c) the description of the system's architecture, explaining how software components build upon or integrate with each other and contribute to the overall processing; the computational resources used to develop, train, test, and validate the AI system; (d) where relevant, the data requirements, including datasheets describing the training methodologies and techniques, and the training datasets used, including a general description of these datasets, information about their origin, scope, and main characteristics; how the data was obtained and selected; labeling procedures (e.g., for supervised learning), data cleaning methodologies (e.g., outlier detection); (e) an assessment of the human oversight measures required under Article 14, including an assessment of the technical measures needed to facilitate the interpretation of the outputs of AI systems by the operators, in accordance with Article 13(3), point (d); (f) where applicable, a detailed description of any predetermined changes to the AI system and its performance, along with relevant information regarding the technical solutions adopted to ensure continuous compliance with the requirements set out in Chapter III, Section 2; (g) the validation and testing procedures used, including information about the validation and testing data and their main characteristics; metrics used to measure accuracy, robustness, and compliance with other relevant requirements in Chapter III, Section 2, as well as any potential discriminatory impacts; test logs and all test reports dated and signed by responsible persons, including for predetermined changes as referenced in point (f); (h) cybersecurity measures implemented.

Thus, it should be ensured (even in terms of the technical specifications outlined in Article 79 and Annex II.5 of Legislative Decree No. 36/2023) that, before being used in certain tenders and to evaluate the resulting technical bids, the AI system is certified as having operated within specific environments and with relevant and adequately representative datasets.

According to Article 30 of the Public Procurement Code, a secure and reliable AI system should be deploying machine learning but be overseen by humans. This, while not eliminating them entirely, significantly reduces complex and opaque outputs that complicate the understanding and interpreting of the results.[27] The European legislator is fully aware of this risk and, indeed, mandates for "high-risk" activities,[28] under Article 14.1, that: "High-risk AI systems shall be designed and developed in such a way, including with appropriate human-machine interface tools, that they can be effectively overseen by natural persons during the period in which they are in use".

---

[27] Borgesius (2018) and Crawford (2016).

[28] AI Act, Art. 6(1–3): 1. Irrespective of whether an AI system is placed on the market or put into service independently of the products referred to in points (a) and (b), that AI system shall be considered to be high-risk where both of the following conditions are fulfilled: (a) the AI system is intended to be used as a safety component of a product, or the AI system is itself a product, covered by the Union harmonisation legislation listed in Annex I; (b) the product whose safety component pursuant to point (a) is the AI system, or the AI system itself as a product, is required to undergo a third-party conformity assessment, with a view to the placing on the market or the putting into service of that product pursuant to the Union harmonisation legislation listed in Annex I. 2. In addition to the high-risk AI systems referred to in paragraph 1, AI systems referred to in Annex III shall be considered to be high-risk. 3. By derogation from paragraph 2, an AI system referred to in Annex III shall not be considered to be high-risk where it does not pose a significant risk of harm to the health, safety or fundamental rights of natural persons, including by not materially influencing the outcome of decision making. The first subparagraph shall apply where any of the following conditions is fulfilled: (a) the AI system is intended to perform a narrow procedural task; (b) the AI system is intended to improve the result of a previously completed human activity; (c) the AI system is intended to detect decision-making patterns or deviations from prior decision-making patterns and is not meant to replace or influence the previously completed human assessment, without proper human review; or (d) the AI system is intended to perform a preparatory task to an assessment relevant for the purposes of the use cases listed in Annex III. Notwithstanding the first subparagraph, an AI system referred to in Annex III shall always be considered to be high-risk where the AI system performs profiling of natural persons.

All. III: High-risk AI systems pursuant to Article 6(2) are the AI systems listed in any of the following areas:

1. Biometrics, in so far as their use is permitted under relevant Union or national law: (a) remote biometric identification systems. This shall not include AI systems intended to be used for biometric verification the sole purpose of which is to confirm that a specific natural person is the person he or she claims to be; (b) AI systems intended to be used for biometric categorisation, according to sensitive or protected attributes or characteristics based on the inference of those attributes or characteristics; (c) AI systems intended to be used for emotion recognition.

Related: Recital 54 and Recital 159 2. Critical infrastructure: AI systems intended to be used as safety components in the management and operation of critical digital infrastructure, road traffic, or in the supply of water, gas, heating or electricity. Related: Recital 55 3. Education and vocational training: (a) AI systems intended to be used to determine access or admission or to assign natural persons to educational and vocational training institutions at all levels; (b) AI systems intended to be used to evaluate learning outcomes, including when those outcomes are used to steer the learning process of natural persons in educational and vocational training institutions at all levels; (c) AI systems intended to be used for the purpose of assessing the appropriate level of education that an individual will receive or will be able to access, in the context of or within educational and vocational training institutions at all levels; (d) AI systems intended to be used for monitoring and detecting prohibited behavior of students during tests in the context of or within educational and vocational training institutions at all levels.

Actually, there is a veto on high-risk activities against AI systems with deep learning capabilities without human oversight.

But does the sector regulate by the Public Procurement Code fall under high-risk activities?

5 High-Risk Activities and the Public Procurement Sector

The answer, considering the provisions of the AI Act itself, is negative.

Given the broad scope of the public procurement sector, it is difficult to identify with certainty which specific activities may qualify as high risk; however, those involving essential public services or critical digital infrastructure could potentially fall within this category, particularly when the use of generative artificial intelligence systems introduces inherent vulnerabilities.

Nonetheless, two aspects, concerning the sufficiency and relevance of the concept of high-risk in public procurement, should be briefly considered. On the one hand, it appears unrealistic to attempt to categorically and preemptively classify all risks—both future and present, whether high or low—and their corresponding sectors, given the unpredictability and fluid nature of the subject matter. On the other hand, the author subscribes to the view that it is not necessarily the sector of use that is inherently risky, but rather the concrete application and use of generative artificial intelligence systems themselves.[29]

The necessary elaboration of this first premise leads to the question of what level of human supervision is required to potentially overturn an automated decision, pursuant to letter (b) of paragraph 3 of Article 30 of the Public Procurement Code, which, as is well known, mandates that algorithmic decisions cannot be exclusive.

The EU's AI Act requires the user to implement controls aimed at correcting potential distortions in usage,[30] as provided for in Article 15.5 of the AI Act:

> The technical solutions to address AI-specific vulnerabilities shall include, where appropriate, measures to prevent, detect, respond to, resolve and control for attacks trying to manipulate the training data set (data poisoning), or pre-trained components used in training (model poisoning), inputs designed to cause the AI model to make a mistake (adversarial examples or model evasion), confidentiality attacks or model flaws.

---

[29] Helberger and Diakopoulos (2023). The author's state: "The alternative scenario would be that all generative AI systems would fall under the high-risk category because it cannot be excluded that they may be used also in a high-risk area. In that case, there may be a serious risk of over-regulation. For this reason, rather than trying to fit general-purpose AI systems into existing high-risk categories, we propose that they should be considered a general-risk category in their own right, similar to the way that chatbots and deep fakes are considered a separate risk category of their own, and subject to legal obligations and requirements that fit their characteristics".

[30] Art. 14, I.A. Act: Human oversight shall aim to prevent or minimize the risks to health, safety or fundamental rights that may emerge when a high-risk AI system is used in accordance with its intended purpose or under conditions of reasonably foreseeable misuse, in particular where such risks persist despite the application of other requirements set out in this Section.

6 The New and Hybrid System of Automation Between Human-in-the-Loop Oversight and Governance Framework

A key aspect is the responsibility of operators, the people who control the machine.[31] These individuals may be "*any natural or legal person, public authority, agency, or other body that uses an AI system under their authority, except where the AI system is used in the course of a personal non-professional activity*".

There is no doubt that when speaking of responsibility and risk management, it pertains to the moment of use and is ultimately placed upon the operator, who is deemed responsible and subject to a considerable range of obligations.[32] Among

[31] Whereas n. 58 A.I. Act: Another area in which the use of AI systems deserves special consideration is the access to and enjoyment of certain essential private and public services and benefits necessary for people to fully participate in society or to improve one's standard of living. In particular, natural persons applying for or receiving essential public assistance benefits and services from public authorities namely healthcare services, social security benefits, social services providing protection in cases such as maternity, illness, industrial accidents, dependency or old age and loss of employment and social and housing assistance, are typically dependent on those benefits and services and in a vulnerable position in relation to the responsible authorities. If AI systems are used for determining whether such benefits and services should be granted, denied, reduced, revoked or reclaimed by authorities, including whether beneficiaries are legitimately entitled to such benefits or services, those systems may have a significant impact on persons' livelihood and may infringe their fundamental rights, such as the right to social protection, non-discrimination, human dignity or an effective remedy and should therefore be classified as high-risk. Nonetheless, this Regulation should not hamper the development and use of innovative approaches in the public administration, which would stand to benefit from a wider use of compliant and safe AI systems, provided that those systems do not entail a high risk to legal and natural persons. In addition, AI systems used to evaluate the credit score or creditworthiness of natural persons should be classified as high-risk AI systems, since they determine those persons' access to financial resources or essential services such as housing, electricity, and telecommunication services. AI systems used for those purposes may lead to discrimination between persons or groups and may perpetuate historical patterns of discrimination, such as that based on racial or ethnic origins, gender, disabilities, age or sexual orientation, or may create new forms of discriminatory impacts. However, AI systems provided for by Union law for the purpose of detecting fraud in the offering of financial services and for prudential purposes to calculate credit institutions' and insurance undertakings' capital requirements should not be considered to be high-risk under this Regulation. Moreover, AI systems intended to be used for risk assessment and pricing in relation to natural persons for health and life insurance can also have a significant impact on persons' livelihood and if not duly designed, developed and used, can infringe their fundamental rights and can lead to serious consequences for people's life and health, including financial exclusion and discrimination. Finally, AI systems used to evaluate and classify emergency calls by natural persons or to dispatch or establish priority in the dispatching of emergency first response services, including by police, firefighters and medical aid, as well as of emergency healthcare patient triage systems, should also be classified as high-risk since they make decisions in very critical situations for the life and health of persons and their property.

[32] AI Act, Article 23 Obligations of importers: 1. Before placing a high-risk AI system on the market, importers shall ensure that the system is in conformity with this Regulation by verifying that: (a) the relevant conformity assessment procedure referred to in Article 43 has been carried out by the provider of the high-risk AI system; (b) the provider has drawn up the technical documentation in accordance with Article 11 and Annex IV; (c) the system bears the required CE marking and is

these is the crucial role of human monitoring and supervision of the use of artificial intelligence systems, explicitly referenced in Article 26 of the A.I. Act. In particular, the Act requires that:

1. "Deployers of high-risk AI systems shall take appropriate technical and organizational measures to ensure they use such systems in accordance with the instructions for use accompanying the systems, pursuant to paragraphs 3 and 6."
2. Deployers shall assign human oversight to natural persons who have the necessary competence, training, and authority, as well as the necessary support.
3. "The obligations set out in paragraphs 1 and 2 are without prejudice to other deployer obligations under Union or national law and to the deployer's freedom to organize its own resources and activities for the purpose of implementing the human oversight measures indicated by the provider".[33]

In our legal system, where administrative actions must be grounded on constitutional values, human control and supervision must always be present within administrative operations.

From this perspective, the Constitution is clear, as established by Articles 28, 97, and 98, which emphasize the functions and responsibilities of public officials, and directly link public action to public employees. Beyond the Constitution, Article 30 of the Public Procurement Code is even more explicit, as it does not allow the use of machines without human supervision, rendering them unusable in its absence. As has been widely discussed, our legal system does not allow the removal of responsibility from the public official, requiring that the human, not merely the official, make decisions and be accountable for their actions.[34]

7 The Governance System

A well-functioning governance system, just like the supervision of automated mechanisms, represents one of the most important factors in ensuring the proper functioning of artificial intelligence systems. This aspect is crucial, especially in public

---

accompanied by the EU declaration of conformity referred to in Article 47 and instructions for use; (d) the provider has appointed an authorised representative in accordance with Article 22.

[33] At the same time, article 26 required that: 5. Deployers shall monitor the operation of the high-risk AI system on the basis of the instructions for use and, where relevant, inform providers in accordance with Article 72. Where deployers have reason to consider that the use of the high-risk AI system in accordance with the instructions may result in that AI system presenting a risk within the meaning of Article 79(1), they shall, without undue delay, inform the provider or distributor and the relevant market surveillance authority, and shall suspend the use of that system. Where deployers have identified a serious incident, they shall also immediately inform first the provider, and then the importer or distributor and the relevant market surveillance authorities of that incident. If the deployer is not able to reach the provider, Article 73 shall apply mutatis mutandis. This obligation shall not cover sensitive operational data of deployers of AI systems which are law enforcement authorities.

[34] Barberio (2023), Gallone (2023), see note 3.

procurement, where it is essential for public administrations to adopt clear, pre-tested systems to ensure that artificial intelligence mechanisms comply with the rules set out in Article 30 of the new Public Procurement Code.[35]

When it comes to governance, there are multiple perspectives, differing approaches, and contrasting visions on the subject, given that this is an entirely new area, which does not easily conform to previous rules. Some authors advocate for complex governance systems, structured in various ways, where responsibility is shared between providers, requiring them to assume responsibility for the systems and to provide all necessary safeguards and protections in the use of such tools.[36]

In this case, the system differs from the one outlined by the AI Act where, as we have seen, responsibility falls directly on the operators and their use of the system.

On the other hand, there is an alternative approach that adopts a different framework. In this governance model, the complexity and novelty of AI systems are highlighted, necessitating new responses that are not currently provided by existing regulations or older systems, which need to be reassessed against the new verification and control methods.[37]

The European AI Act appears to be developing its governance and responsibility framework in a different manner compared to the models currently under study, with adjustments to be made based on practical experiences in the coming years. In fact, as with the responsibility for managing and using these systems, governance is also left to the operators, who, according to Recital 58a, must:

> Establish appropriate governance structures in the specific context of use, such as human oversight arrangements, complaint management procedures, and redress mechanisms, as governance choices may be crucial in mitigating risks to fundamental rights in specific use cases.

They must also, where the system falls within "one or more critical sectors or use cases as outlined in Annex III",[38] conduct a preliminary assessment aimed at

---

[35] Corrado (2023).

[36] Mokander et al. (2023).

[37] "AI cannot be governed like any previous technology, and it is already shifting traditional notions of geopolitical power … the challenge is clear: to design a new governance framework fit for this unique technology. If global governance of IA is to become possible, the international system must move past traditional conceptions of sovereignty and welcome technology companies to the table": Bremmer and Suleyman (2023).

[38] Art. 6, co. 3 A.I. Act: By derogation from paragraph 2, an AI system referred to in Annex III shall not be high-risk where it does not pose a significant risk of harm to the health, safety or fundamental rights of natural persons, including by not materially influencing the outcome of decision making. The first subparagraph shall apply where any of the following conditions is fulfilled: (a) the AI system is intended to perform a narrow procedural task; (b) the AI system is intended to improve the result of a previously completed human activity; (c) the AI system is intended to detect decision-making patterns or deviations from prior decision-making patterns and is not meant to replace or influence the previously completed human assessment, without proper human review; or (d) the AI system is intended to perform a preparatory task to an assessment relevant for the purposes of the use cases listed in Annex III. Notwithstanding the first subparagraph, an AI system referred to in Annex III shall always be considered to be high-risk where the AI system performs profiling of natural persons.

identifying and quantifying the impact of the AI system by drafting a "detailed plan" that outlines, among other things, measures and tools aimed at mitigating risks, as well as gathering relevant information deemed necessary for the impact assessment.

Impact assessment[39] already exists in EU law,[40] and has been envisioned, within the AI Act, as a necessary tool for regulating artificial intelligence in high-risk scenarios and preventing negative effects and potential violations of the fundamental rights of individuals affected by AI mechanisms. The AI Act sets out the general content of the impact assessment, mandating that minimum content be provided to offer adequate responses to the machine's functioning.

On this point, Article 27 outlines the minimum content required to provide appropriate responses both to users and public entities that use AI systems. Indeed, the system is primarily directed at those "providing public services", who are obligated to perform an impact assessment on the effects that the mechanism may have on the fundamental rights of recipients. In particular, the impact assessment must include:

> (a) a description of the deployer's processes in which the high-risk AI system will be used in line with its intended purpose; (b) a description of the period of time within which, and the frequency with which, each high-risk AI system is intended to be used; (c) the categories of natural persons and groups likely to be affected by its use in the specific context; (d) the specific risks of harm likely to have an impact on the categories of natural persons or groups of persons identified pursuant to point (c) of this paragraph, taking into account the information provided by the provider pursuant to Article 13; (e) a description of the implementation of human oversight measures, according to the instructions for use; (f) the measures to be taken in the case of the materialization of those risks, including the arrangements for internal governance and complaint mechanisms.

Only in these terms can the governance system be adapted to ensure the proper functioning of artificial intelligence mechanisms.

The governance system envisioned at the European level is aimed at minimizing risks and maintaining constant control over outcomes, in pursuit of the goal of protecting individuals' fundamental rights. Should the governance system fail to function correctly, resulting in violations of the rules established by the A.I. Act, Article 26 provides that:

> Deployers shall monitor the operation of the high-risk AI system on the basis of the instructions for use and, where relevant, inform providers in accordance with Article 72. Where deployers have reason to consider that the use of the high-risk AI system in accordance with the instructions may result in that AI system presenting a risk within the meaning of Article 79, they shall, without undue delay, inform the provider or distributor and the relevant market surveillance authority, and shall suspend the use of that system. Where deployers have identified a serious incident, they shall also immediately inform first the provider, and then the

[39] Art. 27, co. 1 A.I. Act: Prior to deploying a high-risk AI system referred to in Article 6(2), with the exception of high-risk AI systems intended to be used in the area listed in point 2 of Annex III, deployers that are bodies governed by public law, or are private entities providing public services, and deployers of high-risk AI systems referred to in points 5 (b) and (c) of Annex III, shall perform an assessment of the impact on fundamental rights that the use of such system may produce. For that purpose, deployers shall perform an assessment consisting of.

[40] Like the environmental sector, Directive 85/337/CEE del 27 June 1985; or that of data protection, Art. 35 Regulation UE 2016/679 del 27 aprile 2016.

> importer or distributor and the relevant market surveillance authorities of that incident. If the deployer is not able to reach the provider, Article 73 shall apply mutatis mutandis. This obligation shall not cover sensitive operational data of deployers of AI systems which are law enforcement authorities.[41]

In this context, it is conceivable to adopt a governance system in Italy capable of adapting and revising the European model, particularly concerning data management and its accuracy, as the functioning of machine learning systems relies primarily on the completeness and truthfulness of the data. This is because the reasoning used by the machine is not known, nor is there utility in understanding the source code.[42]

But is the system built within the AI Act truly transparent, making decisions accessible to citizens and providing clear answers with appropriate tools? Or is it a system based on rules that must inevitably adapt to the lack of mechanisms capable of explaining the decision-making process?

8 Conclusion

The Italian and European frameworks laid down a milestone in the regulation of artificial intelligence. Despite significant progress, many doubts remain concerning decisions made in the presence of so-called black-box systems.[43]

In the Italian system, as outlined in the new Public Procurement Code, decisions must necessarily be both understandable and accessible. In this sense, the use of deep learning machine, with LLM tools, could prove revolutionary. The integration of LLMs establishes a dual-layer review mechanism, whereby decisions can be assessed both through the generated textual output, akin to traditional administrative review, and through an additional layer of analysis that examines the underlying rationale deployed by the AI system in the decision-making process. This enables a more thorough and comprehensive review, allowing stakeholders to more effectively dissect and understand administrative decisions.[44]

By contrast, the AI Act, which recognizes the impossibility of direct access to the information needed to understand how the system operates, adopts a "top-down

---

[41] For criticism on the point, see note 14; the author criticizes that "the legal framework mentioned above lies in the fact that it focuses almost exclusively on the risks of discriminatory outcomes and violations of individual rights but does not seem to sufficiently address the issue of erroneous, inaccurate, or incomplete data being returned in public and institutional contexts. It is therefore considered that, insofar as an AI system is involved in a procurement procedure classified as high-risk, the impact assessment could be suitably enhanced by the operator, during the analysis of potential and specific impacts, with additional and varied content aimed at improving the effectiveness and optimization of the artificial intelligence system".

[42] On the point and for further information see Lo Sapio (2021, 2024).

[43] Di Martino (2023).

[44] Carullo (2023).

transparency" approach. This is achieved through obligations to provide instructions for use, communications, and summary documents prepared by the providers themselves.[45]

Initial doubts about transparency arise from Article 13 of the AI Act, which applies to high-risk systems and confirms an informational model that only explains how the machine functions.[46] In this context, transparency is required "in such a way as to ensure that their operation is sufficiently transparent to enable deployers to interpret a system's output and use it appropriately".

However, this required transparency is left largely to the discretion of the providers, with the meaning of transparency open to their expertise, leaving interpretation on this point unresolved.

Communication obligations are further confirmed in Article 50 of the AI Act, particularly when clarifying that a system is not controlled by human beings. The article states that:

> Providers shall ensure that AI systems intended to interact directly with natural persons are designed and developed in such a way that the natural persons concerned are informed that they are interacting with an AI system, unless this is obvious from the point of view of a natural person who is reasonably well-informed, observant and circumspect, taking into account the circumstances and the context of use.

In addition to this obligation, the article also addresses the use of generative artificial intelligence,[47] about which further doubts remain regarding the use of such mechanisms in our legal system when it is not possible to explain their reasoning. Therefore, it appears that providers are not subject to strict information obligations, but instead, are free to select the information made available for the use of AI systems.

[45] The thought on the point for Lo Sapio (2024) is that: "Since it is impossible to have full knowledge of the training data, models, and IT infrastructures behind AI systems, the provider is required to deliver "clear and comprehensible" communication. This obligation, however, is based on vague standards of reasonableness, which leave considerable room for interpretation by those tasked with "explaining" the system and, consequently, selecting the information to be shared".

[46] Recital 72: "To address concerns related to opacity and complexity of certain AI systems and help deployers to fulfil their obligations under this Regulation, transparency should be required for high-risk AI systems before they are placed on the market or put it into service. High-risk AI systems should be designed in a manner to enable deployers to understand how the AI system works, evaluate its functionality, and comprehend its strengths and limitations. High-risk AI systems should be accompanied by appropriate information in the form of instructions of use. Such information should include the characteristics, capabilities and limitations of performance of the AI system".

[47] Art. 50, co. 2, A.I. Act: Providers of AI systems, including general-purpose AI systems, generating synthetic audio, image, video or text content, shall ensure that the outputs of the AI system are marked in a machine-readable format and detectable as artificially generated or manipulated. Providers shall ensure their technical solutions are effective, interoperable, robust and reliable as far as this is technically feasible, considering the specificities and limitations of various types of content, the costs of implementation and the generally acknowledged state of the art, as may be reflected in relevant technical standards. This obligation shall not apply to the extent the AI systems perform an assistive function for standard editing or do not substantially alter the input data provided by the deployer or the semantics thereof, or where authorized by law to detect, prevent, investigate or prosecute criminal offences.

The abstract nature of these requirements raises significant concerns, especially in terms of protecting the recipients of such decisions.

The limitations of the European regulatory framework and its potential application in our legal system are evident from these provisions. By failing to specifically define the obligations concerning the management of such systems, they stand in clear contrast to the principles of transparency and justification in administrative decisions.

Finally, it is crucial to highlight the importance of Article 86, which addresses the "right to explanation" granted to individuals affected by decisions made by AI systems. According to this article, the "Right to explanation of individual decision-making" is established in favor of individuals affected by decisions made using AI systems.[48]

The knowability and clarity of the decision do not refer to the AI system used, but rather to the specific case, targeting the users on the one hand, to ensure they are prepared to explain and justify the "*why*" behind the decision. On the other hand, it acts as a safeguard for individuals affected by the decisions, ensuring that they understand the reasons behind the outcome.

The content of this article can be adapted to Italian administrative law, particularly the new Public Procurement Code, establishing a generalized obligation for public administrations to explain the role that AI systems played in the administrative procedure. This should be reflected in the final decision, with an explanation that is both clear and meaningful.[49]

To ensure the system functions correctly, enabling comprehensibility of decisions and allowing for the effective use of AI tools, it is necessary to strengthen transparency obligations for providers. At the same time, there should be increased scope for using AI, always with human supervision to correct potential distortions or errors.

Undoubtedly, the most significant challenges emerge—and will persist—as long as technology remains incapable of explaining itself, particularly with machine learning and deep learning systems, where the opacity of the reasoning process precludes their use in areas where transparency is mandatory, such as the Italian administrative sector.

The first steps have been taken, but to ensure that artificial intelligence systems can operate in a legal system such as Italy's, or more broadly within the European legal framework defined by the principle of legality, it is essential to develop

[48] Art. 86, A.I. Act: 1. Any affected person subject to a decision which is taken by the deployer on the basis of the output from a high-risk AI system listed in Annex III, with the exception of systems listed under point 2 thereof, and which produces legal effects or similarly significantly affects that person in a way that they consider to have an adverse impact on their health, safety or fundamental rights shall have the right to obtain from the deployer clear and meaningful explanations of the role of the AI system in the decision-making procedure and the main elements of the decision taken. 2. Paragraph 1 shall not apply to the use of AI systems for which exceptions from, or restrictions to, the obligation under that paragraph follow from Union or national law in compliance with Union law. 3. This Article shall apply only to the extent that the right referred to in paragraph 1 is not otherwise provided for under Union law.

[49] See note 33.

advanced procedures. These must ensure that, when infringed, citizens' rights can be protected. The intrinsic opacity of AI decisions and the right to explanation should be two guiding principles to ensure the correct use of artificial intelligence systems in compliance with the law.

References

Auby JB (2019) Il diritto amministrativo di fronte alle sfide digitali. Le istituzioni del federalismo, 3: 619-641

Avanzini G (2019) Decisioni amministrative e algoritmi informatici. Predeterminazione analisi predittiva e nuove forme di intelligibilità, Editoriale scientifica, Naples

Barberio M (2023, June) L'utilizzo degli algoritmi e l'intelligenza artificiale tra futuro prossimo e incertezza applicativa. www.giustizia-amministrativa.it

Barbiero M (2024) L'art. 30 del D.L. vo 36/2023 alla prova dell'A.I. Act dell'Unione Europea. Relazione tenuta al Convegno di Studi presso l'Università degli Studi di Cagliari "L'intelligenza artificiale nel diritto amministrativo". www.giustizia-amministrativa.it

Borgesius FZ (2018) Discrimination, Artificial Intelligence and Algorithmic Decision-Making. Council of Europe, Strasbourg

Bremmer I, Suleyman M (2023) The AI paradox, can states learn to govern artificial intelligence before it's too late? Foreign Affairs, September/October

Carloni E (2008) La qualità dei dati pubblici. In: Ponti B (ed), Il regime dei dati pubblici. Maggioli, Rimini.

Carloni E (2020) I principi della legalità algoritmica. Le decisioni automatizzate di fronte al giudice amministrativo. Diritto amministrativo, 27(2): 273-304

Carullo G (2023) Large language models for transparent and intelligible AI-assisted public decision-making. Ceridap 3:6

Cavallo Perin R (2020) Ragionando come se la digitalizzazione fosse data. Diritto amministrativo, 28(2): 305-328

Chollet F (2021) Deep learning with Python, 2nd edn. Manning, Shelter Island, New York

Colletti G (2024) La ricerca di un (non) perfetto equilibrio tra sistemi di automazione e principi regolatori nel nuovo Codice dei contratti pubblici. In: Cerrillo i Martínez A, Di Lascio F, Martín Delgado I, Velasco Rico CI (eds), Inteligencia artificial y administraciones públicas: una triple visión en clave comparada. Iustel, Madrid, pp. 333-341

Corbino M (2024) Prospettive di digitalizzazione della Pubblica Amministrazione nel settore degli appalti: tra esigenze di efficienza e principio di legalità della regola algoritmica. In: Cerrillo i Martínez A, Di Lascio F, Martín Delgado I, Velasco Rico CI (eds), Inteligencia artificial y administraciones públicas: una triple visión en clave comparada. Iustel, Madrid, pp. 345-353

Corrado A (2023) I nuovi contratti pubblici, intelligenza artificiale e blockchain: le sfide del prossimo futuro. Federalismi.it, 19:128-154

Costantino F (2017) Lampi. Nuove frontiere delle decisioni amministrative tra open e big data, Diritto amministrativo, 25(4): 799-836

Crawford MAK (2016) Seeing without knowing: Limitations of the transparency ideal and its application to algorithmic accountability. New Media & Society, 20(3): 973-989

D'Orlando E, Orsoni G (2019) Nuove prospettive dell'amministrazione digitale: Open Data e algoritmi. Istituzioni del federalismo, 3: 593-617

Delgado IM (2016) La riforma dell'amministrazione digitale: un'opportunità per ripensare la pubblica amministrazione. In: Civitarese Matteucci S, Torchia L (eds), La tecnificazione, Vol. VI. In: Ferrara L, Sorace D (eds), A 150 anni dall'unificazione amministrativa italiana, Firenze University Press, Florence, p. 133 ff.

Delgado IM (2019) Automazione, intelligenza artificiale e pubblica amministrazione: vecchie categorie concettuali per nuovi problemi? Istituzioni del federalismo, 3: 643-662
Delle Cave G (2024) L'amministrazione algoritmica dal punto di vista del controllo: revisori digitali e audit pubblici «a valle» del procedimento automatizzato. In: Cerrillo i Martínez A, Di Lascio F, Martín Delgado I, Velasco Rico CI (eds), Inteligencia artificial y administraciones públicas: una triple visión en clave comparada. Iustel, Madrid, pp. 355-367
Di Martino A (2023) Tecnica e potere nell'amministrazione per algoritmi. Editoriale scientifica, Naples
Falcone M (2023) Ripensare il potere conoscitivo pubblico tra algoritmi e Big Data. Editoriale scientifica, Naples
Fanti V (2022) Intelligenza artificiale e diritto amministrativo: prospettive, limiti, pericoli. Diritto e processo amministrativo, 4: 1001-1014
Floridi L, Chiriatti M (2020, Dec) GPT-3: its nature, scope, limits and consequences. Mind Mach 30(4):681–694
Forte P (2020) Diritto amministrativo e data science. Appunti di Intelligenza Amministrativa Artificiale (AAI). Persona & Amministrazione, 1, p. 247 ff
Galetta DU, Corvalan JG (2019) Intelligenza artificiale per una pubblica amministrazione 4.0? Federalismi.it, 3: 2-23
Gallone G (2023) Riserva di umanità e funzioni amministrative: indagine sui limiti dell'automazione decisionale tra procedimento e processo, Cedam, Padova
Goodfellow I, Bengio Y, Courville A (2016) Deep learning. MIT Press, Cambridge, Massachusetts
Helberger N, Diakopoulos N (2023) ChatGPT and the AI Act. Internet Policy Review, 12(1): 2-6
Lo Sapio G (2021) La black box: l'esplicabilità delle scelte algoritmiche quale garanzia di buona amministrazione, Federalismi.it, 16:114-127
Lo Sapio G (2024) L'Artificial Intelligence Act e la prova di resistenza per la legalità algoritmica, Federalismi.it, 16:265-290
Marongiu D (2020) L'intelligenza artificiale "istituzionale": limiti (attuali) e potenzialità. Eur Rev Digit Adm Law, 1(1–2): 37-53
Masucci A (2020) L'algoritmizzazione delle decisioni amministrative tra Regolamento europeo e leggi degli Stati membri. Diritto pubblico, 3: 943-979
Masucci A (2022) L'automatizzazione delle decisioni amministrative algoritmiche fra big data e machine learning. Verso l'algocratic governance? Diritto e processo amministrativo, 2, p 265 ff
Mohri M, Rostamizadeh A, Talwalkar A (2012) Foundations of machine learning. MIT Press, Cambridge
Mokander J, Schuett J, Kirk HR, Floridi L (2023) Auditing large language models: a three-layered approach. AI Ethics 4, 1085–1115
Patroni Griffi F (2018) La decisione robotica e il giudice amministrativo. www.giustizia-amministrativa.com
Resta G (2019) Governare l'innovazione tecnologica: decisioni algoritmiche, diritti digitali e principio di uguaglianza. Politica del diritto, 2, pp. 199-236
Schweighofer E (2004) An e-Government interface for the director-general – Or: How to Support decision makers with an electronic chief secretary? In: Traunmueller R (ed), Electronic government: Third International Conference, EGOV 2004, Zaragoza, Spain, August 30–September 3, 2004, Proceedings. Lecture Notes in Computer Science, Springer-Verlag, Berlin Heidelberg
Simoncini A (2020) Amministrazione digitale algoritmica. Il quadro costituzionale. In: Cavallo Perin R, Galetta DU (eds), Il diritto dell'amministrazione pubblica digitale. Giappichelli, Turin
Slosser JL (2022). Thoughts on the Black Box: Getting to Cooperative Intelligence in Public Administration. Verfassungsblog: On Matters Constitutional.
Sterpa A (2024) L'ordine giuridico dell'algoritmo. Editoriale scientifica, Naples
Torchia L (2023) Lo Stato digitale. Il Mulino, Bologna

Giuseppe Sferrazzo, Ph.D. candidate in Administrative Law at the University of Rome Tor Vergata. Specialist in public contracts and administrative litigation. Focuses on the intersection between public procurement, technology, and AI regulation.

Open Access This chapter is licensed under the terms of the Creative Commons Attribution 4.0 International License (http://creativecommons.org/licenses/by/4.0/), which permits use, sharing, adaptation, distribution and reproduction in any medium or format, as long as you give appropriate credit to the original author(s) and the source, provide a link to the Creative Commons license and indicate if changes were made.

The images or other third party material in this chapter are included in the chapter's Creative Commons license, unless indicated otherwise in a credit line to the material. If material is not included in the chapter's Creative Commons license and your intended use is not permitted by statutory regulation or exceeds the permitted use, you will need to obtain permission directly from the copyright holder.

Copyright Issues in Deep Generative Models According to European Union Law

Lorenzo Basile, Andrea Mecchina, and Luca Bortolussi

Abstract Over the past decade machine learning witnessed an unprecedented increase in popularity, mainly due to the excellent results achieved by neural networks on a large variety of tasks. Among the subfields of machine learning, Generative Deep Learning stands out for the interest it is lately drawing in the research community and general public. In particular, the last few years marked the dawn of a new era in image and text generation, thanks to new powerful models which are deeply impacting the way we work, communicate and even create art. State-of-the-art text-to-image translation models are now capable of generating novel and photo-realistic images of almost anything, while in the realm of text generative models we are witnessing the overflowing emergence of Large Language Models such as ChatGPT, that are revolutionising the way we work and our daily lives. These developments unveil new vulnerabilities, such as the threat posed by machine-generated art to the work of creative professionals, as well as some relevant legal issues regarding copyright and intellectual property. Firstly, modern generative models are trained on vast datasets, densely populated by copyrighted data in the form of images or texts. Moreover, model owners are usually very opaque when it comes to disclosing details related to training data. Secondly, generative models produce novel data, and it is unclear who can claim copyright protection on them (if anyone), raising an interesting philosophical question: what does it mean for an artwork generated by an algorithm to be original? Machine learning regulations are still largely in the making by European authorities, but in this paper we try to clarify these issues according to the law currently in force in the European Union and from the perspective of the Artificial Intelligence Act.

Keywords Generative models · Machine-generated art · Intellectual property · Copyright · European law

L. Basile
AREA Science Park, Trieste, Italy

A. Mecchina (✉) · L. Bortolussi
University of Trieste, Trieste, Italy
e-mail: andrea.mecchina@phd.units.it

© The Author(s) 2025

C. Amodio and A. Diurni (eds.), *Human Vulnerability in Interaction with AI in European Private Law*, https://doi.org/10.1007/978-3-031-93247-2_17

1 The Rise of Machine Learning

Artificial intelligence (AI) and machine learning (ML) are without a doubt some of the hottest keywords in the contemporary age: the field is growing at an unprecedented rate, both in terms of scientific publications[1] and of generated revenue[2] (Zion Market Research 2022).

This growth is largely due to the peremptory emergence of Deep Learning, a long-neglected subfield of ML that employs very complex and powerful models called artificial neural networks (or simply neural networks) over a large and diverse variety of tasks. Such models are very data-hungry and rely massively on an incredible amount of data which is constantly acquired and processed: as an example, it is estimated that, already back in 2019, more than 2.5 trillion bytes of data were created every day.[3]

Neural networks owe their name to their resemblance with the networks that make up our brains, made of neurons and axons. Just like their biological counterparts, neural networks are made of strongly interconnected computational units that are able to process the input they receive in a very flexible way. A review of the history that led from some simplistic models of the brain to the incredibly versatile and powerful instruments developed nowadays is available.[4]

The name Deep Learning comes from the fact that neural networks are usually *deep*, meaning that the input has to traverse many layers of neurons before reaching the output. The role of these many layers is to allow for modelling complex and non-linear dependencies in the data.

Deep Learning has achieved outstanding results in the last 10 years, especially on predictive tasks, such as image classification,[5] natural language processing[6] and protein structure prediction.[7] What all these models have in common is that they are *discriminative* models, meaning that they are able to take as input some data and learn some hidden properties about them, for example a label telling whether an image contains a cat or a dog. The purpose of these models is indeed learning to associate particular features with specific labels of the input data.

The other main approach in ML is *generative* modeling, in which raw data are processed to learn the probability distribution that generated them, allowing the generation of new data samples that in some way look realistic, as is they were part of the same generating process.

The rest of this article is structured as follows: Section 2 briefly outlines the current state of the art in generative ML, Section 3 focuses on the copyright issues and the

[1] Zhang et al. (2021).

[2] Zion Market Research (2022).

[3] Hackenberger (2019).

[4] Shao and Shen (2023).

[5] Krizhevsky et al. (2012).

[6] Vaswani et al. (2017).

[7] Jumper et al. (2021).

relative European Union (EU) rules, and Section 4 finally concludes and discusses some future perspectives.

2 Overview of Generative ML

While scientific progress in discriminative modeling has been continuous and almost constant over the last decade, research in generative modeling has been mainly marked by a few major breakthroughs. A more detailed review of the distinction between the two paradigms of ML can be found in Jebara (2012).[8]

The first revolution in the field of generative models happened in 2014, thanks to the development of Generative Adversarial Networks (GANs), introduced by Goodfellow et al (2014). GANs are conceptually very simple: there are two models, a generator and a discriminator. The generator, starting from random guesses which look nothing like the data we want to eventually generate, tries to fool the discriminator, whose objective is discriminating between real data and generated data. The two models are trained together and get better over time by fighting against each other. This (hopefully) allows the generator to become so good that, eventually, the novel data that it is generating become indistinguishable from the real data.

Despite having become amazingly popular in the Deep Learning community, GANs are far from perfect. They are very difficult to train and the results they produce (usually images) are often unsatisfactory in terms of quality. GANs suffer from issues such as mode collapse, where the generator fails to capture the full diversity of the training data, and training instability, which can lead to non-convergence or oscillating behavior.

Other classes of generative models have been proposed, such as Variational Autoencoders[9] and Normalizing Flows,[10] but the most prominent breakthroughs since the introduction of GANs happened over the last few years, with the publication of several groundbreaking models. These include DALL·E 2,[11] and GPT-3,[12] both developed by OpenAI. Some other relevant examples are Stable Diffusion[13] by Stability AI, and PaLM,[14] developed by Google.

These models, along with their improved successors like DALL·E 3, GPT-4, and Stable Diffusion XL, have ushered in a new era of generative AI. They leverage massive datasets and novel architectures to produce highly coherent and contextually relevant outputs. In the realm of text-to-image generation, Stable Diffusion has gained

---

8 Jebara (2012).

9 Kingma and Welling (2013).

10 Rezende and Mohamed (2015).

11 Ramesh et al. (2022).

12 Brown et al. (2020).

13 Rombach et al. (2022).

14 Chowdhery et al. (2023).

Fig. 1 Example of image generations obtained with DALL·E, adapted from Ramesh et al. (2022)

significant popularity due to its open-source nature and ability to generate high-quality images with relatively low computational requirements. Midjourney, another text-to-image model, has also garnered attention for its artistic and creative outputs. Some examples of images generated by DALL·E 2 are shown in Fig. 1.

In the domain of large language models, alternatives to GPT-3 and GPT-4 emerged, such as Meta's LLaMA,[15] and its derivatives. These models have demonstrated impressive capabilities in natural language understanding and generation, often with different architectural approaches or training methodologies.

These advancements have not only pushed the boundaries of what's possible in generative ML but have also sparked discussions about the ethical implications,

[15] Touvron et al. (2023).

potential societal impacts, and the importance of addressing some significant legal questions regarding copyright.[16]

In this regard, a first point to address is the possibility to use protected works (such as paintings, poems, novels or code) to train ML models. This issue is not even strictly specific to generative ML, however generative models are particularly data-hungry and increasing the size of training datasets obviously increases the possibility of ending up using copyrighted works.

In addition, deep generative models output novel data, usually in the form of text and images. It is currently far from clear who has the ownership of these works, since the person that does the creative part (the one that prompts the model) does not usually coincide with the owner (and trainer) of the model.

3 Copyright Issues According to EU Law

We shall now try to address to the questions which arose at the end of the previous section. Giving a firm legal answer to these questions is often complicated (if not impossible), since a harmonized international legislation on these aspects is still missing and current rules at the national level differ from one another.

3.1 Usage of Copyrighted Artworks for Training

We will start by evaluating the cases in which using protected works for training a ML model is permitted or not, according to EU law.

In general, it is obviously allowed to use (lawfully acquired) copyrighted data for training in case the access is explicitly licensed by rightholders or if the artwork has fallen in the public domain. According to subparagraphs 1 and 2 of the Copyright Term Directive 2006/116/EC (European Parliament, Council of the European Union 2006), this happens 70 years after the death of the last living author of an artwork. In any other case, the possibility of using a copyrighted artwork is regulated by the Copyright and Information Society Directive 2001/29/EC (European Parliament, Council of the European Union 2001). Articles 2 and 3 provide the authors with the right to prohibit or authorize the reproduction and the right of making available their work respectively. Article 5 provides a partial exception to Article 2, stating that reproductions of copyrighted work "which are transient or incidental [and] an integral and essential part of a technological process" are allowed as long as they have no independent economic significance.

When it comes to generative machine learning, the inclusion of a copyrighted work in the training database can be usually thought of as transient (data are stored in a temporary RAM memory which is later erased), while it is much harder to claim

[16] Novelli et al. (2024).

that it has no economic significance. In fact, the inclusion of a few (or even just one) copyrighted works in the training dataset can significantly improve the performance of a model, increasing its economic worth.

Moreover, it is common for ML practitioners to store the data used for training for longer periods of time to allow model testing and verification, making the requirement on reproduction transience not met anymore. On top of this, a recent research paper[17] proved that it is possible to adversarially extract training data (which may be copyrighted) by querying large ML models, exposing the fact that models may indeed memorize copyrighted data in their weights.

The IS Directive has been amended by the Directive (EU) 2019/790 on Copyright in the Digital Single Market (DSM) (European Parliament, Council of the European Union 2019). The exceptions and limitations provided by this directive aimed at achieving a fair balance between the rights and interests of authors and other rights holders, on the one hand, and users, on the other hand (see Recital 6). Specifically, Article 3 provides an exception to the rights granted by Article 2 of the IS directive (European Parliament, Council of the European Union 2001), regarding the reproduction of protected works: it states that such reproduction is permitted if "made by research organisations and cultural heritage institutions in order to carry out, for the purposes of scientific research, text and data mining of works or other subject matter to which they have lawful access".

While Article 3 is limited to scientific research and does not mention private companies, Article 4 of the DSM directive extends this exception to all text and data mining processes (not limited to research and academic institutions); however, this extension is only granted if the usage of works has not been expressly reserved by their rightholders.

This means that, while in principle Article 4 might be invoked by any ML user, in practice one should seek confirmation on whether the usage of a given work is permitted or not before training any model. This is a costly and time-consuming activity and one of the main reasons why some commentators find the DSM directive as not well-fitting to the needs of the current ML ecosystem or even as a "missed opportunity for true modernization of the European Copyright Law in the digital single market".[18]

In addition, the DSM directive (European Parliament, Council of the European Union 2019) only deals with the extraction and reproduction rights. It does not mention the right of making available copyrighted artworks. This is a crucial point in ML applications, since it is a common practice in research environments to share the training data for verification and reproducibility purposes.[19]

Finally, another potential problem may arise with copyright infringement: it is not impossible that, by training on protected material, a model learns to reproduce that exactly. This issue is being addressed by researchers by trying to build ever more

[17] Nasr et al. (2023).

[18] Chiou (2019).

[19] Franceschelli and Musolesi (2021).

transformative models, that tend to create truly original works, learning nothing more than general patterns from the data they are given.

The application of these regulatory aspects to the context of AI has been partially harmonized by the European Parliament in June 2024 through the approval of the Regulation (EU) 2024/1689 (so called AI Act) (European Parliament, Council of the European Union 2024). Such regulation establishes a uniform legal framework regarding the development, marketing, deployment, and use of AI systems in the EU. In the approved text, among other things, in addition to the definition of an AI system, mechanisms for classifying high-risk AI systems are introduced, along with regulations for models, general-purpose AI systems, and governance, as well as prohibitions and measures to ensure compliance with the law. This is a regulatory document based on a human-centric approach to AI, consisting of a set of rules aimed at protecting fundamental human rights.

With particular regard to copyright protection, the above introduced AI Act restates the following concepts:

• considering that the development and training of large generative models require access to large amounts of text, images, videos, and other data that may be protected by copyright and related rights, any use of copyrighted content by General Purpose AI models requires explicit authorization from the rights holder, except in cases where limitations and exceptions apply (Recital 105). However, in cases covered by the exceptions and limitations introduced by the previously discussed DSM directive, see European Parliament, Council of the European Union (2019), apart from cases of use for scientific purposes, the rights holder may decide to impose a reservation on the use of their work by exercising their right to "opt out" in a "machine-readable" manner in the case of content made publicly available online, as stated in Article 4(3) of the same DSM directive (Recital 105);

• all providers of AI systems marketed in the European market are required to comply with the rules contained in the Regulation itself (and therefore with the implementation of DSM directive on copyright). In particular, the AI act establishes that providers of general-purpose AI models must identify and respect any reservations declared by rights holders under Article 4(3) of the DSM directive, and thus provide adequate information about the materials used for training the model (see Recital 106 and Recital 107). Therefore, consistent with the considerations outlined above, Article 53 of the AI Act establishes that "Providers of general-purpose AI models [. . .] shall implement a policy aimed at complying with Union copyright law and, in particular, at identifying and respecting, also through cutting-edge technologies, a reservation of rights expressed under Article 4(3) of Directive 2019/790". These obligations also apply "to providers of AI models released under free and open-source licenses that allow access, use, modification, and distribution of the model and whose parameters, including weights, model architecture information, and model usage information, are made public".

3.2 Ownership of Generated Works

Deep generative models allow the creation of original artwork, and this poses another interesting copyright question: who owns the data that GPT, DALL·E or similar models generate?

The answer looks far from trivial, given that OpenAI (the company that owns DALL·E and GPT) granted users full rights to reprint, sell, and merchandise generated artworks.[20] On the other hand, OpenAI retains ownership over the original images, as discussed.[21]

At first sight, both positions make sense, since the users and the owners of the models are playing two different but equally crucial roles. The former take care of the creative part of the process, by designing a textual prompt to feed into the model, while the latter created, trained and keep running the model itself, in a manner that some commentators find similar to the interaction between photographers and constructors of digital cameras.[22]

To frame the outlined issue from a more rigorous legal perspective, an important reference is the Berne convention, an international treaty of the World Intellectual Property Organization (WIPO) on the harmonization of copyright law.[23] It does not set any specific requirement for the protection of artistic works, allowing the protection of "every production in the literary, scientific and artistic domain, whatever may be the mode or form of its expression" and leaving plenty of room for variations in the national implementations of copyright law. However, a widely adopted standard requires copyrighted works to be *original.*[24]

It is not trivial to define the concept of originality, but the Copyright Term directive (European Parliament, Council of the European Union 2006), reads that "a photographic work within the meaning of the Berne Convention is to be considered original if it is the author's own intellectual creation reflecting his personality". The concept of originality is thus linked with the presence of a physical author, from whom personality emanates.

For text-to-image generators such as DALL·E and Stable Diffusion or chatbots such as ChatGPT, it may be argued that the creative effort belongs to the user, who provides a textual description of the desired model output; however it is not clear whether this level of human intervention suffices in emanating the personality of the author, thus defining the work as truly original. Moreover, it is much harder to claim that there is human creativity in the generation process of other models that do not accept any input, such as GANs.

Some degree of human intervention is surely required in the training of any ML model, but it is very questionable whether this renders generated artworks the result of the personality of someone, since usually the output does not contain any direct

---

[20] OpenAI (2022).

[21] Forbes (2022).

[22] VentureBeat (2022).

[23] WIPO (1886).

[24] Deltorn (2017).

and unmistakable trace of choices made by humans while training. This means that machine-generated works may end up being unprotected by current rules.

While this issue is not discussed in the AI Act (European Parliament, Council of the European Union 2024), it is now being discussed in the academic community[25] as well as before European policy makers, as proven by a 2020 resolution of the European Parliament on intellectual property rights in AI (European Parliament, Committee on Constitutional Affairs, Committee on Culture and Education, Committee on Legal Affairs, Committee on Transport and Tourism, Committee on the Internal Market and Consumer Protection 2020), whose Article 15 stressed "the importance of creating an operational and fully harmonised regulatory framework in the field of AI technologies", with specific reference to ownership of AI-generated works.

Moreover, some EU Member States, including Italy, in line with the approach of American jurisprudence, have been discussing their own laws in recent months to regulate this issue (Senato della Repubblica XIX Legislatura 2024). In particular, the Italian bill alters a law dating back to 1941 by modifying the definition of a "work of ingenuity" to include "those of human ingenuity of a creative nature, even when created with the aid of artificial intelligence tools, provided that the human contribution is creative, significant, and demonstrable".

4 Conclusions and Perspectives

In this paper we presented an overview of deep generative models and analyzed the legal issues related to their training process and the ownership of their generations. We looked at generative models through the lens of European Union current rules, but similar considerations can be generally made following US law. A more extensive discussion on the same topics, including also references to American law, is available.[26] By analyzing the law that currently regulates ML and, specifically, deep generative models, it is evident that some lawmaking effort is urgently needed: ML is moving forward at an accelerating pace and law needs to follow it closely.

Regarding generative models, the issues related to copyright law are just the tip of an iceberg that includes major privacy and fairness concerns (Naik 2022). Another infamous problem worth mentioning is that of deepfakes.[27] In this sense, the effort demonstrated by the EU institutions with the AI Act (European Parliament, Council of the European Union [2024]) and the aforementioned 2020 resolution (European Parliament, Committee on Constitutional Affairs, Committee on Culture and Education, Committee on Legal Affairs, Committee on Transport and Tourism, Committee on the Internal Market and Consumer Protection 2020), is appreciable and it would surely be very helpful for the ML community if the AI Act could be

[25] Franceschelli and Musolesi (2021), Krizhevsky et al. (2012).

[26] Franceschelli and Musolesi (2021).

[27] Pei et al. (2024).

shortly followed by further European directives or regulations, addressing the issues currently left open.

References

Brown T, Mann B, Ryder N, Subbiah M, Kaplan JD, Dhariwal P Neelakantan A, Shyam P, Sastry G, Askell A and Agarwal S (2020) Language models are few-shot learners. Adv Neural Inf Process Syst 33:1877–1901

Chiou T (2019) Copyright lessons on machine learning: what impact on algorithmic art? JIPITEC 398

Chowdhery A, Narang S, Devlin J, Bosma M, Mishra G, Roberts A, Fiedel N, Barham P, Chung HW, Sutton C, Gehrmann S, Schuh P (2023) Palm: scaling language modeling with pathways. J Mach Learn Res 24(240):1–113

Deltorn JM (2017) Deep creations: intellectual property and the automata. Frontiers in Digital Humanities 4:3

European Parliament, Council of the European Union (2001) Directive 2001/29/ec of the european parliament and of the council of 22 may 2001 on the harmonisation of certain aspects of copyright and related rights in the information society. Official J Eur Union

European Parliament, Council of the European Union (2006) Directive 2006/116/ec of the european parliament and of the council of 12 december 2006 on the term of protection of copyright and certain related rights. Official J Eur Union

European Parliament, Council of the European Union (2019) Directive (eu) 2019/790 of the european parliament and of the council of 17 april 2019 on copyright and related rights in the digital single market and amending directives 96/9/ec and 2001/29/ec. Official J Eur Union

European Parliament, Council of the European Union (2024) Regulation (eu) 2024/1689 of the european parliament and of thecouncil of 13 june 2024 laying down harmonised rules on artificial intelligence and amending regulations (ec) no 300/2008,(eu) no 167/2013, (eu) no 168/2013, (eu) 2018/858, (eu) 2018/1139 and (eu) 2019/2144 and directives 2014/90/eu, (eu) 2016/797 and (eu) 2020/1828 (artificial intelligence act). Official J Eur Union

European Parliament, Committee on Constitutional Affairs, Committee on Culture and Education, Committee on Legal Affairs, Committee on Transport and Tourism, Committee on the Internal Market and Consumer Protection (2020) European parliament resolution of 20 october 2020 on intellectual property rights for the development of artificial intelligence technologies (2020/2015(ini)). Official J Eur Union

Forbes (2022) Forbes: 4 predictions about the wild new world of text-to-image ai. https://www.forbes.com/sites/robtoews/2022/09/11/4-hot-takes-about-the-wild-new-world-of-generative-ai/

Franceschelli G, Musolesi M (2021) Copyright in generative deep learning. arXiv preprint arXiv:2105.09266

Goodfellow I, Pouget-Abadie J, Mirza M, et al (2014) Generative adversarial nets. Advances in Neural Information Processing Systems 27 (NIPS 2014)

Hackenberger BK (2019) Data by data, big data. Croat Med J 60(3):290

Jebara T (2012) Machine learning: discriminative and generative, vol 755. Springer Science & Business Media

Jumper J, Evans R, Pritzel A, Green T, Figurnov M, Ronneberger O, Tunyasuvunakool K, Bates R, Žídek A, Potapenko A Bridgland A (2021) Highly accurate protein structure prediction with alphafold. Nature 596(7873):583–589

Kingma D, Welling M (2013) Auto-encoding variational bayes. arXiv preprint arXiv:13126114

Krizhevsky A, Sutskever I, Hinton GE (2012) Imagenet classification with deep convolutional neural networks. Adv Neural Inf Process Syst 25 (NIPS 2012)

Naik AR (2022) The societal dangers of dall·e 2. Analytics India Magazine. https://analyticsindiamag.com/ai-origins-evolution/the-societal-dangers-of-dall-e-2/. Accessed on 15 Sep 2015
Nasr M, Carlini N, Hayase J, Jagielski M, Cooper AF, Choquette-Choo CA, Wallace E, Tramèr F, Ippolito D, Lee K (2023) Scalable extraction of training data from (production) language models. arXiv preprint arXiv:2311.17035
Novelli C, Casolari F, Hacker P, Spedicato G, Floridi L (2024) Generative ai in eu law: liability, privacy, intellectual property, and cybersecurity. Comput Law Secur Rev 55:106066
OpenAI (2022) Openai: Dall·e now available in beta. https://openai.com/blog/dall-e-now-available-in-beta/
Pei G, Zhang J, Hu M, Zhang Z, Wang C, Wu Y, Zhai G, Yang J, Tao D (2024) Deepfake generation and detection: A benchmark and survey. arXiv preprint arXiv:2403.17881
Ramesh A, Dhariwal P, Nichol A, Chu C, Chen M (2022) Hierarchical text-conditional image generation with clip latents. arXiv preprint arXiv:2204.06125
Rezende DJ, Mohamed S (2015) Variational inference with normalizing flows. arXiv preprint arXiv:1505.05770
Rombach R, Blattmann A, Lorenz D, Esser P, Ommer B (2022) High-resolution image synthesis with latent diffusion models. Proceedings of the IEEE/CVF conference on computer vision and pattern recognition, pp 10684–10695
Senato della Repubblica XIX Legislatura (2024) Disposizioni e delega al governo in materia di intelligenza artificiale. Fascicolo Iter DDL S 1146
Shao F, Shen Z (2023) How can artificial neural networks approximate the brain? Front Psychol 13:970214
Touvron H, Lavril T, Izacard G, Martinet X, Lachaux MA, Lacroix T, Lample G et al (2023) Llama: open and efficient foundation language models. arXiv preprint arXiv:2302.13971
Vaswani A, Shazeer N, Parmar N, Uszkoreit J, Jones L, Gomez AN, Kaiser L, Polosukhin I (2017) Attention is all you need. Adv Neural Inf Process Syst 30 (NIPS 2017)
VentureBeat (2022) Venturebeat: who owns dall·e images? legal ai experts weigh in. https://venturebeat.com/ai/who-owns-dall-e-images-legal-ai-experts-weigh-in/
WIPO (1886) Berne convention for the protection of literary and artistic works, sept. 9, 1886, as revised at paris on july 24, 1971 and amended in 1979. S Treaty Doc No 99–27
Zhang D, et al. (2021) The ai index 2021 annual report. arXiv preprint arXiv:2103.06312
Zion Market Research (2022) Artificial Intelligence (ai) market—global industry analysis

Lorenzo Basile, B.Sc. in Automation Engineering from the Federico II University of Naples in 2019, M.Sc. and Ph.D. in Data Science from the University of Trieste in 2021 and 2025, respectively, currently a postdoctoral researcher at the Laboratory of Data Engineering of Area Science Park in Trieste. His research interests include AI interpretability, focusing on explaining and controlling complex models, and multimodal machine learning, integrating vision, language, and other data for richer representations.

Andrea Mecchina, B.Sc. in Physics from the University of Trieste in 2019, and M.Sc. in Data Science and Scientific Computing from the University of Trieste in 2021, is currently a Ph.D. candidate in Applied Data Science and Artificial Intelligence at the University of Trieste. His research interests include statistical modeling, time series analysis and unsupervised learning.

Luca Bortolussi, Degree in mathematics in Trieste (2003) and Ph.D. in computer science from the University of Udine (2007),Visiting Researcher at the University of Edinburgh (2012), Associate Researcher at CNR-ISTI Pisa (QUANTICOL FP7 Project, 2013–2017), and Professor at Saarland University (2014–2015, Guest 2016, 2018–2021). At the University of Trieste, he was Assistant/Associate Professor (2006–2021) and is now Full Professor, leading the AI Laboratory. His research spans artificial intelligence, bridging symbolic, formal, and applied methods.

Open Access This chapter is licensed under the terms of the Creative Commons Attribution 4.0 International License (http://creativecommons.org/licenses/by/4.0/), which permits use, sharing, adaptation, distribution and reproduction in any medium or format, as long as you give appropriate credit to the original author(s) and the source, provide a link to the Creative Commons license and indicate if changes were made.

The images or other third party material in this chapter are included in the chapter's Creative Commons license, unless indicated otherwise in a credit line to the material. If material is not included in the chapter's Creative Commons license and your intended use is not permitted by statutory regulation or exceeds the permitted use, you will need to obtain permission directly from the copyright holder.

ODR, Reputation by Litigation and (Ex Post) Discrimination

Maria Cecilia Paglietti

Abstract This paper explores how Online Dispute Resolution (ODR) mechanisms reshape traditional justice systems, leading to increased privatization of coercion and the rise of private autonomy in dispute resolution. The emergence of platforms as "online courts" raises concerns about due process guarantees and substantive justice, with platforms acting as powerful private actors exerting regulatory, executive, and judicial authority over vast, heterogeneous communities. The core inquiry is whether ODR on platforms ensures fair access to justice and effective protection, particularly for vulnerable consumers. The analysis delves into how technological functionalities influence adjudicative dispute resolution for individual consumers in high-volume, low-value, and cross-border disputes, especially within online marketplaces where platforms may play a dual role as provider and party. The paper highlights how the digital environment exacerbates power imbalances, questioning if ODR can lead to discrimination in dispute handling and outcomes. It discusses consumer complaining behavior (CCB), noting how online voice empowers consumers, yet platforms' use of consumer profiles and scores can result in ex-post discrimination, favouring profitable consumers and potentially silencing others. Notably, it introduces the concept of reputation by litigation, highlighting how consumers themselves become reputational subjects through their complaint behavior. Finally, the study identifies key vulnerabilities hindering consumer access to justice in the digital realm: redress vulnerability (costs, complex procedures, personal attitude, cross-border issues), economic vulnerability, and digital vulnerability. While ODR may alleviate the first two by offering affordable, accessible solutions, it unfortunately exacerbates digital vulnerability, potentially leading to exclusion for less tech-savvy individuals.

This paper is based on a speech given at the International Conference "Human Vulnerability in Interaction with AI", which was held in Rome on 16-17 May 2024. An earlier version of this contribution is published with the title 'ODR and Discrimination in the Platform Economy' (2024). Journal of European Consumer and Market Law, 5: 217.

M. C. Paglietti (✉)
Roma Tre University, Rome, Italy
e-mail: mariacecilia.paglietti@uniroma3.it

© The Author(s) 2025

C. Amodio and A. Diurni (eds.), *Human Vulnerability in Interaction with AI in European Private Law*, https://doi.org/10.1007/978-3-031-93247-2_18

Keywords Fair access to justice and effective protection · Consumer complaining behavior (CCB) · Ex-post discrimination · Reputation by litigation · Redress vulnerability

1 Introduction

If we look at the debate on the interplay between digital technologies, law and society, "disruption" appears to be the key word.[1]

In the specifics of the enforcement, when a dispute is solved by a technological-data driven out-of-court mechanism handled by private entities (i.e. by Online Dispute Resolution—ODR), technological innovation is considered disruptive as it impacts the legal systems on several levels: that of the theoretical dimension of dispute resolution and the role of the nation-state in the enforcement (in the form of increased privatisation of coercion, given that the administration of justice is no more a monopoly of the apparatus of state courts exercising public powers)[2]; that of the raise of private autonomy in the dispute resolution field; and that of the related issues of potential discrimination among users, either on the procedural and the substantive field.

Even more in detail, the emerging of a wide range of alternative mechanisms redress handled by platforms operating as online courts[3] and the facto disputes managers[4] raises concerns either regarding the possible undermining the values and mechanisms of adjudication (in terms of due process guarantees) and also the possible threatens of the values of substantive justice (in terms of rectitude of the decision).

Assuming a regulatory perspective of the ecosystem of digital platforms, the entrance, over recent years, of ODR in the dispute resolution pyramid[5] can be read as a confirm of the emerging role of digital platforms as private ordering, i.e. as private actors—other than the traditional public authorities—which, due to their economic power and dimensions, have elaborated independent regulatory, executive and judicial power.[6]

Although this is not the first time that private model of protection and users' governance replaced public governance models (let's just think about the example of the diamond and the cotton markets),[7] the peculiarity of this new instances of private

---

[1] Susskind (2010).

[2] Koulu (2018).

[3] Van Loo (2016) and Goanta and Ortolani (2022).

[4] Del Duca et al. (2014).

[5] The dispute resolution pyramid (inspired by Braithwaite's enforcement pyramid: Ayres and Braithwaite (1992)] is an analytic model elaborated by the social science research that illustrates the stages of complaint resolution. At the bottom of the pyramid the disputant will attempt informal negotiation. At the second tier of the pyramid are ADR processes. Litigation occupies the apex of the pyramid: Cortés and de la Rosa (2013, p. 423).

[6] Bassan (2021).

[7] Bernstein (1992).

governance is in their magnitude. It is no limited to sector specific industries and small homogeneous communities, but it affects huge and heterogenous communities.[8]

The question I will pose is whether ODR on platforms assures fair access to justice and provides effective protection—especially for vulnerable consumers.

In terms of specifics, I will try to investigate how the use of ODR on platforms can provide effective protection for consumers in disputes between users and the platform and between users themselves. In particular, I will focus on how technological functionalities affect the adjudicative type of dispute resolution (either automated decision or human-driven) where a single consumer is involved, leaving aside the collective dimension. Therefore, this contribution focuses on high-volume, low-value and potentially cross-border disputes where platforms are the dispute resolution service provider. Sometimes platforms could also play a dual role in these disputes, as, at the same time as the dispute resolution provider, they could also be a party to the dispute. In these cases platforms embrace an adjudicative function. A typical example concerns content moderation, which is common to social media platforms, such as the Facebook Oversight Board. I will instead focus on the online marketplace type of transaction platforms, where a customer (either a consumer or a professional party) orders goods or services in exchange for payment—like ride-platforms (such as Uber and Airbnb).

2 ODR and the Effectiveness of Protection of (Vulnerable) Consumers

ODR schemes do not enjoy a specific definition (which is not even included in the EU Reg. 524/2013[9]).[10] Some claim that they are a digitised version of ADR. Others claim that, due to the digital context in which the dispute resolution takes place and due to the "Fourth Party" role of technology, meaning the influential and disruptive role of technology in the procedure,[11] ODR is a specific type of a dispute resolution that is quite different from its face-to-face counterpart.[12] For this paper I will use a simplified definition considering ADR as the process of out-of-court dispute resolution with ODR understood as ADR employing new technologies.[13] Although it is probably fair to identify ODR as a new dispute resolution paradigm.[14]

[8] Koulu (2018, p. 14).

[9] Regulation (EU) No 524/2013 of the European Parliament and of the Council of 21 May 2013 on online dispute resolution for consumer disputes and amending Regulation (EC) No 2006/2004 and Directive 2009/22/EC (Regulation on consumer ODR).

[10] Menkel-Meadow (2016).

[11] Katsh and Rifkin (2001) and Amsler et al. (2020).

[12] Katsh (2021) and Lodder and Zeleznikow (2010).

[13] For the same approach: Durovic and Lech (2021).

[14] Ortolani (2021).

To start with, I think it would be useful to recall some common ground about the enforcement of consumer rights.

It has been commonly agreed, at least since Cappelletti and Garth, that access to justice is a basic human right, with two main conceptions: the first being the equal accessibility to all citizens that a legal system must assure; the second being the need for results that are individually and socially just.[15]

It has also been commonly accepted, first, that models of justice are, in the modern era, focused on the effectiveness of protection, which is supported by such provisions as Articles 6(1) and 13 of the European Convention of Human Rights (ECHR) and Article 47 of the Charter of Fundamental Rights.[16] Second, in the area of consumer protection[17] access to justice is understood in the sense of "*equality of arms*",[18] an expression that encompasses the need for both substantive and procedural protection and for the removal of any imbalances of powers and asymmetries that preclude access to justice.[19]

From this perspective, beginning in the late 1980s, the main concern of modern civil procedure scholars and associated reforms focused on two topics of substantive and procedural justice and on the accompanying tension between a just decision and a fair procedure.[20]

It has also been commonly held, at least since Menkel-Meadow, that we are in the midst of a shift towards multiple paradigms of justice,[21] where ADR is an integral element of the policies aimed at improving access to justice.[22] The concept of access to justice has evolved into a broader paradigm,[23] it has now entered an era of process pluralism,[24] where citizens seek "appropriate" dispute resolution.[25] We are now dealing with a Three Pillar Model of enforcement of the law.[26]

It has been commonly agreed, moreover, that disputes between consumer and business are characterized by asymmetrical relations: the unbalance of power is not only limited to the substantive side, but also extended on the procedural field.

The consumer, therefore, is considered the weakest party in both the agreement and the process, marking the shift from the isonomic trial, intended as a tool to solve disputes between equal parties based on the neutrality of the judge to a model which

[15] Garth and Cappelletti (1978).

[16] Recently: van Gelder (2022).

[17] Rott (2007).

[18] Garth and Cappelletti (1978).

[19] Cappelletti (1979) and Alphen et al. (2007). See also Article 7(1) Council Directive 93/13/EEC of 5 April 1993 on Unfair Terms in Consumer Contracts [1993] OJ L 95.

[20] Zuckerman (2003).

[21] Menkel-Meadow (2006).

[22] European Commission, 'Green Paper on Alternative Dispute Resolution in Civil and Commercial Law', COM (2002) 196 final, para. 9.

[23] Kramer et al. (2002).

[24] Menkel-Meadow (2006, 2020a).

[25] Menkel-Meadow (2020b).

[26] Hodges (2010).

takes into account that the dispute is between parties with a significant imbalance of powers.

Further common ground is the consensus that challenges undermining the enforcement of consumer rights might be an obstacle to social and financial inclusion.[27]

And finally, we see common ground in consumer protection policies, where there has been a shift from a market-based approach towards a broader human rights approach[28] and where the trend, at least since Micklitz, Reich and Stuyck, has been towards a fragmentation of the notion of consumer[29] and a plurality of consumer images.[30] This, in turn, has introduced, along the "reasonably well-informed and reasonably attentive and circumspect consumer" standard of the average consumer, the new figure of the vulnerable consumer.[31]

Thus, if I had to find a key phrase for what has been said until now, it would be *effectiveness of protection*: this notion refers to the set of guarantees that a legal system should provide, i.e., not only protection but complete and adequate protection.[32]

Having in this way set the scene, it is worth noting that when all these procedural and substantial concerns are applied to a digital environment, imbalances of power and the asymmetries between parties may in fact be exacerbated.[33] This raises the question of how much ODR is "appropriate" in assuring effectiveness of consumer protection. The answer here is complicated by the fact that one must take into account both the substantive and the procedural aspects of justice.

In particular, we can ask ourselves whether ODR might lead to discrimination in the handling of disputes (pre-procedural and procedural justice) and to discrimination in the outcomes (substantive justice).

3 Consumer Complaining Behavior and the Dispute Resolution Cycle

3.1 Consumer Complaining Behavior and Access to Justice

One point should be taken into account: dissatisfied consumers can respond in many different ways to the underperformance of the company, and redress is just one of them.

---

[27] Comparato (2018).

[28] Cherednychenko (2007).

[29] Micklitz (2016).

[30] Stuyck (2015).

[31] Riefa and Saintier (2020).

[32] Snyder (1993).

[33] Sartor (2020); Casarosa and Micklitz (2024).

While legal scholars had been traditionally focusing on the enforcement level (seeking for ADR, notifying the regulator, filling a lawsuit-) there is a broad body of marketing and psychology literature that studies what happens *before* consumer's decision to air his/her grievances outside. In this perspective, it worth recall the shift in the studies of access to justice from focusing on "finding fair and efficient means for resolving those civil disputes that arrived at the courthouse door" to focusing "the social landscape of potential legal disputes and the processes through which these disputes came to the legal system in the first place".[34]

The modern trend in legal scholarship is towards a socio-legal approach to access to justice by the use of empirical research,[35] i.e. a combination of top-down and bottom-up solutions. In fact, it does not only focus on the institutional design (top-down), but also on "barriers that people experience on the ground and have less to do with the design of institutions and more to do with social inequality, and cognitive and cultural barriers"[36] (bottom-up).

There are many different stages of the Dispute resolution cycle, and each of them raise several managerial and public-policy considerations.[37]

Here, I will focus on the first stage, which is once a complain arises but before parties contemplate litigation.

This methodological approach implies also the use of cognitive and behavioural sciences. Consumer Complaint Behaviour (CCB) studies dissatisfied consumers behaviour.[38] For legal scholars the most familiar theoretical model is Hischman's exit-voice-loyalty model[39]: according to this model customers have basically three options, between exit (switching), voice (complaining) and suffer in silent (loyalty).

While "exit" works only in competitive markets and is not possible in concentrated/monopoly markets, in "voice" the customer is willing to address the company, when exit is impossible because there is no alternative to switch to.[40] Thus, voice is more likely to emerge in concentrated markets.[41] Lack of exit options generates voice, so that there is a positive relationship between exit and voice: when exit options increase, voice decreases.[42] Scholars pointed out the theoretical relationships among market structure, quality, and complaints.[43]

Trends had been observed: after having experienced a service failure, the majority of consumer will act privately (boycotting: not confronting the company but not buying the product/service anymore); only a small minority will decide to act publicly, confronting the others. Among those, only a few others will seek redress

---

[34] Albiston and Sandefur (2013).

[35] Creutzfeldt and others (2020).

[36] Creutzfeldt et al. (2021).

[37] Cortés (2023, 317).

[38] Istanbulluoglu et al. (2017).

[39] Hirschman (1970).

[40] Ivi, p 33.

[41] Gans et al. (2021).

[42] Dowding and John (2012).

[43] Beard et al. (2015) and Andreasen (1985).

from the company (talking to the manager, filling a lawsuit, putting negative reviews online).[44]

3.2 Consumers' (Rational) Apathy and Activism

In a legal perspective, this behavior has well-known foundations in the theoretical considerations borrowed from behavioural law and economics, which differentiate types of consumers according to the level of activism they show in entering in a contract (pre-purchase conduct: like reading, understanding comparing prices, quality and terms and eventually negotiating) and/or after it (post-purchase conduct: reactions to events like small charge, late shipping).[45] The highest percentage of consumers is by far composed by passive, due to a wide range of reasons. First, individual consumers' characteristics that affect complaint propensities plays a pivotal role, along with other determinants of consumers' complaints such as awareness of the infringement and apathy.

The latter maybe be either rational or rational.[46] Apathy is considered rational when the costs of taking actions would be higher than the benefits (for instance, the costs of reading—time and efforts—are certain while the benefits are not—given the lack of power to negotiate the contract terms-) or when the expenses (in terms of costs, risks of losing the case and the difficulties in collecting judgements[47]) to sue and bring the claim would be higher of the gain. Apathy is considered irrational when it is due to cognitive limitation and biases (in many cases consumers systemically err).[48]

As a matter of fact, whether complaining, switching, or suing, consumers face transaction costs, particularly in the form of enforcement costs.[49] Making complaints presents a high burden and requires much more effort than "[p]ersonal boycotting".[50]

Once decided to complain, the customer has as well to decide the specific response.

Both brand-switching and voice can be exercised differently depending on whom the actions are directed at: "private response actions," "third party response actions," and "voice response actions".[51]

In the digital environment the "voice" option is easier and much more impactful.

Voice is easier because the burdens of making complaints are alleviate by the simplicity of the gesture of posting a negative comment instead of writing a letter (prior finding to whom it should be address to), reaching out a call-center etc.

---

44 Arbel and Shapira (2019).

45 Ivi, p. 245.

46 Landes and Posner (1975).

47 Arbel and Shapira (2019).

48 Bar-Gill (2008, p. 765).

49 Ramsay (2012).

50 Bolfing (1989).

51 Singh (1988); Beard et al. (2015).

Voice is also more powerful because when a customer decides to take his/her protests online or on platforms, his/her complaints are potentially knew by a wide range (even millions) of other consumers.[52] Both the legal and marketing literature report a plethora of anecdotal evidences that highlight the impact of online complaints in increasing consumer bargaining power. When a single consumer engage a protest following the traditional route of calling the company, she has to talk to a customer service representative hoping to find her in a good day so to be the random recipient of a concession: she confronts the company in a one-on-one basis, with little leverage, has no power and is at the mercy of the company.[53]

On the contrary, online complaints, especially when visible to others, can make the individual consumer's voice heard by thousands of individuals who spend an ever increasing number of hours per day on the internet.

Reviews impact future consumer decisions: as positive reviews are crucial for a seller, as they are proven to increment seller's business, at the same time negative reviews may be potentially very harmful affecting their reputation and, thus, their business.[54] Thus, posting adverse comments on various platforms or discussion forums are a form of electronic word-of-mouth[55] and have considerable detrimental effects on a platform's former, current and potential customers.[56]

The pressure the consumer may exerted on the company gives her a greater power to negotiate solutions, so her bargaining of power at the post-formation disappointment expectations stage it is much higher as it is as the formation stage".[57]

The keyword here is dissemination (of negative information): airing public (whether going to court or posting a negative review) has serious reputational consequences for platforms, and reputational sanctions are as powerful as more widely negative information are diffused.

This creates a new bargaining power of consumers over merchants.

3.3 *Consumer's Scores and (Ex Post) Discrimination*

Platforms of course react and try to mitigate the legal and reputational risks of complains.

They basically have three options: restore the compromised relationship with the dissatisfied consumer; end the contractual relationship and avoid for the future dealing with the complainer customer; give no response.

When choosing between this three options, platforms response strategy will depend on large extent on the assessment of consumer's likely value to them.

---

[52] Barnes (2019).

[53] Barnes (2012, p. 689).

[54] Narciso (2019), Đurović and Kniepkamp (2022), and OECD (2019).

[55] Weitzl (2019).

[56] Weitzl et al. (2018).

[57] Ivi, 690.

They use classification scores and ratings to determine how to treat a given consumer.[58] In the era of big data, platforms may gather a huge amount of information about a given consumer, and applying algorithms and analytical tools can make accurate predictions about future behaviour and propensities and assess how likely he/she would abandon the business, or return items, or will bad-mouth a company or will publicity voice his/her frustration.[59] Platforms can track what consumers shop, how they pay, if they use loyalty cards, their spending habits; they can collect information related to race, family, gender, ethnicity and also ZIP codes.[60] This also raises an issue related to the risk of discrimination among users.[61]

Platforms decision on whether and how respond to complainers and treat them depends on the evaluation of the consumer personal profile and financial history: platforms seek for the most lucrative consumers and thus they will decide what to offer and which remedies each consumer deserves according to how profitable the customer is.

Thus, the assessment of a consumer's profile is based either on the evaluation of how valuable and how risky she is.

Consequently platforms, when trying to restore their relationship with the complainer (through the so-called webcare), will use a different level of efforts depending on the type of consumer they are dealing with.

Wealth consumers or consumers with a high social capital gain are more likely to receive "accommodation responses" such as: acknowledgement that the negative event has been caused by the company; apologies; or even monetary benefits (money refund). On the contrary, those who have a bad financial history or that are identified as serial complainers (i.e. with a high volume and value of past complains) are more likely to receive "defensive responses", such as the company denying that the event was caused by her or no responses at all.[62] In some cases, especially those of serial complainers, the platform may prefer to "silent" them, limiting their ability to make transactions or navigate on the platform: for instance, on Airbnb some hosts refuse to rent their house to consumers who turns out to write negative reviews.[63] It appears here evident that the propensity to litigation is deeply interconnected with reputation.

Thus, also consumers have reputation, in the form of the reputation by litigation.

The early identification of the type on consumer and the subsequent personalisation of the platforms responses have significant consequences.

They may lead to discrimination among consumers, in the form of ex-post discrimination.[64] Platforms, once identified the type of consumer they are dealing with, will select and offer different remedies to different consumers. In particular, by according preferential treatments to consumers depending on how wealthy (and thus profitable),

[58] Schmitz (2014, p. 1419).

[59] Arbel and Shapira (2020), pp. 963–964.

[60] Schmitz (2014, p 1413 and 1454).

[61] Katz (2015).

[62] Weitzl et al. (2018, p 317).

[63] Shapira (2021).

[64] Becher and Zarsky (2008, pp. 309 and 348).

platforms contribute to the growing gap between the "haves" and the "have nots". At the same time, active consumers, and especially serial complainers, would benefit of a tailored treatment if they are assessed as prone to spend money.

Moreover, this form of silencing active consumers prevents the economics theoretical "informed minority".[65]

This difference in recovery strategies marks the shift from a model where costumers are the ones deciding with whom they want to be in a contractual relationship to a new model, where platforms decide to whom they want to be in a contractual relationship.[66]

According to what has been previously said, the online context brings interesting twists to the issue of the balance of power between companies and consumers.

On one hand, easy dissemination of negative information (whether they would be mere negative reviews or public complains) gives an impressive power to consumers, which have now leverage to exert pressure on the platform and make it sit at the table ready to deal with the consumer, now considered a troublesome adversary.

On the other hand, the early identification of the type of consumer based on both the propensity to spend and the reputational risks raised by each consumer (CCB) may have consequences even on the access to justice side and on the substantial justice of the outcomes of a dispute. Platform may tend to treat benevolently wealthy or assertive consumers, while they may prefer to ignore or even silent less lucrative yet complaining costumers, preventing them by using the platform or giving them no responses to their complains.

4 Obstacles to Accessing Justice and, specifically, Online Justice

The current pathways in the demand for justice are speed, simplicity and self-representation.[67]

When a consumer has a dispute with her online counterparty or with the platform itself, she may experience three main sources of vulnerability on the enforcement side: redress vulnerability; economic vulnerability, and digital vulnerability.

4.1 Redress Vulnerability

Whereas legal scholars have been intensively investigating the different sources of vulnerability for consumers on the substantive side, not the same can be said for the

[65] Schmitz (2014, p. 281).

[66] Arbel and Shapira (2020), p. 975.

[67] Kramer et al. (2002), p. 2.

enforcement side. Redress vulnerability is a dimension which, if perhaps not entirely neglected, has at a minimum been subject to less debate.[68]

Redress vulnerability refers to the difficulties consumers may face in seeking redress as well as to the multiple barriers faced when attempting to access justice. These barriers are mainly related to the cost of a judicial procedure; to the availability of adequate procedures; to the personal attitude towards pursuing redress; and to the potential cross-border nature of the dispute.

Costs: Cost is one of the main barriers for consumers in accessing justice (and thus one of the main sources of redress vulnerability). Below a certain value threshold, consumers are likely to refrain from taking action at all[69] ("only a lunatic or a fanatic sues for $30").[70] The costs of litigation may not only outweigh any potential benefit from a victorious action (as in most consumer litigation cases), but they may also be prohibitively expensive for economically disadvantaged. This is the well-known issue of the "rational apathy", where individual losses are too small compared to the costs and efforts of bringing a claim against a trader and thus prevent consumers from exercising their rights.[71]

Also, in most legal systems the "loser-pays rule", applies, meaning that the non-prevailing party in a lawsuit is typically required to bear the winner's legal costs.[72]

From this perspective, ADR schemes may mitigate the problem to the extent that "the disparity between individual costs and benefit is decreased",[73] which will be further elaborated on in the next paragraph. In the economic analysis of law perspective, ADRs are in fact considered tools to lessen consumers rational apathy and encourage them to raise their claims.[74]

Adequate procedures. The technical and formal requirements of existing procedural mechanisms are a significant obstacle to obtaining restorative or compensatory protection.[75] Even in those legal systems that are described as 'advanced', the resolution of civil disputes is at the same time, antiquated and unintelligible to ordinary people,[76] and comprehension asymmetries are at their peak.[77]

---

[68] The expression of redress vulnerability has been coined by Cartwright (2015, p. 123) in his paper which was one of the first attempt to elaborate a taxonomy of consumer vulnerability.

[69] Civic Consulting Dg Sanco, Study Regarding the Problems Faced by Consumers in Obtaining Redress for Infringements of Consumer Protection Legislation, and the Economic Consequences of Such Problems (26 August 2008: so-called Redress Problems Study. A relevant part of Trebilcock's access to justice scholarship is focused on the costs topic—from a consumer welfare perspective—including a concern not only for low-income individuals but also for the middle class: Trebilcock (2008).

[70] In Judge Posner's words in the decision Carnegie v. Household Int'l, Inc., 376 F.3d 656, 661 (7th Cir. 2004).

[71] Engel (2016).

[72] Hodges et al. (2010) and Reimann (2012).

[73] Civic Consulting DG SANCO (2008), p. 82.

[74] Luzak (2016).

[75] Benöhr (2019).

[76] Susskind (2019).

[77] Wagner (2019).

One of the main difficulties in obtaining redress is that of proving one's claim. Very often consumers lack evidence of the damage suffered as it is highly unlikely that they retained evidence of the transaction (such as an invoice).[78] It is well-known that the allocation of the burden of proof is central to the outcome of a decision and that the principle of party disposition (meaning that the subject-matter of a case is delimited by the parties—an idea common to all legal systems) is, in its purest formulation, inappropriate in the situation of disputes between unequal parties, as it will work against the weaker one. Even where there is not a total *relevatio ab onere probandi* (legitimate only where provided for by the law), ODR may, given its nature, allow for a flexible system capable of alleviating the burden of proof by making use of judicial presumptions (drawing inferences from established facts).

From this perspective, ADR is most valuable for low- to medium-value claims[79] as a way of rebalancing an asymmetry of positions.

Personal attitude. Consumers may lack the capacity and inclination to pursue redress. This can stem from several reasons, ranging from socio-demographic reasons—marginalized groups tend not to complain[80]—to an individual's high adversity to conflict. There is evidence, from marketing and psychology literature, that vulnerability affects the complaining behaviour of consumers, i.e., the vulnerable are less likely to be dissatisfied and less likely to complain.[81] Empirical studies confirm that demographics such as age (older people are less likely to report an unsatisfactory experience),[82] education (the more consumers are aware of their rights the more they are in the position of enforcing them), income (despite the fact that low-income parties have more to lose, they are less likely than others to complain)[83] and race (members of minority groups have lower levels of trust than whites) are strong predictors of the types of consumer complaints that will potentially be brought.[84] Other psychological reasons that may determine the capacity to pursue redress are internalized litigation culture, the personal attitude (whether active or passive and a serial- or non-complainer: more in detail see next paragraph),[85] a (perceived) imbalance of power (which in turn depends on whether the complainer is a repeat player or one-shotter[86]), systemic power asymmetries (typically the case of elder law), and pressure exerted by the seller.

Dealing with consumer complaints is considered a business strategy to keep consumers happy. While litigation in courts is considered costly and disruptive for the user/platform relationship, amicable resolution of the dispute has the potential to preserve the relationship and prevent customer to switch to another network (and

[78] Civic Consulting DG SANCO (2008), p. 82.

[79] Ibid.

[80] See, e.g., Schmitz (2012) and Willis (2015).

[81] Andreansen and Manning (1990).

[82] Soberon and Ferrer (1999). More recently, Meiners et al. (2024).

[83] Andreansen and Manning (1990).

[84] Raval (2020).

[85] Arbel and Shapira (2020).

[86] Galanter (1974).

disseminate negative word-of-mouth[87]—see next paragraph). Thus, platforms have a more benevolent approach towards online complaints than the ones in courts and for this reason consumers may experience less hostility towards their complaints.

Consumers may also have a low level of trust in the system, which translates into a low expectation of success in any litigation.

From the perspective of one's personal attitude towards pursuing redress, ODR schemes appear a means of at least alleviating, if not eliminating, this source of vulnerability.

The potential cross-border nature of the dispute. Given the inherently cross-border nature of technology, online dispute resolution aligns perfectly with the intent of removing this type of vulnerability source.

Digital literacy (which will be discussed further).

In the context of redress vulnerability, the guiding model of the individualistic and responsible consumer who exercises his/her rights and, as necessary, goes to court, is outdated.

4.2 *Economic Vulnerability*

While all consumers suffer from the dynamic of economic deterrence, it is clear that those who suffer from it the most and for whom, therefore, redress vulnerability is most pronounced are those economically disadvantaged.[88] We should thus point to the intersection between social policies and consumer law and to the potential applicability of EU non-discrimination law to vulnerable consumers.[89]

Going beyond the traditional approach whereby economic vulnerability was considered exclusively a public law topic, both North American and European scholars have turned their attention to exploring the connections between private law and poverty law. This led to scholars linking the topic of vulnerability to the economic situation of the consumer, adopting a census-based perspective and using Caplovitz's theories on 'ghetto consumers' with modern nuances.[90]

In this perspective, the traditional issues of the costs of dispute resolution and the quest for affordable justice overlap with the concepts of redress and economic vulnerability.

In this context, ODR helps to remove access-to-justice barriers and correct consumers' redress vulnerability as related to poverty and a low-income because,

---

[87] Weitzl et al. (2018, pp. 316–317).

[88] United Nations Guidelines for Consumer Protection GA Res 248, 39 UN GAOR (106th plen. Mtg), UN Doc A/Res/39/248 (1985), p 180, referencing the need of governments to enable consumers "to obtain redress through formal or informal procedures that are expeditious, fair, inexpensive and accessible. Such procedures should take particular account of the needs of low-income consumers".

[89] Mulder (2021) and Meers (2024).

[90] Garth and Sarat (1998).

given its essentially free-of-charge nature, it also allows non-wealthy consumers to enforce their rights.[91]

5 Digital Vulnerability

Digital vulnerability has been described as "a universal state of defencelessness and susceptibility to (the exploitation of) power imbalances that are the result of increasing automation of commerce, datafied consumer-seller relations and the very architecture of digital marketplaces".[92]

The attempt to settle a dispute online can exacerbate digital vulnerability. Even though we are dealing with a digitally savvy consumer who has already bought goods or services online and undertaken a digital purchase, this does not mean that the consumer is digitally savvy enough to engage in an online dispute. There is a difference between completing a transaction, in an online platform where, eventually, credentials are memorised, and initiating and handling an online dispute. ODR requires a higher degree of digital skills as consumers need to be able to navigate all the different steps of the dispute resolution process. Thus, whereas ODR schemes may primarily benefit high profile, tech-savvy users, it may limit accessibility for less digitally savvy consumers, leading to the exclusion of certain groups within society, especially older generations and persons living with disabilities.[93]

It is widely accepted that in the digital environment the source of vulnerability associated with old age relates to the generational barriers in understanding and dealing with digital tools.[94] These obstacles appear predestined to increase with the advancing level of required technological skills.

Thus, ODR schemes do not help to eliminate consumers' digital vulnerability. To the contrary, they exacerbate the state of defencelessness and susceptibility to (an exploitation of) power imbalances, and may lead to digital exclusion.

6 Benefits of ODR in Relation to Redress Vulnerability and Economic Vulnerability

At least three (costs, adequate procedures, potential cross-border nature of the dispute) out of five sources of redress vulnerability are potentially removed by ODR procedures. Economic vulnerability is also potentially removed. Thus, ODRs may be conceived as inclusive rather than a discriminatory dispute resolution schemes

---

[91] See Ramsay (2003), who, adopting a socio-legal approach, claims that individual redress mechanisms serve the lower-income class less than the middle class.

[92] Helberger et al. (2021), Calo (2014), and Grochowski (2024).

[93] Casarosa (2024, p. 126).

[94] Rabitti and Paglietti (2022).

because they are a means of dispute resolution for disputes that are not suitable for court litigation. Consequently, they promote affordable justice. The typically low value at dispute and the significant costs that litigation would entail, especially in cases where the parties are located in different jurisdictions, makes it unrealistic that consumers will seek judicial redress on a large scale. ODR schemes, conversely, offer speed and easy-to-use procedures to obtain restorative or compensatory protection. They are helpful in cases where the dispute has a cross-border nature, given the digital dimension of dispute resolution. Further, they alleviate personal aversion to pursuing redress and being subject to the judicial system.

Conversely, ODR schemes do not help in remedying consumers' digital vulnerability.

7 Concerns

ODR has numerous detractors. Some of these critics' concerns pertain to all types of ADR, e.g., regarding the quality of justice they promote. There are, however, also concerns specific to ODR, e.g., as to the opaque nature of the decision-making process and neutrality. There is an on-going debate, among scholars and practitioners, on the need of the adoption of Ethical Principles for Online Dispute Resolution, i.e. as an articulation of shared values, that would further increase trust in ODR.[95]

7.1 *Quality of Justice*

Among the generic concerns, the quality of justice promoted by ADR is probably the most important. It is a well-known issue the distrust of a part of the legal literature towards Alternative Disputes Resolution schemes,[96] seen as tools out of public control that may undermine the protection of the rights of weaker party,[97] perpetuating social inequalities either by "privatizing" dispute resolution[98] (individualized redress procedures have a distributional tilt against lower-income and disadvantaged groups)[99] and by "disaggregating" claims of collective injustice.[100] ADR schemes, by creating a homogenised discourse, may exacerbate social inequalities,[101] particularly in case where repeat players are involved.[102] Scholars claim that ADRs are a

[95] Wing (2016) and Wing et al. (2021, 2022).
[96] Resnik (2003).
[97] Abel (1982) and Resnik (2015).
[98] Nader (1979) and Delgado et al. (1985).
[99] Ramsay (2003).
[100] Fiss (1984).
[101] Auerbach (1983).
[102] Galanter (2014).

second class justice[103]; a 'Trojan horse in the [access to justice] paddock, a cuckoo in the dispute resolution nest'.[104] The 'triumphant industry of ADR' then no longer constitutes an alternative to judicial decision-making, because, in the name of a 'forced harmony'[105] the protection of rights is replaced by a compromise, which, however, effectively precludes access to justice. The "ADR market",[106] especially in the view of the legal anthropology studies, aims to pursue harmony over justice,[107] discouraging parties from "insisting" on asserting their rights and making them give up the legal dispute.[108]

In the specifics of ODR schemes, concerns are related to the role of law, opacity, neutrality, and the legality both of the decisions and the procedures.

While in early 90s debate on the interplay between out-of-court and litigation in courts some scholars claimed for a loss of protection for poor litigants,[109] then for a "loss of law",[110] then for the erosion of substantive law,[111] the debate focuses nowadays on the possible "death of law", meaning that in the future there will be no room for law viewed as a systematic body of though.[112]

Nowadays, scholars and practitioners insist on the need to learn from the ADR experience and adopt some procedural safeguards in order to avoid the drifts that have occurred with adr,[113] using the vulnerabilities identified in ADR processes in the past as prescient warnings about how ODRs can be manipulated to the detriment of less advantaged members of the society[114]

7.2 *Opacity*

Opacity refers to the opaque nature of the decision-making process. In particular, there is no transparency as to how platforms decide cases, especially whether and how they apply mandatory consumer law, in either automated or human-driven decisions-systems.

---

[103] Wagner (2019) and Moscati et al. (2020) and cited bibliography.

[104] Lindblom (2008).

[105] Nader (2003).

[106] Cooper (1991).

[107] Nader and Grande (2002).

[108] Ivi.

[109] Nader and Grande (2002, p 590).

[110] Hofrichter (1987).

[111] Glover (2015).

[112] Lucy (2022); the death of law is of course not a new formula, but in Lucy's case refers explicitly to modern law's judgment and technological management.

[113] Welsh (2016) and Wing (2012).

[114] Dwight (2021).

In AI-driven systems, their manner of function remains a black box, with scholars advocating transparency and explanation as a means of combating the adverse effects of the "black box society".[115] The risk here is one of algorithm discrimination.

In human-driven systems, by contrast, there are generally no guidelines related to any conflict of interests.

On the substantive level, opacity and legality may impact the quality, whether real or perceived, of the involved decision-making and produce distrust in consumers. The consequence thereof will be discussed at the end of this contribution.[116]

On the procedural level, opacity impacts the equality of arms principle, due to the knowledge asymmetry it creates between parties. Further, it influences the adversarial principle and also the right of a reasoned decision in those cases where algorithms or humans neither explain nor justify how a particular decision has been reached.[117] Regarding this latter issue, the main question legal scholars are addressing is whether procedural quality standards should be embedded in ODR procedures, so that ODR can become both an accessible and a just pathway for consumer redress. Although Article 47 CFR and Article 6(1) ECHR partially apply to ADR, they do not in the case of ODR—because the applicability of ODR is based on a civil contract.[118]

Though the debate is still raging, it is worth noting that scholars have recently been pointing out the "procedural turn" in platform dispute resolution regulation.[119] The need for procedural safeguards can be considered, by now, a common ground.[120]

Since the two Directives on ADRs[121] and ODRs,[122] the EU regulator has started to set quality requirements and guarantees that out-of-court dispute settlement mechanisms should have had (legality, liberty, speed, impartiality). This trend was confirmed by the Regulation 2019/1150 ("P2B Regulation"),[123] which represents a step forward in regulating ODRs. It not only aims to assure appropriate transparency, fairness and effective redress possibilities[124] but also expressly requires platforms either to provide an internal system for handling the complaints of business users (Article 11) or a mediation system (Article 12). Through these two provisions the

115 Pasquale (2015).

116 Carvalho and Carvalho (2016).

117 Palmiotto (2020).

118 Ebers (2022, p 162).

119 Busch (2020).

120 See the suggestions in Welsh (2016), Van Loo (2021), and Cortés and Cole (2018).

121 Directive 2013/11/EU of 21 May 2013 on alternative dispute resolution of consumer disputes and amending Regulation (EC) No 2006/2004 and Directive 2009/22/EC [2013] OJ L 165/63.

122 Regulation (EU) 524/2013 on online dispute resolution for consumer disputes and amending Regulation (EC) 2006/2004 and Directive 2009/22/EC (Regulation on consumer ODR) [2013] OJ L 165/1.

123 Regulation (EU) 2019/1150 of the European Parliament and of the Council of 20 June 2019 on promoting fairness and transparency for business users of online intermediation services [2019] OJ L 186/57.

124 Art. 1(1), Regulation (EU) 2019/1150.

concept of procedural fairness in the relationship between platform and their business users had made its entrance in ODR schemes.[125]

More recently the Digital Services Act (DSA)[126] confirms the willingness, in EU policy, to regulate ODR schemes more intrusively in order to control the quasi-judiciary power of platforms, establishing requirements for the design model and implementing procedural quality standards. It has been observed that the DSA "inaugurates a system of private enforcement through tort liability and judicial remedies that is supplemented by important elements of alternative, i.e. out-of-court, dispute resolution".[127]

Solving disputes on platforms is progressively becoming a system with its own architecture, designed to encourage parties to settle earlier.[128] There is an initial "procedural" stage when users should negotiate directly with their counterparty through the internal complaint-handling system (Article 20). The second potential phase is that of mediation, with the assistance of dispute certified settlement body which must satisfy specific requirements of expertise, professionalism, impartiality, easy accessibility and must decide according to clear and fair rules of procedure that are easily and publicly accessible (Article 21). The third and final stage disputes may reach is that of adjudication.

Thus, tripartism seems to be the way the EU regulator tries to solve the issue of the digitalised access to justice. The transformation of a grievance into a proper legal dispute follows a tri-phasic procedure, where consumers may gradually escalate their complaint in an enforcement pyramid that leads up to more costly and time-consuming processes, with judicial review at the apex of the pyramid.

In the online dispute resolution pyramid each stage of complaint resolution is designed to avoid the next one, with some scholars dividing ODR into dispute avoidance and dispute resolution.[129] This mechanism reminds that of the 'prior exhaustion of remedies', according to which the claimer should exhaust his/her remedies/stages before taking his/her grievances to the next level.[130]

Behind these policy options is an important cultural issue. The preference for a procedural approach underpins the issue of whether the requirements of substantive justice should prevail over the formal compliance with the rules that regulate the process (procedural justice).

The analysis of the European legal systems shows that in the modern age priority has consistently been given to the substantive regularity of the decision over its formal regularity. This principle informs the British reform of Lord Wolf, as well.[131] This

[125] Busch (2020, p. 134).

[126] Regulation (EU) 2022/2065 of the European Parliament and of the Council of 19 October 2022 on a Single Market For Digital Services and amending Directive 2000/31/EC (Digital Services Act) [2022] OJ L 277.

[127] Eifert et al. (2021).

[128] Van Loo (2021, p. 829).

[129] Cortés (2011).

[130] Bassan (2021, p 97).

[131] Jolowicz (2003).

may and must be influenced by considerations with regard to the appropriateness of the decision, i.e., a merits-based strategy.

On the contrary, as observed, the trend in regulating how to solve disputes in digital platforms is that of proceduralization of intermediary responsibility.[132] In this perspective, ODRs stand in a countertrend position to the evolutionary trajectories found in the field of jurisdiction, because of their being a less mature system, which must first establish certain procedural minimum standards.

7.3 Neutrality

The neutrality of ODRs is also questioned. A crucial issue to be taken into account is that even though platforms act as "arbitrators", online platforms are private entities with commercial interests. Profit has a pivotal role even in the handling of complaints. Dispute management is regarded by platforms as a tool of corporate strategy, one from which they should derive the maximum possible profit. Platforms tend to tailor their decisions in ways that maximize their expected utility, their having the aim not to provide an accurate approximation of legal outcomes, but to reward valued customers.

Assuming a dispute prevention strategy, through the use of big data and predictive tools as relates to a given manner of consumer behaviour, companies are at an early stage able to identify the type of the customer they will be dealing with (behavioural patterns and personality, future preferences, etc.) and decide to either avoid selling to certain customers or offer them preferential treatment.[133]

Platforms also may tend to handle the complaint process and the outcomes differently depending on the type of consumers with whom they know to be dealing with. Namely, they will be inclined to accommodate the demands of wealthy consumers who have large sums of money to spend on the platform. Conversely, poor customers who have very little to spend will be treated with indifference or even neglect.[134]

This may potentially lead to discrimination, not only in the handling of the procedure or merely in terms of the outcomes but also as regards accessibility to justice. Likely, this would exacerbate mainly census-based discrimination, i.e., between low-income and wealth consumers.

---

[132] Busch (2020, p. 133).

[133] Eidenmueller and Wagner (2021); Van Loo (2021, p. 844).

[134] Eidenmueller and Wagner (2021, p 241).

8 ODR as a Trust-Enhancer (Fairness and Decision Acceptance)

Instead of being a mere tool of profit, platforms should embrace a new perspective on ODRs and begin considering them as a means of ensuring a relatively high level of consumer protection. From this perspective, ODRs are considered a reputational system.[135] Recent studies have proven that the business model of a platform ultimately depends on the platform's ability to build trust. Thus, platforms should embrace mechanisms that play the role of trust-enhancers in the marketplace they aim to create.[136]

From this perspective, it is worth noting how research has shown that positive perceptions of procedural fairness led to a better acceptance of decisions, to a more positive view of individual courts and of the justice system, and to a greater compliance with court orders. According to these rigorous evaluations, both the acceptance of court decisions and overall approval of the court system are much more closely connected to perceptions of procedural fairness than to outcome favourability (*Did I win?*) or outcome fairness (*Did the right party win?*).

According to Tyler's models on consumers' decision acceptance, people are responsive to evaluations of the fairness of procedures, even if authorities do not provide the outcomes they hoped for.[137] There is empirical evidence that people will accept an adverse outcome if the procedure was experienced as fair.[138]

9 Conclusions

In the light of what previously said regarding the three main sources of vulnerability on the enforcement side (redress vulnerability, economic vulnerability and digital vulnerability), ODRs seem to be a strategic tool to remove economic vulnerability and the source of redress vulnerability related to costs because of their essentially free-of-charge nature. Although all consumers would benefit from this, ODR are a "game changer" for non-wealthy consumers.

ODRs would also help removing another source of redress vulnerability, the one related to the adequateness of procedures. Specifically, as ODRs provide an informal procedure with very low level of technical requirements, they would help to rebalance asymmetries in comprehension where most of the consumers may not fully understand the technicalities of the court system.

---

[135] Koulu (2018).

[136] Ortolani (2021, p 149).

[137] Tyler and Huo (2002).

[138] Lind and Tyler (1998).

Also, ODRs would help alleviating redress vulnerability related to personal attitude and in particular to the pressure exerted by platforms because consumers may experience less hostility towards their complaints.

Finally, online dispute resolution, given the inherently cross-border nature of technology, aligns perfectly with the intent of removing the type of vulnerability source related to the potential cross-border nature of the dispute.

On the other hand, ODRs schemes do not help removing digital vulnerability. On the contrary, there may exacerbate it and discriminate those customers who may experience generational (due to age) or personal (due to disabilities) barriers in using digital tools which require some level of digital savviness.

Above all, the main concern about ODRs schemes appears to be the neutrality of the decision, because, despite the "procedural turn" (intended as an ongoing process of proceduralisation aiming to assure a certain level of transparency) ODRs are and remain a tool of corporate strategy to maximise profit by which they tend to rewarding profitable consumers offering them preferential treatment, while treating with indifference or even neglecting those customers who have very little to spend.

Thus, while ODRs are an effective and strategic tool to remove redress and economic vulnerability, as they promote affordable (removing census-based discrimination in accessing justice) and inclusive (resolving disputes that are not suitable for court litigation) justice, they may led to "ex post discrimination",[139] which implies that platforms may actively discriminate between valuable or assertive consumers—who will be granted relief after a dispute arises—and "low revenue, high cost customers" who will not.[140]

One of the main outcome of this work is, thus, that not only firms have reputation but also consumer do, a specific form of reputation: reputation by litigation.

References

Abel R (1982) The contradictions of informal justice. In: Abel R (ed) The politics of informal justice. Academic Press, New York, p 267

Albiston C, Sandefur R (2013) Expanding the empirical study of access to justice. Wisconsin L Rev 101:103

Amsler LB, Martinez JK, Smith SE (2020) Dispute system design: preventing, managing, and resolving conflict. Stanford University Press, Stanford

Andreansen AR, Manning J (1990) The dissatisfaction and complaining behavior of vulnerable consumers. J Consum Satisf 3(12):15

Andreasen AR (1985) Consumer responses to dissatisfaction in loose monopolies. J Consum Res 12:135–141

Arbel YA, Shapira R (2019) Consumer activism: from the informed minority to the crusading minority twenty-fifth annual clifford symposium on tort law and social policy: rising stars: a new generation of scholars looks at civil justice: articles & essays. DePaul L Rev 69:233, p 235

[139] Becher and Unger-Aviram (2018, p. 207).

[140] Becher and Zarsky (2009, p. 309).

Arbel YA, Shapira R (2020) Theory of the Nudnik: the future of consumer activism and what we can do to stop it. Vanderbilt L Rev 73:929
Auerbach JS (1983) Justice without law? Resolving disputes without lawyers. Oxford University Press, Oxford
Ayres I, Braithwaite J (1992) Responsive regulation: transcending the deregulation debate. Oxford University Press, Oxford
Bar-Gill O (2008) The behavioral economics of consumer contracts. Minnesota L Rev 92(3):749–802.
Barnes WR (2012) Social media and the rise in consumer bargaining power. U Pa J Bus L 14:661
Barnes WR (2019) The good, the bad, and the ugly of online reviews: the trouble with trolls and a role for contract law after the consumer review fairness act. Georgia L Rev 53(2):549–612
Bassan F (2021) Digital platforms and global law. Edward Elgar Publishing, Cheltenham
Beard TR, Macher JT, Mayo JW (2015) Can you hear me now: exit, voice, and loyalty under increasing competition. JL Econ 58(3):717
Becher I, Zarsky TZ (2008) E-contract doctrine 2.0: standard form contracting in the age of online user participation. Mich Telecommun Tech L Rev 12:303–366.
Becher SI, Zarsky TZ (2009) E-contract doctrine 2.0: standard form contracting in the age of online user participation. Mich Telecomm Tech L Rev 14:303
Becher SI, Unger-Aviram E (2018) The law of standard form contracts: misguided intuitions and suggestions for reconstruction. Depaul Bus Comm L J 8:199
Benöhr I (2019) Collective redress in the financial sector and the new EU deal for consumers'. Eur Rev Priv L 6(1345):1349
Bernstein L (1992) Opting out of the legal system: extralegal contractual relations in the diamond industry. J Leg Stud 21:115
Bolfing CP (1989) How do customers express dissatisfaction and what can service marketers do about it? J Servs Mark: 5, 7
Busch C (2020) The P2B Regulation (EU) 2019/1150: towards a "procedural turn" in EU platform regulation? J Eur Consum Mark L: 133
Calo R (2014) Digital market manipulation. George Washington L Rev 82:995
Cappelletti M (1979) Access to justice and the welfare state: an introduction. In: cappelletti and others (eds) Access to justice, Vol I: a world survey, and Vol. III: emerging issues and perspectives. Sijthoff & Noordhoff, Alphen aan den Rijn; Giuffrè Editore, Milan.
Cartwright P (2015) Understanding and Protecting Vulnerable Financial Consumers. J Consum Policy 38, 119–138. https://doi.org/10.1007/s10603-014-9278-9
Carvalho JM, Carvalho JC (2016) Online dispute resolution platform. Making European contract law more effective. In: De Franceschi A (ed) European contract law and the digital single market: the implications of the digital revolution. Intersentia, Cambridge. pp 245, 255
Casarosa (2024) Access to (digital) justice: is there a place for vulnerable people in online dispute resolution mechanisms? J Eur Consum Mark L 13:3
Casarosa F, Micklitz H-W (2024) Addressing vulnerabilities in online dispute resolution. In De Franceschi A and others (eds.), The new shapes of digital vulnerability in european private law. Nomos, Baden-Baden, p 343
Cherednychenko O (2007) Fundamental rights, contract law and the protection of the weaker party. Sellier, München
Civic Consulting (2008) Study regarding the problems faced by consumers in obtaining redress for infringements of consumer protection legislation (Final Report). European Commission, Directorate-General for Health and Consumers (DG SANCO). civic-consulting.de
Comparato G (2018) The financialisation of the citizen: social and financial inclusion through European private law. Bloomsbury Academic, London.
Cooper A (1991) Do the merits matter: a study of settlements in securities class actions. Stanford L Rev 43:497, 575–577
Cortés P (2011) Online dispute resolution for consumers in the European Union. Routledge, London

Cortés P (2023) Embedding alternative dispute resolution in the civil justice system: a taxonomy for ADR referrals and a digital pathway to increase the uptake of ADR. Leg Stud 43(2):312–330.
Cortés P, Cole T (2018) Legislating for an effective and legitimate system of online consumer arbitration. In: Piers M, Aschauer C (eds) Arbitration in the digital age: the brave new world of arbitration. Cambridge University Press, Cambridge, p 209
Cortés P, de la Rosa FE (2013) Building a global redress system for low-value cross-border disputes. Int Compar L Q 62(2):407
Creutzfeldt N and others (eds.) (2020) Routledge handbook of socio-legal theory and methods. Routledge, Abingdon.
Creutzfeldt N, Gill C, Cornelis M, McPherson R (2021) Access to justice for vulnerable and energy-poor consumers: just energy? Hart, Oxford
Del Duca FL, Rule C, Rimpfel K (2014) EBay's de facto low value high volume resolution process: lessons and best practices for ODR systems designers. Arbitration L Rev 204:205
Delgado R et al (1985) Fairness and formality: minimizing the risk of prejudice in alternative dispute resolution. Wisconsin L Rev:1359–1404
Dowding K, John P (2012) Exits, voices and social investment: citizens' reaction to public services. Cambridge University Press, Cambridge
Đurović M, Kniepkamp T (2022) Good advice is expensive—bad advice even more: the regulation of online reviews. L Innov Tech 14(1):128–156
Durovic M, Lech F (2021) Legal tech in ADR. In: Di Matteo LA and others (eds) The Cambridge handbook of lawyering in the digital age. Cambridge University, Cambridge, p 99 ff.
Dwight G (2021) A prescient warning of the vulnerabilities in ADR. In: Hinshaw A, Kupfer Schneider A, Rudolph Cole S (eds) Discussions in dispute resolution. Oxford University Press, Oxford, pp 308 ff
Ebers M (2022) Automating due process: the promise and challenges of AI-based techniques in consumer online dispute resolution. In: kramer XE, Hoevenaars J, Kas B, Themeli E (eds) Frontiers in Civil Justice: Privatisation, Monetisation and Digitisation. Edward Elgar Publishing, Cheltenham, pp. 142–168.
Eidenmueller H, Wagner G (2021) Law by algorithm. Mohr Siebeck, Tübingen
Eifert M, Metzger A, Schweitzer H, Wagner G (2021) Taming the giants: the DMA/DSA package. Comm Mark L Rev 58(987):1019
Engel D (2016) The myth of the litigious society—why we don't sue. The University Chicago Press, Chicago
Fiss OM (1984) Against settlement. Yale L J 93(1073):1085–1087
Galanter M (1974) Why the "Haves" come out ahead: speculations on the limits of legal change. L Soc Rev 9:95
Galanter M (ed) (2014) Why the Haves come out ahead: the classic essay and new observations. Quid Pro Books, New Orleans
Gans JS, Goldfarb A, Lederman M (2021) Exit, Tweets, and loyalty. Am Econ J Microecon 13(2):68–112
Garth B, Cappelletti M (1978) Access to justice: the newest wave in the worldwide movement to make rights effective. Buffalo L Rev 27:181–182
Garth B, Sarat A (1998) Justice and power in law and society research: on the contested careers of core concepts. In: Garth B and others (eds) Justice and power in sociolegal studies. Northwestern University Press, Evanston, IL.
Glover JM (2015) Disappearing claims and the erosion of substantive law. Yale Law Journal 124:3052–3092
Goanta EC, Ortolani P (2022) Unpacking content moderation. The rise of social media platforms as online civil courts?. In: Kramer XE, Hoevenaars J, Kas B, Themeli E (eds) Frontiers in civil justice. Privatisation, monetisation and digitisation. Edward Elgar Publishing, Cheltenham, p 192 ff.

Grochowski M (2024) Digital vulnerability in a post-consumer society. subverting paradigms? In: Crea C, De Franceschi A (eds) (2024) The New Shapes of Digital Vulnerability in European Private Law. Nomos, Baden-Baden, p 187 ff.
Helberger N, Lynskey O, Micklitz H-W, Rott P, Sax M, Strycharz J (2021) EU consumer protection 2.0: structural asymmetries in digital consumer markets, March. https://www.beuc.eu/sites/default/files/publications/beuc-x-2021
Hirschman AO (1970) Exit, voice, and loyalty. responses to decline in firms, organizations, and states. Harvard University Press, Cambridge, MA.
Hodges C (2010) Collective redress in Europe: the new model. Civil Just Quar 29:370
Hodges C, Vogenauer S, Tulibacka M (2010) Costs and funding of civil litigation: a comparative perspective. CH Beck, München.
Hofrichter R (1987) Neighborhood justice in a capitalist society: the expansion of the informal state. Greenwood Press, New York
Istanbulluoglu D, Leek S, Szmigin I (2017) Beyond exit and voice: developing an integrated taxonomy of consumer complaining behaviour. Eur J Mark 51:5/6, 1109–1128
Jolowicz JA (2003) Adversarial and inquisitorial models of civil procedure. Int Compar L Quar 52:281
Katsh E (2011) Online dispute resolution (ODR): a look at history. In: Abdel Wahab MS, Katsh ME, Rainey D (eds) Online Dispute Resolution: Theory and Practice. A Treatise on Technology and Dispute Resolution. Eleven International Publishing, The Hague, p 21-33
Katsh E, Rifkin J (2001) Online dispute resolution. Resolving conflicts in cyberspace. Jossey-Bass, San Francisco.
Katz V (2015) Regulating the Sharing Economy. Berkeley Technol L J 30:1067, p 1118
Koulu R (2018) Law, technology and dispute resolution. Privatisation of coercion. Routledge, Abingdon.
Kramer X, Hoevenaars J, Themeli E (2002) Frontiers in civil justice—privatising, digitising and funding justice. Front Civil Just (1)2
Landes WM, Posner RA (1975) The private enforcement of law. J Legal Stud 4(1):33
Lind EA, Tyler TR (1998) The social psychology of procedural justice. Plenum Press, New York.
Lindblom P (2008) ADR—the opiate of the legal system? Eur Rev Priv L 16:1, 63, p 66
Lodder AR and Zeleznikow J (2010) Enhanced dispute resolution through the use of information technology. Cambridge University Press, Cambridge
Lucy W (2022) The death of law: another obituary. Cambridge L J 81(1):109–138
Luzak J (2016) The ADR Directive: designed to fail? A hole-ridden stairway to consumer justice. Eur Rev Priv L 24:1, 81–101
Meers (2024) Discrimination at the interface: the equality act 2010 and platform interface design. Mod L R 87(3):640–669
Meiners N, Reucher E, Khan H (2024) Consumer (non) complaint behavior: a comparative study of senior consumers in germany before and after the Covid-19 pandemic. J Consu Satisfact Dissatisfact Complain Behav 37:1
Menkel-Meadow C (2006) Peace and justice: notes on the evolution and purposes of plural legal processes. Georgetown L J 94:553–580
Menkel-Meadow CJ (2016) Is Odr Adr? Reflections of an adr founder from 15th ODR conference. Int J Online Disp Resolut 3:1, 4–7
Menkel-Meadow C (2020a) Hybrid and mixed dispute resolution processes: integrities of process pluralism. In: Palmer M, Roberts, Moscati M (eds) Comparative dispute resolution research handbook. Edward Elgar Publishing, Cheltenham
Menkel-Meadow CJ (2020b) What is an appropriate measure of litigation? Quantification, qualification and differentiation of dispute resolution. Oñati Socio-Legal Ser 11(2):321
Micklitz H-W (2016) The consumer: marketised, fragmentised, constitutionalised. In: Leczykiewicz D, Weatherill S (eds) The Images of the Consumer in EU Law: Legislation, Free Movement and Competition Law. Hart Publishing, Oxford, pp 21 ff.

Moscati MF, Palmer M, Roberts M (2020) Comparative dispute resolution. Edward Elgar Publishing.
Mulder J (2021) What is vulnerability anyway? Tracing the EU notion of the vulnerable consumer through the eyes of EU non discrimination law. Eur L Rev 46:6, 719
Nader L (1979) Disputing without the force of law. Yale L J 88(998):1007–1008
Nader L, Grande E (2002) Current illusions and delusions about conflict management—in Africa and elsewhere. L Soc Inq 27(3):577
Nader, L (2003) Le Forze vive del diritto. Un'introduzione all'antropologia giuridica, ESI, Naples
Narciso M (2019) The regulation of online reviews in European consumer law. Eur Rev Priv L 27(3):557–582
Ortolani P. (2021) Digital Dispute Resolution: Blurring the Boundaries of ADR. In: DiMatteo LA, Janssen A, Ortolani P, de Elizalde F, Cannarsa M, Durovic M (eds) The Cambridge Handbook of Lawyering in the Digital Age. Cambridge University Press, Cambridge, p. 140–56
OECD (2019) Good practice guide on online consumer ratings and reviews—protecting consumers in ECommerce, September 9. www.oecd-ilibrary.org/docserver/0f9362cf-en.pdf?
Palmiotto F (2020) The Black Box on trial: the impact of algorithmic opacity on fair trial rights in criminal proceedings. In: Ebers M, Cantero Gamito M (eds) Algorithmic Governance and Governance of Algorithms: Legal and Ethical Challenges. Springer, Cham, p 61 ff
Pasquale F (2015), The Black Box society: the secret algorithms that control money and information. Harvard University Press, Cambridge, MA.
Rabitti M, Paglietti MC (2022) A matter of time. Digital-financial consumers' vulnerability in the retail payments market. Eur Bus L Rev 33:4, 581
Ramsay I (2003) Consumer redress and access to justice. In: Rickett CEF, Telfer TGW (eds) International Perspectives on Consumers' Access to Justice. Cambridge University Press, Cambridge, p 38 ff.
Ramsay I (2012) Consumer law and policy, 3rd edn. Hart Publishing, Oxford.
Raval D (2020) Whose voice do we hear in the marketplace? Evidence from consumer complaining behavior. Mark Sci 39(1):168
Reimann M (2012) General report. In: Reimann M (ed) Cost and fee allocation in civil procedure. Springer, Dordrecht, p 35 ff.
Resnik (2015) Diffusing disputes: the public in the private of arbitration, the private in courts, and the erasure of rights. Y L J 124:2804
Resnik J (2003) For Owen M. Fiss: some reflections on the triumph and the death of adjudication. Univ Miami L Rev 58:173
Riefa C, Saintier S (eds) (2020) Vulnerable consumers and the law: consumer protection and access to justice. Routledge, Abingdon
Rott P (2007) Effective enforcement and different enforcement cultures. In: Wilhelmsson T, Paunio E, Pohjolainen A (eds) Private Law and the Many Cultures of Europe. Kluwer Law International, Alphen aan den Rijn, p 291 ff.
Sartor G (2020) New Aspects and Challenges in Consumer Protection: Digital Services and Artificial Intelligence. European Parliament, Brussels, PE 648.790
Schmitz AJ (2012) Access to consumer remedies in the squeaky wheel system. Pepperdine L Rev 39:279
Schmitz AJ (2014) Secret consumer scores and segmentations: separating "haves" from "have-nots". Mich St L Rev 1411
Shapira R (2021) Comprehensibility and accountability. Oxford J Leg Stud 41:4, 1227–1248
Singh J (1988) Consumer complaint intentions and behavior: definitional and taxonomical issues. J Mark 52(1):93
Snyder F (1993) The effectiveness of European community law: institutions, processes, tools and techniques. Mod L Rev 156(19):9, 22
Soberon LJ, Ferrer H (1999) An empirical analysis of elderly consumers' complaining behavior. Fam Consum Sci Res J 27(3):341

Storskrubb E, Ziller J (2007) Access to justice in European comparative law. In: Francioni F (ed) Access to justice as a human right. Oxford Academic, Oxford, pp. 177 ff.
Stuyck J (2015) Consumer concepts in EU secondary law. In: Klinck F, Riesenhuber K (eds) Verbraucherleitbilder: Interdisziplinäre und europäische Perspektiven. De Gruyter, Berlin/ Boston, p 115 ff.
Susskind R (2010) The end of lawyers? Rethinking the nature of legal services. Oxford University Press, Oxford
Susskind RE (2019) Online courts and the future of justice. Oxford University Press, Oxford
Trebilcock MJ (2008) Legal Aid Review (Toronto: Ministry of the Attorney General), online: https://wayback.archiveit.org/16312/20210402061121/http://www.attorneygeneral.jus.gov.on.ca/english/about/pubs/trebilcock/
Tyler TR, Huo YJ (2002) Trust in the law: encouraging public cooperation with the police and the courts. Russell Sage Foundation, New York
van Gelder EM (2022) Consumer online dispute resolution pathways in Europe: analysing the standards for access and procedural justice in online dispute resolution procedures. Eleven International Publishing, The Hague
Van Loo R (2016) The corporation as courthouse. Yale J Reg 33:547
Van Loo R (2021) Federal rules of platforms procedure. Univ Chic L Rev 88:4, 829
Wagner W (2019) Incomprehensible: a study of how our legal system encourages incomprehensibility, why it matters, and what we can do about it. Cambridge University Press, Cambridge
Weitzl W (2019) Webcare's effect on constructive and vindictive complainants. J Prod Brand Manage 28:3, 330–347, p 330
Weitzl W, Hutzinger C, Einwiller S (2018) An empirical study on how webcare mitigates complainants' failure attributions and negative word-of-mouth. Comput Hum Behav 89:316–327
Welsh N (2016) ODR: a time for celebration and the embrace of procedural safeguards. In: Conference presentation at the International Forum for Online Dispute Resolution, The Hague, May. Available at: www.adrhub.com/profiles/blogs/procedural-justice-in-odr
Willis LE (2015) Performance-based consumer law'. Univ Chic L Rev 82(1309):1326
Wing L (2012) Intersectionality and conflict resolution pedagogy. In: Pliner S, Banks C (eds) Teaching, learning, and intersecting identities in higher education. Peter Lang Publishers, New York, p 49 ff.
Wing L (2016) Ethical principles for online dispute resolution: a GPS device for the field. Int J Online Disp Res 3:1, 12–29, at 17
Wing L, Martinez J, Katsh E, Rule C (2021) Designing ethical online dispute resolution systems: the rise of the fourth party. Negotiation J 37:1, Special Issue: Artificial Intelligence, Technology, and Negotiation, 49–64.
Wing L, Rainey D, Obi-Farinde M, Elisavetsky A, Cortes P (2022) ODR ethics and standards: the revised NCTDR and ICODR standards. Int J Online Disp Resol 9(2):124–132
Zuckerman AAS (2003) Civil justice in crisis: comparative perspectives of civil procedure. Oxford University Press, Oxford.

Maria Cecilia Paglietti, Associate Professor of Private Comparative Law, Department of Law, Roma Tre University. Former member (2015–2021) of the Banking and Financial Ombudsman (ABF) at the Bank of Italy. Lawyer, PhD in "Consumers and Market," and Director of the Clinical Program at Roma Tre Law School. Teaches European Digital Platform Law and runs one of Italy's first Legal Clinic on small savers' protection.

Open Access This chapter is licensed under the terms of the Creative Commons Attribution 4.0 International License (http://creativecommons.org/licenses/by/4.0/), which permits use, sharing, adaptation, distribution and reproduction in any medium or format, as long as you give appropriate credit to the original author(s) and the source, provide a link to the Creative Commons license and indicate if changes were made.

The images or other third party material in this chapter are included in the chapter's Creative Commons license, unless indicated otherwise in a credit line to the material. If material is not included in the chapter's Creative Commons license and your intended use is not permitted by statutory regulation or exceeds the permitted use, you will need to obtain permission directly from the copyright holder.

Insurance Robo-Advisors Under EU Law

Szymon Skalski and Piotr Tereszkiewicz

Abstract This paper investigates the regulatory treatment of AI-driven robo-advisors in the insurance sector under European Union law. It analyses the interaction between the European Union Insurance Distribution Directive (IDD), which provides a sector-specific framework for consumer protection, product oversight, and distributor conduct, and the European Union Regulation on artificial intelligence (the EU AI Act), which introduces a horizontal, risk-based regime for AI systems. The paper argues that while both frameworks share core objectives—risk management, transparency, and accountability—their regulatory logics diverge. The IDD relies on human oversight, personalised suitability assessments, and conflict-of-interest safeguards, whereas the AI Act prioritises technical compliance, quality management, and conformity assessments for high-risk AI systems, including those used in underwriting and pricing. These differences may give rise to regulatory fragmentation and gaps in consumer protection when AI-driven distribution tools operate across both regimes. The paper identifies areas of convergence, potential conflicts, and unresolved questions surrounding algorithmic decision-making, liability, and supervisory coordination. It concludes by recommending greater harmonisation, including sector-specific guidance and enhanced cooperation between insurance and AI regulators, to ensure that innovation in AI-based insurance distribution aligns with the EU's legal standards and fundamental rights protections.

Keywords Robo-advisors · Insurance · Insurance distribution · Consumer protection · The EU AI Act · The EU Insurance Distribution Directive

This chapter was written within the framework of the research project funded by the Polish National Science Centre (NCN), grant no. 2018/29/B/HS5/01281.

S. Skalski · P. Tereszkiewicz (✉)
Jagiellonian University, Krakow, Poland
e-mail: piotr.tereszkiewicz@uj.edu.pl

© The Author(s) 2025
C. Amodio and A. Diurni (eds.), *Human Vulnerability in Interaction with AI in European Private Law*, https://doi.org/10.1007/978-3-031-93247-2_19

1 Introduction

The insurance industry has undergone significant changes since the emergence of artificial intelligence (AI) and its applications in the financial services sector.[1] One notable development is the proliferation of AI-driven robo-advice, which uses advanced algorithms and machine learning techniques to deliver customised insurance advice, optimise product offers, and improve client relations by employing targeted insurance counsel.[2] This technological breakthrough presents numerous legal issues despite promising a better customer experience and higher efficiency. Policymakers and business leaders must ensure that, in line with strict consumer protection criteria, the use of artificial intelligence encourages innovation. Two crucial regulatory frameworks have emerged in the European Union's dynamic environment: the Insurance Distribution Directive (referred to as IDD) and the Artificial Intelligence Act (referred to as the AI Act).[3] The IDD focuses on the governance of insurance distribution, implementing comprehensive organisational and behavioural rules to enhance risk management, openness, and consumer protection within the insurance industry. Comprising strict suitability assessments and the criteria for Product Oversight and Governance (POG), IDD provisions ensure that insurance products are tailored to meet consumer needs and that conflicts of interest are adequately addressed.

On the other hand, the AI Act employs a technology-oriented, risk-based approach to regulate the use of artificial intelligence in various areas,[4] including high-stakes fields such as life and health insurance.[5] The AI Act classifies obligations imposed on providers by dividing AI systems into 'high-risk' and 'limited-risk' categories. Therefore, it includes strict quality control and documentation requirements for high-risk systems as well as transparency and accountability mechanisms for lower-risk applications. This horizontal approach to artificial intelligence governance aims to mitigate risks associated with automated decision-making and foster an environment conducive to technological progress.

[1] Insurance Europe (2021), Hielkema (2023), and European Insurance and Occupational Pensions Authority (EIOPA) (2024).

[2] See most notably: Baker and Dellaert (2018), Schwarcz et al. (2024), and Krueckeberg (2020).

[3] Regulation (EU) 2024/1689 of the European Parliament and of the Council of 13 June 2024 laying down harmonised rules on artificial intelligence and amending Regulations (EC) No 300/2008, (EU) No 167/2013, (EU) No 168/2013, (EU) 2018/858, (EU) 2018/1139 and (EU) 2019/2144 and Directives 2014/90/EU, (EU) 2016/797 and (EU) 2020/1828 (Artificial Intelligence Act) (Text with EEA relevance). OJ L 2024/1689, 12 July 2024. Available via EUR-Lex. https://eur-lex.europa.eu/eli/reg/2024/1689/oj/eng.

[4] See recitals 1, 2, 3, 6, 7, and 8 of the AI Act.

[5] However, for a critique of the true nature of the 'risk-based approach', see Ebers (2024).

1.1 Preliminary Remarks on the Definition of AI

One of the issues worth noting at the outset is the definition of the subject under analysis. The primary focus of the study is the structure of the two EU regulations mentioned above. However, underlying this is the main subject of the survey: artificial intelligence in the insurance sector. In the current state of regulation, from a legal perspective, only the secondary (or compliance) significance of this type of system has a technical definition. The AI Act defines artificial intelligence systems and general-purpose artificial intelligence systems. It would seem that this solves the issue, but the necessity to publish extensive guidelines[6] for the very definition of an AI system undermines this thesis. Before undertaking a close analysis, we briefly examine these definitions and relevant legal acts.

According to the AI Act, the definition includes a machine-based system designed to operate with varying levels of autonomy and that may exhibit adaptiveness after deployment. The system infers, from the input it receives, how to generate outputs such as predictions, content, recommendations, or decisions that can influence physical or virtual environments (Article 3 (1) of the AI Act) for explicit or implicit objectives.

The definition adopts a lifecycle-based approach, recognising two primary phases: the pre-deployment or 'building' phase and the post-deployment or 'use' phase.[7] This encompasses everything from emerging quantum computing technology to traditional computing designs.[8] Autonomy—understood as the capacity of an artificial intelligence system to operate somewhat independently of human intervention—is an essential component of the concept.[9] One of the primary distinguishing characteristics of artificial intelligence systems is their ability to perform inference, enabling them to process inputs and generate outputs, including recommendations or forecasts.[10] This sets artificial intelligence systems apart from more straightforward, rule-based programs that run predefined instructions.[11] While not a necessary quality, adaptability is the system's capacity to change its behaviour over time through self-learning processes.[12] The AI Act also ensures that AI systems can operate with clearly stated goals developed by their creators or with implicit aims arising from the interactions between the system and its surroundings.[13]

AI system categorisation primarily depends on inference, as it determines the system's capacity to produce outputs from given inputs. Along with logic- and knowledge-based approaches depending on encoded rules or symbolic representations, the AI Act describes several methodologies enabling inference, including

[6] European Commission (2025).

[7] Ibid. points 11–12.

[8] Ibid. point 13.

[9] Ibid. point 14–15.

[10] Ibid. points 26–27.

[11] Ibid. point 40.

[12] Ibid. points 22–23.

[13] Ibid. points 24–25.

machine learning approaches such as supervised, unsupervised, self-supervised, and reinforcement learning.[14] Beyond simple data processing, artificial intelligence systems incorporate reasoning, knowledge, or modelling, thus different from conventional software.[15]

Not all computer systems, in the meantime, fit the concept of an artificial intelligence system. Eliminated are conventional optimisation techniques, rudimentary statistical studies, and simple rule-based algorithms lacking advanced inferencing capability.[16] For instance, the AI system characteristics are not met by simple data processing tools, including spreadsheets that run specified computations.[17] Similarly, basic prediction models based on stationary estimate methods—that is, those based on past averages to project future results—do not show the adaptive, inferential powers unique to artificial intelligence systems.[18] Another component of the concept is that the outputs of an artificial intelligence system have to be able to affect either virtual or real surroundings.[19] This encompasses forecasts, content creation, suggestions, and automated decision-making that may impact actual systems, including autonomous driving technologies, financial transactions, or healthcare diagnostics.[20]

The AI Act's concept of artificial intelligence covers a spectrum of technologies and approaches with limits that distinguish it from traditional software. The extent of regulatory responsibilities under the AI Act depends on this description, since not all artificial intelligence systems are subject to rigid legal restrictions.[21] Using a risk-based approach, the Act regulates high-risk AI applications that raise significant ethical or social concerns.[22] Additionally, under independent examination are general-purpose AI models, whose regulatory issues outlined in Chapter V of the AI Act, require specific attention.[23] Analysing AI's influence in the insurance industry depends on how one understands this definition since risk assessment and regulatory compliance rely on whether a particular system meets the parameters of the AI Act. The interpretation of this term affects not only the legal framework for AI governance but also the broader discussion on the responsible development and implementation of artificial intelligence in key sectors, such as insurance.

On the other hand, there is a definition of a general-purpose artificial intelligence system which under the AI Act is distinct from the definition of an AI system itself: while the definition of AI systems refers exclusively to systems, the provisions on general-purpose AI cover both models and systems. A general-purpose AI model is an AI model, including those trained with large-scale self-supervision on vast

[14] Ibid. points 30–39.

[15] Ibid. points 26–27.

[16] Ibid. points 40–51.

[17] Ibid. point 46.

[18] Ibid. points 49–50.

[19] Ibid. points 52–60.

[20] Ibid. points 54–58.

[21] Ibid. points 61–63.

[22] Ibid. point 63.

[23] Ibid. point 64.

amounts of data, that exhibits significant generality and is capable of competently performing a wide range of distinct tasks, regardless of its market positioning. These models can be integrated into various downstream systems or applications, except when used solely for research, development, or prototyping purposes prior to market deployment.

This distinction is fundamental to understanding the AI Act's regulatory structure. While an AI system is a fully operational entity that includes models alongside other necessary components, such as interfaces, rule-based mechanisms, or integration layers, to perform specific functions, a general-purpose AI model is a standalone component that can be embedded into multiple AI systems.[24] AI models do not constitute AI systems on their own; instead, they must be integrated with additional elements to become part of a functioning system. However, once a general-purpose AI model is embedded into a system that maintains its broad applicability across multiple functions, the resulting system is classified as a general-purpose AI system.[25] Another essential regulatory distinction concerns high-impact capabilities and systemic risks. The AI Act recognises that specific general-purpose AI models possess high-impact capabilities, meaning their performance matches or exceeds the most advanced general-purpose AI models.[26] These models have the potential to introduce systemic risks, defined as risks specific to high-impact capabilities that can propagate at scale across the value chain, leading to significant effects on public health, safety, security, fundamental rights, or the economy. Systemic risks may arise from factors such as model reach, misuse potential, bias, security vulnerabilities, or the ability of models to replicate or interact with physical systems.[27]

A general-purpose AI system is an AI system based on a general-purpose AI model, designed to serve multiple purposes, either directly or by integrating with other AI systems. Unlike standard AI systems, which often have a well-defined intended purpose, general-purpose AI systems can be applied flexibly across a wide range of use cases, making their governance more complex. Large generative AI models, including those used to create text, audio, images or video, are considered typical examples of general-purpose AI models because they can be adapted for various applications.[28] The distinction between models and systems is essential for understanding regulatory obligations under the AI Act. General-purpose AI models are subject to specific obligations once they are placed on the market, even before they are integrated into AI systems.[29] However, when a provider integrates its general-purpose AI model into an AI system made available on the market, that model remains subject to the AI Act's model-specific obligations in addition to any obligations that apply to the AI system itself.[30]

---

[24] Recital 97 of the AI Act.

[25] Recital 100 of the AI Act.

[26] Recital 110 of the AI Act.

[27] Recital 110 of the AI Act.

[28] Recital 99 of the AI Act.

[29] Recital 97 of the AI Act.

[30] Recital 97 of the AI Act.

The AI Act's definitions of both AI systems and general-purpose AI models aim to encompass a broad range of technological capabilities, from narrowly focused machine-learning applications to comprehensive, multipurpose generative models. Nevertheless, understanding these definitions in isolation does not suffice to address the unique regulatory questions arising when such systems are deployed in the insurance sector. The very breadth of the AI Act's classifications—and the obligations they impose—reveals the potential for overlap or even tension with the IDD's insurance-specific framework. Indeed, reconciling the AI Act's risk-based governance of AI technology with the IDD's longstanding focus on consumer protection, suitability assessments, and market conduct raises fundamental questions about how best to regulate AI-driven insurance distribution. It is precisely these questions—on aligning two distinct yet intersecting legal regimes, identifying shared objectives, and pinpointing gaps and challenges—that guide the comparative analysis in the following sections.

The difference between the IDD's insurance-specific approach and the general AI governance model outlined in the AI Act raises important questions about the optimal control of AI-driven insurance distribution. Essential research questions guiding this chapter include: How do the IDD and the AI Act regulate the use of AI in insurance distribution? Where do their needs coincide or differ, and what are the shortcomings and challenges to reaching effective compliance across both systems? This chapter compares the IDD and the AI Act by examining their fundamental concepts, operational frameworks, and legal implications for the insurance industry. It clarifies areas of convergence—such as risk management, openness, and consumer protection—as well as some apparent differences and regulatory gaps. These cover differences in sector specificity, the balance between algorithmic decision-making and human supervision, and the unique testing procedures for insurance products relative to artificial intelligence systems. Through recommendations for regulatory harmonisation, the study aims to strike a balance between the insurance-centric focus of the IDD and the broad, technologically oriented character of the AI Act, thereby building a coherent framework that promotes both innovation and consumer welfare in the AI-driven insurance sector.

2 The EU Insurance Distribution Directive Framework

The IDD provides a comprehensive framework for the internal organisation, governance, and compliance of insurance distributors.[31] This structure aims to ensure that institutions and their staff possess the necessary knowledge, skills, and ethical standards to operate in a market driven by consumers and competition. The IDD emphasises continuous professional development, strict internal controls, and transparent approaches for assessing and maintaining competency, thereby supporting a sustainable risk management culture within the industry. Two fundamental ideas

[31] Marano (2021, pp. 68–72) and Marano and Li (2023).

underlie these organising principles: professional competency, as stated in Article 10 of the IDD, and control over product development and marketing, as outlined in Article 25 of the IDD. Article 10 of the IDD requires insurance and reinsurance distributors and their staff to maintain a minimum level of professional competence through mandatory training (at least 15 h per year) and, if relevant, certification.[32] Furthermore, it emphasises the need for ongoing professional growth tailored to the complexity of the given products and the need for staff members to keep a clear record of excellent standing. These requirements establish a benchmark for the ethical and professional standards of market players.

2.1 Product Oversight and Governance Under the IDD

Most importantly, Article 25 of the IDD introduces the concept of Product Oversight and Governance (POG), a significant development under the IDD that affects insurance companies and their regulatory authorities. POG marks a significant shift from past regulatory approaches by requiring insurance companies and intermediaries to incorporate client protection into the development and lifecycle of insurance products.[33] Modelled after the MiFID II framework, the POG framework has evolved to address challenges in the insurance industry that former regulatory systems could not adequately handle. Article 25 of the IDD mandates that every insurance product, or any significant alteration thereto, undergo a rigorous product approval process before being sold. This technique aims to define a target market for every product, ensuring thorough risk analysis and a good fit for the intended consumers. Firms must produce a documented 'product oversight and governance policy', which includes methods for product design, monitoring, and review. Under regular review, this policy must be incorporated into the company's internal control systems and updated to reflect changes in product efficacy or market conditions.

It has been suggested that POG align with the anticipatory supervisory structure established under Solvency II.[34] POG helps prevent the spread of unsuitable products by requiring a methodical evaluation of products throughout the design stage, thereby enhancing the transparency of the product development process for regulatory authorities. This realisation helps authorities respond quickly should a product's design or performance deviate from its intended customer protection objectives. Moreover, the POG's approach requires producers to document every aspect of the product life—from initial design to ongoing monitoring—and to share this data with distributors and, if necessary, with supervising authorities.

---

[32] LexisNexis (2018) and BIPAR (2024).

[33] Marano (2021, p. 55).

[34] Ibid. pp 55–56, 61–62; See also: EIOPA (2018, 2020, 2021, 2022a, 2022b, 2023, 2025).

2.2 *Business Conduct Regulations: Protecting Customers Under the IDD*

Under the IDD, the business conduct rules govern the marketing, sales, and advisory practices related to insurance products, thereby protecting customers. From initial consultations to post-sale correspondence, these rules govern all aspects of customer interaction, ensuring that openness, fairness, and prioritising client interests take precedence over business goals. As such, they build a structure that calls for moral behaviour and responsibility in providing insurance products, thereby fostering a more reliable relationship between insurers and their customers.

Article 14 of the IDD on complaint handling is essential for these rules, laying down a framework for addressing clients' complaints regarding distributors.[35] This article emphasises the need for developing procedures that enable consumers and consumer groups to report issues effectively, ensuring that problems are resolved promptly and fairly. These steps are essential for building responsibility and confidence as they provide a methodical structure for consumers to seek compensation and for businesses to demonstrate their willingness to address problems fairly and honestly.

Emphasising the need to prioritise the customer's best interest, Articles 17(1) and (3) of the IDD aim to improve the existing complaint management system.[36] Under this open-ended standard, insurance distributors must conduct all sales and advisory activities honestly, fairly and professionally. Article 17(1) of the IDD explicitly prohibits sales targets or incentive plans that promote products based solely on commission rather than on the appropriateness of the product for the consumer's needs. This ban is necessary to protect customer interests against commercial pressures, thereby enhancing the ethical foundation of the distribution mechanism. Furthermore, Article 27 of the IDD addresses the prevention of conflicts of interest.[37] Insurance distributors must establish comprehensive organisational structures to identify, prevent, and manage disputes that could compromise consumer interests. The article calls for consumers to be specifically informed about the type and source of conflicts when their eradication is impossible. Maintaining confidence depends on this openness, as it allows consumers to make informed decisions about the recommendations and products they receive. Article 30 of the IDD ensures that the advice provided to them is suitable and acceptable, taking into account their financial situation and needs. Specific means to achieve this objective include utilising comprehensive client assessments, which require intermediaries to gather detailed information about a customer's investment acumen, experience, financial capacity, and risk tolerance. This information mandates intermediaries to recommend products that fit the customer's profile. Furthermore, if a product is deemed unsuitable,

[35] Defever (2021).

[36] Noussia (2021) and Siri (2021).

[37] Insurance Europe (2025).

the intermediary must notify the customer immediately, retain thorough evaluation documentation and provide advised guidance.

3 The AI Act: Responsibilities for High-Risk and Limited-Risk AI Providers

The AI Act categorises artificial intelligence systems as either high-risk or low-risk, depending on their potential impact on individuals and society, employing a risk-based approach for their regulation (Article 6 of the AI Act). Among other uses, high-risk artificial intelligence systems are employed in critical sectors such as life and health insurance, where the consequences of any failure or bias could be severe. On the other hand, limited-risk artificial intelligence systems emphasise openness and detailed documentation to ensure their activities are understandable and responsible, as their governance is subject to less strict regulations. Under the AI Act, providers of high-risk artificial intelligence systems are subject to significant obligations. Article 16 of the AI Act defines the essential responsibilities of these suppliers and requires adherence to all set high-risk criteria before market launch. This includes creating a quality management system, as Article 17 of the AI Act mandates that providers must develop written policies and procedures to guide the design, development, and post-market surveillance of their artificial intelligence systems. These systems must be integrated through testing and validation procedures and techniques to ensure regulatory compliance, mitigate risk, and facilitate continuous system performance evaluation.

Furthermore, in line with Article 18 of the AI Act, providers must maintain thorough technical documentation and records for an extended period to support regulatory control and post-market surveillance. Furthermore, Article 19 of the AI Act requires providers to maintain automatically generated logs by their artificial intelligence systems, enabling a swift analysis of operational disparities. Article 20 of the AI Act requires providers to identify non-compliance or dangers and respond immediately with corrections, including system withdrawal, deactivation, or recall, along with prompt notice to relevant authorities and distributors. Under Article 21 of the AI Act, providers assist competent authorities by providing all necessary information and documents to confirm the conformance of their systems, therefore increasing the general transparency and integrity of the regulatory system.

More specifically, providers must ensure that their high-risk AI systems are identifiable and traceable (Article 16(b) of the AI Act) by affixing on the system—or, where that is not feasible, on its packaging or accompanying documentation—the provider's name, registered trade name or trademark, and a contact address.[38] This measure promotes transparency and accountability, particularly in the event of a system recall or the need for corrective action (Article 16(b) of the AI Act). Providers must also ensure that their systems undergo the relevant conformity assessment procedures

[38] Tsipras (2024).

before market launch and subsequently bear an EU declaration of conformity and the CE marking—clear indicators of compliance with all applicable requirements (Articles 16(f),[39] 16(g), and 16(h) of the AI Act).[40] In addition, providers are obligated to register their high-risk AI systems and maintain comprehensive technical documentation, including automated logs, throughout the system's lifecycle, thereby ensuring that any operational discrepancies or emerging risks can be identified and addressed (Articles 16 (i), 18, and 19 of the AI Act). Finally, providers must act immediately upon identifying any non-compliance or potential hazards by implementing corrective measures—such as system withdrawal or deactivation—and by providing all necessary documentation upon a reasoned request from the competent authorities, thus ensuring effective and transparent regulatory oversight (Articles 16(k) and 20 of the AI Act).

Concerning liability, limited-risk AI systems are subject to somewhat less strict obligations. Unless this is obvious, the Article 50 of the AI Act requires providers to satisfy transparency criteria, including notifying individuals when they interact with an artificial intelligence system. Providers of GPAI models are additionaly subject to documentation obligations under Article 53 of the AI Act. Moreover, Article 54 of the AI Act attaches significant responsibility to authorised representatives. It requires providers outside the Union to appoint a representative within the EU, ensuring ongoing compliance with the designated legal duties. The designated person is responsible for confirming the suitability of the technical documentation and ensuring that the AI system meets the criteria outlined in the AI Act.

Based on those provisions, the AI Act establishes a transparency framework for AI systems. For example, providers of interactive AI systems must design them to inform users that they are engaging with an AI, except when the non-human nature is apparent[41] or when the system is used for law enforcement purposes.[42] Similarly, content–generating system providers must integrate technical marking solutions (e.g., watermarks or embedded metadata) to ensure that any generated or manipulated output is machine-readable and identifiable.[43] Deployers of emotion recognition and biometric categorisation systems are also required to inform individuals about the operation of such systems, with a specific exemption provided for law enforcement applications.[44] These transparency obligations are cumulative, meaning that if an AI system performs multiple functions, all relevant requirements must be met simultaneously.[45] The regulatory framework requires that these transparency obligations be supported by documentation and periodic evaluations, with key roles assigned to the AI Office and the Commission. These bodies are empowered to develop codes of practice, issue guidelines, and adopt implementing acts

[39] See more in Ozkayagan Prandl and Kwiatkowska (2024).

[40] Tsipras (2024).

[41] Gils (2024).

[42] Ibid. pp 790–791.

[43] Ibid. pp. 792–795.

[44] Ibid. pp. 800–802.

[45] Ibid. pp. 797–798.

to clarify the obligations and ensure their uniform application across the Union.[46] Finally, enforcement measures, including administrative fines, are provided to ensure compliance and to protect public trust in AI systems.[47]

Insurance undertakings that use—but do not place on the market—an AI-based underwriting, pricing, or claims-handling tool are considered deployers under Article 3(4) of the AI Act. Annex III point 5(c) of the AI Act designates AI tools used to set or adjust life- or health-insurance premiums as high-risk systems. When an insurer merely uses such a tool—rather than placing it on the market—it qualifies as a deployer of a high-risk system. That status activates the deployer-specific duties outlined in Articles 26 and 27 of the AI Act, which include operating the system in accordance with the provider's instructions, ensuring effective human oversight and data-quality controls, retaining logs, and completing a Fundamental-Rights Impact Assessment prior to first use. The EU insurance supervisor has already underlined this point and mapped those duties onto the familiar Solvency II governance framework.[48]

In practice, Article 26 of the AI Act requires insurers to run the system exactly as instructed by the provider, appoint staff who can override outputs in real-time, ensure that any input data under their control are relevant and representative, pause use and notify authorities if a serious incident arises, and store automatically generated logs for at least six months. They must also tell employees and customers whenever an AI-assisted decision produces legal or similarly significant effects (Article 26(7) and (11) in conjunction with Article 50 of the AI Act). Before an insurer can put a high-risk AI pricing or underwriting system into service, Article 27 of the AI Act requires the firm, as a deployer, to draw up a Fundamental Rights Impact Assessment (FRIA).[49] The assessment must describe how and where the system will be used, identify the individuals or groups who may be affected, analyse concrete risks to fundamental rights such as discrimination or unfair exclusion, spell out the human-oversight arrangements (including who can pause or override the model) and set out the fallback measures that will be triggered if those risks materialise. It needs to be completed before the tool goes live and kept up to date whenever any of those elements change. Where the insurer has already prepared a GDPR data-protection impact assessment, the two exercises may be combined, provided that every FRIA element is covered. The AI Act outlines duties based on a proportionality criterion. For high-risk systems, the provider is treated almost like a regulated manufacturer; it must embed a formal quality-management system, prove ex-ante conformity through a notified body, register the system, preserve design documentation and logs for supervisory audit, conduct post-market monitoring and, where necessary, trigger withdrawal or recall while cooperating with market-surveillance authorities. For limited-risk systems, the legislature relies on visibility and traceability instead. Here, the provider's obligations are reduced to three core elements: disclosure that the user is engaging with AI, technical marking of synthetic output, and maintaining sufficient

[46] Ibid. pp. 815–817.

[47] Ibid. pp. 818–819.

[48] EIOPA (2024, 2025a, 2025b).

[49] Mantelero (2024).

records, as well as the appointment of an EU representative when the provider is based abroad.

4 Comparative Analysis of IDD and the AI Act in the Field of AI-Driven Insurance

In the context of AI systems, one can view the regulatory approaches outlined in the IDD and the AI Act as distinct yet mutually reinforcing. The IDD prioritises consumer protection, rigorous internal controls, and targeted risk management within the insurance distribution landscape, ensuring that products and services are aligned with the needs of consumers. Conversely, the AI Act employs a technology-focused, risk-based framework aimed at mitigating the broader challenges posed by advanced AI systems. A closer examination reveals several areas of overlap, indicating that integrating these frameworks could yield a more robust regulatory environment that addresses both the sector-specific nuances of insurance and the complex risks associated with AI technologies.

4.1 Risk Management and Oversight

Both regulatory tools emphasise the importance of risk management and monitoring as crucial components of their systems. The IDD mandates that insurance entities and distributors meticulously assess and consistently oversee insurance products before their market introduction as stipulated in Article 25 of the IDD on Product Oversight and Governance (POG) provisions.[50] This entails identifying a target market, performing risk evaluations throughout product development, and establishing systems for ongoing review. These organisational principles prevent potential hazards and ensure that products consistently meet client needs.

The AI Act concurrently enforces risk management mandates on suppliers of high-risk AI systems as outlined in Article 9 of the AI Act and further detailed in its Articles 16–21.[51] Providers of high-risk AI must establish robust quality control systems, maintain thorough technical documentation, and perform regular conformity evaluations. These procedures ensure that AI systems, particularly those used in critical areas such as life and health insurance, undergo continuous supervision and that any operational or safety hazards are mitigated. Both regulatory measures, the IDD and the AI Act, aim to create an environment where risk management is a fundamental component of the product development and deployment process rather than an afterthought. This convergence improves regulatory clarity and fosters a more secure market for consumers.

---

[50] Marano (2021, pp. 68–72).

[51] See recitals 79, 80, and 81 of the AI Act.

4.2 Transparency and Comprehensibility

Both regulatory systems underscore transparency and explainability, albeit through divergent approaches. Under the IDD, strict suitability and appropriateness assessments (Article 30 IDD) require insurance intermediaries to collect comprehensive data on clients' financial capacity, risk tolerance, and investment knowledge.[52] This systematic, data-driven methodology is designed to document and justify product recommendations, thereby identifying and flagging mismatches between clients and products. While these measures serve to protect consumers, they also aim to instil a degree of procedural clarity in insurance advisory practices. Conversely, the AI Act imposes transparency standards on limited-risk AI systems (Article 50 of the AI Act) by requiring providers to ensure that their systems' operations and decision-making processes are transparent and understandable.[53] This includes labelling outputs as artificially generated and providing accessible, machine-readable information on system capabilities and limitations. The intent is to demystify the inner workings of AI systems, enabling stakeholders—from consumers to legislators—to assess the factors that drive automated decisions critically.

Although the IDD and the AI Act operationalise transparency via different instruments—client assessments versus technical documentation and labelling—they both rely on transparency as a cornerstone for accountability. However, their different procedural frameworks may complicate efforts to harmonise oversight, particularly at the intersection where the complexities of algorithmic decision-making meet sector-specific insurance advisory practices.

4.3 Consumer Protection

The IDD and the AI Act are committed to consumer protection within their frameworks, albeit through distinct mechanisms. The IDD explicitly addresses potential conflicts of interest, mandating that insurance intermediaries adhere to strict organisational procedures designed to identify, avoid, and mitigate conflicts that could compromise customer interests.[54] This includes the early disclosure of unavoidable conflicts and the prohibition of commission-based incentives, which collectively ensure that product recommendations align with consumer preferences. Conversely, the AI Act aims to mitigate algorithmic bias and reduce undesirable outcomes in AI-driven decisions by implementing rigorous quality management and risk assessment requirements for high-risk systems.[55] While the AI Act does not explicitly frame these measures as addressing conflicts of interest, its provisions aim to prevent

[52] Paras 1 and 2 of Article 30 of the IDD, also Siri (2021, p. 124).

[53] See the literature cited above and recitals 132–137 of the AI Act.

[54] See recital 2 IDD.

[55] Kuśmierczyk (2022), Bosoer et al. (2023), and Massarotto (2023).

systemic injustices by ensuring that AI systems are developed and maintained under controlled conditions.

The convergence between these regulatory approaches lies in their shared recognition that adequate consumer protection demands proactive, preventive measures rather than reactive responses to adverse events. The IDD achieves this through detailed procedural safeguards in product design and delivery, while the AI Act relies on continuous monitoring, adversarial testing, and corrective actions to uphold standards. However, this alignment also highlights a broader challenge: integrating ethical considerations and fairness into a framework that addresses sector-specific practices and general AI compliance.

5 Integration and Consequences for a Coordinated Regulatory Framework

The IDD and the AI Act also diverge in ways that could lead to regulatory conflicts in AI-driven insurance. Although both frameworks prioritise proactive risk management, transparency, and consumer protection, their underlying approaches differ significantly. The IDD's insurance-specific model emphasises tailored risk assessments, detailed suitability evaluations, and human oversight, ensuring each product aligns with individual consumer profiles. Conversely, the AI Act applies a broader, risk-based framework, favouring standardised compliance procedures, which may overlook unique challenges of the insurance sector.

This divergence may lead to regulatory fragmentation since a generic AI governance approach may not adequately address sector-specific risks. At the same time, the emphasis on automation in the AI Act could conflict with the IDD's assumption of human accountability. Consequently, this misalignment raises questions about effective oversight, especially when automated decisions obscure the origins of potential errors.[56] Ultimately, reconciling these differences is crucial to prevent consumer protection gaps while fostering innovation in a regulated environment.

5.1 Principal Conflicts and Regulatory Deficiencies

Notwithstanding a high degree of convergence between the IDD and the AI Act, significant conflicts and regulatory flaws still demonstrate two different regulatory philosophies guiding each system. Examining the degree of regulatory monitoring, the balance between algorithmic decision-making and human responsibility, and different testing procedures used for insurance products compared to artificial intelligence systems helps one to flesh out the differences between both regimes.

[56] On establishing an effective AI oversight regime, see Novelli et al. (2024), Rankin (2025), Politico (2024), and Shrishak (2024).

One main area of change is regulatory fragmentation. Emphasising the need to create, approve, and market insurance products to prioritise consumer welfare, the IDD aims to reduce hazards peculiar to the insurance sector. The rules are subtly entwined into the operational complexities of the insurance industry, emphasising tailored evaluations, including conflict of interest protections and appropriateness assessments. On the other hand, the AI Act employs a comprehensive, technologically based governance approach designed to regulate AI applications across various fields. This all-encompassing approach yields a general framework that may not be sufficient to address the sector-specific risks unique to the insurance sector, particularly those related to client protection and financial stability. The differences in focus lead to a regulatory structure whereby a generalised AI governance model may not be able to control insurance-related challenges effectively, therefore generating shortcomings in the supervision.

5.2 *Algorithmic Decision-Making Versus Human Oversight*

Another area of conflict is the balance between human oversight and algorithmic decision-making. The IDD rests on the assumption that insurance customers should be responsible for their own transactional decisions. Nevertheless, it calls on insurance distributors to take responsibility for providing client advice, ensuring that final decisions result from individual assessments of product suitability in view of clients' needs and wishes.[57] In cases of incorrect or biased product recommendations, this human-centric approach fosters customer confidence and lays groundwork for the provider's liability. The AI Act acknowledges the growing importance of automation by allowing entirely automated decision-making procedures to be subject to strict system protection only. This approach risks weakening responsibility even if it could increase scalability and efficiency.[58] Reliance on automated processes may obscure the cause of judgment errors, complicating the identification of whether a failure stems from the system's architecture, its data sources, or the monitoring systems. This discrepancy raises questions about the effectiveness of corrective actions and the ability of regulatory authorities to respond promptly to manifest consumer harms.

5.3 *Suitability Assessment Against AI Compliance*

The third significant difference results from the different approaches taken in testing and compliance. Under the IDD, consumer protection depends mainly on individual appropriateness evaluations. Insurance intermediaries must holistically examine the

[57] On personalisation in insurance, see Tereszkiewicz et al. (2024) and Pałka and Wiśniewska (2022).

[58] Fink (2025) and Laux (2023).

client's financial situation, risk tolerance, and investment objectives. This customised evaluation ensures that product recommendations precisely fit every client's needs and circumstances. On the other hand, the AI Act generally emphasises the compliance of artificial intelligence systems rather than particular interactions and requires a broader risk management approach. Although this comprehensive compliance framework helps develop standardised artificial intelligence systems, it may not be sufficient for the complex and unique assessments required in the insurance industry. The discrepancy between tailored suitability assessments and the standardised risk management rules of the AI Act highlights a major conflict: the need to maintain thorough consumer protections in insurance while harnessing the creative power and efficiencies of AI. The challenge is to combine these two approaches so that AI-driven systems are sufficiently suited to the unique financial profiles of specific clients and efficient in their risk assessment processes.

In essence, whereas the IDD and the AI Act aim at risk management, openness, and consumer protection, their differing regulatory approaches lead to various conflicts and shortcomings despite pursuing the same goals. Regulatory fragmentation means that sector-specific threats may not be sufficiently addressed within a comprehensive AI governance structure. An unresolved equilibrium between algorithmic decision-making and human supervision creates challenges for responsibility and effective intervention. The differences between suitability assessments and general AI compliance criteria reveal a clear gap in ensuring that AI systems in insurance efficiently meet the specific needs of individual customers. Resolving these conflicts and eliminating these gaps requires coordinated efforts for regulatory harmonisation, utilising sector-specific suggestions that combine the benefits of both systems and thereby mitigate their respective flaws.

6 Conclusion

In conclusion, while the AI Act and the Insurance Distribution Directive are committed to risk management, transparency, and consumer protection, they diverge significantly in their regulatory focus. The AI Act primarily functions as a product safety regulation, emphasising quality management, comprehensive documentation, and risk assessment protocols for high-risk AI systems. This approach ensures that AI-driven products meet rigorous safety and compliance standards. In contrast, the IDD is tailored to the insurance sector, concentrating on regulating specific types of companies through detailed product monitoring, suitability assessments, and human oversight. While comprehensive in intent, this dual regulatory framework may lead to practical conflicts. The AI Act's generalised, technology-oriented framework may not fully capture the risks inherent to the insurance industry, and its product-centric safety measures clash with the IDD's focus on the operational and behavioural aspects of insurance companies. As a result, entities within the industry fulfil multiple, sometimes conflicting, roles—acting simultaneously as product safety regulators and as sector-specific market overseers.

To resolve these conflicts, it is essential to harmonise the frameworks by developing sector-specific guidelines that integrate thorough customer assessments and product monitoring into the broader AI risk control structure. Moreover, enhanced coordination among supervisory bodies—such as EIOPA and AI regulatory authorities—is crucial for developing a flexible and cohesive framework that can adapt to the evolving challenges of AI-driven insurance while ensuring robust consumer protection.

References

Baker T, Dellaert BGC (2018) Regulating robo advice across the financial services industry. All Faculty Scholarship 1740, pp 721–724. Available via the University of Pennsylvania. https://scholarship.law.upenn.edu/faculty_scholarship/1740

BIPAR (2024) Insurance Distribution Directive (IDD). Available via BIPAR, pp 4. https://www.bipar.eu/images/uploads/general/IDD-en-24052024.pdf

Bosoer L, Cantero Gamito M, Rubio-Marin R (2023) Non-discrimination and the AI Act. In: casadei (ed) Law and Digitalization. Arazandi, pp 10–12. Available via SSRN. https://ssrn.com/abstract=4666071

Defever KM (2021). Enaction of Chapter VII of the Insurance Distribution Directive: what can member states learn from the enforcement failures of the United States? In: Marano P, Noussia K (eds) Insurance distribution directive: a legal analysis. AIDA Europe Research Series on Insurance Law and Regulation, vol 1. Springer, Cham, p 200. https://doi.org/10.1007/978-3-030-52738-9

Ebers M (2024). Truly risk-based regulation of artificial intelligence—how to implement the EU's AI Act. Available via SSRN, pp 11–20. https://ssrn.com/abstract=4870387 or https://doi.org/10.2139/ssrn.4870387

EIOPA (2018) Decision on the cooperation of competent authorities under the IDD. Published on 10 October 2018. Available via EIOPA. https://www.eiopa.europa.eu/publications/decision-cooperation-competent-authorities-under-idd_en

EIOPA (2020) EIOPA's approach to the supervision of product oversight and governance. Published on 8 October 2020. Available via EIOPA. https://www.eiopa.europa.eu/publications/eiopas-approach-supervision-product-oversight-and-governance_en

EIOPA (2021) Supervisory statement on assessment of value for money of unit-linked insurance products under product oversight and governance. Published on 30 November 2021. Available via EIOPA. https://www.eiopa.europa.eu/publications/supervisory-statement-assessment-value-money-unit-linked-insurance-products-under-product-oversight_en

EIOPA (2022a) Methodology to assess value for money in the unit-linked market. Published on 31 October 2022. Available via EIOPA. https://www.eiopa.europa.eu/publications/methodology-assess-value-money-unit-linked-market_en

EIOPA (2022b) Supervisory statement on exclusions in insurance products related to risks arising from systemic events. Published on 22 September 2022. Available via EIOPA. https://www.eiopa.europa.eu/publications/supervisory-statement-exclusions-insurance-products-related-risks-arising-systemic-events_en

EIOPA (2023) Supervisory statement on differential pricing practices in non-life insurance lines of business. Published on 16 March 2023. Available via EIOPA. https://www.eiopa.europa.eu/publications/supervisory-statement-differential-pricing-practices-non-life-insurance-lines-business_en

EIOPA (2024) Factsheet on the regulatory framework applicable to AI systems in the insurance sector, July 15. https://www.eiopa.europa.eu/publications/factsheet-regulatory-framework-applicable-ai-systems-insurance-sector_en

EIOPA (2025) Consumer Protection Department: EIOPA warns insurers and banks to address issues with high remuneration and conflicts of interest from the sale of credit protection insurance or face possible supervisory action. Available via EIOPA. https://www.eiopa.europa.eu/document/download/86343478-edb9-46d1-acc2-5375fa709305_en?filename=EIOPA%20warning%20to%20insurers%20and%20banks%20on%20Credit%20Protection%20Insurance.pdf

EIOPA (2025) Impact assessment of EIOPA's opinion on AI governance and risk management, February 11. https://www.eiopa.europa.eu/document/download/197892cf-5100-4cba-9f10-143b5e893559_en

European Commission (2025) The commission publishes guidelines on the definition of AI systems to facilitate the application of the first AI Act's rules. Available via: https://digital-strategy.ec.europa.eu/en/library/commission-publishes-guidelines-ai-system-definition-facilitate-first-ai-acts-rules-application

European Insurance and Occupational Pensions Authority (EIOPA) (2024) Report on the digitalisation of the European insurance sector. EIOPA-BoS-24/139. Available via EIOPA. https://www.eiopa.europa.eu/document/download/6ca9e171-42b9-44d7-a2e6-beaf0134ecb8_en?filename=Report%20on%20the%20digitalisation%20of%20the%20European%20insurance%20sector.pdf

Fink M (2025) Human oversight under Article 14 of the EU AI Act, pp 10–13. Available via SSRN. https://ssrn.com/abstract=

Gils T (2024) Article 50: transparency obligations for providers and deployers of specific AI systems. In: pehlivan CN, Forgó N, Valcke P (eds) The EU Artificial Intelligence (AI) act: a commentary. Wolters Kluwer Law International Alphen aan den Rijn, p 788

Hielkema P (2023) AI in the insurance sector: industry adoption and regulatory developments. European Insurance and Occupational Pensions Authority (EIOPA). Available via EIOPA. https://www.eiopa.europa.eu/document/download/b56434a2-dd9a-41de-8f0d-de08cca04080_en?filename=eurofi-magazine_septembre-2023-AI%20in%20the%20insurance%20sector%20industry%20adoption%20and%20regulatory%20developments.pdf

Insurance Europe (2021) Artificial intelligence (AI) in the insurance sector. Available via Insurance Europe https://www.insuranceeurope.eu/publications/2608/artificial-intelligence-ai-in-the-insurance-sector/

Insurance Europe (2025) Comments template on the consultation paper on technical advice on possible delegated acts concerning the Insurance Distribution Directive, Question 9. Available via Insurance Europe, p 15 https://www.insuranceeurope.eu/publications/1904/response-to-eiopa-consultation-on-idd-delegated-acts/

Krueckeberg S (2020) Situating robo-advisory. In: Scholz P (ed) Robo-advisory—investing in the digital age. Palgrave Macmillan, New York, pp 2–4. Available via SSRN https://ssrn.com/abstract=3589348

Kuśmierczyk M (2022) Algorithmic bias in the light of the GDPR and the proposed AI Act. In: olejnik M, Morawska W (eds) (In)equality. Faces of modern Europe. Wydawnictwo Centrum Studiów Niemieckich i Europejskich im. Willy'ego Brandta, Wrocław (forthcoming), pp 2–4. Available via SSRN. https://ssrn.com/abstract=4117936 or https://doi.org/10.2139/ssrn.4117936

Laux J (2023) Institutionalised distrust and human oversight of artificial intelligence: toward a democratic design of AI governance under the European Union AI Act. Available via SSRN, pp 8–12. https://ssrn.com/abstract=4377481 or https://doi.org/10.2139/ssrn.4377481

LexisNexis (2018) The Insurance Distribution Directive (IDD) introduces CPD requirements (Art 10) for insurance distribution. Published by a LexisNexis Financial Services expert, 28 August 2018. Available via LexisNexis. https://www.lexisnexis.co.uk/legal/guidance/the-insurance-distribution-directive-idd-introduces-cpd-requirements-art-10-for-insurance-01

Mantelero A (2024) The Fundamental Rights Impact Assessment (FRIA) in the AI act: roots, legal obligations and key elements for a model template. SSRN Working Paper, pp 13–15. Available at https://papers.ssrn.com/sol3/papers.cfm?abstract_id=4782126

Marano P (2021) The contribution of product oversight and governance (POG) to the single market: a set of organisational rules for business conduct. In: marano P, Noussia K (eds) Insurance distribution directive: a legal analysis. Springer Nature, Cham, pp 61–64

Marano P, Li S (2023) Regulating robo-advisors in insurance distribution: lessons from the Insurance Distribution Directive and the AI Act. Risks 11(1):12, pp 3–4. https://doi.org/10.3390/risks1101 0012

Massarotto G (2023) What is algorithmic bias and why antitrust agencies should care. CPI Antitrust Chronicle, June 2023. U of Penn, Inst for Law & Econ Research Paper No. 23–39, pp 3–5. Available via SSRN. https://ssrn.com/abstract=4625894

Noussia K (2021) The IDD and its impact on the life insurance industry. In: marano P, Noussia K (eds) Insurance distribution directive: a legal analysis. Springer Nature, Cham, pp 78 88

Novelli C, Hacker P, Morley J, Trondal J, Floridi L (2024). A robust governance for the AI Act: AI Office, AI Board, Scientific Panel, and national authorities. Eur J Risk Regul [https://doi.org/10.1017/err.2024.57], pp 10–15. Available via SSRN. https://ssrn.com/abstract=4817755 or https://doi.org/10.1017/err.2024.57

Ozkayagan Prandl H, Kwiatkowska K (2024) Article 43: conformity assessment. In: pehlivan CN, Forgó N, Valcke P (eds) The EU Artificial Intelligence (AI) act: a commentary. Wolters Kluwer Alphen aan den Rijn

Pałka P, Wiśniewska K (2022) Normative considerations in data-driven personalisation of consumer insurance contracts. In: Poncibò C, Tereszkiewicz P (eds) European insurance contract law: the promises and perils of digitalization. Springer International, pp 3–5. Available via SSRN. https://ssrn.com/abstract=4391650 or https://doi.org/10.2139/ssrn.4391650

Politico (2024) The EU's AI bans come with big loopholes for police. Available via Politico. https://www.politico.eu/article/ai-deepseek-chatgpt-openai-eu-bans-series-of-ai-practices-but-with-loopholes/

Rankin J (2025) EU accused of leaving 'devastating' copyright loophole in AI Act. The Guardian, 19 February 2025. Available via The Guardian https://www.theguardian.com/technology/2025/feb/19/eu-accused-of-leaving-devastating-copyright-loophole-in-ai-act

Schwarcz D, Baker T, Logue KD (2025) Regulating robo-advisors in an age of generative artificial intelligence. Wash & Lee L Rev 82(2):775–858

Shrishak K (2024) A false start is not an option for the EU AI Office. Euractiv, July 10. Available via Euractiv https://www.euractiv.com/section/tech/opinion/a-false-start-is-not-an-option-for-the-eu-ai-office/

Siri M (2021) Insurance-based investment products: regulatory responses and policy issues. In: Marano P, Noussia K (eds) Insurance distribution directive: a legal analysis. Springer Nature, Cham, p 123 ff

Tereszkiewicz P, Południak-Gierz K, Walczak P (2024) The digital vulnerability of insurance consumers and personalised pricing of insurance products. In: crea C, De Franceschi A (eds) The new shapes of digital vulnerability in European private law. Nomos, pp 4–8. Available via SSRN https://ssrn.com/abstract=4965865 or https://doi.org/10.2139/ssrn.4965865

Tsipras S (2024) Article 16: obligations of providers of high-risk AI systems. In: pehlivan CN, Forgó N, Valcke P (eds) The EU Artificial Intelligence (AI) Act: a Commentary. Wolters Kluwer, Alphen aan den Rijn pp 411–413

Szymon Skalski, Ph.D. candidate at the Doctoral School of Social Sciences, Jagiellonian University. Researches tort law, emerging technologies, and insurance law. Member of expert groups on AI law implementation. Visiting Scholar at Indiana University. Advises companies in critical infrastructure on EU cybersecurity regulations and is a certified lead auditor for ISO 27001 and ISO 22301.

Piotr Tereszkiewicz, Professor of Private Law at the Jagiellonian University in Kraków, Poland, and Senior Research Affiliate at KU Leuven, Belgium. Research and teaching Fields include Comparative Private Law, International Commercial Contracts, Digitalisation of Law, and Insurance Law.

Open Access This chapter is licensed under the terms of the Creative Commons Attribution 4.0 International License (http://creativecommons.org/licenses/by/4.0/), which permits use, sharing, adaptation, distribution and reproduction in any medium or format, as long as you give appropriate credit to the original author(s) and the source, provide a link to the Creative Commons license and indicate if changes were made.

The images or other third party material in this chapter are included in the chapter's Creative Commons license, unless indicated otherwise in a credit line to the material. If material is not included in the chapter's Creative Commons license and your intended use is not permitted by statutory regulation or exceeds the permitted use, you will need to obtain permission directly from the copyright holder.

Artificial Intelligence and Data Protection: Seeking Sustainable Development

Annamaria Iandoli

Abstract Personal data are now commonly perceived as an external manifestation of the individual's personality. This distinctive identity also influences the GDPR, whose strength lies precisely in having provided transversal principles that regulate personal data processing, regardless of the wider scenario wherein data processing occurs. This is exactly why these principles pose challenges for artificial intelligence, which needs free, secure, robust and quality data, including personal ones, in order to be competitive in the market. Undoubtedly, since the free market requires circulation and sharing of data, even before artificial intelligence emerged, conflicts between principles were evident and demand a broader contextualisation. Understanding how to balance the free flow and broad accessibility of such data, which AI systems need in order to be trained, with the security and confidentiality criteria that must be guaranteed during personal data processing becomes a general challenge shared in the digital market. Assuming that the circulation of data is encouraged by their negotiability, a manifestation of the peculiar patrimonial character that characterises them, it is necessary to point out that the principles of lawfulness, purpose limitation and minimisation, cornerstones of data protection, are essential even in AI-driven operations. Inspired by the purpose of balancing individuals' self-determination with demanding development needs, this paper aims to reflect on the legal "infrastructures" used by current AI systems (such as ChatGPT) to process personal data. In this context, it should also take into account the perspectives offered by current contracts for the provision of digital goods and services (referred to in Directive No. 770/ 2019).

Keyword Artificial intelligence · Personal data · Contracts for the provision of digital goods and services

A. Iandoli (✉)
University of Rome Tor Vergata, Rome, Italy
e-mail: annamaria.iandoli1996@gmail.com

© The Author(s) 2025

C. Amodio and A. Diurni (eds.), *Human Vulnerability in Interaction with AI in European Private Law*, https://doi.org/10.1007/978-3-031-93247-2_20

1 The Advent of Generative Artificial Intelligence

Society as we know it today is the result of the modernisation of social customs, the evolution of employment dynamics and the gradual adoption of cutting-edge tools in daily life. Since the Industrial Revolution—which can be credited with the initial impetus of today's production processes—innovation has grown exponentially, driven by technological progress and, more recently, Artificial Intelligence (AI).[1]

Setting aside the conceptual classification of artificial intelligence within computer science, technology, or emerging taxonomies,[2] it is evident how swiftly certain forms of AI—particularly generative AI—have permeated our daily lives.

Therefore, before proceeding with a purely legal assessment, it is useful to consider certain systemic factors. It should be noted that there are different types of artificial intelligence,[3] distinct operating mechanisms, and separate methodologies underlying the training of an AI algorithm. These systems can be approached from various research perspectives. While the developers of AI systems have not become enmeshed in the narrative of so-called generative AI, legal experts have expressed a certain wariness. The autonomy of such systems, their human-like capacity to provide answers, and their self-learning ability (as discussed below) have been the main causes for concern.

These capabilities of generative AI systems are precisely what make them so appealing to web users. It is no accident that, since the rise of a well-known chatbot powered by generative AI ("ChatGPT"), scientific discourse has increasingly focused on such systems. In fact, within two months of its launch, ChatGPT registered over 100 million users, bringing generative AI to the forefront of media and political attention. It is clear, therefore, that generative AI systems are spreading rapidly and pervasively. Although the advent of AI dates back to 1956,[4] it operated discreetly for many years, at least in civil society. By contrast, the advent of generative AI has brought about a substantial surge in users, considerable media resonance, and mixed public sentiments, ranging from apprehension to curiosity.

The extraordinary nature of generative AI lies in its ability to perform so-called "divergent thinking", creating associations between disparate concepts, reworking

---

[1] For a broader and general reconstruction, please refer to Groppi (2020, pp. 666–674), Kissinger et al. (2023), Llano-Alonso (2021, pp. 327–348), Morcellini (2024, pp. 175–183).

[2] From a legal perspective G. Alpa (2021, pp. 115).

[3] It should be noted that, at the scientific level, three types of artificial intelligence are commonly distinguished: Artificial Narrow Intelligence, Artificial General Intelligence, and Artificial Superintelligence. Artificial Narrow Intelligence, also referred to as weak or restricted intelligence, can perform specific tasks by learning from a dataset tailored to that purpose and operating within predefined parameters. Examples of such technology include Google Assistant, Siri, and Alexa. The next level is Artificial General Intelligence, i.e. technology capable of understanding and learning to perform tasks like humans. The final category is Artificial Super Intelligence, technology expected to surpass the human cognitive abilities (although there are currently no predictions regarding its potential development, which may lie decades or even centuries in the future).

[4] The first official text on Artificial Intelligence was published in 1956: the proceedings of the Dartmouth Conference (Hanover, New Hampshire). See McCarthy et al. (1956).

information by focusing on the most relevant, and reaching plausible and compelling solutions. This is because generative AI employs machine-learning algorithms for so-called autonomous learning, enabling it to generate content that imitates human thought.[5]

This type of AI, which relies on machine-learning algorithms, feeds on massive amounts of data. The autonomy of artificial intelligence systems (upstream) and their performance (downstream) are directly proportional to the volume and quality of the datasets on which these models are trained or train themselves autonomously. The best-known model based on large datasets is undoubtedly the Large Language Model (LLM),[6] used by generative artificial intelligence systems to interpret human language. Notable examples include OpenAI's flagship product, ChatGPT, and the corresponding chatbot developed by Google, Gemini.[7] These products are based on so-called foundation models.[8] Foundation models process vast amounts of data, which the systems acquire and repurpose to generate new content that is syntactically and logically coherent—though not necessarily accurate from a conceptual or scientific standpoint. In doing so, these models rely on what are known as transformers[9]: a type of neural network architecture[10] that enables the system to learn the "long-range dependency relationships between the words of a sequence",[11] just like a human mind processes language. This fact is conclusive: the idea that generative artificial intelligence system can reproduce humanlike reasoning mechanisms, albeit at an indisputably faster speed, undermines the possibility of substantiating, explaining, and justifying the nature of its inferential processes. As a result, even the developers of such systems are often unable to explain why the AI generated a specific outcome rather than another. In fact, machine-learning systems[12] operate through inferential processes of such infrastructural complexity that they are not only difficult to identify[13] ("black box effect"[14]), but altogether indiscernible. The issue

---

[5] In this regard, we must consider the terms of the debate concerning the 'innovative' or 'creative' nature to be attributed to the outputs produced by artificial intelligence systems. Campione et al. (2024, pp. 131–156), Kissinger et al. (2023).

[6] Barreto et al. (2023).

[7] It should be noted that while ChatGPT is Open AI's generative artificial intelligence chatbot, Google's analogous chatbot is Gemini. However, whereas ChatGPT has suffered from limitations and defects due to information not being updated properly, with results therefore being obsolete, Gemini can benefit from Google's intensive data assets.

[8] For a detailed study on this topic, see Schneider et al. (2024, pp. 221–231).

[9] Regarding the Transformers, please consider Kolides et al. (2023).

[10] See Kumar et al. (2024).

[11] The scientific definition results from the research conducted by the Artificial Intelligence Observatory of the Polytechnic University of Milan, whose studies are available at: https://www.osservatori.net/it/ricerche/osservatori-attivi/artificial-intelligence.

[12] For an in-depth study on this topic, see Mahesh (2020, pp. 381–386).

[13] In this regard, see Brkan (2019, p. 91), Mitrou (2018), Pellecchia (2019, p. 1209), Sartor and Lagioia (2020).

[14] On this topic, Casonato (2021, pp. 359–365), Pasceri (2023, pp. 21–41), Peruzzi (2021).

is further exacerbated by the degree of algorithmic opacity, especially in the case of unsupervised machine learning.[15]

The lack of immediate understanding of the aforementioned processes raises significant concerns among legal scholars. This is due to two main reasons. Firstly, there is widespread hesitation and scepticism towards AI systems, which possess a considerable degree of autonomy closely linked to the vast amounts of data with which the algorithms are trained.[16] Upon closer examination, jurists are particularly concerned about selection criteria and methodologies used in collecting the training data, which shape and constrain the output generated by AI. Secondly, there is a need to establish clear authorship for the results produced by such systems.

It is therefore evident that generative AI exhibits a sort of "skillfulness" that surpasses the earlier, more narrowly defined types of artificial intelligence—demonstrating the capacity to create and generate *quid novis* with the same intellectual refinement that, until recently, belonged exclusively to the human mind.[17]We have moved beyond the original designs of utilising AI for static tasks, such as facial recognition. The dynamic nature of this new type of artificial intelligence has captivated society. The qualities of generative artificial intelligence may be compared to those of a conductor that moves faster than 'ociety's ability to absorb the energy it transmits: generative AI operates in a manner and at a speed that no human mind can replicate.

Looking back, the societal impact and vibrancy associated with the advent of artificial intelligence are comparable to those brought about by the invention of electricity. Like electricity, AI's greatest strength lies in its usability. The "user-friendly"[18] interface of AI systems does not require any particular technical expertise, therefore facilitating its introduction into social customs. Artificial intelligence is clearly set to influence all aspects of life, not just daily activities. Indeed, some advocates argue that AI can serve as a tool for managing and, most importantly, preventing crucial issues and problems.[19]

Hence, the distinctive features and widespread applications of generative AI have shifted the debate: the central question is no longer merely how such systems should be used, but how they should be governed.

[15] For more on unsupervised machine learning, see Gentleman and Carey (2008).

[16] As clarified in these sources: https://arstechnica.com/science/2023/07/a-jargon-free-explanation-of-how-ai-large-language-models-work/; https://www.heinz.cmu.edu/media/2023/July/generative-ai-is-a-math-problem-left-unchecked-it-could-be-a-real-problem; https://www.nngroup.com/articles/how-ai-works/.

[17] The study conducted to demonstrate how generative AI can now compete with human creativity, stimulating divergent thinking, challenging insider prejudices, and helping to convey and refine ideas, is remarkable. In this regard, see Eapen et al. (2023).

[18] The reference is taken from Zinno (2023).

[19] In an interview about Microsoft's incredible transformation into an AI-driven company, Kurt Del Bene said: "In the past, the best we could do was to react as quickly as possible. Instead, now, with artificial intelligence we can prevent problems, from bad contracts to computer intrusions".

2 What Role Does Data Play?

The following legal considerations will focus on the complex relationship between the training, development, and operation of artificial intelligence systems and the protection of personal data—one of the many concerns raised by the use of AI systems.[20] Although the issue can be examined from multiple perspectives,[21] this analysis will prioritize the European Union context, not the least given the need to refer to shared legal categories, taxonomies, and systems.

The need to investigate the balance between AI advancement and personal data protection arises in large part from the detailed explanatory memorandum accompanying the European Directive on Artificial Intelligence, the so-called AI Act.[22] The European Parliament recognizes the importance of guaranteeing robust, transparent, well-documented, and traceable operating mechanisms, particularly in the case of high-risk AI systems where human supervision is essential.[23] The Act also underscores the necessity of using high-quality data to train such algorithms. This contribution seeks to move beyond a purely data-centric perspective to focus on the deeper connection between the availability of data—no longer a mere informational resource—and the widespread adoption of AI systems. According to legal doctrine,[24] the increasing internet accessibility is among the key factors driving the ever-growing popularity of artificial intelligence systems. Since the 1990s, the advent of the internet and digital technologies has transformed public and private activities, making information far more accessible. As a result, the concept of data has undergone a significant transformation. In particular, personal data—once considered an expression of individual personality[25]—is now recognized as an autonomous asset, subject to economic exploitation and central to a new dimension: the digital data market.[26]

Upon closer examination, this novel and economically significant understanding of data cannot be separated from the rise of new technologies and, in particular, artificial intelligence. AI systems depend on data, including personal information. Indeed, as suggested by authorative literature, it is precisely due to the increasing

[20] Concerning some observations on the current relevance of the issue, see Van Den Hoven Van Genderen (2017, p. 338), Fred et al. (2018, p. 289); Pizzetti (2018).

[21] Refer to Finocchiaro (2024).

[22] The regulation was approved on 21 May 2024. The digital version is available at the following link https://eur-lex.europa.eu/resource.html?uri=cellar:e0649735-a372-11eb-9585-01aa75ed71a1.0001.02/DOC_1&format=PDF.

[23] See the Explanatory Memorandum of the AI Act, p.7.

[24] Finocchiaro (2019a).

[25] The traditional approach, which determined the current protection framework, viewed personal data as an expression of the individual's identity, and as such argued that they should be covered by the prerogatives of fundamental rights. In this regard, see Alpa (2017, pp. 723–727), Modugno (1995), Resta (2005, pp. 209), Rodotà (1997, p. 583).

[26] See Raganella (2024, pp. 1–33), Ricciuto (2018, pp. 689–726).

availability of data[27] that artificial intelligence, despite having potentially been usable for some time, has only recently started to be exploited more substantially.[28]

Among other factors, the increasing availability of data has, to date been accompanied by a substantial degree of gratuity. Very often, users of digital services become unwitting contributors to the supply of such data.[29] Data represents the true lifeblood of such systems: the more quality data the developer has, the greater the competitiveness of the AI system in the market. This dynamic explains the growing financial interest in data and justifies its designation as the "new oil" or as the central asset of a data-driven digital economy.[30]

However, reducing data—and above all personal data—to a purely economic resource, and thus emphasizing its commercial and negotiable value while overlooking its inherent significance, requires that an additional profile be considered: the protection of the individual.[31] In order to reflect on this issue, it is helpful to identify three decisive moments in the training of algorithms. Initial training takes place during the programming phase and is entrusted to the expertise of developers. Using large datasets[32] provided by so-called data owners, developers conduct the initial coding and basic training of AI systems. Subsequently, before being launched on the market, these systems undergo rigorous testing: the resulting data is subject to oversight and evaluation by IT professionals responsible for system refinement. Once finalized and made available to the general public, a further phase may occur. If programmed accordingly, AI systems can continue learning autonomously, drawing on datasets available online and/or data provided by users during their use of the service (a process referred to as self-training).

[27] As claimed by Mantelero (2019). This report was provided to the Consultative Committee of the Convention for the Protection of individuals with regard to automatic processing of personal data.

[28] "The current expansion of AI is fuelled by the availability of large data sets combined with increases in computing power and connectivity", as stated by the Commission in its Communication entitled "A Coordinated Plan on Artificial Intelligence" to the European Parliament, the Council, the European Economic and Social Committee and the Committee of the Regions on 7 December 2018 (n.795).

[29] The allusion is clearly to the reality of social networks (Facebook, Instagram and Google) where it is estimated that there are billions of users who, more or less consciously, provide data worldwide every day.

[30] As stated in the Journal "The Economist" in May (6th) 2017, the world's most valuable resource is no longer oil, but data. In this regard, Bergè et al. (2018), see Tremolada (2002), Zuboff (2019, pp. 77–78; pp. 92–93).

[31] In this regard, please consider Franzoni (2021, pp. 4–20).

[32] Precisely because big data is an essential prerequisite for algorithm training, it plays a fundamental role. It is worth noting that data collection often constitutes a core activity for many business. In this regard, reference should be made to the cognitive survey on big data carried out in 2020 by the Italian Independent Authorities (the Data Protection Authority, the Communications Regulatory Authority, and the Competition and Market Authority), which is available, in Italian, at the following link https://www.agcm.it/dotcmsdoc/allegati-news/IC_Big%20data_imp.pdf. In addition, Mantelero (2018, pp. 289–305).

This paper examines the issues surrounding data protection, particularly in the context of self-training—that is, the relationship that develops between users and AI-driven digital platforms. There are three key reasons for focusing on this phase: firstly, the unique characteristics of the user profile involved; secondly, the current issues surrounding the use of generative AI systems; and thirdly, the need to investigate and clarify sensitive aspects regarding web user privacy and data protection. The matter has also been addressed by the Italian Data Protection Authority,[33] especially in relation to events concerning ChatGPT.[34]

The delicate question of the *an* and *quomodo*—whether and how—OpenAI's increasingly well-known flagship product should be used has been the subject of a heated global debate. Originally offered as a free online tool, ChatGPT[35] has attracted a wide range of users: students who rely on it for their homework, curious individuals using itthe same blithe confidence once reserved for the Oracle of Delphi, even professionals[36] employing it for questionable purposes, as has been reported in the news.[37] Taken together, key factors justify a more in-depth legal analysis of the relationships between users and the artificial intelligence systems that supply digital services. These factors include the widespread reliance on chatbots, their increasing use across all demographics, the mix of trust and scepticism users place in them, and the growing media attention they attract. On closer inspection, it is evident that anyone using the internet interacts with services that may or may not rely on AI systems; as such, everyone inevitably becomes –often unknowingly—a provider of their data.

Consequently, this paper will focus on reflections directly related to this dynamic. The first two training phases, as well as the legal frameworks governing the acquisition of large datasets[38] used by developers to train artificial intelligence systems, will not be explored in detail here.

Although this issue will not be subject to analysis, there remains a shared need to ensure effective transparency regarding the data sources employed by the AI algorithm developers, even at this stage.

---

[33] The Italian Authority for Personal Data Protection—also known as the Privacy Authority—is an independent Italian administrative authority established by Law No. 675 of 31 December 1996. Its purpose is to ensure that personal data is processed with respect for the rights, fundamental freedoms, and dignity of natural persons. On this subject, Merusi and Passaro (2002).

[34] Acronym for "Generative Pretrained Transformer".

[35] See D'Onofrio (2023, pp. 26–36), Radice (2024).

[36] The publishing industry has also been impacted by ChatGPT, so much so that it has begun to actively engage in the phenomenon, notably through the publication of practical guides for professionals—such as lawyers and accountants—on how to use ChatGPT in their work.

[37] Consider, for example, the well-known case of the American lawyer who relied on ChatGPT to conduct legal research for a case filing. As reported by the US press, not all of the legal precedents turned out to be real: ChatGPT had 'created' case law that did not exist. This incident is only the most notorious of the many cases in which OpenAI's new tool has been used unknowingly. For a more comprehensive account, see coverage in leading newspapers.

[38] See Mayer Shonberger and Cukier (2013), Zeno-Zencovich (2018).

3 Critical Aspects in the Initial Training of Algorithms: Researching and Identifying the Critical Vulnus

As established, the analysis of data protection issues will focus on the dynamics that characterise the so-called self-training phase of generative AI algorithms, particularly with respect to their impact on the safeguarding of personal data. In this regard, examining a concrete case is useful, as a practical example can help clarify the reflections that follow. Since early 2023, the well-known ChatGPT platform has collected and processed users' personal data to train its underlying algorithm using a machine-learning system.[39] This data collection and processing occurred without an appropriate legal basis. While the legal implications of such processing will be addressed later, it is important to emphasise that artificial intelligence systems require a continuous flow of data, including personal data. This data must be secure, reliable (i.e. robust[40]), and of high quality.[41] As stated, generative AI systems operate by aggregating and using a considerable amount of data in addition to that originally provided by developers—specifically, data acquired during the system's ongoing operation. The sophisticated analytical abilities and inferential processes underlying AI systems[42] inherently expose personal data to the risk of unlawful processing. This scenario calls for an investigation of how technological development—or the natural operation of artificial intelligence systems—can be reconciled with the fundamental provisions governing personal data protection.

In the case of ChatGPT, the platform functioned by accessing users' personal data for the purpose of training its algorithm, without a suitable legal basis to legitimise such acquisition. The United States-based company merely stated in its so-called "General Terms of Use" that it would collect and process users' personal data, without requiring an explicit expression of consent, thereby violating the provisions of the GDPR. Consequently, users were effectively deprived of the opportunity to refuse this processing, both initially and retroactively, and could not, therefore, exercise their right to withdraw consent, as guaranteed under Article 7 of the GDPR. Moreover, the chatbot presented the collection and processing of users' personal data as a true *condicio sine qua non* for accessing the service—that is to say, as an indispensable and non-negotiable prerequisite for use.

---

[39] On the events involving ChatGPT and the Italian Privacy Authority, see Pacini (2023, pp. 649–651), Riva (2024, pp. 153–176).

[40] As stated in the official version of the Annex of the Commission communication n. 795/2018, "The Coordinated Plan on Artificial Intelligence".

[41] As stated in the Annex of the Commission communication—The Coordinated Plan on Artificial Intelligence—addressed to the European Parliament, the Council, the European Economic and Social Committee and the Committee of the Regions of 7 December 2018 (n.795), "Making secure, robust and quality data to a wide range of users across borders is one of the cornerstones of European policy" (section E—Data: a cornerstone for AI—Creating a Common European Data Space, available at the following link https://eur-lex.europa.eu/legal-content/EN/TXT/HTML/?uri=CELEX:52018DC0795). In this regard, please consider what was observed by Finocchiaro (2019a).

[42] Concerning the relationship between artificial intelligence and data protection, see Lorè and Musacchio (2024), Pin and Scaffardi (2024).

Such data processing was therefore characterised by illegitimate, unrestricted, and unconditional access to users' personal data, resulting in multiple and evident violations of the GDPR,[43] to the point of consisting of an inevitably unlawful and *contra ius* processing. *In primis*, the generative AI employed by ChatGPT invalidated the principle of informed consent. The impossibility of establishing *a priori* the outcomes of the operations requiring the use of personal data significantly weakened the informational frameworks which, if not deficient, were at best vague and generic. *In secundis*, the inability to predetermine the purposes of the processing carried out by the AI system at the time of data collection resulted in an evident breach of the principle of purpose limitation (Article 5(1)(b) GDPR). On the contrary, the collection of such data should occur for specific, explicit, and legitimate purposes, and its processing should comply with the principle of data minimization (Article 5(1)(c) GDPR),[44] meaning the data should be used soly for the expressed purposes.[45]

The principle violated—just like all the provisions of the GDPR, in fact—proceed from the assumption that personal data constitutes an expression of an individual's identity. The provisions governing data processing, grounded in the logic of consent, are therefore intended to safeguard the right to self-determination.[46] This ensures that the circulation of data results exclusively from conscious and voluntary choices. Despite the unparalleled usefulness of artificial intelligence, any system that undermines the foundations of self-determination cannot be ontologically conceived or even accepted. The rationale behind the GDPR provisions is unequivocal. It emphasises both the inalienability of the principles at stake and the challenge reconciling the unrestricted data access required for autonomous machine learning with compliance[47] with European data protection standards.

Although based on the specific case of ChatGPT, the above discussion illustrates more generally how, in the absence of sufficient oversight and regulatory safeguards, personal data may be processed unlawfully with relative ease. Such processing stems

[43] For the sake of completeness, it is worth noting that the chatbot's conduct—specifically, the collection and storing of users' personal data to train the algorithm underlying the platform's operation, in absence of a suitable legal basis—did not go unchallenged. This conduct led to the suspension of the service by the Italian Data Protection Authority (Garante per la Protezione dei Dati Personali), with reactivation contingent upon the provision of an adequate notice informing users about the use of their data.

[44] This principle requires that the data processing must be limited to the "minimum necessary" for the provision the service; in other words, data must be processed strictly within the scope required to achieve the stated purposes.

[45] For the sake of completeness, it should be mentioned that the principle of purpose limitation in data processing is rooted in Article 8(2) of the Nice Charter (Charter of Fundamental Rights of the European Union), which states: "Such data must be processed fairly for specified purposes and on the basis of the consent of the person concerned or some other legitimate basis laid down by law […]".

[46] While it is well known and widely accepted that the ratio behind the GDPR is to ensure the individual's right to self-determination, it was soon observed that this logic is poorly suited to large-scale data processing—particularly in cases where artificial intelligence systems process such data. On this point, please see Sica (2018, p. 162).

[47] See, El Hamdani et al. (2021, pp. 40–49).

from the unrestricted access to a continuous stream of data that the AI system collects, processes, and learns from—in other words, from the modus operandi of generative artificial intelligence systems used in the provision of digital services. Stepping back from the ChatGPT case to outline general considerations, it is clear that that the continuous availability of data—including personal data—required by these systems poses a structural threat to the principles of purpose limitation and data minimisation that are essential for lawful processing.[48]

It is imperative to provide appropriate notice, as required by the GDPR.[49] This is part of the informational foundation on which the data subject bases their consent.[50] Nonetheless, any platform that employs generative artificial intelligence or machine-learning for self-learning is naturally inclined to compromise the legitimate data processing purposes previously agreed upon by users. This is because these systems are naturally reactive to external environmental stimuli, which can cause them to adapt or expand their processing in ways that diverge from the original purposes. The self-training process is thus intrinsically inclined to alter the processing of personal data in ways that no longer align with the purposes initially accepted by the user. This occurs not only when there is a lack of specific indications of the purpose of training the algorithm, but also when such a purpose has been stated. As will be further discussed, the risk of deviation from legitimate processing can also arise under conditions of apparent compliance.

Accordingly, the ChatGPT case demonstrates a critical, non-isolated issue that is deeply ingrained in the working mechanisms of today's generative AI systems. In particular, highlights the difficulty, if not impossibility, of accurately and effectively predetermining the purposes of data processing at the time consent is given. In other words, even when acting within the bounds of lawfulness or relying on validly obtained consent, generative artificial intelligence systems are inherently exposed to a natural and uncontrolled violation of both the principle of purpose limitation and the minimisation of data processing. This is due to their reliance on inferential processes that operate on data collected during use and its various combinations—potentially even including data the data subject has neither provided nor disclosed.[51]

We have outlined the difficult challenge of identifying a regulatory model that can guarantee the protection of personal data belonging to the users of online services without obstructing technological development. At this point, it is important to make a further preliminary clarification. Although the terminology[52] employed thus far may

[48] For further information on this issue, see Tani (2018, pp. 35–65).

[49] In addition to the modalities of the data process, the information notice should also indicate the tools of protection of the person concerned by the process, such as, by way of example, the possibility of requesting the deletion of one's own personal data (Article 17 GDPR), of obtaining a restriction of the data process (Article 18 GDPR) or, finally, of opposing the data process itself.

[50] Most recently, on the role performed by consent, Gatt et al. (2016, p. 67).

[51] Cf. Gallo (2022a).

[52] The issue stems from the use of the expression "artificial intelligence", which recalls a deeper meaning, even though the metaphorical use of the word "intelligence" is well known. On the importance of language in this regard, see Galgano (2010).

have suggested the attribution of legal subjectivity to artificial intelligence systems—such as plying their capacity to independently own or conduct data processing—there is, in fact, no consensus on recognizing such legal status; the debate is still ongoing. Although assigning legal subjectivity to artificial intelligence may raise legitimate concerns, this potential misunderstanding has been, to some extent, tolerated in the discussion. This is due to the need to shed light on the specific interactions between the *modus operandi* of AI systems and the personal data of individuals. In a global context, however, it has been clearly established that artificial intelligence systems do not enjoy legal subjectivity and that they cannot be imputed with legal will; rather, they are conceived as tools at the service of the human mind.[53] The human agent who uses an artificial intelligence system bears the responsibility for its output. Nonetheless, the rapid proliferation of such systems and the diverse range of sectors they are used in has led some commentators to suggest that alternative interpretations or legal reconstructions may not be entirely implausible.[54]

4 Reflections on Prospective Legislation

Continuing to draw on the ChatGPT case to propose systematic considerations of a broader scope, it is worth recalling that, in the face of an obvious violation of GDPR[55] provisions by OpenAI (the data controller operating the chatbot), the Italian Data Protection Authority ordered the provisional restriction of processing activities involving data improperly collected by the US-based company. The reactivation[56] of the service was made conditional upon strict compliance with seven specific requirements.[57]

One of the essential requirements was suitable information,[58] meaning that the company needed to inform all concerned individuals and explicitly request their

[53] For a more comprehensive study on the configurability of a legal subjectivity to artificial intelligence, see Picaro (2020, pp. 1485–1522), Rizzuti (2020, pp. 285–288).

[54] For a more comprehensive study on the configurability of legal subjectivity to artificial intelligence, see Picaro (2020, pp. 1485–1522), Rizzuti (2020, pp. 285–288).

[55] With regard to the territorial scope of these provisions, it should be noted that the regulation applies to all companies, businesses and professionals whose activities involve the collection of personal data and processing of individuals located in the European Union. On this point, see Article 3 of Regulation (EU) 2016/679.

[56] On April 5th 2023, a videoconference took place between the Italian Privacy Authority and the OpenAI company. The latter confirmed its intention of collaborating with the former with the aim of finding a solution to the critical issues raised by the Italian Privacy Authority regarding ChatGPT. The extract of the minutes is available, online, on the website of the Privacy Authority, at the following link < < https://www.gpdp.it/web/guest/home/docweb/-/docweb-display/docweb/9872832 > >.

[57] Order of 11 April 2023, available at the following link https://www.gpdp.it/web/guest/home/docweb/-/docweb-display/docweb/9874702#english.

[58] In particular, ChatGPT was required to publish a transparent and easily accessible notice on its website that would appear, for users connected from Italy, before the conclusion of the registration

consent regarding how their personal data would be processed. With regard to the specific purpose of using personal data to train the algorithm powering the platform, the Authority presented two alternative approaches to OpenAI. The logical assumption for the Authority was that the processing of personal data for such purposes could be lawful, provided that it was based on freely given and informed consent from the data subjects.

The Authority's provisions highlight that the need to protect personal data—an essential component of any kind of legitimate processing—cannot be hindered or altered by the purpose of training algorithms used provide digital services. As previously discussed, the GDPR provisions—based on the assumption that personal data constitutes an expression of individual identity—are intended to ensure that the circulation of data is always the result and consequence of the self-determination of individuals. Therefore, the distinction between lawful and unlawful algorithmic training based on users' personal data lies in the explicit communication of this purpose within the privacy notice. Only when users are fully informed can they validly consent to the use of their data for training purposes.

In this regard, the Authority instructed the US company OpenAI to modify:

> the legal basis of the processing of users' personal data for the purpose of algorithmic training, by removing any reference to contract and relying on consent or legitimate interest as legal bases by having regard to the assessment the Company is required to make from an accountability perspective.[59]

The Authority's decision serves as a reference point for future reflection. It underscores the need to distinguish between the various purposes of processing personal data. It also recommends that a separate and independent legal basis be adopted when the data is processed specifically for the purpose of algorithmic training.

The Authority expressed the view that the legitimate legal basis for such processing could not be the contract under which OpenAI has been providing the digital service since 2023. Instead, a different legal basis should be considered: either *ad hoc* consent (specifically given for that purpose) or so-called legitimate interest,[60] which the company eventually opted for.

---

phase; as for users who were already registered, the notice was required to appear, on the relevant webpage, with the first access following reactivation of the service.

[59] Concerning the accountability principle, please see, Amore (2014, p. 414), Arcella (2018, pp. 393), Butterworth (2018, pp. 257–268), Bistolfi (2016, p. 323), Camardi (2022, p. 25), Faccioli and Cassaro (2018, p. 561), Finocchiaro (2019b, p. 2778), Siano (2022, p. 236).

[60] For this purpose, one should assume that the legitimate interest is not a suitable legal basis for data processing unless it is concrete, effective, and not subordinate to the individual's interests, rights, or fundamental liberties, and ensures no lower level of data protection. In this regard, please consider The Art. 29 Working Group on Data Protection, Opinion No. 6/2014, on the concept of legitimate interest of the data controller under Article 7 of Directive 95/46/EC, 9 April 2014, available at www.ec.europa.eu. Legitimate interest is anchored in value-based canons and not dogmatic notions. Therefore, reference must be made to canonical values that enable the substance of the legitimate interest to be assessed only through an appropriate balancing test, whereby there are no disproportionate effects on the data subject, particularly given the nature of the data acquired and processed. Even "apparently harmless" data, when collected on a large scale and aggregated, could give rise to deductions on personal data. As a result, it is therefore not always easy to determine

It should be noted that the provisions of the GDPR show an implicit logic of "accountability", intended to guide the choice of the legal basis for data processing activities, including those related to algorithm training. This principle requires the data controller to carry out a preliminary assessment and careful examination of all possible processing methods, to guarantee effective data protection.[61]

The specific aspects of this case raise a number of questions. It is crucial to ascertain whether the objective of algorithm training—now explicitly identified as a purpose of the processing (pursuant to the Authority's provision—meets the GDPR's requirements of specificity, transparency, and legitimacy.[62]

As mentioned in the preceding paragraph, there are grounds to believe that, while the formal criteria for the lawful processing of personal data may be fulfilled, the substantive legitimacy is not necessarily guaranteed. The Authority repeatedly sanctioned the vague and general nature of the information provided to users, which cannot be justified merely by ascribing it to training. In other words, a new cause for concern arises if the principles of the GDPR, including purpose limitation and data minimisation, are to govern the legitimate processing of personal data: that these principles may not be effectively upheld when the information notice merely states the purpose of training the AI algorithm used for providing the service. Indeed, it is understood that the uncontrolled inferential mechanisms that characterise machine-learning algorithms are likely to process data that was not subject to prior informed consent. When it comes to effective compliance with the principles of purpose limitation and data minimisation, such concerns cannot be dismissed. Such inferential processes operate based on user data collected during interaction, and through its combination with other data, may lead to the processing of information that the data subject did not intend to disclose or make available.

Given the critical issues inherent in the training of today's AI systems, it may be more appropriate to consider the Authority's decision as a transitional measure; aimed at ensuring that data protection obligations do not obstruct technological innovation. Furthermore, the rapid development of artificial intelligence systems, often outpacing legislative efforts, necessitates the rethinking of traditional data governance models and the adoption of new solutions.[63] The issue is complex and cannot be sufficiently addressed in just a few sentences, but readers should be encouraged to consider hitherto unexplored analytical tools and fresh approaches to envisage further, dynamic forms of protection for users' data. These are inevitably involved in this continuous "open-air" training of generative artificial intelligence systems.

---

whether a given processing operation can be permitted on the basis of the legitimate interest. On this aspect, please consider Dell'Utri (2019).

[61] See Greco (2017, p. 254).

[62] The Italian Court of Appeal also ruled along these lines in its judgment No. 14381 of 25.5.2021. In this respect, consider Lafratta (2022, p. 153). Moreover, see Genovese (2023).

[63] Conversely, see Finocchiaro (2019a, p. 1670) where it is emphasised that very often the Legislator has succumbed "to the media appeal and the flattery of consensus that can be obtained with an easy answer". Rather, it is considered reasonable that a valid solution can be reached by applying a "systematic vision and an interpretative method", as "peculiarities of the jurist's work, which should be proudly revalued".

5 Negotiation Perspectives

The specific case involving ChatGPT served as a valuable starting point for reflections on the complex interactions between artificial intelligence and personal data protection, particularly regarding the critical issues encountered so far. It is precisely for this reason that the same legal dispute will be used to examine the intricate relationship between the protection of personal data, the use of generative AI systems and the digital platforms using them.

It is widely acknowledged that merely accessing a digital platform does not equate to the automatic acceptance of data processing by the underlying AI systems. Further considerations are essential. Following the reactivation of the service and the designation of algorithm training as one of the purposes for processing users' personal data, ChatGPT resumed operation. In so doing, OpenAI effectively gained access to user data, including personal data, under the basis of legitimate interest.

This situation brings to the forefront the relevance of contractual frameworks governing the provision of digital services in exchange for personal data, rather than monetary payment. These types of contracts are addressed at the EU level by Directive (EU) 2019/770, transposed into national law in 2021 and now expressly regulated under Article 135-octies, paragraph 4, of the Italian Consumer Code, which closely adheres to the Directive's provisions.[64]

Undoubtedly, this contractual model has codified an economic dynamic that was well established in practice. In such arrangements, the processing of personal data is not an secondary element of the contractual arrangements, but rather the core function of new negotiation models aimed at enabling the aggregation and processing of vast data volumes required by advanced technological systems, particularly those based on AI. The formal recognition of this model—where access to a digital good or service is conditioned upon the user's consent to data collection and processing (the so-called "free digital services")—has conferred legal visibility to a phenomenon that had been occurring in practice without appropriate regulatory safeguards, now being gradually instituted.

It is therefore important to examine the real-world scenarios in which such contracts may be formed, in order to assess whether such models are applicable in cases like ChatGPT, where a digital service provider or web platform gains de facto control over—and uses for its own purposes—the personal data of users in exchange for the services offered.

Thus far, the guiding principle of the analysis has been to consider whether the so-called self-training of AI algorithms can indeed be compliant with GDPR principles, focusing on the direct, bilateral relationship between generative AI and personal data. Nevertheless, as previously mentioned, this perspective has been adopted to highlight the peculiarities and criticalities of personal data processing, but it is not the only feasible line of inquiry. To ensure effective user protection online, we must consider an additional layer of analysis. Specifically, it becomes necessary

[64] Cf. Basunti (2020, pp. 860–895), Camardi (2019), Gallo (2022b, pp. 1054–1092), Pagliantini (2022, p. 1500), Ricciuto (2022), Solinas (2022), Versaci (2020b).

to consider whether the legal relationship that emerges between the user—who, by giving consent, effectively provides personal data—and the professional—who uses generative AI systems to deliver services—can be characterised in consumer law terms. Professionals who leverage digital infrastructures and platforms governed by AI systems (at least in the cases under consideration) receive compensation for their services not in the form of money, but through the ongoing and unrestricted availability of users' personal data. The ongoing, unrestricted availability of personal data has an intrinsic value that far exceeds what might be imagined, due to the possibility of aggregations and analyses.

This economic model, based on the proprietary nature of data, solidifies a system of exhange n which a genuine contract can be identified. The contractual obligations consist, respectively, of the provision of the digital service and the user's authorisation for data processing.

By distinguishing these two lines of inquiry, generative artificial intelligence emerges as a tool used for delivering a service and/or producing an output, yet it lacks legal subjectivity. Thus, it does not prevent the establishment of consumer contracts between the user and the digital professional who, as the data controller of the consumers' personal data, employs AI systems to provide the service.

5.1 Contractual Assumptions

The need to determine whether contracts can be established in these cases stems from the premise that when an individual user is both a data subject and a contracting party, they may benefit from the protections afforded by both the GDPR and consumer law. Therefore, the rationale behind this analysis is to evaluate further tools available to the consumer affected by data processing when using digital services provided through generative AI systems.

To assess whether such contracts can be formed, it is necessary to adopt a civil law perspective, focusing on the consensual basis of contractual agreements—even where consent may be obtained only in a formal sense, such as in "tying" arrangements involving unsuspecting users.

Therefore, it is necessary to examine whether two declarations of intent are required in order for such agreements to take place: (i) consent for data processing (permissive in nature), and (ii) consent to enter into a contract (instrumental to its fulfilment). If this were not the case, it would be imperative to consider "unity", assuming that negotiation dynamics would occur during the processing itself or, on the other hand, that the contractual relationship would include the authorization to process data.

On this point, legal opinion is divided. Some scholars[65] observe that, although from a practical standpoint the two moments may coincide temporally and be

[65] In this sense, see Caggiano (2018, p. 67), Morace Pinelli (2022, pp. 1322–1333).

expressed concurrently,[66] contractual consent cannot and should not in any way be confused with the informed (and therefore "reinforced") consent required for processing personal data.[67] According to this view, it is essential to identify precisely when each form of consent is expressed. However, this approach[68] is not shared by those who advocate for a unified model of consent. They maintain that the very act of concluding the contract implies authorisation for data processing—especially when the contract itself centres on the "exchange" of personal data.

Far from being resolved, the ongoing debate is further complicated by a significant interpretive element. Article 135-octies, paragraph 4 of the Italian Consumer Code—implementing Directive (EU) 2019/770—seeks to recognise the economic value of what was previously presented as gratuitous conduct, leaving data subjects without adequate protection. The general consensus is that such contracts were codified to safeguard consumers, who were often unaware of the underlying transactional dynamics. This suggests that contracts might be considered valid even in the absence of express contractual consent, relying instead on the authorisation given for data processing.

Therefore, this reflection is based on the "core" of consent, whether "informed" or negotiated, leading to a legal transaction or a contract. The complexity does not end with whether such contracts are conceptually viable, but extends to the *quomodo*—that is, the manner in which they are formed. In other words, alongside the question of prerequisites for contract formation, there is the challenge of reconciling consumer law with data protection regulation. This leads us into relatively unexplored legal terrain, where numerous questions emerge. A starting point must be the primacy of the GDPR, which prevails not only in matters of personal data processing, but also in the context of contractual termination—as established in Article 135-novies-decies, paragraph 3 of the Consumer Code.[69]

---

[66] In this regard, for the purpose of completeness, mention should be made of Irti (2021).

[67] In this regard, see Court of Cassation, 2.7.2018, no. 17278 where it has been clarified that, with regard to the data process, "strengthened" consent is required by virtue of the need to "remedy the inherent situation of weakness of the data subject, both from the perspective of the evident information asymmetry and from the perspective of protection against possible aggressive or suggestive commercial techniques. This regulation, therefore, arises from the need to address the risks to the individual caused by the mass process of personal data, as made possible by technological evolution". Moreover, in this sense, consider also the European Data Protection Board (EDPB) Guidelines No. 2/2019 (Guidelines On the Processing of Personal Data Pursuant to Article 6, § 1(b) of the GDPR, Brussels, 8 October 2019, available at www.edpb.europa.eu), where, in paragraph 20, it is emphasised that "it is important to distinguish between the acceptance of terms of service for the purposes of concluding a contract and the provision of consent within the meaning of Article 6(1)(a), as these concepts have different requirements and legal consequences".

[68] Cf. Ricciuto (2023).

[69] Article 135-novies-decies (3) of the Consumer Code regulates the termination of contract for the supply of digital goods and services. In the first and second paragraphs, it deals with the repetition of services, and then, in the third paragraph, it provides that "With regard to the consumer's personal data, the trader shall comply with the obligations arising from Regulation (EU) 2016/679 as well as Legislative Decree No. 101 of 2018".

The non-derogable nature of the GDPR provisions, as established by the legislator, prompts other questions, where we can find reflections on data protection or on the advantage of placing data processing within a consumer dimension.

is the primary issue to understand how the withdrawal of consent during the execution of the contract might affect the validity of the contractual relationship itself. Under the GDPR, withdrawal of consent prohibits future processing without affecting the lawfulness of past operations. However, this approach conflicts with contractual situations where data processing constitutes the user's obligation. In such cases, termination of the contract would nullify the causal basis for data processing. Such processing results from the supply of data to which the consumer is obliged. In other words, this processing depends, upstream, on the fulfilment of a contractual obligation which, by virtue of its termination, would no longer have any causal justification. Nevertheless, the pathological development of the negotiation, in terms of resolution, would entail further questions—relating, for example,[70] to the potential occurrence and attitude of the contractual service repetition.[71]

Answering this question clearly implies understanding how placing the processing of users' personal data within a negotiation dimension may represent a choice favoring online users. In any case, the questions raised are only an example of the more complex reflection required by this subject. However, it is the writer's aim to offer readers only the key outlines to give them an idea of the disparate consequences of placing personal data processing within a negotiated dimension—not alongside the main performance but as the actual object of the contractual obligation.

6 Notes on Legitimate Interest

Different considerations and reflections arise if, on the other hand, data processing is based on so-called legitimate interest.[72] This is the case of ChatGPT which, following the reactivation of the chatbot, indicated that the legal basis for the processing of users' personal data—not essential to the use of the service[73]—was the legitimate interest of the controller (OpenAI) in training the algorithm underlying the digital

[70] In a completely different perspective, the same consumer dimension in which the matter is set would also prompt useful reflections in the physiological context of the contract. The possible supply of untruthful or inaccurate data would raise the question of the not insignificant nature of the breach of contract. Conversely, dissatisfaction on the part of the professional due to the amount of data collected during the use of the service could invalidate the continuation of the relationship.

[71] Versaci (2023, p. 2244).

[72] With regard to the configurability of the contracts in question in cases where the processing of personal data takes place on the basis of the so-called legitimate interest, it should be, first of all, mentioned that Directive No. 770/2019 excludes from its scope those cases where personal data, provided by the consumer, are processed exclusively for the platform purpose of providing digital content or service.

[73] It should be noted that Directive (EU) 2019/770 excludes from its scope those cases where personal data, provided by the consumer, are processed exclusively for the platform purpose of providing digital content or service.

platform. In an attempt to safeguard themselves against interested parties revoking their consent, which could potentially jeopardise future processing of their personal data or alter the economic consistency of consumer compensation, professionals and digital platforms often opt to use so-called legitimate interest (as referred to in Article 6(1)(f) of the GDPR) in lieu of the principle of consent.

It is therefore necessary to understand what is meant by "legitimate interest".[74] For this purpose, it should be assumed that it is impossible to arrive at a dogmatic notion. We must refer to canonical values that allow the substance of the legitimate interest to be assessed only through an appropriate balancing test,[75] whereby there are no disproportionate effects on the data subject, particularly given the nature of the data acquired and processed. As a result, legitimate interest is not a suitable legal basis for data processing unless it is concrete, effective, and not subordinate to the individual's interests, rights, or fundamental liberties, and unless it does not provide a lower level of data protection.[76]

It is therefore rather complex to establish, *a priori*, whether and when the so-called legitimate interest of the data controller can constitute a suitable legal basis for the processing of personal data. Moreover, it is even more challenging to determine whether negotiating profiles can actually be identified. Nevertheless, Recital 47 of the GDPR offers guidance on this specific issue. The text rules out the controller's legitimate interest constituting a suitable legal basis when personal data is processed in circumstances in which the subjects could not reasonably have expected further processing.

The overall scenario does not appear crystal-clear and the prerequisites for the admissibility of such processing are tied to multifactorial elements. This makes it even more complex to understand whether the contracts concerned are conceivable in those cases where the professional supplies the digital service and, at the same time, processes the users' personal data on the basis of legitimate interest.[77]

For a preliminary analysis,[78] the terminology used by the legislator—which is anything but accurate and refers to 'cases' rather than 'contracts' in describing the dynamics at hand—suggests that the configurability of the contractual relationship referred to in Article 135-octies, paragraph 4, of the Consumer Code should not be limited solely to cases in which prior consent had been given as a legal prerequisite for a potential contractual agreement.

However, this view is not universally shared. A different school of thought[79] expresses serious concerns about the possibility of recognizing the elements of a contract for the supply of digital content or services in cases where the processing of

---

[74] Cf. Proietti (2022, p. 890).

[75] Cf. Dell'Utri (2019).

[76] The Art. 29 Working Group on Data Protection, Opinion No. 6/2014, on the concept of legitimate interest of the data controller under Article 7 of Directive 95/46/EC, 9 April 2014, (available at www.ec.europa.eu), already stated in these terms.

[77] See Trigo Kramcsák (2023).

[78] Cf. Angiolini (2023, p. 55 ff.).

[79] In this sense Versaci (2020a, pp. 282). Id (2019).

users' data takes place on the basis of the trader's legitimate interest. The absence of a clear intention by the parties poses an obvious obstacle to recognizing a contractual dispute. In these cases, the legal basis for processing is not rooted in any unified consent—expressed, in principle, for the purpose of using the main service—but rather in the data controller's own interest, as stated in the privacy notice. It follows that this may not be considered sufficient—at least in this interpretation—to constitute a negotiating dynamic which, by contrast, would require independent consent. Therefore, the true vulnerability of the issue lies in the question of whether implicit or explicit consent—a prerequisite for the conclusion of the contracts referred to in Article 135-octies, paragraph 4, of the Consumer Code—can be waived.

The issue is undoubtedly complex, especially given the widespread use of legitimate interest as a legal basis for data processing, not only by OpenAI but by virtually all digital platforms and web professionals. Nevertheless, for the purposes of this discussion, excluding the configurability of such contracts for the supply of digital services when data processing is based on legitimate interest would mean disregarding a potential contractual framework—one that could open the way to the additional protections discussed above.

7 Final Considerations

This examination has aimed to highlight the critical issues arising from the interaction between generative artificial intelligence systems and personal data, due to the distinctive characteristics of machine-learning algorithms. The problems identified should not be considered as mere criticism. Rather, they should be understood as a stimulus to develop innovative solutions that reconcile technological development with the fundamental protection of personal data.

This investigation aimed to explore how and to what extent the self-training phase characterizing generative AI systems could align with the obligation to uphold the principles of the GDPR. It started from an anthropocentric perspective, emphasizing the importance of safeguarding individuals and their personal data as expressions of their identity. Additional motivation stemmed from the will to identify further contractual protections for users, particularly concerning the possible contractual implications that may arise when data processing is based on user consent.

All the considerations presented here are part of a broader effort to find an ideal solution: one that safeguards personal data while also allowing for the continued advancement of generative AI systems relying on the continuous autonomous training based on the progressive accumulation of user data.

References

Alpa G (2017) L'identità digitale e la tutela della persona. Spunti di riflessione. Contratto e impresa 33(3):723–727

Alpa G (2021) L'intelligenza artificiale. Il contesto giuridico 115 ff

Angiolini C S (2023) Una riflessione critica sulla complementarietá fra norme sulla protezione dei dati personali e diritto dei consumatori nella disciplina dei profili patrimoniali del rapporto fra interessato e titolare del trattamento. In: Angiolini C S, Santarpia D (eds) La fattispecie "liquida": quattro casi sintomatici, Edizioni Scientifiche Italiane, Naples, p. 7 ff

Amore G (2014) Fairness, Transparency e Accountability nella protezione dei dati personali. Studium Iuris 4:414 ff

Arcella G (2018) GDPR: il Registro delle attività di trattamento e le misure di accountability. Notariato 393 ff

Barreto F, Moharkar L, Shirodkar M, Sarode V, Gonsalves S, Johns A (2023) Generative artificial intelligence: opportunities and challenges of large language models. In: Balas VE, Semwal VB, Khandare A (eds) Intelligent computing and networking. IC-ICN 2023. Lecture notes in networks and systems, vol 699. Springer, Singapore https://doi.org/10.1007/978-981-99-3177-4_41

Basunti C (2020) La (perduta) centralità del consenso nello specchio delle condizioni di liceità del trattamento dei dati personali. Contratto e Impresa 2:860–895

Bergè JS, Grumbach S, Zencovich VZ (2018) The "datasphere", data flows beyond control and the challenge for law and governance. Eur J Comp Law Gov V(2):144–178. Conversely

Bistolfi C (2016) Le obbligazioni di compliance in materia di protezione dei dati. Principi da osservare. In: bolognini L, Pelino E, Bistolfi C (eds) Il regolamento privacy europeo. Commentario alla nuova disciplina sulla protezione dei dati personali, Giuffrè Editore, Milano, p 323 ff

Brkan M (2019) Do algorithms rule the world? algorithmic decision-making and data protection in the framework of the GDPR and beyond. Int J Law Inf Technol 27(2):91–121 ff

Butterworth M (2018) The ICO and artificial intelligence: the role of fairness in the GDPR framework. Comput Law Secur Rev. 34(2), April 2018:257–268. https://doi.org/10.1016/j.clsr.2018.01.004

Caggiano IA (2018) Il consenso al trattamento dei dati personali nel nuovo Regolamento europeo. Analisi giuridica e studi comportamentali. Osservatorio di diritto civile e commerciale, p 67 ff

Camardi C (2019) Prime osservazioni sulla Direttiva (UE) 2019/770 sui contratti per la fornitura di contenuti e servizi digitali. Operazioni di consumo e circolazione di dati personali. Giustizia Civile 3

Camardi C (2022) Liability and accountability in the "digital relationships". In Senigaglia R., Irti C., Bernes A. (eds) Privacy and data protection in software services, Springer, Singapore, p 25 ff

Campione F, Catena E, Schirripa A, Caligiore D (2024) Creatività umana e intelligenza artificiale generativa: similarità, differenze e prospettive. Sistemi Intelligenti, Rivista Quadrimestrale di Scienze Cognitive e di Intelligenza Artificiale 1:131–156 https://doi.org/10.1422/109012

Casonato C (2021) Giustizia e intelligenza artificiale: considerazioni introduttive. BioLaw Journal-Rivista di BioDiritto (2):359–365

D'Onofrio C (2023) Legal Design e Intelligenza Artificiale: nuove prospettive per il futuro del diritto. i-lex, Rivista di Scienze Giuridiche, Scienze Cognitive ed Intelligenza Artificiale 16(1):26–36 https://doi.org/10.6092/issn.1825-1927/17198

Dell'Utri M (2019) Principi generali e condizioni di liceità del trattamento dei dati personali. In Cuffaro V., D'Orazio R. e Ricciuto V. (eds) I dati personali nel diritto europeo, Giappichelli Editore, Turin, 149–276

Eapen TT, Finkenstad DJ, Folk J, Venkataswamy L (2023) How Generative AI Can Augment Human Creativity. Harvard Business Review, 57–64

El Hamdani R, Mustapha M, Restrepo Amariles D, Troussel A, Meeùs S, Krasnashchok K (2021) A combined rule-based and machine learning approach for automated GDPR compliance checking.

In: Proceedings of the eighteenth international conference on artificial intelligence and law (ICAIL '21), New York, NY, USA, 40–49, https://doi.org/10.1145/3462757.3466081
Faccioli E, Cassaro M (2018) Il GDPR e la normativa di armonizzazione nazionale alla luce dei principi: accountability e privacy by design. Diritto Industriale, pp 561 ff
Finocchiaro G (2019a) Intelligenza Artificiale e protezione dei dati personali. Giurisprudenza italiana, 7, pp 1670-1677
Finocchiaro G (2019b). Il principio di accountability in GDPR tra novità e discontinuità. Giurisprudenza Italiana, 12, p. 2778–2783
Finocchiaro G (2024) Intelligenza Artificiale. Quali regole?, Il Mulino, Bologna
Franzoni M (2021) Lesione dei diritti della persona, tutela della privacy e intelligenza artificiale, Jus civile, 1, pp 4–20. https://hdl.handle.net/11585/815686
Fred HC, Kuner C, Lynskey O, Millard C, Loideain NN (2018) Expanding the artificial intelligence-data protection debate. Int Data Priv Law, 8(4): 289–292
Galgano F (2010) Le insidie del linguaggio giuridico. Il Mulino, Bologna
Gallo P (2022a) Dati personali (Diritto allo sfruttamento economico). Leggi d'Italia Legale
Gallo P (2022b) Il consenso al trattamento dei dati personali come prestazione. Rivista di Diritto Civile 6:1054–1092
Gatt L, Montanari R, Caggiano I A (2017) Consenso al trattamento dei dati personali e analisi giuridico-comportamentale. Spunti di riflessione sull'effettività della tutela dei dati personali. Politica del diritto 48(2):337–353
Genovese A (2023) Trattamento dei dati personali e consenso dell'interessato. In: morace Pinelli A (ed) La circolazione dei dati personali: persona, contratto e mercato, Pacini Giuridica, Pisa
Gentleman R, Carey VJ (2008) Unsupervised machine learning. In: bioconductor case studies. Use R!. Springer, New York, NY https://doi.org/10.1007/978-0-387-77240-0_10
Groppi T (2020) Alle frontiere dello Stato costituzionale: innovazione tecnologica e intelligenza artificiale. Consulta Online 3:666–674
Irti C (2021) Consenso "negoziato" e circolazione dei dati personali, Giappichelli Editore, Turin
Kissinger HA, Schmidt E, Huttenlocher D (2023) L'era dell'Intelligenza Artificiale. Il futuro della società umana, Mondadori Editore, Rome
Kolides A, Nawaz A, Rathor A, Beeman D, Hashmi M, Fatima S, Berdik D, Al-Ayyoub M, Jararweh Y, (2023) Artificial intelligence foundation and pre-trained models: fundamentals, applications, opportunities, and social impacts. Simul Modell Pract Theory 126. https://doi.org/10.1016/j.simpat.2023.102754
Kumar V, Srivastava P, Dwivedi A, Budhiraja I, Ghosh D, Goyal V, Arora R (2024) Large-Language-Models (LLM)-based AI chatbots: architecture, in-depth analysis and their performance evaluation. In: santosh K, et al. Recent trends in image processing and pattern recognition. RTIP2R 2023. Communications in computer and information science, vol 2027. Springer, Cham https://doi.org/10.1007/978-3-031-53085-2_20
Greco L (2017) I ruoli: titolare e responsabile. In: Finocchiaro G (ed). Il nuovo Regolamento europeo sulla privacy e sulla protezione dei dati personali, Zanichelli, Turin, pp 251–286
Lafratta D (2022) Algoritmo reputazionale tra requisiti normativi e dignità della persona (note to Cass. Civ., Sez. I, 14381/2021). Il lavoro nella giurisprudenza, 2:153–159
Llano-Alonso FH (2021) L'etica dell'intelligenza artificiale nel quadro giuridico dell'Unione europea. Ragion pratica, 2:327–348 https://doi.org/10.1415/102317
Lorè F, Musacchio P (2024) Intelligenza Artificiale, tra profili di responsabilità e protezione dei dati personali: aspetti de jure condito e prospettive de jure condendo. Amministrativ@mente, 4(1):1–50
Mahesh B (2020) Machine-learning algorithms-a review. Int J Sci Res (IJSR) (9):381–386
Mantelero A (2018) La gestione del rischio nel GDPR: limiti e sfide nel contesto dei Big Data e delle applicazioni di Artificial Intelligence. In: mantelero A, Poletti D (eds) Regolare la tecnologia: il Reg. UE 2016/679 e la protezione dei dati personali. Un dialogo fra Italia e Spagna, Pisa University Press, pp 289–305

Mantelero A (2019) Report on artificial intelligence. Artificial intelligence and data protection: challenges and possible remedies, https://rm.coe.int/report-on-artificial-intelligence-artificial-intelligence-and-data-pro/16808e6012
Mayer Shonberger V, Cukier K (2013) Big data, Giuffrè editore, Milan
McCarthy J, Minsky ML, Rochester N, Shannon EC (1956) A proposal for the Dartmouth summer research project on artificial intelligence, https://it.scribd.com/document/458760481/1904-Article-Text-1900-1-10-20080129-pdf
Merusi F, Passaro M (2002) Independent authorities. Enc Dir (VI)
Mitrou L (2018) Data protection, artificial intelligence and cognitive services: is the General Data Protection Regulation (GDPR) 'artificial intelligence-proof'? Available at SSRN:https://doi.org/10.2139/ssrn.3386914
Modugno F (1995) I "nuovi diritti" nella giurisprudenza costituzionale. Giappichelli, Turin
Morace Pinelli A (2022) La circolazione dei dati personali tra tutela della persona, contratto e mercato. La nuova giurisprudenza civile commentata (6):1322–1333
Morcellini M (2024) La magnitudo sociale dell'Intelligenza artificiale. ParadoXa 8(2):175–183
Pacini F (2023) La controversia tra Garante della privacy e OpenAI, nel contesto della regolazione dell'intelligenza artificiale. Quaderni costituzionali (3):649–651
Pagliantini S (2022) L'attuazione minimalista della dir. 2019/770/ue: riflessioni sugli artt. 135 octies -135 vicies ter Cod. Cons. La nuova disciplina dei contratti b-to-c per la fornitura di contenuti e servizi digitali. Le nuove leggi civili commentate 6:1500 ff
Pasceri G (2023) Le scienze argomentative tra stereotipi e veri pregiudizi: la black box. Ciberspazio e diritto, 24(73):21–41
Pellecchia E (2019) Profilazione e decisioni automatizzate al tempo della black box society: qualità dei dati e leggibilità dell'algoritmo nella cornice della responsible research and innovation. Nuove leggi civili commentate, 5, pp 1209 ff
Peruzzi M (2021) Il diritto antidiscriminatorio al test di intelligenza artificiale. Labour & Law Issues 7(1) https://doi.org/10.6092/issn.2421-2695/13117
Picaro R (2020) Relazioni consumeristiche, intelligenza artificiale e nuove identità. Rassegna di diritto civile 4:1485–1522
Pin A, Scaffardi L (2024) Tra protezione dei dati e intelligenza artificiale, in Europa e oltre. DPCE Online 64(2) https://doi.org/10.57660/dpceonline.2024.2212
Pizzetti F (2018) Intelligenza artificiale, protezione dei dati personali e regolazione. Giappichelli Editore, Turin
Proietti G (2022) Algoritmi e interesse del titolare del trattamento nella circolazione dei dati personali. Contratto e Impresa 3:890 ff
Radice GA (2024) Nihil est enim simul et inventum et perfectum. Intelligenza artificiale nel diritto tra prospettive attuali e sperimentazioni romanistiche. Rivista di diritto romano, 24:373–386
Raganella E (2024) Le nuove tecnologie e la Data Economy. Bilanciamento tra privacy ed esigenze di mercato. In: la monetizzazione dei dati personali, pp 1–33
Resta G (2005) Autonomia privata e diritti della personalità, Jovene Editore, Naples
Ricciuto V (2018) La patrimonializzazione dei dati personali. Contratto e mercato nella ricostruzione del fenomeno. Dir. Inf, 4–5, pp 689–726
Ricciuto V (2022) L'equivoco della privacy. Persona VS dato personale, Edizioni Scientifiche Italiane, Napoli
Ricciuto V (2023) Il consenso negoziale nella circolazione dei dati personali In: Morace Pinelli A. La circolazione dei dati personali: persona, contratto e mercato, Pacini Giuridica, Pisa.
Riva GM (2024) Diritto e intelligenza artificiale generativa: l'istruttoria del Garante per la protezione dei dati italiano su OpenAI e ChatGPT. In: Ciberspazio e diritto, 1:153–176
Rizzuti M (2020) Il peculium del robot. Spunti sul problema della soggettivizzazione dell'intelligenza artificiale. In: dorigo S (ed) Il ragionamento giuridico nell'era dell'intelligenza artificiale. Pacini giuridica, Pisa, pp 285–288
Rodotà S (1997) Persona, riservatezza, identità. Prime note sistematiche sulla protezione dei dati personali. Rivista critica di diritto privato (4):583

Sartor G, Lagioia F (2020) The impact of the General Data Protection Regulation (GDPR) on artificial intelligence, Brussels: European Parliament https://doi.org/10.2861/293

Schneider J, Meske C, Kuss P (2024) Foundation models. Bus Inf Syst Eng 66:221–231 https://doi.org/10.1007/s12599-024-00851-0

Siano M (2022) Voce "Art. 24" in GDPR e normativa Privacy. In: Belisario E, Riccio GM e Scorza G (eds) GDPR e Normativa Privacy Commentario, Wolters Kluwer, Milan, p 236 ff

Sica S (2018) La responsabilità' civile per il trattamento illecito dei dati personali. In: Poletti D, Mantelero A (eds) Regolare la tecnologia: il Reg. UE 2016/679 e la protezione dei dati personali. Un dialogo tra Italia e Spagna, Pisa University Press, Pisa, p 162 ff

Solinas C (2022) Autonomia privata e regolazione pubblica nel trattamento dei dati personali, Cacucci Editore, Bari

Tani T (2018) L'incidenza dei Big data e del machine learning sui principi alla base del Regolamento Europeo per la tutela dei dati personali (2016/679/UE) e proposte per una nuova normativa in tema di privacy. In: bonavita S (ed) Società delle tecnologie esponenziali e General Data Protection Regulation: profili critici nella protezione dei dati, Ledizioni, Milan, p 35–65 https://doi.org/10.4000/books.ledizioni.3946

Tremolada L (2002) I dati non sono il petrolio e neppure oggetti fisici (ma i governi non la pensano così). Guida al Diritto (5)

Trigo Kramcsák P (2023 April) Can legitimate interest be an appropriate lawful basis for processing artificial intelligence training datasets? Comput L Secur Rev 48 https://doi.org/10.1016/j.clsr.2022.105765

Van Den Hoven Van Genderen R (2017) Privacy and data protection in the age of pervasive technologies in AI and robotics. Eur Data Prot L Rev 3:338 e ff

Versaci G (2019) Dati del consumatore tra persona e contratto. Una prospettiva italo-europea (PhD Thesis University of Foggia)

Versaci G (2020a) Dati personali e contratto tra Reg. (Ue) 2016/679 e dir. 2019/770/Ue. In: pagliantini S. (ed) Ricerche di diritto europeo tra sostanza e processo, Edizioni Scientifiche Italiane, Naples, p 282 ff

Versaci G (2020b) La contrattualizzazione dei dati personali dei consumatori, Edizioni Scientifiche Italiane, Naples

Versaci G (2023) GDPR e consumerizzazione dei dati personali - Contratti di fornitura di contenuti e servizi digitali: scioglimento, restituzioni e obbligazioni post-contrattuali. Giurisprudenza Italiana 175(10):2244–2253

Zeno-Zencovich V (2018) Dati, grandi dati, dati granulari e la nuova epistemologia del giurista. MediaLaws 2:32–38.

Zinno R (2023) Strategie, modelli di leadership e organizzazioni, La rivoluzione dell'intelligenza artificiale. Harvard Business Review Italia

Zuboff S (2019) The age of surveillance capitalism. The fight for the future at the new frontier of power, public affairs book, PublicAffairs, New York

Annamaria Iandoli, Ph.D. candidate in Theory of Contracts, Services and Markets at the University of Rome Tor Vergata (private law curriculum). Author of several publications in civil, administrative, and internet law. Former research grant holder at the Ministry of Economic Development and intern at the Supreme Cassation Court. Licensed lawyer and civil mediator.

Open Access This chapter is licensed under the terms of the Creative Commons Attribution 4.0 International License (http://creativecommons.org/licenses/by/4.0/), which permits use, sharing, adaptation, distribution and reproduction in any medium or format, as long as you give appropriate credit to the original author(s) and the source, provide a link to the Creative Commons license and indicate if changes were made.

The images or other third party material in this chapter are included in the chapter's Creative Commons license, unless indicated otherwise in a credit line to the material. If material is not included in the chapter's Creative Commons license and your intended use is not permitted by statutory regulation or exceeds the permitted use, you will need to obtain permission directly from the copyright holder.

Emerging Risks and the European Liability Framework in AI-Based Market Manipulation

Andrea Mecchina, Lorenzo Basile, and Luca Bortolussi

Abstract Artificial Intelligence (AI) is rapidly reshaping global economics and this transformation is particularly impacting banks and investments firms, as they started to develop and adopt AI-assisted trading algorithms. Because of the very nature and cutting-edge complexity of these new technologies, they are also bound to give rise to new and unprecedented risks, particularly affecting individuals and human competitors. Industries adopt AI-based solutions in their working pipelines in order to deliver efficiency gains and produce more profit. Due to their exponentially rapid development, these new solutions are acting as increasingly independent agents. Despite having been developed by humans, such forms of AI might misbehave in ways which are unacceptable to a human competitor, even without being explicitly programmed to do so. Adequate legal instruments are required to prevent potential threats resulting from concurrent human–machine interactions. Nonetheless, AI-trading solutions are difficult to fit into the current European Union legal framework concerning market manipulation, especially when trying to assess liability under traditional legal concepts such as *intent*, *causation* and *foreseeability*, which were originally developed when dealing with human-only agents. Rules struggling to keep up the pace with technological innovation is a documented and well-known phenomenon that has been observed at least since the rise of industrial capitalism. The main current European Union regulatory instruments to contrast AI-based harms in this context are the European Market Abuse Regulation (EU) No 596/2014 and the Market Abuse Directive 2014/57/EU, which date back to 2014. Technological progress comes accompanied by a continuous blurring of the boundary between humans and machines. Addressing the liabilities of the new machine agents that coexist and interact with humans calls for an up-to-date legal framework. This paper aims to highlight emerging human vulnerabilities and critically investigate the current European Union legal framework.

A. Mecchina (✉) · L. Bortolussi
University of Trieste, Trieste, Italy
e-mail: andrea.mecchina@phd.units.it

L. Basile
AREA Science Park, Trieste, Italy

© The Author(s) 2025

C. Amodio and A. Diurni (eds.), *Human Vulnerability in Interaction with AI in European Private Law*, https://doi.org/10.1007/978-3-031-93247-2_21

Keywords Artificial intelligence · Vulnerability · Market manipulation · Liability · Algorithmic trading

1 Introduction

The challenge of regulatory systems struggling to keep pace with technological innovation is a well-documented and long-standing phenomenon, present since the rise of industrial capitalism, the era that gave rise to modern finance.[1]

The development of AI and its application in the field of algorithmic trading allowed to draw some causal inference conclusions about how these new technologies impact in a positive manner the quality of the market itself.[2] On the other hand, AI-driven approaches to algorithmic trading introduce a new set of unprecedented risks, with the most sophisticated involving complex forms of market manipulation.

European Union laws offer regulators and enforcers a clear definition of market manipulation, which will be discussed further. Additionally, there are tools available to assess liabilities. However, legal frameworks often become outdated quickly, primarily due to the rapid advancements in AI and algorithmic technologies.[3]

New and unprecedented vulnerabilities emerge for competing agents operating alongside these new technologies. Building upon the work of Azzutti,[4] this paper critically investigates them, in the perspective of the current European Union rules. The rest of this contribution is organised as follows: Sect. 2 presents various forms of AI-based market manipulation and explores the emerging risks; Sect. 3 presents the current European Union regulatory framework, with a focus on liability issues; finally, Sect. 4 provides a summary and conclusion.

2 AI-Based Market Manipulation

A first legal definition of market manipulation is provided in the Market Abuse Regulation (EU) No 596/2014 (European Parliament, Council of the European Union (2014b)). Quoting Article 12: "[…] market manipulation shall comprise the following activities:

(a) entering into a transaction, placing an order to trade or any other behaviour which:

[1] Fenwick et al. (2016).

[2] Boehmer et al. (2021).

[3] Dutta (2018).

[4] Azzutti (2022).

(i) gives, or is likely to give, false or misleading signals as to the supply of, demand for, or price of, a financial instrument, a related spot commodity contract or an auctioned product based on emission allowances; or
(ii) secures, or is likely to secure, the price of one or several financial instruments, a related spot commodity contract or an auctioned product based on emission allowances at an abnormal or artificial level; [...]

(b) entering into a transaction, placing an order to trade or any other activity or behaviour which affects or is likely to affect the price of one or several financial instruments, a related spot commodity contract or an auctioned product based on emission allowances, which employs a fictitious device or any other form of deception or contrivance;

(c) disseminating information through the media, including the internet, or by any other means, which gives, or is likely to give, false or misleading signals as to the supply of, demand for, or price of, a financial instrument, a related spot commodity contract or an auctioned product based on emission allowances or secures, or is likely to secure, the price of one or several financial instruments, a related spot commodity contract or an auctioned product based on emission allowances at an abnormal or artificial level, including the dissemination of rumours, where the person who made the dissemination knew, or ought to have known, that the information was false or misleading;

(d) transmitting false or misleading information or providing false or misleading inputs in relation to a benchmark where the person who made the transmission or provided the input knew or ought to have known that it was false or misleading, or any other behaviour which manipulates the calculation of a benchmark. [...]"

The reported definition is quite general, as it identifies as forbidden market practices also those behaviours which are not explicitly programmed to manipulate the market, but which are also "likely to" do it. Such broad definition is meant to encompass also manipulations arising from the developing field of AI, which are to be discussed next.

2.1 Emerging Manipulation Scenarios

The adoption of AI systems translates into delegating cognitive decisions to a new set of tools which we define "intelligent", with the ability to self-learn and adapt autonomously to the environment through their experience, while pursuing a predefined goal.[5] This very new autonomy brings unprecedented risks and comes accompanied by new ethical and legal questions, which regulators need to address. We also refer to Annunziata for an additional discussion on how recent developments in the

[5] Dellermann et al. (2019).

AI field affect the enforcement of rules in the European Union to prevent market abuse.[6]

Algorithmic trading is used to refer to any technology-based instrument which assists and automates, completely or even partially, any task within the trading cycle.[7] With the advent of AI, the paradigm of algorithmic trading shifted from an "if/then" logic, thought of as a tool to assist human experts, to much more advanced systems able to self-learn without the need of human supervision. This step forward has been possible mainly thanks to the development of Machine Learning (ML), building upon the exponentially increasing data availability and the progress in technological computational power.[8]

In the risk framework defined by European Parliament, Council of the European Union (2024), AI-based trading methods are not labelled as "high-risk", despite coming accompanied by the typical risks of data-driven ML applications, most notably: they are built upon very complex and interconnected domain-specific knowledge, they are "autonomous", as their behaviour is not explicitly programmed by the human experts who realised the systems, and they are often considered "black-boxes", in the sense that not even the experts who developed these methods are able to explain in full detail why and how a particular result was obtained.[9]

Such technical aspects are mentioned to shed some light upon the difficulties a classical liability framework could face when trying to prevent and punish AI trading misconduct and potential harm.[10] Neglecting the case of a system whose functioning is compromised by some external party, it is possible to summarise two distinct possible scenarios of market manipulation:

- the misbehaviour of a system might be due to its developers, either through their negligence, in the form some sort of code "bugs", or their intentional actions;
- the AI system may self-learn to perform market manipulations thanks to its "intelligent" component, drawing its conclusions from the data it is trained on, while pursuing its predetermined goal, even without an explicit human design.

It is also worth pointing out that law enforcement authorities would be required to possess some sophisticated manipulation diagnostic instruments, together with advanced and specific knowledge of the both the financial and the AI sectors. Moreover, in the current fast and ubiquitous market systems, manipulations could take the form of flash-crashes and ultra-fast and extreme events,[11] thus complicating their detection tasks even more.

[6] Annunziata (2023).

[7] Kirilenko and Lo (2013).

[8] Koshiyama et al. (2020).

[9] Burrell (2016).

[10] Azzutti (2022).

[11] Johnson et al. (2013).

2.2 A View on Reinforcement Learning

Reinforcement learning is a machine learning paradigm which can be used to improve the efficiency and performance of decision-making strategies. Here, a brief overview of reinforcement learning is given,[12] with a focus on its relationship with a more traditional point of view on trading markets.

Reinforcement learning is based on training an agent how to operate in an environment based on a system of rewards. In the context of trading, an example would be an agent that learns how to optimise a portfolio based on metrics like profit, loss, volatility, and so on. Some crucial features of any reinforcement learning systems are:

- Agent: the trained AI system, which interacts with the environment;
- Environment: anything which gives us back an observable state;
- State: the current position of the agent;
- Action: the optimal decision taken by the agent, based on the current state;
- Reward: a quantity returned by the environment, which may evaluate positively or negatively on the action taken by the agent.

The general idea behind reinforcement learning is trying to train the agent to take actions in order to maximise some function of the rewards.

Through the rewards it receives from the environment, the agent collects information and learns a strategy which is not explicitly programmed, following an "if/else" logic, by its developer.

The above definitions are quite general; in the context of trading, they can take some more precise meanings: the agent is a trader, the environment is the market, the state is related to some statistics about the market itself which are observed, which may be daily log-returns, volumes of assets and so on, an action might be going long or short on certain assets and the reward might be profit, volatility or more complex measures such as the Sharpe ratio.

One major point of reinforcement learning is that the agent will not learn to give a prediction like some expected values of some relevant financial quantities or the sentiment of a document, but rather it will try to maximise a reward function, which might be, for example, related to the expected return of a portfolio and so on.

It is worth pointing out that reinforcement learning is not an isolated method, but it can be easily integrated with other ML techniques such as deep learning, giving even higher freedom to the agent. In particular, it is possible to use neural networks, such as LSTM networks,[13] which are particularly suited to work with time series, thus exploiting in an efficient way the natural structure of financial data.

In general, neural networks can be used to obtain more precise expectations, which will be then fed to the reinforcement learning algorithm with the goal of optimising its performance. This interconnection between reinforcement learning and neural

[12] Foy (2021).

[13] Viera (2019).

networks makes AI-based training algorithms even more complex, due to the typical "black-box" nature of deep neural models.

The above considerations stress the considerable amount of autonomy those systems have. Such new technologies have the potential of transforming the financial industry, as to some extent is already happening, calling for more dedicated rules, able to counter the misbehaviour of AI-based agents.

3 Current European Union Rules

A first legal instrument available for European Member States, under the European Union law, is the aforementioned Market Abuse Regulation (EU) No 596/2014 (European Parliament, Council of the European Union (2014b)). As stated in Article 1, such regulation explicitly prohibits market manipulations, as it reads: "This Regulation establishes a common regulatory framework on insider dealing, the unlawful disclosure of inside information and market manipulation (market abuse) as well as measures to prevent market abuse to ensure the integrity of financial markets in the Union and to enhance investor protection and confidence in those markets."

The definition of market manipulation reported in Sect. 2 suggests that the legislators opted for an "effect-based" specification, due to the adoption of broad expressions such as "entering into a transaction" or "disseminating information". The definition does not take into account any subjective component: the specific intent of the manipulator is not considered to be relevant.

It is worth recalling the distinction, as it will be discussed more extensively in the following subsections, between a natural and a legal person, in the jurisdictional context:

- a natural person is a human person; in the financial context, a natural person might be the employee of an investment firm;
- a legal person is, in the broader meaning, any "thing" that can do the same things a human person can do; in the financial context, a legal person might be an investment firm.

Article 15 of the Market Abuse Regulation (EU) No 596/2014 explicitly states that "A person shall not engage in or attempt to engage in market manipulation."; such definitions puts on equal grounds any manipulative intent, notwithstanding its successful implementation.

The above definition refers both to natural and legal persons, but for the purposes of the discussed regulation, it is not clear whether an AI-based system might be considered a "person" in such sense. As it emerges from the subsection dealing with reinforcement learning, it is clear that AI-systems might share some features of natural or legal persons; nonetheless, they possesses some unique aspects which make them difficult to fit into traditional frameworks, which will be discussed next.

3.1 Administrative Liability Framework

Violations of market through non-manipulative conduct, if not extremely serious and harmful, can be addressed in the framework of administrative liability, which is regulated explicitly by the Market Abuse Regulation (EU) No 596/2014 (European Parliament, Council of the European Union (2014b)).

Article 22 states that "Without prejudice to the competences of the judicial authorities, each Member State shall designate a single administrative competent authority for the purpose of this Regulation. [...] The competent authority shall ensure that the provisions of this Regulation are applied on its territory, regarding all actions carried out on its territory, and actions carried out abroad relating to instruments admitted to trading on a regulated market, for which a request for admission to trading on such market has been made, auctioned on an auction platform [...]." Thus, the regulation states that administrative liability should be enforced by national competent authorities of Member States.

Moreover, Article 16(1) requires market operators to adopt procedures aimed at preventing and detecting market manipulations Article 16(2) requires the same operators to report to the competent authorities every reasonable suspicion of market manipulation they may encompass.

Article 30(2) tries to define a set of administrative sanctions which each Member State should be able to dispose of: "Member States shall, in accordance with national law, ensure that competent authorities have the power to impose at least the following administrative sanctions and to take at least the following administrative measures [...]:

(a) an order requiring the person responsible for the infringement to cease the conduct and to desist from a repetition of that conduct;
(b) the disgorgement of the profits gained or losses avoided due to the infringement insofar as they can be determined;
(c) a public warning which indicates the person responsible for the infringement and the nature of the infringement;
(d) withdrawal or suspension of the authorisation of an investment firm; [...]
(h) maximum administrative pecuniary sanctions of at least three times the amount of the profits gained or losses avoided because of the infringement, where those can be determined; [...]"

Moreover, such article prescribes pecuniary sanctions both with respect to natural and legal persons. In the context of an AI-trading system, the enforcement of point (a) seems particularly challenging, as it would require the developers to alter the same trading system, which may not have been developed with the goal of committing any infringement at all.

Additionally, Article 23(2) also specifies that each national competent authority should enjoy a certain number of investigatory powers: "In order to fulfil their duties under this Regulation, competent authorities shall have, in accordance with national law, at least the following supervisory and investigatory powers:

(a) to access any document and data in any form, and to receive or take a copy thereof;
(b) to require or demand information from any person, including those who are successively involved in the transmission of orders or conduct of the operations concerned, as well as their principals, and if necessary, to summon and question any such person with a view to obtain information; [...]
(d) to carry out on-site inspections and investigations at sites other than at the private residences of natural persons;
(f) to refer matters for criminal investigation;
(g) to require existing recordings of telephone conversations, electronic communications or data traffic records held by investment firms, credit institutions or financial institutions; [...]"

Most critically, Article 13 provides a list of accepted market practices, which may be of use of investment firms: if they could prove that an alleged manipulative behaviour was indeed compliant with the accepted practices, they could prevent being subject to administrative liability. In particular Article 13(2) reads: "A competent authority may establish an accepted market practice, taking into account the following criteria:

(a) whether the market practice provides for a substantial level of transparency to the market; [...]
(c) whether the market practice has a positive impact on market liquidity and efficiency; [...]
(e) whether the market practice does not create risks for the integrity of, directly or indirectly, related markets, whether regulated or not, in the relevant financial instrument within the Union; [...]"

In order to ease the work of law enforcement authorities, the Market Abuse Regulation (EU) No 596/2014 provides in Annex I two sets of indicators which could raise a presumption of manipulation. In particular, indicators related to "false or misleading signals" suggest to investigate the "extent to which orders to trade given or transactions undertaken" relate to some meaningful indicators such as the daily transactions volume in the related financial instrument or the time of day around which the transactions happen. Complementarily, in order to discover manipulations related to "deception or contrivance" instead, it is suggested to deem as suspect those trade orders preceded by the dissemination of any misleading information or investment recommendation by the same persons undergoing the trade or by other persons close or linked to those undergoing the trade. Again, it seems that such indicators were created having in mind the activity of a person, be it natural or legal; it is therefore hard to apply the same indicators to an AI-driven activity.

3.2 Criminal Liability Framework

The Market Abuse Regulation (EU) No 596/2014, at Article 30(1) subparagraph 2 states that Member States are allowed not to apply the administrative sanctions prescribed by the regulation itself, as long as the same infringements are subject to criminal sanctions in the national laws. On the other hand, if a state opted for both administrative and criminal sanctions for the same infringement, it must ensure to respect the jurisdictional principle of "ne bis in idem", stating that a person cannot be subject to a criminal proceeding for which the same person has already been judged.[14]

The legal instrument available to Member States to address criminal liability, and in general to provide a set of common rules for the most dangerous market manipulation cases, is the Market Abuse Directive 2014/57/EU (European Parliament, Council of the European Union (2014a)). In particular, Article 5(1) reads:

1. Member States shall take the necessary measures to ensure that market manipulation […] constitutes a criminal offence at least in serious cases and when committed intentionally.
2. or the purposes of this Directive, market manipulation shall comprise the following activities:
    (a) entering into a transaction, placing an order to trade or any other behaviour which:
        (i) gives false or misleading signals as to the supply of, demand for, or price of, a financial instrument or a related spot commodity contract; or
        (ii) secures the price of one or several financial instruments or a related spot commodity contract at an abnormal or artificial level;

        unless the reasons for so doing of the person who entered into the transactions or issued the orders to trade are legitimate, and those transactions or orders to trade are in conformity with accepted market practices on the trading venue concerned;
    (b) entering into a transaction, placing an order to trade or any other activity or behaviour which affects the price of one or several financial instruments or a related spot commodity contract, which employs a fictitious device or any other form of deception or contrivance;
    (c) disseminating information through the media, including the internet, or by any other means, which gives false or misleading signals as to the supply of, demand for, or price of a financial instrument, or a related spot commodity contract, or secures the price of one or several financial instruments or a related spot commodity contract at an abnormal or artificial level, where the persons who made the dissemination derive for themselves or for another person an advantage or profit from the dissemination of the information in question; or

[14] Bošković and Kostić (2020).

(d) transmitting false or misleading information or providing false or misleading inputs or any other behaviour which manipulates the calculation of a benchmark.

Point 2 provides a definition of market manipulation which mimics that of the Market Abuse Regulation (EU) No 596/2014. The only difference is that in the above one, the expression "is likely to" do not figure. A "preponderance of the evidence" of market manipulation, as required by the Market Abuse Regulation (EU) No 596/2014 to constitute an administrative offence, does not suffice for the Market Abuse Directive 2014/57/EU, which requires the manipulation to be ascertained "beyond a reasonable doubt" in order to be deemed as a criminal infringement.[15]

Anyway, a precise definition of the term "serious" is not provided; Article 6(1) also states that: "1. Member States shall take the necessary measures to ensure that inciting, aiding and abetting the offences referred to in Article 3(2) to (5) and Articles 4 and 5 is punishable as a criminal offence. [...]" Therefore, Member States are required also to act in a preventive manner. Article 7(1) requires the criminal penalties enforced by Member States to be "effective, proportionate and dissuasive" and Article 7(2) requires the offences to be punishable "by a maximum term of imprisonment of at least four years".

Mimicking again the prescription of the Market Abuse Regulation (EU) No 596/2014, Article 8(1) of the Market Abuse Directive 2014/57/EU extends criminal liability also to legal persons for offences committed for the benefit of the legal persons themselves by any person playing a leading role within the legal persons.

The Market Abuse Directive 2014/57/EU, since it does not differ considerably from the dispositions of the Market Abuse Regulation (EU) No 596/2014, suffers from the same problems of applicability already highlighted, when the agents are neither natural nor legal persons, but rather AI-driven agents.

4 Conclusions

The rationale behind the presented European Union legal framework is to establish a common level between Member States, to uniform and provide national competent authorities with some instruments to fight AI-based trading market manipulation. The current liability framework, as presented in the Market Abuse Regulation (EU) No 596/2014 and the Market Abuse Directive 2014/57/EU, does not fit in a straightforward manner to all categories of AI algorithms, mainly because of their very "black-box" nature. On top of this, also detecting increasingly complex and sophisticated forms of AI trading manipulations is a challenging task for market supervising authorities.

Moreover, for investment firms, it suffices to produce an annual self-assessment to show their compliance to the current AI-based trading rules, as can be read in Article 9

[15] Azzutti (2022).

referenced from European Commission, Directorate-General for Financial Stability, Financial Services and Capital Markets Union (2017). This requirement might not be strict enough to ensure that the described rules are successfully enforced.

Moreover, it is worth adding that the outlined rules suffer from the issue of "divided interpretation": prohibitions are free to be enforced in different ways by any national competent authority. As a consequence, these uneven legal frameworks also expose markets to some complex forms of cross-border manipulations, while preventing the successful creation of a single European market.

We can add to the "divided interpretation" problem some other factors which could postpone the adoption of an effective anti-manipulation regime. First of all, some uncertainty in the prohibitions themselves, even if left over on purpose in order to extend the application scope of the legislations, could not be enough to prevent some new forms of manipulation to simply circumvent the current regulatory system.

The purpose of this paper was to present the current legal framework related to market manipulation, with a focus on the problem arising when trying to fit such framework to the current system of liability, both administrative and criminal. The current approach, as outlined, might be flawed in preventing AI-based trading market manipulation. The two most vulnerable aspects seem to be the lack of a truly aligned European Union legal framework, together with that of a new liability paradigm, more up-to-date with the current developments of ML technologies.

References

Annunziata F (2023) Artificial intelligence and market abuse legislation: a European perspective. Edward Elgar Publishing

Azzutti A (2022) Ai trading and the limits of EU law enforcement in deterring market manipulation. Comput Law Secur Rev 45:105690

Boehmer E, Fong K, Wu JJ (2021) Algorithmic trading and market quality: international evidence. J Fin Quantitat Anal 56(8):2659–2688

Bošković MM, Kostić JŽ (2020) The application of the NE BIS in Idem related to financial offences in the jurisprudence of the European courts. NBP J Criminal L 25(2):67–77

Burrell J (2016) How the machine 'thinks': understanding opacity in machine learning algorithms. Big Data & Society

Dellermann D, Ebel P, Söllner M et al (2019) Hybrid intelligence. Bus Inf Syst Eng 61(5):637–643

Dutta S (2018) An overview on the evolution and adoption of deep learning applications used in the industry. Wiley Interdiscip Rev Data Min Knowled Discov 8(4):e1257

Fenwick M, Kaal WA, Vermeulen EP (2016) Regulation tomorrow: what happens when technology is faster than the law. Am U Bus L Rev 6:561

Foy P (2021) Deep reinforcement learning for trading: strategy development & AutoML. https://medium.com/@Lidinwise/trading-through-reinforcement-learning-using-lstm-neural-networks-6ffbb1f5e4a5

Johnson N, Zhao G, Hunsader E et al (2013) Abrupt rise of new machine ecology beyond human response time. Sci Rep 3(1):2627

Kirilenko AA, Lo AW (2013) Moore's law versus Murphy's law: algorithmic trading and its discontents. Journal of Economic Perspectives 27(2):51–72

Koshiyama A, Firoozye N, Treleaven P (2020) Algorithms in future capital markets. https://papers.ssrn.com/sol3/papers.cfm?abstract_id=3527511

Viera A (2019) Trading through reinforcement learning using LSTM neural networks. https://blog.mlq.ai/deep-reinforcement-learning-trading-strategies-automl/

Andrea Mecchina, B.Sc. in Physics from the University of Trieste in 2019, and M.Sc. in Data Science and Scientific Computing from the University of Trieste in 2021, is currently a Ph.D. candidate in Applied Data Science and Artificial Intelligence at the University of Trieste. His research interests include statistical modeling, time series analysis and unsupervised learning.

Lorenzo Basile, B.Sc. in Automation Engineering from the Federico II University of Naples in 2019, M.Sc. and Ph.D. in Data Science from the University of Trieste in 2021 and 2025, respectively, currently a postdoctoral researcher at the Laboratory of Data Engineering of Area Science Park in Trieste. His research interests include AI interpretability, focusing on explaining and controlling complex models, and multimodal machine learning, integrating vision, language, and other data for richer representations.

Luca Bortolussi, Degree in mathematics in Trieste (2003) and Ph.D. in computer science from the University of Udine (2007),Visiting Researcher at the University of Edinburgh (2012), Associate Researcher at CNR-ISTI Pisa (QUANTICOL FP7 Project, 2013–2017), and Professor at Saarland University (2014–2015, Guest 2016, 2018–2021). At the University of Trieste, he was Assistant/Associate Professor (2006–2021) and is now Full Professor, leading the AI Laboratory. His research spans artificial intelligence, bridging symbolic, formal, and applied methods.

Open Access This chapter is licensed under the terms of the Creative Commons Attribution 4.0 International License (http://creativecommons.org/licenses/by/4.0/), which permits use, sharing, adaptation, distribution and reproduction in any medium or format, as long as you give appropriate credit to the original author(s) and the source, provide a link to the Creative Commons license and indicate if changes were made.

The images or other third party material in this chapter are included in the chapter's Creative Commons license, unless indicated otherwise in a credit line to the material. If material is not included in the chapter's Creative Commons license and your intended use is not permitted by statutory regulation or exceeds the permitted use, you will need to obtain permission directly from the copyright holder.

Human Vulnerability in Interaction with AI: Conclusions

Reiner Schulze

Abstract This article discusses some of the main features and key topics of the research presented at the conference in Rome on 16–17 April 2024, on which this volume is based. These include, in particular, the cross-cutting nature of this research, which results from the relevance of the interaction between human vulnerability with artificial intelligence for numerous social areas and fields of law and the interaction of legal doctrine with both informatics and social sciences according to the interplay of technological and social aspects in this topic. On this basis, attention is initially focused on defining the role of artificial intelligence between the autonomy attributed to it with the concept of 'autonomous system' on the one hand and the functional descriptions under the concept of 'agency' on the other (including the associated legal issues such as the problem of legal subjectivity, the application of principles of representation or the adaptation of the doctrines of defects of will to the use of artificial intelligence as a 'tool' in the conclusion of contracts). From this starting point, the tension between the concept of autonomy with regard to artificial intelligence and the autonomy of the individual person and their vulnerability to artificial intelligence is considered. Among other things, emotional vulnerability and—with regard to the example of medicine—the potential impact of artificial intelligence in terms of both vulnerability and healing are also included. Finally, the focus is on the task of developing concrete proposals in further research on how legislation and case law can remedy digital vulnerability.

R. Schulze (✉)
University of Münster, Münster, Germany
e-mail: reiner.schulze@uni-muenster.de

© The Author(s) 2025

C. Amodio and A. Diurni (eds.), *Human Vulnerability in Interaction with AI in European Private Law*, https://doi.org/10.1007/978-3-031-93247-2_22

1 Introduction

The conference in Rome,[1] from which this volume emerged, focused on the relationship between human vulnerability and artificial intelligence. The vulnerable human being has created this artificial construct in order to shift the boundaries of his understanding and action outwards. This has created a point of reference with which his vulnerability interacts, as the title of the conference suggests. Artificial intelligence can help to remedy human vulnerabilities and weaknesses and, to a certain extent, allow people to grow beyond themselves. But it can also create new vulnerabilities and contribute to exploiting and deepening weaknesses, thereby increasing vulnerability in human interaction.

Against the background of the discussions at the underlying conference, the essays in this volume illuminate numerous facets of the interaction between human vulnerability and artificial intelligence. They also focus in particular on the question of how humans can influence this interaction with artificial intelligence by means of the law that they have also created or will create in such a way that the vulnerabilities caused by artificial intelligence are minimised and its positive effects promoted. The following remarks cannot adequately reflect the richness of these considerations and cannot even mention all the aspects that would be worth mentioning with regard to the results of the conference. Therefore, they cannot and should not spare the reading of every single contribution to this volume. Rather, they can only recall a few impressions of the meeting in Rome from a very subjective point of view by explaining the research context and referring to some of the main features and topics of the discussions there, which are reflected in this volume.

2 Research Context

With regard to the research context of this volume and the underlying conference, its role as the second part of a trilogy must be considered in particular. It was preceded by the conference in Ferrara,[2] which is documented in the volume 'The New Shapes of Digital Vulnerability in European Private Law'.[3] The third part—and the completion of the DiVE project,[4] which spans all three meetings—is a conference in Trieste on 'Remedies to Digital Vulnerability in European Private Law'.[5] The research in the first part was primarily focused on defining the contours of the object of investigation and establishing the framework for further work. The view was directed towards three

[1] Human Vulnerability in Interaction with AI, on 16 and 17 May 2024 at Tor Vergata University of Rome. The following article essentially reflects the closing remarks at this conference unchanged, supplemented by footnotes and some adaptations to the present volume.

[2] Digital Vulnerability in European Private Law, 15 and 16 June 2023.

[3] Crea and De Franceschi (2024a).

[4] Crea and De Franceschi (2024b).

[5] Trieste, on 10 and 11 April 2025; conference proceedings in Crea and Infantino (2025).

main areas: firstly, digital vulnerability as a paradigm for consumer law; secondly, the conceptualisation of digital vulnerability, also beyond consumer law; and thirdly, contexts and images of digital vulnerability subjects. As a result of these analyses, the new shapes of digital vulnerability in European private law emerged as presented in the conference proceedings.

In many respects, this first part of the research in the DiVE project laid the foundations for the subsequent investigations, including the new issues that came into focus in the second part with regard to the relationship between human vulnerability and artificial intelligence. Just one example should be emphasised to illustrate this: the focus on the cross-cutting nature of digital vulnerability. In this respect, the Ferrara conference proceedings show that the 'broad scope and diversity of the consequences of digitalisation [...] preclude attributing digital vulnerability' to a single specific risk situation or a single type of potentially harmful actions. Rather, research in this field will have to consider different types and causes of such vulnerability (or of such 'vulnerabilities') and different concepts of 'vulnerability' in the digital world.[6] This results in the assessment: 'The wide spectrum of digital vulnerability, as a phenomenon that encompasses many areas of society in the digital age, is reflected at the level of law as a cross-cutting challenge for almost all areas of law, branches of courts and disciplines of legal doctrine. Just as for national law, it is therefore necessary for European private law to look at the multiple types of digital vulnerability across the breadth of private legal relationships, taking into account the context of the respective branches of private law'.[7]

3 Cross-Cutting Perspective

As thus foreshadowed in the framework of the first part of the project, the contributions in this volume make it evident that human vulnerability in interaction with artificial intelligence is a broad cross-cutting issue. From a factual point of view, in addition to and in conjunction with gender-related aspects of digital vunerability, social circumstances in particular come into consideration, which can favour a specific vulnerability of groups of people through digitalisation. This involves, among many other things, issues of education, income, and social role allocation, which can have a negative impact on the participation in digital communication, the ability to utilise information and the protection of one's own interests in the digital world for the groups of people concerned.

Not least, with regard to the relevant factual circumstances, it must also be taken into account that human vulnerability in interaction with digitalisation as a cross-cutting issue can be based on specific problems in certain phases of life—from 'child vulnerability' (in many respects, for example, from certain products for young children, such as 'smart toys', to digitally produced and distributed forgeries of

[6] Schulze (2024), Casarosa and Micklitz (2024), and Rodríguez de las Heras Ballell (2024).

[7] Schulze (2024).

images and other digital bullying at school[8] to the problems of digital transformation for the elders.[9] Incidentally, even with death, digital vulnerability does not end. The 'eternal memory' of the internet outlives the individuals and allows access to what they wanted to guard for themselves personally during their lives. And the manipulative power of artificial intelligence can change posterity's image of him or her (literally and figuratively, for example, what he or she wrote or painted); in other words, post-mortem—so to speak—fiction takes the place of the real personality, without the person whose personality has been violated being able to defend himself or herself.

This wide spectrum of vulnerability as a phenomenon that encompasses many areas of society in the digital age is reflected at the level of law as a cross-cutting challenge for almost all areas of law. They comprise, for example, the consumer law, the rules on Unfair Commercial Practices,[10] the labour law with regard to the digital vulnerability of employees,[11] but also the online dispute resolution[12] or the Private International Law.[13] For all these and other areas across private law and neighbouring fields of law, research is faced with the task of analysing the new problems that arise in the digital age with regard to human vulnerability and considering appropriate solutions.

Following on from the discussions in Ferrara, this research includes looking at some of the steps taken by the European Union in this regard in its recent legislation a few years after the enactment of the General Data Protection Regulation,[14] alongside other regulatory frameworks at national and European level. This European legislation on digital challenges covers a wide range of matters and is, in a sense, cross-cutting in itself. Some of this legislation concerns very specific issues with regard to digitisation, including the use of artificial intelligence. From this new perspective, however, it also touches on traditional central issues of civil law such as contract law and non-contractual liability and includes tasks of protection against digital vulnerability (for example, by extending the regulation on standard terms to cover the protection of minors with regard to the digital vulnerabiliy by obliging providers of online intermediary services that are primarily aimed at minors or are predominantly used by minors to explain the conditions and restrictions on the use of the service in question in such a way that minors can understand them; Art. 14

[8] Pera and Rigazio (2024a).

[9] See Gardella Tedeschi (2024).

[10] Durovic and Kaprou (2024).

[11] Wildhaber and Ebert (2024).

[12] Paglietti (2025).

[13] Goh Escolar (2024).

[14] Regulation (EU) 2016/679 of the European Parliament and of the Council of 27 April 2016 on the protection of natural persons with regard to the processing of personal data and on the free movement of such data, and repealing Directive 95/46/EC (General Data Protection Regulation) (L 119 p. 1); on its significance with regard to digital vulnerability, see for example, Shabahang A (2024, p. 181 et seqq).

(4) Digital Services Act).[15] In addition to the Digital Services Act,[16] which contains important and, in some cases, innovative approaches to countering serious forms of digital vulnerability such as the dissemination of illegal content and unsubstantiated messages, this recent legislation includes in particular the Digital Markets Act[17] with its orientation towards adapting competition law to the problems of digital markets; the Data Act[18] with its focus on fair data access and fair data use; the adaptation of product liability[19] to the risks resulting from software in many forms, including artificial intelligence; and last but not least, the Artificial Intelligence Act.[20]

4 Interdisciplinary Approaches

Analysing this broad spectrum of factual circumstances that can give rise to digital vulnerability and the related provisions from many different areas of law requires the cooperation of various disciplines. From the perspective of legal doctrine, the primary concern may be to reconsider the legal conditions that can favour or reduce digital vulnerability and to ask about legal conceptual and regulatory approaches in order to limit this vulnerability or manage its consequences for the respective situations. However, the focus of the entire 'Digital Vulnerability in European Private Law' project on *digital* vulnerability already points to the need to consider the technological reference field addressed as an integral part of the research and to incorporate the findings of the relevant disciplines, in particular informatics. This applies even more when the focus is on human vulnerability in interaction with artificial intelligence and the diverse, complex and rapidly advancing developments in the field of artificial intelligence take centre stage. The inclusion of the perspectives and knowledge of informatics and other technical disciplines is indispensable for this topic, because without them, the peculiarities of the new technology and thus also the interaction of human behaviour with artificial intelligence cannot be understood.

At first glance, the attention for this interaction may seem to be just a new version of an old topic: the interaction between humans and the technology they have created.

[15] More details on the provisions of the DSA with regard to minors Casarosa and Micklitz (2024, p. 369 ff). Addressing Casarosa and Micklitz (2024).

[16] Regulation (EU) 2022/2065 of the European Parliament and of the Council of 19 October 2022 on a Single Market For Digital Services and amending Directive 2000/31/EC (Digital Services Act) (L 277 p. 1).

[17] Regulation (EU) 2022/1925 of the European Parliament and of the Council of 14 September 2022 on the contestable and fair markets in the digital sector and amending Directives (EU) 2019/1937 and (EU) 2020/1828 (Digital Markets Act) (L 265 p. 1).

[18] Regulation (EU) 2023/2854 of the European Parliament and of the Council of 13 December 2023 on harmonised rules on fair access to and use of data and amending Regulation (EU) 2017/2394 and Directive (EU) 2020/1828 (Data Act) (L 2023/2854 p. 1).

[19] Directive (EU) 2024/2853 of the European Parliament and of the Council of 23 October 2024 on liability for defective products and repealing Council Directive 85/374/EEC.

[20] See, for example, Mantelero (2024).

This topic has accompanied mankind through various phases of its history. In the 19th century, it arose under the auspices of the Industrial Revolution, and in the second half of the 20th century, the emphasis was on nuclear technology in particular. In each case, the relationship between creators—human beings—and what they have created was under consideration, and this regularly includes the sub-topic of whether and how the creators can be burdened and harmed by what they have created. 'Technology – a blessing or a curse'—this has been a favourite topic for school essays for generations.

But is 'human vulnerability in interaction with AI' really just a simple continuation of this much-discussed—and now perhaps somewhat boring—topic? 'New wine in old bottles', so to speak? This assumption would fail to recognise the peculiarities of artificial intelligence compared to earlier technological innovations—and thus the new challenges that now arise in the digital age in the relationship between humans and a technology originally created by them, but which must be attributed its own kind of intelligence, and its own creativity based on that—with characteristics such as the ability to learn and the unpredictability of its independent development (the 'black box' feature) and with a role description not only as a 'tool' but as an 'autonomous system'.[21]

Some contributions in this volume illustrate this difference from earlier technologies, for example, with regard to the 'delegation of decision-making' to artificial intelligence.[22] A number of other articles also address the peculiarities of this new technology from various perspectives, combining legal considerations with references to these peculiarities. These include, to name just a few examples, the question of whether artificial intelligence should be recognised as a legal entity,[23] the admissibility of AI simulation,[24] and the risk of risk regulation.[25]

Such references to the specific character of artificial intelligence in no way preclude consideration of profound differences between human intelligence, learning and understanding on the one hand, and artificial intelligence and its learning and 'machine understanding' on the other.[26] Nevertheless, it is essential to recognise the peculiarities of this new technology—and its constant developments—by combining legal approaches with the perspectives of informatics and other technical disciplines when considering the challenging relationship between human vulnerability and artificial intelligence.

However, the topic of the interaction between human vulnerability and artificial intelligence requires not only this attention to technical disciplines but also the cooperation of legal doctrine and disciplines of the humanities, including social sciences, such as philosophy, sociology and psychology. Linking legal research in this field with the humanities is not only an obvious step because the very formulation of the topic places *human* vulnerability in relation to artificial intelligence. Rather, as

---

[21] Zech (2019).

[22] Rodríguez de las Heras Ballell (2024).

[23] Legerén-Molina (2024).

[24] Pasquale (2025).

[25] Smorto (2025).

[26] Bertolaso and Marinucci (2025).

far as philosophy is concerned, for example, standards with regard to the protection of human dignity and personality against 'automated' discrimination, "deepfakes" and other impairments by means of artificial intelligence should be based on both ethics and law. The contribution of philosophy is also required, for instance, when the concern of 'technological humanism' is considered as a background to regulatory considerations.[27]

In particular, the involvement of sociology—or, more generally, the empirical social sciences—is indispensable because the search for legal answers to the problems of digital vulnerability must first analyse the factual situations in which such vulnerability exists or can arise (as already mentioned in connection with the cross-cutting perspective of the research).[28] This analysis is particularly dependent on the conceptual instruments and empirical methods of the social sciences. Therefore, the legal assessment of digital vulnerability is to be accompanied with a sociological lens in order to consider the effects of digital technologies, for example, with regard to topics such as inclusion or exclusion, discrimination and 'social sorting'.[29]

By focusing on such interdisciplinary approaches,[30] the research documented here in this part of the project has opened up a rich store of knowledge and inspiration for further efforts to find legal responses to the challenges of digital vulnerability. In doing so, it has set an important course for the project as a whole to achieve sustainable results. Only in this interdisciplinary way will it be able to arrive at an in-depth analysis and ultimately provide long-term stimuli for the future development of positive law in the face of the challenges of the digital age.

5 Research Topics

5.1 Autonomy, Subjectivity and Agency

In the following, a few brief references to three research topics should illustrate the range and some of the focal points of these interdisciplinary studies on 'human vulnerability in interaction with artificial intelligence' from which the present volume has emerged. Firstly, the attention is focused on the relationship between 'autonomy' and 'agency', which—in the wording of the title of the first section of the Rome conference—is linked to issues of identity and legal subjectivity. The meaning of these two terms—'autonomy' and 'agency'—obviously challenges legal theory as well as philosophy and other disciplines. As far as the interaction between human vulnerability and artificial intelligence is concerned, 'autonomy' has become a core

[27] Bertolaso and Marinucci (2025).

[28] See above under Sect. 3.

[29] Sorice and Volterrani (2025).

[30] The prominent role of medicine and psychology in interdisciplinary cooperation, in addition to the approaches just mentioned, is discussed separately below under Sect. 5.4.

concept for the latter side of this relationship—artificial intelligence—which distinguishes it from other, conventional information technology system. The autonomy of artificial intelligence—and the corresponding labelling as an 'autonomous system' in contrast to other information technology systems—is essentially based on the ability of artificial intelligence to self-learn. Autonomous systems therefore take on external influences in a way and with results that are not completely predictable, and the decisions they make are, in this respect, beyond the control of their producers and operators. In short, an 'autonomous system can change its behaviour without human intervention, i.e., it can change the rules governing its behaviour independently'.[31]

However, this characterisation of artificial intelligence through the concept of autonomy is contrasted with the description of the relationship between artificial intelligence and the natural or legal persons who operate it as an 'agency' or even the use of a 'tool'. The discussions that address this tension reflect different approaches, including at the legal level. For example, as discussed in detail in the conference,[32] the concept of the autonomy of artificial intelligence at the legal level could be extended to the extreme of attributing legal subjectivity to certain forms of artificial intelligence. From this approach, it is obvious to consider granting artificial intelligence the role of a representative of a natural person or of another legal person (even including another artificial intelligence with legal personality).

If one does not follow the—indeed questionable[33]—approach of attributing legal subjectivity to artificial intelligence (for example, because one generally does not want to recognise autonomy based on the ability to learn as a decisive criterion for legal subjectivity, neither for artificial intelligence nor for other potential 'subjects' such as animals capable of learning), another approach is up for discussion; however, in order to treat certain forms of artificial intelligence legally as representatives of their respective operator it is suggested that the past could be made fruitful for the future by recourse to a model of ancient Roman slave law. The operator of artificial intelligence could then be considered liable for its actions, including the conclusion of contracts, just like the owner of a slave with human intelligence but without legal capacity.[34] However, this would require profound changes to the terminology and systematics in those current legal systems that reserve the status of representative to natural and legal persons.

At least within the framework of such legal systems, approaches could therefore be preferable that dispense with the construction of a representative position for artificial intelligence and attribute the declarations made and actions taken by it directly to the respective operator as its own actions (for example, by modifying the theory of the declaration of intent in such a way that the operator does not necessarily have to know and want the relevant specific declarations which he issues by means

---

31 Zech (2019).

32 On this topic, Legerén-Molina (2024).

33 Report of the Expert Group on Liability for Artificial Intelligence (2019, p. 37 et seq.); and the Policy and investment recommendations for trustworthy AI of the High-Level Expert Group on Artificial Intelligence (2019), point 29.7.

34 Staudenmayer et al. (2017).

of artificial intelligence). From such a perspective, artificial intelligence has neither legal subjectivity nor the status of a legal representative in the context of any agency for a natural or legal person. Rather, despite its ability to act autonomously, its role is limited to that of a highly developed technical *tool* of its operator.

Beyond these fundamental questions of the legal nature of autonomous systems and their function as a representative or as a mere 'tool', further discussion about the 'agency role' of artificial intelligence will have to focus in particular on issues that are conventionally assigned to the problem of errors or more generally to the theory of defects of will and which have taken on a new shape with regard to artificial intelligence, in particular through the problem of 'unexpected outcomes'.[35] These questions, which are crucial for the legal practice, will ultimately likely have a significant impact on which of the fundamental approaches to understanding the legal character of artificial intelligence will prevail in legislation and judiciary.

5.2 *Digital Vulnerability of Autonomy*

As far as the concept of autonomy is concerned, it should also be noted that it can be relevant in the context of the topic discussed here not only for characterising artificial intelligence as an autonomous system but also with regard to the reference field of digital vulnerability. Digital vulnerability can be based, among other things, on the fact that the use of digital information technology, in particular artificial intelligence, impairs the self-determination of the individual and thus his or her autonomous personal behaviour.

Expressed in legal categories, digital vulnerability can arise from factual or legal restrictions on private autonomy in the use of digital information technologies. The spectrum of problematic situations here ranges from algorithms that 'conceal' alternative courses of action from users of digital information services to the use of 'dark patterns' when concluding contracts with artificial intelligence and the discriminatory or manipulative design of personalised advertising and contractual offers.[36] In the relationship between contracting parties, asymmetries that have traditionally been addressed by consumer law[37] or labour law[38] in particular may be exacerbated and new problems may arise with regard to contractual parity. The concern to ensure protection against digital vulnerability therefore also includes the need to guarantee the prerequisites of private autonomy, such as freedom of action and a certain parity of the contracting parties, against possible restrictions in the use of digital technologies and, in particular, in artificial intelligence contracting.

However, as it is always the case with such protective provisions, the protection of private autonomy with regard to the digital vulnerability of one party may imply

[35] European Law Institute (ELI) (2022), see also Metzger (2020).

[36] Skalski and Tereszkiewicz (2025).

[37] Goanta et al. (2024).

[38] Wildhaber and Ebert (2024).

that the other party's freedom of action, in particular the freedom to determine the content of contracts, must be restricted (as shown, for example, by the discussions on numerous provisions in the recent legislation mentioned above,[39] from the Online Intermediary Services Regulation to the Digital Services Act and the Data Act). As with the traditional situations of protecting vulnerable or 'weaker' parties, it will be essential to find the right ways and the right measures to achieve the goal of protecting against digital vulnerability as far as possible without compromising the basic patterns of self-determination and private autonomy more than necessary.

5.3 *Artificial Intelligence and Emotional Vulnerability*

However, protection against digital vulnerability is not limited to the question of how vulnerable people and groups of people can be protected from suffering material losses in the context of the use of new technologies. Rather, an important finding of this volume is that the problems of using artificial intelligence in relation to human emotionality should not be underestimated. In this respect, it is to be noted that autonomous systems can use personalised approaches to have an emotional impact on certain groups of people who may be particularly sensitive or vulnerable in that regard, for example, through promises of (pseudo) emotional care, and that they may ultimately lead to deep emotional harm. In particular, on the one hand, this concerns the far-reaching possibilities for recognising emotions with the help of artificial intelligence[40] and the use of such findings to control behaviour, for example, in the context of advertising and sales strategies. Emotion-related personal data can thus be a relevant trading commodity in the data economy.

On the other hand, in the course of the development of virtual worlds with the help of artificial intelligence, the fiction of reference persons for emotional needs is becoming increasingly important, such as artificial intelligence as a dialogue partner for certain life situations, as a substitute for a parent or child and, above all, for a girlfriend or boyfriend.[41] In this way, autonomously acting intelligence not only replaces the lack of human emotional affection. It also manipulates the emotions of the human recipient of attention without being bound to a similar emotionality on its part and without associated 'filters' such as empathy, etc. Such emotional vulnerability of humans in their interaction with emotionless artificial intelligence poses more than just a major challenge for philosophical and psychological reflection. Rather, if the manipulation of emotions by artificial intelligence leads to dependencies that individuals can hardly control themselves, regulatory tasks for legislation and jurisdiction—similar to the danger of addictions to gambling or drugs—may also have to be considered in this respect.

---

[39] See above under Sect. 3.

[40] Confortini (2025).

[41] Pera and Rigazio (2025).

However, as just emphasised,[42] it must also be considered here that any regulation should ultimately take into account the aim of protecting self-determination. Self-determination also includes the right to expose oneself to risks that can be harmful and damaging when viewed objectively. Under certain circumstances, digital vulnerability can therefore also be based on recognisable self-determination, and protective legislative measures must not lead to paternalistic over-regulation. In this respect, the problems of emotional dependence on artificial intelligence confirm just how delicate ethical and legal assessments can be in the face of digital vulnerability.

5.4 Vulnerability and Healing

Last but not least, there is another focal topic to emphasise among several others: The contributions in this volume reflect the fact that the discussions at the conference in Rome were not limited to the vulnerability of humans due to artificial intelligence (as is often the focus of considerations on legal responses to digitalisation) but also included the 'healing effects' of artificial intelligence on human vulnerability. This aspect of the interaction of human vulnerability and artificial intelligence concerns the 'healing effects' in both a figurative and a literal sense.

In the first, figurative sense, it refers to the protective and strengthening effects of the use of artificial intelligence, for example, in favour of consumers. This concerns, for example, the use of artificial intelligence, which is geared towards the needs and interests of consumers, by consumers themselves or consumer organisations when drafting and concluding contracts. However, it also includes the possibility of imposing legal obligations on artificial intelligence operators or digital intermediary services to use appropriate technologies such as 'filters' to prevent certain types of consumer detriment.[43]

In the other, literal sense, the benefits of artificial intelligence to healing people in the context of its use for medical purposes are taken under consideration. Artificial intelligence is being used on a large and constantly growing scale and for many different purposes in almost all areas of medicine—in research institutes as well as in hospitals and medical surgeries. In these areas, it can help to minimise people's physical vulnerability through preventive measures and heal existing physical injuries.

Against this background, the contributions to the conference and this volume show how the ambivalence of the effects of artificial intelligence with regard to human vulnerability is taking on clear contours, particularly in the field of medicine. They focus on the changes associated with the use of the new technologies in medical treatment methods and in the structure of medical facilities, on the resulting opportunities for the preventive and curative tasks of medicine, but also on the resulting risks and responsibilities. This concerns, among other aspects, the issues of the institutional

[42] See above under Sect. 5.2.

[43] Schulze (2024).

framework for ensuring the appropriate use of artificial intelligence for health,[44] the collection and collation of data in the application of artificial intelligence for medical purposes and the resulting risks of social control[45] and the role of ethical standards in the use of artificial intelligence in healthcare, as well as of bodies that monitor its utilisation.[46] Overall, this research confirms that AI, even when used for the purposes of healthcare and medical treatment, encounters human vulnerability of many kinds, both in regard to the people whose health it is intended to serve and with regard to others. It therefore indicates that, in this area as in other areas, it is necessary to embed this interaction between human vulnerability and artificial intelligence in a normative framework that includes ethical and legal rules for the production, operation and use of autonomous systems, also with regard to human vulnerability and the resulting needs for protection.

6 Outlook

On the basis of the conference in Rome and the results presented in this volume, a key challenge for further research is likely to be to contribute to the further development of this normative framework. This includes continuing to analyse existing legal approaches at European and national level with regard to digital vulnerability. However, it also leads to the task of developing concrete proposals based on the description of deficits and the need for improvement, which should primarily concern European private law within the context of the 'DiVE' project. This task also concerns the adaptation of the doctrine of European private law to new technological circumstances and new protection needs. However, it extends no less to considerations and concrete suggestions for legislative measures and for the application of current and future law in the relevant areas by the courts.

To put the context of these research tasks in simple terms: In the first step, Ferrara defined the conceptual and legal framework ('digital vulnerability' and 'European private law'). In the second step, Rome substantiated this theoretically and concretised it with regard to artificial intelligence. In the third step, the final part of this project, the focus now shifts to the legal-pragmatic task of providing legal doctrine, legislation and judiciary with suggestions for the further development of private law in view of the manifold vulnerabilities associated with the new digital technologies, which have created new needs for protection and require corresponding remedies in European private law.

[44] Cascini (2025).

[45] Konnoth (2025).

[46] Ferrari (2024).

References

Bertolaso M, Marinucci A Human Vulnerability in interaction with AI—Toward a technological humanism. In this volume

Casarosa F, Micklitz H-W (2024) Addressing vulnerabilities in online dispute resolution. In: Crea C, De Franceschi A. (eds), The new shapes of digital vulnerability in European private law, Nomos, Baden-Baden, pp 351–380

Cascini F EU institutions and competent authorities dealing with the revolution of Artificial Intelligence for health. In this volume

Confortini C Emotions recognition systems and the data economy. In this volume

Crea C, De Franceschi A (2024a) The new shapes of digital vulnerability in European private law. Nomos, Baden-Baden

Crea C, De Franceschi A (2024b) Digital vulnerability in European private law—towards a digital fairness. In: Crea C, De Franceschi A (eds) The new shapes of digital vulnerability in European private law. Nomos, Baden-Baden, p 17 et seq

Crea C, Infantino M (2025) Remedies to Digital Vulnerability in European Private Law: Pathways towards Fairness, Springer Cham

Durovic M, Kaprou E (2024) The new concept of digital vulnerability and the European rules on unfair commercial practices. In: Crea C, De Franceschi A (eds) The new shapes of digital vulnerability in European private law. Nomos, Baden-Baden, pp 127–144

European Law Institute (ELI) (2022) Guiding principles for automated decision-making in the EU, ELI innovation paper

Ferrari I (2024) AI in health care and ethical committee perspective. Presentation at the conference Human Vulnerability in Interaction with AI, in Rome

Gardella Tedeschi B. (2024) Digital transformation and the elders. Presentation at the conference Human Vulnerability in Interaction with AI, in Rome.

Goanta C, De Gregorio G, Spanakis J (2024) Consumer protection and digital vulnerability: common and diverging paths. In: Crea C, De Franceschi A (eds) The new shapes of digital vulnerability in European private law. Nomos, Baden-Baden, pp 31–52

Goh Escolar G (2024) Private international law and developments in artificial intelligence. In: Crea C, De Franceschi A (eds) The new shapes of digital vulnerability in European private law. Nomos, Baden-Baden

Konnoth C AI implants and self-enstrangement. In this volume

Legerén-Molina A (2024) Should AIs be recognized as legal persons? Presentation at the conference *Human Vulnerability in Interaction with AI*, in Rome

Mantelero A (2024) Facing the challenges of AI. Keynote speech at the conference Human Vulnerabilty in Interaction with AI, in Rome

Metzger A (2020) Market model for personal data: state of play under the new directive on digital content and digital services. In: Staudenmayer D, Schulze R, Lohsse S (eds) Data as counter-performance—contract law 2.0?: Münster colloquia on EU law and the digital economy V. Nomos, Baden-Baden, pp 25–46

Paglietti MC ODR, reputation by litigation and (ex post) discrimination. In this volume

Pasquale F AI and electoral manipulation: from misinformation to demoralization. In this volume

Pera A, Rigazio S (2024) Let the children play. Smart toys and child vulnerability. In: Crea C, De Franceschi A (eds) The new shapes of digital vulnerability in European private law. Nomos, Baden-Baden, pp 413–438

Pera A, Rigazio S Emotional vulnerability and AI girlfriends: a gender perspective. In this volume

Rodríguez de las Heras Ballell T (2024) Digital vulnerability and the formulation of harmonized rules for algorithmic contracts: a two-sided interplay. In: Crea C, De Franceschi A (eds) The new shapes of digital vulnerability in European private law. Nomos, Baden-Baden, pp 259–292

Schulze R (2024) Digital vulnerability in European private law—conclusions. In: Crea C, De Franceschi A (eds) The new shapes of digital vulnerability in European private law. Nomos, Baden-Baden, pp 528–530

Skalski S, Tereszkiewicz P Robo-advisory services in the insurance sector and EU Law. In this volume

Smorto G Human vulnerability and AI. The risk of risk regulation. In this volume

Sorice M, Volterrani A Beyond liminality: digital technologies between inclusion and citizenship. In this volume

Staudenmayer D, Schulze R, Lohsse S (2017) Contracts for the supply of digital content: regulatory challenges and gaps—an introduction. In: Staudenmayer D, Schulze R, Lohsse S (eds) Contracts for the supply of digital content: regulatory challenges and gaps: Münster colloquia on EU Law and the digital economy II. Nomos, Baden-Baden, pp 11–30

Wildhaber I, Ebert IL (2024) From digital vulnerability to data anxiety: the situation of employees in digitally permeated workplaces. In: Crea C, De Franceschi A (eds) The new shapes of digital vulnerability in European private law. Nomos, Baden-Baden, pp 469–498

Zech H (2019) Liability for autonomous systems: tackling specific risks of modern IT. In: Staudenmayer D, Schulze R, Lohsse S (eds) Liability for artificial intelligence and the internet of things: münster Colloquia on EU Law and the digital economy IV. Nomos, Baden-Baden, pp 187–200

Reiner Schulze, Professor of Law at the University of Münster and Director of the Centre for European Private Law. Founding member of the European Law Institute. Specialist in European private law, consumer and commercial law, and civil law history. Member of several prestigious academies, including the Italian Accademia Nazionale and Spanish Real Academia de Jurisprudencia y Legislación.

Open Access This chapter is licensed under the terms of the Creative Commons Attribution 4.0 International License (http://creativecommons.org/licenses/by/4.0/), which permits use, sharing, adaptation, distribution and reproduction in any medium or format, as long as you give appropriate credit to the original author(s) and the source, provide a link to the Creative Commons license and indicate if changes were made.

The images or other third party material in this chapter are included in the chapter's Creative Commons license, unless indicated otherwise in a credit line to the material. If material is not included in the chapter's Creative Commons license and your intended use is not permitted by statutory regulation or exceeds the permitted use, you will need to obtain permission directly from the copyright holder.

MIX
Papier aus verantwortungsvollen Quellen
Paper from responsible sources
FSC® C105338

FSC
www.fsc.org

If you have any concerns about our products,
you can contact us on
ProductSafety@springernature.com

In case Publisher is established outside the EU,
the EU authorized representative is:
Springer Nature Customer Service Center GmbH
Europaplatz 3, 69115 Heidelberg, Germany

Printed by Libri Plureos GmbH
in Hamburg, Germany